an account.

M000165493

198-99
206
238
239 - pragmatic appeal
       - rhetoric
       - neutrals

267
329

138
140 - public opin
149 - (,
152
181-82
186

p. 40
43 - 44
88
108: public opinion does not
137 grace laut

weakened
Russia

necessity
reprisal
change of
circum-

- meaningless
- instrument
- indecisive

& Hull focuses on nothing else

less clear what
her view is
"in the eyes
of society" (p. 50)

political/
public
opinion ?

was guilt
(p. 9)?

Q: Why didn't anyone argue the
invasion of France violated IL?

A Scrap of Paper

A SCRAP OF PAPER

*Breaking and Making International Law
during the Great War*

ISABEL V. HULL

CORNELL UNIVERSITY PRESS
Ithaca and London

Copyright © 2014 by Cornell University

First published 2014 by Cornell University Press

Printed in the United States of America

Library of Congress Cataloging-in-Publication Data

Hull, Isabel V., author.
    A scrap of paper : breaking and making international law during the Great War / Isabel V. Hull.
        pages cm
    Includes bibliographical references and index.
    ISBN 978-0-8014-5273-4 (cloth : alk. paper)
    1. War (International law)—History—20th century.   2. Humanitarian law—
History—20th century.   3. World War, 1914–1918—Law and legislation.   I. Title.
    KZ6795.W67H85   2014
    341.609'041—dc23   2013042450

Cloth printing   10 9 8 7 6 5 4 3 2 1

For My Beloved Michiganders
(in order of acquaintance)
Gayle, Lynn, and Vicki

Contents

Preface

This book began with a small research project on the interpretation of military necessity in Imperial Germany before World War I.[1] It discovered an enormous cleft between the latitudinarian views current in Germany and the narrow interpretation common in most other Western countries. Military necessity and the laws of war are on opposite ends of a seesaw—the more power you grant to military necessity, the less the law applies or is obligatory, so the stakes at issue are very high. The difference between Germany and other European states was so great that I wondered if it could possibly be true in practice. Finding out meant comparing the actual conduct of war. The obvious comparison seemed to be the great land power (Germany) fighting on land versus the great naval power (Britain) at sea, since states especially tend to minimize the restrictions of international law in the areas of their greatest strength. So, I began to study the British blockade during the Great War as the most apt comparison to Germany's war on land.

As anyone who has visited the British National Archives knows, on your way to your seat you pass a large card cabinet, actually several cabinets together, measuring perhaps twenty feet in length. Now itself classified as a document (FO 370), these index cards rubricized the Foreign Office's documents after 1910 and throughout the war. As I searched for blockade documents, I discovered a large number of rubrics and a staggering number of files dealing directly with issues of international law during the war. Each file revealed extensive correspondence inside the Foreign Office and between it and the War Office, the Admiralty, the attorney general, and others, arguing about what was permissible in the war and why. Obviously, international law was of more importance to how the war was fought than a mere comparison of the blockade to Germany's land warfare would

---

1. Isabel V. Hull, "'Military Necessity' and the Laws of War in Imperial Germany," in *Order, Conflict, Violence,* ed. Stathis Kalyvas, Ian Shapiro, and Tarek Masoud (Cambridge, 2008), 352–77.

uncover. Consequently, I widened the project to other areas: prisoners of war, automatic contact mines, reprisal, civilian detainees, aerial bombardment, hospital ships, etc. It became important to discover not just the differences between states, but the extent to which international law affected the conduct of the war.

There was a second problem, as well. It was hard to tell if the differences between how Britons and Germans understood law did not simply reflect the difference between the common law and its ways of thinking and those of the Continental civil law tradition. Adding Britain's ally, France, provided a way to check, for when France disagreed with Britain and interpreted law similarly to Germany, we may conclude that their respective positions reflected the common law / Continental law divide and not deeper divisions over the nature of law and war.

The resulting comparative project, covering so many different subjects over four and a half years of war, outstripped the capacity of a single researcher in a single lifetime and was furthermore impossible to distill into a single volume that covered all aspects of the laws of war. Consequently, I have chosen two foci for this book. The first is the original question: How different (or similar) was Imperial Germany from the Western Allies in its interpretation of international law?[2] The second is simply to demonstrate to modern readers a fact that post-1919 writings, academic and popular, have resolutely denied or obscured, namely, that international law was central to how and why the Great War was fought. The first chapter explores why we no longer know this.

Finally, I have chosen to discuss those rubrics that seem most likely to demonstrate in detail these foci. This book therefore does not cover the entire range of subjects concerning international law during the war. James W. Garner's two-volume work, *International Law and the World War,* published in 1920, is still the best compendium of and commentary on the legal issues raised by the war.[3] Garner lacked access to internal governmental correspondence, but the reader will still find his work extremely valuable. It is not a flattering commentary on our times that no scholar has attempted to update Garner's work. Throughout, I have been careful to avoid the anachronistic practice of reading backward our own, often quite different, legal standards. That is why most of the legal writings cited in this book are the old ones, contemporary to the war or before.

I must also admit another motive in writing this book. I have been deeply dismayed by the lawlessness of my own country in its pursuit of the "war on terror." But I am a historian, and not even of the United States. Like most historians, I work out my preoccupations by trying to understand why the dead did what they did when they were as quick, and as responsible, as we are now. I hope that the reader, without misapplying contemporary standards to the past, will still find it helpful to contemplate the choices available when war and law meet.

---

2. For the most part "international law" will refer to what was then known as the "laws of war," now called "international humanitarian law." But the fact that the laws of war had recently been codified into convention or treaty law, together with Germany's violation of Belgian neutrality, means that, for the Allies and for this book, "international law" must also be understood more widely as the laws regulating interstate behavior in peace and in war.

3. James Wilford Garner, *International Law and the World War* (London, 1920).

Acknowledgments

I am grateful to the staffs of the archives and libraries listed in the bibliography for their help and friendliness, and in particular Annegret Wilke and Dr. Gerhard Keiper of the Politisches Archiv des Auswärtigen Amtes. I would like to thank Sophie de Schaepdrijver for her help with the chapters on Belgium and her generosity and encouragement, the members of the Cornell History Colloquium and audiences at Oxford University and the Eric Castrén Institute, Helsinki, Finland, for their spirited discussion of earlier versions of this work, and John Ackerman and Lynn Eden for their editorial acumen. I have very much missed talking to Hans W. Gatzke, whose knowledge and judgment would have helped me a great deal. He was right about lots of things.

Abbreviations

AA	Auswärtiges Amt (German Foreign Ministry)
AA/PA	Auswärtiges Amt, Politisches Archiv
AJIL	*American Journal of International Law*
AKO	Allerhöchstes Kabinettsorder (Imperial Edict)
BAB	Bundesarchiv Berlin-Lichterfelde
BayKrA	Bayerisches Kriegsarchiv
BD	*British Documents on Foreign Affairs: Reports and Papers from the Foreign Office Confidential Print.* Part II: From the First to the Second World War.
BPNL	*Bescheiden Betreffende de Buitenlandse Politiek van Nederland 1848–1919, Derde Periode 1899–1919, Vierde Deel, 1914–1917.*
CIL	customary international law
CRB	Committee for the Relief of Belgium
DDFr	France. Foreign Office. Commission de publication des documents diplomatiques français. *Documents Diplomatiques Français*
DoL	Declaration of London (*1909*)
FO	Foreign Office (Great Britain)
FOPD	Foreign Office Prisoners of War and Aliens Department
FRUS	United States. Department of State. *Papers Relating to the Foreign Relations of the United States; 1914–1918; Supplement: The World War.*
GG	General Government
GP	Germany. Foreign Office. *Die grosse Politik der Europäischen Kabinette, 1871–1914. Sammlung der Diplomatischen Akten des Auswärtigen Amtes.*
Hansard	*Hansard's Parliamentary Debates*
ICRC	International Committee of the Red Cross

ILC	International Law Committee (Britain, *1918*)
KEO	Kriegs-Etappen-Ordnung
MAE	Ministère des affaires étrangères (French Foreign Ministry)
MP	Member of Parliament
NOT	Netherlands Overseas Trust
OHL	Oberste Heeresleitung (German high command)
RGDIP	*Revue Générale de Droit International Public*
RMG	Reichsmilitärgericht
SHAT	Société historique de l'armée de terre (French army archives)
Sten.Ber.	*Stenographische Berichte über die Verhandlungen des Reichstags*
StGB	*Strafgesetzbuch*
TNA	The National Archives (Great Britain)
UA	Germany. National Constitutional Assembly. *Das Werk des Untersuchungs-ausschusses der Verfassunggebenden Deutschen Nationalversammlung und des Deutschen Reichstages, 1919–1928, Verhandlungen, Gutachten, Urkunden.*

A Scrap of Paper

Prologue

What We Have Forgotten

Precisely four years after the beginning of the First World War, the British minister of blockade, Robert Cecil, approved an internal memorandum written by the Political Intelligence Department of the Foreign Office setting out, among other things, why the Allies fought and how they had explained the war to neutrals and to their enemies. It summarized "the principles at stake in the war" as the destruction of "Prussian militarism" and the triumph of "the ideal of a peaceful settlement based on the rights of small nations, on the reign of international law, and on the introduction into all civilised States of the principle of democratic responsible government."[1] The memo might almost have cited Prime Minister Herbert Asquith speaking to Parliament four years earlier, when he explained that Britain fought "to fulfil a solemn international obligation" against "material force" that threatened to crush "small nationalities" "in defiance of international good faith."[2] "International obligation" and "international good faith" were synonyms for international law. During the entire war those aims had remained the same. They were expressed equally commonly in private letters and in public statements and propaganda. They were so obvious that the (London) *Times* arranged its *Documentary History of the War* into these sections: diplomacy, naval, military, overseas, and international law. Few would have quarreled with Sir Graham Bower (formerly of the Admiralty) that the Allies were "engaged in the defense of international law and justice," or with the most renowned international lawyer of the day, France's Louis Renault, when he wrote

---

1. Robert Cecil to Committee on Economic Defence and Development, Aug. 1, 1918, *BD*, ser. H, vol. 8: 322, 324.

2. J. A. Spender and Cyril Asquith, *Life of Herbert Henry Asquith, Lord Oxford and Asquith* (London, 1932), 2:114.

(1917) that "the goal of the present war must be to affirm the sanctity of treaties, the destruction of the German theory that necessity justifies the violation of all the laws of war, the guarantee of the existence of small states, the development of arbitration."[3]

International law was so central to how contemporaries interpreted the war because law was a linchpin and guarantee of the post-Napoleonic European state system that the war seemed to be destroying. Many international-legal norms, especially humanitarian ones, long predated 1815; others were the precipitate of the security interests, needs, and mutual claims of the large and small states that defined themselves as the community of self-styled "civilized" states. The legal system they created was set down in treaties and visible in customary practices that had come to be recognized as obligatory. They included rules of war. Beginning in 1856, the rules of war began to be codified. The successful agreement on the rules of land warfare concluded at the Hague Peace Conferences of 1899 and 1907, and the creation of the Permanent Court of Arbitration (1899) and the International Prize Court (1907) seemed to usher in an era of progressive development in which the rule of law would more and more displace the resort to war. August 1914 shattered that hope. More important, violations of treaty law and the laws of war in the opening weeks challenged the international legal system that had defined Europe and held it together. Leaders and public opinion in Great Britain and France were the first to see the war as a titanic struggle over law, a kind of European civil war. Germany almost immediately reciprocated; both sides henceforth vied with one another to claim the international-legal high ground. This was not just or even mostly a public relations battle. Meters and meters of internal documents and diplomatic correspondence record the central role of law in forming war policy, justifying that policy to neutrals, judging one's enemies, and measuring the existential danger they posed. The Allies had two interpretations of the clash of legal systems. The more common one condemned Imperial Germany as a criminal state that disregarded law altogether. International lawyers like Renault instead saw in Germany's actions an alternative "German theory" of law rooted in (military) necessity. As we shall see, there were actually several competing German theories. Judging from their vantage points, it was the Allies who appeared as scofflaws or as self-interested promoters of obsolete or unrealistic legal principles. Therefore, three main objects of this book are, first, to analyze and compare the belligerents' legal assumptions; second, to explore their implications for international law and how it operated and changed *in extremis;* and, not least, third, to examine the effect of international law on the actual conduct of war—that is, on the major governmental decisions on how the war was to be fought (not on atrocities or war crimes committed by individuals).

Three weeks after the Armistice, Britain's attorney general and its law officers issued a report on how to rebuild the legal system after the "dangerous challenge to the fundamental

---

3. Graham Bower, "The Laws of War: Prisoners of War and Reprisals," *Grotius Society, Problems of the War: Papers Read before the Society in the Year 1915* 1 (1916): 24; Louis Renault, *Les premières violations du droit des gens par l'Allemagne, Luxembourg et Belgique* (Paris, 1917), 81. Renault was, in turn, citing the British international jurist Pearce Higgins.

principles of public law" that defeated Germany had posed.[4] Like the leaders and France, they favored trials of the Kaiser and his generals. Attorney General E. Smith was confident that "common people" everywhere saw what was at iss... things are very easy to understand, and ordinary people all over the world u.......... them very well." In November 1918, Smith was undoubtedly correct, but in a few short years, what was so completely obvious to contemporaries had become just as completely erased.

That erasure continues to this day in both academic writing and popular culture. It has robbed the war of meaning. The Great War has come to stand for tragic senselessness (*Oh! What a Lovely War*) and pointless mass death. A further aim of this book is to restore international law to its rightful place in the conflict, to recall the great stakes at issue in 1914–18, as well as to explore the complexities of international law during belligerency.

Before beginning that task, we must examine why and how international law became forgotten. This subject deserves an entire book, because many of the misconceptions driving the erasure process continue to mislead us about what international law is and how it works, and about its relation to power and high politics. Here, we can only briefly survey the matter.

Forgetting was an active process that began with a threefold disillusionment. First, pacifists were frustrated that the laws of war codified at the Hague Peace Conferences had not prevented war altogether. That, of course, was not the mandate of those laws, which was rather to "mitigate the severity [of war] as far as possible."[5] Second, the laws of war did little to prevent the shocking carnage among soldiers. Artillery shells and machine guns, the two main causes of combat death, were perfectly legal when used against regular troops. Four and a half years of killing, ten million soldiers' deaths, were simply appalling. As Adam Roberts writes, "law [had] got separated from some of the real causes of moral concern" to the public.[6] Third, the very clash of legal views among the belligerents produced confusing claims and counterclaims of violations that seemed easiest to sum up as a tit-for-tat process of destruction. Even U.S. Secretary of State Robert Lansing (a lawyer) despaired in December 1916 that "every new breach begat another, which in turn begat others, until the standards of right sanctioned by treaties and usage, were torn to bits."[7]

But building on these disappointments, the eclipse of international law's reputation among the public after 1919 was most strongly determined by two propaganda campaigns: paradoxically, the successful British one during the war, and the successful German one afterward. The first made international law the centerpiece of attention, the second erased it.

---

4. Imperial War Cabinet meeting No. 39, Nov. 28, 1918; the appendix is the full report, G.T.-6411, TNA CAB 23/42. Hereafter, TNA will be omitted; all archival signatures beginning with CAB, FO, WO, and ADM are from The National Archives, Great Britain.

5. Preamble to Convention (IV) Respecting the Laws and Customs of War on Land [the Hague Rules], in *Documents on the Laws of War,* 3rd ed., ed. Adam Roberts and Richard Guelff (Oxford, 2004), 69.

6. Adam Roberts, "Land Warfare: From Hague to Nuremberg," in *The Laws of War: Constraints on Warfare in the Western World,* ed. Michael Howard, George Andreopoulos, and Mark Shulman (New Haven, CT, 1994), 125.

7. Lansing memo of Dec. 1, 1916, United States, *Papers Relating to the Foreign Relation of the United States: The Lansing Papers, 1914–1920,* 2 vols. (Washington, DC, 1939), 1:229.

Although both the French and German foreign offices had press sections, Britain entered the war with none. Its propaganda effort developed from scratch; in the formative days of August and September 1914, it simply reacted to widespread shock at Imperial Germany's methods of warfare, relying on volunteers to put into words and images what Britain's leaders and the Allied and neutral public already felt.[8] Already on August 2, a liberal Belgian paper used the word "barbarism" to describe the German campaign. Repeated by French philosopher Henri Bergson in Paris on August 8, barbarism versus civilization became the organizing epithet of the struggle, with its suggestion that Germany had left the community of the civilized.[9] As Britain belatedly assembled its propaganda apparatus, it adopted several rules that responded to the ill repute of propaganda in a liberal society. Its propaganda would be based on facts, not lies, nor on heavy censorship at home; it would primarily target neutral public opinion; and it would be subtly contoured to its foreign audience rather than an ostentatious display of government opinion.[10]

The resulting British propaganda campaign was massive, successful, and partly secret. In less than a year, Wellington House, the coordinating organ, had issued two and a half million publications; two years into the war, it ran six semimonthly newspapers, had published three hundred books and pamphlets, commanded three hundred distribution centers in Latin America alone, and circulated four thousand photos each week to newspapers.[11] One of the most influential publications was the "German crimes' calendar," devoted to striking violations of the laws of war. As one German observed regarding the effects of this deluge on opinion in America, "Today we may say that the three names Louvain, Reims, Lusitania, almost in equal measure, have wiped out sympathy with Germany."[12]

Together with the facts, however, exaggerations and untruths also circulated, some under government cover but most via the popular press. These myths later discredited the entire campaign. The most notorious legend concerned the allegation that German soldiers had hacked off the hands of infants and children in Belgium and Northern France. No genuine eyewitnesses or mutilated corpses were ever found.[13] The severed-hands myth

---

8. Prime Minister Herbert Asquith to King George V, Aug. 31, 1914, CAB/41/35/38; Asquith to King, Sept. 5, 1914, ibid., CAB 41/35/41; Alan Kramer, *Dynamic of Destruction: Culture and Mass Killing in the First World War* (Oxford, 2007), 13–14; Michael L. Sanders and Philip M. Taylor, *British Propaganda during the First World War* (London, 1982), 25–35, 37; Gary S. Messinger, *British Propaganda and the State in the First World War* (Manchester, 1992), 33–36.

9. Daniel H. Thomas, *The Guarantee of Belgian Independence and Neutrality in European Diplomacy, 1830s–1930s* (Kingston, RI, 1983), 495; Kramer, *Dynamic of Destruction,* 183; Sophie De Schaepdrijver, *La Belgique et la Première Guerre Mondiale* (New York, 2004), 73.

10. Messinger, *British Propaganda,* 37–39, 90, 123; Sanders and Taylor, *British Propaganda,* 143; Marion Girard, *A Strange and Formidable Weapon: British Responses to World War I Poison Gas,* Studies in War, Society and the Military (Lincoln, UK, 2008), 129–30. In fact, the foreign offices of Britain, France, and Germany all tried to check facts before issuing public statements, though the armies and navies were variously cooperative and mostly rather slow to respond.

11. Messinger, *British Propaganda,* 40–41.

12. Kramer, *Dynamic of Destruction,* 30; Sanders and Taylor, *British Propaganda,* 119.

13. John Horne and Alan Kramer, *German Atrocities, 1914: A History of Denial* (New Haven, CT, 2001), 202–4, 212–25; Trevor Wilson, "Lord Bryce's Investigation into Alleged German Atrocities in Belgium, 1914–1915," *Journal of Contemporary History* 14, no. 3 (July 1979): 369–83.

was at least partly the creation of the free press, which heedlessly multiplied the rumor. Newspapers often rushed ahead with "squalid forms" of propaganda unsanctioned and in many cases condemned by the government's own propaganda agencies.[14] Later critics lumped them together, tarring the government with the brush of yellow journalism.

More troublesome than lurid false stories was secrecy. The existence of Wellington House was unknown to the public for two years, and one of the most successful British propagandists working in the United States, Gilbert Parker, did so under cover.[15] Secrecy made credible later claims of lying government manipulation.

By emblazoning international law and a stable, peaceful postwar order on their escutcheon ("The War that will end War"—H. G. Wells, September 1914), the Allies set very high standards for themselves and raised equally high expectations among their increasingly exhausted publics. It is remarkable how quickly after the Armistice liberal British newspapers measured their government against its own public standards and found it wanting. The pivotal issue was the continuance of the blockade after November 1918. Britain and France, unsure of the degree of their military victory or the constancy of their American ally, and above all unsure that Germany might not resume fighting, decided to keep the blockade in order to force Germany to sign the peace treaty. As reports trickled out on the parlous health of German civilians, the British government, but not the French, favored relaxing the blockade. By March 1919, liberal journals in Britain pilloried their government in the same register as wartime propaganda. "The failure to raise the blockade has been a political and moral failure," wrote the *Nation*. It claimed that "Germany is being turned into one vast concentration camp," and the rest of the press was hushing up the truth.[16] The following week it asked, "Will history, assigning to Germany the guilt of making the war, assign to the victorious Allies the equal guilt of making a peace which is no peace, but is sown thick with the seeds of hate and future strife?"[17]

These sentiments revived the criticisms of radical liberals and pacifists briefly silenced in August 1914. Some of them had founded the Union of Democratic Control (UDC) to protest Britain's entry into the war, which they saw as the predictable result of Foreign Minister Sir Edward Grey's dishonest, covert policy of entente with France.[18] One UDC member, E. D. Morel, radical liberal and gifted muckraker, in 1916 published *Truth and the War*, setting out this alternate view of the war. Honing a standard radical-liberal criticism of Britain's foreign-policy makers, he argued that the war was the product of secret, antidemocratic diplomacy and its ill-begotten alliance machinery.[19] In 1919 this

---

14. Messinger, *British Propaganda*, 76.

15. Ibid., 38, 54–68.

16. "The Infamy of the Blockade," *Nation*, Mar. 8, 1919, cited in *The Blockade of Germany after the Armistice, 1918–1919: Selected Documents of the Supreme Economic Council, Superior Blockade Council, American Relief Administration, and Other Wartime Organizations*, ed. Suda Lorena Bane and Ralph Haswell Lutz (Stanford, CA, 1942), 724–25.

17. *Nation*, Mar. 15, 1919, ibid., 732. The *Nation*'s campaign was joined by the *Daily News* and the *Daily Herald*, ibid., 770, 785, 794.

18. John Viscount Morley, *Memorandum on Resignation August 1914* (London, 1928).

19. Annika Mombauer, *Origins of the First World War: Controversies and Consensus* (New York, 2002), 89–93.

well-developed line of radical attack merged with war fatigue, suspicion of war-swollen government, shame at the very success of the blockade and hate-inducing propaganda, and the relaxation made possible by victory.[20] It made some Britons (and isolationist, pacifist, and some self-styled progressive Americans, but fewer French people) susceptible to the unmasking of putative government lies, including the propaganda campaign's claims about international law. In the most influential political book of 1919, the economist John Maynard Keynes added his authority to the growing disillusionment by referring to "so-called international law" in the course of his bitter critique of the economic provisions of the Versailles Treaty.[21] The controversial treaty quickly came to epitomize the seeming falsity of Allied claims about law. For the treaty contained a theory of the origins of the war ("the aggression of Germany and her allies"—article 231), an indictment of the Kaiser and others on war crimes (articles 227–30), and was itself the legal cornerstone of the postwar world and a succinct expression of Allied diplomacy—in short, it was a perfect icon of international law, and, if one opposed the treaty, a perfect icon of all that ailed international law.[22] By the spring of 1919, the grounds were thus set among the victors and some neutrals for a radical revision of the history and meaning of the World War.

This perfect storm of opinion and emotion opened up exciting possibilities to a German state trying to escape the consequences of its defeat. During the war, Germany had become hypersensitive to propaganda. It had been first off the blocks in August 1914, inundating Europe with tendentious news about the war.[23] That early advantage soon vanished as Germany's conduct of the war in Belgium and Northern France became known through refugee and eyewitness reports. By the end of August, the German foreign office (Auswärtiges Amt, or AA) was scrambling to counteract stories in the Allied and neutral press about mass executions, the burning of Louvain and other towns and villages, pillage, shelling of cultural monuments (the cathedral of Reims), and so on.[24] Germany's ambassadors begged for "quick denials with as concrete details as possible in order to stop the planting of lies," but that method often backfired.[25] The *démentis* too often proved false, or significant details were wrong, discrediting the denials altogether. Germany then switched to general denials and *tu quoque* charges—you are as guilty as we are—against the Allies. But these also rested on information provided by the military, and, worse, they often incorporated tough, military language unconvincing or even repulsive to neutrals, the main audience in the propaganda wars. By April 1915, legation secretary Bruno Wedding of the

---

20. Archibald C. Bell, *A History of the Blockade of Germany and of the Countries Associated with Her in the Great War, Austria, Bulgaria, and Turkey, 1914–1918* (London, 1937), 554; Avner Offer, *The First World War: An Agrarian Interpretation* (Oxford, 1989), 398–401.

21. John Maynard Keynes, *The Economic Consequences of the Peace* (New York, 1920), 71–72; Étienne Mantoux, *The Carthaginian Peace; or, the Economic Consequences of Mr. Keynes* (London, 1946).

22. The Treaty of Versailles, June 28, 1919, available through the Avalon Project, Yale University, http://avalon.law.yale.edu/subject_menus/versailles_menu.asp.

23. Messinger, *British Propaganda*, 33–34, 36; Poincaré diary entries of Aug. 11, 12, and 14, 1914, in *The Memoirs of Raymond Poincaré, 1914,* trans. George Arthur (Garden City, NY, 1929), 34–35, 42–43, 48, 105; Ambassador Beau to Delcassé, Bern, Oct. 29, 1914, *DDFr* 1: doc. 440.

24. Jagow to AA, GHQ, Aug. 29, 1914; Zimmermann to Jagow, Berlin, Aug. 31, 1914, AA/PA R 22382.

25. Ambassador Beau, Bern, in Zimmermann to Jagow, Berlin, Nr. 1427, Oct. 4, 1914, AA/PA, R 22383.

AA had despaired; in his view, Germany had lost the propaganda war.[26] Gary Messinger, a historian of British propaganda, argues that the German propaganda campaign was handicapped not only by organizational bifurcation characteristic of Imperial German government, but also by the "failure to understand foreign audiences." The "bluntness," "extreme nationalism," and "blustering mannerisms" that characterized German propaganda were, he maintains, "the consequences of growing up in an autocratic culture, where...practice in listening to opposing points of view was limited."[27]

Cosmopolitan Germans fretted about precisely these shortcomings. The Catholic Center Party leader Matthias Erzberger, a propaganda activist during the war, noted that Germany's violation of Belgian neutrality made Belgium "the darling of the world"; the éclat concerning the Belgian deportations (1916) finished off all German hopes: "Germany lost the game completely," he concluded.[28] Unable to defend how it conducted the war, Germany was equally unable to provide positive reasons why neutrals should hope for a German victory. The claim of higher German *Kultur* rang hollow. Theodor Wolff, editor of the *Berliner Tageblatt,* complained in November 1914 that "presenting German culture as the savior of world culture is not exactly flattering for the neutrals."[29] By 1918 nothing had changed. In that year the future chancellor Max von Baden observed that "to date our claim to power has been grounded only on securing Germany's existence and vital interests," which meant, as Erich Volkmann summarized for the Reichstag investigating committee after the defeat, that "the Central Powers never developed an idea that could unite peoples like the [Allied claims of justice and freedom]."[30]

As a result, Germany, but especially the AA, learned to answer the Allies in their own coin. During the war, the AA founded institutes dedicated to counteracting the Allies' legal barrage: the War Archive of International Law (Kriegsarchiv des Völkerrechts) in Kiel, the Research Institute for the History of the War (Forschungsinstitut für die Geschichte des Krieges) and the War Archive (Kriegsarchiv) in Jena, and the German Society for International Law (Deutsche Gesellschaft für Völkerrecht).[31] It paid journalists and established useful foreign contacts. And it learned from Britain's oblique techniques. An especially good learner was Bernhard Wilhelm von Bülow, a jurist and former attaché in Washington. In June 1918, Legation Secretary Bülow found himself in charge of containing the damage from the Allied contention that Germany had started the war. Dissatisfied

---

26. Wedding to Grünau, Berlin, April 10, 1915, AA/PA, R 22386.

27. Messinger, *British Propaganda,* 18.

28. Matthias Erzberger, *Erlebnisse im Weltkrieg, von Reichsfinanzminister a. d. M. Erzberger* (Stuttgart/Berlin, 1920), 8.

29. Diary entry of Nov. 16, 1914, *Theodor Wolff. Tagebücher 1914–1919; Der Erste Weltkrieg und die Entstehung der Weimarer Republik in Tagebüchern, Leitartikeln und Briefen des Chefredakteurs am "Berliner Tageblatt" und Mitbegründer der "Deutschen Demokratischen Partei,"* ed. Bernd Sösemann (Boppard am Rhein, 1984), 1:119.

30. Prince Max von Baden, *Erinnerungen und Dokumente* (Stuttgart, 1927), 253; Archivrat im Reichsarchiv Major Erich Volkmann, report on "Die Annexionsfragen des Weltkrieges," in *UA* 4:12, 19.

31. Ernst Stenzel, *Die Kriegführung des deutschen Imperialismus und das Völkerrecht; zur Planung und Vorbereitung des deutschen Imperialismus auf die barbarische Kriegführung im Ersten und Zweiten Weltkrieg, dargestellt an den vorherrschenden Ansichten zu den Gesetzen und Gebräuchen des Landkrieges (1900–1945)* (Berlin, 1973), 52.

with mere short-term efforts, Bülow already in the summer of 1918 developed the basic idea that shaped Germany's propaganda efforts during the Weimar Republic: Germany would influence public opinion through scholarship. The campaign would ostensibly be run by a "politically trained" historian with no seeming governmental contact. In reality, he was to enjoy "a special relationship of trust" with the AA.[32]

Because of the crush of events following the Armistice, it took several years before Bülow's idea could be put into practice. The AA first poured its energy into trying to avoid the coming reparations bill. That effort helped establish the later template for Weimar-era propaganda. First, Bülow was put in charge of sifting diplomatic documents to build a legal case disproving Germany's "war guilt." The AA thus joined the fight on the same terrain and using the same legal language as the Allies. Second, Bülow's office became institutionalized as the "Guilt Office," or Schuldreferat. The Schuldreferat coordinated propaganda into the 1930s. Third, the AA used moderate professors with good reputations among the neutrals to present to the Peace Conference as their own scholarship a "professor's memorandum" on Germany's innocence that was in fact produced by the AA. None of them had read the material before they signed it.[33] Nevertheless, this first postwar propaganda campaign failed; it halted neither reparations nor the rest of the Versailles Treaty.

The effort now shifted to revising the entire treaty. Bülow was again *spiritus rector.* Although the Allies had pointed out that the Treaty of Versailles could indeed be modified, either through the League of Nations or in collective negotiation, Bülow fastened on a third, more absolute way.[34] He sought to discredit the treaty by convincing world opinion that "the whole treaty has been built upon a lie, namely on the forced confession of Germany's sole guilt for [starting] the war."[35] If one could disprove war guilt, one could expose the treaty as invalid and get it annulled.

The AA's propaganda plan was entirely in the service of German foreign policy. Continuity of personnel and decisions by early Weimar cabinets not to make a clean break with the Kaiserreich produced continuity in foreign policy, insofar as the struggle to revise the Treaty of Versailles aimed to roll back Germany's defeat, recoup its great power status, and recommence its prewar policies of prestige and power.[36] The key to this plan was treaty

---

32. Bülow to Smend, June 20, 1918, cited in Erich J. C. Hahn, "The German Foreign Office and the Question of War Guilt," in *German Nationalism and the European Response,* ed. Carole Fink, Isabel V. Hull, and MacGregor Knox (Norman, OK, 1985), 47.

33. Holger Herwig, "Clio Deceived: Patriotic Self-Censorship in Germany after the War," in *Forging the Collective Memory: Government and International Historians through Two World Wars,* ed. Keith Wilson (Providence, RI, 1996), 93–94.

34. Reply of the Allied and Associated Powers to the Observations of the German Delegation on the Conditions of Peace (Clemenceau to Ulrich von Brockdorff-Rantzau), Paris, June 16, 1919, in *FRUS, Paris Peace Conference,* 6:935; art. 19 of the Covenant of the League of Nations, contained in the Treaty of Versailles, Avalon Project, Yale University, http://avalon.law.yale.edu/imt/parti.asp.

35. Bernhard Wilhelm von Bülow, "Völkerfrieden" unpublished manuscript, cited in Ulrich Heinemann, *Die verdrängte Niederlage; Politische Öffentlichkeit und Kriegsschuldfrage in der Weimarer Republik* (Göttingen, 1983), 57.

36. Peter Krüger, *Deutschland und die Reparationen 1918; Die Genesis des Reparationsproblems in Deutschland zwischen Waffenstillstand und Versailler Friedensschluss* (Stuttgart, 1973).

revision. A weakened Germany aimed to use history to discredit the legal underpinnings of the treaty by attacking the "war guilt" clause. Historians have since disagreed about whether war guilt could bear such a legal burden.[37] The AA's campaign against *Alleinschuld* (Germany's sole war guilt) assumed that the Allies justified the reparations burden as a legal rather than a political measure, that is, that reparations were due as punishment for launching aggressive war in violation of international law, rather than as the usual political price of losing a major war. In fact, politics and law were inextricably entwined. Article 231 of the Versailles Treaty said that "Germany accepts the responsibility of Germany and her allies for causing all the loss and damage [to the victors]...as a consequence of the war imposed upon them by the aggression of Germany and her allies."[38] The treaty made two charges: the legal one of violating treaty law and the laws of war, and the political one of launching an aggressive war, which the Allies regarded as a "crime against humanity" and which had vast legal implications because the aggression was undertaken against a state order partly guaranteed by law. *Alleinschuld* focused on the second as *pars pro toto*—the part taken for the whole.

In targeting war guilt Bülow merely followed the lead of Germany's head diplomat at Versailles, Ulrich Count von Brockdorff-Rantzau. On May 24, 1919, Rantzau had laid down the main argument against the reparations bill: Germany had signed the Armistice on the basis of President Woodrow Wilson's promise that it would be "a Peace of Right," not Might, and therefore that "the President demanded the unconditional restitution of the violated Right."[39] Under that rubric, Germany admitted to violating Belgian neutrality and via that breach to entering Northern France; it indirectly admitted waging aggressive war: "It was for this aggression," Rantzau wrote, "that the German Government admitted Germany to be responsible: it did not admit Germany's alleged responsibility for the origin of the war or for the merely incidental fact that the formal declaration of war had emanated from Germany." If the Allies now wanted to saddle Germany with reparations for the entire war, then Germany must respond by demanding reparations for the "immeasurable injury" that German civilians suffered "owing to the Blockade, a measure opposed to the Law of Nations." Five days later, the German delegation submitted an eighty-four-page rebuttal of the draft treaty. By asking for an impartial inquiry into both responsibility for the war and "culpable acts in its conduct," Rantzau's cover letter questioned Germany's responsibility for both.[40]

The Allied reply put violations of international law at the heart of the war and therefore of the proposed peace treaty. The cover letter was drafted by Philip Kerr (of the British delegation) and went out over the signature of the French prime minister, Georges

---

37. Fritz Dickmann, *Die Kriegsschuldfrage auf der Friedenskonferenz von Paris 1919* (Munich, 1964) argues that it could not.

38. Clearly, the Allies also included Austria-Hungary in "responsibility," as one insider in AA operations admitted: internal report by Major Alfred von Wegerer, head of the Center for the Study of the Causes of the War, cited in Heinemann, *Verdrängte Niederlage*, 230.

39. Brockdorff-Rantzau to Clemenceau, Versailles, May 24, 1919, *FRUS, Paris Peace Conference, 1919*, 6:38.

40. Brockdorff-Rantzau to Clemenceau, Versailles, May 29, 1919, ibid., 6:798–99.

Clemenceau.[41] Historians who minimize the legal weight of article 231 point out that the cover letter was "not at all an official interpretation of Art. 231," but merely a compromise designed to paper over internal Allied disagreements over reparations.[42] There were certainly disagreements, and the reply was certainly a compromise, but it is all the more striking that Britain, France, the United States, and Italy continued to agree so fully on the central issues at stake: the violation of international laws.

The cover letter began by pointing out Germany's failure "to understand the position in which Germany stands today," "as if this were but the end of some mere struggle for territory and power," that is, as if it were merely political.[43] Instead, the war was, in the judgment of "practically the whole of civilised mankind," "the greatest crime against humanity and the freedom of peoples that any nation, calling itself civilised, has every consciously committed." Germany, it said, had dedicated itself to the "doctrine that might was right in international affairs," and had set out to achieve "predominance in Europe by force." "Germany's responsibility, however is not confined to having planned and started the war. She is no less responsible for the savage and inhuman manner in which it was conducted." There followed a paragraph listing the methods and weapons that the Allies viewed as clear violations of international law. The letter then repeated a number of statements by Wilson, British prime minister David Lloyd George, and Clemenceau naming the chief Allied war aim as to "make Right the law of the world," quoting Wilson (speech of April 6, 1918). "Justice, therefore, is the only possible basis for the settlement of the accounts of this terrible war," and "reparation for wrongs inflicted is of the essence of justice." The Allies modified some economic and financial sections of the draft treaty but stuck by the reparations section. At the end, they announced that "in its principles they [the Allies and Associated powers] stand by the Treaty."

The lengthy official reply that followed was entirely consistent with its cover letter. In both the Allies pursued a dual process. On the one hand, they charged Imperial Germany with violations of international law, a clearly judicial matter pertaining mostly to how Germany had waged the war. On the other, they poured political content into legal forms. That is, as victors in a great war, they set about creating deterrents, mechanisms, guarantees, and precedents designed to establish "that reign of law among nations which it was the agreed object of the peace to set up" (962)—the legal order was meant to maintain peace in a stable European state system. The official reply and the cover letter both accorded with the private views of Wilson, Lloyd George, and Clemenceau.[44]

41. Michael Graham Fry, "British Revisionism," in *The Treaty of Versailles: A Reassessment after 75 Years*, ed. Manfred H. Boemeke, Gerald D. Feldman, and Elisabeth Glaser (Cambridge, 1998), 581.

42. Heinemann, *Verdrängte Niederlage*, 230, following Fritz Dickmann and Klaus Schwabe: Dickmann, *Kriegsschuldfrage*; Schwabe, "Versailles Nach 60 Jahren," *Neue Politische Literatur* 24 (1979): 446–75, esp. 451n17, where Schwabe points out how very interested Britain was in pursuing war crimes trials.

43. Reply of the Allied and Associated Powers to the Observations of the German Delegation on the Conditions of Peace (Clemenceau to Brockdorff-Rantzau), Paris, June 16, 1919, *FRUS, Paris Peace Conference 1919*, 6:926–35, here 926.

44. On Wilson's views on German guilt: Manfred F. Boemeke, "Woodrow Wilson's Image of Germany, the War-Guilt Question, and the Treaty of Versailles," in Boemeke, Feldman, and Glaser, *Treaty of Versailles*, 603–14; Lloyd George: Fry, "British Revisionism," 581–83, 598.

The ensuing "innocence campaign" redefined guilt in ways that made it easier to defend Germany (and the AA itself for its complicity in the July Crisis).[45] First, by focusing on "war guilt"—that is, on who began the war—the enormous question of how the war was conducted dropped from sight. For it was in the conduct of the war, beginning with the violation of Belgian neutrality, that most observers saw the clearest evidence of repeated and obvious violations of international law—starting an aggressive war was not yet an actual infraction of positive law (hence the reference to "international morality," instead of "law" in the Allied reply). The narrow focus on "war guilt" obscured Germany's more fundamental challenge to the legal order. Second, the AA's campaign displaced attention from the July Crisis, where it was easiest to see Germany's and Austria's bellicosity, to the complicated and often obscure diplomatic history of preceding decades.

Less than a month after Germany signed the treaty (June 28, 1919), the German cabinet approved the first phase of the campaign to revise it: the publication of Germany's prewar diplomatic documents (1871 to 1914).[46] The Schuldreferat controlled access to the documents and exercised veto power over publication. These forty volumes appeared from 1922 to 1927, the first of any nation's records to be open to historians. Formative in setting the standard historical record, *Die Große Politik* was tendentious and based in part on the suppression and destruction of records.[47] The *Grosse Politik* was just the beginning. The Schuldreferat also fed documents and legal briefs to the Reichstag committee investigating the war; orchestrated the suppression, delay, or timely publication and distribution of its lengthy, detail-ridden reports; created front organizations to combat the "war-guilt lie" in Germany and abroad (for example, in Norway, the Netherlands, Austria, Hungary, and Bulgaria) and secretly funneled government money to these organizations; arranged countless conferences and public lectures; published and translated books and pamphlets; falsified memoirs; and altogether dominated the public relations and the historical scholarship on the origins of the war during the entire interwar period.[48] It did these things clandestinely, and, because it was active in many countries, produced an international synergy of revisionist works in which the various recipients of its largesse reinforced one another and seemed part of an inexorable groundswell of enlightened opinion.

Through the well-financed Center for the Study of the Causes of the War (1921) led by the energetic Alfred von Wegerer, the "innocence campaign" especially targeted the

45. Hahn, "German Foreign Office," 69.

46. Germany and Auswärtiges Amt, *Die grosse Politik der Europäischen Kabinette, 1871–1914. Sammlung der Diplomatischen Akten des Auswärtigen Amtes,* ed. Johannes Lepsius, Albricht Mendelssohn Bartholdy, and Friedrich Thimme (Berlin, 1922–27).

47. Heinemann, *Verdrängte Niederlage,* 78–87; Herwig, "Clio Deceived," 95–98.

48. An early account of this clandestine activity: Hahn, "German Foreign Office." Now the best documented study: Heinemann, *Verdrängte Niederlage.* See also Herwig, "Clio Deceived"; Wolfgang Jäger, *Historische Forschung und politische Kultur in Deutschland; Die Debatte 1914–1980 über den Ausbruch des Ersten Weltkrieges* (Göttingen, 1984); Herman Wittgens, "Senator Owen, the Schuldreferat, and the Debate over War Guilt in the 1920s," in *Forging the Collective Memory: Government and International Historians through Two World Wars,* ed. Keith Wilson (Providence, RI, 1996), 128–50; Ellen L. Evans and Joseph O. Baylen, "History as Propaganda: The German Foreign Ministry and the 'Enlightenment' of American Historians on the War-Guilt Question, 1930–1933," in Wilson, *Forging the Collective Memory,* 151–77. My account follows these studies.

United States and American historians. The United States was important because the AA hoped to bring a revisionist America, which moreover never ratified the treaty, back into European politics on its side.[49] The center was guided by the Schuldreferat and aided by German embassies and consulates, each of which had a trained staff person dedicated to combating the "war-guilt lie" and ordered to provide lists of promising persons whom the center might influence.[50] In the United States, this list included major historians, of whom the most useful proved to be Sidney B. Fay (Harvard) and Harry Elmer Barnes (Smith). The AA's desired message was subtle: Germany bore some responsibility for the war, but it was shared with other powers. Gradually that message solidified into the theory that out-of-control, entangling alliances had caused Europe to slide into war; thus, no state was responsible. That was the conclusion of Fay's influential 1928 *The Origins of the War,* heavily based on the German documents; it was so useful that the AA bought a hundred or more copies, distributed them for free, and underwrote the French translation.[51] The enormous clandestine activity directed at American historians is well documented.[52] It was remarkably successful. The German consul in New York reported in June 1933 that most influential historians in the United States held views similar to Fay's—for example, scholars at Harvard (two), Princeton, Columbia, Virginia, and Stanford—whereas only one, Bernadotte E. Schmitt (Chicago), demurred.[53] In the words of one scholar, by 1929 "the Germans had largely won the battle of history."[54] The historian Holger Herwig notes that the success of revisionism "retarded critical appraisal of the origins of the war until the 1960s."[55] In fact, revisionism still dominates U.S. high school history textbooks and reappears in recent works presenting themselves as revisionist.[56] And, in a vicious cycle, revisionism encouraged isolationism and appeasement, and vice versa.[57]

For our purposes, however, the important point is that the innocence campaign's triumph necessarily obliterated from consciousness the legal interpretation against which it struggled with such success. Gone was the central importance of international law, both to how contemporary leaders (including Germans) fought the war, and to what they thought was at stake in it. Claims of systematic violations were now dismissed as mere war propaganda, and the shock at what happened to law during the war and the Allies' heated

---

49. Heinemann, *Verdrängte Niederlage,* 68, 232; Evans and Baylen, "History as Propaganda."

50. Heinemann, *Verdrängte Niederlage,* 112.

51. Sidney B. Fay, *The Origins of the World War* (New York, 1928), 2:250; Herwig, "Clio Deceived," 105; cf. Evans and Baylen, who say one hundred: Evans and Baylen, "History as Propaganda," 154. On Fay: Selig Adler, "The War-Guilt Question and American Disillusionment, 1918–1928," *Journal of Modern History* 23, no. 1 (March 1951): 11, 23.

52. Evans and Baylen, "History as Propaganda"; Adler, "War-Guilt." See also Jeff Lipkes, *Rehearsals: The German Army in Belgium, August 1914* (Leuven, 2007), ch. 15.

53. Evans and Baylen, "History as Propaganda," 168–69.

54. Adler, "War-Guilt," 21, cited in Evans and Baylen, "History as Propaganda," 170.

55. Herwig, "Clio Deceived," 119.

56. For example, Niall Ferguson, *The Pity of War: Explaining World War I* (New York, 1998), and Christopher Clark, *The Sleepwalkers: How Europe Went to War in 1914* (New York, 2012).

57. Adler, "War-Guilt," 27.

insistence on refounding an international legal order at Versailles and in the League of Nations became mere cant, or a fig leaf for Allied imperialism.[58]

For the most part, historians have accepted this state of affairs. Few modern histories of the First World War even mention international law in the index.[59] Few historians any longer recognize the importance of the violation of Belgian neutrality, either to Britain's entry into the war, or to setting the parameters by which contemporaries began to judge the conflict. Faced with claims and counterclaims concerning violations of the laws of war, too many historians despair of getting to the bottom of things and making a reasonable judgment. Instead, they refuse to judge; they fall back on the *tu quoque* defense. That position generally rests on the unspoken (and rarely examined) premise that every violation was equal, that every decision of statesmen or military leaders to break the law was taken for the same reasons, or taken as easily or thoughtlessly, or was arrived at in the same way, following the same procedure, or was justified or explained to themselves or the world with the same arguments, or in the same language. In fact, all of these things could, and often did, differ. These differences are critical to understanding why state leaders did what they did, what they thought was permissible, and why. Understanding these differences goes to the heart of what they thought the order of (European) states actually was and what it ought to be. Uncovering and analyzing these differences are major goals of this book.

The legacy of revisionism is even stronger in political science. There, international law disappeared even more completely because it disappeared theoretically, in the "realist" theory of international relations. One of the twin foundations of IR theory was the "realism" of the 1930s in such writings as those of E. H. Carr, whose rejection of what he identified as Wilsonian idealism led him, in the words of Stanley Hoffmann, to "swallow some of the 'tough' arguments which the revisionist powers such as Mussolini's Italy, Hitler's Germany, and the militaristic Japan had been using against the order of Versailles— arguments aimed at showing that idealism served the interests of the status quo powers."[60] The other foundation was the work of Hans Joachim Morgenthau, an international lawyer who fled Nazi Germany and who founded international relations theory in the United States after 1945.[61] This is not the place to rehearse Morgenthau's enormous and complicated

---

58. Key to demoting violations to propaganda: Arthur Ponsonby, *Faleshood in War-Time* (London, 1928), and James Morgan Read, *Atrocity Propaganda, 1914–1919* (New Haven, CT, 1941). The classic account of law as a cover for Allied imperialism: Carl Schmitt, "Völkerrechtliche Formen des modernen Imperialismus (1932)," in *Positionen und Begriffe im Kampf mit Weimar-Genf-Versailles 1923–1939* (Berlin, 1994), 184–203.

59. Of twenty recent works owned by Cornell University, only three devoted enough attention to the subject to list it in the index: Volker R. Berghahn, *Der Erste Weltkrieg* (Munich, 2003); Hew Strachan, *The First World War*, vol. 1, *To Arms* (Oxford, 2001); and Daniel Marc Segesser, *Der Erste Weltkrieg* (Wiesbaden, 2010).

60. Stanley Hoffmann, "An American Social Science," in *Janus and Minerva: Essays in the Theory and Practice of International Politics*, ed. Stanley Hoffmann (Boulder, CO, 1987), 5. Edward Hallett Carr, *International Relations since the Peace Treaties* (London, 1937); Edward Hallett Carr, *The Twenty Years' Crisis, 1919–1939: An Introduction to the Study of International Relations* (London, 1940); E. H. Carr, *Propaganda in International Politics* (New York, 1939).

61. On the influence of Weimar thinkers on U.S. political science: Martti Koskenniemi, *The Gentle Civilizer of Nations: The Rise and Fall of International Law, 1870–1960* (Cambridge, 2001), 465–67.

influence, especially on American political science.[62] But, briefly, the "six principles of political realism" that Morgenthau identified in his seminal book *Politics among Nations* (1954) accept fundamental assumptions about states, the international system, and hence about international law that characterized Imperial Germany and its Weimar apologists. It is not too much to say that Imperial Germany became a kind of model state for theory. The political realist, wrote Morgenthau, believes in "objective laws that have their roots in human nature," which, on the state level, meant "the concept of interest defined in terms of power."[63] The state was in essence the power state (*Machtstaat*) of Wilhelminian conviction.[64] In a sentence that might have summed up the Weimar critique of the Treaty of Versailles, Morgenthau's fifth principle was that "political realism refuses to identify the moral aspirations of a particular nation with the moral laws that govern the universe" (10). Politics was an independent sphere following its own laws, autonomous from those of the economy, law, and morality (10). A collection of states running on these principles was perforce anarchic. Although Morgenthau never denied the existence of international law, and indeed recommended it to statesmen as prudent, in a system of power states it inevitably became demoted from an obligatory system of rules created by the state community to an expression of morality or ethics coming from outside the power-state system, an expression of the "moral reluctance to use unlimited violence as an instrument of international politics" (216). Its efficacy depended on "complementary interests of individual states and the distribution of power among them. Where there is neither community of interests nor balance of power, there is no international law" (252). Morgenthau remained ambivalent about international law, for on the one hand, he thought the actual community of interest among states sufficient for them to comply voluntarily with the law most of the time (271–72), but on the other, his theory of power/interest meant that law had no real ground or worth in itself—it remained always contingent and likely to be swept away in the first, inevitable power struggle. Many of Morgenthau's followers were less ambivalent; in their writings international law became more ephemeral and contingent, and therefore it was rarely a factor in international relations.[65] On this view, international law could hardly have played an important role in the First World War.

The chapters that follow return to the voluminous internal governmental and diplomatic correspondence to show both how critical international law was to the conduct of the war and to what the conflict was about. Out of the sea of controversies we examine seven central issues that illustrate how law constrained decision makers, when and why it did not, and how law actually operated and changed. The method is for the most part

---

62. An excellent introduction: William E. Scheuerman, *Morgenthau,* Key Contemporary Thinkers (Malden, MA, 2009).

63. Hans J. Morgenthau, *Politics among Nations* (New York, 1954), 4, 5.

64. Hoffmann, "American Social Science," 7, on Morgenthau's borrowings from Heinrich von Treitschke and Max Weber.

65. See the discussions of: Stanley Hoffmann, "International Systems and International Law," in *The International System: Theoretical Essays,* ed. Klaus Knorr and Sidney Verba (Princeton, NJ, 1961), 205–37; Stanley Hoffmann, "Is There an International Order?" in Hoffmann, *Janus and Minerva,* 85–121; Morton A. Kaplan and Nicholas deB. Katzenbach, *The Political Foundations of International Law* (New York, 1961), esp. ch. 1, 3–29.

comparative and pays close attention to the inner workings of governmental decision making. Unfortunately, chronology forces us to handle first three subjects—the violation of Belgian neutrality, land warfare, and occupation—that early on set the legal arguments that defined the war. These three subjects do not lend themselves to comparison because they overwhelmingly involve Imperial Germany's policies and not those of the Western Allies. The other four subjects permit comparison: the blockade versus unrestricted submarine warfare, the introduction of new weapons, and the use of reprisals. We turn to the first great shock to international law, the violation of Belgian neutrality.

Belgian Neutrality

The First World War began with an international crime: Germany's violation of Belgian neutrality. The issue considered in this chapter is not why Germany went to war in 1914. I have excluded the controversies over the origins of the war, Germany's role in starting it, and its war aims, in order to focus squarely on international law during the conflict itself. In any case, in 1914 launching an aggressive war was not forbidden in international law, though public and state opinion were changing. The avalanche of documents each government immediately published to prove its innocence and the Allied charge at the peace treaty that German aggression had violated "international morality" show the growing condemnation of aggressive war that has indeed become law in our own time.[1] But in 1914 the first incontrovertible issue of law raised by the war was Germany's violation of Belgium's guaranteed neutrality. That act, epitomized in Chancellor Theobald von Bethmann Hollweg's phrase "scrap of paper," instantly became a staple of Allied propaganda. The postwar reaction against the propaganda campaign has helped to erase the importance of Belgian neutrality as a matter over which the war was fought, as a cause of Britain's entrance into the war, and as an indicator of the role of international law in the war. At issue was the legal order of the European state system. This chapter examines what the invasion of Belgium put at risk.

---

1. Art. 227 of the Versailles Treaty arraigned Wilhelm II "for a supreme offence against international morality and the sanctity of treaties," thus combining the charge of launching an aggressive war with violating the treaty guaranteeing Belgium's neutrality. Treaty of Versailles, available on the Avalon Project website at http://avalon.law.yale.edu/subject_menus/versailles_menu.asp. For the "colored books" of diplomatic correspondence: Luigi Albertini, *The Origins of the War of 1914* (Oxford, 1952–57), 3:703–8; also, Annika Mombauer, *Origins of the First World War: Controversies and Consensus* (New York, 2002), 23, 24, 27, 32, 41.

The Treaty of 1839

The 1830 revolution in Paris sparked the Belgian provinces to break away from the Kingdom of the Netherlands. The resulting power struggle between France, which would have liked to dominate the new state, and the Netherlands, which wanted to retain the provinces, caused the great powers to intervene. They created in 1831 an independent Belgium. Not until 1839 did the Netherlands agree to that creation. In two separate treaties signed in London on April 19, 1839, the five European great powers (France, Britain, Russia, Prussia, and Austria) and Belgium and the Netherlands set down the final borders and conditions for Belgian independence. The treaty said that "under the auspices of the Courts of Great Britain, Austria, France, Prussia, and Russia," Belgium became "an Independent and perpetually Neutral State...bound to observe such Neutrality towards all other States."[2] Thus the great powers became guarantors of Belgium's independence and neutrality *in their own interest*. Belgium's interest was that the independence it was unlikely to be able to defend by itself was guaranteed by major military powers, but at the cost of giving up an entirely independent foreign policy. Belgian neutrality was a European creation, a way to end war over the issue of its independence and above all to prevent any great power, especially France at this juncture, from becoming hegemonic in the region.

The Treaty of London of 1839 was a strong treaty. Every major European power was a signatory. It was a "lawmaking" treaty, setting down international borders, recognizing a new state, and enacting major foreign-policy conditions for all states in future (that is, all states having intercourse with Belgium were to do so within the confines of its neutrality). Because it occurred under the "auspices" of the major military and naval powers, it suggested the strong sanctions that threatened violators. It also contained two trajectories of legal development: first, the principle of the right of small states to exist, and second, the rejection of Continental hegemony as an acceptable foreign policy for any European state.[3] As a fundamental, lawmaking treaty, the Treaty of London would not be annulled by the outbreak of war; it retained its validity.[4] For all these reasons, the treaty of 1839 was a paradigmatic example of positive international law, the sort of treaty that even contemporary skeptics accepted as having the qualities of law.

The Treaty of London was a cornerstone of European international law. It was part of the international system developed in the wake of the Napoleonic Wars to regularize and contain state relations and conflict through law. That principle was famously stated in the Declaration of the 1818 Congress of Aix-la-Chapelle, in which the leaders of the great powers promised "to observe as the fundamental basis [of their relations] their invariable

---

2. Edward Hertslet, *The Map of Europe by Treaty; Showing the Various Political and Territorial Changes Which Have Taken Place since the General Peace of 1814* (London, 1875), art. 1 and art. 7 of Annex, pp. 981 and 985.

3. On incompatability of a hegemon with international law: Franz von Holtzendorff, *Handbuch des Völkerrechts. Auf Grundlage europäischer Staatspraxis*, vol. 1, Einleitung in das Völkerrecht (Berlin, 1885), 52, 66–67.

4. On lawmaking treaties: Lassa Oppenheim, *International Law: A Treatise* (London, 1905), 1:518 [para. 18], 2:108 [para. 99], and 1:563–68.

resolution never to deviate, neither among themselves nor in their relations with other states, from the strictest observation of the principles of the laws of nations [*droit des gens*]" which they regarded "as the only effective guarantee of the independence of each government and the stability of the general association."[5]

Making law the basis of inter-state relations contained several principles or assumptions worth examining. First, statesmen (and jurists) considered international law to be formed by the community of European states acting together. No state could form law by itself; the independence and development of each could occur only inside the community.[6] As a result, second, international law was in the states' interest; that is, state self-interest and the legal restraints emanating from the community did not fundamentally conflict.[7] No one denied that states might disagree about its content, or that particular state interests might change, but nineteenth- and early twentieth-century legal writers shared the view that the *legal state system* was "necessary" for every state.[8] Third, treaties (especially general treaties intended to set law for the future) were thought to be especially clear instances of law because as written documents they were often easier to interpret than binding custom, and they more closely resembled codified state law that positivists and Continental lawyers recognized. Fourth, while jurists and statesmen disagreed about many things (the relation of treaty to customary law, the bindingness of general treaties on non-signatories, the validity of reservations to treaty articles, and ratification requirements), no one doubted that treaty law presupposed a rule binding states to fulfill their treaty obligations. That requirement was often called "good faith"; it acquired the Latin tag *pacta sunt servanda*—agreements must be kept.[9] This rule was understood to be a necessary foundation of international life without which normal relations would be simply impossible; it was a general duty to the community as a whole, not simply to one's contracting partner. Good faith played a critical role during the World War, as leaders judged whether their enemies could be trusted to keep their word.

But everyone also recognized that occasionally changed circumstances justified voiding treaty obligations. Before 1914, jurists generally identified three cases: when changed conditions made fulfillment actually impossible; when changes in shared values invalidated the basis of previous treaties (for example, concerning slavery); or when the preconditions or assumptions behind a treaty had changed so radically that it no longer made

---

5. Johann Caspar Bluntschli, *Le droit international codifié,* trans. C. Lardy (Paris, 1874), 55n2; Oppenheim, *International Law,* 1:66; Henry Bonfils, *Manuel de droit international public (droit des gens) aux étudiants des facultés de droit et aux aspirants aux fonctions diplomatiques et consulaires* (Paris, 1912), para. 809.

6. Representative: Bluntschli, *Droit international,* 54; Holtzendorff, *Handbuch,* 7; Heinrich Triepel, *Völkerrecht und Landesrecht* (Leipzig, 1899), 32; Bonfils, *Manuel* (1912), 23.

7. John Westlake, *International Law; Part II: War* (Cambridge, 1907), 1:15; Bonfils, *Manuel* (1912), para. 47.

8. Holtzendorff, *Handbuch,* 20–21, 45, 65, 81; William Edward Hall, *A Treatise on International Law* (Oxford, 1904), 5–6; Bonfils, *Manuel* (1912), 23.

9. Hugo Grotius, *The Rights of War and Peace Including the Law of Nature and of Nations,* A. C. Campbell (Chestnut Hill, MA, 2003), ch. 19, para. 1, and ch. 21, para. 1; Vattel: Hans Wehberg, "Pacta Sunt Servanda," *American Journal of International Law* 53, no. 4 (October 1959): 779; Holtzendorff, *Handbuch,* 61; Pasquale Fiore, *Nouveau droit international public, suivant les besoins de la civilisation moderne* (Paris, 1885–86), para. 971; Hall, *International Law,* 43, 55; Oppenheim, *International Law,* 1:519–20; Bonfils, *Manuel* (1912), para. 845.

sense.[10] Some writers seemed to recognize broader justifications in the interest of states' development.[11] But writers commonly acknowledged the dangers posed by the claim of changed circumstances (known as *rebus sic stantibus*—things standing thus). If it were elevated to equal status with *pacta sunt servanda,* then "all obligation would cease," as Swiss jurist Johann Caspar Bluntschli noted; it "would make the existence of conventional international law impossible."[12] And so writers before the war (and since) described *rebus* as a "clause," "condition," "doctrine," or "exception," but not generally as a "rule" or "principle"—the words used for *pacta.* Among the limits commonly placed on the *rebus* exception were these: states were not supposed to exercise it by fait accompli; instead, they were to articulate their objections, and if necessary renegotiate with their treaty partner(s). Some writers suggested that *rebus* might only be claimed for certain classes of treaties.[13]

State practice also strongly favored *pacta sunt servanda* over *rebus sic stantibus* in the nineteenth century. Britain's influential jurist Lassa Oppenheim noted how few states used the clause, apparently for fear that doing so "would certainly destroy all [a state's] credit among the nations."[14] The most famous case involved Russia's 1870 renunciation of the clauses in the 1856 Treaty of Paris that banned Russian warships from the Black Sea—a price for Russia's loss in the Crimean War. As Europe became preoccupied by the Franco-Prussian War, Russia claimed that changed circumstances and occasional violations of the treaty entitled it to declare the clauses null and void.[15] Britain protested strongly, not because it feared Russian warships—even seven years later Russia had still stationed none on the Black Sea—but because of the acidic consequences of the *rebus* principle.[16] Foreign Secretary George Leveson-Gower, Earl Granville, did not dispute the possibility that changed circumstances might lead to renegotiation of an out-of-date treaty; doing so unilaterally, however, as "the only judge," was "a very dangerous precedent as to the validity of international obligations."[17] Supported by the other great powers, Britain forced Russia to the conference table. There, Russia received what it wanted, but only after the agreement of all other signatories. In agreeing to the conference, Russia renounced the *rebus* claim. More important, Russia, Britain, France, (North) Germany, Austria, Italy, and Turkey all signed a protocol stating "that it is an essential principle of the Law of Nations that no Power can liberate itself from the engagements of a Treaty, nor modify the stipulations thereof, unless with the consent of the Contracting Powers by means of an amicable arrangement."[18]

---

10. Fiore, *Nouveau droit international public,* para. 1052; Hall, *International Law,* 350; Bonfils, *Manuel* (1912), paras. 856–57.

11. See Hall on Bluntschli and Fiore: Hall, *International Law,* 358–59.

12. Bluntschli, *Droit international,* para. 456, p. 259; Oppenheim, *International Law,* 1:550–53, para. 539.

13. Westlake, *International Law,* 1:304–5.

14. Oppenheim, *International Law,* 1: para. 539, p. 551.

15. Hertslet, *Map of Europe,* 3: nos. 429–31 and 433.

16. A. J. P. Taylor, *The Struggle for Mastery in Europe, 1848–1918* (Oxford, 1954), 215–16.

17. Granville to Sir A. Buchanan, London, Nov. 10, 1870, cited as no. 431 in Hertslet, *Map of Europe,* 3: 1898–1900.

18. Protocol of Jan. 17, 1871, signed by the powers above (Germany was in the process of unification, so its signature appears as "North Germany"): Hertslet, *Map of Europe,* 3: 1904. See Hall, *International Law,* 351–57; Henry Bonfils and Paul Fauchille, *Manuel de droit international public (droit des gens)* (Paris, 1908), paras. 857–58.

The 1839 treaty guaranteeing Belgian neutrality was therefore a strong document deeply embedded in the European legal order. However, it did not specify the nature of the guarantee. A joint, or joint and several, guarantee would have obligated each guarantor separately to intervene to uphold the treaty, even if the other guarantors shirked their duty. A collective guarantee required all guarantors to act together; none was obligated to act alone. However, even a collective guarantee permitted a single guarantor to uphold the treaty itself. Collective guarantees were weaker, and in the immediate years after 1839, European statesmen interpreted the guarantee as collective.[19] But after mid-century, attitudes hardened, especially among British leaders. By 1867 Prime Minister Edward Stanley, Lord Derby, flatly, and incorrectly, informed the House of Lords that the Belgian treaty "was binding individually and separately upon each of the Powers."[20] Derby's statement shows that in the intervening years British policy was determined to uphold Belgian neutrality even alone.

Three years later, the Franco-Prussian War provided a test-run for 1914. Both France and the leader of the German forces, Prussia, announced that they would respect Belgium's neutrality unless the other violated it first. That vow was insufficient for Britain. Prime Minister William Ewart Gladstone concluded two identical treaties with France and Prussia pledging that Britain would join with the unoffending power using "her naval and military forces to insure [the] observance" of Belgium's neutrality and integrity, without however engaging in "the general operations" of war. He explained to the House of Commons that the government had intended to head off a dual violation in which both powers blamed the other for acting first: it was "the combination, and not the opposition, of the two Powers which we had to fear."[21] Britain was thus erasing another misstatement of law that Lord Derby had announced in 1867, namely that if a guarantor violated a treaty, it was nullified, freeing the other guarantors from their duty. Since the guarantors of Belgium and Luxembourg (neutralized by treaty in 1867) were for military and geographical reasons also the most likely potential violators, Derby's construction would have eviscerated the whole project of guarantee. The former foreign minister and prime minister, John, Earl Russell, had corrected Derby at the time, but Gladstone's treaty made Britain's position clear.[22]

As they did in 1914, radical liberals split over the issue in 1870. Radical leader Jacob Bright excoriated the new treaty as a "quixotic expedition"; in his view Britain had to

---

19. Subsequent investigators have agreed with them: Ernst Satow, "*Pacta Sunt Servanda* or International Guarantee," *Cambridge Historical Journal* 1, no. 3 (1925): 295–318; Daniel H. Thomas, *The Guarantee of Belgian Independence and Neutrality in European Diplomacy, 1830s–1930s* (Kingston, RI, 1983), 586–87.

20. Great Britain, Parliament, *Hansard's Parliamentary Debates,* vol. 183, House of Lords debates, June 20, 1867, 150 (hereafter *Hansard*), available at http://hansard.millbanksystems.com/. The next foreign minister, the Earl of Clarendon, agreed with Derby's interpretation, which seemed uncontroversial; ibid., 152. On the hardening interpretation of Belgian guarantee: Horst Lademacher, *Die belgische Neutralität als Problem der europäischen Politik, 1830–1914* (Bonn, 1971), 483–88; Thomas, *Guarantee,* 580–87. Derby partly quoted in Lademacher, *Belgische Neutralität,* 221.

21. Gladstone, House of Commons, August 10, 1870, *Hansard,* 3rd ser., vol. 203:1788.

22. Russell in House of Lords, June 20, 1867, *Hansard,* 3rd ser., vol. 183:158. See also Oppenheim's refutation of Derby: Oppenheim, *International Law,* 1:575 (para. 576).

remain "entirely free from Continental entanglements" and to engage in no Continental war "on any pretext whatever."[23] His followers tried to diminish Britain's obligations under the 1839 treaty, arguing that they were merely collective and not individual.[24] One railed against "secret diplomacy," declaring that "I have myself lost all faith in diplomacy."[25] But this same speaker revealed the radicals' dilemma, for he thought that even so it might be necessary to fight "to maintain not only our honour, but our liberties"—that is, to fight for law's sake as well as for security interests.

It was in response to the radicals' criticisms that Prime Minister Gladstone made his longest speech explaining the relation between law and British interests. He made four points. First, he rejected the characterization of Britain's interest in upholding Belgian neutrality as "the specially distinct, separate, and exclusive interest" of Britain alone. "It is the same as that of every great Power in Europe. It is contrary to the interest of Europe that there should be unmeasured aggrandizement."[26] Belgian neutrality was thus a *European* interest.

Second, he responded to the radicals' fear that treaty engagements might automatically pull Britain into a Continental war. He denied that a treaty of guarantee was "binding on every party to it irrespectively altogether of the particular position in which it may find itself at the time." Some historians have thought that Gladstone's remark gave radicals in 1914 an opening to deny the treaty's obligation.[27] But given the context in which Gladstone pressed strongly and unequivocally for intervention, it seems likely that the prime minister was not announcing a doctrine of policy over legality, but simply noting that legal obligation is always subject, as the American jurist James Wilford Garner wrote, to "the conceivable inability of one of the guaranteeing powers at a given moment, resulting from exceptional circumstances, to fulfil the obligations imposed by the treaty."[28]

This interpretation is strengthened by Gladstone's next point, that Belgium's good government based on the "liberty of the people" would disappear without the guarantee. The day that it was absorbed by another power would sound the death knell "of public right and public law in Europe."[29] This was a strong identification of Britain's, and the Liberals', interest with law per se.

Gladstone then continued, "We have an interest in the independence of Belgium which is wider than that"—to avoid the moral ignominy of having quietly stood by as a witness to "the perpetration of the direst crime that ever stained the pages of history, and thus becom[ing] participators in the sin."[30] Gladstone's rhetoric had climbed the ladder from the European interest to prevent aggrandizement, to the practical obligations of treaties, to the sanctity of law, to morality. He had laid out the palette of reasons that decision

23. Bright, House of Commons, Aug. 9, 1870, *Hansard, 3rd ser., vol. 203*:1740.

24. Sir Wilfrid Lawson, House of Commons, Aug. 9, 1870, ibid.

25. Osborne, House of Commons, Aug. 10, 1870, ibid., 1777–78.

26. Ibid., 1786.

27. Thomas, *Guarantee,* 511; Keith M. Wilson, "Britain," in *Decisions for War, 1914,* ed. Keith M. Wilson (New York, 1995), 189.

28. James Wilford Garner, *International Law and the World War* (London, 1920), 2:229.

29. Gladstone, House of Commons, Aug. 10, 1870, *Hansard,* 3rd ser., vol. 203:1788.

30. Ibid.

makers in 1914 debated again. And for Gladstone, as for most British leaders in his time and later, these reasons coincided and reinforced one another.

Britain was the strongest supporter of the legal obligation to protect Belgium's independence and neutrality. But in 1870 both France and Prussia quickly agreed to Gladstone's supplementary treaty, and Austria and Russia indicated their approval.[31] The European interest in preventing the emergence of a Continental hegemon inevitably using war to achieve that position, and their interest in orderly, regular (legal) relations, remained very strong. Belgian neutrality was the result and symbol of that intertwined interest.

Only once did Britain hesitate in its policy of guarantee. That was in 1887 when France, egged on by the unstable populist war minister Georges Ernest Boulanger, appeared ready to attack Germany through Belgium. Britain's default policy is visible in the immediate assurances of its ambassadors to Brussels and Vienna that Britain would automatically come to Belgium's aid. The exasperated prime minister, Robert Gascoyne-Cecil, Third Marquess of Salisbury, reined them in. "It is very difficult to prevent oneself from wishing for another Franco-German war," he sighed, "to put a stop to this incessant vexation."[32] Boulanger's removal ended the crisis before the British government had to make up its mind. Salisbury's unique view was based on his expectation that Germany would defeat France by itself, without help from Britain, and that Chancellor Otto von Bismarck's "satiated," conservative foreign policy meant that Germany would never annex Belgium or infringe on its postwar independence.[33] By 1914 neither of those latter assumptions was true.

Germany and Belgian Neutrality

Imperial Germany's legal obligation to respect Belgian neutrality was universally acknowledged by German statesmen and diplomats. They understood the new German state to be the legal successor to Prussia and bound by its treaties. In 1887 Bismarck repeated Germany's pledge not to violate Belgian neutrality. During and even after the First World War, the AA's official position was always that Germany was bound by the 1839 treaty. In his unpublished legal brief defending the invasion, the chief of the AA's legal division, Johannes Kriege, admitted that Germany's action broke the 1831 and 1839 treaties and the firm principle of customary international law establishing the inviolability of neutral territory.[34] But after Wilhelm II dismissed Bismarck in 1890, military planning soon diverged from legal principle.

---

31. Gladstone, House of Commons, Aug. 8, 1870, ibid., 1701.

32. William E. Lingelbach, "Belgian Neutrality: Its Origin and Interpretation," *American Historical Review* 39, no. 1 (October 1933): 69.

33. This is also the view of Thomas, *Guarantee,* 586–87, 591. Both Bismarck and Chief of the General Staff Helmuth von Moltke publicly guaranteed Belgium's neutrality during the crisis: Gerhard Ritter, *The Schlieffen Plan: Critique of a Myth* (London, 1958), 80–81.

34. Johannes Kriege, "Entwurf einer Denkschrift über die Verletzung der belgischen Neutralität durch Deutschland für den Parlamentarischen Untersuchungs-Ausschuss des Reichstages," no date, 9, AA/PA, Kriege Papers, vol. 4, no. 25; Frhr v. Mumm to K. A. Fuehr, Berlin, Jan. 6, 1915, BAB R 901 86588, copy.

It is important to underscore that all governments "plan," or rather discuss, policy options across the widest spectrum, including potential treaty violations, and militaries tend to plan for the worst-case scenarios, regardless of legal limits. In the prewar period one can find British and French military leaders, and even high-ranking civilians, favoring quick troop movements through Belgium to strike at the (German) enemy. As Jonathan Steinberg writes, the difference between these discussions and those in Germany was that Germany put its plans into practice.[35] But there are other differences, too—some commonly remarked upon, others more obscure, visible only in the patterns of decision making over time. These differences concern the structure of government and the political culture it produced, the quality of the Kaiser's leadership, and governing assumptions about international law, most famously about military necessity, but also about fundamental issues of state sovereignty, neutrality, and the relation of military power to international law.

The Schlieffen Plan

General Alfred von Schlieffen became chief of the general staff in 1890. The following year he began considering Belgium the key to solving Germany's geographical problem in a possible two-front war against France and Russia. A quick strike at France via Belgium, sweeping north of the heavily fortified Franco-German border, might destroy France before Russia was fully mobilized; a disastrous two-front war would thus be converted into two, quick one-front wars in which Germany could use its full strength against each foe. By 1897, Schlieffen had formally incorporated the invasion of Belgium into the plan, where it remained the core of German military strategy for the next seventeen years.[36] Actually, Schlieffen's plan called for violating three neutral countries, two guaranteed by international convention (Belgium and Luxembourg) and one pursuing its own neutral policy (the Netherlands). Around 1908, Schlieffen's successor, General Helmuth von Moltke (the younger), dropped the invasion of the Netherlands, concentrating all of Germany's troops through Belgium and Luxembourg.[37]

Germany's constitutional structure conspired to prevent coordinated decision making between its military and civilian parts. Lacking a cabinet and possessing a privileged military whose prerogatives included direct personal access to the Kaiser without the chancellor or foreign secretary, Imperial Germany had no formal venue in which the

---

35. Jonathan Steinberg, "A German Plan for the Invasion of Holland and Belgium, 1897," in *The War Plans of the Great Powers, 1880–1914,* ed. Paul J. Kennedy (Boston, 1985), 160. Germany's later *tu quoque* defense claimed that the Allied invasion of Salonika in 1915 was the equivalent of Germany's violation of Belgian neutrality. The two cases are quite different. The complexity of the Greek case deserves and requires a full account impossible within the confines of this book. For a beginning see Garner, *International Law,* 2:241–55.

36. Gerhard Ritter, *Staatskunst und Kriegshandwerk; Das Problem des "Militarismus" in Deutschland* (Munich, 1964), 2:247.

37. Annika Mombauer, *Helmuth von Moltke and the Origins of the First World War* (Cambridge, 2001), 94–97.

general staff's military plans were vetted for their political, economic, legal, or other deficiencies. Between 1890 and 1914 no joint meeting was ever held to discuss the army's plans.[38] Instead, three years after the Belgian invasion had been formally adopted into Germany's military plan, Schlieffen for the first time privately sent an intermediary, Count Bogdan von Hutten-Czapski, to the foreign office's head of political affairs, Baron Friedrich von Holstein. Schlieffen had told Hutten-Czapski of his conclusion that in a two-front war, Germany "could not let its operations be limited by existing international agreements."[39] Informed of Schlieffen's views, Holstein replied: "If the chief of the general staff and especially a strategic authority like Schlieffen says such a measure is necessary, then it is the diplomat's duty to adjust to it and prepare for it if possible." The next day Holstein and Hutten-Czapski went together to Chancellor Chlodwig von Hohenlohe, who said nothing. Hohenlohe may, or may not, have discussed the issue directly with Schlieffen at a dinner party that Hutten-Czapski arranged a few days later.

In 1905, outgoing chief of staff Schlieffen prepared a long memorandum on his plan that of course included the violation of the three neutral states; one draft of this document bears the notation "discussed with the chancellor," who was by then Hohenlohe's successor, Bernhard von Bülow.[40] Bülow is notorious for his troubled relationship to the truth, and after the war he struggled to present himself as a wise critic of the plan. He admitted in a 1921 interview that, had he been chancellor in 1914, "perhaps I would have allowed myself to be convinced of the military expediency of a march through Belgium...but certainly not until the enemy had invaded first, or the Belgian attitude had been proved to be hostile."[41] However, the week after the invasion, Bülow had more candidly told the editor of the *Berliner Tageblatt,* Theodor Wolff, "that he considered the march through Belgium and the violation of neutrality as correct."[42] Gerhard Ritter is surely right to conclude that, when Bethmann Hollweg became chancellor in 1909, he must have felt that he had inherited a military plan long accepted by his two predecessors.[43]

The high point, if one may call it that, of civil-military cooperation in planning occurred between 1911 and 1914, as real war threatened. Chief of Staff von Moltke (the younger) wanted the diplomats to prepare the ground for the coming invasion. On December 21, 1912, Kaiser Wilhelm reported to Moltke and Bethmann his recent conversation with King Albert in which the Kaiser had assured the Belgian monarch that in a coming war Germany wished merely to protect its right flank. On that same day, Moltke sent the only written notification the general staff ever produced of its invasion plan, one copy going to the chancellor and the other to the Prussian war minister.[44] Three weeks later, Gottlieb von

---

38. Ritter, *Staatskunst,* 2:254; Ritter, *Schlieffen Plan,* 92.

39. Bogdan von Hutten-Czapski, *Sechzig Jahre Politik und Gesellschaft* (Berlin, 1936), 371, 371–73; see also the account in Ritter, *Staatskunst,* 2:255, and Ritter, *Schlieffen Plan,* 91–92.

40. Ritter, *Schlieffen Plan,* 79.

41. Cited ibid., 92.

42. Diary entry of Aug. 12, 1914, *Theodor Wolff. Tagebücher 1914–1919; Der Erste Weltkrieg und die Entstehung der Weimarer Republik in Tagebüchern, Leitartikeln und Briefen des Chefredakteurs am "Berliner Tageblatt" und Mitbegründer der "Deutschen Demokratischen Partei,"* ed. Bernd Sösemann (Boppard am Rhein, 1984), 72.

43. Ritter, *Schlieffen Plan,* 94, and Hutten-Czapski, *Sechzig Jahre,* 372–73.

44. Mombauer, *Moltke,* 157–58.

Jagow became foreign secretary. Jagow made the sole concerted effort by the civilian leadership to change the plan. In early February 1913, Jagow met with Moltke and objected that Germany's violation of Belgian neutrality would cause Britain to enter the war.[45] Neither Moltke nor his fellow army leaders were unduly troubled, because they had long believed that Britain would fight against them in any case. Jagow pressed the issue, insisting that it should come before the Kaiser. Moltke used his military prerogative and met with the Kaiser without Jagow or the chancellor, so no complete, political reconsideration occurred. Furthermore, Jagow recorded no support for his intervention from the chancellor. Nevertheless, Wilhelm's remark to Jagow, "yes, I've spoken with Moltke that the operation plan should be changed," suggests that the Kaiser and military leaders did rethink the matter one last time.[46] Jagow learned that Moltke had canvassed "a group of high-ranking officers," and significantly, a minority favored changing the war plan. But most clung to operational wisdom that "victory over Russia *and* France was only possible if the latter were defeated *quickly* before Russia could become completely able to act.... So the march through Belgium was unfortunately unavoidable."[47] That was the state of affairs in August 1914.

The above pattern has a number of remarkable characteristics. First, only the chief of the general staff's perception that he needed something from another ministry (diplomatic preparation from the AA, increased troops from the war minister) moved him to contact them formally. Otherwise, "discussions" were informal, oral, random, and seriatim—that is, never in groups where strategic synergy or debate might occur. Second, no chancellor appears ever to have taken the initiative to find out what the military planned to do in the event of war. Third, all the civilian leaders, except possibly Jagow, were prepared to subordinate their misgivings to military expertise. That subordination had two aspects: it reflected the habit of Wilhelminian governance that allowed a maximum of autonomy and a minimum of interference for bureaucrats operating inside their own sphere (called *Ressortpartikularismus* by its critics); and it embodied the general subordination of civilian to military matters. The latter meant that after Bismarck, who had never adopted that precept, civilian leaders granted to the military the right to define national security, which it did in a narrowly technical fashion stripped of nonmilitary considerations. The rubric under which the military construed its purview was "military necessity."

Military Necessity and Preemptive Self-Defense

In international law, military necessity is the general cover for wartime acts that, for example, makes killing soldiers lawful, rather than criminal (murder).[48] During the Bismarckian and Wilhelminian eras, Germany developed a uniquely robust doctrine of

---

45. This account follows Mombauer: ibid., 159–60. See also Ritter, *Staatskunst*, 2:271.

46. AA/PA, Nl. Jagow, vol. 8, pt. 1, "Politische Aufsätze," "Der Durchmarsch durch Belgien," fol. 50.

47. Ibid., fols. 50–51; emphasis in original.

48. This discussion follows my previous article, Isabel V. Hull, "'Military Necessity' and the Laws of War in Imperial Germany," in *Order, Conflict, Violence*, ed. Stathis Kalyvas, Ian Shapiro, and Tarek Masoud (Cambridge, 2008), 352–77.

military necessity thought to apply to many levels of action from the tactical (combat), to operational (battle), and at the level of the state itself (war and peace). We shall examine the development of "military necessity" regarding the first two levels in the next chapter. The violation of Belgium—that is, harming a third party in the course of pursuing a war against another enemy—belongs to the highest category of military necessity, or simply the necessity of self-defense. Self-defense remained Germany's official justification, from the chancellor's speech to the Reichstag on August 4, 1914, to the AA's (unpublished) legal defense in the 1920s. We will examine that justification in greater detail below; here we must briefly consider the international legal limits to state self-defense and the internal mechanisms predisposing the Kaiserreich to override them.

Self-defense is a valid international-legal argument. Self-defense (taking up arms to defend against actual or imminent military attack) ought to be distinguished from the wider concept of self-preservation. Because all prewar legal texts took the state as the atomic unit of international law, most repeated that the preservation of states is a necessary function of international law; some went further, granting to states "a right of existence" that authorized them "to have recourse to all natural measures to safeguard their physical and moral integrity so as to avert all actual or possible [*éventuel*] dangers."[49] Fearful that such a wide writ would undermine law entirely, other jurists defined self-preservation as merely a "governing condition" of international law, not a "source of specific rules";[50] that is, it was not a law-generating principle. Oppenheim's definition (1905) addresses the problem posed in 1914: "It is frequently maintained that every violation is excused as long as it was caused by the motive of self-preservation, but it becomes more and more recognised that violations of other States in the interest of self-preservation are excused in cases of *necessity* only."[51] An unreal danger or one that could be averted otherwise would not excuse such action. Despite the fact that disagreement over where to draw the line continues today, prewar customary law had developed fairly well-defined limits to the plea of necessary self-defense.[52]

Since Hugo Grotius (1583–1645), statesmen and international lawyers had accepted necessity as excusing inherently unlawful actions, but only under the following circumstances: the state must be responding to a vital, imminent danger; must respond proportionately, not excessively; and must offer restitution for damages. Unanimity of opinion among such diverse thinkers as Grotius, Machiavelli, Hobbes, Montesquieu, and Vattel shows how firmly entrenched in customary law were these limits.[53] The nineteenth century further defined them. The prewar customary law of necessity was famously expressed by Secretary of State Daniel Webster to Alexander Baring, Lord Ashburton, in 1842 as the United States and Great Britain settled their claims in the *Caroline* case. Webster wrote that a state claiming this excuse must show a "necessity of self-defence, instant,

---

49. A. Méringhac, "De la sanction des infractions au droit des gens commises, au cour de la guerre européenne, par les empires du centre," *Revue générale de droit international public* 24 (1917): 19.

50. Hall, *International Law,* 269.

51. Oppenheim, *International Law,* 1: para. 130; also Bonfils, *Manuel* (1912), para. 242.

52. Today: Martin Dixon, *Textbook on International Law* (Oxford, 2000), 299–303.

53. Burleigh Cushing Rodick, *The Doctrine of Necessity in International Law* (New York, 1928), ch. 1.

overwhelming, leaving no choice of means, and no moment for deliberation."[54] It must do "nothing unreasonable or excessive; since the act, justified by the necessity of self-defence, must be limited by that necessity, and kept clearly within it." A war plan of seventeen years' duration hardly fit these strictures.

Nonetheless, the subjective conviction of necessity probably did exist in Berlin in the summer of 1914, but it was largely of the Kaiserreich's own making and imagination. Civilian and military leaders all agreed that none of the Entente nations—Britain, France, or Russia—intended to invade Germany in 1914.[55] Instead, the subjective peril they faced came from the convergence of two strands of policy making. One reacted to the isolation, or "encirclement," that Germany's own bumptious foreign policy had created and which political leaders feared might thwart Germany's justified development into a world power on a par with Britain. The second came from Germany's military establishment. Since unification, Germany had developed a strong, institutionalized military culture with peremptory convictions about the nature of war, prescriptions (like the Schlieffen Plan) for waging it, and absolute standards of victory.[56] The resulting pseudo- or hyper-realism created "necessities" that swept away the limits to exceptional necessity imposed by customary international law. It proved hard to maintain proportionality in the face of the requirement of the absolute victory of military force, or of the Prusso-German way of waging war by breakneck speed, terrific risk, and the concentration of force.[57] The felt necessity to risk everything to produce absolute victory produced existential danger where objectively there was none. A lost day of mobilization, the inevitable "friction" slowing down the fulfillment of scheduled objectives, the diversion of forces to occupation—these commonplaces threatened the fleeting windows of opportunity on which apparently complete success or utter failure depended. Real, immediate, and vital danger thus proliferated in the minds of Germany's military leaders (and, differently, in those of many of its civilian leaders) and easily fulfilled for them the stringent conditions of military necessity enumerated since Grotius. Danger became anticipatory, and vital interest was no longer confined to self-preservation, but expanded to include victory, or even mere military convenience.

It took World War I to finish the development of military necessity into a virtually law-obliterating principle. Yet despite the imperatives of military necessity, it cannot be said that German military leaders were simply oblivious to international law. They were

---

54. Webster to Ashburton, July 27, 1842, cited in R. Y. Jennings, "The *Caroline* and McLeod Cases," *American Journal of International Law* 32, no. 1 (1938): 89.

55. Jagow to Theodor Wolff, July 24, 1914: Wolff, *Tagebücher*, 64; Bethmann to Ambassador Heinrich v. Tschirschky, July 28, 1914, cited in Imanuel Geiss, *July 1914: The Outbreak of the First World War: Selected Documents* (New York, 1968), 259; Max v. Montgelas on Germany's "preventive war": Mombauer, *Origins*, 27; on Prussian war minister Erich v. Falkenhayn's views: Holger Afflerbach, *Falkenhayn: Politisches Denken und Handeln im Kaiserreich*, Beiträge zur Militärgeschichte, vol. 42 (Munich, 1994), 161, 163; on Chief of Staff Helmuth von Moltke, Bethmann, the Kaiser, and others: Mombauer, *Moltke*, 186–93.

56. Isabel V. Hull, *Absolute Destruction: Military Culture and the Practices of War in Imperial Germany* (Ithaca, NY, 2005).

57. Dennis Showalter, "From Deterrence to Doomsday Machine: The German Way of War, 1890–1914," *Journal of Military History* 64 (July 2000): 679–710.

alive to the advantages it might offer under certain circumstances. Moltke's decision to drop the invasion of Holland from the Schlieffen Plan shows this possibility.

Taking office after 1905, Moltke faced a strategic situation somewhat different from that faced by Schlieffen. As Russia recovered from the Revolution of 1905, as the Entente linking Britain, France, and Russia solidified, as Germany's potential enemies strengthened and Germany's ally Austria weakened, Moltke contemplated the possibility of a longer war and the heightened need to keep Germany's troop strength as great as possible relative to its enemies. These developments meant that he paid more attention to extra-military factors than Schlieffen had done. Moltke explained in 1915 that he had "preferred to take on the great technical difficulties" of squeezing the German armies through only Belgium and Luxembourg in order to avoid adding Dutch troops to Germany's enemies and having to peel off German troops to cover Holland.[58] But more than that, Moltke foresaw how international law was likely to intersect with world politics, and with what military consequences. In a memorandum in 1911 Moltke explained,

> A hostile Holland at our back could have disastrous consequences for the advance of the German army to the west, particularly if England should use the violation of Belgian neutrality as a pretext for entering the war against us. A neutral Holland secures our rear, because if England declares war on us for violating Belgian neutrality, she cannot herself violate Dutch neutrality. She cannot break the very law for whose sake she goes to war.

Moltke counted on British entry over the Belgian treaty of guarantee, and he foresaw the limits that law would impose on British policy during the war. He also predicted a British blockade that could be subverted using neutral American ships plying their transfer trade to Germany through neutral Dutch harbors. The Netherlands would "be the windpipe that enables us to breathe."[59] Violating Dutch neutrality was therefore no longer a military necessity; indeed, international law could be used to Germany's advantage as a belligerent.

But that legal advantage was instantly counteracted by a further military necessity: squeezing a greater number of German troops through the narrow Belgian-Luxembourg gate required immediate capture of the Liège forts just over the German-Belgian border. German troops would have to cross that border on the first day of mobilization, *before* a declaration of war, in order to ensure the least friction-producing Belgian resistance.[60] The Liège surprise was another example of how German military culture produced military necessities that were taken to supersede law.

The easy violation of neutral countries appears many times in prewar German military and naval planning. In 1897, for example, Corvette-Captain August Ludwig von Schröder, one of the section chiefs of the Admiralty staff, developed a plan for a possible war against Britain that called for seizing Antwerp and the Dutch and Belgian forts along the Scheldt

---

58. Moltke to General v. Freytag-Loringhoven, July 26, 1915, cited in Mombauer, *Moltke,* 94.

59. Moltke memorandum of 1911, cited ibid., and 94n231.

60. Mombauer's nice discussion: Mombauer, *Moltke,* 95–98, 161.

River, thus violating the neutrality of both Belgium and Holland, and furthermore doing so without a preceding declaration of war.[61] Despite the chief of the admiralty's judgment that the plan was too "adventurous and impractical," he nonetheless submitted it to the Kaiser, who approved its further development in tandem with the general staff. None of the naval or military figures who vetted the plan objected to the violations of law at its heart. Schröder clearly expressed the theory of law at its base. A war with England, he wrote, would involve "perhaps our very existence as a state.... In the face of such considerations, clinging to artificially constructed clauses of international law would be far more reprehensible from an ethical point of view than merely bending the law because circumstances force us to do so. If the life of the nation is at stake, disregarding the neutrality of Belgium and the Netherlands need not dismay us."[62]

Schröder was thus not ignorant of the law; he considered it "artificial," which we may take to mean incongruent and external to laws derived from the nature of warfare itself, and subservient to vital state interests. These vital interests are merely assumed ("perhaps"), and furthermore that assumption occurred before Britain's entente with France and before the establishment of Germany's naval rivalry with Britain. That is, the existential nature of the potential conflict was a basic assumption of warfare, not a reflection of political, diplomatic, or military reality.[63]

The Kaiser also provided no principled objection to violating neutral countries. He had favored attacking France through Belgium since 1894.[64] Between 1899 and 1904 Wilhelm II four times approved naval plans to occupy neutral Denmark in case of war with Britain.[65] In December 1904 he explained to the German ambassador to Denmark that one must simply "pass over" (*hinweggehen*) international treaties.[66]

The Kaiser, to whom the constitution gave the final decision on military and foreign-political matters, revealed many times before the war that he did not recognize even the strongest form of international law, treaty law, as necessarily binding or of intrinsic worth. Wilhelm told Belgium's King Leopold II in January 1904 that if Belgium refused to aid Germany in a European war, the Kaiser would decide matters "according to strategic considerations."[67] But several times Wilhelm also adduced a novel interpretation of the international law of neutrality that had nothing to do with putative strategic considerations. He told the brother of Denmark's King Christian IX that neutralization of Denmark and its territorial waters "was only possible, if Denmark was also in a military position to force every great power, including England, to respect it."[68] Queen Wilhelmina of the Netherlands learned from Wilhelm in early 1904 that "if the Netherlands and Denmark

---

61. Steinberg, "German Plan."

62. Schröder, "Memorandum: An Operation against Antwerp," Nov. 1897, ibid., 163.

63. Steinberg makes this point: Steinberg, "German Plan," 162.

64. Mombauer, *Moltke*, 76n138.

65. John C. G. Röhl, *Wilhelm II. Der Weg in den Abgrund 1900–1941* (Munich, 2008), 343, 344, 354, 358–59, 361–62. Hereafter *Wilhelm 3*.

66. Röhl, *Wilhelm 3*, 428.

67. Ibid., 349.

68. Ibid., 345.

were not in a position to defend their neutrality adequately, they would receive twenty-four hours' notice" to decide if they were for or against Germany in the event of war.[69] These and other remarks permit the conclusion that Wilhelm interpreted international law and the rights of states as mere reflections or results of military power. Militarily weaker states had to accommodate themselves to the requirements of greater ones. Clearly, the Kaiser provided no principled hindrance to military policies based on the violation of neutrality.

In the absence of firm limitations from the Kaiser, the navy's Danish plans (1903–5) illustrate on what bases such plans could be idled and by whom. The pattern of planning was this: the Admiralty staff worked out its plans alone. When the Kaiser approved them the first time, he ordered the navy to consult with the army general staff but notably not with the war minister, navy minister, chancellor, or foreign office (AA). After the general staff worried about diverting troops to occupy Denmark, the Kaiser ordered it nevertheless to get on with the practical planning, which it did. It took from April 1903 until January 1905 before the chief of the Admiralty staff, Admiral Wilhelm Büchsel, realized that the other ministries must be notified. "The chancellor must know the general framework of the operational plan and the view that the war leadership wants to take of the international legal questions, so that national policy may if necessary take our intentions into account."[70] The now enlightened chancellor and AA raised political, not legal, objections; they feared international reaction from the other great powers. As a result of these hesitations, Wilhelm abandoned the plan he had already approved. Law therefore played either no role, or a very indirect one in the decision-making process: at most, it was other powers' concern to uphold the legal neutrality of small nations that weighed against risky, offensive military/naval planning.

France provided the most famous counterexample of political-military decision making on Belgian neutrality. S. R. Williamson has explored this subject in depth, and we need only summarize his findings.[71] The first difference to the German pattern was Chief of Staff Joseph Joffre's conviction that political and diplomatic considerations, including treaty commitments, provided the necessary parameters to military planning. Military planning was based on politics and diplomacy, not on military necessity. It was Joffre himself who insisted on meeting with French foreign office officials (October 1911) to learn what legal and diplomatic limits constrained military policy. Second, Joffre told the foreign office that the French general staff had never contemplated violating Belgian neutrality first, because that policy would have been "a denial of our signature," and it would have alienated Russia and Britain.[72] Joffre thus noted France's legal obligation first, and then political interest. Third, the foreign office replied in a memorandum that first observed that "it is our duty" not to initiate a violation; that is, French foreign policy too was set inside the legal parameter. But the Quai d'Orsay hastened to say that it expected that Germany

---

69. Ibid., 351.

70. Büchsel report to Kaiser, Jan. 31, 1905, cited ibid., 359.

71. This account follows Samuel R. Williamson, "Joffre Reshapes French Strategy, 1911–1913," in *The War Plans of the Great Powers, 1880–1914* (Boston, 1985), 205–27.

72. Joseph Joffre, *The Personal Memoirs of Joffre, Field Marshal of the French Army,* trans. T. Bentley Mott (New York, 1932), 1:41.

would attack Belgium first, permitting France to strike back quickly.[73] Fourth, when Joffre returned to the subject in February 1912, he argued "the strictly military point of view, which my duty obliged me to make clear to the Government"—that is, that France's purely military interests demanded a quick, preemptive strike through Belgian territory. Joffre moreover received the support of Naval Minister Théophile Delcassé and War Minister Alexandre Millerand. But his advice was still predicated on the assumption, as he explained, "*that no other consideration prevented such a course and that we could come to an understanding with the Belgian Government beforehand.*"[74] That is, Joffre and his backers saw French military plans as unfolding largely within the parameters of the 1839 treaty: intervention would be at the request of the Belgian government together with another guarantor, Britain. Nevertheless, Premier Raymond Poincaré rejected the idea; he felt both assumptions were false, and he was proved right. Tentative soundings of Belgian military and political leaders elicited the vehement response that Belgium would defend itself; and, at the end of 1912, France learned in no uncertain terms through British chief of staff General Henry Wilson that Britain opposed any first violation. British foreign secretary Edward Grey had sent Wilson to warn against a French first violation, because that would cause the Belgian army to join with Germany "and the British Government would then be called upon to defend [Belgian] neutrality" against France.[75] Grey foresaw the strong public pressure that any violation of Belgian neutrality (French or German) would unleash. Poincaré's decision against a first violation remained French military policy down to August 1914. Finally, these decisions were made at joint meetings of the military leaders, the civilian heads of the naval and war ministries, the foreign office, and the premier. French military policy was thus the syncretic result of legal, political, diplomatic, and military calculation. When these clashed, the first three trumped the last.

In Germany, the last trumped the first three. In the waning days of July 1914, Chancellor Bethmann Hollweg's attempt to establish Germany as a world power either by fracturing the Triple Entente or by risking a successful, limited war by Germany's ally Austria-Hungary careened out of his control. As Russia held firm, the small Austro-Serbian conflict (declared on July 28) threatened to mutate into a grand European war, and policy initiative switched from the chancellor to the chief of the general staff. Moltke anticipated both Russian mobilization (in response to an Austrian declaration of war against Serbia) and British entry into a general European war (in response to Germany's invasion of Belgium). Thus, two days *before* the Austrian declaration of war, Moltke (not the AA) had already drafted the German ultimatum to Belgium.[76] It gave the Belgian government twenty-four hours to declare whether it would permit German troops to cross Belgium into France. If Belgium demonstrated what Moltke termed "benevolent neutrality," Germany guaranteed to restore at war's end its territorial integrity and independence; further, Germany dangled

---

73. Ibid., 1:42–43.

74. Ibid., 1:50; emphasis in the original.

75. Cited ibid., 1:54.

76. Max Montgelas and Walter Schücking, eds., *Die deutschen Dokumente zum Kriegsausbruch; Vollständige Sammlung der von Karl Kautsky zusammengestellten amtlichen Aktenstücke mit einigen Ergänzungen. Im Auftrage des Auswärtigen Amtes nach gemeinsamer Durchsicht mit Karl Kautsky* (Charlottenburg, 1919), 2: doc. 376.

the prospect of expansion at the expense of France. If Belgium defended itself, however, it would be treated as an enemy.

Wilhelm von Stumm (head of the political section of the AA) made minor stylistic corrections to Moltke's draft. Bethmann, Jagow, and undersecretary of the AA Arthur Zimmermann approved it on July 29. Later that night, Moltke decided that Germany must use its last good chance to win a complete military victory; it must go to war now.[77] The next day (July 30), Bethmann acceded to Moltke's pressure and, together with War Minister Erich von Falkenhayn, agreed to mobilize by midday on the thirty-first. As most readers probably know, the Kaiser caused a brief hiccup in the proceedings by his last-ditch attempt to prevent Britain from entering the war; he suddenly ordered an attack eastward, against Russia.[78] After a brief delay, Moltke prevailed, because by this time Germany had only a single war plan, and it went west, through Belgium. By August 2, German troops entered neutral Luxembourg; on the morning of August 4, they were in Belgium.

Both the ultimatum to Belgium and the mobilization decision contained important assumptions about international law that were shared by both military and civilian decision makers. First, both were anticipatory; the draft ultimatum preceded the Austrian declaration of war by two days, and mobilization was decided upon following military calculations, a half day before news of Russian mobilization reached Berlin.[79] The decisions were therefore not reactive. One might argue that the decision makers were simply certain that the precipitating events would occur, but of course they could not *know* it. The press of military necessity was therefore subjective, not actual.

Second, the ultimatum contained an interpretation of "benevolent neutrality" that nowhere existed in international law, even regarding "voluntary" neutrals, much less for those states whose neutrality was internationally guaranteed as a perpetual political status. As the jurist Lassa Oppenheim summarized in 1905, "neutrality is an attitude of impartiality, it excludes such assistance and succour to one of the belligerents as is detrimental to the other," including "the transport of troops, war materials, and provisions."[80] By allowing the passage of German troops, Belgium would have violated the treaties that had created it. The Belgian cabinet united on August 2 around this very point. As one recent historian has written, Belgium owed its existence "to the primacy of international law over the law of force. The attachment of the country to the principle of international law was less a question of merit than of self-defense. For Belgium, honor and security perfectly coincided. Basing their policy on the irrefutable juridical argument of Belgian obligations," the cabinet decided for war.[81] The official Belgian reply stated that Germany's proposal was "a flagrant violation of the rights of nations" and to accept it "would be to sacrifice the honour of a nation."[82]

---

77. I follow the excellent account of Mombauer, *Moltke,* ch. 4.

78. Harry F. Young, *Prince Lichnowsky and the Great War* (Athens, GA, 1977), 114–22; Mombauer, *Moltke,* 216–26.

79. Mombauer, *Moltke,* 205–7.

80. Oppenheim, *International Law,* 2:317, 324.

81. Sophie De Schaepdrijver, *La Belgique et la Première Guerre Mondiale* (New York, 2004), 59.

82. Edward Grey (Viscount Grey of Fallodon), *Twenty-Five Years, 1892–1916* (London, 1925), 2:326.

Because Germany's demand of Belgium would have destroyed the protection of permanently neutral status, Germany's guarantee of independence and territorial integrity in fact spelled the end of Belgian sovereignty. Most contemporary observers knew that in the event of a German victory, Belgium, like most neighboring small states, would surely fall into Germany's orbit, as the Kaiser had predicted in 1903–4 regarding Denmark.[83]

Third, Moltke's draft of July 26 began with the allegation that "reliable news" "left no doubt that France intends to march through Belgian territory," that is, that France was or would be the first violator.[84] There was no such news, of course. At most, Moltke might have assumed that France would put military necessity above all other considerations, just as he did. More likely, this allegation was supposed to provide legal cover for the Schlieffen Plan—a weak nod to the law, since Moltke even on paper dared not wait for a genuine breach; an excuse, not a justification, was all he sought.

British Entry into the War

Annika Mombauer correctly sums up the current historiography: "Few historians would still maintain that the 'rape of Belgium' was the real motive for Britain's declaration of war on Germany."[85] Instead, the role of Belgian neutrality is variously interpreted as an excuse to mobilize the public, to provide embarrassed radicals in the cabinet with a justification for abandoning their principled pacifism and thus for staying in office, or, in the more conspiratorial versions, to cover for naked imperial interests.[86] Denigrating the importance of Belgian neutrality appeals particularly to those who believe that Britain should never have entered the war, or indeed that the war should never have been fought; the basis for this view is the belief that Imperial Germany was not a danger either to Britain's security or to Europe's.[87] Significantly, specialists in German history do not generally share these views.[88]

Careful historians know of course that Britain's decision, like most important acts of state, was multi-determined. Skeptics on the role of Belgian neutrality emphasize two arguments: that most cabinet members chose war for reasons of security, not legal

---

83. Röhl, *Wilhelm 3*, 1173.

84. Montgelas and Schücking, *Die deutschen Dokumente*, 2:98, doc. 376.

85. Mombauer, *Origins*, 197.

86. Cf. Keith M. Wilson, "The British Cabinet's Decision for War, 2 August 1914," *British Journal of International Studies* 1 (1975): 148–59; Hubert Gebele, *Großbritannien und der Große Krieg: Die Auseinandersetzung über Kriegs- und Friedensziele vom Kriegsausbruch 1914 bis zu den Friedenschlüssen von 1919/1920* (Regensburg, 2009), 2; Cameron Hazlehurst, *Politicians at War, July 1914 to May 1915: A Prologue to the Triumph of Lloyd George* (London, 1971), 67–68; Niall Ferguson, *The Pity of War: Explaining World War I* (New York, 1998), 164–68.

87. Recent representatives of this view are Niall Ferguson and John Charmley: Ferguson, *Pity of War*, 169–73, 458–62; Charmley, *Splendid Isolation? Britain and the Balance of Power, 1874–1914* (London, 1999).

88. Mombauer, *Origins*, 198; Richard F. Hamilton and Holger Herwig, *Decisions for War, 1914–1917* (Cambridge, 2004), 145; Stig Förster, "Im Reich des Absurden: Die Ursachen des Ersten Weltkrieges," in *Wie Kriege entstehen: Zum historischen Hintergrund von Staatenkonflikten*, ed. Bernd Wegner (Paderborn, 2003), 215–17.

obligation; and that Prime Minister Herbert Asquith and Foreign Minister Grey fell back upon Belgian neutrality as the only way to assemble a majority cabinet decision for a war that radical members would not support for the sake of France or the Entente. In order to assess the issue properly and thus to understand the role that international law played in the decision, one must do two things. First, one must avoid the conceptual error that rigidly dichotomizes law and security. Second, one must ask, why was it precisely the guarantee of Belgian neutrality, and only that issue, that was capable of getting majority support in the Liberal cabinet?

Turning to the first problem, the view that legal obligation and security interests are opposed or of a different order encourages the search for "real" reasons behind state behavior, which are then usually taken to be security or material interest. This is a common, but caricatured, view of political science "realism" that has found its way easily into the historiography of foreign affairs.[89] It seems at first glance to describe the results of the first cabinet meeting (July 29, 1914) held to discuss Britain's obligations regarding Belgian neutrality. Only five of nineteen cabinet members (Grey, Prime Minister Asquith, War Secretary Richard Haldane, First Lord of the Admiralty Winston Churchill, and India Secretary Robert Crewe-Milnes) favored British military intervention on the Continent to oppose what they identified as a German bid for hegemony that would crush France as a great power.[90] In their view, protecting France was so obviously in Britain's security interest that they needed no formal obligation (to France by the Entente of 1904 or to Belgium by the treaty of 1839) to authorize war, though many or perhaps all of them believed that Britain also had such obligations. But they faced a group of radical Liberals whose priorities lay with domestic reform and whose foreign policy principles were those of Richard Cobden and Jacob Bright: no entangling alliances and no wars, especially in Europe. Their pacifism and isolationism had caused them to view with dismay Britain's increasingly formal agreements with Japan, France, and Russia. Their distrust of "secret diplomacy" and Grey's strong support for France during the Second Moroccan Crisis in 1911 energized them to form a parliamentary oversight committee for foreign affairs. To quiet their anxiety, Grey had revealed to Parliament (1912) his correspondence with French ambassador Paul Cambon stating explicitly that Franco-British military and naval conversations did not commit either nation to come to the aid of the other.[91] By July 1914, therefore, the radicals for years had regarded the central issue of British European policy to be maintaining a free hand versus becoming enslaved to formal obligation. They spared no effort to ensure the former against the latter, which is why the question of obligation tended to dominate cabinet discussions during the crisis.

Belgian neutrality began to emerge as the central issue of cabinet discussion after Grey failed on July 27 to persuade his radical colleagues to go to war for France. Two days later, the cabinet discussed Belgium for the first time, fortified with reading material that Grey had provided them: the debates that in 1870 had led to Britain's re-guarantee in the face of a

---

89. A typical example: Lademacher, *Belgische Neutralität*, 477.

90. David French, *British Strategy and Wars Aims, 1914–1916* (Oxford, 1986), 23.

91. *BD* 10:2, nos. 413–17.

previous German-French war. No protocol of cabinet meetings was kept in those days, so historians have relied on Asquith's terse, summary letter to King George V and on the participants' memoirs. Asquith told the king that the cabinet "had reviewed the obligations" of 1839 and 1870 and concluded that it was doubtful "how far a single guaranteeing State is bound" by the 1839 treaty to "maintain Belgian neutrality if the remainder abstain or refuse. The Cabinet consider that the matter if it arises will be rather one of policy than of legal obligation."[92] Cameron Hazlehurst interprets the meeting as having focused narrowly on law, and having rejected it.[93] It would be more accurate to say that the cabinet correctly interpreted the collective guarantee of 1839.[94] But the meeting had begun with a warning from the prime minister that in the event of war Germany would surely violate Belgian neutrality. Those in the cabinet who either had reached this conclusion on their own or who now seriously entertained that possibility placed great weight on Belgian neutrality and on Britain's obligation. But, as Hazlehurst writes, "there were those who did not want to believe."[95] When others pressed the issue of Britain's own security in the event of a German violation, Minister of Education Joseph Albert Pease hit upon a happy way to avoid dissension: "we should not in conversation allude to a possible German invasion of Belgium."[96] Thus, the cabinet position of the twenty-ninth on legal obligation, which Asquith told the king was a concession to the peace party,[97] was taken on the purely theoretical ground that no such occasion would ever arise. It was a decision to postpone a decision; it was not a statement of principle. That is clear from the conviction of President of the Privy Council John Morley, one of the strongest peaceniks in the cabinet, a confirmed "little Englander," and in the end one of only two cabinet members to resign over Britain's entry into the war. Morley always accepted the fact that Britain owed a legal obligation to maintain Belgium's neutrality; his policy was to prevent that obligation from covering a war that in his view would actually be fought to support France or the chimera of a balance of power.[98]

Bethmann Hollweg now inadvertently moved matters along. On the morning of the July 30, the Foreign Office in London received a telegram from the British ambassador to Germany, Sir Edward Goschen. It reported the chancellor's bid for British neutrality in a European war. Bethmann promised that Germany would not "crush" France, would not annex French territory except perhaps in the colonies, and would not violate Dutch neutrality. Regarding Belgium, he refused to say "what operations Germany might be forced [to take] by the action of France," but he promised that if Belgium "did not take sides against Germany, her integrity would be respected after the conclusion of the war." As Sir Eyre Crowe minuted, "Germany practically admits the intention to violate Belgian neutrality."[99] Crowe

---

92. Herbert Henry Asquith, *Memories and Reflections, 1852–1927* (London, 1928), 81.

93. Hazlehurst, *Politicians at War,* 75.

94. Satow, "Pacta," 301–18.

95. Hazlehurst, *Politicians at War,* 74.

96. Ibid., 73–74.

97. Wilson, "Cabinet's Decision," 149n1.

98. Morley's editor, F. W. Hirst on Morley, and then Morley himself: John Viscount Morley, *Memorandum on Resignation August 1914* (London, 1928), xiii, 6, 13.

99. *BD* 11, doc. 293.

and Grey were incensed at what both regarded as a dishonorable proposition. Grey turned it down instantly, telling Asquith that "without cabinet sanction he could not bargain treaty obligations away."[100] The next day, the thirty-first, he reported Bethmann's offer to the cabinet. His report had three results. First, the cabinet upheld Grey's rejection; it, too, did not "bargain treaty obligations away." Second, it authorized Grey to inquire directly of both France and Germany whether they guaranteed Belgian neutrality. Third, several radicals now began to abandon their uncompromising pacifism. Solicitor-General Sir Stanley Owen Buckmaster recalled that he and three others (Attorney General John Simon, Colonial Secretary Lewis Harcourt, and Pease) who "had intended to resign if we became involved" in the war now changed their minds as a result of Bethmann's proposal.[101] Historian Keith M. Wilson is right to note that Buckmaster's statement did not "fit the facts," insofar as the first resignation (John Burns) and the private discussions among radicals about whether to resign occurred on August 2, two days after the cabinet meeting at which Germany's offer was discussed. Wilson calls Buckmaster's statement "nonsense," and rejects it together with all the radicals' claims that Belgium was important to changing their minds (Simon, Harcourt, Lloyd George), calling them mere "argument[s] of convenience."[102] But it is hard to see why an argument of convenience made after August 3 would not simply cite Germany's actual violation, rather than its earlier offer. Whatever Buckmaster's inner motives, he seems to have recalled the first movement among radicals reacting to Germany's own policies. Grey noted too that by August 1, the cabinet's views were changing.[103]

So was public opinion. The liberal press had begun to shift against Germany by the twenty-ninth, probably in response to the Austrian ultimatum to Serbia (July 28).[104] The increasingly clear danger to Belgium began to galvanize public opinion, which by August 2 seemed prepared for war.[105] As Zara Steiner writes, Belgium was a "catalyst which unleashed the many emotions, rationalisations and glorifications of war which had long been part of the British climate of opinion."[106] It was impossible for Britain to go to war without the full backing of the public, though it did not go to war on that account. Nevertheless, the centrality of Belgium to this prerequisite for British entry into the war cannot be overestimated. After receiving Germany's evasive reply on whether it would respect Belgium neutrality, the cabinet authorized Grey to warn German ambassador Karl Prince von Lichnowsky (July 31) that "our attitude would be determined largely by public opinion here, and the neutrality of Belgium would appeal very strongly to public opinion here."[107]

---

100. Hazlehurst, *Politicians at War,* 182.

101. Wilson, "Cabinet's Decision," 157.

102. Ibid., 158.

103. Grey, *Twenty-Five Years,* 2:2.

104. Wilson, "Britain," 180–81.

105. C. J. Lowe and M. L. Dockrill, *The Mirage of Power* (Boston, 1972), 1:153.

106. Zara S. Steiner, *Britain and the Origins of the First World War* (New York, 1977), 233.

107. Grey to Goschen, Foreign Office, Aug. 1, 1914, *BD* 11, doc. 448, partly cited in Steiner, *Britain and the Origins,* 233.

By August 1, Asquith noted that "the main controversy pivots upon Belgium and its neutrality."[108] Matters came to a head the next day because by then Belgium had declared that it would defend itself, and Germany had invaded Luxembourg—a clear indication that Belgium was next.[109] The radicals were still not prepared to go to war for France, but they were open to considering the defense of Belgium. At several private meetings they debated their position. Harcourt doubted whether the 1839 treaty was "necessarily binding," and Simon remarked that "eighty years had created wholly different circumstances."[110] However, by late morning both of them had agreed with Lloyd George, First Commissioner of Works William Lygon (Earl Beauchamp), Pease, and president of the Board of Agriculture Walter Runciman that "a wholesale invasion of Belgium" might be a casus belli.[111] By "wholesale" they meant an invasion of the entire country, not just passing through its southern tip. At noon, president of the Local Government Board Herbert Samuel informed the prime minister that he thought "the Belgium issue might decide the matter for almost all the Cabinet."[112]

Samuel worked out the formula that united all the radicals except for Morley and Burns, who resigned as the cabinet decided for war.[113] Samuel believed that Britain would be "justified in joining the war" for either of two reasons.[114] One was defending the French Channel coast, which Britain's naval agreement with France had left bereft of French warships and thus under the protection of the Royal Navy. Radicals, whose foreign policy was founded on the principle of the free hand, might not have regarded protecting the French coast as an actual obligation. At any rate, Samuel described his position not as an obligation but in security terms: "We could not afford to see [the French coast] bombarded by the German fleet and occupied by the German army." At its morning meeting on the second of August, the cabinet authorized Grey to assure France of British naval protection should the German fleet enter the Channel or attack the French coast or shipping. Britain did not formally promise to go to war, however.[115] Because naval operations in the Channel played no part in Germany's war plans, Germany agreed not to attack the French coast.[116]

That left the second part of Samuel's formula, maintaining Belgian independence. Here Samuel argued both legal obligation and security: "We were bound by treaty to protect [Belgium] and...again we could not afford to see [it] subordinated to Germany."[117] Samuel repeated the radical principle that Britain had no obligation "for the sake of our goodwill for France, or for the sake of maintaining the strength of France and Russia against

---

108. Asquith, *Memories*, 84.

109. G. R. Clerk minute to F. Villiers to Grey, Brussels, Aug. 2, 1914, *BD* 11, no. 476.

110. Pease diary, Aug. 2, 1914, Hazlehurst, *Politicians at War*, 71.

111. Pease diary, Aug. 2, 1914, ibid., 166.

112. Herbert Viscount Samuel, *Memoirs* (London, 1945), 104.

113. Wilson, "Cabinet's Decision," 151; Steiner, *Britain and the Origins*, 230, 235.

114. Samuel to Beatrice Samuel, Aug. 2, 1914, in Lowe and Dockrill, *Mirage of Power*, 489–91.

115. Grey to Bertie, Foreign Office, Aug. 2, 1914 (4:45 p.m.), *BD* 11, doc. 487; Lowe and Dockrill, *Mirage of Power*, 150.

116. Communication from the German embassy, Aug. 3, 1914, *BD* 11, doc. 531.

117. Samuel to Beatrice Samuel, Aug. 2, 1914, in Lowe and Dockrill, *Mirage of Power*, 489–91.

that of Germany and Austria." He reported that his views on the Channel coast and Belgium were "shared by the majority of the Cabinet with various degrees of emphasis on the several parts of it." Indeed, the discussions were difficult, but at the evening meeting on the second, the cabinet, following the decision the radicals had arrived at privately in the morning, agreed that "a substantial violation" of Belgium "would place us in the situation contemplated as possible by Mr. Gladstone in 1870, when interference with Belgian independence was held to compel us to take action."[118]

The next day, the third, the cabinet reviewed its position and prepared for Grey's afternoon speech to Parliament that would explain it to the nation. Before he could give it, the news of Germany's ultimatum to Belgium arrived. Asquith told the king that Grey's speech "presents, exactly and exhaustively," the cabinet's position.[119] The kaleidoscope of events prevented Grey from writing his speech; he spoke from notes and frequently read from diplomatic documents. He enjoined his listeners to focus on "British interests, British honour, and British obligations."[120] He began with obligations, that point of greatest contention between Grey, who believed that the entente with France had produced an obligation despite the fact that it was not an alliance, and many of his fellow Liberals, who did not. He left it up to "every man [to] look into his own heart ... and construe the extent of the obligation" (314). Grey's main argument, the bulk of his speech, was that interests, honor, and obligation converged. He reported the cabinet's conclusion that they did so regarding France's northern coasts. But "the more serious consideration," he said, was "the question of the neutrality of Belgium" (317). He quoted at length Gladstone and Granville from 1870, both of whom used "honour" and "interest" in a single breath (317–19). Grey emphasized that the treaty of 1839 was concluded "in the interests of those [states] who guarantee the neutrality of Belgium. The honour and interests are, at least, as strong today as in 1870" (318). He reported Belgium's request (of that day) for diplomatic intervention from the guarantors. He cited Gladstone's characterization of the violation of Belgian neutrality as a "crime," and then predicted the domino effect that would begin with the disappearance of an independent Belgium, followed by the Netherlands and France: "If Belgium fell under the same dominating influence, and then Holland, and then Denmark, then would not Mr. Gladstone's words come true, that just opposite to us there would be a common interest against the unmeasured aggrandisement of any Power?" (321).

Having laid out the imperative security interests that Britain shared with France and the small states of Europe, Grey then repeated the cabinet's contention that interest, honor, and obligation were identical. If "we run away from those obligations of honour and interest as regards the Belgian Treaty, I doubt whether, whatever material force we might have at the end [of the war], it would be of very much value in face of the respect that we should have lost" (322). If Britain did nothing as "the whole of the West of Europe opposite us ... [fell] under the domination of a single Power, ... I am quite sure that our moral

---

118. Crewe to King, Aug. 2, 1914, in Asquith, *Memories*, 82. Difficult: Asquith, *Memories*, 85, 91.

119. Asquith to King, Aug. 3, 1914, in Asquith, *Memories*, 82.

120. The speech is appendix D to Grey, *Twenty-Five Years*, 2:308–26. Hereafter cited parenthetically in text by page number.

position would be such as to have lost us all respect" (322)—a sentiment he repeated once more (324).

After Grey had finished, word arrived that Belgium had rejected Germany's ultimatum. The official Belgian announcement echoed Grey's description of the "sacredness" of the rights guaranteed in 1839 (317). He read it aloud. It called Germany's policy "a flagrant violation of the rights of nations," to accept which "would be to sacrifice the honour of a nation. Conscious of its duty, Belgium is firmly resolved to repel aggression by all possible means" (326).[121]

Grey's speech "satisfied, I think, all the House, with perhaps three or four exceptions, that we were compelled to participate," reported the Liberal Christopher Addison. For himself, Addison's diary entry emphasized security first, adding "apart altogether from the fact that we were pledged, as much as a nation could be, to defend Belgium."[122] Addison, a member of pacifist Arthur Ponsonby's "Foreign Affairs Group," responded like many other Liberal critics of Grey's prewar foreign policy who now concluded, as another said, "that the Government is in honour bound to go in."[123] The sudden collapse of Liberal neutralist opposition angered those few who remained steadfast. In 1928 Morley published his suspicion that Belgium was just an excuse to enter the war in order to save France.[124] Some later historians have built on Morley's suspicions and argued that Belgium was merely a "pretext for an otherwise humiliating *volte face*" that permitted the radicals to remain in office.[125] This conviction has caused them to discount the unanimous explanations that cabinet members made at the time citing Germany's violation of Belgian neutrality as casus belli. Some (Masterman, Hobhouse, and Beauchamp, for example) emphasized security, particularly when they argued with former fellow neutralists; some (Asquith, Lloyd George, Runciman, Harcourt, Loreburn, Pease, Buckmaster, and Simon) stressed the violation itself, suggesting that legal obligation was a decisive factor; and some (again Asquith, Grey, and Samuel) explicitly cited both equally.[126] But even a list such as this is incomplete and misleading, since positions changed rapidly in the week before Britain went to war on August 4. And even those who were prepared to fight for the sake of France (Grey, Asquith, Crewe, Haldane, and Churchill) were just as determined that a

---

121. Davignon to v. Below Saleski, Brussels, Aug. 3, 1914, in *Diplomatic Documents Relating to the Outbreak of the European War,* ed. James Brown Scott (New York, 1916), no. 22.

122. Diary entry Aug. 3, 1914, Christopher Addison, *Four and a Half Years: A Personal Diary from June 1914 to January 1919* (London, 1934), 1:32. Addison did not know that he was about to replace Burns in the cabinet.

123. John Dillon (and Gilbert Murray), as reported by Mair to Charles Prestwich Scott early on Aug. 4, 1914, in Charles Prestwich Scott, *The Political Diaries of C. P. Scott, 1911–1928,* ed. Trevor Wilson (Ithaca, NY, 1970), 95.

124. Morley, *Memorandum,* 3, 10, 13.

125. Pretext: Hazlehurst, *Politicians at War,* 68, 68–74. Wilson argues most strongly for opportunism: Wilson, "Cabinet's Decision."

126. Hazlehurst, *Politicians at War,* 55–56, 58, 59, 60, 66, 71, 73–74, 82, 97–99, 109–10, 113; J. A. Spender and Cyril Asquith, *Life of Herbert Henry Asquith, Lord Oxford and Asquith* (London, 1932), 85, 112; Scott, *Political Diaries,* 96–98; Morley, *Memorandum,* 24; Addison, *Four and a Half Years,* 35; Grey, *Twenty-Five Years,* 2:27, 46, 330–31; Wilson, "Cabinet's Decision," 152, 159; Samuel, *Memoirs,* 102; Steiner, *Britain and the Origins,* 234, 236.

German violation of Belgian neutrality was equally a cause for war.[127] Belgian neutrality and independence was the one issue capable of uniting the cabinet, because since 1839 it had combined Britain's security interests with legal obligation and thus with honorable duty. One might stress one aspect or the other, but they were two sides of the same coin in a world in which law served the interest of Britain (and France, Belgium, and the other small states of Europe). It is therefore hardly surprising that a Liberal government, with its principled devotion to the rule of law in the international sphere, should have agreed on Belgian neutrality as casus belli in August 1914.

I have extracted the role of Belgium from the very complicated foreign and domestic negotiations leading to war not in order to deny other motives (including clinging to office), but to clarify the unique salience and multi-determined quality of this one issue. When Prime Minister Asquith on August 6 laid out before Parliament the reasons why Britain had entered the war, he made three broad points, all concerning Belgium.[128] He devoted a great deal of time to Bethmann's neutrality proposal, calling it "infamous" (112); it was impossible to accept "a promise given by a Power which was at that very moment announcing its intention to violate its own Treaty obligation and inviting us to do the same" (113). He used the same language of simultaneous honor and interest that Gladstone and Granville had used in 1870. Accepting Bethmann's offer, he told Parliament, would have covered Britain "with dishonour. We should have betrayed the interests of this country of which we are the trustees" (113). Asquith summarized Britain's war aims: "to fulfil a solemn international obligation...not only of law, but of honour"—to uphold the law against force (114–15).

Asquith's interpretation of the war as a conflict over the rule of law remained Britain's policy throughout (not just its propaganda self-presentation). At the end of the war, the attorney general made exactly the same points in an internal report to the government Committee on Breaches of the Laws of War: "Our own view is that an aggressive War was forced upon the world by an ambitious and unscrupulous power, and that the challenge so developed involved the whole future of the Public Law of States."[129] Germany "care[d] nothing for all the doctrines of International Law," and, had it won the war, "public law and the sanctity of treaties would have disappeared in our day and our generation from the world."

The government's steadfast position built upon a long tradition of self-understanding shared by both leaders and the public. Before Grey or Asquith had uttered a word, public opinion, measured by both the press and the crowds in the street, had concluded the same thing. Before the launching of Britain's propaganda campaign and without government manipulation of the press, the British public sphere condemned Germany's impending

---

127. Conservatives agreed. Bonar Law promised the government Conservative support on July 31, 1914: "If war came, and especially if the Germans ignored the international treaty of 1839 guaranteeing the neutrality of Belgium." R. J. Q. Adams, *Bonar Law* (Stanford, CA, 1999), 169.

128. Reprinted in Spender and Asquith, *Asquith,* 111–16. Hereafter cited parenthetically in text by page number.

129. Attorney general's address, first interim report from the Committee of Enquiry into Breaches of the Laws of War, Jan. 13, 1919, 6, Oxford Bodleian Library, Pollock Papers, MS ENG. Hist. d. 431.

violation.[130] Permanent Undersecretary Arthur Nicolson observed the swing of public opinion and reported to Charles, Lord Hardinge, on August 5, "The whole country is now united and the German behaviour in Belgium has raised a feeling against her the depth and fervour of which cannot be estimated."[131] The difficult cabinet negotiations in the last week of peace reflected the enormous Liberal reluctance to wage war, but they did not signal a breach in the common identification of Britain as a defender and beneficiary of international law. Postwar revisionists and "realist" skeptics deny the importance of Belgium as an actual cause of war (for Britain), preferring explanations of imperialism or balance-of-power politics (overlooking the common argument among "realist" political scientists that a balance of power produced the optimum conditions for upholding international law).[132] If one regards the Belgian question as merely a means to unite the country behind war for other reasons and not as a substantial reason in itself, one cannot understand why Britain fought or why the British public remained so staunchly behind the war effort—Britain's war becomes inexplicable. It is not necessary to claim that Belgium was the sole reason, for its importance came precisely from the fact that it combined four reasons in one: security, self-interest, the principle of law, and public reputation (honoring obligation). There were other, important reasons (upholding France and the Entente) and more that developed during the war, but Belgium defined the central issues, and that is why it was the sole "catalyst" capable of symbolizing Britain's war from the beginning to the end. We might close this argument by citing Dutch ambassador R. de Marees van Swinderen, who asked Grey privately in March 1915 if Britain had truly joined the war on account of Belgium. "The Secretary answered the question emphatically confirming his word."[133]

The Scrap of Paper

Germany's violation of Belgian neutrality ruined its reputation in world public opinion.[134] Allied and neutral public opinion alike condemned Germany's actions. The Dutch public

---

130. Steiner, *Britain and the Origins* (1977), 167–68, 233; Lowe and Dockrill, *Mirage of Power*, 1:153; Wilson, "Britain," 181; Hamilton and Herwig, *Decisions*, 142.

131. Cited in Lowe and Dockrill, *Mirage of Power*, 3:492.

132. One of the first and most influential deniers of the importance of Belgium: Sidney B. Fay, *The Origins of the World War* (New York, 1928), 1:557–58. Balance of power and international law: Stanley Hoffmann, "International Systems and International Law," in *The International System: Theoretical Essays,* ed. Klaus Knorr and Sidney Verba (Princeton, NJ, 1961), esp. 221; Morton A. Kaplan and Nicholas deB. Katzenbach, *The Political Foundations of International Law* (New York, 1961), 30–55.

133. *BPNL* 4:340. On Aug. 5, 1914, Grey told German ambassador Prince Karl v. Lichnowsky that "the disregard of internationally recognized treaties ... made it impossible for him to stand aside any longer," Young, *Lichnowsky*, 126.

134. Germany sent at least four spokesmen to the United States, Sweden, and Holland in the second week of the war to counter the upswelling of anti-German sentiment: Theodor Wolff, diary entry of Aug. 12, 1914, in Wolff, *Tagebücher*, 74.

turned instantly anti-German; Germany's wartime ambassador to the United States later told the Reichstag investigating committee that "throughout the entire war, the Belgian question was the one which interested Americans most and which was most effective in working up American public opinion against us."[135] The nascent Allied propaganda effort had an easy time selling Germany as the world's scofflaw, and nothing summed it up better than Bethmann Hollweg's notorious phrase "scrap of paper."

In several meetings with Foreign Secretary Jagow and one with Chancellor Bethmann Hollweg on August 4, British ambassador Goschen heard from both men how devastated they were at the "crumbling" of their entire foreign policy, which had been to draw closer to Britain (they did not say in order to detach it from the Entente).[136] That failure and the unremitting pressure of the July Crisis explain the high degree of agitation in which Goschen found Bethmann a little after 7 p.m. on August 4. The chancellor "harangue[d]" the ambassador for twenty minutes. Goschen summarized Bethmann's words: "He said that the step taken by His Majesty's Government was terrible to a degree; just for a word—'neutrality,' a word which in war time had so often been disregarded—just for a scrap of paper Great Britain was going to make war on a kindred nation who desired nothing better than to be friends with her"; "it was like striking a man from behind while he was fighting for his life against two assailants. He held Great Britain responsible for all the terrible events that might happen." Goschen "protested strongly," arguing that just as Jagow had presented Germany's "strategical reasons" for thinking itself in a life-or-death situation, it was also

> a matter of "life and death" for the honour of Great Britain that she should keep her solemn engagement to do her utmost to defend Belgium's neutrality if attacked. That solemn compact simply had to be kept, or what confidence could anyone have in engagements given by Great Britain in the future? The Chancellor said, "But at what price will that compact have been kept. Has the British Government thought of that?" I hinted to his Excellency as plainly as I could that fear of consequences could hardly be regarded as an excuse for breaking solemn engagements.[137]

The chancellor never denied his words (though he regretted having said them), and T. G. Otte has recently examined this famous conversation from every angle and concluded that Goschen's summary was correct.[138] Perhaps because "scrap of paper" became such a cliché, historians no longer take it seriously. They should. Surely it is significant that at their very

---

135. Marc Frey, *Der Erste Weltkrieg und die Niederlande: Ein neutrales Land im politischen und wirtschaftlichen Kalkül der Kriegsgegner,* Studien Zur Internationalen Geschichte (Berlin, 1998), 70; German National Constituent Assembly, *Official German Documents Relating to the World War,* trans. Division of International Law Carnegie Endowment for International Peace (New York, 1923), 1:253–54.

136. Goschen to Grey, London, Aug. 8, 1914, printed in Great Britain, *Great Britain and the European Crisis: Correspondence, and Statements in Parliament, together with an Introductory Narrative of Events* (London, 1914), no. 160, pp. 110–14. This telegram was based on an earlier one written on the fourth, which was never sent. Goschen's original letter is in FO 371/2164, file 30342, no. 41041.

137. Goschen to Grey, London, Aug. 8, 1914, in Great Britain, *Great Britain and the European Crisis,* 111.

138. T. G. Otte, "A 'German Paperchase': The 'Scrap of Paper' Controversy and the Problem of Myth and Memory in International History," *Diplomacy and Statecraft* 18 (2007): 53–87.

last meeting the two spokesmen for Britain and Germany argued about international law. Jagow had spelled out to Goschen the strategic requirements of the Schlieffen Plan and summarized the situation by saying "that the safety of the Empire" required the advance through Belgium. Bethmann's remark about "fighting for [one's] life" repeated that view, and it was the same argument he used to explain Germany's action to the Reichstag. Both men understood safety or security in a military manner, both imagined a world of aggressive enemies, and both judged that in that situation, law would be swept away. Bethmann's phrase was drastic, but accurate: the Wilhelminian interpretation of self-defense permitted or even required the abrogation of treaty law. Goschen summarized Britain's position equally clearly: regardless of consequences, Britain must uphold its international agreements or else lose the good faith and credit it enjoyed in the world. Goschen used the word "honor" in the same way as the cabinet members had done, as an amalgam of legal, moral, and security considerations. If Britain's word counted for nothing, it would be unable to build the thousand arrangements and understandings with other nations and economic actors on which its own security relied; that is why international law was equally a "life or death" issue for Britain. The "scrap of paper" was an adequate summary of what the war was actually about.

Self-Defense versus State of Emergency: *Notwehr* versus *Notstand*

Earlier on August 4, before he spoke to Goschen, Bethmann had explained Germany's situation to the Reichstag.[139] His speech was the only time during the war that a German spokesman acknowledged publicly that Germany had broken international law. He began by saying that "a powerful fate [*Schicksal*]" had broken over Europe, that "in peaceful work we have become strong and mighty and therefore envied," and that "covered by the allegation that Germany was warlike, enmities in East and West...had forged chains against us"—phrases that reflected the leadership's conviction that war was inevitable (fate) if Germany tried to break those chains preventing it from becoming as "strong and mighty" as possible. These hints about the expansion of German power then disappeared in Bethmann's rehearsal of the diplomatic events leading to "a war forced upon us by Russia and France." Russian mobilization forced Germany to launch the war, lest it leave "the time of attack to the powers between whom we are wedged in." Using general staff allegations of the kind already contained in the draft ultimatum to Belgium of July 26, Bethmann accused France of "actually having attacked us." Admitting to one border violation by Germany, the chancellor accused French troops of having attacked German border guards and French planes of having bombed targets in South Germany. Germany later dropped all of these allegations.[140] But in August, they provided the basis for Bethmann's legal argument. He said:

---

139. *Sten.Ber.*, Legislaturperiode 13, 2. Session, vol. cccvi (Berlin, 1914), 5–7.

140. Garner, *International Law*, 2:210–11; Lademacher, *Belgische Neutralität*, 464. Various sections of government tried for years to find evidence of Allied violations of Belgium's neutrality; they ultimately gave up: see BAB R 901 86587–86593.

Gentlemen, we are now in a situation of self-defense [*Notwehr*]; and necessity knows no law! [*Not kennt kein Gebot*] Our troops have occupied Luxembourg, and perhaps have already entered Belgian territory. Gentlemen, that contradicts international law. The French government has declared to Brussels that it will respect Belgian neutrality so long as the enemy does. But we knew that France stood ready to attack. France could wait, we could not! A French attack on our flank on the lower Rhine could have become disastrous [*verhängnisvoll*]. So, we were forced to override the legitimate protest of the governments of Luxembourg and Belgium. This injustice [*Unrecht*]—I speak openly—this injustice that we are doing, we will seek to make good as soon as our military goal is reached. Whoever is as threatened as we are and who fights for his most important goals [*sein Höchstes*], can only think about how he shall hack his way through! [Long tumultuous applause and clapping in the entire house and on the rostrum.]

This is a succinct statement of the primacy of military necessity over international law. Why did the chancellor admit so openly Germany's violation of law? Did Bethmann's admission reflect his own unease at Germany's military methods? Probably not, for this famous passage was not Bethmann's at all. The press chief of the AA, Otto Hammann, added it to induce the Social Democrats to support the war.[141] At least part of Hammann's surmise was correct; throughout the war, the strongest voices raised in the Reichstag for upholding international law came from Social Democrats. As for the chancellor, his regard for international law seems to have been mostly instrumental.

Notstand and *Notwehr*

Although the chancellor used *Notwehr*, or self-defense, as Germany's legal cover, the correct legal term was *Notstand*, as many jurists noted.[142] *Notstand* remained Germany's official defense, repeated by Chancellor Georg von Hertling in late September 1918 and by the AA's jurist, Johannes Kriege, after the war.[143] What is the difference? In German municipal law, *Notwehr* is the force a person may legally use to defend himself against an unjust attack. *Notstand*, a condition of necessity, excuses a person from having harmed the rights of third parties in the course of defending himself; it does not require a preceding injustice. But *Notstand* was not a concept in international law. In fact, as Kriege later admitted, "only a few [non-German states had concepts] close to that standpoint" in

141. AA/PA, Nl. Jagow, vol. 8, pt. 1, "Politische Aufsätze," "Der Durchmarsch durch Belgien," fols. 52–53.

142. Georges Kaeckenbeeck, "Divergences between British and Other Views on International Law," *Grotius Society, Problems of the War: Papers Read before the Society in the Year 1918* 4 (1918): 229. The Kaiser's speech to the Reichstag on August 4 also cited "Notwehr": Röhl, *Wilhelm 3*, 1175.

143. Georg Graf v. Hertling to the Reichstag, Sept. 24, 1918, in *Der Hauptausschuss des Deutschen Reichstags 1915–1918*, Quellen zur Geschichte des Parlamentarismus und der Politischen Parteien, ed. Reinhard Schiffers, Manfred Koch, and Hans Boldt (Düsseldorf, 1981–83), 4:2291; Kriege, "Entwurf."

their own municipal laws.[144] Josef Kohler, editor of the leading German international-legal journal, *Zeitschrift für Völkerrecht,* was reduced simply to insisting that *Notstand* "must also hold in international law" for "all cases where a justified or unjustified attack and a defense are possible."[145]

Notstand was indeed a slender reed. In 1913, the Swiss jurist Max Huber, later a distinguished justice on the Permanent Court of International Justice, carefully parsed the different forms of necessity inhering in the laws of war.[146] Despite Huber's adherence to General Julius von Hartmann's famous views on the exceptional quality of war and on the equation of all modern wars with existential threat, he nonetheless concluded that *Notstand* was not relevant to international law. He explicitly recognized the right of neutrals to defend themselves, and he underscored the binding strength of treaties guaranteeing permanent neutrality to states like Belgium. To abrogate those, he wrote, one would have to have recourse to what he called "reasons of state" (*Staatsnotwendigkeit*) or "war necessity" (*Kriegsnotwendigkeit*), which he carefully distinguished from mere military necessity. But he thought such abrogations would be extremely rare, since the legal road was open to denounce treaties that no longer served the state's interest. Of course, for seventeen years Germany's military plans had called for abrogating Belgian neutrality, yet it had never taken the legal route of renunciation, nor did the German government ever claim that changed circumstances (*rebus sic stantibus*) had voided the treaty.

During the 1920s, the AA's former chief legal officer Johannes Kriege labored at a draft defense of Germany's violation of Belgian neutrality. He hewed closely to the official line: Germany found itself in *Notstand,* and only the Schlieffen Plan could have saved it.[147] Because his report represents the most closely reasoned legal defense of Germany's violation of Belgian neutrality, we shall examine it in some detail.

In order to maintain that *Notstand* was recognized in international law, Kriege followed the usual practice of trying to discover its principles in the municipal laws of many states, in the writings of jurists, and/or in state practice. He was not altogether successful. He relied heavily on analogy to the German penal law, in which he claimed the concept was developed most fully. Yet it contained no paragraph on *Notstand;* paragraph 54 of the penal code simply listed conditions under which illegal acts affecting innocent third

144. Johannes Kriege, "Der deutsche Einmarsch in Belgien, eine Notstandshandlung (Ausarbeitung über den Begriff des Notstandes im Strafrecht, Völkerrechte und in der Staatenpraxis)," Kriege papers, vol. 4, no. 21, AA/PA; Charles de Visscher, "Les lois de la guerre et la théorie de la nécessité," *Revue général de droit international public* 24 (1917): 92.

145. Josef Kohler, "Notwehr und Neutralität," *Zeitschrift für Völkerrecht* 8, no. 1 (1914): 578. Cf. the admission by Allfeld in "Der Lusitania-Fall," *Zeitschrift für Völkerrecht* 9 (1916): 151.

146. Max Huber, "Die kriegsrechtlichen Verträge und die Kriegsraison," *Zeitschrift für Völkerrecht* 7 (1913): 351–74.

147. Johannes Kriege, "Der deutsche Einmarsch in Belgien, eine Notstandshandlung (Ausarbeitung über den Begriff des Notstandes im Strafrecht, Völkerrechte und in der Staatenpraxis)," AA/PA, Kriege papers, vol. 4, no. 21, 40–43. No. 25 is a second, more polished draft titled "Entwurf einer Denkschrift über die Verletzung der belgischen neutralität durch Deutschland für den Parlamentarischen Untersuchungs-Ausschuss des Reichstages." Neither draft is dated, but "Entwurf" is filed together with a letter dated March 29, 1929, suggesting that it dates from that year.

parties might be excused.[148] A survey of other states' laws revealed enormous diversity (including utter absence), making "it impossible to arrive at a uniform concept of *Notstand*." Nevertheless, he concluded that the concept was present in all nations and thus potentially applicable in international law.[149] Despite calling *Notstand* a "basic concept" of international law, Kriege could find it in international-legal writings only by including references to a right to self-preservation whose limits we have already examined. Finally, without adducing extraneous cases (involving, for example, claims of *rebus sic stantibus,* pursuit of alleged revolutionaries or criminals, or declarations of independence), Kriege was hard-pressed to find examples of state practice showing that *Notstand* existed as an international usage. His two most apposite cases were Frederick the Great's invasion of Saxony in 1756 and Japan's virtual annexation of Korea in 1904—both highly controversial examples of expansive adventurism.[150]

In the end, Kriege's concept of *Notstand* thus approximated the older doctrine of self-defense or self-preservation. But Kriege included only some of the limits that customary law placed on self-defense. He recognized just three necessary conditions: "existential danger," no other possible means of averting it, and no responsibility for creating the emergency situation on the part of the state claiming it. These are the same three conditions contained in German penal code paragraph 54.[151] Kriege omitted the limitations imposed by customary international law that required that the danger be immediate and real (not the result of assumption or imagination), the response proportionate, and compensation mandatory. Kriege insisted that compensation was voluntary.[152] Thus, this concept of *Notstand* significantly weakened the limits on acts of self-defense contained in customary law.

Kriege's elastic interpretation of existential danger was equally noteworthy. It included threats to "the existence of a state, its current territory or population, or its state power ... or independence to such a degree that its ability to function in the international legal sphere would be entirely ended or reduced to a minimum."[153] This language suggests that mere reduction of territory or relative power, as might occur in a lost war, was enough to trigger *Notstand* and suspend law. It also seemed to equate state participation in the international legal community with power, as if less powerful states were less able or less entitled to participate in the international legal arena. And it defined the state's existence broadly as current power or status. These assumptions led to this conclusion: "Every norm of international law can only be binding for each state if following it does not threaten its *Bestand*," a word that means "existence" but also "duration," or "current substance."[154] Kriege concluded that state practice had recognized *Notstand* "as an international-legal

---

148. Kriege, "Entwurf," 45–46; Germany, *Strafgesetzbuch für das Deutsche Reich. Mit Commentar von Hans Rüdorff* (Berlin, 1871), para. 54.

149. Kriege, "Entwurf," 51.

150. He also listed Britain's shelling of Copenhagen and seizure of the Danish fleet in 1807, which occurred during wartime. On the legal status of that action see Hall, *International Law,* 273–74.

151. Kriege, "Entwurf," 46; Germany, *StGB,* para. 54.

152. Kriege, "Entwurf," 73.

153. Ibid., 69.

154. Ibid., 58.

emergency right, an exceptional right [*Ausnahmerecht*] that supersedes all other rights" in the international-legal order.[155]

Kriege's case for *Notstand* summarized many of the operative assumptions of the late Kaiserreich. It conceived of state security in narrow military terms. It conflated state existence with relative state power and therefore inflated the international dangers it faced. It granted wide emergency powers to individual states, excusing them from obligations to treaty law and thus to the community. In doing so, it revealed a conception of the state system as coordinate; that is, it stressed sovereign authority over the state community and its lawmaking powers.

Appropriately enough, it fell to a Belgian jurist to deliver the most complete refutation of this point of view. Charles de Visscher had taught at Ghent and then fled to Britain during the war. Like Max Huber, de Visscher later helped to develop international law as a judge on the Permanent International Court of Justice. In 1917, he examined the various theories of necessity and their capacity to suspend or breach law. For our purposes, there are three important parts to his analysis. First, like most jurists, de Visscher found that *Notstand* in its various guises (which he combined together as *Notrecht*) did not exist in international law.[156] There were only two justifications for violating international law: reprisal and self-defense, Both were predicated upon a preceding injustice or illegal act, a central qualification missing from *Notstand*. De Visscher recognized in *Notstand* merely the recrudescence of what he took to be an older view of the unlimited right of states to do what they wanted. Second, the reduction of the state to its military capacity was neither descriptive of reality nor a proper basis for international relations: "The immediate object, the defeat of the enemy, is confused with the defense of the supreme interests of the belligerent state."[157] The military's needs were not synonymous with the good of the state. Third, and most important, the nature of the international community and its laws was entirely different from the narrow confines of mere coordination. Taking the Hague Conventions as his example, de Visscher wrote that such lawmaking treaties showed "a collaboration of states founded on the consciousness of a durable legal community of interests. By the sole fact of their participation in these conventions, states necessarily engage in subordinating the pursuit of their particular interests to the realization of a common end which is the object and the reason for their collaboration."[158] In this widespread view, there actually were abiding common interests among states that produced laws binding on them all and which took precedence over claims to sovereignty. Breaking such fundamental laws could be justified only by a prior violation of them and, I would add, only in order to reconstitute the community by protecting its state units. Claiming "necessity," de Visscher summarized, "is the negation of the principle on which international collaboration rests."[159]

---

155. Ibid., 67.

156. De Visscher, "Lois de la guerre," 87.

157. Ibid., 97.

158. Ibid., 102.

159. Ibid.

Aftermath

The Allied view that Germany's invasion of Belgium violated fundamental norms of international law and life seemed cogent to most observers outside Germany. Inside Germany, the invasion's devastating effect on official and public world opinion came as a surprise. Few Germans publicly accepted that the invasion was a legal wrong; among the exceptions were just two jurists, Hans Wehberg and Walter Schücking, and the leaders of Social Democracy.[160] The groundswell of anger at the chancellor's (or Hammann's) admission that Germany had broken international law was so strong (Bernhard von Bülow: "I would certainly not have talked before the assembled Reichstag about a wrong done to Belgium!") that the chancellor retracted the words on December 2, 1914.[161] Officials, Reichstag deputies, and jurists devoted much effort and imagination trying to show that France or Britain had violated Belgium's borders first, or that Belgium had violated its own neutrality by defending itself or by engaging in unofficial military conversations with Britain before the war, or that treaties guaranteed Belgium's neutrality but not its "inviolability," or that Belgium's colonial wealth made it ineligible for neutral status.[162] In the end, it was fruitless. Germany had to drop its allegations and legalisms.[163] The Weimar-era AA suppressed Kriege's postwar draft report. No official defense of Germany's invasion was ever published after the war.[164]

Despite their greater sensitivity to international law, neither Bethmann nor the AA could conceive of a state acting from legal obligation. In a famous interview with the Associated Press on January 24, 1915, Bethmann tried to minimize the damage from the "scrap of paper." He repeated his conviction that "England drew the sword only because it believed its own interests demanded it. Just for Belgian neutrality it would never have entered the war."[165] This false dichotomy of interest versus law was fundamental to

160. Ernst Stenzel, *Die Kriegführung des deutschen Imperialismus und das Völkerrecht; zur Planung und Vorbereitung des deutschen Imperialismus auf die barbarische Kriegführung im Ersten und Zweiten Weltkrieg, dargestellt an den vorherrschenden Ansichten zu den Gesetzen und Gebräuchen des Landkrieges (1900–1945)* (Berlin, 1973), 52.

161. Bülow: Ritter, *Schlieffen Plan*, 92; also, diary entry of Dec. 11, 1914, in Wolff, *Tagebücher*, 135. Bethmann's Dec. 2, 1914, speech: *Sten.Ber.*, vol. 306, 17–20. For a typical negative reaction to Bethmann's earlier admission, see Maj. Gen. Gerhard Tappen, cited in Mombauer, *Moltke*, 230.

162. See Garner's complete discussion of the German jurists' claims: Garner, *International Law*, 2: ch. 29; Josef Kohler, "Die Neutralität Belgiens und die Festungsverträge," *Zeitschrift für Völkerrecht* 9 (1916): 298–309; Kohler, "Notwehr und Neutralität"; Hermann Kreth (Conservative Party) in Reichstag 3 May 1917, Schiffers, Koch, and Boldt, *Hauptausschuss*, 3:1416, 1419.

163. Garner, *International Law*, 2:205–6; Thomas, *Guarantee*, 580.

164. Ulrich Heinemann, *Die verdrängte Niederlage; Politische Öffentlichkeit und Kriegsschuldfrage in der Weimarer Republik* (Göttingen, 1983), 197. Germany's postwar official legal defenses against Allied claims appeared in the published Reichstag investigation reports: Germany. Nationalversammlung, *Das Werk des Untersuchungsausschusses der Verfassungsgebenden Deutschen Nationalversammlung und des Deutschen Reichstages 1919–1928, Verhandlungen/Gutachten/Urkunden*, ser. 1, vols. 3 (1927), 10 (1930), 11 (1930); ser. 3, vols. 2–4 (1927); ser. 4, vols. 1–7 (1925–28) (Berlin, 1925–30).

165. "The Neutrality of Belgium," *American Journal of International Law* 9, no. 3 (July 1915): 717.

policy-making assumptions in Berlin. However, a number of influential Germans rejected that assumption. Among them was Theodor Wolff, the liberal editor of the *Berliner Tageblatt*. Again and again he returned to the subject in wartime interviews with government leaders. In December 1915, Wolff exclaimed to Bethmann that "the breach of international law that we committed by marching into Belgium weighs like a burden on German history. One can only remove it by restoring Belgium's complete independence." Bethmann refused to consider it because his military construal of Germany's security concerns made a return to the legal status quo ante impossible.[166] Like Wolff, Germany's last ambassador to Britain, Prince Karl von Lichnowsky, rejected Bethmann's concept of security guarantees, which in Lichnowsky's view "could only mean the erection of a military dictatorship in Belgium and Poland."[167] "A system based entirely on force," he continued, could have no "lasting success among civilized Europeans."

The view of Wolff and Lichnowsky was ultimately inscribed into the Covenant of the League of Nations, which saw security as dependent on "the maintenance of justice and a scrupulous respect for all treaty obligations" among states.[168] The principle that treaties, as sources of international law, must be upheld (*pacta sunt servanda*) has ancient roots and robust continuing development in customary law, the legal expectations of states (*opinio juris*), state practice and declarations, court decisions, and the United Nations Charter.[169] International relations cannot really be conceived without it. It is therefore in the fundamental and abiding interest of states that international law, including treaties, should exist and function. In 1928, Max Huber, whom we have already met, famously explained the intersection of law and interest in his decision in the *Palmas* arbitration case. "International law, like law in general, has the object of assuring the coexistence of different interests which are worthy of legal protection."[170] Interests and law are not antithetical; they are joined. If it is true that international law in 1914 coincided better with Britain's avowed interests than with Imperial Germany's, it also incorporated the interests of Belgium, Luxembourg, France, Holland, Denmark, etc. The broad protections inhering in the 1839 treaty covered much more than mere British security, though they also helped to shield that. As Lichnowsky pointed out in 1915, a more realistic, longer-term understanding of Imperial Germany's own interest would have recognized that "we must wish

---

166. Diary entry of Dec. 9, 1915, Wolff, *Tagebücher,* 322–23. See Bethmann's plans to make Belgium a "tributary state": Bethmann to Zimmermann, GHQ, Oct. 18, 1914, BAB R 901 85345.

167. Young, *Lichnowsky,* 144. Cf. "Aufzeichnung über die Behandlung Belgiens nach dem gegenwärtigen Kriege im Falle eines entscheidenden deutschen Sieges," appendix to Bethmann to Zimmermann, GHQ, Oct. 18, 1914, BAB R 901 85345, which also rejected Bethmann's plans as impossible to maintain against Belgian and world opinion.

168. Covenant of the League of Nations, available through the Avalon Project at http://avalon.law.yale.edu/20th_century/leagcov.asp.

169. For a succinct and learned synopsis: Wehberg, "Pacta"; cf. Vienna Convention on the Law of Treaties (1969), art. 26 *"Pacta sunt servanda,"* at http://untreaty.un.org/ilc/texts/instruments/english/conventions/1_1_1969.pdf.

170. Island of Palmas (Mangias) case (Netherlands/USA), April 4, 1928, Permanent Court of Arbitration, 2 U.N. Report of International Arbitral Awards, vol. 2, 829–71, here 870, http://untreaty.un.org/cod/riaa/cases/vol_II/829–871.pdf.

to create *lasting* and not temporary conditions," for "we need one another in this society of peoples."[171]

As it was, the "scrap of paper" and all it stood for seemed to condemn Imperial Germany in the eyes of that society. The next test of the writ of international law followed almost immediately, with Imperial Germany's conduct of the war in Belgium and Northern France and its administration of the occupied zones.

---

171. Young, *Lichnowsky,* 144.

The "Belgian Atrocities" and the Laws of War on Land

The opening days of combat instantly made the laws of war the center of public attention. Whether belligerents' conduct upheld or broke international law became hugely important to policy makers and to world public opinion. For the Western Allies, Imperial Germany's methods confirmed the impression of lawlessness produced by its violation of Belgian neutrality. For Germany, the disputes over lawful means of warfare revealed the cleft that seemed to separate it from many states whose militaries operated differently. For us, the inner European disagreement on lawful combat, especially regarding treatment of civilians, shows the enormous complexities involved in how international law develops, and underscores some of the most important issues at stake in the war.

World War I opened with the massacre of Belgian (and later, French) civilians by the German armies. These began on the first day of invasion, as soon as German troops encountered unexpected armed resistance from the Belgian army.[1] General Otto von Emmich, a veteran of the Franco-Prussian War given the critical task of immediately seizing the forts around Liège, issued a prepared proclamation as soon as his troops crossed the Belgian border on August 4. It repeated the offer Germany had made to Belgium and that Belgium had rejected: if Belgians permitted Germany unhindered crossing, no harm

---

1. John Horne and Alan Kramer, *German Atrocities, 1914: A History of Denial* (New Haven, CT, 2001), 13. Besides Horne and Kramer's book, the best-researched and most detailed accounts are by Lothar Wieland, *Belgien, 1914: Die Frage des belgischen "Franktireurkrieges" und die deutsche öffentliche Meinung von 1914 bis 1936* (Frankfurt, 1984), and Jeff Lipkes, *Rehearsals: The German Army in Belgium, August 1914* (Leuven, 2007). My account generally follows theirs. First day: Sophie De Schaepdrijver, *La Belgique et la Première Guerre Mondiale* (New York, 2004), 80; Wieland, *Belgien*, 20.

would come to them, and damage and requisitions would be recompensed. But it threatened that "the destruction of bridges, tunnels, and railways will be regarded as hostile acts. Belgians! It is for you to choose."[2]

The Schlieffen Plan, and doubtless most officers and their troops, had assumed that a weak, neutral, unprepared state like Belgium would permit the German army to cross it unhindered. Chief of Staff Helmuth von Moltke, Chancellor Theobald von Bethmann Hollweg, and the Kaiser knew differently. On December 19, 1912, the Belgian king had told Wilhelm in no uncertain terms that Belgium would fight to protect itself from an invader, and it was planning to increase its army to do just that. But that increase was unfinished in August 1914, and Moltke judged that beforehand, "Belgium would probably be too weak to defend her neutrality with arms."[3] Moltke's view reflected among other things the widespread conviction that small states were negligible, even nonviable entities because the measure of a state was military power. Recall Kaiser Wilhelm's repeated expostulation that he would honor neutrality only if the neutral state could defend itself. "Military realism" also expected the weak to recognize their subordinate status and to give in to the inevitable facts of force. Belgium was obviously no match for Imperial Germany. General Karl von Einem expressed the astonishment widespread among officers and troops that Belgium would fight: "It would mean their ruin," he exclaimed.[4] And it did. As the Belgian army and militia (and later, French and British troops) successfully disrupted the smooth unfolding of the Schlieffen Plan, junior officers reacted with a wave of violence.

This first phase of violence took seven forms: executions (850 civilians were shot between August 5 and 8); arson (one hundred houses in a single incident on August 5, three hundred in another); burning of whole villages (Micheroux on the sixth, Louveigné on the seventh); hostage taking; use of human shields (sometimes in groups of two hundred to four hundred civilians at once); killing unarmed prisoners of war; and pillage. By August 8, every one of the thirteen infantry regiments investing the fortresses at Liège had engaged in such acts.[5] The motive seems to have been primarily revenge (together with indiscipline and drunkenness) in retaliation for reverses suffered at the hands of the Belgian army defending the Liège forts.[6] However, from the first (already on August 4), Emmich's interpretation was that "civilians have fired on our troops."[7]

After the city of Liège (though not all its forts) fell on August 8, opening the passage for the bulk of Germany's troops, there was a momentary lull in violence against civilians. During this period Imperial Germany tried again to get the Belgian government to stop its resistance, but was once more rebuffed (August 10). Two days later, Germany announced its official policy in an order by Chief of Staff Moltke that in effect covered the events that

---

2. Lipkes, *Rehearsals,* 39.

3. Theobald v. Bethmann Hollweg memorandum, Dec. 22, 1912, cited in Annika Mombauer, *Helmuth von Moltke and the Origins of the First World War* (Cambridge, 2001), 162.

4. Einem diary, Sept. 13, 1914, Karl von Einem, *Ein Armeeführer erlebt den Weltkrieg; persönliche Aufzeichnungen,* ed. Junius Alter (Leipzig, 1938), 38.

5. Horne and Kramer, *German Atrocities,* 10–23.

6. Ibid., 17–18; Lipkes, *Rehearsals,* 44, detailed account: 39–124.

7. Lipkes, *Rehearsals,* 94.

had already occurred. He claimed that civilians had fired on German soldiers, which "contravenes international law." He warned that any nonuniformed person resisting the German advance "will be treated as a franc-tireur and immediately shot according to martial law." "If the conduct of war should thus assume an especially harsh character, Germany is not responsible. France [Belgium] alone is responsible for the streams of blood that it will cost."[8]

Moltke's order appears to have gone out to every army, for all of them now acted in concert.[9] Planned reprisal displaced spontaneous actions, and to the executions, arson, systematic pillaging, and hostage taking was added expulsion/deportation—by February 1915, between thirteen thousand and fourteen thousand Belgian and ten thousand French civilians had been deported to Germany.[10] During this second phase after mid-August, the policy of reprisal was invoked variously after incidents of friendly fire, panicky drunkenness, frustration at having to retreat, or surprise by well-camouflaged French or Belgian troops. The result was major massacres in Andenne (262 dead), Dinant (674), Aarschot (156), Ethe (218), and Tamines (383), culminating in the fiery destruction of much of the university town of Louvain with its priceless medieval library and the deaths of 248 civilians.[11] By the time trench warfare had frozen movement on the Western front, 6,427 Belgian and French civilians had been purposely killed; half of the three hundred regiments involved in the invasion had participated in civilian massacres.[12] The aerial bombardment by zeppelin of Antwerp (August 25) and the shelling of the French medieval cathedral of Reims (September 17–19), which the Germans suspected was an observation post, capped Germany's opening campaign and cemented its reputation as brutal and lawless.

News of Germany's war conduct traveled fast. French president Raymond Poincaré had learned of hostage taking by August 7 and civilian executions by the eleventh; he heard about Louvain just four days after it happened.[13] The newly arrived secretary to the United States legation, Hugh Gibson, inspected Louvain while it was still being destroyed. An officer told him that Germany was destroying the town "under definite orders": "We shall make this place a desert. We shall wipe it out so that it will be hard to find where Leuven used to stand. For generations people will come here to see what we have done, and it will teach them to respect Germany and to think twice before they resist her."[14] The Belgian government (August 7), France (September 23, 1914), and Britain (December 15, 1914) appointed official commissions to investigate German conduct.[15] By mid-September, Belgium had already published three volumes detailing German actions,

---

8. Moltke to AA, no. 1605, Berlin, Aug. 12, 1914, AA/PA R 20880; partly cited in Horne and Kramer, *German Atrocities*, 95.

9. Horne and Kramer, *German Atrocities*, 70.

10. Ibid., 29, 39, 40, 52, 72, 76–77.

11. Ibid., 24–53, and appendix 1.

12. Ibid., 74, 76.

13. Raymond Poincaré, *The Memoirs of Raymond Poincaré, 1914,* trans. George Arthur (Garden City, NY, 1929), 16, 22, 34, 112.

14. Hugh Gibson, *A Journal from Our Legation in Belgium* (Garden City, NY, 1917), 172, 162–63.

15. David Stevenson, *French War Aims against Germany* (Oxford, 1982), 235n6; Gary S. Messinger, *British Propaganda and the State in the First World War* (Manchester, 1992), 71; Gerd Hankel, *Die Leipziger*

France produced twelve by the war's end, and Britain sold its 360-page Bryce Report (1915) for a mere one pence to guarantee the widest circulation.[16] By August 20, France had drafted a notice to all neutral nations telling them that Germany had now added to its original "crime against civilization" (violating Belgian neutrality) "barbarous" war conduct. France enumerated especially acts expressly forbidden by the Hague rules of land warfare: "killing the wounded, firing on ambulances and Red Cross personnel, bombarding non-defended towns, placing French wounded on the German front lines, misusing Belgian and French uniforms and flags, using dumdum bullets, murder, arson, imprisoning consuls, violating neutrality."[17] More important was the French charge that these acts were not isolated atrocities, but a "system, ordered by the heads of the German army." "The triumph of the German system," it concluded, "would be the total negation of law and the independence of nations." On the twenty-eighth France sent its appeal to thirty-seven neutral and Allied nations.[18]

This official activity was probably unnecessary; revulsion was instantaneous and widespread. Even the pro-German former president of Switzerland confided to the French ambassador that he thought these were the "acts of savages."[19] The "Belgian atrocities," as they quickly became known, apparently also helped to poison Italy's already strained relations with its alliance partners.[20] The unanimous foreign reaction was not lost on Germany. Theodor Wolff of the *Berliner Tageblatt,* himself sickened by the news of Louvain, instantly knew that "the impression abroad will be completely disastrous [*höchst übel*]."[21] That same day (August 28), the commander of the German Sixth Army, Bavarian Crown Prince Rupprecht, forbade further acts of village burning, thinking it counterproductive, unfair, and dangerous to troop discipline. When Antwerp fell to the Germans in October, the Kaiser wanted no troops to enter it, in order to prevent a second Louvain.[22] In any event, once the war of movement stopped, so did the occasion for reprisals of this kind. The damage to Germany's international reputation had already been done. Bergson's

---

Prozesse: Deutsche Kriegsverbrechen und ihre strafrechtliche Verfolgung nach dem Ersten Weltkrieg (Hamburg, 2003), 168n251.

16. Belgium and Official Commission of the Belgian Government, *Reports on the Violation of the Rights of Nations and of the Laws and Customs of War in Belgium* (London: HMSO, 1914); Foreign Office, France, *Les violations des lois de la guerre par l'Allemagne* (Paris, 1915); Great Britain, *Report of the Committee on Alleged German Outrages Appointed by His Britannic Majesty's Government and Presided Over by the Right Hon. Viscount Bryce* (London, 1914). One pence: Michael L. Sanders and Philip M. Taylor, *British Propaganda during the First World War* (London, 1982), 120.

17. "Memorandum of an appeal to neutral powers," Cabinet of the Foreign Office, no. 9, Aug. 20, 1914, *DDFr* 1: doc. 101.

18. *DDFr* 1: doc. 137.

19. Amb. Beau to For. Min. Delcassé, Bern, Nr. 263, Aug. 30, 1914, in *DDFr* 1: doc. 141.

20. Alan Kramer, *Dynamic of Destruction: Culture and Mass Killing in the First World War* (Oxford, 2007), 15.

21. Wolff diary, Aug. 28, 1914, *Theodor Wolff. Tagebücher 1914–1919; Der Erste Weltkrieg und die Entstehung der Weimarer Republik in Tagebüchern, Leitartikeln und Briefen des Chefredakteurs am "Berliner Tageblatt" und Mitbegründer der "Deutschen Demokratischen Partei,"* ed. Bernd Sösemann (Boppard am Rhein, 1984), 1:94.

22. Rupprecht diary of Aug. 28, 1914, in Rupprecht Kronprinz von Bayern, *Mein Kriegstagebuch,* ed. Eugen von Frauenholz (Munich, 1929), 1:65; Pohl diary of Oct. 13, 1914, Hugo Pohl, *Aus Aufzeichnungen und Briefen während der Kriegszeit* (Berlin, 1920), 77.

epithet of August 8—"the struggle of civilization against barbarism"—circulated for the rest of the war.[23]

Germany never denied its actions. It contended throughout the war and afterward that Belgian civilians had illegally engaged in hostilities against the German occupation; it had been a criminal "people's war" against which Germany was entitled to respond by reprisal.[24] Reprisal was Germany's earliest legal claim and remained its main cover. For example, on the very first day of invasion, one German colonel told the mayor of Herve, whom he was taking hostage: "Since our entry into this country, our troops have been fired upon.... The laws of war authorize reprisals; burning, shooting."[25] On the same day General Emmich made the same charge at Visé, where twelve civilians were executed after Belgian troops destroyed a bridge.[26] In other incidents, high-ranking officers cited a right of self-defense, deterrence through collective punishment, or military necessity.[27]

There are broadly four explanations for the "Belgian atrocities": (1) there was a "people's war" in which Belgian and French citizens took up arms; (2) there was none, but German troops acting under a mass delusion believed there was; (3) Germany's military culture predisposed its leaders, first, to interpret setbacks encountered in militarily inferior countries as the result of perfidy, and second, in any case to place such a premium on victory that civilian lives were readily sacrificed to military convenience; and (4) German purposely launched a reign of terror to cow potential resistance. The second and third possibilities are interrelated, and both together achieve the results of the fourth. Let us briefly examine them.

The sheer scale of Germany's reprisals has suggested to some that there must have been some truth to its claim of a "people's war." Or, perhaps troops mistook the Belgian civil guard, with its partial uniforms, for civilian fighters?[28] Belgium did call up the non-active civil guard on August 5; it informed Germany on August 8 how they were uniformed; it disbanded them on August 15 (before the worst massacres), either to make any claims of mistaken identity impossible, or because they stood no chance against the vastly superior German army.[29] Even during their brief call-up, the non-active civil guard mostly functioned as policemen, not soldiers. The active civil guard, which clearly fulfilled the Hague Rules defining legitimate soldiers, did fight the Germans at Liège and elsewhere in the beginning days of the war. As the elder Moltke had done in 1870–71, German units interpreted them as illegal combatants.[30] As we shall see, the prewar discussion at the Hague Conventions had forewarned the Belgian government that Germany was likely to expect

---

23. Cited in Kramer, *Dynamic of Destruction*, 183.

24. Germany and Foreign Office, *Die völkerrechtswidrige Führung des belgischen Volkskriegs* (Berlin, 1915).

25. Cited in Horne and Kramer, *German Atrocities*, 13.

26. Lipkes, *Rehearsals*, 94.

27. Horne and Kramer, *German Atrocities*, 15, 17–18, 33, 64.

28. This is Hankel's surmise, without evidence. He assumes that, given the preceding discussions at the Hague Conference in 1899 (which are analyzed below), there might well have been a people's war: Hankel, *Leipziger Prozesse*, 279, 279n616.

29. Horne and Kramer, *German Atrocities*, 125–29; Gibson, *Journal*, 96.

30. Horne and Kramer, *German Atrocities*, 129. In August 1870, Moltke had declared that franc-tireurs were liable to the death penalty, despite the fact that they were uniformed: Helmuth von Moltke, *Militärische*

franc-tireurs and to react accordingly. Therefore, on August 4 it warned every commune in the country (2,700 of them) to tell its citizens "not to fight; To utter no insulting or threatening words; To remain within their houses and close the windows, so that it will be impossible to allege that there has been any provocation" that "might serve as a pretext for measures of repression . . . or the massacre of the innocent population."[31] In many localities mayors collected their citizens' guns to make sure no incidents occurred. Careful studies at the time and since, including two recent examinations using archival evidence, have established that no "people's war" ever took place in Belgium (or Northern France, where German troops committed the same pattern of reprisal), either in the form of a *levée en masse* before the arrival of German troops, or an insurrection after occupation.[32]

There were German doubters, too. Even as he ordered reprisals for nighttime attacks on his troops, General von Einem nevertheless chalked up Germany's heavy losses before Liège to friendly fire, not devious civilians.[33] Germany's own investigations do not seem to have upheld its official view. When 416 alleged franc-tireurs from Dinant were finally released from prison in mid-November 1914, General von Longchamps told one of them that his investigation had shown that no civilians had fired weapons. But perhaps, he thought, "French soldiers in civil clothing" might have done so, but in any case he admitted that "under the press of events, the right balance is often exceeded."[34] At the war's end, as Germany prepared to negotiate with the Allies, the head of the legal division of the foreign office (AA), Johannes Kriege, advised against offering to submit to a neutral investigation of the "Belgian atrocities," because "then we will get the entire war reparations dumped on us"—a view he would hardly have held had Germany had good evidence of its claim.[35]

One of the most intriguing explanations for the massacres is mass delusion. In the words of historians John Horne and Alan Kramer, the franc-tireur myth was "a massive case of collective self-suggestion, probably unparalleled in a modern army."[36] It is certainly true that even officers who admitted that some men "might have seen ghosts" still believed in the reality of the franc-tireurs.[37] It was a myth long in the making. France's *levée en*

Korrespondenz aus den Dienstschriften des Krieges 1870/71, 1st section, 3rd part, ed. General Staff Germany (Berlin, 1896), doc. 193, pp. 241–42.

31. Minister of the interior circular of Aug. 4, 1914, cited in Gibson, *Journal,* 31.

32. Horne and Kramer, *German Atrocities;* Wieland, *Belgien;* Belgium, Ministère de la justice, *Réponse au livre blanc allemand du 10 mai 1915,* "Die völkerrechtswidrige Führung des belgischen Volkskriegs" (Paris, 1916). On the accuracy of the Belgian reply, see Horne and Kramer, *German Atrocities,* 246 and 513n95; Lipkes, *Rehearsals.*

33. Diary entry of Aug. 9, 1914, Einem, *Armeeführer,* 36.

34. Cited in Carl Ernst, *Der große Krieg in Belgien; Beobachtungen seinen ehemaligen hannoverschen Landsleuten gewidmet* (Gembloux, Belgium, 1930), 66.

35. Cited in Prince Max von Baden, *Erinnerungen und Dokumente* (Stuttgart, 1927), 458. See also General Max v. Hoffmann's interpretation of Germany's refusal to show France its court-martial protocols of alleged franc-tireurs in exchange for France's documents on French treatment of German prisoners of war: diary entry Oct. 12, 1915, Max von Hoffmann, *Die Aufzeichnungen des Generalmajors Max Hoffmann,* ed. Karl-Friedrich Nowak (Berlin, 1929), 1:96.

36. Horne and Kramer, *German Atrocities,* 77. Also, Wieland, *Belgien,* 11–16.

37. Ghosts: Max von Gallwitz, *Meine Führertätigkeit im Weltkriege 1914/1916: Belgien—Osten—Balkan* (Berlin, 1929), 29. Believers: Gen. Hans v. Plessen to Countess Brockdorff, Sept. 10, 1914, in *Kaiser Wilhelm II.*

masse in 1870–71 had been one of the formative lessons of the German army. The frustration and cost of indecisive guerrilla warfare and the rejection of democratic methods of warfare in favor of the superior discipline that the general staff associated with itself joined to make the franc-tireurs of 1870 into an object lesson taught to officers down to 1914. The discussions at the Brussels Convention (1874) and at The Hague (1899) on the legality of the *levée en masse* also kept the memory alive. But the myth was not self-perpetuating. The specter of franc-tireurs was purposely reignited in a press campaign beginning on August 9 (after the first phase of violence); it primed German troops just crossing the border to interpret regular battle as criminal resistance.[38] Officers and the patriotic shapers of public opinion thus instrumentalized a claim that conveniently excused taboo-breaking violence that had already occurred.

There is no question that the franc-tireur myth was at work in August-September 1914. But it cannot by itself explain what happened. I have argued elsewhere that Imperial Germany's military culture was fundamental to precipitating the "Belgian atrocities."[39] A particularly strong variant of organizational culture, Germany's military culture defined and pursued warfare in ways that were distilled into the Schlieffen Plan. That plan's burden of an inexorable, unrealistic timetable, requiring great risk and huge sacrifices, its guarantee of a single "prescription for victory" that by applying the greatest force to the smallest area would lead to the swift and total annihilation of the enemy's forces, its discounting of "friction" such as Belgian armed resistance, set the stage for draconian measures to fulfill its impossible demands. The Schlieffen Plan flowed from a broader set of organizational habits and assumptions that included the concentration on combat and battle at the cost of logistics (thus requiring heavy requisitions and frequent contact with civilians), and of all other considerations (like law or economics); the demand that even its junior officers act independently, decisively, and prophylactically in excess of what a situation required (the so-called "mission system"); the conviction that the only acceptable victory was total destruction of the enemy; a disdain for mere civilians and thus a propensity to instrumentalize them for military ends, etc.[40] These habits, scripts, and assumptions made excessive force likely, though not inevitable. The franc-tireur myth, with its rigidly dichotomous model of disciplined, law-abiding uniformed soldiers versus treacherous, criminal civilians, thrived in this atmosphere, and the Kaiserreich's military culture, with its goal of quick, complete victory and its obliviousness to the real obstacles to achieving it, created just the military necessities and frustration that both required and fed such a myth. Regarding the "Belgian atrocities," the franc-tireur myth and Imperial German military culture reinforced each other.

---

als Oberster Kriegsherr im Ersten Weltkrieg; Quellen aus der militärischen Umgebung des Kaisers 1914–1918, ed. Holger Afflerbach (Munich, 2005), 659; Wilhelm Kronprinz von Preußen, *Meine Erinnerungen aus Deutschlands Heldenkampf* (Berlin, 1923), 49; Fritz von Loßberg, *Meine Tätigkeit im Weltkriege 1914–1918* (Berlin, 1939), 13, 17, 18–19.

38. Wieland, *Belgien,* 10–31, 39–44.

39. Isabel V. Hull, *Absolute Destruction: Military Culture and the Practices of War in Imperial Germany* (Ithaca, NY, 2005), 208–12, but passim.

40. Ibid., chs. 6–7.

Already on August 5, Moltke wrote to Austrian chief of staff Franz Conrad von Hötzendorf that "our procedure in Belgium is certainly brutal, but for us it is a matter of life and death and whoever gets in our way must bear the consequences." On the same day he repeated to Foreign Minister Gottlieb von Jagow, "the serious situation in which the fatherland finds itself makes it a duty to use every means that can harm the enemy."[41] Coming one day after the chancellor, using the same phrase "life or death," had told the Reichstag that "necessity knows no law," Moltke's letters strongly suggest that perceived military necessity was behind a policy of brutality that found a convenient excuse in the myth of the franc-tireur.

The Allies interpreted Moltke's military necessity as premeditated terror for military purposes.[42] State terror subsequently became a common Allied interpretation of other methods of warfare, such as aerial bombing of cities, occupation policies, and unrestricted submarine warfare.[43]

For our purposes, the important question is what the German army and government believed legal under the international laws of war. In all of the practices that together made up the "Belgian atrocities"—the reach of military necessity, the proper scope of reprisals, hostage taking and hostage killing, burning villages, collective fines, the question of who was a proper combatant, the definition of genuine occupation, the right to requisition and levy taxes, etc.—Germany had disagreed with most other European states on the law for almost fifty years. From the standpoint of international law, the "Belgian atrocities" had been prefigured for decades. There is every reason to believe that Imperial Germany thought its actions legal, permissible, or at least excusable; this is why it never denied them.

Germany was not alone in many of its interpretations of law; the "arch-occupier" Russia frequently voted with it.[44] Austria-Hungary, which appears to have faced large contingents of irregular troops (*comitadji*) in 1914, reacted with the same palette of immediate executions, deportation, mass internment of civilians, hostage taking, collective fines, and

---

41. Both citations in Wieland, *Belgien,* 7.

42. Horne and Kramer, *German Atrocities,* 165, 235–37; A. Méringhac, "De la sanction des infractions au droit des gens commises, au cour de la guerre européenne, par les empires du centre," *Revue générale de droit international public* 24 (1917): 11.

43. République Française, Documents relatifs à la guerre 1914–1915–1916–1917: Rapports et procès-verbaux d'enquéte de la commission instituée en vue de constater les actes commis par l'ennemi en violation du droit des gens (Décret du 23 Sept. 1914), vol. 8 (Paris, 1917), 15 [in SHAT 6N1]; Louis Rolland, "Les pratiques de la guerre aérienne dans le conflit de 1914 et le droit des gens," *Revue générale de droit international public* 23 (1916): 537; Antoine Pillet, "La guerre actuelle et le droit des gens," *Revue générale de droit international public* 23 (1916): 428; Lassa Oppenheim, "The Legal Relations between an Occupying Power and the Inhabitants," *Law Quarterly Review* 33, no. 4 (October 1917): 370; Robert Lansing to Ambassador James Gerard, Washington, Oct. 19, 1914, in United States, *Papers Relating to the Foreign Relation of the United States: The Lansing Papers, 1914–1920* (Washington, DC, 1939), 1: no. 445.

44. Best's phrase and analysis: Geoffrey Best, *Humanity in Warfare: The Modern History of the International Law of Armed Conflicts* (New York, 1980), 180–81.

arson.[45] Many of the disputes during the prewar codification process pitted the great land powers against smaller nations, large land powers with small armies (Britain), or large land powers whose recent history made them capable of conceiving of themselves as the occupied rather than the occupier (France). But Germany was indeed alone in holding some positions, it was more vociferous and vocal than Russia or Austria-Hungary, and it was the only power that held *all* of the views that became synonymous with "militarism."

Fundamental disagreements among the European states meant that the codified laws of war (the Hague Rules) were silent on important issues. That silence increased the importance of rules of interpretation: What was customary law (that is, binding law that was not yet written down)? How did one think law developed? How could one recognize it? Making matters more difficult was the fact that the international law of war was changing rapidly from 1870 to 1914. One can observe that change in such developments as these: the movement away from simple acceptance of war as another tool of state policy and a nascent rejection of aggressive war (in the requirement that war be preceded by a declaration or ultimatum explaining the grounds); recognition of the patriotic feelings of modern citizens who were no longer mere subjects (the rejection of oaths of allegiance required of occupied civilians, their protection against having to collaborate in their enemy's military efforts, the legality of the *levée en masse* in unoccupied areas); the recognition of the integrity of states within the Western community (occupied territory did not automatically become annexed to the occupant); and basic rights of occupied civilians (no collective punishments, detailing the protections of family and honor to be upheld by occupants).

Horne and Kramer conclude that "the German army had no intention of accepting the provisions of Convention IV [the Hague rules of land warfare] in spirit or in letter."[46] Their judgment rests on Germany's actions in 1914 and on an important prewar service manual. But the possible evidence base is much larger than this because, in addition to other manuals, law books, and commentaries, Germany's military representatives played an important role in drafting the Hague Rules, during the course of which they revealed important assumptions about both law and war. Even an intention to violate raises questions: Did Germany's representatives negotiate in bad faith (on the analogy with the decades-long public charade that Germany would not violate Belgian neutrality)? Did they simply not take law seriously? Or, did they understand the law differently? And of course, it was the German state, not the general staff, that signed the Hague Conventions; we must ask if the famously polycratic nature of the German state did not also produce a split view of legal interpretation and obligation.

The following sections examine the discussions among first the European states in 1874 and then a wider group of states in 1899. They reveal that Imperial Germany had developed a different understanding of international law from that of its neighbors regarding

---

45. Jonathan E. Gumz, *The Resurrection and Collapse of Empire in Habsburg Serbia, 1914–1918,* Cambridge Military Histories (Cambridge, 2009), 21, 33n18, 38, 42, 45–61, 102, 202–3; Andrej Mitrovic, *Serbia's Great War, 1914–1918,* Central European Studies (West Lafayette, IN, 2007), 73–78, 218, 236, 276.

46. Horne and Kramer, *German Atrocities,* 149.

both material law (i.e., the content of the rules) and the nature of law, its development, and obligatoriness. These differences already were well developed by 1914.

Germany at the Brussels Conference (1874)

Russia invited the other European states to meet in Brussels in 1874 to codify the international laws of war. Until then, European armies had operated according to customary rules developed gradually from state practices that states had come to regard as binding. Codification promised that disagreements might be laid to rest or at least clarified, thus at the same time extending legal protections and making command decisions easier. At Brussels, the diplomatic/legal and military experts of thirteen states eventually revised an original Russian draft code; their result was nonbinding but intended to provide the model for similar national codes. In fact, the final Brussels draft became the template for the Hague Convention of 1899.

Military input was strong, even predominant according to some interpreters. Belgium's diplomatic representative Auguste Baron Lambermont regretted that the conference had spent more time on material rather than moral concerns and had stressed security issues at the expense of others.[47] Nevertheless, one can see a steady movement toward limiting the use of force in war. There are many examples: the list of weapons and methods absolutely forbidden (245); the suppression of a section originally permitting "the destruction of everything that hinders the success of operations of war" (40); the same for a section listing rather wide-ranging belligerent permissions (247–48). In addition, requisitions were restricted proportionately to the ability of the occupied area to raise them (164); "contributions" (levies in excess of taxes) and fines were not to be expropriative or self-enriching, but restricted to defraying the occupant's expenses (164); mere conquest was not annexation (206–7); and spies could no longer be shot out of hand—they had to be tried first (52–53).

Although both Germany and Russia defended belligerent military rights most strongly, neither opposed codification; after all, Russia had convened the conference in the first place. Military men of both powers favored detailed positive laws to give field commanders more guidance, for example, concerning what one could take as requisitions (213, 167–68). But there was profound disagreement on what constituted real occupation, who was a legitimate combatant, the rights of occupied citizens, and the use of reprisals. These were exactly the areas defining the "Belgian atrocities."

---

47. Best on the height of the "arch-occupier" influence: Best, *Humanity in Warfare*, 183–84. The protocols of the conference: Brussels, Conference, 1874, *Actes de la Conférence de Bruxelles (1874)* (Brussels, 1899), available through Hathitrust, http://hdl.handle.net/2027/wu.89101297448. Hereafter, *Actes*, or cited in text by page number. Lambermont quote, 198.

Occupation

Both Russia and Germany were concerned that a stringent definition of genuine occupation would force them to leave too many active troops in the occupied zone. Therefore, both argued that an invader need not exercise a large, visible presence in order to establish legal occupation (239). They clashed with the majority view that wanted to apply to occupation the same criterion that the Pact of Paris had applied to blockade in 1856, in the first international codification of the laws of (maritime) war, namely, that it should be "real" and not "paper." Troops should be present in such quantity as to guarantee that they could exercise genuine control (129–31). Russia was closer to the majority view than Germany. Russian general Geinrikh Antonovich von Leer thought occupation was real when one part of the army had established its positions and lines of communication with the rear (129). German general Konstantin Bernhard von Voigts-Rhetz warned that requiring visible presence would only "provoke insurrections" that would be "followed by cruel repression and war would become atrocious" (129). Voigts-Rhetz had experience in this realm: he had helped suppress the Revolution of 1848 in Germany and was a veteran of the Franco-Prussian War with its sharp response to guerrilla warfare. In his view, real occupation occurred when the population was disarmed, "or when columns have crossed the country and established relations with the local authorities" (132). Germany's loose standards meant that it would tend to consider areas "occupied," and thus subject to the rules of occupation, when other nations would consider them still part of the front, governed by very different rules. The definition of occupation determined the difference between the *levée en masse* and insurrection.

The *levée en masse* and the Qualities of Legal Combatants

France had resorted to this general call-to-arms during the Franco-Prussian War. Smaller states, like Belgium and the Netherlands, or even larger ones without large standing armies relied on this possibility to boost their numbers. Given the recent French precedent, even Germany and Russia accepted relatively quickly that the *levée* was legal in unoccupied areas. Disagreement erupted over how such volunteers should be organized (168–80). Germany and Russia insisted that they share the four conditions that defined regular combatants: they be led by a responsible person, they wear a visible mark or sign (in lieu of a uniform), they carry arms openly, and they follow the laws of war. These four conditions were customary law, as the Italian military representative pointed out (168). Germany wished to go further, however. Voigts-Rhetz wanted volunteers to be under regular army command and to have been organized and trained already in peacetime; otherwise, he argued, they would descend into brigandage (171). The German position thus recognized as legitimate combatants only those who approximated as much as possible regular soldiers of a standing army—that is, its own military model. Belgium's Baron Lambermont replied that smaller states needed to be able to defend themselves using patriotic volunteers without previous training (175). He added that the press of time might make it hard to have them all wear [the same] distinctive sign and impossible to place them under the commander of the army (176). In the end, the delegates kept the four conditions for regular armies, militias, and "corps of volunteers" (article 9) but added a tenth article saying that a population spontaneously rising against an approaching enemy were legitimate combatants even if they had not had time to conform to the conditions, so long as they followed international law. The smaller states thus had won the argument, but the fundamental clash between the standing army versus militia/*levée* models was clear, with all its implications for 1914.

Although Germany's military representative had accepted the legitimacy of the *levée en masse* in principle, he was obviously ambivalent.[48] One representative asked what would happen when an occupant was forced to retreat from a village that then rose up as the former occupant advanced again? Voigts-Rhetz thought that "all military men" would agree that "generals or army commanders would punish an insurrection that broke out in occupied territory" (132). Apparently he was wrong, since Greece's Colonel Manos immediately pointed out that once you had admitted the legality of the *levée*, you had to accept its legality also in this instance. Voigts-Rhetz's reply is interesting for several reasons. First, he assumed a uniformity of military interest common to all countries, thus implicitly projecting his own organization's culture onto others. Second, he clearly believed that once a territory was occupied, it remained so, even after the occupant had lost control of it. Third, his use of the word "punish" (*punirait*) suggested a punitive, rather than a strictly military motive, or perhaps better, the tendency to make the military the executor of its own law.

Insurrection

To avoid confusion, let us refer to uprisings under legitimate occupation as insurrections, saving the *levée en masse* for popular risings in the not-yet-occupied areas. The original Russian draft recognized the latter, but criminalized insurrections, whose participants might "be referred to justice" (20, section 46). In a fascinating debate, Europe divided over the issue. Significantly, the delegates argued back and forth, mixing the *levée* and the insurrection, because many states believed that both forms of defense were a right (199–204). They cited history, the insurrections against Napoleon, and what they took to be the logical extension of popular sovereignty—that is, that citizenship brought with it patriotism and a laudable desire to defend one's country, which the law ought to recognize. The disagreement was so fundamental that section 46 had to be dropped. In place of the clarity that both sides had wanted to inscribe in positive law, there was now silence. Two basic issues now arose: What was the relation between practices of war and law, or in other words, what was customary law? and how ought one to interpret the silence of positive law?

---

48. On the *levée en masse* in German military thinking: Michael Geyer, "Insurrectionary Warfare: The German Debate about a *Levée en Masse* in October 1918," *Journal of Modern History* 73 (September 2001): 459–527.

The military representatives habitually argued that the (often harsh) permissions of the laws of war "asked nothing more than that which already exists in reality," as Voigts-Rhetz put it (170). In other words, the law did and should simply reflect existing martial practice. Against this view Belgium's Baron Lambermont replied that "there are things done in war, and that will always be done, that we must probably accept. But that does not mean we must convert them into law, into positive international prescriptions" (198). In short, in this view positive law was not a mere compendium of usages or facts. Switzerland's Colonel Hammer seemed to agree (202).

In calling for the law to prefer silence to ratification of odious practice, Baron Lambermont felt he was leaving the contested matter in the purview of a stronger law of nations (199). Indeed, he felt that the law of nations had a clear content; in this case, it protected citizens rising up against an enemy. His French colleague de Baude agreed that such civilians were not "outside the law" (*hors la loi*) (197). Speaking of individual resisters (not groups), Lambermont went on to explain that "if no clause covers them, one cannot conclude by an argument *a contrario* that they are outside of the law"; their special case "will rest, like lots of others, in the unwritten law" (200–201). To this, Voigts-Rhetz responded that one could not legislate with the unwritten law. "He observed that there were lots of things admitted in war that were not written down. If one did not want to regulate them, fine; but one could not say that one wanted the contrary of that which is recognized and consecrated by usage" (201).

Beneath the argument about substance was a deeper argument about the nature of international law. Belgium and other states thought that there was operative outside of positive (written) law a strong, customary international law that was more than a mere collection of usages; indeed, it could be contrary to these. Germany argued that usages became law (it was not clear from these debates how that occurred, that is, how long and how widespread usage had to be to become law, or what happened if a usage contravened important principles of international law).[49] Modern commentators agree that customary law is determined by a combination of widespread and persistent state practice plus *opinio juris sive necessitatis,* or simply *opinio juris*—that is, the assumption that a particular practice is indeed lawful. Both conditions must exist to create customary law. But even applying these two principles leaves the identification of customary law an uncertain undertaking.[50] However, the Brussels debates underscored the fundamental disagreement between those states strongly emphasizing *opinio juris* and general principles that could never be nullified by state practice regardless how widespread, and those tilting toward state practice. As we shall see, Imperial German writers developed a theory of law creation that in effect

---

49. On customary law: Brian D. Lepard, *Customary International Law: A New Theory with Practical Applications* (Cambridge, 2010).

50. On customary law see the recent book and helpful bibliography of Lepard, *Customary International Law,* 381–96; Anthony A. D'Amato, *The Concept of Custom in International Law,* foreword by Richard A. Falk (Ithaca, NY, 1971); Hugh W. A. Thirlway, *International Customary Law and Codification: An Examination of the Continuing Role of Custom in the Present Period of Codification of International Law* (Leiden, 1972); and Michael Byers, "Custom, Power, and the Power of Rules: Customary International Law from an Interdisciplinary Perspective," *Michigan Journal of International Law* 17 (1995–96): 109–80.

made *opinio juris* a function of state (wartime) practice. The Brussels proceedings suggest that Voigts-Rhetz might have thought that, in the absence of positive limits, there were none at all. That is, he might have seen positive law as a mere patchwork of proscriptions beyond which armies were free to develop practices/usages as convenient. In a sense, that view was the pendant to his desire that positive law be as detailed and specific as possible. Both he and Russia's head of delegation, Alexander Jomini, worried that abuses would proliferate in a legal vacuum (142, 239–40). And a legal vacuum was exactly the fate of Russia's efforts to rein in reprisal.

Reprisal

Reprisal was the main legal cover for Germany's acts during the "Belgian atrocities." In international law, reprisal is the use of otherwise illegal means against a state that has broken the law, in order to force it to abide by law in future. It is both exceptional and an important institute of international law, one of its most obvious sanctions.[51] By 1874, it was also a major embarrassment. Reprisals, as everybody saw, might easily spiral out of control, they hit the innocent with the guilty, and they seemed to place the repriser on the same illegal plane as his adversary. In the course of centuries, the interaction of European states in wartime had developed four principles that by the mid-nineteenth century most states recognized as binding in customary law. These were: (1) reprisals were not revenge or punishment, but means "of obliging [a miscreant] to observe the law of war."[52] (2) They should be resorted to "cautiously" and only "after careful inquiry into the real occurrence."[53] (3) They should not be "unjust or inconsiderate," that is, they should remain in proportion to the offense.[54] And (4) they should "not violate the fundamental principles of humanity," that is, there were absolute limits to the means one might employ.[55]

The Russian draft on reprisal was based on these principles. Article 69 admitted reprisal only "in extreme cases, observing as much as possible the laws of humanity," when it has been "indiscutably proved" that the target of reprisal has broken the laws and customs of war "and that he has used means condemned by the law of nations" (24). Article 69 set a high bar. It made reprisals an extreme exception, entered into only after a high standard of proof, if possible following the laws of humanity, and in any case only if the state had both broken the law *and* done so in an especially heinous way. Article 70 laid down that the means must be proportionate to the offense: "Reprisals disproportionately severe are

---

51. Lassa Oppenheim, *International Law: A Treatise* (London, 1905), 2:34–42.

52. Emmerich de Vattel, *The Law of Nations, or, Principles of the Law of Nature, Applied to the Conduct and Affairs of Nations and Sovereigns* (London, 1797), 348.

53. Francis Lieber, *Instructions for the Government of Armies of the United States in the Field, General Orders No. 100, 24 April 1863*, in *The Laws of Armed Conflicts: A Collection of Conventions, Resolutions and Other Documents*, ed. Dietrich Schindler and Jiri Toman (Geneva, 1988), art. 28.

54. Ibid.

55. Johann Caspar Bluntschli, *Das moderne Kriegsrecht* (Nördlingen, 1866), art. 56.

contrary to the rules of the law of nations" (24). Article 71 restricted them to orders of the commander in chief, the highest responsible military officer.

Despite these strictures, the delegates of many states felt that reprisals were repellent. Russia's diplomat Alexander Jomini set about redrafting the section and hit upon an unfortunate way to ground reprisal in law. He wrote, "violations of the laws and customs of war by one belligerent party dispense the other party from observing them" (238). Dispensation would account for why the law-abiding party was permitted to use illegal means against the miscreant, but it would also annihilate international law by making alleged violation sufficient to end a state's obligation to follow the law. Italy's Colonel Lanza instantly pointed out Jomini's error (238).[56] Aside from this faux pas, Jomini mostly kept the original draft's curbs, but added another, further limiting the means of reprisal to those permitted by the penal code of the enforcer (238).

Most of the delegates associated reprisal with upholding occupation, as reprisal had last been used in that way by Germany in 1870–71. Until the delegates came to discuss reprisal, the conference had been quite amicable; it now became embittered.[57] Belgium's delegate refused to enshrine "odious" reprisals in positive law. The argument about the unwritten law flared anew. Baron Lambermont introduced an early version of the Martens Clause (see below) to underscore the principled point that beyond positive law was the more powerful, dynamic, and progressive law of nations. He again argued for leaving this matter "in the domain of the unwritten law, under the sanction of the public conscience, waiting until the progress of science and of civilization shall bring forth a completely satisfactory solution." He proposed "to sacrifice the article on the altar of humanity" (239). Belgium prevailed. The articles were withdrawn. Reprisal was now not to be curbed by positive law.

Voigts-Rhetz was not opposed to regulating reprisals. He would have preferred to govern them by Germany's newly minted military penal code.[58] Among other things, it prescribed the death penalty for civilian acts against the authority of the occupant (*Kriegsverrat*), but at least the penal code mandated a trial first. As it was, silence permitted the counterargument that there was no unwritten law, only military usages. Voigts-Rhetz's suggestion to regulate reprisal by Germany's military code again suggests how strongly Imperial Germany associated reprisal with punishment, rather than as a way to return a state to following law. In the context of occupation, of course, the chief objects of reprisal likely would be civilians, not agents of the state; the punishment model fit them much better than the international-legal model.

Two issues closely connected with reprisal in the minds of the delegates—hostage taking and forcing civilians to act as guides against their own country—followed reprisal into the realm of silence: guides at Russia's suggestion (240), and hostages at Belgium's (239). Therefore, the European disagreement on the law meant that the Brussels Declaration gave no guidance on the most controversial issues—insurrection, reprisal, hostage taking

---

56. See also Westlake, writing against Carl Lueder: John Westlake, *International Law; Part II: War* (Cambridge, 1907), 112–14.

57. Best, *Humanity in Warfare*, 172, 348n70.

58. A. Romen and Carl Rissom, eds., *Militärstrafgesetzbuch für das Deutsche Reich vom 20. Juni 1872 nebst dem Einführungsgesetz* (Berlin, 1916).

and hostage killing, and forced guides. In interpreting these issues, everything depended on how one understood that silence: as a realm of no limits, of purely self-imposed limits, or of limits imposed by the law of nations, the public conscience, or humanity.

There were other signs in 1874 of Germany's principled stance in favor of military power and discretion. We will discuss two that had implications far beyond 1914: treatment of prisoners of war and raising money from the occupied zones.

The original Russian draft had sketched the principles of modern treatment of prisoners of war, who were now thought of as honorable opponents and citizens of sovereign states: they were to be subjected to "no *violence* or bad treatment"; they were not to be treated as criminals; they might be made to work, but not on jobs "with a direct relation to the operations of war," or below their social status; escapees might be shot at or killed, but once recaptured were subject only to disciplinary, not criminal prosecution; and their food and lodging were subject to agreement between the parties (16–17). The delegates extended two of these points in a humanitarian direction. The final code said that prisoners "must be treated with humanity," and in the absence of mutual agreement, "and as a general principle," prisoners' food and clothing must be provided "on the same basis as those of the government's own troops" (380–81).

Throughout the discussions, Voigts-Rhetz pressed against limitations to the military's discretion to use force against prisoners and against requirements to spend more money on their upkeep. On the first issue, he worried that forbidding the use of "violence" against prisoners would harm security if they disobeyed orders, to which Russia's General von Leer opined that even if they committed a crime, violence should never be used against them (69). Voigts-Rhetz appears to have chafed even at Prussia's own military code, which mandated trials for recalcitrant prisoners. During a battle, he said, trials were impossible; that left only the resort to violence (69). The same was true for prisoners who refused to move back to their depot during a battle: "It is necessary to force them. Foreseeing insubordination is the duty of every officer," he said (69). That suggestion roused Spain's Marshal Servert to ask for language forbidding escorts outright from killing prisoners even if circumstances prevented the escorts from fulfilling their duty to bring the prisoners back to camp (70). Servert made clear what was at stake in these debates on "violence": killing unarmed prisoners. Voigts-Rhetz wanted to keep that option open.

Voigts-Rhetz also wanted to protect the widest latitude for using resources. So, for example, he enunciated the principle that prisoners of war could not be better treated than the captor's own troops; the French and Spanish delegates reformulated his negative language to say that they should be treated equally (75). He wanted to be able to deduct immediately from their wages the salaries prisoners were due to receive at the war's end from their own states, even though these deductions would likely jeopardize their standard of living, as one delegate pointed out (74). On the matter of raising taxes in the occupied zone, most delegates wanted these capped at prewar levels, while Voigts-Rhetz wanted them to rise with any increased outlays undertaken by the unoccupied area in a longer war (139–42). All these examples of toughness were ways to compensate for Prussia's relative lack of manpower (to guard and control prisoners) and financial resources (to pay for war and its incidental costs, such as prisoner upkeep).

Military Necessity

These examples show that on some fundamental matters Germany's military favored a tougher line than did its colleagues, including in Russia. While Voigts-Rhetz favored specifying law for the guidance of commanders, he also wanted to preserve the widest purview of force regarding actual combat (reprisals), prisoners, and the occupied zones (civilians). One could enlarge the military's freedom of decision in several ways: by keeping codification narrow and specific, by construing the resulting realm of silence either as a legal vacuum (no limits), or as governed by "usages" that were merely military decisions already taken in the past, or by preparing for exceptions to the written rules on grounds of "military necessity." As Voigts-Rhetz put it, "it is necessary to proclaim the [legal] principle, but to reserve the inevitable exceptions" (166). All four methods were in operation in 1874, but, though historians have seen the Brussels Conference as occurring at the apex of the doctrine of military necessity in nineteenth-century Europe, that doctrine was seldom explicitly discussed.[59]

In 1898 Russia again issued invitations, this time to a much larger contingent of twenty-six states, whose representatives met at The Hague the following year to discuss arms control, arbitration, and codification of the laws of war. The Brussels draft was the basis for the Hague discussions. As a result, reprisal, insurrection, hostage taking and hostage killing were not debated again, but the identical disagreements over the content and the principle of the laws of war still existed, or had grown even more pronounced. The Hague Conference therefore reprised many of the same arguments, which we shall examine below. But since Brussels, Imperial Germany had developed military necessity into a more principled, or at least doctrinal and explicit legal cover for its stance on the laws of war.[60]

In 1874 Jomini had remarked that "one would perhaps be able to add after each article: 'except for necessities of war,'" but he already cautioned that doing so "would inflame public opinion" (150–51). In the intervening twenty-five years public opinion and most jurists had been moving toward limiting the writ of military necessity. In the majority view, military necessity was what permitted killing and destruction in war at all. Francis Lieber, writing the U.S. military code of 1863, had expressed the usual variant of this broader view of the concept: "Military necessity, as understood by modern civil nations, consists in the necessity of those measures which are indispensable for securing the ends of the war, and which are lawful according to the modern law and usages of war."[61] Thus, military necessity was what made causing death in combat permitted killing and not murder. But as the second part of Lieber's sentence made clear, the permission covered by military necessity was embedded in and thus limited by the larger parameter of law.

---

59. Best, *Humanity in Warfare*, 48, 161–62, 184.

60. Important for the background of military necessity: Manfred Messerschmidt, "Völkerrecht und 'Kriegsnotwendigkeit' in der deutschen militärischen Tradition," in *Was damals Recht war. NS-Militär- und Strafjustiz im Vernichtungskrieg*, Manfred Messerschmidt (Essen, 1996), 191–230.

61. Lieber, *Instructions*, art. 14.

Military necessity was therefore not an exception to law; only reprisal was that. Older German writers, like the Swiss-born Johann Caspar Bluntschli and Felix Dahn, agreed with the writers of other nations that military necessity did not suspend the laws of war, even in the case of danger to one's troops or to the success of a mission.[62] Lassa Oppenheim, summing up in 1905 the European legal literature and the majority view at the Hague Conference, wrote that "many legal rules of warfare are so framed that they do not apply to a case of necessity"; and "there are...many rules which know nothing of any exception in case of necessity." In other words, most laws of war were a priori beyond the reach of a claim to military necessity. Only "mere usages, in contradistinction to laws, may be ignored in case of necessity," he continued.[63] (Oppenheim understood "usages" to be practices that had become customary or usual, but not yet binding, i.e., not yet *customary law.*)[64] Thus, in the modern view military necessity could be claimed only regarding those laws of war that explicitly recognized that exception. Laws that did not mention it could not be abrogated for any reason, except in legitimate reprisal. In the twentieth century, international law has continued to develop in this direction, whittling down military necessity to a mere excuse, not a justification, in specific cases where the exception was theoretically permitted and where unforeseen circumstances prevent the actor physically from fulfilling the letter of the law.[65]

Meanwhile, Imperial Germany was moving in the opposite direction. Three years after the Brussels Conference, General Julius von Hartmann pungently expressed the German military's point of view in a three-part article widely cited by subsequent German jurists.[66] Hartmann complained that Brussels had mentioned military necessity just three times, and then only "as an aside and superficially" (87). He filled this lamentable lacuna by developing a two-level definition of military necessity.

The first level occurred as an exception to concrete rules of war conduct. In Hartmann's view, this particular military necessity was so protean, so dependent upon unforeseeable circumstance, that it was incapable of being hedged around by regulation. Therefore, instead of offering "abstract concepts," he provided a phenomenological account of specific instances of military necessity as they had appeared in Europe's last war, so as to permit readers and jurists to get a "theoretical understanding of the phenomena of war in real life" (456).

In the course of his phenomenology, Hartmann exculpated Germany's most controversial actions in France in 1870–71. For example, during a mobile war, he wrote, requisitioning could neither distinguish state from private property, any more than it could be

---

62. Oppenheim, *International Law,* 2: para. 69; Felix Dahn, *Das Kriegsrecht; Kurze, volksthümliche Darstellung für Jedermann zumal für den deutschen Soldaten* (Würzburg, 1870), 3–4; Bluntschli, *Das moderne Kriegsrecht,* para. 25.

63. Oppenheim, *International Law,* 2: para. 69.

64. Ibid.

65. H. McCoubrey, "The Nature of the Modern Doctrine of Military Necessity," *Revue de droit militaire et de droit de la guerre* 30, nos. 1–4 (1991): 215–55.

66. Julius von Hartmann, "Militärische Nothwendigkeit und Humanität; ein kritischer Versuch," *Deutsche Rundschau* 13–14 (1877–78): 13:111–28 and 450–71, 14:71–91. Hereafter cited parenthetically in text by page number.

limited without harming the "military ability to act" (458). A proportional limit on requisitions was undesirable, because in modern warfare between nation states, it was good for civilians to feel the press of war (459). Against the *levée en masse,* "terrorism becomes a military necessity" (462). Executing spies without trial, forcing guides, destroying infrastructure, huge collective punitive fines, hostage taking, and forcing occupied civilians to serve their enemy's army were harsh measures, he argued, but "military realism, when it observes them, shrugs its shoulders silently" (462).

This was military necessity on the tactical or perhaps operational level. But Hartmann advanced a much more profound definition that went to the heart of the laws of war themselves. Although he greeted some international agreements on war as practical and largely beneficial, such as the new Geneva Convention (1864) on wounded and sick soldiers, he rejected the attempt to create positive laws of war. He pitted "modern international law" against "military realism" (111). International law was "theoretically constructed," "academically construed," he complained; it was simply ignorant of the reality of warfare (112, 113). Moreover, it was outdated. The political and military revolutions of Napoleon and modern technology had completely transformed the necessities of war, and "insofar as the modern laws of war have cut themselves loose from military empiricism, they have lost the firm foundation on which their edifice of [legal] derivations is built" (127). Modern jurists mistakenly clung to the narrow view of military necessity as "a single, albeit powerfully determinative agent" in war, whereas military realists knew that it determined "the entire external phenomenon of war" (120).

In short, military necessity *was* the law of war. "The grand goal of war [is] conquering the enemy's energy...and will. This *single* goal rules absolutely, it dictates law and regulation. The concrete form of this law appears as military necessity" (453–54). This definition differs from the usual view that military necessity is what excuses acts of killing and destruction. Hartmann's definition is instead a claim about the nature of reality and consequently the nature of law. For Hartmann, the essence of war was dictated by battle, not by the political, legal, or other reasons for which a state might ostensibly fight: war "is nothing other than battle [*Kampf*]" (121). Therefore, nonmilitary considerations were simply irrelevant to conducting war, and thus also to limiting it. Hartmann's "realism" was in fact highly idealistic; it sundered war from its political, economic, diplomatic, and other contexts, reducing it to the techniques necessary to defeat an enemy that Hartmann moreover insisted included the entire populace (126–27).[67] Hartmann derived his positivistic principles from an artificially narrow base. His same assumptions about the priority of combat and the autonomy of the military were those that had pitted Chief of Staff Helmuth von Moltke (the elder) against Prime Minister Otto von Bismarck in 1870–71 and that dominated the views of Germany's officer corps through the World War and beyond.[68] In this view, "once war has begun, only the commands of military necessity may take effect" (471).

---

67. Moltke expressed this same conviction in his famous letter to Bluntschli of Dec. 11, 1880, in Helmuth von Moltke, *Moltke; Vom Kabinettskrieg zum Volkskrieg: Eine Werkauswahl,* ed. Stig Förster (Bonn, 1992), 634.

68. Hull, *Absolute Destruction,* pt. 2.

Hartmann thought himself neither cruel nor uncivilized. On the contrary, he favored the possibilities for humanitarianism that flowed uniquely from superior military organization (suppressing the atrocities born of indiscipline), technological innovation (railroads that whisked the wounded and prisoners to better care), and above all, the moral convictions of civilized officers and soldiers (116–18, 71–77). But his definition of broad military necessity had two enormous implications for international law.

First, Hartmann flatly contradicted the dominant view, as expressed by Bluntschli, that "the modern international law of civilized peoples recognizes no absolute right of military force," either over occupied civilians or enemy troops (124). That view recognized absolute limits to weapons and methods that armies might use—for example, outlawing poison, cruelty, torture, the infliction of unnecessary suffering—or as Lieber put it, "Military necessity does not include any act of hostility which makes the return to peace unnecessarily difficult" (article 16). For Hartmann, odious methods were condemned by usages among experienced armies and their leaders, but not at all by law, which disappeared as soon as war began (114). "War interrupts the legal conditions of peace explosively and during its activity completely suspends the entire legal norms characteristic of peace. If the power of war recognizes duties, it does so [voluntarily] out of its own sovereignty [*Machtvollkommenheit*]; it is not compelled to do so from the outside" (124). In other words, there was by definition no law applicable to war. Moreover, where other (legal) positivists postulated complete state sovereignty, Hartmann applied sovereignty during wartime not to the state, but to the power of war (*Kriegsgewalt*) itself, as if the state had become a mere agent of war, or perhaps as if the essence of state sovereignty were the ability to wage war—an idea that Erich Kaufmann expressed directly for the first time in 1911.[69] For our purposes, the important point is that Hartmann's construal of military necessity made the laws of war expressly impossible.

Second, Hartmann's expansive view of military necessity negated even treaty law, which most late nineteenth-century legal positivists and even extreme skeptics took to be the nearest thing to international law. Civilian positivists agreed that sovereign states might limit themselves through treaties, though they argued over whether such treaties were utterly binding; after all, voluntary acquiescence could presumably be just as voluntarily withdrawn. But military realism took a doubly harder view. First, it insisted that such treaties had to reflect the real essence of war (pure combat), not will-o'-the-wisp humanitarianism or legal-theoretical principles. "States must not let themselves be led by general legal principles;...they are thoroughly dependent on the peculiarity of real conditions, as war creates them, that is, they depend on military necessity" (124–25). Second, war eliminated the community of states that others imagined created the legal order in the first place. Again, Hartmann rejected Bluntschli's typical description of international law as "the legal [and] necessary recognized order which the relations of states regulate among themselves" (128). No, no—"war suspends this community; it takes as its starting point the most one-sided, harshest standpoint of the individual [state]; it thus removes itself

---

69. Erich Kaufmann, *Das Wesen des Völkerrechts und die clausula rebus sic stantibus* (Tübingen, 1911), 146.

from the basis of legal settlement" (128). In this dream of total enmity and singularity, Hartmann anticipated Carl Schmitt.[70]

I have characterized Hartmann's view as positivistic—one might call his theory "war positivism" on the analogy to legal positivism. Legal positivism was a widespread theory of law in the nineteenth century and virtually hegemonic in Germany from Bismarck to the World War.[71] Like the positivism of Auguste Comte, it purported to take the world as it existed and to analyze or typologize it objectively, without inserting value judgments or politics. Law existed as a fact, regardless of whether it was just. Historians often interpret legal positivism in Germany as an accommodation to Bismarck's defeat of liberalism, for positivists gave up using the law as a political weapon to establish a liberal constitution in order to limit monarchical power and establish the rule of civil rights, and instead devoted themselves to applying logic to parse the status quo of already written (positive) law. Hartmann (and his many followers) claimed to do the same for the laws of war, that is, to "discover" them already existing in the objective "reality" of warfare. But war positivism was in one way more powerful than legal positivism. Because the latter took the written law as given, because it was premised on a constitution and set of laws already existing, it could not account for (indeed, it ignored) how that constitution came to be, that is, whence the power invested in it flowed (from popular sovereignty? from somewhat limited absolutism? from "the monarchical principle," as it was called?). But war positivism could do just that. Law was simply a logical derivative of war. It was an epiphenomenon of a more powerful underlying reality, and in this way one could say that war positivism "solved" a central dilemma of broader legal positivism.

The general staff may have asked General Hartmann to write his piece;[72] in any event, he presented his views, probably accurately, as those of the military. They entered German jurisprudence in the widely used handbook of Carl Lueder (1889). Despite his reputation among contemporary Anglo-Saxons as a militarist, Lueder struggled against the deniers of international law and fought for its acceptance, more or less along the lines in which the Brussels Declaration had outlined it.[73] Lueder was sensitive to military leaders' "mistrustful rejection of codification and humanizing" of the laws of war (275). Presumably to mollify them, he adopted Hartmann's admonition against "any a priori, subjective

70. For example: Carl Schmitt, "Der Begriff des Politischen (1927)," in *Frieden oder Pazifismus? Arbeiten zum Völkerrecht und zur internationalen Politik 1924–1978*, ed. Günter Maschke (Berlin, 2005), 194–239; Carl Schmitt, "Das Doppelgesicht des Genfer Völkerbundes (1926)," in *Positionen und Begriffe mit Weimar-Genf-Versailles 1923–1939* (Berlin, 1994), 48–50; or Carl Schmitt, "Völkerrechtliche Probleme im Rheingebiet (1928)," in *Positionen und Begriffe mit Weimar-Genf-Versailles 1923–1939* (Berlin, 1994), 111–23.

71. Leslie Green, "Legal Positivism," in *The Stanford Encyclopedia of Philosophy (2009 Edition)*, ed. Edward M. Zalta (Stanford, CA, 2009), http://plato.stanford.edu/entries/legal-positivism/; Ernst-Wolfgang Böckenförde, *Gesetz und gesetzgebende Gewalt: Von den Anfängen der deutschen Staatsrechtslehre bis zur Höhe des staatsrechlichen Positivismus* (Berlin, 1981), 211–20; Michael Stolleis, *Geschichte des öffentlichen Rechts in Deutschland* (Munich, 1988), 2:276–78, 341–48, 351–55.

72. James Wilford Garner, *International Law and the World War* (London, 1920), 1:279n4.

73. Westlake, *International Law*, 115–17; Garner, *International Law*, 2:196n2—cf. Carl Lueder, "Krieg und Kriegsrecht im Allgemeinen," in *Handbuch des Völkerrechts*, ed. Franz von Holtzendorff (Hamburg, 1889), 4:188–91, 256–57, 268–69, 325, 329–30. Hereafter cited parenthetically in text by page number.

construction, or desire to build a new, 'reasonable' law of war," instead "of discovering what the law of war actually is" (275). "Humanity can only be recognized in war to the degree that the nature and goal of war permit" (276). Lueder followed Hartmann's positivism in imagining that the laws of war were "a *lex lata naturae* [located] in the nature and history of the phenomenon" itself (176). The nature of war was "unlimited force [*Gewalt*], the dominion of the sword and of military necessity" (186). Law must be consonant with the essence of war.

But unlike Hartmann, Lueder believed that these limits were binding law, not just historical usages (188). In order to have expansive military necessity and binding law at the same time, Lueder turned to the analogy of self-defense and emergency (*Notwehr* and *Notstand*). He imagined war as existential, thus throwing the state into a situation of self-defense in which only it could decide which measures to take; thus it "cannot be limited by the rule of law" (187). In such times of self-defense, Lueder found it impossible to believe that a state "would voluntarily accept defeat, perhaps even ruin, simply in order not to violate formal law" (255).

But having granted the principle of binding law, Lueder hastened to subordinate it to military necessity. He wrote that the law of war could be broken in only two cases: "the most extreme necessity," and reprisal, when the other side had violated the law (254). Citing Hartmann, Lueder declared that "on the basis of this necessary recognition of [law-breaking] reason of state, one can find union with the demand of the military that in case of doubt military necessity must absolutely have priority.... In a true conflict, one must decide not in favor of the letter of the law, but of the goal of war and military necessity." But he insisted, "such a conflict will be rare" (257).

Lueder's textbook took the Brussels Declaration as its model, so it was progressive in many respects. But where it differed, it did so mostly following Voigts-Rhetz's official lead. For example, Lueder accepted that military necessity excused the killing of unarmed prisoners of war if one "could not feed or hold them and could not let them go without endangering oneself, or because they would for some other reason become a danger one could not otherwise surmount" (437). Like Voigts-Rhetz, Lueder accepted the legality of hostage taking, forced guides, and mass destruction or arson for such reasons as "to show the folly of continuing the war and forcing [the enemy] to sue for peace" (471, 475–77, 484).[74] Lueder somewhat exceeded Voigts-Rhetz on rejecting proportional limits on requisitions (502–3). In general, however, Lueder's textbook took its lead from Imperial Germany's policy in the Franco-Prussian War and its position at the Brussels Conference.

---

74. Voigts-Rhetz recognized only two rules limiting the requisitions in kind or service that an occupier could raise. One was that requisitions could not harm the honor or patriotism of the inhabitants (i.e., humiliate them or force them to work against their own country). But he did not remark upon, and in the end he accepted the final draft of art. 40, which said that requisitions must be in proportion to the country's resources. Brussels, Conference, 1874, *Actes,* 213, 382. Lueder, however, refused to set a limit because of possible military necessity: Carl Lueder, "Das Landkriegsrecht im Besonderen," in Holtzendorff, *Handbuch des Völkerrechts* (Hamburg, 1889), 4:502–3.

The Hague Convention, 1899

Ten years after Lueder's book, when the Hague Convention met, it largely replayed the arguments of 1874. We shall focus on the three most important issues of principle: military necessity, the relation of facts to lawmaking, and interpreting silences in the positive law (i.e., interpreting the Martens Clause).

The crystallization of military necessity as a doctrine, and the general movement in opinion outside Germany that it must be curbed, meant that the delegates now debated military necessity specifically. The occasion was what became article 46, which enjoined belligerents to respect the honor and rights of occupied civilian families and their religious expression. As he had done on numerous other occasions, Germany's military representative, Colonel Karl Julius von Gross, genannt von Schwarzhoff, asked that the military necessity exception be explicitly contained in the article. His Austrian colleague expressed astonishment that such matters as these could ever be contravened by military necessity. Belgian representative Édouard Descamps declared that "it is contrary to the spirit of the Brussels project to introduce into specific articles a special clause pertaining to military necessity. It is impossible to admit as a legal thesis the destruction of individual rights, even though occasionally one will have recourse to it."[75] Descamps thus repeated the principle that his predecessor had enunciated in 1874: facts of force did not by virtue of their facticity produce law in contravention of larger legal principles. Édouard Rolin Jaequemyns, charged with writing to the plenary council the report of the (second) commission that was drafting the laws of war, asked Schwarzhoff to withdraw his motion: "It is not necessary to weaken the principle by putting it in the form of a dubitative declaration," he argued.[76] Schwarzhoff replied that "although not entirely sharing this opinion, he would retract his amendment, so long as Chevalier Descamps's declaration was accepted as giving the exact interpretation of the article." In other words, Schwarzhoff believed that (1) military necessity did indeed undermine general principles; and (2) the convention had recognized (and thus accepted) the fact that armies might occasionally break the law/principle. Schwarzhoff's position was thus identical to Voigts-Rhetz's in 1874.[77]

But Schwarzhoff had not actually succeeded; the second commission proceeded to debate the question whether facticity constituted law. The relation of inconvenient facts of force to law is an ancient dilemma for international law, because to be effective, the law must be realistic, while upholding at the same time general principles or specific content that will inevitably at some time be broken. Belgium's first representative, Auguste Marie François Beernaert, repeated at length his country's objections from 1874. "It is better to abandon [codification of controversial issues, like the rights of occupiers] to the domain of the rights of man, as vague as those are. One must not transform facts into law" (3:112). The official report of Louis Renault to the plenary session of the conference upheld Beernaert's

---

75. Ministry of Foreign Affairs Netherlands, *Conférence Internationale de la Paix, La Haye 18 Mai–29 Juillet 1899* (The Hague, 1899), 3:98. This volume contains four parts, so 3:98 means part 3, p. 98.

76. Ibid.

77. Brussels, Conference, 1874, *Actes,* 166, 264–65.

position, explicitly denying that the Hague Rules recognized "the law of force" (1:196). The president of the second commission, the Russian Fyodor Martens, walked the tightrope when he tried to calm both Beernaert and the proponents of military necessity. Martens compared international law to a mutual insurance company against disaster: "One is not at all legalizing these disasters, one is merely recognizing that they exist. On the other hand, that does not contravene the necessities of war; it is uniquely directed, I repeat, gentlemen, against the *abuse* of force" (3:125). Unmollified, Beernaert insisted on suppressing several articles entirely; his colleagues enthusiastically applauded his speech and had it printed for wider distribution (3:113). As Jomini had done in 1874, Martens countered that by leaving controversial matters in silence, one abandoned the field to the belligerents, who were then free to exercise "the unlimited right to interpret the laws of war in their fashion and according to their convenience" (3:115). This possibility is probably why Schwarzhoff, unlike his predecessor at Brussels, embraced Beernaert's method of leaving the law silent on matters of disagreement (3:136, 157).

Insurrection, the right to rise up against an occupant (as opposed to the *levée en masse*—the right to rise up in advance of occupation), was the greatest of these disagreements. The impasse was so obvious that the president of the second commission, Martens, did not even permit discussion before he had proposed an interpretation of the inevitable legal silence that he knew would result. His compromise became the famous Martens Clause. For issues not included in the current regulations, he wrote, "populations and belligerents remain under the safety and the empire of the principles of the law of nations as these result from the usages established among civilized nations, the laws of humanity, and the exigencies of the public conscience. It is in this sense that one should understand articles 9 and 10 [later 1 and 2] adopted by the conference" (3:152). Those articles defined who was recognized as a legitimate belligerent, set out the four conditions that militiamen and volunteers must meet to enjoy legal protection, and permitted the *levée en masse* before occupation. The silence concerned the right of insurrection.

Switzerland and then Britain tried to put the conference on record as permitting insurrection, or at least not denying it as a right (3:145, 154). Both motions were hopeless, given the opposition of Germany and Russia (joined by the Netherlands). In order to assuage the other powers, the Martens Clause was formally affixed to the final protocol, adopted unanimously by the second commission, and in its final version became part of the preamble of the Hague Rules, itself adopted unanimously in plenary session (3:158–9; 1:49–50, 197). But how did the delegates understand their vote?

Belgium's two representatives expressed the widespread belief that by leaving some issues uncodified in law, the conference encouraged progressive legal development. Beernaert had asked if it were not better rather than inscribing into law interests that ill fit the goals of the convention, instead "by relating these matters to the law of nations and to that unceasing progress of the conference's true ideas... to strongly encourage these" (3:113). Descamps also thought it preferable "to wait for the results of the progressive mellowing of morals" (3:136). In this view, the Martens Clause therefore helped international law avoid recognizing the exceptional use of force and to develop in a progressive direction.

More specifically, Léon Bourgeois (the first delegate of France), Beernaert, and Abraham Pieter Cornelis van Karnebeek (former Dutch foreign minister and plenipotentiary to the conference) seemed to believe that the scope of the Martens Clause encompassed the right to insurrection that they thought inhered in the law of nations (3:158). When Britain's representative, General Sir John Ardagh, retracted his motion defending such a right, he said that he did so because "the principle which it developed had received unanimous approbation" (3:159).

Schwarzhoff explicitly denied this interpretation, referring to Ardagh's proposition as "an eel under the rock" by which delegates proposed "to enlarge the means of defense given to the population" (3:159). Martens did publish Ardagh's motion in the protocol, but he included all the arguments for and against it, thus showing that the matter was not decided (3:159). Nevertheless, the Martens Clause occupied a prominent place in the preamble, where it stayed in 1907, together with the sentence saying that it governed the intepretation of articles 1 and 2 on belligerency and the *levée en masse* in the unoccupied zone.[78]

There are three salient points to take from the Hague discussions. First, Germany's disagreements with most other nations on material law—that is, on the actual rules of law—were explicit and, if anything, becoming more pronounced. For example, Schwarzhoff tried and failed to get the conference to excise the sentence "occupation extends only to territories where such authority has been established and can be exercised" (3:117). But Germany's low standards of occupation meant that for it the fighting front turned almost instantly into the occupied zone, making practically impossible even the legally permitted *levée en masse*. Unlike many European governments, Germany rejected insurrection as criminal, raising the specter of reprisal. Because reprisal (and allied methods such as hostage taking) were not governed by positive law, Germany felt free to follow the usages it recognized as legal and had used itself in 1870–71. Germany was not on record concerning the four limiting conditions for reprisal that constituted binding customary law; it is unclear whether before 1914 military officials recognized these limits as obligatory. There were other disagreements on material law concerning occupation, and we will discuss these in the next chapter.

Second, Germany's military and jurists had developed military necessity into a robust doctrine that constituted a wild-card exception to positive law and one that was perhaps more far-reaching than the only genuine exception recognized by most other powers: reprisal. Although the conference rejected Germany's desire to insert that exception into most articles, Germany's interpretation was quite public and studded the protocols. Together, reprisal for infractions unrecognized by other powers and military necessity were powerful tools opening the road to military discretion.

Third, Germany interpreted the silence of law and the Martens Clause differently from other powers. Schwarzhoff made clear that when positive law was silent, the remaining

---

78. Adam Roberts and Richard Guelff, eds., *Documents on the Laws of War* (Oxford, 2004), 70. The Second Hague Convention of 1907 added that volunteers in the *levée* had not only to follow the laws of war but also to carry their arms openly.

realm was simply the customary usages of great military powers, not a law of nations derived from laws of humanity or dictates of the public conscience. There was no engine of humanitarian principles or progressive development operating outside the sphere of positive law. There were only the facts of force. This matter arose again regarding Germany's opposition to the proportional limit on requisitions (where the conference again held fast). Schwarzhoff cited what he called the "axiom: 'war feeds war'"—that is, an occupant may take from the occupied area what he needs to pursue the war—declaring that it was "recognized in all the large armies of Europe and one will never make it disappear"; the conference should stop trying. "For his part, he agreed with the advice of Excellency Beernaert that one should keep silent about the things over which one disagreed. The fact exists. One must not speak of it, but it is impossible to forbid it; that would go too far" (3:136). These facts *were* law. Schwarzhoff's war positivism was thus founded on the principle opposite to that adopted by the conference, that its rules did not recognize "the law of force" (1:196).

Germany's Jurists on the Laws of War

Germany's civilian leaders did not challenge the arguments made by its military representatives to international legal conferences. Their views stood as official policy.[79] Germany's interpretation of military necessity was unique; it was held by no other nation or by other national jurists.[80] Germany's prewar international lawyers followed their government, but one can see them struggling to reconcile the German view with the law as set down in the Hague Rules.

Albert Zorn, the son of Philipp Zorn, who had been Germany's legal representative to the first Hague Convention, published the first attempt to interpret the new codification. Albert Zorn fully accepted that the Hague Rules were binding law for Germany.[81] But following Lueder (who followed Hartmann), he was a self-proclaimed apostle of "military realism" (19), and therefore the law he affirmed with one hand, he erased with the other. "More than peace does, war shows that facts are the basis of law and that law and power

---

79. Despite the agreement during the conference, devised in order to encourage free discussion, that speakers expressed only their personal views: Netherlands, *Conférence*, 3:90.

80. The exception was the "Swiss-Belgian" Rivier—see Oppenheim, *International Law,* 2: para. 269. On Germany's uniqueness: Heinrich Albrecht Schütze, *Die Repressalie unter besonderer Berücksichtigung der Kriegsverbrecherprozesse* (Bonn, 1950), 96; Burleigh Cushing Rodick, *The Doctrine of Necessity in International Law* (New York, 1928), 59–60; Geoffrey Best, "How Right Is Might? Some Aspects of the International Debate about How to Fight Wars and How to Win Them, 1870–1918," in *War Economy and the Military Mind,* ed. Geoffrey Best and Andrew Wheatcroft (London, 1976), 129–30; Best, *Humanity in Warfare,* 174; George Winfield Scott and James Wilford Garner, eds., *The German War Code Contrasted with the War Manuals of the United States, Great Britain, and France* (Washington, DC, 1918), 4; Oppenheim, *International Law,* 2: para. 69; Garner, *International Law,* 2:197–98; Westlake, *International Law,* 115–17.

81. Albert Zorn, *Das Kriegsrecht zu Lande in seiner neuesten Gestaltung; Eine kritische Untersuchung* (Berlin, 1906), 4n3. Hereafter cited parenthetically in text by page number.

in the end amount to the same thing" (15). "Absolute, unlimited force [*Gewalt*] is determinant in war, which clearly expresses the power and the law of the stronger. Therefore, everything, even the apparently worst breach, is legally untouchable, so long as it is an act of imperative military necessity" (15–16).

The next year, Christian Meurer published the most influential German-language account of the Hague Conference. He, too, was adamant that the Hague Rules were binding law.[82] But he, too, followed Lueder, proposing to define military necessity juridically in this way: "There is no violation of the laws of war if the act was undertaken to preserve the troops, or to protect them from a danger that could not be averted in any other way, or which is necessary to carry out a legitimate operation of war, or to secure its success" (14). As John Westlake pointed out, such a definition adopted mere success as the criterion of necessity.[83] But Meurer struggled to get the genie back in the bottle: "Whoever cites military necessity while violating the laws of war," he wrote, "will have to prove genuine *Notstand*" (15).

For writers who followed Hartmann, Lueder, Albert Zorn, and Meurer in their war positivism, it was impossible to fend off the inevitable conclusion that military necessity was the *ultima ratio* that waived the law. The Jewish liberal Karl Strupp had almost finished his account of international law when the war broke out. He hurried his manuscript into print in the autumn of 1914. Like his predecessors, he fully accepted the binding nature of the Hague Rules, but like them he also wrote that legal rules could "*in no way*" hinder the goal of "the complete defeat of the enemy."[84] But Strupp was clearly unhappy with the inevitable consequences for the law. He insisted that even military necessity did not rob the Hague Rules of their character as binding law.[85] Strupp also followed the dominant trend among non-German writers in recognizing the sway of military necessity only in those articles in which it was specifically mentioned. But he still felt compelled to introduce a larger variant of military necessity, *Notstand,* in its place. *Notstand* permitted the momentary annulment of the positive laws of war under the same conditions that Meurer had allotted to military necessity: that it was "the *only* possibility of carrying out an operation of war, or ensuring its success, or when that operation appeared necessary to protect the troops or portions of them (even a single soldier)" (8).

The enormous pressure that German jurists felt to adopt the military's view on military necessity is nowhere better illustrated than in the young, pacifist Hans Wehberg. Wehberg quickly distinguished himself as a freethinker who left the convenient path of his colleagues. In November 1914 he resigned as associate editor of the *Zeitschrift für Völkerrecht* when its chief editor, Josef Kohler, defended in the intemperate terms of the daily press Germany's violation of Belgian neutrality, and in doing so "advocated certain ideas that would ultimately have led to the denial of international law as a whole," as Wehberg put

---

82. Christian Meurer, *Die Haager Friedenskonferenz,* vol. 2, *Das Kriegsrecht der Haager Konferenz* (Munich, 1907), 11, 17–19.

83. Westlake, *International Law,* 117.

84. Karl Strupp, *Das internationale Landkriegsrecht* (Frankfurt, 1914), 3; emphasis in original.

85. Ibid., 4; emphasis in original.

it in a public letter to the *Berliner Tageblatt*.[86] But in his handbook on international law (1910), the young Wehberg felt constrained to present the German view that "war necessity stands above the law of war. This view is generally recognized in the German legal literature, but is rejected by practically all foreign writers."[87] Calling a spade a spade, he concluded that "in a situation of necessity this view holds that every rule of the law of war may be broken" (14–15).

Emanuel von Ullmann is another good example of how hard contemporary jurists found it to avoid the dogma of military necessity. Ullmann rejected the dominant view among his colleagues that international law was a quasi- or weak form of law conceded provisionally by the will of the sovereign state. For him, international law was produced by a really existing international community, whose "real life circumstances have created a mutual dependency of states."[88] Law flowed not from morally indifferent "facts" but directly from the "necessity of the international community and the solidarity of interests of its members" (9). International law was real law (19–26), which had produced a "uniform complex of norms," including in the laws of war (470–71); "the law is followed because it is law" (23n2). Ullmann's is thus a robust, liberal view of international law, very similar to the writings of his colleagues in France and Britain. Nevertheless, Ullmann recognized two ways in which international law could be legitimately broken: by reprisal resulting from a prior violation by the enemy, and by "a situation of extreme necessity in which…he faced the choice of conscientiously following the rules of law at the cost of achieving the goal of war or giving up his own existence" (470). Ullmann covered this view (which he did not call "military necessity") by analogy to *Notstand* in criminal law (470n1). But he hedged this admission in two ways: he noted that the German view "was not generally accepted," and it did not apply to "*absolutely binding* laws of civilized peoples," such as those listed in Hague article 23 on forbidden weapons.[89]

The Views of the German Officer Corps

Officers were unlikely to have read the German academic literature on the laws of war. If they had done so, they would hardly have been challenged in their views. But we have two good examples of works they might well have read, and these give us a much better sense of what professional officers thought the laws of war were in 1914.

Unlike its opponents, Germany lacked an official military manual of the laws of war. That omission might well signal the army's preference to operate as much as possible in

---

86. Sept. 24, 1915, trans. in *American Journal of International Law* 9, no. 4 (Oct. 1915): 924–27, here 926; also Garner, *International Law*, 2:221n1.

87. Hans Wehberg, *Die Abkommen der Haager Friedenskonferenzen, der Londoner Seekriegskonferenz nebst Genfer Konvention* (Berlin, 1910), 14.

88. Emanuel von Ullmann, *Völkerrecht*, Das Öffentliche Recht der Gegenwart (Tübingen, 1908), 6. Hereafter cited parenthetically in text by page number.

89. Ibid., 470 (emphasis in original), 470n2.

the freedom of the unwritten. But the historical division of the general staff had commissioned in 1902 a semiofficial work printed in the series *Kriegsgeschichtliche Einzelschriften.* Major Rudolf von Friederich wrote *Kriegsbrauch im Landkrieg* in just six weeks, relying on the libraries of the war academy and the general staff, supplemented with his own books.[90] After the war, he explained that his goal had been to "reprise in broad strokes the general opinion of the most well regarded personalities [writing] in the literature of war. In essence, I collated."[91] *Kriegsbrauch* is thus particularly valuable for the historian, because its author intended "to describe and ground the views current in Germany."[92] It was also clearly designed to be a practical handbook: it tells its readers such things as how to word capitulation agreements, how to train officers sent to make agreements with the enemy, and even how big to make the Red Cross symbol.

Even before the war, German jurists noted that *Kriegsbrauch* was in many places seriously out of step with the Hague regulations that Germany had approved three years earlier.[93] Friederich told the postwar Reichstag investigating committee that he had known of the Hague Rules only from a newspaper account.[94] Nevertheless, his book mentions the Hague Rules nine times and once alludes to their wording.[95]

The theory of law visible in *Kriegsbrauch* is an interesting example of war positivism. The book claims that the attempts to codify the customary practices of war had "completely failed," leaving only the tenuous "agreement [between enemies] resting on reciprocity" (2). Reciprocity was a weak reed, of course, for it meant that any violation nullified the rule. Apparently, custom could be set by a single state: Germany's practices in 1870 are presented as sufficient to do so (5). The criterion determining customary law was military success. For instance, regarding the use of civilian hostages to protect railroads, Friederich wrote that its "war-legal justification" lay in the fact that it was preceded by warnings, "but more so in that this means had the most complete success" (50). He relegates the Hague Rules to mere "moral recognition" of norms—thus, they were not binding law in his view (3). Yet, where positive law protected soldiers, as in the Geneva Convention, *Kriegsbrauch* completely accepted it (25). It is unclear whether to read this discrepancy as the fruit of mere convenience, or of the greater age of the Geneva Convention (1864 versus 1899). Friederich did not define military necessity and in the end seemed to equate it with might makes right. Regarding forced requisitions, for example, he wrote that they were simply necessary, and "whether one grounds them legally through military necessity or merely through the might of the stronger is irrelevant for practice" (61).

Kriegsbrauch directly violated important Hague Rules. It permitted forcing civilians to give military information against their own country, raising unlimited requisitions, imposing collective fines without safeguards, killing unarmed prisoners of war for reasons

---

90. *UA* 3:1, 47–48.

91. Ibid., 47.

92. Ibid., 48.

93. Zorn, *Kriegsrecht*, 4n3; Meurer, *Haager Friedenskonferenz*, 17n2; Strupp, *Landkriegsrecht*, 3, 28, 44n1.

94. *UA* 3:1, 47.

95. Großer Generalstab Germany, *Kriegsbrauch im Landkriege,* Kriegsgeschichtliche Einzelschriften (Berlin, 1902), 3, 7, 14, 15, 18, 21, 24, 31, 67. Hereafter cited parenthetically in text by page number.

of security or because they could not be fed, shooting peace negotiators who had been warned that one did not want to receive them, and killing spies without trial (16, 26, 31, 48, 62, 63). Shooting unwanted, prewarned peace negotiators had been permitted in 1874 but forbidden in 1899 at Germany's own suggestion.[96] The point is not that *Kriegsbrauch* caused German officers to hold these views on law (which the investigating committee was at pains to deny), but that it reflected what they already believed and what they thought the reality of war dictated.[97]

If *Kriegsbrauch* was important because of its semiofficial nature and its avowed purpose to reflect what every officer already knew, Karl Endres's treatise is important because it is the only attempt from inside the officer corps to interpret the Hague Rules before 1914.[98] Endres was judicial adjutant (*Kriegsgerichtsrat*) to the general command of Bavarian Army Corps II. He intended his book for the "quick orientation" of army and naval officers (3). Thus, it represents an informed, legal view of the state of international law.

Like other professional jurists, Endres accepted the Hague Rules as in general binding law, and he began by citing the Martens Clause, though without comment (9, 12–13). For the most part, he gives a clear summary of the rules and accepts them. But his departures from them, mostly on the grounds of military necessity, sometimes by citing previous authorities, and occasionally by frankly bizarre interpretations of the law, describe almost perfectly the most controversial acts that German troops later committed in August 1914 and thereafter in the occupied zones.

Concerning the legality of the *levée en masse,* Endres acknowledged articles 1 and 2, but followed Meurer in raising the bar to legal recognition so high that no real *levée* would be acceptable. He notes that "military necessity" would permit measures protecting the troops against "abuse of this article" (16). After noting that article 2 did not require participants in a legitimate *levée* to fulfill all four conditions of recognition demanded of militias, he continues, "necessity can make a heightening of these [conditions] an incontestable duty" (16). That is, military necessity could override the law by adding additional (legal) requirements—by subjecting the *levée* to the higher standards of the militia, for example. Furthermore, Endres clearly anticipated abuse: "The fulfillment of the third requirement of Art. 2, obeying the laws of war, will actually only be present when there is [prior] organization. Lawless bands will soon violate them and lose the right to be treated as legal combatants" (17).[99] Endres therefore reflected exactly the repeated official German arguments in 1874 and 1899 that only units trained in advance were bona fide soldiers.

Endres confirmed the drift to ever looser definitions of legitimate occupation. Again, he acknowledged that the law required the ability to exercise power continuously, but following Schwarzhoff's remarks in the protocol of 1899, he argued that the mere "advance into enemy territory and the occupation in a military sense must be viewed as equal" to the

---

96. Netherlands, *Conférence,* 1:56–57.

97. *UA* 3:1, 28.

98. Karl Endres, *Die völkerrechtlichen Grundsätze der Kriegführung zu Lande und zur See* (Berlin, 1909). Hereafter cited parenthetically in text by page number.

99. The original Russian draft of the Brussels Convention had mentioned the danger of such "bands," a paragraph removed at French insistence: Brussels, Conference, 1874, *Actes,* 167–68.

legal view, even in cases of retreat (16–17). Endres therefore directly contradicted the position of Russia's General Leer at Brussels, who had made working communication lines the sine qua non of genuine occupation.[100] Similarly, after noting the proportional limitation to requisitions, Endres again followed Schwarzhoff's speech in the protocol, that "military necessity will be determinant" (29).

Endres was sure that military necessity covered the use of civilian hostages to safeguard railroads (39), though Meurer and Liszt (1913) had followed most jurists' opinions and rejected that practice (while Ullmann was uncertain and Albert Zorn held Endres's view).[101] But Endres nevertheless recognized "general international-legal principles" as governing the fate of hostages, given the Hague's silence. He thought their position was analogous to that of prisoners of war (77–78). However, general international-legal principles were in Endres's view hardly bulletproof safeguards, for military necessity permitted the killing of unarmed prisoners of war if they presented a danger and one was unable to feed or transport them (41). Endres therefore followed *Kriegsbrauch,* but added that such an eventuality would rarely occur, and killing prisoners would cause great bitterness and reprisals (41). Still, it was legal. He therefore recognized that military necessity contravened even absolute principles of law—killing prisoners was forbidden under article 23(c), which listed methods "especially forbidden."[102]

The almost limitless elasticity of mere practice is clear in two other examples, too. Concerning levying collective fines, the Hague Rules had restricted them to cases where the population was "jointly and severally responsible" (article 50). That high bar Endres undercut by including "failure to report criminal plans or to stop them from being carried out" as sufficient to establish guilt (30). That interpretation virtually ensured that any act interpreted as sabotage would permit collective fines.

Reprisal was the main cover for the "Belgian atrocities," and thus Endres's views on that subject are of great importance. He now wrote that reprisal "will probably never" be limited in positive law, "because reprisal as an act of retaliation does not permit itself to be incorporated in limited legal rules since its use will always depend on the kind and extent of the military necessity produced by self-preservation" (49). Obviously, Endres did not see reprisal as a legal institute, permitted at all only as a sanction to enforce the law. Instead, he saw it as a retaliatory measure of military necessity bordering on *Notstand* (i.e., magnified by self-preservation, which decades of German legal writing had identified with the stronger exceptional power of *Notstand*). Thus the "kind and extent" of reprisal were not proportional to the enemy's offense, but to one's own assumed military necessity understood in the more urgent register of self-preservation. Reprisal was thus unlimited, unlimitable, and available for use as a military tool.

Both *Kriegsbrauch* and Endres's volume strongly suggest that Germany's actions in August 1914 (and thereafter) had been long preprogrammed; it would have been astonishing

---

100. Ibid., 129.

101. Meurer, *Haager Friedenskonferenz,* 244–45; Liszt thought only reprisal covered the practice: Franz von Liszt, *Das Völkerrecht systematisch dargestellt* (Berlin, 1913), 305–6; Ullmann, *Völkerrecht,* 496, 496n2; Zorn, *Kriegsrecht,* 281–82.

102. Roberts and Guelff, *Documents,* 77–78.

if they had not occurred. But did Germany actually intend or plan to ignore the Hague Rules during wartime? In other words, was Germany's signature in 1899 and 1907 simply in bad faith?

One could doubtless find many examples of high-ranking military men who openly expressed scorn at the whole idea of international law. In Germany they included General-Major Erich von Gündell, Germany's military representative to the Second Hague Conference. He shared his caste's contempt for "weak-minded pacific proposals" (*friedensduselige Anträge*) and its conviction of the unchanging nature of war.[103] Gündell praised his Japanese military colleague's "natural understanding, unmarred by sentimentality, of reality, of war with all its unavoidable ruthlessness and hardness."[104] More disturbing is Gündell's post-conference audience with the Kaiser. Gündell recorded his pleasure that his ruler spoke of the Hague "with the disdain that I expected and desired." The Kaiser told Gündell that "he would do what he wanted, despite all the Hague agreements."[105]

However, such views were not terribly different from those, for example, expressed by Britain's First Sea Lord and Admiral of the Fleet (and delegate to the First Hague Conference) John A. Fisher, who thought that "the inevitable result of Conferences and Arbitrations is that we always give up something. It's like a rich man entering into a conference with a gang of burglars."[106] In 1908 Eyre Crowe informed Foreign Minister Edward Grey that "Sir J. Fisher told me personally three days ago that in the next big war, our commanders would sink every ship they came across, hostile or neutral, if it happened to suit them. He added, with characteristic vehemence, that we should most certainly violate the Declaration of Paris and every other treaty that might prove inconvenient."[107] Expostulations such as these reveal underlying attitudes especially of military men, but not necessarily government policy. Furthermore, they seem typical of all late nineteenth-century militaries, not just Germany's, and one must recall that both Colonels Schwarzhoff (Germany) and J. Gilinsky (Russia) explicitly spoke on behalf of the military profession and its supposed technical requirements in their interventions at the Hague Conference in 1899.[108]

One should also be wary of automatically extending to the Hague Rules Germany's utter rejection of two other issues raised at the Hague Conferences: disarmament (actually, arms control) and arbitration. The Allies later took Germany's vociferous opposition to both as a sign of its bellicosity and international truculence. After the war, Johannes Kriege spent many pages explaining and defending Germany's position.[109] The historian Jost Dülffer has concluded that Imperial Germany's uniquely sharp and undiplomatic double rejection did indeed indicate that it had drifted into opposition to the European

---

103. Erich von Gündell, *Aus seinen Tagebüchern: Deutsche Expedition nach China 1900–1901, 2. Haager Friedenskonferenz 1907; Weltkrieg 1914–1918 und Zwischenzeiten,* ed. Walter Obkircher (Hamburg, 1939), 98.

104. Ibid., 99.

105. Ibid., 107.

106. Avner Offer, *The First World War: An Agrarian Interpretation* (Oxford, 1989), 271.

107. Eyre Crowe to Grey, minute of Dec. 24, 1908, FO 371/794, fol. 146, cited in Offer, *First World War,* 277. Fisher later (1912) retracted some of his most bloodcurdling remarks: Kramer, *Dynamic of Destruction,* 97.

108. Netherlands, *Conférence,* 3:122, 123.

109. Johannes Kriege, "Die Haltung Deutschlands auf den Haager Friedenskonferenzen," *UA* 1:5, 161–221.

state system and to the international legal institutions that that system was developing, among other things, through the Hague Conferences.[110] The findings of this study confirm Dülffer's view, but even that confirmation does not necessarily mean that Germany planned simply to overthrow the law when war broke out.

A better test is how far Germany fulfilled the Hague's injunction that signatories "issue instructions to their armed land forces which shall be in conformity with the Regulations."[111] Here, Germany's record was significantly worse than that of its neighbors. The general staff never issued an official military handbook of regulations for the army. It took until 1911 for the Hague Rules to be reprinted without commentary in the field service manual (*Felddienstordnung*) and until 1914 for the general staff to issue regulations for its officers that contained excerpts of the Hague Rules. Those regulations were secret, however.[112] The war academy did not teach the laws of war at all from 1907 to 1911, after which it devoted a single hour per week to (mostly domestic) law.[113] In December 1911 military leaders decided to compile a summary of the Geneva and Hague Conventions to be handed to troops upon mobilization (but not before).[114] Before the war German jurists had noted discrepancies between the 1872 military penal code and the Hague Rules (concerning punishment for escaped prisoners, treatment of recaptured spies, the use of hostages to protect trains, and forcing inhabitants to act as guides), but these were not corrected.[115] The instructions for the rear and occupied areas (Kriegs-Etappen-Ordnung, or KEO) also violated the Hague Rules on collective fines; the Prussian war ministry knew this in 1903 but did not correct the KEO until 1916.[116] The same was true of the Imperial Edict of December 28, 1899, regulating the punishment of prisoners of war and enemy civilians in occupied territory; it also was finally brought into conformity in 1916.[117] Even the Reichstag investigating committee, which on the whole completely rejected Allied allegations of German illegal war conduct, had to admit that other states had been far more assiduous in preparing their officers and men to follow international law.[118]

Britain and Russia made their first attempts to incorporate the Hague and Geneva Rules into their own military manuals in 1904.[119] Not until respectively 1912 and 1913 did Britain

---

110. Jost Dülffer, *Regeln gegen den Krieg? Die Haager Friedenskonferenzen 1899 und 1907 in der internationalen Politik* (Berlin, 1981), passim, and conclusion, 329–48.

111. Hague Convention IV (1907), art. 1: Roberts and Guelff, *Documents*, 70.

112. Kriege writing to the German embassy in Copenhagen, on behalf of the chancellor, Berlin, June 4, 1915, copy, IIIa 9402/74842, "Streng vertraulich," BAB R 901 86663.

113. Ernst Stenzel, *Die Kriegführung des deutschen Imperialismus und das Völkerrecht; zur Planung und Vorbereitung des deutschen Imperialismus auf die barbarische Kriegführung im Ersten und Zweiten Weltkrieg, dargestellt an den vorherrschenden Ansichten zu den Gesetzen und Gebräuchen des Landkrieges (1900–1945)* (Berlin, 1973), 36–37.

114. Ibid., 37.

115. Meurer, *Haager Friedenskonferenz*, 133–34, 188–89, 244–45, 246–47.

116. *UA* 3:1, 35. For more examples: Hull, *Absolute Destruction*, 226–27.

117. *UA* 3:1, 35, 43–45.

118. *UA* 3:1, 35–36.

119. The British attempt was private, by Thomas E. Holland: Thomas Erskine Holland, *The Laws and Customs of War on Land, as Defined by the Hague Convention of 1899* (London, 1904). In 1908 Holland chided Russia's attempt as incomplete: Holland, *The Laws of War on Land* (Oxford, 1908), 2n, 6n.

and France complete that task and thus explicitly fulfill their obligation as signatories according to article 1 of Hague Convention IV (1907) and article 26 of the Geneva Convention (1906).[120] I am unaware of any similar project in Germany. Both the French and British manuals were (co)written by international lawyers. Britain's most distinguished international lawyer, Lassa Oppenheim, coauthored its manual together with Colonel J. E. Edmonds (a nonlawyer), while Louis Renault, the premier international jurist of the Continent and one of the French representatives to the Hague Conferences in 1899 and 1907, provided the introduction to the French manual, actually written by Lieutenant Robert Jacomet, who had received his doctorate of law with a study on war and treaties.

Both manuals incorporated the Hague and Geneva Rules, plus the St. Petersburg and Hague (1907) declarations governing explosive and dumdum bullets, bombardment, and asphyxiating gases, and they supplemented the actual wording with commentary and with customary law where positive law was silent. Both included practical information, ready-made forms, and detailed instructions clearly designed for actual use in the field. And both were official publications of their respective general staffs, and in the British case, of the War Office.

Neither manual was utopian or unrealistic. They both adduced the military necessity exception where it had been noted (and occasionally elsewhere). The French manual explicitly made the rules binding only on condition of reciprocity.[121] That view had severe consequences once the war began.[122] Nevertheless, both manuals freely accepted as binding many rules regarding which German writers, official, semiofficial, and civilian, had caviled: the recognition of fighters in the *levée en masse* should be "generously interpreted";[123] in case of doubt no officer or soldier should decide for himself to execute a suspected unlawful belligerent ("No law authorizes them to have him shot without trial, and international law forbids summary execution absolutely");[124] suspected spies had to be tried ("No officer, regardless of rank or command, is authorized to order the summary execution of individuals accused of espionage");[125] recaptured spies were not subject to prosecution;[126] prisoners of war could not be killed for any other reasons than attempts at escape or outright revolt—military convenience was explicitly rejected as a valid ground;[127] requisitions must be proportionate to the resources of the occupied area (Edmonds gave detailed instructions on how much food must be left to civilians,[128] while Jacomet set

---

120. Colonel J. D. Edmonds and Lassa Oppenheim, *Land Warfare: An Exposition of the Laws and Usages of War on Land, for the Guidance of Officers of His Majesty's Army* (London, 1912), iii; and Robert Jacomet, *Les lois de la guerre continentale* (Paris, 1913), 14–15.

121. Jacomet, *Lois de la guerre,* 26.

122. See chapter 9 on reprisals.

123. Edmonds and Oppenheim, *Land Warfare,* para. 30; Jacomet, *Lois de la guerre,* art. 5, p. 29.

124. Edmonds and Oppenheim, *Land Warfare,* para. 37.

125. Jacomet, *Lois de la guerre,* art. 68.

126. Ibid., art. 68; Edmonds and Oppenheim, *Land Warfare,* paras. 169–70.

127. Jacomet, *Lois de la guerre,* art. 8, p. 33; Edmonds and Oppenheim, *Land Warfare,* para. 80.

128. Edmonds and Oppenheim, *Land Warfare,* paras. 416–22; Jacomet, *Lois de la guerre,* art. 104.

down the rule that French troops should conduct themselves abroad as they would at home);[129] occupants were forbidden to use forced civilian labor on fortifications.[130]

There were several places where British and sometimes French views were closer to those of Germany on controversial issues: (1) Edmonds and Oppenheim accepted the Hague conditions for real occupation, but wrote that "flying columns" could still constitute genuine occupation, so long as the inhabitants had been disarmed and arrangements for administration had been made.[131] (2) Forcing civilians to act as guides was still considered illegal, though Edmonds and Oppenheim noted that "in practice patrols will seek information as heretofore";[132] Jacomet thought that the numerous reservations to that rule meant it was probably not binding.[133] (3) Edmonds and Oppenheim recognized the legality of destruction (for example, of houses) for illegal acts of civilians, but cautioned that "care must, however, be taken to limit the destruction to the property of the guilty."[134] (4) Whereas Jacomet recognized absolutely the Hague ban on collective punishment (article 109), the British writers acknowledged the legality of collective reprisal against localities in some cases (§458).

Despite these areas of concurrence, the prewar British and French manuals laid out on their side the principled areas of disagreement that erupted once the war began.

Neither manual made a fetish of military necessity—in fact, neither manual defined it or included it in the index.[135] Edmonds wrote, "The question in what circumstances a necessity arises cannot be decided by any hard and fast rule" (§434). And both volumes ventured to fill the silences of the Hague on important issues such as hostages and reprisals.

Jacomet laid down the "principle" that hostage taking was forbidden, but he left a loophole for "absolute necessity" if it were "ordered by the troop commander and, if possible, by the commander of the army" (article 92). Thus, he tried to keep the practice out of the hands of subordinates. The British felt that hostages probably should not be taken at all, and certainly could not be killed. Despite Lord Frederick Roberts's brief foray into the German practice during the Boer War, Edmonds and Oppenheim flatly rejected using hostages to protect trains, and noted that Roberts's order had been rescinded within a week (§461).

Jacomet mentioned reprisals only once, as one of the sanctions upholding international law (24). Edmonds and Oppenheim went into much greater detail. They, too, regarded it as a purely legal institution, and thus explicitly "not a means of punishment, or of arbitrary vengeance" (§452). Reprisals "must not exceed the degree of violation committed by the enemy," and once his infraction had stopped, so must they (§459–460). The writers'

---

129. Jacomet, *Lois de la guerre*, annex 3, p. 106.

130. Ibid., art. 94; Edmonds and Oppenheim, *Land Warfare*, para. 391.

131. Edmonds and Oppenheim, *Land Warfare*, para. 351. Cf. Holland, *Laws of War* (1904), art. 68, p. 33.

132. Edmonds and Oppenheim, *Land Warfare*, para. 382.

133. Jacomet, *Lois de la guerre*, art. 95. Holland agreed: Holland, *Laws of War* (1908), 53.

134. Edmonds and Oppenheim, *Land Warfare*, para. 414.

135. Holland had defined military necessity in the usual way, as Lieber had done, as that justification of measures to secure the object of war "provided that they are not inconsistent with the modern laws and usages of warfare." Holland, *Laws of War* (1904), para. 6, p. 3; Lieber, *Instructions*, art. 14.

discomfort is especially clear in section 456, which took the reader through all the steps of scrupulous investigation and notification before one resorted to this distasteful method. Even after this lengthy procedure, they enjoined commanders to consider whether the enemy "is not more likely to be influenced by a steady adherence to the laws of war on the part of his adversary" (§457).[136]

The French and British manuals were not identical. The British were less sensitive to the possible excesses of occupation than were the French, who had recently been occupied themselves. The biggest difference related to the question of reciprocity. Whereas Jacomet set down the widespread view in France that reciprocity was the condition for making the international laws of war binding, Edmonds and Oppenheim were much more careful: "A belligerent is not justified in at once dispensing with obedience to the laws of war on account of their suspected or ascertained violation on the part of his adversary."[137]

But the disagreements between the French and British manuals were of a different order of magnitude from those separating them both from German writers. There can be no question that the Entente partners regarded the Hague and Geneva rules as generally binding on themselves and others. Though the distance between their own and Germany's apparent expectations was quite visible, few observers anticipated that the differences of 1874–1907 would be reflected so perfectly in practice. It would seem that Europeans believed that Germany intended to uphold the Hague Rules, and there were many reasons for them to hold that view.

Although Germany preferred bilateral agreements to general conventions and staunchly opposed the disarmament and arbitration efforts at the Hague Conventions, its military representatives had dominated the discussions of the rules of warfare.[138] Chancellor Bernhard von Bülow reported his satisfaction that the Hague Rules of 1899 were a success.[139] In the 1906 conference to revise the Geneva Convention, Germany followed the same tack as it had in 1899 and did again in 1907: "In almost all matters of too far reaching demands we succeeded in adding limitations like 'so far as circumstances permit' or 'according to the decision of the responsible military office' etc."[140] Even the German military had reason to be satisfied that the resulting rules did not limit it significantly.[141]

And while the *political* section of the German foreign office had been in charge of the 1899 Hague negotiations, it was the *legal* section that prepared Germany's case for 1907.

---

136. Before them Holland had also listed the usual restrictions on reprisal: careful inquiry, genuine redress unobtainable, authorization only by the commander in chief "unless under very special circumstances," proportionate to the offense, and not barbarous. Holland, *Laws of War* (1904), art. 100, p. 46.

137. Jacomet, *Lois de la guerre,* 26; Edmonds and Oppenheim, *Land Warfare,* para. 53. Holland had written that reprisals were the "painful exception to the rule that a belligerent must observe the laws of war, even without reciprocity on the part of the enemy": *Laws of War* (1904), para. 99, pp. 45–46.

138. Bilateral: Paul Cambon to Léon Bourgeois, Aug. 29, 1906, France, Min. des affaires étrangères, Service Juridique, Fonds Fromageot 2. Domination: Amb. Count Münster to Chlodwig v. Hohenlohe-Schillingsfürst, Nr. 88, Scheveningen, July 17, 1899, *GP* 15: doc. Nr. 4351, pp. 354–59.

139. Bülow to Kaiser, June 21, 1899, *GP* 15: doc. 4320.

140. Manteuffel to Pr. War Min., Report no. 7, Halberstadt, July 21, 1906, BAB R 901 28907. Manteuffel listed seven such articles.

141. Best, *Humanity in Warfare,* 142–48, 153, 161–62, 166.

That shift suggests that Germany had realized in the interim that law would play an important role in any coming war and that Germany must influence such law.[142]

Germany also held the obligatory inter-ministerial meetings to reconcile its domestic laws with those of the Hague and Geneva. The Naval Office early pointed out that German law needed some revision to be consonant with two Geneva articles: misuse of the Red Cross symbol needed to be criminalized, and other criminal punishments might need strengthening.[143] Nevertheless, the bureaucratic correspondence dragged on until the 1912 deadline neared. The federal interior secretary clearly preferred to rely on German domestic law.[144] In the end, Germany satisfied the Geneva requirement by listing domestic laws already on the books.[145] It did the same with the Hague Rules. Neither dilatoriness nor reliance on domestic legislation was unusual among the signatories to the Geneva and Hague Conventions, but there were unexpected legal consequences to this tactic during the war. It was politically comfortable to assert that there were no collisions between German and international law because in that case it was unnecessary to submit either Geneva or the Hague Rules to the Reichstag for ratification; they became binding German law by virtue of the Kaiser's acceptance of them and their publication in the *Reichsgesetzblatt*. That was the interpretation of a major meeting held after the Second Hague Convention between representatives of the foreign ministry (AA), the federal offices of the interior, justice, post office, and navy, and the Prussian ministries of trade, justice, war, and the general staff. But forgoing formal ratification had unfortunate consequences during the war. In 1915, the president of the imperial military court (Reichsmilitärgericht, or RMG) and the chief prosecutor discovered discrepancies, most seriously concerning which law applied to prisoner-of-war escapees. The German military code was harsher than the Hague Rules. Despite AA entreaties, the RMG and prosecutor stuck to their position that in cases of conflict, German domestic law overruled international law that apparently in their view had never been properly ratified through the Reichstag and Bundesrat. This position made it seem to the outside world that Germany had broken its word (and the law).[146]

Nevertheless, the documents give no hint that high-ranking German officials, including the representatives of the military, directly intended to disregard the law; at most, they intended to force it into familiar bottles. In reply to a U.S. query in August 1914, the German government declared that the Hague Rules of 1907 were binding law in Germany, but that "special regulations for their application were not drawn up for the time being, but were saved for that time when a practical need arose and the particular circumstances

---

142. *UA* 1:5:1, 165–67.

143. Imperial Naval Office (RMA) to AA, G. III. 1048, Berlin, Apr. 27, 1907, BAB R 901 28909.

144. Graf Posadowsky to AA, Nr. IA 3243, Berlin, Apr. 29, 1907, BAB R 901 28909.

145. Lentze memo, IIIa 12993, Sept. 18, 1912, BAB R 901 28914.

146. Jagow to Pres. of Reichsmilitärgericht, IIIb 16866/88988, Berlin, June 30, 1915, "Vertraulich!"; Memo of Simons, Berlin, June 25, 1915, "Vertraulich!" "Aufzeichnng über die Bestrafung entwichener Kriegsgefangenen," Bethmann to Kaiser, Nr. IIIb 17932/2881, copy, Berlin, July 7, 1915, Jagow to Pres. of RMG, Nr. IIIB 18124/104002, July 27,1915, all in BAB R 901 86664.

were clear."[147] This response again suggests the preference for improvisation unhindered by positive law that characterized the military and which the civilian leadership did nothing to gainsay.

Even the general staff appears to have assumed that the Hague Rules would provide the outlines for its own conduct. In 1914 it issued (secret) instructions whose section on occupation cited the Hague articles 42 to 56 governing the rights, limitations, and obligations of occupants. There were no further such instructions.[148]

The "Belgian atrocities" were probably not the result of a concerted plan or intent simply to throw out the law. They reflected long-standing and publicly defended interpretations of the laws of war as Imperial Germany, led by its military, but followed by its civilian leaders and academics, interpreted them. Imperial Germany believed that its actions were lawful or permitted. The Allied and neutral shock could hardly have been due to ignorance of the well-publicized German position; it was due instead to the cleft between it and the interpretations of law and community held by most other European states.

The Development of International Law and the Persistent Objector

There are several ways in which we might try to understand the legal divide of 1914. One focuses on the disagreements among European states as evidenced in different state practices and different views of interpretation; it emphasizes the unsettled or patchwork nature of the laws of land warfare and the consequent permission of many methods of warfare that were later forbidden. This is a common view of post-1945 writers, who are struck by the difference between then and now.[149] In this view, the disputes over violations were simply the unfortunate result of international law's relatively primitive development. Another interpretation would say that the Hague Conventions expressed considerable state agreement on the legal status of many rules and principles, but that areas covered by (noncodified) customary international law remained indistinctly regulated or subject to much interpretive contention, again leaving latitude for many warlike extremes.[150] That view would refocus our attention to problems of interpreting customary law. A third would argue that the codification process had done what codifications often do: it had caused states to become clearer about the customary law that they were now setting down in writing; by defining more exactly and by compromising in order to reach consensus, it had inevitably changed some rules of custom, which through ratification then received the imprimatur of binding law; and it had offered the opportunity for states to contest some principles of

---

147. Verbal note to the U.S., copy, Nr. IIIa 891/61068, Berlin, Aug. 21, 1914, BAB R 901 86663.

148. Kriege writing to German embassy in Copenhagen, on behalf of chancellor, Berlin, June 4, 1915, copy, IIIa 9402/74842, "Streng vertraulich," BAB R 901 86663.

149. Best, *Humanity in Warfare*, 128–48 and passim.

150. On the difficulties of interpreting customary international law: Byers, "Custom"; D'Amato, *Concept of Custom;* Thirlway, *International Customary Law;* Lepard, *Customary International Law,* pt. 1.

settled customary law.[151] By doing all these things, the turn-of-the-century codifications revealed broadly two different developmental possibilities for modern international law, which were then explicitly fought out in the World War. This third interpretation brings into sharper focus what happened in 1914–18.

At issue was much more than simply answering the question of which state broke what law, for, as Anthony D'Amato puts it, "an 'illegal' act by a state contains the seeds of a new legality. When a state violates an existing rule of customary international law, it undoubtedly is 'guilty' of an illegal act, but the illegal act itself becomes a disconfirmatory instance of the underlying rule. The next state will find it somewhat easier to disobey the rule, until eventually a new line of conduct will replace the original rule by a new rule."[152]

If we take seriously the possibility that both sides believed they were in the right, or should have been in the right, then one of the greatest stakes at issue in the war was the very constitution of postwar international law with all its implications for the modern community of states.

In order to judge the belligerents' claims and counterclaims, we must briefly take stock of the status of codified law in 1914 and examine the rules for interpreting customary international law.

All the belligerents had ratified the Hague codification of 1899. The Second Hague Convention of 1907 (Convention IV) contained minimal changes to the rules governing land warfare, the most important of which were two requirements (that belligerents pay compensation for violations committed by their armed forces [preliminary article 3], and that in addition to following international law, participants in a *levée en masse* carry their arms openly [article 2]), and one prohibition (on forcing occupied enemy civilians to serve as guides [article 44]). However, since Turkey, Montenegro, and Serbia had failed to ratify them by 1914, the 1907 rules were nonbinding for all belligerents (preliminary article 2). But no state had denounced the 1899 codification, therefore it still bound them all (article 4 of Hague Convention IV, 1907). The Hague Convention of 1899 was thus in effect for the entire First World War.[153] No power had reserved any of its articles.[154]

Customary international law (CIL) governed those areas on which the codified law was silent or unclear. CIL is widespread state practice that the community of states recognizes as "legally necessary or legally right," in Oppenheim's words—that is, customary law is state practice and *opinio juris*.[155] Interpreting CIL is an art, not a science, and conflicting views are common, as is true for all forms of law. Concerning state practice, no clear interpretive rule sets the necessary duration or extent, or determines when recent practices supplant older ones. Greater interpretive problems surround *opinio juris*. Jurists

---

151. Contesting "settled" matters: Thirlway, *International Customary Law*, 115.

152. D'Amato, *Concept of Custom*, 97.

153. Garner, *International Law*, 1:17–21.

154. James Brown Scott, *The Hague Conventions and Declarations of 1899 and 1907, Accompanied by Tables of Signatures, Ratifications and Adhesions of the Various Powers and Texts of Reservations....* Publications of the Carnegie Endowment for International Peace, Division of International Law, Washington, DC (New York, 1918), 130. Scott's edition conveniently compares 1899 and 1907 in double columns.

155. Oppenheim, *International Law*, vol. 1, para. 17, p. 23.

then and now have been skeptical of government statements, which are often made for political purposes. For this reason they tend to accept treaties, declarations, and protocols more readily as evidence of state belief that some practice is obligatory.[156] However, official statements, including justifications for infractions, would fail in their political purpose if they did not reflect or address the community's legal expectations. They are therefore good mirrors of what governments think other governments want to hear—and that is often strong indication of *opinio juris.* So are justifications that backhandedly acknowledge a broken rule. Furthermore, historians' greater access to the confidential speech of policy makers permits one to test the congruence between secret and public utterances and to judge real belief—that is, the assumptions that actually guide policy.

But a second and more far-reaching problem concerns the ambit of *opinio juris.* Does it mean that states believe their action is already binding law (*lex lata*)? Or does it include the opinion that it ought to be law, that it is "right" in the sense of just? The latter view is a statement of *lex ferenda* (law in the making), sometimes called "soft law," which indicates the direction in which states or their agents wish to see international law develop. Modern writers disagree on whether *opinio juris* should be construed widely or narrowly.[157] The inclusion of a moral imperative would hasten legal change and extend the writ of law as against the narrower view. The same effect would occur if one weighed *opinio juris* more strongly than state practice in judging which rules had become customary law.

Modern scholars believe that in our world of extensive codification, where statements (General Assembly resolutions, official declarations, treaties and codifications) outstrip the record of state practice, *opinio juris* counts more heavily in determining the law than does state practice. They imagine that the reverse was true in the era we are studying. However, both the heated philosophical debates in 1874 and 1899 that we have examined and the writings of the most famous contemporary international jurists show that the argument among statesmen and lawyers over the balance of state practice and *opinio juris* and over how far the latter included the moral "ought," *lex ferenda,* was lively and quite "modern."

Most prewar jurists did not use the phrase *opinio juris*—their judgments on law interpretation were often couched in discussions of sources. We can discover their views in two ways: in their definitions of international law (which list the attributes required to prove the existence of an obligatory rule) and in their discussion of state recognition of binding rules. For example, the Swiss jurist Bluntschli (1874) discovered gradually changing

---

156. Anthony D'Amato proposed the stringent view that official statements are speech acts stating belief, but are not actual belief. I think most historians would say that careful scrutiny of internal and private documents allows reasonable conclusions about actual belief. D'Amato, *Concept of Custom,* 33–41.

157. The narrower construction: D'Amato, *Concept of Custom,* 73; Jean-Marie Henckaerts, "Study on Customary International Humanitarian Law: A Contribution to the Understanding and Respect for the Rule of Law in Armed Conflict," *International Review of the Red Cross* 87, no. 857 (March 2005): 181. The wider construction, including *lex ferenda:* Anthea Roberts, "Traditional and Modern Approaches to Customary International Law: A Reconciliation," *American Journal of International Law* 95, no. 4 (2001): 763–64, 768. Thirlway proposes a two-stage progression of *opinio juris* from the point when states articulate that they have acted in some way because they think the action ought to be law, to a second stage, when they think it has become law: Thirlway, *International Customary Law,* 53–54.

customary law in the combination of "the improvement and elevation of spirit and the tendencies which emerge in the usages of nations," suggesting that he took some account of *lex ferenda*.[158] His German contemporary August Wilhelm Heffter (1867) did so more explicitly. He noted that international law was mostly customary (*ius non scriptum*) and "consisted" of "consensual laws" recognized (as obligatory) in different ways, sometimes in treaties, sometimes as "convergent state practices," as "abstractions from the essence of useful institutions, and also from the convergent morals [*Sitte*] and education of nations, such that those things held here to be unjust can hardly be considered just for states or their leaders."[159] Holtzendorff (1885) advised his readers that correctly interpreting customary law required "considering not just the logical, but also the ethical and political aspects of law creation." "In the interests of durability, security, and effectiveness," he wrote, "positive law must already in the moment of its birth be examined to see if its content coincides with the requirements of the common ethical conscience of civilized nations [*Culturnationen*]" as these were expressed, for example, in official writings, treaties, and public opinion.[160] On the other side were William Edward Hall (1889) and Henry Bonfils (1912) who tilted much more strongly toward judging the legal primarily according to state practice. Hall stated more clearly than many of his contemporaries the dual character of customary international law as combining recurrent state practices with recognition of "certain moral obligations, which are recognized as being the source of legal rules." But actual obligation inhered solely in *lex lata*, not in "practices which the contracting parties wish to incorporate into the usage of law, but which they know to be outside the actual law."[161] Obviously, prewar jurists described approximately the same latitude for interpretation of the binding law as exists today.

In an influential article, Anthea Roberts has suggested a useful way of weighing state practice against *opinio juris* in interpreting hard cases where state practice is mixed or inconclusive. She begins by observing that not all international-legal conflicts are equal; some bear on strong normative principles. In those cases, she writes, *opinio juris*, understood as "what the law is or should be," should be more definitive than state practice when it violates these norms.[162] Oscar Schachter makes the same point: where rules "express deeply-held and widely shared convictions as to the unacceptability of the prohibited conduct.... Contrary and inconsistent [state] practice would not and should not defeat their

---

158. Johann Caspar Bluntschli, *Le droit international codifié*, trans. C. Lardy (Paris, 1874), para 14, p. 60.

159. August Wilhelm Heffter, *Das Europäische Völkerrecht der Gegenwart auf den bisherigen Grundlagen* (Berlin, 1867), 16–17.

160. Franz von Holtzendorff, *Handbuch des Völkerrechts. Auf Grundlage europäischer Staatspraxis*, vol. 1, Einleitung in das Völkerrecht (Berlin, 1885), 48, 62–63.

161. William Edward Hall, *A Treatise on International Law* (Oxford, 1904), 5–6. The 1904 edition is identical to the 1889 edition, save for additions in brackets by the editor, J. B. Atlay. The above quotations are Hall's, not Atlay's. Bonfils had little to say about what we would call *opinio juris:* Henry Bonfils, *Manuel de droit international public (droit des gens) aux étudiants des facultés de droit et aux aspirants aux fonctions diplomatiques et consulaires* (Paris, 1912), paras. 46–54.

162. Roberts, "Traditional and Modern Approaches," 776–83, citation at 778.

claims as customary law."[163] Interpretations using this method will be controversial, but the reasons behind this choice seem cogent.

This modern discussion helps us appreciate the great importance of the facticity versus lex ferenda arguments at Brussels and The Hague. The German position leaned heavily toward prioritizing state (military) practice in determining CIL, while the opposing view, expressed in the Martens Clause, leaned toward opinio juris, which included progressive development of the law (lex ferenda) in a humanitarian direction ("the laws of humanity, and the dictates of the public conscience"). Because the Martens Clause was passed unanimously and placed so conspicuously in the preamble, together with Renault's report rejecting the lawmaking capacity of mere force, the state community appears to have accorded greater weight to opinio juris than to state practice alone, at least concerning important norms.

The debate over reprisal epitomized this issue. If one's guiding star was recent state practice, then Germany's actions in France in 1870–71 set the template. (Of course, there were immediate state protests, so an opposing view might claim that these prevented the practices from recognition as lawful.[164]) Nevertheless, there was a long history of state reprisals, including against civilians. There was also a long history of restraints dating from the seventeenth century and most recently incorporated in Lieber's United States Manual (1863), Bluntschli's code, and the Russian draft code of 1874: reprisals must be rare and exceptional, and to be permitted they require definite proof of violation, proportionality, and "as far as possible" consonance with "the laws of humanity." Germany's representative seemed prepared to accept the revised Russian draft, meaning that the big land powers expressed the view that these limits were customary (opinio juris).[165] Belgium's idealist objections then prevented them from being codified, but as customary international law, they remained binding on all states regardless. If we grant that German troops and their leaders were convinced that they faced an illegal insurrection that legitimized reprisal, the ensuing reprisal campaign nonetheless failed the test of customary law. It was widespread policy, not an exception; alleged civilian crimes were almost never proved and seldom investigated with vigor before reprisals were taken; and the draconian mass shooting and massive destruction were disproportionate.[166] (The rejection of all reprisals against the defenseless articulated so vociferously by Belgium and other states in 1874 later became codified international law, in 1929 regarding prisoners of war and the wounded, and in 1949 regarding civilians.[167])

But reprisal raised other legal issues. As we have seen, German military leaders on the spot explained their measures variously as reprisal, self-defense, deterrence, and military

---

163. Ibid., Schachter cited on 783.

164. On the difficulty in interpreting protests: D'Amato, Concept of Custom, 98–102.

165. Voigts-Rhetz offered an emendation to the draft on reprisal but never voiced opposition to regulating it: Brussels, Conference, 1874, Actes, 239.

166. Hankel, Leipziger Prozesse, 229–40, 256, 269, 274, 280, 309–20.

167. Art. 2 of the July 27, 1929, Geneva Convention; art. 33 of Geneva Convention IV of 1949. For a convenient list of all articles in codified international law regulating reprisal see the ICRC website: http://www.icrc.org/ihl. nsf/WebSearch?SearchView&Query=reprisal&SearchFuzzy=TRUE&SearchOrder=4.

necessity. Each of these arguments has a different legal valence. Self-defense and reprisal make no claim for the legality of the actions taken; on the contrary, they admit their illegality and claim exception. Deterrence and military necessity are prophylactic (not reactive) and far-reaching. They assert that measures taken under their aegis are legal. In his study of the postwar war crimes trials in Germany, Gerd Hankel notes that the Imperial Court (Reichsgericht) avoided the term "reprisal" regarding the "Belgian atrocities" precisely because of its admission that the actions were illegal. Instead, the court preferred the stronger claims, including that of *Kriegsbrauch*—customary law of war—which insisted on their legality and asserted at the same time a contrary customary legal tradition based solely on state practice.[168] This assertion brings us to the larger issue of military necessity.

The international legal interpretation of military necessity was undergoing change: the Hague Convention signaled development in the direction of greater limitation, while Imperial German views were moving oppositely. The colloquy over section 46 suggests that most states already accepted the view that exceptions of military necessity were limited to those articles specifically permitting the exception. Schwarzhoff's remarks and German juristic writing clearly rejected this understanding. Of course, Germany signed the Hague Convention and published its annex as law, and thus was on record as having approved it. But arguably the interpretive point was not contained in the code, but in the protocols, and there Germany had disagreed with the majority view. As a thought experiment, let us consider this state of affairs under the rubric of what has become known as the "persistent objector."

Although the term persistent objector is anachronistic, the concept is not. First used by the International Court of Justice in 1950, it has entered the legal arena since the 1970s and 1980s to describe a state that clearly articulates its objection to a developing customary law (*lex ferenda*).[169] The United States has recently used the term to describe its position regarding several issues. Jurists disagree whether it is a genuine legal concept or simply a subterfuge.[170] If it does exist, it holds that a single state may object to a new law as it is developing (but not afterward), and consequently, when that law has become *lex lata*, the objector is not bound by it, except for normative principles so fundamental that they are held to be universally binding, no matter what (*jus cogens*).[171]

In their discussion of the formation of new international-legal rules, nineteenth-century writers recognized the phenomenon, which we might regard as analogous to reservations to a multilateral treaty or protests against a disapproved action. They seem to have thought of it as a consequence of the voluntary theory of international lawmaking that held that

168. Hankel, *Leipziger Prozesse*, 309–10. On the elastic use of "Kriegsbrauch" in German law: Andreas Toppe, *Militär und Kriegsvölkerrecht: Rechtsnorm, Fachdiskurs und Kriegspraxis in Deutschland* (Munich, 2008), 89–97, 124, 428; Endres, *Völkerrechtliche Grundsätze*, 18, 47.

169. Ted L. Stein, "The Approach of the Different Drummer: The Principle of the Persistent Objector in International Law," *Harvard International Law Journal* 26, no. 2 (1985): 457–82.

170. Patrick Dumberry, "Incoherent and Ineffective: The Concept of Persistent Objector Revisited," *International and Comparative Law Quarterly* 59, no. 3 (2010): 779–802.

171. Bradley Curtis and Mitu Gulati, "Withdrawing from International Custom," *Yale Law Journal* 120 (2010–11): 205.

states only agreed to limits on their sovereignty voluntarily. Bluntschli disapproved, calling the concept "vague and dangerous," but Hall thought that "the refusal of a single state to accept a change in the law prevents a modification agreed upon by all other states from being immediately compulsory, except as between themselves." In other words, the objector was exempt from obligation. But he thought that a rule finding acceptance by all but one state was "an unusually solid foundation of usage" that could become law very quickly.[172] Westlake wrote similarly, describing "sufficiently general" approbation as "an element in determining the limit of the forbearance to be shown to a state which persists in resisting the change or addition."[173]

Persistent objector accurately describes Imperial Germany's role in the first phase of land war codification (but not the codification of naval rules, where Germany voted with the majority). The point of this exercise is not to determine definitively what rules were binding on Germany, but instead to locate its position in the lawmaking community. Persistent objection normally applied to material law, the substantive rules that develop or disappear over time. But as we have seen, Germany's objections went deeper in two ways. First, the facticity / *lex ferenda* debate went to the heart of how law was thought to develop and what, at base, it was. The issue was how strong, or indeed whether, the "ought" expressed in the Martens Clause as coming from "the principles of the laws of nations, as they result from the usages established among civilized peoples, from the laws of humanity, and the dictates of the public conscience" should determine law, as opposed to military practices, usages, or weapons. Second, the military necessity debate (and to some degree reprisal) posed the question of the balance between the law and the exception. The Kaiserreich came down strongly on the side of the exception, grounded variously on the principle of self-preservation or more grandly on the assertion of the law-giving positivity of the nature of war. Behind disagreements about the content of rules therefore loomed these much larger issues. If one views this first period of legal codification as a transitional moment in the history of international law in which two different theories of law vied with each other, then one recognizes the enormous stakes involved in the First World War.

---

172. Bluntschli, *Droit international,* para. 14, p. 60; Hall, *International Law,* 12–13.
173. Westlake, *International Law,* 1:16–7. See also Bonfils, *Manuel* (1912), para. 53, p. 25.

Occupation and the Treatment of Enemy Civilians

The partial success of the Schlieffen Plan placed between nine and ten million enemy civilians under Germany's control, some seven million in Belgium and over two million in France.[1] By the end of 1915 Erich Falkenhayn's defeat of Russia brought another three million Poles, Lithuanians, and others to this number.[2] After the defeat of Romania in 1916, the collapse of the Russian Empire, and the Treaty of Brest-Litovsk in 1918, many millions more were added.[3] Imperial Germany was therefore the Great War's greatest occupant. In comparison, France administered a tiny sliver of Alsace near the Swiss border, Austria occupied Serbia, Montenegro, and part of Poland after 1915, and Russia twice took over Galicia (1914 and 1916) and occupied part of the Ottoman Empire. A real comparison of Germany's policies would therefore be with its ally, Austria, or with Russia, not with the Western Allies, the basis of this study. But there is an even more fundamental problem in offering a full analysis of occupation and the law—no complete examination of the occupation of any place in World War I exists. Occupation is the stepchild of Great War historiography; only now are historians laboring to

---

1. Herbert Hoover, *An American Epic*, vol. 1, *Introduction: The Relief of Belgium and Northern France, 1914–1930* (Chicago, 1959), 388; Ludwig Köhler, *Die Staatsverwaltung der besetzten Gebiete. Volume: Belgien*, Carnegie Foundation for International Peace (New Haven, CT, 1927), 13; Sophie De Schaepdrijver, *La Belgique et la Première Guerre Mondiale* (New York, 2004), 87.

2. Aba Strazhas, *Deutsche Ostpolitik im Ersten Weltkrieg; der Fall Ober-Ost, 1915–1917* (Wiesbaden, 1993), 13n5; Vejas Liulevicius, *War Land on the Eastern Front: Culture, National Identity, and German Occupation in World War I* (Cambridge, 2000), 21, 30.

3. Herbert Hoover, in charge of relief administration, estimated the number in Eastern Europe at perhaps fifteen million: Hoover memo, London, Feb. 21, 1916, in George I. Gay, *Public Relations of the Commission for Relief in Belgium: Documents* (Stanford, CA, 1929), 2:108.

uncover what happened to civilians caught up in the vortex of war. Their task is hard because the documentary base is fragmented, uneven, and often simply nonexistent. The temporary and often ad hoc nature of occupation, the chaos of invasion and subsequent retreat, and the destruction caused by the Second World War have often left only ephemeral and chaotic traces. The following account attempts to outline the relation of international law to practice regarding Imperial Germany, as far as we know it. That relation is clearest in Belgium and Northern France, where Germany first worked out its occupation policies and which occasioned the most complete internal discussions of international law.[4]

Law and Expectations

The law governing the treatment of civilians under occupation was considerably less detailed than that on soldiers active, prisoner, or hors de combat. The laws of war focused on operations and those who carried them out, and it assumed that occupations were temporary, thus perhaps making it seem less crucial to regulate them so minutely. Nevertheless, delegates to the Brussels and Hague Conferences discussed certain aspects of occupation with great precision, furthermore with many of the same fundamental disagreements about the nature of law and war that divided Germany (and sometimes Russia) from other European states. We will not repeat those debates, but instead focus on the content and principles of the law, which also announced the expectations of most European states in 1914. Five topics are particularly central.

The Basic Principles Governing the Treatment of Occupied Civilians

These were set down in the Hague articles 44–46. Article 46 said: "Family honor and rights, the lives of persons, and private property, as well as religious convictions and practice, must be respected. Private property can not be confiscated." As we saw, this was the article that touched off the great debate about military necessity after Germany's military delegate, Colonel von Schwarzhoff, insisted on inserting that exception into the article. That debate ended ambiguously. The reporter for the second commission, the Belgian delegate Édouard Rolin Jaequemyns, expressed the view of apparently every nation except Germany, that legal principles of such a fundamental kind as life, honor, and property should not be "enervated" by announcing exceptions to them, while Schwarzhoff clung to his view that one must recognize, as another delegate had admitted, that under certain

---

4. I am very grateful to Sophie De Schaepdrijver for her criticisms and generosity, especially regarding this chapter.

circumstances a state might have recourse to such exceptions.[5] But Schwarzhoff retracted his amendment, leaving the field free for the (vast) majority view that these were the basic principles that must guide state actions. To these was added a fifth, the recognition of patriotism or identification with one's own state, in the requirement that an occupant could require no oath of allegiance (article 45) nor extort information about the occupied country's army or defenses (article 44). Germany, Austria-Hungary, Russia, Japan, and Montenegro all reserved article 44, signaling that they would continue to rely on forced civilian guides as their armies moved through enemy territory.[6] Finally, Imperial Germany opened one further escape hatch from the limits imposed by articles 44–46. Schwarzhoff observed, apparently without contradiction, that "these restrictions should not be taken to fetter the belligerent's freedom of action in certain extreme situations which might constitute legitimate defense."[7] That was ominous, for we have already seen that the German legal definition of *Notstand* or *Notwehr* was practically unlimited.

Whose Law Governed the Occupied Territories?

The question whether local law or the occupant's own law should be authoritative in the occupied zones was hotly debated and became unhelpfully entangled in the larger question of whether an occupant's military victory gave him a legal "right" to govern, or whether his power to govern rested merely on fact. The Brussels Declaration in the end called for occupants "to maintain the peacetime laws in effect and not to modify, suspend, or replace them except when necessary" (article 3). Exactly the same arguments erupted anew at the Hague; Belgium's delegate again favored suppressing all articles recognizing

---

5. See chapter 3; Netherlands, Ministry of Foreign Affairs, *Conférence Internationale de la Paix, La Haye 18 Mai–29 Juillet 1899* (The Hague, 1899), 3:97–98.

6. The Hague Rules contained a seeming contradiction between art. 24, which permitted "measures necessary for obtaining information about the enemy and the country," and art. 52, which prohibited forcing inhabitants to render services that involved them in military operations against their own country. The issue here was forced guides. At Brussels, disagreement had resulted in silence, at Russia's suggestion. But Brussels had adopted the main principle that inhabitants must not be forced to aid the enemy directly in military operations (art. 36). Rolin Jaequemyns's final report made clear that the Hague Convention of 1899 had developed the main principle and subordinated the lesser. He reported that critics had pointed out that the wording of art. 24 might support the mistaken conclusion that any and all measures to obtain information were permitted, including forcing civilians to act as guides. Such an interpretation was false. Methods of information-gathering "would cease to be 'licit' if they contravened an imperative rule contained elsewhere," he wrote (1:55). The Brussels draft had originally cited exactly that imperative rule prohibiting belligerents from forcing inhabitants to aid the enemy army. Because there were other, similar imperatives, the Hague drafters had omitted an exhaustive list, but Rolin Jaequemyns's report made clear their intent: forced guides were now forbidden. That prohibition was made explicit in 1907 and elicited the reservations of Germany, Austria-Hungary, Russia, Japan, and Montenegro. Brussels, Conference, 1874, *Actes de la Conférence de Bruxelles (1874)* (Brussels, 1899), 240; Netherlands, *Conférence,* 1:55; James Brown Scott, ed., *The Hague Conventions and Declarations of 1899 and 1907, Accompanied by Tables of Signatures, Ratification and Adhesions of the Various Powers and Texts of Reservations* (New York, 1915), 131–32.

7. Rolin Jaequemyns's final report of second commission, Netherlands, *Conférence,* 1:59.

an occupant's legal power in occupied territory. To break the deadlock, the Swiss delegate and secretary of the International Committee of the Red Cross, Édouard Odier, suggested making explicit that any changes would be permitted only "in the measure and for the time when they are necessary to maintain order" (3:122). Schwarzhoff replied that he thought "it would be difficult for military men to accept such an amendment." He was seconded by his Russian colleague, Colonel Gilinsky, who, speaking in his capacity as technical delegate, laid down the principle that "for considerations of military order, the laws of an occupied country may only be maintained so long as they do not contradict the military laws of the invader" (3:123). Schwarzhoff and Gilinsky were announcing two rules: first, that "order" was much broader and longer lasting than the mere regulation of incidents (and hence could not be limited in the way Odier suggested), and second, that the occupant's military law automatically superseded conflicting local law. Schwarzhoff hinted that Germany would have trouble ratifying a convention limiting an occupant in the way Odier had suggested (3:127). France's second delegate, Pierre Bihourd, suggested the compromise that bridged over these difficulties. The final wording said: the occupant "shall take all measures in his power to restore, and ensure, as far as possible, public order and safety [*l'ordre et la vie publique*], while respecting, unless absolutely prevented, the laws in force in the country" (article 43). The Hague colloquy thus presaged major problems once war broke out.

Requisitions, Taxes, Contributions, and Collective Fines

These are the four means of raising money or its equivalent from the occupied zone. Requisitions are goods or services (i.e., civilian labor) taken directly from the inhabitants by the occupation army; taxes refer to those duties already in effect when the occupation army arrives; contributions are tax-like levies in addition to normal taxes; and collective fines are monetary penalties exacted on whole communities for infractions of the occupied order. The main issue was how much an occupant could defray his war expenses at the cost of enemy civilians. That question was enormously controversial, as shown by the lengthy deliberations in the second commission, by the number of times "military necessity" or its equivalent figured in the final articles (of the five times it was used in the section on occupation, three concerned this issue), and by the necessity to form an editorial subcommittee to thresh out the final wording.

In the end, Rolin Jaequemyns reported to the plenary council widespread agreement on three limiting rules: extraordinary contributions should be raised only by order of the commander, the amount should be based on existing taxes, and a receipt must be given.[8] But behind these rules were broader principles that he also named and which made up the final articles: (1) requisitions of goods and services could only be used for the army of occupation (not for the larger war effort); (2) they must be proportionate to the resources of the territory; (3) they must not be such as to force the inhabitants to

---

8. Ibid.

contribute to the operations of war; (4) contributions must not be meant to enrich the occupant; and (5) collective fines must be levied for truly collective acts, not in retaliation for those of individuals (1:60–61). Articles 49 to 52 were passed unanimously, except for Switzerland, which held out for an explicit right to reimbursement, not merely a receipt. The law now held that occupants might use the resources of the occupied zone for their own upkeep (which included occupation expenses and repairing infrastructure indirectly useful to the occupant's own war effort), but not as a material or capital reserve to pay for the larger war—that had to be paid by the belligerent or by the loser(s), if the victor forced inclusion of such a provision in the peace settlement. Therefore, expropriation, including under the guise of collective fines, was illegal (3:138).

Germany's military delegate Schwarzhoff explicitly rejected limits to requisition of goods and services. He thought the entire attempt to limit them quixotic, indeed "contrary to the essence of war," and he endorsed the "axiom: war nourishes war," meaning that belligerents had always relied on confiscation to pay for war (3:136). This was simply a fact; "one must not speak of it, but it is impossible to prohibit it; that is going too far."

International law had long recognized a belligerent's right to take and use his opponent's state property and wealth for his own war effort, if he could capture it, or, subject to reimbursement, private property needed for transport or communication (article 53). But the principles of private property and the prohibition on forcing civilians to contribute to their enemy's war operations offered a higher level of protection to civilian property than to state property. Those two principles were already in the Russian draft at Brussels in 1874 and were recognized by Schwarzhoff's predecessor, General Voigts-Rhetz.[9] Schwarzhoff was thus announcing the contrary principle that private property was equally subject to expropriation, such that enemy civilians would wind up paying for the war effort against themselves and relieving their enemy of that burden.

Destruction of Property

The Hague Rules dealt with destruction in four ways. Destruction of private property during combat was covered under the larger concept of military necessity, that is, if it constituted a legitimate military object (for example, because troops used a house for cover) or became unavoidably damaged during a legitimate operation. But pillage, the wanton destruction or theft of property by individual soldiers, was prohibited in all cases, uncontroversially (article 47). An occupant's permission to use state buildings, lands, and forests was limited to usufruct, that is, the occupant was enjoined to "safeguard the capital of these properties"; he could not simply expropriate them (article 55). And finally, state property of cultural or educational value was protected as if it were private property (article 56). Apart from Schwarzhoff's statement that the articles protecting occupied civilians (including article 47 prohibiting pillage) must not be interpreted "to shackle the

---

9. Brussels, Conference, 1874, *Actes,* 213.

belligerent's freedom of action in certain extreme eventualities [to engage in] legitimate [self] defense" (1:59), Germany did not reserve or demur in voting for these articles.

Civilian (Forced) Labor

Forced labor turned out to be the most odious aspect of occupation in World War I, yet it was barely regulated save for an aside in article 52. That article held that "requisitions in kind *and services* shall not be demanded from municipalities or inhabitants except for the needs of the army of occupation," they shall be in proportion, and shall not force inhabitants to take "part in military operations against their own country." The Russian draft at Brussels in 1874 had suggested a wider prohibition against forcing civilians to "contribute to the goals of war" against their own state (article 48). General Voigts-Rhetz, seconded by Colonel Lanza of Italy, persuaded the delegates to drop this wording because it contradicted other articles permitting occupants to force civilians to pay taxes and levies to the occupant (which obviously aided his war effort), and because occupants depended on civilian labor to repair roads and transport facilities.[10] At the Hague, General Gilinsky of Russia wanted to make sure that it was only illegal to make civilians work *directly* in military operations (3:97). He surely had in mind the analogy to prisoner-of-war labor, equally barred from engaging in military operations, but free for use on other military projects not at the front—an interpretation that Alexander Jomini in 1874 had called self-evident.[11] Against Gilinsky's military view, delegates from Belgium and the Netherlands defended a broader prohibition of using civilians even indirectly in military operations, except for such things as surrendering their horses or cars (3:97). Schwarzhoff favored a middle position; he interpreted the article to apply only to the population as a whole, leaving the army free to use individuals as necessary (3:97). Since Gilinsky did not insist on making the article narrower, it passed in its broader form. Schwarzhoff's opening later served as a wedge to weaken the prohibition of article 52.

An observer of the Brussels and Hague discussions could have predicted that Imperial Germany might well claim military necessity to overturn or weaken the basic principles of protecting civilian life, property, honor, and religious observance; that it would consider its military law as superseding local law; that it might ignore the proportionality rule regarding requisitions and services; and that it might tend to use individual civilian laborers on military projects outside the combat zone. These were all positions Schwarzhoff had openly maintained. But the observer would have imagined that the laws governing pillage, the usufructuary status of the occupant, banning expropriation for enrichment of the occupant, and protecting cultural/educational buildings were firm. As it was, most contemporaries seem to have thought that the Hague Rules on occupation, especially the principles set out in articles 45 to 47, were the minimum legal guidelines for state policy in wartime.

---

10. Ibid., 205–6.
11. Ibid., 72.

If Imperial Germany entered the war with no official war manual laying down the rules of fighting, it did have newly revised regulations for the rear/occupied zones (the Kriegs-Etappen-Ordnung, or KEO).[12] Although the KEO was revised in March 1914, it neither mentioned the Hague Rules, nor did it provide general guidelines for treatment of (enemy) civilians. Indeed, in places it contradicted international law. For example, it called for collective fines to punish any sabotage in an area, whereas Hague article 50 required that the population actually be "jointly and severally responsible" for the act. In the next sentence the KEO underscored that "it is important that every threat be carried out" (68). In a universe where nineteenth-century state practice and legal writing both tended to reduce or even eliminate hostage taking and, if it occurred, to grant hostages prisoner-of-war protections, the KEO unhesitatingly recommended using notable hostages to protect railways and, more curiously, taking hostages as a preventive measure in areas about to be attacked by enemy troops (69).[13] It is unclear how they might have been useful in this last situation, since an attack by regular soldiers constitutes legal combat, in which, even according to a latitudinarian interpretation of hostage taking, hostages had no place.

---

12. Prussia and War Ministry, *Kriegs-Etappen-Ordnung* (March 12, 1914) (D.V.E. Nr. 90) (Berlin, 1914).

13. Hostage taking was not covered by the Hague Rules, but states had largely abandoned the practice by the late eighteenth century. Napoleon reintroduced it, but no state in the nineteenth century executed hostages. Using hostages to protect railways was a *novum* of the U.S. Civil War, repeated by German troops in 1870–71, and briefly by Britain in the Boer War—a policy rescinded after a week, as illegal. By 1900, most legal writers thought hostage taking unlawful. Thus, customary law governing hostage taking was in the process of changing, a change noted in the French and British war manuals, but not in the KEO. German jurists were split: Meurer and Liszt (1913) condemned it, while Ullmann and Zorn (1906) recognized it as a state practice. Lueder noted that hostage taking had declined and that using hostages to protect railroads was universally condemned by writers, though he defended it as lawful. In 1914, Russia engaged in widespread hostage taking among its own (Jewish) population. When some French officers took hostages in August 1914, President Raymond Poincaré was incensed: "I cannot understand how French officers could have had so stupid an idea as to molest inoffensive people, and I am urging that exemplary penalties should be inflicted": *The Memoirs of Raymond Poincaré, 1914,* trans. George Arthur (Garden City, NY, 1929), 116. See the excellent discussion in James Wilford Garner, *International Law and the World War* (London, 1920), 1:298–311. Manuals: Robert Jacomet, *Les lois de la guerre continentale* (Paris, 1913), art. 92; Colonel J. D. Edmonds and Lassa Oppenheim, *Land Warfare: An Exposition of the Laws and Usages of War on Land, for the Guidance of Officers of His Majesty's Army* (London, 1912), paras. 461, 463, and p. 99; German legal texts: Christian Meurer, *Die Haager Friedenskonferenz,* vol. 2, *Das Kriegsrecht der Haager Konferenz* (Munich, 1907), 244–45; Franz von Liszt, *Das Völkerrecht systematisch dargestellt* (Berlin, 1913), 305–6 (permits hostage taking as reprisal only); Emanuel von Ullmann, *Völkerrecht,* Das Öffentliche Recht der Gegenwart (Tübingen, 1908), 496; Albert Zorn, *Das Kriegsrecht zu Lande in seiner neuesten Gestaltung; Eine kritische Untersuchung* (Berlin, 1906), 281–82 (covered by military necessity); Karl Endres, *Die völkerrechtlichen Grundsätze der Kriegführung zu Lande und zur See* (Berlin, 1909), 77–78; Carl Lueder, "Das Landkriegsrecht im Besonderen," in *Handbuch des Völkerrechts,* vol. 4, ed. Franz von Holtzendorff (Hamburg, 1889), 476. Russia: Eric Lohr, "The Russian Army and the Jews: Mass Deportation, Hostages, and Violence during World War I," *Russian Review* 60, no. 3 (July 2001): 404–19. Heinrich Albrecht Schütze, *Die Repressalie unter besonderer Berücksichtigung der Kriegsverbrecherprozesse* (Bonn, 1950), 95; Gerd Hankel, *Die Leipziger Prozesse: Deutsche Kriegsverbrechen und ihre strafrechtliche Verfolgung nach dem Ersten Weltkrieg* (Hamburg, 2003), 269–74; John Westlake, *International Law; Part II: War* (Cambridge, 1907), 102; Lassa Oppenheim, *International Law: A Treatise* (London, 1905), 2:271–73.

Despite these examples, the KEO was not a blustering or bloodthirsty document, but simply a technical manual drily laying out the bureaucratic skeleton of occupation. Its significance lies in revealing the basic principles rear officers were to follow. Two of these we have seen above: the assumption of collective responsibility for any acts undertaken against the occupation authority, and the right to instrumentalize civilians and their lives for military convenience (not for necessity). However, they derived from more fundamental assumptions with far-reaching effects. First, the manual said that "the entire activity of the rear must be directed to relieving the field army to such an extent that its operations are never hindered or made impossible by logistical considerations. . . . Ensuring the readiness of the field army has complete precedence over the welfare of the rear/occupation zone" (52). Second, in fulfilling this task, the rear "must foresee coming needs and making use of all possibilities must make such extensive preparations that they may be immediately adequate to meet upcoming tasks" (52–53). Third, "to relieve replacements from home, the rear must make the widest use of means available in the rear zone, especially if it lies in enemy territory. Food, tools of all kinds, motor vehicles, factory and construction materials . . . are all to be collected beyond the current needs of the army" (57–58). Fourth, "even in enemy territory one will be able to use the (local) civil authorities, medical personnel and civilian laborers" for one's needs (58). In short, battle had priority over all other considerations, the rear was to provide materials and labor in preference to raising them at home, and the rear authorities were prophylactically to go beyond actual need in taking supplies, making no distinction between state and private goods, including food.

Strictly speaking, the KEO applied only to that portion of occupied territory directly behind the operation areas. In fact, during the war there were four institutions of German occupation: the front armies (whose field administrations assumed occupation responsibilities); the rear (run by a rear inspectorate); the general governments of (most of) Belgium and Poland (run by military governors general who answered directly to the Kaiser); and in the East, the headquarters of the commander of the eastern front (Ober-Ost).[14] For the front and rear, the chief of the general staff through the quartermaster general was to set the general parameters of policy making, sure (following the precepts of "mission tactics") "to leave full freedom for independent activity" to subordinates.[15] But the four occupation authorities were not coordinated, though in practice they followed very similar policies, largely mirroring the principles and assumptions set out in the KEO.

The Occupation Statute

The decisive role of the military in curtailing the international-legal protections for enemy civilians is nowhere clearer than in the struggle over the occupation statute for Belgium.

14. Isabel V. Hull, *Absolute Destruction: Military Culture and the Practices of War in Imperial Germany* (Ithaca, NY, 2005), 226–28.

15. Prussia and War Ministry, *Kriegs-Etappen-Ordnung* (1914), 10.

Taking the KEO and Germany's occupation of France in 1870–71 as guidance,[16] Chief of Staff Moltke and the Prussian war ministry began, independently and in ignorance of the other, preparing occupation guidelines. Neither met the legal standards upheld by the AA. The war ministry draft acknowledged two Hague articles: article 43, which held the occupant to restoring order as far as possible keeping local laws, and article 53, permitting seizure of state property and four categories of private property (means of transport, communication, arms, and munitions).[17] Moltke's draft aimed unabashedly at treating Belgium as a "base of operations" to be exploited for the German army and, among other things, called for deporting large numbers of the Belgian working class.[18] While the AA intervened with the war ministry and extracted modifications from them, Chancellor Bethmann Hollweg, apart from making deportation a "possibility," appears to have accepted most of Moltke's plans.[19] When the war ministry learned of the Moltke draft, it tried to "weaken and specify" its terms, but produced a document still quite at odds with the Hague Rules.[20] The AA again intervened "to try as far as possible to make the draft consistent with the Hague Rules."[21] It succeeded in adding the sentence that "in executing his power [the governor general] will take into consideration the instructions of the Hague Rules of Land Warfare of 18 Oct. 1907"—a crucial point in the later fight over mass deportation.[22] But it permitted commanders to set the amount of collective fines and extra taxes (contributions); although it made the general government responsible for the "regular provisioning" of the civilian population, it also admonished him "whenever possible to make supplies available for our own land"; it called for saturating Belgium with German workers and managers so that "everywhere the German element is to be brought into the land to make it readily disposable for our goals"; and it envisioned the possibility of mass deportation of Belgian workers across the front into Allied hands. The Kaiser

---

16. Köhler, *Staatsverwaltung,* 4; Frank Wende, *Die belgische Frage in der deutschen Politik des Ersten Weltkrieges* (Hamburg, 1969), 21.

17. Anweisung für den General-Gouverneur besetzter feindlicher Landesteile, n.d. (Aug. 26, 1914), AA/PA R 22421.

18. Helmuth von Moltke, "Grundzüge über die militärische und wirtschaftliche Ausnutzung des Königreichs Belgien," cited in Wende, *Die belgische Frage,* 21, and Jens Thiel, *"Menschenbassin Belgien": Anwerbung, Deportation und Zwangsarbeit im Ersten Weltkrieg* (Essen, 2007), 37. The AA's legal director Johannes Kriege, writing on behalf of the chancellor, claimed that secret general staff occupation guidelines of 1914 cited the Hague occupation articles (42 to 56): Kriege to German embassy in Copenhagen, Berlin, June 4, 1915, copy, IIIa 9402/74842, "streng vertraulich," BAB R 901 86663. That is certainly not true for the guidelines approved by the Kaiser and sent to the first governor general: Falkenhayn to von der Goltz, GHQ, Aug. 30, 1914, AA/PA RZ 202, R 22421.

19. Wende, *Die belgische Frage,* 21.

20. Weaken and specify: Werner Freiherr v. Grünau memorandum, Aug. 29, 1914, zu A.H. 404, AA/PA R 22421.

21. Ibid.

22. Anhaltspunkte für die Geschäftsführung des General-Gouverneurs in Belgien, Aug. 29, 1914, AA/PA R 22421, no. 933.

approved this draft, and the war ministry sent it to the first governor general, Colmar von der Goltz, on August 30, 1914.[23]

The internal dispute over how much law should govern occupation policies continued throughout the war. The winner was most often the military. We will examine these policies under five headings: the legal parameters, requisitions/expropriation, feeding civilians, forced labor, and deportation.

Law under Occupation

The Hague Rules called on occupants to retain local law "unless absolutely prevented" (article 43). Judging by the final guidelines to the governor general, Germany intended to follow the Hague rule. The governor could change criminal laws and police regulations if they contravened the Prussian law of siege of June 4, 1851, but civil matters were to remain subject to Belgian law.[24] In Belgium, the governor general at first left both Belgian law and the Belgian legal and judicial establishment in charge of legal matters, and in the lands ruled by Ober-Ost, the commanders used a Russian legal code of 1903, which, though it had not yet been adopted for (Congress) Poland, was at least not German law.[25]

But these efforts clashed with a peculiar feature of German law that elevated it automatically over local law. In an occupied area, the kind of authority the occupant possesses rests upon the fact of (temporary) military conquest; it is military authority. Therefore, the legal basis of his authority is martial law.[26] International law called upon the occupant's military code to coexist with local law wherever possible. But Germany's military penal code of 1872 (MStGB) held that "A foreigner or German, in an area occupied by German troops, who commits a punishable offense according to the laws of the German Empire against German troops or members of the armed forces or against an office founded by Imperial order shall be punished as if the act had occurred in Germany" (article 161).[27] It automatically treated inhabitants as if Germany had annexed their territory. And it made them subject to Germany's laws against treason. In articles 87, 89, and 90 the (civilian) German criminal code (RStGB) criminalized a range of acts intended to harm Germany or its allies during wartime.[28] Article 91 said that "foreigners [who fall afoul of] articles 87, 89, 90 are to be handled according to the customs of war [*Kriegsgebrauche*]," meaning

---

23. Falkenhayn to v.d. Goltz, GHQ, Aug. 30, 1914, AA/PA R 22421.

24. Anhaltspunkte, para. 2.

25. Liulevicius, *War Land,* 76–77.

26. Lassa Oppenheim, "The Legal Relations between an Occupying Power and the Inhabitants," *Law Quarterly Review* 33, no. 4 (1917): 364; see also Francis Lieber, *Instructions for the Government of Armies of the United States in the Field, General Orders No. 100, 24 April 1863,* in *The Laws of Armed Conflicts: A Collection of Conventions, Resolutions and Other Documents,* ed. Dietrich Schindler and Jiri Toman (Geneva, 1988), art. 1.

27. Kurt Elsner von Gronow and Georg Sohl, eds., *Militärstrafrecht für Heer und Marine des Deutschen Reichs; Handbuch für Kommando- und Gerichtsstellen, für Offiziere und Juristen* (Berlin, 1906), 217.

28. Ibid., 926.

they were to be summarily executed, whereas, if they had committed identical acts in Germany, they would have faced lesser sentences.[29] According to the interpretation of Bavarian jurist-soldier Karl Endres, article 91 had been superseded by Germany's military code, which called for trials for all serious offenses, and in fact, his view appears to have been authoritative: once occupation was under way, Germany used trials, not summary executions. Nevertheless, occupied civilians found themselves in certain circumstances subject to German domestic law.

The military code (article 160) punished Germans and foreigners alike for "war treason" (*Kriegsverrat*), which it defined as "treason committed on the battlefield" (article 57).[30] The odd part here, of course, was that articles 57 to 59 and 134 were obviously intended to apply to soldiers serving in the German army (whose members might include foreigners). But in the occupied zone, German military law held enemy civilians to the same standards it set for its own soldiers. Therefore, in these two ways (once in the criminal law and once in military law), the legal status of occupied inhabitants anticipated outright annexation, that is, they were already subject to German domestic law.

A third, parallel legal avenue also potentially regulated enemy civilians in the occupied zone. The Imperial Edict (AKO) of December 28, 1899 (August 21, 1900, for the sea) went beyond the written law by giving military commanders the authority to punish foreign civilians with death for aiding the enemy, harming German interests, or disobeying (military) ordinances or orders. The AKO called for a regular court-martial, except for those caught red-handed, who were subject to summary execution according to "the customs of war" (*Kriegsbrauch*); the AKO thus reintroduced summary execution (which the RStGB had permitted, but the later MStGB had superseded).[31]

The concept of "war treason" became quite controversial during the war. Several Allied writers considered it an evil German invention, an illicit bleeding of militarism into the legal realm. In his learned self-defense against charges that he had "smuggled" the term into English-language jurisprudence, Lassa Oppenheim uncovered "war treason's" probable origin.[32] The 1845 Prussian military code mentioned it, and from there it appears that Francis Lieber, who would probably have known Prussia's code in his native Germany, introduced it into the 1863 U.S. war code. It remained common in American writing even after 1900. The influential Swiss international jurist Johann Kaspar Bluntschli used the term in 1868, and later German and French international-legal writers followed him. It entered British usage in 1876 via Sir Edward Creasy, but remained more controversial in

---

29. Endres makes clear that *Kriegsgebrauch* or *Kriegsbrauch* meant summary execution: Endres, *Völkerrechtliche Grundsätze*, 18.

30. Elsner von Gronow and Sohl, *Militärstrafrecht*, 216.

31. Heinrich Dietz, "Das Militärstrafrechtswesen im Kriege," in *Der Weltkampf um Ehre und Recht*, vol. 8, *Die Organisationen der Kriegführung, Dritter Teil: Die Organisationen für das geistige Leben im Heere*, ed. Max Schwarte (Leipzig, 1931), 136; John Horne and Alan Kramer, *German Atrocities, 1914: A History of Denial* (New Haven, CT, 2001), 160–61. Dietz notes that the ordinances or orders were required to be within international law and treaties, "insofar as these were still in effect" (137).

32. Lassa Oppenheim, "War Treason," *Law Quarterly Review* 33, no. 3 (1917): 266–86.

Britain and France than Oppenheim's famous textbook admitted.[33] John Westlake, Amos S. Hershey, J. H. Morgan, and in France Antoine Pillet, all objected to it.[34]

At issue was the degree of obedience owed by civilian inhabitants to the occupant. Critics of "war treason" held that it required an obedience tantamount to allegiance (forbidden under Hague article 45) and repugnant to modern national sensibility. It seemed to these writers like a holdover from the discredited older view that military success gave the conqueror immediate legal title to the occupied area—in Morgan's words, it was a "relic of the bad times when occupation operated as conquest."[35] Oppenheim is probably right to observe that critics confounded war treason's limited demand for temporary obedience with the stronger, moral requirement that domestic laws against treason apply to citizens.[36] Nevertheless, Oppenheim's textbook covered a wider range of acts forbidden under "war treason" than were contained in the official manuals of either Britain or France. Indeed, the French manual did not mention war treason, and the British handbook (of which Oppenheim was coauthor) confined it to passing harmful information, as Lieber's code had done.[37] In his textbook Oppenheim went much further; he listed as forbidden supplying the army of one's own nation with information, money, clothing, provisions, or the like, or helping one's own side by bribing soldiers or officials, freeing prisoners of war, conspiracy, or circulating "enemy proclamations" (propaganda), in addition to acts of sabotage.[38] While Morgan might have been incorrect about Oppenheim's "smuggling," he did catch Oppenheim providing much wider permission for occupation authorities to criminalize inhabitants than was usual among non-German writers.

The stakes in "war treason" were not so much about the unfortunate term with its misleading moral connotations, as about the legal relationship between occupant and inhabitants. Given the heated disputes in 1874 and 1899, it is hardly surprising that they erupted again during the war. Perhaps the most famous case of "war treason" involved the execution of Edith Cavell on October 12, 1915. It illustrates how the Allies, neutrals, and the German military used the law to fashion and cover for deeper disputes about policy and morality.

Cavell was a British nurse who had lived and worked in Belgium for many years when the war broke out. She admitted, and subsequent research has confirmed, that she helped at least eighty to one hundred Allied soldiers, trapped by the swift German occupation, escape to Holland.[39] As a neutral, Holland was bound to intern belligerent soldiers found

---

33. Cf. Oppenheim, *International Law*, 2:268–70.

34. Oppenheim, "War Treason," 279; J. H. Morgan, "War Treason," *Grotius Society, Problems of the War: Papers Read before the Society in the Year 1916* 2 (1917): 161–73; and Garner, *International Law*, 2:93–94.

35. Morgan, "War Treason," 161.

36. Oppenheim, "War Treason," 284–85.

37. Jacomet, *Lois de la guerre*; Edmonds and Oppenheim, *Land Warfare*, arts. 166–67; Lieber, *Instructions*, arts. 90–92. Bonfils's widely used French international-legal textbook also understood war treason to apply to information: Henry Bonfils and Paul Fauchille, *Manuel de droit international public (droit des gens)* (Paris, 1908), para. 1154, p. 705.

38. Oppenheim, *International Law*, 2:268–69.

39. The most recent account, with full bibliography: Katie Pickles, *Transnational Outrage: The Death and Commemoration of Edith Cavell* (Basingstoke, 2007). The number of escapees might have been much greater: 28–29.

on its territory; nevertheless, many of these men made it safely to England to fight again.[40] Her activities obviously harmed German interests, and no occupied power could have been expected to countenance them. That insight accounts for the British Foreign Office's dilatoriness after Cavell was arrested in August 1915: E. A. Warner feared that "Miss Cavell will get a heavy sentence. There seems to be nothing to do"; his colleague Horace Rumbold agreed, "I am afraid we are powerless."[41]

Because Cavell was charged with "war treason," she faced a court-martial under the jurisdiction of the new military governor of Brussels, Brigadier General Traugott Martin von Sauberzweig. In accord with military procedure, Cavell's Belgian lawyer was permitted to see neither his client nor the evidence against her prior to the trial, which was held October 7–8, 1915. Cavell was found guilty; paragraph 58 of the military code called for the death penalty in war treason cases. The court pronounced that sentence on Monday, October 11, at 5 p.m. Within hours, Sauberzweig had confirmed the sentence and set the execution time for before dawn the next day. American and Spanish diplomats intervened with the head of the political department of the general government, Oscar Freiherr von der Lancken-Wakenitz, who reluctantly called Sauberzweig—in vain. Sauberzweig's military and legal authority ran directly from the Kaiser; he was immune to intercession from German civilian or diplomatic authorities. Sauberzweig upheld his own order, and Cavell was executed by firing squad as scheduled.[42]

Outrage was immediate and universal. Three motives reinforced each other. Previously, the German occupiers had executed a handful of people for spying, but no one for Cavell's offense.[43] The British Foreign Office was stunned that the "heavy sentence" was actually execution. Second, there were Cavell's gender and occupation—it seemed wrong to execute a woman, and doubly wrong to kill a nurse who had also aided the German wounded. Britain's policy had long been to imprison but not to execute convicted female spies. France was tougher, but the thirteen women it dispatched during the war it executed for spying, not for war treason, which made a difference in Allied public sentiment.[44] The third reason was the shocking speed of the execution. Robert Cecil exclaimed, "What devils these

---

40. Garner argues that funneling escapees to Holland, rather than directly back to the lines, frees Cavell of legal responsibility for harming the occupant's interest: Garner, *International Law,* 2:100–101.

41. Warner minute and Rumbold minute of Oct. 1, 1915, Page to Grey, Sept. 28, 1915, FO 383/15, file 119156, no. 141378.

42. This account follows the contemporary American documents as printed in United States, *Papers Relating to the Foreign Relation of the United States: The Lansing Papers, 1914–1920,* 2 vols. (Washington, DC, 1939), 48–67, and Page to Grey, Oct. 13, 1915, FO 383/15, file 119156, no. 150476. Pickles suggests that the Americans and their Belgian lawyer might have condensed the time frame in order to hide their dilatoriness in intervening to save Cavell, but she offers no better evidence to undergird her own account: Pickles, *Transnational Outrage,* 32–43, esp. 41, 43. (There is probably an error in G. de Leval's letter to Whitlock, Oct. 12, 1915—"Thursday" must mean "Tuesday"; United States, *Lansing Papers,* 1:60.)

43. Sadi Kirschen, *Devant les conseils de guerre allemands. Affaires: Cavell; Blanckaert; Boël; Franck-Backelmans; Parenté; Colon; Mus; Kugé; Freyling; Bosteels; Libre Belgique; Bril; Feyens; Monod* (Brussels, 1919), 86. My thanks to Sophie De Schaepdrijver for bringing this to my attention.

44. Garner, *International Law,* 2:100–104; Pickles, *Transnational Outrage,* 52–54; Rumbold minute of Oct. 14, 1915, to Page to Grey, Oct. 13, 1915, FO 383/15, file 119156, no. 150476.

Germans are!" He made sure the king saw Cavell's case file.[45] Despite apparently recognizing the weakness of their legal case—Sir Edward Grey noted that worldwide revulsion rested "upon higher considerations" and "deeper feeling than mere illegality," and Cecil advised not pursuing "the legal niceties"—British leaders referred to the case as a "savage murder under legal forms," and threatened to try those responsible after the war.[46] The Allies continued to weigh prosecuting the "assassin of Miss Edith Cavell" as late as September 1919.[47] After the violation of Belgian neutrality and the "Belgian atrocities," the Allies were primed to imagine that every controversial German deed was frankly illegal.

Giving vent to his emotions about Cavell's execution, the Dutch foreign minister, John Loudon, told the British ambassador that "the German policy of frightfulness was more than a crime. It was a stupidity and a stupidity which alienated neutral sympathizers."[48] Stupid, but not illegal. Cavell's execution was the first act in a wave of repression using the law that was inaugurated by the new military governor of Brussels. Sauberzweig thus applied the letter of the law, and he did so immediately in order to shock the occupees and therefore deter "dangerous" patriotic deeds like nurse Cavell's.[49] This was the policy of terror, or "frightfulness," to which Loudon referred, and it was successful in the short term in flushing four thousand more Allied soldiers from their hiding places in Belgium.[50] But it produced one of the abiding martyrs of the war and confirmed Germany's reputation among the Allies and neutrals as brutal. Germany's military attaché to the Netherlands concluded that the backlash "proves once more that the theory of pure deterrence has its doubtful sides" (the Kaiser's marginal comment: "correct"). The attaché recommended in future weighing "usefulness and damage," especially regarding measures taken against women and measures that "fall under the heading 'unavoidable cruelties of war.'" The Kaiser agreed with that conclusion, too.[51] Meanwhile, the highest-ranking diplomat of the general government, von der Lancken, pressured the AA to get Sauberzweig removed, because his "pretty capricious measures" of repression were harming regular administration in Belgium and, in one case, had broken an earlier German ordinance (against quartering).[52] But Sauberzweig remained in office for six more months. Nevertheless, for a time, Germany tried to avoid producing similar cases, and the Kaiser ordered (January 15, 1916)

---

45. Cecil minute, Oct. 19, 1915, to Hugh Gibson's report of Oct. 12, 1915, FO 383/15, file 119156, no. 153206.

46. Grey's response to the query of MP Sir J. D. Rees of Oct. 28, 1915, Cecil's minute of Oct. 27, 1915, FO 383/15, file 119156, no. 164903; and Cecil's reply to MP Ronald M'Neill of Oct. 27, 1915, ibid., no. 161753.

47. Clemenceau, protocol of discussion of Sept. 15, 1919, in Oxford, Pollock Papers, MS. ENG. Hist. C. 943, fols. 6–7.

48. Alan Johnstone to Foreign Office, The Hague, no. 236, Oct. 24, 1915, FO 383/15, file 119156, no. 158412. Former chancellor and longtime diplomat Bernhard v. Bülow, referring to the Cavell case, denounced "the stupid ineptness of our 'frightfulness,'" Bernhard von Bülow, *Denkwürdigkeiten* (Berlin, 1920), 2:22.

49. "Dangerous" was Governor General Moritz v. Bissing's term in his personal report to the Kaiser of November 29, 1915, AA/PA, R 20899–1, frames 30–33; "imperative" was Lancken citing Sauberzweig on the evening of the eleventh, Gibson to Whitlock, Brussels, Oct. 12, 1915, in United States, *Lansing Papers*, 1:53.

50. Pickles, *Transnational Outrage*, 52.

51. Oberstlt. Renner to AA, The Hague, Anlage zu A 30810, Oct. 23, 1915, AA/PA R 20898–2.

52. Lancken to Zimmermann, Brussels, "secret and confidential," Dec. 15, 1915, Belgian State Archives, Klein Papers—again my thanks to Sophie De Schaepdrijver for this document.

that no women were to be executed without his permission.[53] But the deeply ingrained expectations and habits of commanders and military lawyers alike pulled strongly in the opposite direction.

The case of Captain Charles Fryatt (which will be discussed later) reprised many features of the Cavell trial. Fryatt, a merchant marine (not a naval) captain who had evaded a U-boat by steaming directly at it, was charged with attempted ramming and thus being an illegal combatant, a maritime franc-tireur. Found guilty, he was executed immediately after receiving his sentence, destroying efforts by the AA and the German Admiralty to spare his life. Fryatt joined Cavell in the ranks of Allied martyrs. The postwar Reichstag investigating committee recognized the enormous damage done to Germany's reputation, but stumbled again over the law. The military tribunal had followed the AKO (of August 21, 1900, the naval equivalent of the AKO of December 28, 1899, for land forces) that called for "immediate" execution of the sentence; it simply followed the letter of the law. The committee noted further that the AKO swore court officials to "administer justice in accordance with [their] conscientious convictions." In their view the AKO's injunction meant subordinating onself to "the unwritten Laws of Warfare born of the hard necessities of that state." Fryatt's death sentence was "an outcome of the very nature of warfare and is in accordance with the general and immemorial acceptation [*sic*] of the right of a Belligerent Army to proceed with the utmost rigour against all actions calculated to endanger its aims."[54]

In a sense, the Reichstag committee recognized that the subjective views of officers (their "conscientious convictions") were in fact likely to reflect the "unwritten law" of "Military Interests" that covered far more than the "fragments" of positive, Hague law.[55] Or, put another way, the AKO gave to all officers, including junior grades, the same kind of legal latitude that the mission system gave them in combat, and with the same expectations of energetic, crisp action.

Beyond this ex post facto recognition of the actual behavior of officers exercising legal duties, there was a larger presumption that German law and military interest set the foundations of legal action in wartime. In December 1917 the Imperial Military Court (Reichsmilitärgericht, RMG) held (regarding a prisoner-of-war case) that the Hague Rules "are not law; their regulations are rather confirmed only as behavioral rules and declared as service regulations which are to serve the army as guides."[56] The only international laws valid in Germany, they ruled, were those recognized by Germany. Their judgment was consonant with that of the president of RMG, who in 1915 had rejected the entreaties of the chancellor and AA and held that the Hague Rules had never been ratified by the Bundesrat and Reichstag.[57] Both judgments gave primacy to German over international law. Where

---

53. Memo of the Prisoner Department of the Foreign Office, ca. July 31, 1916, FO 383/195, file 123628, no. 151547; Dietz, "Militärstrafrechtswesen," 138.

54. English translation of the Reichstag Committee of Inquiry (1919), in the papers of the Committee of Enquiry into Breaches of the Laws of War, PRO 383/497.

55. Ibid., 573.

56. RMG Urteil 1167/17, Nr. 1126 A.R., Dec. 18, 1917, BayKrA, M Kr. 11172.

57. See preceding chapter.

there was a conflict inside German law, the RMG held that the more expansive Imperial Edict of December 28, 1899, canceled legal protections offered by the code of military procedure (Militärstrafprozeßordnung of December 1, 1898). On March 11, 1915, the RMG noted that the AKO's purpose was to "create a 'summary, accelerated process' appropriate to the peculiarity of wartime conditions."[58] Courts choosing to operate under the AKO were entitled, among other things, to streamline the hearing of witnesses and to drop the right of appeal altogether. Thus the dual legal avenues of military penal code and AKO allowed significant room for caprice even within Germany's own legal system. Governor General Moritz von Bissing took advantage of that latitude; in June 1915 he stopped publicizing politically sensitive trials, and he forbade defense attorneys from seeing evidence or even talking to their defendants before the hearing. When Belgian lawyers protested, Bissing cited convenience, military necessity, and interests of state.[59]

In the Cavell case, both the chief civilian political administrator, von der Lancken, and the governor general, von Bissing, approved using the law's full repressive force. In internal reports they rejected the view that political or diplomatic considerations ("weighing usefulness and harm"), for example concerning neutral public opinion, should affect legal policy. Bissing thought Britain was behind the "hypocritical anger"—hypocritical because Belgium had executed a female spy in August 1914. In any case, Bissing saw no reason to diminish Germany's legal rights: "The administration of law in the conquered areas must be handled in the first instance from a German standpoint."[60]

The German standpoint expressed itself legally in a flood of decrees, orders, regulations, and ordinances emanating from the military command authority of the occupant.[61] Persons falling afoul of these landed not before Belgian courts, but before courts-martial administering German military law. The problem was actually not "war treason," which in the year following September 1915 accounted for only 0.48 percent of convictions, but the sheer number of regulations that produced hundreds of thousands of scofflaws— Whitlock claimed that in one year over six hundred thousand Belgians were convicted of one infraction or another.[62] The dense grid of military control replaced Belgian law in effect without officially doing so. For example, an edict of May 25, 1916, permitted the

---

58. Germany, Reichsmilitärgericht, *Entscheidungen des Reichsmilitärgerichts* (Berlin, 1902–19), 19:129.

59. Bissing to Victor Bonnevie, Brussels, Jan. 28, 1916, cited in Victor Bonnevie, *La défense des Belges devant les tribunaux de guerre allemands* (Brussels, 1919), 23–25. My thanks to Sophie De Schaepdrijver for this information.

60. Lancken to AA, Brussels, Nov. 29, 1915, AA/PA R 20899–1, frame 29; Bissing personal report to the Kaiser, Brussels, Nov. 29, 1915, ibid., frames 30–33.

61. J. Pirenne and M. Vauthier, *La législation et l'administration allemandes en Belgique,* Carnegie Endowment for International Peace, Belgian Series (New Haven, CT, 1925), 24–32, 129–44.

62. 0.48 percent: Garner, *International Law,* 2:96; Brand Whitlock, *Belgium: A Personal Narrative* (New York, 1919), 1:463. Whitlock's figure is very large and may refer to charges later dropped, or to fines levied without trial. Mitrany writes that from the end of 1916 to mid-June 1918, Germany issued 19,797 ordinances: David Mitrany, *The Effect of the War on Southeastern Europe,* Carnegie Endowment for International Peace (New Haven, CT, 1936), 150. According to De Schaepdrijver, during the four years of war, 1,135 active members of the Belgian resistance were executed or died in prison or while resisting arrest: De Schaepdrijver, *La Belgique,* 242. "In Lithuania at least 1,000 executions took place" under German occupation: Liulevicius, *War Land,* 76.

military at its discretion to assume charge of cases covered by Belgian law that concerned economic, commercial, or public health issues. The result of these parallel legal avenues among which the governor general and the German military could choose was a system of "purely arbitrary acts," as Belgian lawyers put it.[63] Finally, in 1918 Belgian lawyers revolted against this displacement, and the Belgian government protested that military administration of this kind violated the Hague Rules by de facto substituting German for Belgian law without having been compelled to do so by military necessity.[64]

The original intention to use the Hague Rules as guidelines was thus swiftly undermined by Germany's own military and civilian law, by prewar imperial decree (the AKO of 1899) and most of all, by the military's rigid conception of order, which tried to control all of civilian life through minute regulations. The assumption common to all these de facto founts of law in the occupied zone was that Germany had a legal right to establish order convenient to its military interests as a belligerent. Its administrators could reasonably interpret article 43, which recognized the military necessity exception ("as far as possible"), as confirming that right. And as Bissing said, no other considerations should be permitted to reduce Germany's full use of the law, which became a powerful weapon in wartime, and which the Allies wielded so successfully on their side.[65]

Expropriation

The Hague Rules had set important principles safeguarding the property of private citizens: requisition of their goods and services was limited both to the costs of occupation and to the resources at hand (article 52), and "contributions" beyond the regular taxes were limited to the "needs of the army or of the [occupation] administration" (article 49). The requirement of proportionality (to resources) had been accepted without debate already at Brussels in 1874, expressed in the draft as the necessity to avoid "the ruin of the population."[66] In 1899, Rolin Jaequemyns's final report summed up the underlying principle that "it is forbidden to raise contributions in order to enrich oneself."[67]

But Germany's occupation manual (*Kriegsetappenordnung*) ran counter to these principles by demanding that materials be raised in the occupied zone in preference to at home; that the "coming needs" of the army be filled, not just its current, actual needs; and that the combat readiness of the field army "has absolute precedence over the occupied zone."[68] In 1914 (and after), Germany followed its own rules. Massive, ad hoc requisitions

---

63. Albert Henry, *Le ravitaillement de la Belgique pendant l'occupation allemande*, Publications of the Carnegie Endowment for International Peace, Belgian Series (Paris, 1924), 67–68, 72.

64. Whitlock, *Belgium*, 1:476–84; Garner, *International Law*, 2:84–96.

65. One scholar of the law sums up this attitude as "a stubborn insistence on one's own right": Andreas Toppe, *Militär und Kriegsvölkerrecht: Rechtsnorm, Fachdiskurs und Kriegspraxis in Deutschland* (Munich, 2008), 128.

66. Brussels, Conference, 1874, *Actes*, art. 40, and p. 21.

67. Netherlands, *Conférence*, 1:60.

68. Prussia and War Ministry, *Kriegs-Etappen-Ordnung* (1914), 52–54, 57–58.

of food and other goods during the invasion gave way to systematic inventories of all property followed by locust-like devourment of everything from inkwells and blankets to mattresses and ovens.[69] Already in the winter of 1914–15 the Prussian war ministry had "seized and transported to Germany all Belgian machinery and raw materials" useful to the war.[70] As Germany expanded to the east in 1915 it honed its expropriation machinery. In the German-occupied areas of Russia and (briefly) Serbia, the same pattern prevailed: thorough dismantling of machinery and factories and almost limitless expropriation of food and raw materials.[71] By August 1916, as German troops were defeating Romania, the German high command (OHL), civilian government, and Germany's allies had perfected expropriation. The expressed goal was "the fullest exploitation of the occupied part of Romania in order to secure and export as quickly as possible everything which would be useful for war purposes and for the provisioning" of Germany's allies. The scholar of this "rational ruthlessness" correctly surmised that it would "no doubt offer a model for future use."[72] A memo from October 1917 emphasized the widespread despair at "completely capricious requisitions" in Lithuania. "Grain, horses and cattle and other requisitions were forcibly taken without any consideration for the most pressing needs of Lithuanian agriculture and without consideration for feeding the Lithuanian population."[73] Requisitions to the point of starvation together with forced labor finally incited partisan warfare against the German occupation in the East.[74] General Ludendorff later acknowledged that "the occupied territories were of decisive help to us, both at the front and at home."[75] Imperial Germany's policy was therefore exactly what Colonel Schwarzhoff had declared in 1899: it fed itself and its war machine from the occupied areas. From time to time the chancellor, some ministries, the civil administration of the general government, and members of the Reichstag protested against these policies, for the most part in vain.[76] They ran up against the argument of military necessity: Germany was too weak to pursue a world war on its own resources. That fact was obvious. Already on August 19, 1914, Admiral Alfred von

69. Georges Gromaire, *L'occupation allemande en France (1914–1918)* (Paris, 1925), chs. 4 and 6; Helen McPhail, *The Long Silence: Civilian Life under the German Occupation of Northern France, 1914–1918* (New York, 2000), 48; Thaer diary of Feb. 6, 1915, Albrecht von Thaer, *Generalstabsdienst an der Front und in der O.H.L.,* Abhandlungen der Akademie der Wissenschaften in Göttingen, philologisch-historische Klasse, Dritte Folge, Nr. 40, ed. Siegfried Kaehler (Göttingen, 1958), 25.

70. Gerhard Ritter, *The Sword and the Scepter: The Problem of Militarism in Germany,* trans. Heinz Norden (Coral Gables, FL, 1969–73), 3:360. Thiel emphasizes post-1916 dismantling of factories: Thiel, *"Menschenbassin Belgien,"* 43–46.

71. Imanuel Geiss, *Der polnische Grenzstreifen, 1914–1918* (Lübeck, 1960), 40. Serbia: Jonathan E. Gumz, *The Resurrection and Collapse of Empire in Habsburg Serbia, 1914–1918* (Cambridge, 2009), 148; Andrej Mitrovic, *Serbia's Great War, 1914–1918,* Central European Studies (West Lafayette, IN, 2007), 205–7.

72. Lisa Mayerhofer, *Zwischen Freund und Feind: Deutsche Besatzung in Rumänien 1916–1918* (Munich, 2010), 118; Mitrany, *Effect of the War,* 141.

73. Memo concerning the most important grievances in Lithuania, Oct. 20, 1917, cited in Werner Basler, *Deutschlands Annexionspolitik in Polen und im Baltikum 1914–1918* (East Berlin, 1962), 279.

74. Strazhas, *Deutsche Ostpolitik,* 29–48; Liulevicius, *War Land.*

75. Erich Ludendorff, *My War Memories, 1914–1918* (London, 1922), 1:348.

76. De Schaepdrijver, *La Belgique,* 135; Strazhas, *Deutsche Ostpolitik,* 29, 39–40; Mayerhofer, *Zwischen Freund und Feind,* 175.

Tirpitz noted that Germany required "occupied land in the West to squeeze dry," or else it could not last more than a year.[77]

What was true for food, machinery, and raw materials was equally true for money. The Allies (Britain, France, and Russia) enjoyed a 60 percent greater combined national income than Germany and Austria-Hungary. Britain's wealth alone outstripped Germany's by 3:1.[78] And the Allies' creditworthiness meant that Wall Street's coffers were open to them, but closed to the Central Powers. As a result, Germany removed the financial burden of the war as far as possible onto the occupied territories. It used several methods. It manipulated the currencies and exchange rates in the occupied zones, issuing scrip that in effect drained the territories of their wealth.[79] It "paid" for requisitions with worthless chits and for outright purchases with scrip such that, in Northern France for example, all municipalities sank into debt, which the French government had to assume after the war.[80] It levied enormous contributions to defray occupation costs: 40 million francs per month from Belgium, rising to 60 million in mid 1917.[81] The criminalization of the inhabitants (via minute regulation) raised large amounts of money from fines and punishments of individuals and from court costs. Ober-Ost had planned a profit of over 20 million marks from court fees alone in 1917, but actually netted 47 million.[82] Collective fines of localities was another huge source of revenue; in 1914, Brussels, Antwerp, and Liège were fined over 100 million francs. The Belgian government reckoned after the war that contributions and fines together had cost 2.575 billion francs.[83] Collective fines were obviously not restricted to collective acts (Hague article 50), or even meant primarily as punishment, but as simple taxation.[84]

Civil and military leaders disagreed about the methods and even the goals of expropriation. The military almost always focused on raising the means to continue to fight the war, a short-term goal. After the first three weeks of war, civilian leaders considered longer-range plans to establish German political, economic, and military hegemony over the Continent, either through outright annexation, or more realistically, via permanent economic subjugation of at least Belgium, Poland, Austria-Hungary, and the Baltic regions. The magnet of *Mitteleuropa*, it was hoped, would then draw in defeated or greatly weakened France and Russia, as well as the neutral states of the Netherlands and Scandinavia.[85]

---

77. Alfred von Tirpitz, *Politische Dokumente: Deutsche Ohnmachtspolitik im Weltkriege* (Hamburg, 1926), 58.

78. Niall Ferguson, *The Pity of War: Explaining World War I* (New York, 1998), 248–49.

79. Reinhold Zilch, *Okkupation und Währung im Ersten Weltkrieg; die deutsche Besatzungspolitik in Belgien und Russisch-Polen 1914–1918* (Goldbach, 1994); Strazhas, *Deutsche Ostpolitik,* 31; Grey to Page, Dec. 31, 1915, in Gay, *Public Relations,* 1:137; John G. Williamson, *Karl Helfferich, 1872–1924: Economist, Financier, Politician* (Princeton, NJ, 1971), 117.

80. Gromaire, *L'occupation allemande en France,* 180–81.

81. Garner, *International Law,* 2:112. Northern France's total indebtedness from contributions was over 184 million francs: Gromaire, *L'occupation allemande en France,* 162.

82. Strazhas, *Deutsche Ostpolitik,* 30, 33.

83. Garner, *International Law,* 2:108–9, 113n3.

84. See edicts setting in advance fines for localities: Pirenne and Vauthier, *Législation,* 73–74.

85. Still fundamental: Fritz Fischer, *Germany's Aims in the First World War* (New York, 1967); and Hans W. Gatzke, *Germany's Drive to the West* (Baltimore, 1966).

These schemes ebbed and flowed with the prospects of victory, but they often clashed with the imperative military demands for immediate confiscation, since, as Governor General Bissing remarked, "a squeezed lemon has no value," and postwar absorption into Germany's sphere of influence was made harder by ruthless expropriation and the anger it engendered.[86]

But civilian leaders also argued with the military specifically on international law. On August 21, 1914, Foreign Secretary Jagow asked his legal section to explain the international law of contributions (extraordinary taxes) and how much Belgium could be expected to pay.[87] That query spurred a meeting of representatives of the AA, the imperial interior, treasury, and justice offices, the Prussian war ministry, trade office, and Reichsbank, which issued guidelines that followed the Hague Rules and clashed with the Prussian war ministry's original intention to let the governor general and army general intendant set fines and contributions without limit.[88] Figuring the yearly tax at about 80 francs/head, the meeting felt that a moderate tax increase due before 1915 would be acceptable and would cover occupation costs estimated at about 6 million marks per army corps. The meeting noted that the Hague Rules limited such contributions to occupation expenses, but collective fines for violation of international law could be used by the regular army. But the guidelines were more rigorous than the Hague Rules, for they subjected collective fines (*Strafkontributionen*) to a proportionality limit not contained in article 50, and they ignored the loophole for military necessity contained in articles 48 and 51 (on taxes and contributions). The guidelines were obviously designed to curb the military. But they failed, for the next day the Kaiser overruled the meeting and gave OHL (and the individual army commanders) authority to set contributions, which they did extravagantly.[89] Prussian War Minister Erich von Falkenhayn refused to transmit the meeting's guidelines to his commanders, arguing that they interpreted the Hague Rules too narrowly, and anyway "war necessity demanded the most far-reaching use possible of the economic resources of conquered enemy territory."[90] He informed the civilians that 25 percent of the sums raised went into a general war ministry fund and the rest was divided up between the army corps that had set the fine "and all parts of the mobile field army." That is, collective fines helped finance the fighting army.

In October 1914 Jagow complained to Falkenhayn that the military's unlimited contributions in Belgium harmed the zone's economy and threatened Germany's as well; they also left Germany open to Allied reprisal.[91] In November 1914 the AA's representative to OHL, Werner Freiherr von Grünau, a trained lawyer, listed Germany's violations: (1) the

---

86. Cited in Gatzke, *Germany's Drive to the West*, 88; orig. in Köhler, *Staatsverwaltung*, 104.

87. Wende, *Die belgische Frage*, 22.

88. Grünau memo, unsigned, Nov. 24, 1914, A.H. 1760/14, AA/PA R 22384; AA to chancellor, tel., Berlin, Aug. 28, 1914, Notiz zu IIIa. 10466/10886, BAB R 901 86663; Wende, *Die belgische Frage*, 21–23; "Anweisung," para. 9.

89. Wende, *Die belgische Frage*, 23; cf. Williamson, *Helfferich*, 117. Extravagantly: Oscar Freiherr von der Lancken-Wakenitz, *Meine Dreissig Dienstjahre, 1888–1918, Potsdam—Paris—Brüssel* (Berlin, 1931), 120.

90. Grünau memo, Nov. 24, 1914, AA/PA R 22384.

91. Jagow to Falkenhayn, Oct. 12, 1914, cited in Wende, *Die belgische Frage*, 23.

AOK of August 28, 1914, did not recognize the Hague limits to fines and did not distinguish between regular contributions and collective fines; (2) contributions had been levied illegally, because they were not justified as punishment (either because collectivities were held responsible for individual acts or because no illegal acts had occurred) or (3) because the fines were disproportionate to the resources of the area. Instead of rolling back the AOK, Grünau thought it better to issue executive orders that would bring it in line with legality by (1) restricting collective fines to genuinely collective misbehavior, (2) restricting contributions to the needs of the occupation army and to the resources of the community, and (3) under the guise of contributions "in no case to permit property confiscation or a complete destruction of economic life." The chancellor initialed Grünau's memo, but it had little effect. While enormous collective fines were mostly characteristic of the first six months of war, contributions rose to 60 million francs/month—far in excess of the 12 million or so that the estimate of August 28 would have predicted for an occupation force of only four divisions, and way out of line with Belgium's rapidly disappearing economy (in February 1917 OHL closed all "nonessential" factories, and ultimately only 3,013 firms out of an original total of 260,000 were operating).[92]

The triumph of military practice relegated the AA's legal department to providing legal cover to the realities emerging on the ground.[93] So, for example, in December 1914, the head of the legal department, Johannes Kriege, held that goods seized for immediate use were not requisitions and therefore not subject to compensation.[94] When Belgian banks protested a September 18, 1914, decree subjecting them to controls that, in their view, broke local law, Kriege defined the measure as "an economic-police measure, not a civil-legal step," and thus not a violation of Hague article 43. To their insistence that control measures required a preceding criminal trial, Kriege replied that the measures were administrative, not criminal.[95] Redefinition became a common way to escape the letter of inconvenient law.[96] Nevertheless, one may observe the residue of the efforts of the AA and the chancellor to follow international law in the forms produced by the quartermaster general's office in July 1916 outlining how to raise forced payments from unwilling occupees. Its first paragraph read: "Forced appropriations [*Zwangsauflagen*] decreed legally and with consideration for the ability to pay of the communal unit (town, province, etc.) must be collected, in the interest of the reputation of the military, *with*

---

92. Four divisions: De Schaepdrijver, *La Belgique,* 87. It is hard to reconstruct the exact number of occupation troops, which in any event fluctuated during the war. OHL later claimed that contributions had not offset occupation costs: Prussia, Kriegsministerium, and Oberste Heeresleitung, *Die deutsche Kriegführung und das Völkerrecht; Beiträge zur Schuldfrage* (Berlin, 1919), 46. By the estimate of the inter-ministerial conference, 60 million francs ought to have covered 240,000 troops; four divisions would have been about 60,000–80,000 men. Firms: Isabel V. Hull, "'Military Necessity' and the Laws of War in Imperial Germany," in *Order, Conflict, Violence,* ed. Stathis Kalyvas, Ian Shapiro, and Tarek Masoud (Cambridge, 2008), 232.

93. Notiz zu IIIa. 13350, Oct. 7, 1914, BAB R 901 86663.

94. Memo of the commissarial discussion of Dec. 14, 1914, IIIa 21392, BAB R 901 86663.

95. Kriege to chancellor, Berlin, Nov. 24, 1914, Nr. IIIa 18525/92950, BAB R 901 86663.

96. For another example, see Hankel, *Leipziger Prozesse,* 367.

all international-legally permitted means."[97] It listed these as fines, seizure (*Pfändung*), enforcement, arrest or firing of communal authorities, and, against individuals, as forcible quartering, limits on movement, hostage taking of notables, and forced labor in non-war-related work.

As with the "Belgian atrocities," Germany never denied its policy of expropriation. Civilian leaders and their allies in the general government knew that expropriation contravened the Hague Rules. But they had lost the struggle with the military, which claimed military necessity and older usages of war (state practice). After the war, OHL and the Prussian war ministry explained publicly that "it became increasingly difficult to uphold international regulations...because, under the growing economic pressure of the illegal blockade, important offices at home demanded ever stricter exploitation of these territories by the military."[98] Germany's policies, they insisted, were "natural and corresponded to the international-legal concept of war necessity." Denying the Allies' charge of plunder, they replied that Germany's actions had been systematic, "according to plan," a "goal-oriented use of resources of the occupied areas in the interest of the German army and of the war economy at home."[99] Exactly the systematic nature that the Allies thought proved German lawlessness they offered as proof of the contrary. The open admission that Germany used foreign resources for its domestic war industry confirmed Germany's adherence to the principle, rejected at the Hague, that "war feeds war."

Feeding Civilians

No article in the Hague Rules nor any prewar discussion of the laws of war mentioned a duty to feed civilians under occupation. That duty was assumed—it is visible in the proportionality rule for requisitions and in the call for the occupant to restore "public order and safety," conditions impossible to imagine together with mass starvation. The British manual of war noted "the usual practice" of leaving at least a three days' supply of food with households subject to requisitions.[100] Both Moltke's original "principles" for the Belgian occupation of August 23, 1914, and the occupation guidelines for Belgium of August 29, 1914, ordered that "the General Government must care for the regular provisioning of the occupying troops and the local population by means of continuous markets, price regulation, etc."[101] The head of the political division of the general government in Belgium,

97. Quartermaster general to Ober-Ost, Heeresgruppen Mackensen and Prinz Leopold, all army high commands, the governors general of Belgium and Warsaw, the governor of Metz, GHQ, July 1916, secret, draft, BAB R 901 84022. Emphasis in original.

98. Prussia, Kriegsministerium, and Oberste Heeresleitung, *Deutsche Kriegführung,* iv.

99. Ibid., 26–27.

100. Edmonds and Oppenheim, *Land Warfare,* para. 416. Cf. J. M. Spaight, *War Rights on Land* (London, 1911), 405.

101. Anhaltspunkte, para. 5; Moltke to Bethmann, Aug. 23, 1914, cited in Wende, *Die belgische Frage,* 21. See also Prussia and War Ministry, *Kriegs-Etappen-Ordnung* (1914), appendix 7, p. 93.

the diplomat Oscar Freiherr von der Lancken-Wakenitz, refers in his memoirs to the "duty of the occupant under the Hague Convention to see to the feeding of the population."[102] But those views swiftly changed.

Densely populated Belgium imported four-fifths of its food, much of it wheat. Few stockpiles, heavy German requisitions, and the siege of its main port, Antwerp, meant that food stores rapidly dwindled. By late August, there were already severe food shortages. The invading Bavarian Sixth Army was under orders to feed enemy civilians only as exceptions in cases "of proven emergencies."[103] As supplies vanished, attitudes hardened. On August 31, 1914, the Prussian finance minister, August Lentze, told the chancellor that "it's better the Belgians starve than that we do. Let the Belgians ask their allies to send them food." Unlike Lentze, Bethmann recognized the occupant's legal duty, but he began to hedge. With the occupation, he replied to Lentze, "we have taken over the self-evident duty of satisfying the most pressing needs of the population, as far as it is compatible with our own needs."[104] Subordinating legal duty to one's own need put the chancellor on the same page as the KEO ("the readiness of the field army has complete precedence over the welfare of the rear/occupation zone").

Toward the beginning of September, efforts by Belgian communal authorities and relief organizations dovetailed with the interest of General Colmar von der Goltz, the newly appointed governor general of Belgium, to address the threat of looming starvation. Both together pressed the United States to intervene with Britain to permit aid to pass through the blockade.[105] Von der Goltz agreed with alacrity (September 17) not to tax or requisition food aid from abroad destined for Belgian civilians.[106] At first he insisted that Germany would distribute the food itself, a demand that Britain, mindful of the "scrap of paper," rejected out of hand. Von der Goltz gave way, the German government backed him, and on October 22, 1914, the Committee for the Relief of Belgium (CRB) was officially established. Headed by Herbert Hoover and aided by American and Spanish diplomats and volunteers, the CRB took over the gargantuan task of funding, buying, shipping, and distributing food, clothing, and other aid to all of occupied Belgium and Northern France—between nine and ten million people—for the duration of the war.[107] In Belgium the CRB worked together with the Belgian National Committee (Comité National de Secour et d'Alimentation), which became a center of national resistance against German administration.[108] Foreign aid alone kept the people of Belgium and Northern France alive during the war. In many respects, including legal ones, the

---

102. Lancken-Wakenitz, *Meine Dreissig Dienstjahre*, 199.

103. v. Hartz (War Ministry), Ic no. 12/15, St. Avold, Aug. 16, 1914, BayKrA, AOK 6 Bund 28.

104. Bethmann to Lentze, Sept. 4, 1914, and Lentze to Bethmann, cited in Wende, *Die belgische Frage*, 24, 24n2.

105. Whitlock to Bryan, Brussels, Oct. 16, 1914, cited in Gay, *Public Relations*, 1:11.

106. Von der Goltz to Brand Whitlock, Brussels, Sept. 17, 1914, cited in Gay, *Public Relations*, 1:6.

107. Numbers: Hoover, *American Epic*, 388. The CRB began feeding Northern France on April 9, 1915: Gromaire, *L'occupation allemande en France*, 192. Because of the almost complete impoverishment of Belgium owing to occupation economic policies, the CRB fed about six million people by war's end: De Schaepdrijver, *La Belgique*, 109.

108. Köhler, *Staatsverwaltung*, 64; Henry, *Ravitaillement*, 37, 44.

CRB was the most remarkable institution of World War I. It raises two questions: why did the Allies agree to this arrangement? and would Imperial Germany really have permitted the entire population to starve?

In November 1914, France's foreign minister Théophile Delcassé expressed the view of all French and British officials, that "after all, it is up to the Germans to provide food for the lands they occupy."[109] Therefore, a scheme like the CRB simply "relieve[d] our enemies of responsibilities which are rightly theirs" (Eustace Percy, November 1916).[110] Even Hoover, who strove mightily to avoid judgments that might seem unneutral, admitted that the CRB worked to Germany's military advantage.[111] Britain's War Office explained that "a starving population" in occupied territory placed the occupant "on the horns of a dilemma, since, if he leaves the population unfed, he must allot a larger force for their control, and, if he prefers to provide foodstuffs, he must deplete further his own supplies. Any measure, therefore, that tends to help the enemy out of this difficulty is tantamount to granting him direct assistance, either in men or in military resources."[112]

Britain tried to keep this inevitable effect to a minimum by making sure that the Americans (and later, Spanish) controlled all aid and by wringing from Germany the promise not to requisition foodstuffs in Belgium—otherwise, the CRB would simply function as "a method of replacement instead of one of relief."[113] As Germany nonetheless continued to requisition food and raw materials from Belgium, to export pigs and the agricultural harvest to Germany, to graze eighty thousand German cattle on Belgian pastures (thus circumventing the blockade of fodder), and so on, Britain tightened restrictions until CRB imports into Belgium were strictly rationed according to population.[114] Renegotiations with the CRB (and through them, with Germany) caused both belligerent sides to engage in brinksmanship. Matters became worse under unrestricted submarine warfare, when neutral CRB ships were sunk along with the rest, reducing the amount of food and clothing reaching Belgium by as much as 50 percent after 1917.[115]

The CRB was unprecedented, deeply controversial, and fraught with complex administrative problems. Britain (and France) only acquiesced to it because they believed that Germany truly would let the Belgian and French civilians starve to death. The unlimited requisitions of August and afterward suggested that end. High-ranking officers said so: General Walther Freiherr von Lüttwitz, the first military governor of Brussels, heatedly

---

109. Delcassé to Paul Cambon, tels. 719–20, Bordeaux, Nov. 20, 1914, *DDFr* 1: doc. 555; Gay, *Public Relations*, 1:135.

110. Eustace Percy minute, Nov. 22, 1916, FO 382/618, file 88, no. 234793.

111. Hoover to Bryan, London, Jan. 26, 1915; Hoover note to proposed agreement, Feb. 4, 1915; Hoover memo, Berlin, Feb. 6, 1915, in Gay, *Public Relations*, 236–37, 243–44, 246.

112. War office to foreign office, Apr. 22, 1916, *BD*, ser. H, 7: doc. 96. Germany was well aware of the enormous military advantage provided by the CRB: Bethmann to AA, GHQ, Oct. 29, 1914, no. 86 zu AH 1915, AA/PA R 22421.

113. Grey to Page, Dec. 31, 1915, *BD*, ser. H, 6: doc. 219.

114. Gay, *Public Relations*, 1:117–213; Henry, *Ravitaillement*, 44–45. British allegations were confirmed in internal German correspondence: Bissing to Bethmann, Brussels, Aug. 15, 1916, J. N. 98, BAB R 1501/102797; Treutler to Bethmann, GHQ, Mar. 6, 1916, no. 126, AA/PA, R 22422.

115. Gay, *Public Relations*, 1:179, 185, 287. List of CRB sinkings: Garner, *International Law*, 1:519–22.

told an American diplomat on October 14 (two days before von der Goltz signed the CRB agreement) that "the allies are at liberty to feed the Belgians. If they don't, they are responsible for anything that may happen. If there are bread riots, the natural thing would be for us to drive the whole civil population into some restricted area, like the Province of Luxembourg, build a barbed wire fence around them, and leave them to starve in accordance with the policy of their allies."[116] Hoover believed that Lüttwitz's views were common. The future head of the CRB told Ambassador Page in London that "it was certain that the occupying army" would not feed the Belgians, and furthermore, after confirmation from a U.S. correspondent he had sent to Berlin for that purpose, Hoover was sure that German public opinion, incensed at the Belgians "for spoiling their plan of campaign," would support the most draconian policies.[117] Grey possessed this information as he made his decision. During one of the (many) low points regarding the CRB, Eyre Crowe asked for an "authoritative ruling" as to "whether our material or moral interest in saving the Belgian population from starving is or is not sufficient to justify us in continuing" with it.[118] The answer was always yes; presumably it was primarily the moral interest that outweighed the enormous military disadvantage in relieving Germany of its responsibilities as occupant.[119] In 1918 the Allied Supreme War Council made feeding Belgium a "war measure," elevating it to a military goal.[120]

The polycratic nature of German government makes it hard to know if the Allies were right that Germany would have let the Belgians and French starve. They were in any event wrong about the chancellor in autumn 1914. Evidently, he could not believe that the Allies would agree to a measure so patently at odds with their military interest. As the talks setting up the CRB dragged on in London, Bethmann received word from Brussels that Belgium had run out of food and that desperate people were attacking bread transports. On October 23, he wrote to Prussian vice president Klemens von Delbrück that if Britain rejected the CRB, "then we must take care of feeding Belgium in time"; he ordered Delbrück to begin preparations.[121] Feeding Belgium meant not just jettisoning the military's goal of using Belgium as a supply depot (paragraph 4 of the occupation guidelines), but diverting Germany's own produce and/or food imports. That was what Finance Minister von Lentze had objected to, and even the chief of the general government's civil administration, Max von Sandt, who had just pleaded for food shipments to stop a potential hunger revolution, insisted that "no international-legal obligation exists for an occupant to feed from its own supplies an occupied people who cannot provision themselves from their own."[122] Aware of the strong pushback from within the civil administration, Bethmann defended his

116. Hugh Gibson, *A Journal from Our Legation in Belgium* (Garden City, NY, 1917), 272.

117. Hoover to Page, Oct. 20, 1914, in Gay, *Public Relations*, 1:15–16; Hoover, *American Epic*, 23.

118. Crowe memorandum, "Position of Native Industries in Belgium under the Present Policy of His Majesty's Government," June 8, 1915, *BD*, ser. H., 5: doc. 175.

119. See Cabinet discussions: Asquith to King, Oct. 22, 1914, CAB 41/35/54; Dec. 4, 1914, CAB 41/35/62; Jan. 31, 1915, CAB 41/36/1.

120. Gay, *Public Relations*, 1:292.

121. Bethmann to Delbrück, GHQ, Oct. 23, 1914, zu A.H. 1813, tel. in code, AA/PA R 22421.

122. Sandt to general governor, Brussels, Oct. 22, 1914, J. no. V-288, forwarded to Bethmann, AA/PA R 22421.

willingness to do so not on legal, but "on military and political grounds": to prevent unrest in Germany's rear lines, to avoid encouraging Britain to believe that its blockade was effective, and to avoid "severely compromising [Germany's] administration of Belgium and the regulation of future things," that is, successful annexation or tributary status.[123]

Germany's position on the legal obligation appears to have been set down in December 1914 by Colonel Zöllner, chief of staff of the quartermaster of the western armies. Endorsing von Sandt's interpretation and consonant with Bethmann's earlier observation that the legal obligation must be "compatible" with the occupant's needs, Zöllner wrote to the chancellor: "The laws and customs of land warfare nowhere require a belligerent to provide for the population of an occupied territory out of his own stores. Such a duty could even less be recognized in the current war, when our enemies plan…to starve us out by cutting off imports. Every feeling of human pity with the hungry enemy must yield to the earnest duty to protect our own people from a coming emergency. Food questions are consequently to be primarily decided by military interests."[124] But Zöllner explained that military interests and humanitarianism coincided insofar as disease and hunger riots must be avoided in the army's rear. The army therefore would give some food to localities. Zöllner hoped these actions would be widely publicized because they were "voluntary" and showed both that "we are trying to wage the war according to the principles of humanity" and that the blockade had not harmed Germany enough to prevent such action.

Imperial Germany therefore recognized only a qualified legal obligation to feed occupied civilians. That was quite at odds with the Allied view. Almost simultaneously with Zöllner's letter, Prime Minister Herbert Asquith informed King George that the cabinet "were strongly of opinion that the duty of feeding the population rests upon the Germans who have occupied and assumed the government of the country."[125] The French government refused to permit Swiss food shipments to occupied Northern France and hesitated for weeks to agree to the extension of the CRB to those areas because it opposed setting a precedent that denied Germany's international-legal responsibility to feed those under its occupation authority.[126] Germany's ally Austria-Hungary interpreted the law like the Allies. In 1915, its chief of staff, General Franz Conrad von Hötzendorf, contemplated letting Serbian civilians under Austria's control starve, but then relented. State policy recognized the legal obligation and consequent loss of international prestige if Austria violated it. Consequently, Austria fed the Serbs, partly from its own, domestic stores.[127]

---

123. Just five days earlier, Bethmann had asked the AA to prepare legal documents to set up such tributary status: Bethmann to Zimmermann, R.K. 369, GHQ, Oct. 18, 1914, BAB R 01 85345.

124. Zöllner to chancellor, Ia Nr. 6512, GHQ, Dec. 2, 1914, AA/PA R 22385. Writing in 1915, the international lawyer Christian Meurer agreed with Zöllner: "No regulation of the Hague Rules says that the army must give its necessary food reserves to the population," Christian Meurer, *Die völkerrechtliche Stellung der vom Feinde besetzten Gebiete* (Tübingen, 1915), 43.

125. Asquith to King, Dec. 4, 1914, CAB 41/35/62.

126. Jagow to Treutler, Berlin, March 16, 1915, Nr. 130 AA/PA R 22422.

127. Gumz, *Resurrection and Collapse*, 25, 149–58.

After the CRB was set up, several crises pitted its continuance against German war policy, testing Germany's commitment to feeding Belgian and French civilian occupees. The first occurred in early 1915 when the CRB was running out of funds and had to turn to Allied and neutral governments to continue its operations. Britain initially refused to do so unless Germany stopped exacting the monthly 40 million franc contribution from Belgium. In effect, Britain offered to trade its monetary subsidy for Germany's right under the Hague Rules to defray occupation expenses from the occupied territory. The AA, banking leaders, and the chancellor rejected the idea out of hand. Imperial Treasury Secretary Karl Helfferich gave Hoover three reasons: (1) the intricate civil-military modus vivendi involving "the rights of local generals" could not be undone; (2) "it would be equivalent to the German Government paying for the food of the Belgians"; and (3) Germany would lose face by backing down.[128] Helfferich's reply was consistent with Germany's rejection of an absolute duty to feed occupied civilians.

By February 1915, the chancellor was aware of the first potential food shortages in Germany.[129] When he rejected the British offer to swap British government funding for Belgian contribution payments, Hoover warned that Britain might close down the CRB "and the Germans would be faced with ten million starving people on their hands." The chancellor replied that he realized that and hoped to find alternate funding.[130] But as of February he valued contributions over the CRB.

In internal deliberations, however, the chancellor valued the CRB more highly. Beginning in January 1915 and consistently thereafter, Bethmann used the CRB as a bludgeon against the navy's plan to launch unrestricted submarine warfare. Submarine warfare, he told Admiral Tirpitz, would cause the United States to suspend aid, and then "we would have a hunger emergency in Belgium or we would have to feed them from Germany. The latter is impossible now because of the state of our reserves."[131] Although we lack evidence for the decision on February 1–2, 1915, to go ahead with submarine warfare, the historian of that decision believes that somehow Chief of the Admiralty Hugo Pohl must have assured the chancellor, Chief of Staff Falkenhayn, and Secretary of Interior Delbrück that CRB ships could safely reach port.[132] Since mid-November 1914 the chancellor had tried to speed up CRB shipments from America, so he could build up provisions in case unrestricted submarine warfare caused Britain to close down the CRB.[133] When new, more restrictive orders were issued to U-boat commanders in September 1915, CRB ships

---

128. Hoover memo, Berlin, Feb. 6, 1915, in Gay, *Public Relations,* 246–47.

129. Germany began grain rationing on Feb. 1, 1915, Archibald C. Bell, *A History of the Blockade of Germany and of the Countries Associated with Her in the Great War, Austria, Bulgaria, and Turkey, 1914–1918* (London, 1937), 117.

130. Hoover memo, Berlin, Feb. 7, 1915, in Gay, *Public Relations,* 255. In the end, Britain caved in; David Lloyd George pushed the government subsidy through the cabinet over the military objections of the Admiralty and War Office (Winston Churchill and General H. H. Kitchener). By war's end, government subsidies (of the Allies and the United States) had paid for 78 percent of the cost of the CRB: Gay, *Public Relations,* 1:258, 262, 215–16.

131. Tirpitz notes of a conversation with Bethmann, Jan. 27, 1915, in Tirpitz, *Politische Dokumente,* 302.

132. Arno Spindler, ed., *Der Handelskrieg mit U-Booten,* Der Krieg zur See 1914–1918 (Berlin, 1932–34), 1:60, 85.

133. Bethmann to v. Sandt, GHQ, Nov. 12, 1914, AAHQ Nr. 2264, AA/PA R 22421.

were expressly forbidden as targets.[134] The internal battle between civilian and naval and military leaders over unrestricted submarine warfare raged throughout 1916. In a famous memorandum of February 1916, Bethmann staved off the fateful decision by listing seven disadvantages that would accrue to Germany, of which stopping the CRB was number five.[135] As in his remarks to Tirpitz, Bethmann did not seem to envision that Germany would feed the Belgians, but simply that "the insecurity of conditions behind our front would surely increase if the Belgians must go hungry." Presumably, had it been policy to feed the Belgians, he would have argued that Germany's stores would be even further reduced. Ultimately, the chancellor ran out of arguments, and the combined services forced through unrestricted submarine warfare in January 1917.

The CRB also figured in the decision to deport hundreds of thousands of Belgian workers to Germany as laborers in war industry. The Prussian war minister first raised this idea in March 1916. Governor General Bissing killed it, arguing, among other things, that it would end the CRB.[136] Heavy industrialists and the newly appointed chief of staff of the OHL, General Paul von Hindenburg, and his energetic quartermaster general, Erich Ludendorff, revived the idea in September 1916 and pushed it through, over the repeated and vehement objections of Bissing and his aide von der Lancken-Wakenitz. Loss of the CRB was central to their arguments made in writing and in person.[137] These arguments failed. The chancellor later explained that he had given in to "military necessity." His correspondence with Bissing does not indicate how Bethmann proposed to handle Belgian starvation, if it happened, though he might have hoped that careful administrative handling could successfully finesse the problem.[138] In the event, the deportations were disastrous, but the CRB continued. However, though the CRB felt forced to feed some deportees on their way to Germany, it cut off aid to workers and their families once they arrived there.[139] The war ministry made good the shortfall by garnisheeing 30–40 percent of the workers' wages for that purpose, following the principle that "the least possible [German] funds are to be tapped."[140]

These examples show that, though German leaders valued the CRB, they were prepared to risk it to pursue military or industrial plans they thought necessary for victory.[141] Civilian leaders and those closest to the possible damage were more likely to defend the CRB.

---

134. Spindler, *Handelskrieg*, 2:286.

135. Bethmann memo, Feb. 29, 1916, in Spindler, *Handelskrieg*, 3:94–101, and Theobald von Bethmann Hollweg, *Betrachtungen zum Weltkrieg*, vol. 2, *Während des Weltkrieges* (Berlin, 1922), 264–67.

136. Bissing to Bethmann, Brussels, Mar. 14, 1916, and Apr. 12, 1916, *UA* 3:1, 334–35.

137. Bissing to Hindenburg, Brussels, Sept. 15, 1916, *UA* 3:1, 343; Bissing to Bethmann, Brussels, Sept. 26, 1916, BAB R 901 84022; protocol of conference of Oct. 6, 1916, *UA* 3:1, 358–59.

138. Bethmann to Bissing, Oct. 6, 1916, BAB R 901 84022.

139. Dana C. Munro, George C. Sellery, and August C. Krey, eds., *German War Practices, Part 1: Treatment of Civilians* (Washington, DC, 1917), 56. The CRB may have continued to aid families of Belgians who volunteered to work in Germany: Bissing to Bethmann, Brussels, Aug. 15, 1916, J.N. 98, BAB R 1501/102797.

140. Prussian war ministry / war office to, among others, AA, Berlin, Dec. 10, 1916, BAB R 901 84023.

141. Hoover reported that "German authorities apparently carefully weighed the possibility that this [the Belgian deportations] might result in breaking down Relief but determined to proceed in any event": Hoover to CRB in New York, London, Nov. 20, 1916, in Gay, *Public Relations*, 2:59.

But even Bissing, whose defense was more vehement and principled than the chancellor's, found that arguments from duty or humanitarianism had little purchase in decision-making circles; he was driven to arguing that if Britain ended the CRB, more freight room would be available to the Allied war effort.[142]

The same arguments about feeding the Belgians recurred in relation to the Poles, who had come under German and Austrian jurisdiction after a devastating scorched-earth retreat by Russia in late 1915. After difficult negotiations with its own allies, Britain reluctantly agreed to a modified U.S. scheme for relief modeled after the CRB.[143] But Britain attached the condition that Germany and Austria must undertake "adequately to supply and care for the populations of Serbia, Albania, and Montenegro, all of which countries are now being reduced to a state of starvation through the removal" or requisitioning of supplies.[144] Germany declined, arguing not unreasonably that it did not run these areas and could not contract for its ally, Austria.[145] Britain's action was clearly an attempt to make the Central Powers admit in practice the rule of occupant responsibility.

If Imperial Germany, on the one hand, rejected on principle the absolute legal and humanitarian duty to feed occupied civilians and at various times risked causing starvation by goading the neutrals and/or Allies into stopping aid, on the other hand, it never adopted an outright policy that occupied civilians should actually starve. Calls for such a policy at the beginning (Lentze, Lüttwitz) and again at the end of the war seem like outbursts of anger and frustration. For example, on July 29, 1918, despite having just three U-boats available for the task, Admiral Henning von Holtzendorff called for the extension of unrestricted submarine warfare to the U.S. coast. Von der Lancken protested that it would mean that 1.5 million French and Belgian workers would not be fed. Holtzendorff replied "that the welfare of Belgians does not concern us, in the first instance only German interests matter." Kaiser Wilhelm rejected Holtzendorff's advice since three U-boats would be ineffective, and starving workers might rise up in Germany's rear. Like every other German leader, the Kaiser agreed that "our feeding the Belgians is out of the question."[146] As a second example, three weeks before the end of the war, Ludendorff told Prince Max von Baden's reform cabinet that Germany should cancel the CRB and let the Belgians suffer—part of his fantastically punitive "plan" to salvage his own and Germany's "honor" by going down fighting.[147] The government declined this suggestion, too. Germany's willingness to play with the starvation of others was not far removed from Ludendorff's and Hindenburg's (and others') willingness to let all Germans incapable of work starve, as well. As

---

142. Bissing to Bethmann, Sept. 26, 1916, *UA* 3:1, 361.

143. *DDFr*, 1: doc. 560; 2: doc. 70; 3: docs. 635, 655. James W. Gerard, *My Four Years in Germany* (New York, 1917), 214–15.

144. Grey to Spring-Rice, May 11, 1916, *BD*, ser. H, 7:193–94.

145. Gerard to Page, Berlin, June 1, 1916, in Gay, *Public Relations*, 2:115–16.

146. Holtzendorff and Kaiser Wilhelm cited in Bernhard Schwertfeger's report in *UA* 4:2, 350, 352.

147. Cabinet meeting minutes of Oct. 17, 1918, in Erich Matthias and Rudolf Morsey, eds., *Die Regierung des Prinzen Max von Baden*, vol. 2 of *Quellen zur Geschichte des Parlamentarismus und der politischen Parteien, Erste Reihe* (Düsseldorf, 1962), 239–41; Hull, *Absolute Destruction*, 309–19; Michael Geyer, "Insurrectionary Warfare: The German Debate about a *Levée en Masse* in October 1918," *Journal of Modern History* 73 (September 2001): 459–527.

Hindenburg told the chancellor in September 1916, "the motto 'who does not work, shall not eat' is more than justified in our situation, *even for women.*"[148]

Not until the 1949 revision of the Geneva Convention did positive international law recognize the occupant's explicit duty of "ensuring the food and medical supplies of the population," if necessary by importing them and by refraining from requisitions for its own needs unless the population's need had already been met (article 55).[149] However, this duty was limited by the phrase "to the fullest extent of the means available to it." If those means were inadequate (as they became in 1916–17 because of food shortages in Germany), article 59 required the occupant to agree to relief along the lines of the CRB, and it required blockaders to permit relief shipments, but granted them the same powers of search, control over distribution, and protection against diversion that Britain had insisted on in World War I (articles 59–62). The World War accomplished two things. Although Imperial Germany did not publicly deny the occupant's duty to feed the population, its actions to the contrary elicited the Allies' specific enunciation of that duty, thus sharpening assumptions that were inherent but not explicit in previous positive law. And the ad hoc solution of the CRB became the template for the law and future expectations.[150]

Forced Labor and Deportation

The Hague Rules devoted only part of a single article (article 52) to regulating civilian labor. It held that requisitions of services could be demanded only "for the needs of the army of occupation," should be proportionate to its resources, and could not "involve the inhabitants in the obligation of taking part in military operations against their own country." The very brief discussion in 1899 suggests that delegates were thinking mostly of civilians providing private transport or doing other immediate but temporary work. Delegates do not seem to have imagined masses of civilians working for extended periods of time.

Prewar manuals and legal commentaries tended to be equally terse and unenlightening. Where they mentioned specifics, most agreed that "purely military work," especially work on trenches or fortifications, was illegal.[151] Most also agreed that repair of roads,

---

148. Hindenburg to Bethmann, GHQ, Sept. 13, 1916, in Erich Ludendorff, *Urkunden der Obersten Heeresleitung über ihre Tätigkeit 1916/18* (Berlin, 1921), 66; emphasis in original. Apparently, most of the opposition to Hindenburg's suggestion concerned forced labor, not its tie to food: Feldman, *Army, Industry, and Labor,* 173–78. Catholic Center Party leader Matthias Erzberger apparently agreed with Hindenburg's food policy: Erzberger to Frühwirth, Oct. 25, 1916, cited in Thiel, *"Menschenbassin Belgien,"* 184.

149. Adam Roberts and Richard Guelff, eds., *Documents on the Laws of War* (Oxford, 2004), 319–20.

150. The 1949 Geneva accords have since been declared customary law, and in 1977 the provisions relating to feeding occupied civilians have been strengthened further. See Charles A. Allen, "Civilian Starvation and Relief during Armed Conflict: The Modern Humanitarian Law," *Georgia Journal of International and Comparative Law* 19, no. 1 (1989): 1–85; René Provost, "Starvation as a Weapon: Legal Implications of the United Nations Food Blockade against Iraq and Kuwait," *Columbia Journal of Transnational Law* 30 (1992): 577–639.

151. "Purely": Zorn, *Kriegsrecht,* 279. Fortifications: ibid., 279n1; Edmonds and Oppenheim, *Land Warfare,* 84; Jacomet, *Lois de la guerre,* 76; Spaight, *War Rights,* 151. The semiofficial German manual permitted work on

infrastructure, and public buildings was permitted.[152] Other services listed in some books included burying the dead and transporting the wounded and military supplies.[153] Beyond that, it was hard to distinguish, because, as Albert Zorn noted, all work that an occupant was liable to require "would have some relation to military proceedings."[154] Many prewar German works, including the manual of occupation (KEO) and Endres's guide, did not specify what types of civilian work were legal.[155] That omission was especially unfortunate, because the occupant was permitted to use force against civilians who refused to perform legal tasks. The degree and kind of force were also unclear.

Both the French and British manuals of war acknowledged the right to use force, but recommended paying volunteers instead as more effective and humane.[156] And that was Germany's main problem. The Allies could call on their colonies for manpower, and when that proved not entirely suitable, they had the money to hire foreign volunteers, including 140,000 Chinese skilled and unskilled laborers.[157] Germany could do neither, and lack of manpower was one of its most critical deficits. Labor is another example of greater power (resources) making lawful behavior easier. Although the Hindenburg Program of late 1916 attempted partly to address that deficit by conscripting Germany's own men and women, in fact Germany had long since grasped at another solution: prisoners of war and captive civilians.[158] Together, those two groups provided two million unfree workers inside Imperial Germany during the war.[159] Of the civilian laborers, between 500,000 and 600,000 (perhaps as many as 750,000) were Russian Poles, over 200,000 were Belgians, about 34,000 were Lithuanians or other Balts.[160] These numbers refer only to workers deported

---

trenches: Großer Generalstab Germany, *Kriegsbrauch im Landkriege*, Kriegsgeschichtliche Einzelschriften (Berlin, 1902), 47.

152. Oppenheim, *International Law*, 2:175; William Edward Hall, *A Treatise on International Law* (Oxford, 1904), 34; Jacomet, *Lois de la guerre*, 76; Germany, *Kriegsbrauch*, 47; Bonfils and Fauchille, *Manuel* (1908), 702; Karl Strupp, *Das internationale Landkriegsrecht* (Frankfurt, 1914), 112.

153. Strupp, *Landkriegsrecht*, 112; Edmonds and Oppenheim, *Land Warfare*, 83.

154. Zorn, *Kriegsrecht*, 279, 279n1.

155. Meurer, *Haager Friedenskonferenz*, 294; Ullmann, *Völkerrecht*, 496; Liszt, *Völkerrecht*, 314; Prussia and War Ministry, *Kriegs-Etappen-Ordnung* (1914), 57–58; Endres, *Völkerrechtliche Grundsätze*, 29.

156. Jacomet, *Lois de la guerre*, 75; Edmonds and Oppenheim, *Land Warfare*, 84.

157. Guoqi Xu, *China and the Great War: China's Pursuit of a New National Identity and Internationalization* (Cambridge, 2005), 49, 240.

158. The Reichstag prevented the limitless conscription envisioned by OHL, and Germany never moved (middle-class) women into the workforce as much as the Allies did: Feldman, *Army, Industry, and Labor*, 197–249; Ute Daniel, "Women's Work in Industry and Family: Germany, 1914–1918," in *The Upheaval of War: Family, Work and Welfare in Europe, 1914–1918*, ed. Richard Wall and Jay M. Winter (Cambridge, 1988), 267–96, whose data disprove Ferguson's assertions: Ferguson, *Pity of War*, 267–68. On prisoners of war, see chapter 9 of this volume.

159. Ulrich Herbert, *Geschichte der Ausländerbeschäftigung in Deutschland 1880 bis 1980; Saisonarbeiter, Zwangsarbeiter, Gastarbeiter* (Berlin, 1986), 112.

160. Ibid., 91, 99; Lothar Elsner, "Ausländerbeschäftigung und Zwangsarbeitspolitik in Deutschland während des Ersten Weltkrieges," in *Auswanderer-Wanderarbeiter-Gastarbeiter; Bevölkerung, Arbeitsmarkt und Wanderung in Deutschland seit der Mitte des 19. Jahrhunderts*, ed. Klaus J. Bade (Ostfildern, 1984), 528–29, 537, 539–40, 542–45; Friedrich Zunkel, "Die ausländischen Arbeiter in der deutschen Kriegswirtschaftspolitik des 1. Weltkriegs," in *Entstehung und Wandel der modernen Gesellschaft; Festschrift für Hans Rosenberg zum 65.*

to or held captive in Germany, not to the hundreds of thousands more who performed forced labor in the occupied areas.

To some degree, forced labor had been planned before the war. Between 1912 and 1914, large landowners in Prussia's eastern provinces had pressured the state secretary of the interior to prevent seasonal agricultural workers from returning home if war broke out. He agreed. Consequently, on August 4, 1914, the deputy commanding generals in charge of these areas forcibly kept three hundred thousand Russian Poles from leaving Germany.[161] Traditions of authoritarian treatment now mixed with the inevitable results of outright repression to unleash a dynamic of resistance and counter-resistance that swiftly led to sequestering Polish workers, arresting them, keeping them under curfew, forbidding them to change jobs, lowering their wages, and so on.[162]

In the occupied territories forced-labor decrees came from the commanders of the rear areas. They typically began targeting draft-age men, but quickly expanded to include everybody, including children. For example, the rear commander of the First Army (in France) on October 29, 1914, made anyone not working liable for conscription in a forced-labor column; on March 25, 1915, Lieutenant General Bockelberg at Saint-Quentin ordered all men, women, and children to work.[163] Similar forced labor decrees engulfed the East after it was occupied in autumn 1915.[164] Georges Gromaire describes how in Northern France motorcycle corps checked to make sure people were working in the fields at the correct times.[165] Troops east and west conducted razzias, grabbing people off the streets to fill work columns.[166] From the beginning, the military used forced labor.[167]

Civilians did all sorts of work, from street cleaning to mining, unloading supplies to railroad repair, shoveling snow to out-and-out military work. Civilian forced laborers repaired guns, dug trenches, brought military supplies up to the front, and strung barbed wire. Army officials reported that 515,150 allegedly "free workers overwhelmingly from the occupied territories," plus another 18,800 unfree occupied civilian laborers, built the Siegfried line—54 percent of the total workers.[168] By any measure, these last kinds of work were all violations unless performed by genuine volunteers.

Geburtstag, ed. Gerhard A. Ritter (Berlin, 1970), 282; and Division of International Law Carnegie Endowment for International Peace, *Violations of the Laws and Customs of War: Reports of the Majority and Dissenting Reports of American and Japanese Members of the Commission of Responsibilities, Conference of Paris, 1919*, pamphlet no. 32 (Oxford, 1919), 33.

161. Elsner, "Ausländerbeschäftigung," 530–32; Herbert, *Geschichte der Ausländerbeschäftigung*, 87–88.

162. Herbert, *Geschichte der Ausländerbeschäftigung*, 90–91, 95; Christian Westerhoff, *Zwangsarbeit im Ersten Weltkrieg: Deutsche Arbeitskräftepolitik im besetzten Polen und Litauen 1914–1918* (Paderborn, 2012), 44.

163. Gromaire, *L'occupation allemande en France*, 209–10.

164. Strazhas, *Deutsche Ostpolitik*, 38–40; Liulevicius, *War Land*, 73.

165. Gromaire, *L'occupation allemande en France*, 216.

166. Heinrich Wandt, *Etappe Gent* (Vienna/Berlin, 1926), 175; Basler, *Annexionspolitik*, 155–56.

167. Jens Thiel, *"Menschenbassin Belgien": Anwerbung, Deportation und Zwangsarbeit im Ersten Weltkrieg*, 330; Westerhoff, *Zwangsarbeit im Ersten Weltkrieg*, 124.

168. Reichsarchiv, *Der Weltkrieg 1914 bis 1918* (Berlin, 1925–44), vol. 14: Beilage 41. At a high-level meeting in Berlin on Sept. 28, 1916, Colonel Ernst v. Wrisberg (General War Department of the Prussian war ministry) and

The conditions under which many forced civilian laborers lived and worked were disastrous, especially for those in work gangs. They rose before dawn; their diet was wholly inadequate to their heavy labor—ersatz coffee, thin soup, small portions of bread, very rarely meat; their barracks or tents, if they had them, were ill-heated; their clothing and shoes seldom if ever replaced; medicine was virtually nonexistent; beatings were common, and other punishments readily inflicted.[169] Even for those who were not paid in chits, wages were low, often below subsistence.[170] The result of these conditions was high disease and mortality rates; for example, in one work camp in Lithuania in the fall of 1916 only 35 percent of inmates were capable of working at all.[171] To counter these inevitable effects, the army developed a rotation system whereby exhausted workers were sent to the countryside where there was more food in order to recover before being returned to their old work.[172]

In France (and this was true also for Belgium), Georges Gromaire discerned nine categories of laborers, only one of which was not forced: (1) real volunteers; (2) those forced to sign "voluntary" contracts; (3) draft-age men; (4) boys approaching draft age; (5) regular work gangs paid in chits and not housed in camps; (6) temporary levies; (7) evacuees from directly behind the front; (8) prisoners of war; and (9) civilian labor battalions (ZABs)—companies of the most harshly treated forced laborers.[173] The Germans recognized fewer categories. Draft-age men were basically assimilated to prisoner-of-war status, which ought to have put them under the protection of Hague article 6 that permitted paid work, so long as it was not "excessive" and had "no connection with the operations of war."[174] Civilians from an area might be conscripted for work in their district, so long as it was for the occupation troops, not the fighting army in the field. Like prisoners of war, they were protected (by article 52) from work connected with military operations. Under international law, therefore, only volunteers were permitted to do the work Germany most needed, building trenches and fortifications and manufacturing munitions. For this reason a third category of civilian became important: criminals. In their attempt to find more disposable laborers, German leaders debated who was a criminal and how criminals might be used.

General v. Sauberzweig had said two hundred thousand civilians were needed to work on military facilities in the rear: protocol of meeting in *UA* 3:1, 353–54.

169. Gromaire, *L'occupation allemande en France*, 232–34, 366–67; Liulevicius, *War Land*, 73–74; Herbert, *Geschichte der Ausländerbeschäftigung*, 101; Elsner, "Ausländerbeschäftigung," 537–38, 548; Basler, *Annexionspolitik*, 280–82; McPhail, *Long Silence*, 163–64, 174–75, 178; Spanish embassy to German government, Berlin, Aug. 8, 1917, IIIb 35108, BAB R 901 84072; Westerhoff, *Zwangsarbeit im Ersten Weltkrieg*, 175, 178, 208, 210, 219–22; Thiel, "*Menschenbassin Belgien*," 125, 128–30.

170. Herbert, *Geschichte der Ausländerbeschäftigung*, 86; Lothar Elsner, "Der Übergang zur Zwangsarbeit für ausländische Arbeiter in der deutschen Landwirtschaft zu Beginn des 1. Weltkriegs," *Wissenschaftliche Zeitschrift der Wilhelm-Pieck-Universität Rostock, Gesellschafts- und Sprachwissenschaftliche Reihe* 26, no. 3 (1977): 298; Zunkel, "Die ausländischen Arbeiter," 288; Strazhas, *Deutsche Ostpolitik*, 39–40; Westerhoff, *Zwangsarbeit im Ersten Weltkrieg*, 153.

171. Liulevicius, *War Land*, 74.

172. Gromaire, *L'occupation allemande en France*, 214, 230.

173. Ibid., 208, 212, 220, 222–24, 230–31, 238–46, 435.

174. See chapter 9 of this volume on reprisals for a detailed discussion of prisoner-of-war work in practice.

The harsh, even lethal, conditions of work were set by different instances: the army (sometimes OHL, or camp commandants, or subalterns at work sites), heavy industry, and individual landowners. There were other Germans, however, who opposed them and who pressed instead to give laborers higher wages and better conditions. This group included Reichstag representatives (especially among the Socialists and Catholic Center Party), the general governments, the imperial interior ministry, and occasionally the Prussian war minister. In the East, the Russian Revolution changed the political climate and apparently helped opponents of the worst aspects of forced labor to mitigate some conditions there.[175] The same was not true of the western front.

Forced labor scandalized the Allied and neutral world, which was mostly unaware of efforts inside Germany to stop it or to improve conditions. The best known and most shocking instance was the Belgian deportations of 1916–17. This decision provoked the only systematic internal discussion of Germany's international-legal obligations regarding the forced labor and deportation of occupied civilians. The policies themselves were not unique to Belgium and Northern France. They occurred throughout the German occupied zones, but concerning the Belgian problem we have a record of the legal thinking behind these policies.

The Belgian Deportations

The deportation of masses of civilians began in August 1914 on both fronts. The Russian army immediately deported draft-age enemy aliens from behind the front, and swiftly moved on to its own citizens, Jews or those of German ancestry; in the end Russia banished perhaps one million people to the interior under harsh circumstances.[176] For similar reasons of putative security and as punishment, the German army also removed large groups of civilians in Belgium and Northern France and some twenty-three thousand more to camps in Germany.[177] A third type of deportation was suggested in December 1914 by the provincial president of East Prussia, Adolf Batocki, who wanted Germany to annex an adjoining strip of Poland and clear its inhabitants for German colonization.[178]

But deportation for forced labor did not cross the German administrative mind until early 1916. Indeed, until June 1915 security concerns had outweighed need, and thereafter efforts first concentrated on enticing volunteers.[179] But these failed in the West for several reasons. Patriotism stopped many Belgians and French from aiding the German war effort, even indirectly, and CRB food allotments, however meager, lessened the impetus to work. Germany's lack of resources encouraged it to keep wages low, and it was reluctant

---

175. Elsner, "Ausländerbeschäftigung," 549–50.

176. Eric Lohr, *Nationalizing the Russian Empire: The Campaign against Enemy Aliens during World War I* (Cambridge, MA, 2003); Lohr, "Russian Army and the Jews."

177. Horne and Kramer, *German Atrocities*, 166; Hull, *Absolute Destruction*, 211–12, 235–42, 253–57.

178. Adolf T. v. Batocki-Friebe to Arnold Wahnschaffe, Dec. 20, 1914, cited in Geiss, *Grenzstreifen*, 76.

179. Ernst von Wrisberg, *Heer und Heimat, 1914–1918* (Leipzig, 1921), 104.

to grant foreign workers the same rights as those enjoyed by Germans, even in the case of Austrian seasonal workers.[180] When the needed workers failed to materialize by themselves, German policy became to force "volunteers" by making the alternatives worse. Governor General von Bissing took the first steps in that direction in August and September 1915 with three decrees threatening with prison unemployed Belgians who refused to accept work "in the public interest or demanded by the German authorities."[181]

When by March 1916 only a disappointing twelve thousand Belgians had volunteered, Deputy War Minister General Franz von Wandel suddenly called for the forcible deportation of four hundred thousand Belgian civilians to Germany, where they would free German munitions workers for front service.[182] Wandel's intervention typified the military's default solution to problems: it was imperative, hasty and thus badly thought out, and huge.[183] It was the governor general's principled legal opposition to Wandel's request that launched the discussion of international law.

The first discussion took place on March 3, 1916, between Lieutenant Colonel Scherenberg, chief of staff of the general government (GG), and two representatives of the Prussian war ministry. The Prussian war ministry acknowledged what they called "the great political difficulties" raised by forcible deportation, the first of which involved "consideration for the Hague convention."[184] Significantly, that consideration appears only in Scherenberg's report, not in that of the war ministry, which strongly suggests that the war ministry did not raise this subject, but rather responded to the legal concerns of Bissing and the general government.[185] The war ministry was prepared to admit that volunteers were better, but it insisted that if they were not forthcoming, then forcible deportation was the only alternative. The report suggested that if the CRB ended, that would increase "volunteers" seeking work in Germany.

Bissing informed the chancellor that such a move would not only incense the United States, neutrals, and especially the Netherlands, but "it would be especially difficult to avoid an open violation of the Hague Convention."[186] Bissing made it an issue of legality; he may also have thought that the Hague Rules provided the strongest, most clear-cut argument against the war ministry's demand. But the chancellor did not clearly endorse

180. Elsner, "Ausländerbeschäftigung," 543, 545.

181. Decrees of Aug. 14 and 15, 1915, and Sept. 4, 1915: Köhler, *Staatsverwaltung,* 144.

182. Ritter, *Sword and Scepter,* 3:361; Köhler, *Staatsverwaltung,* 148.

183. On the military culture producing such solutions, see Hull, *Absolute Destruction.*

184. Anlage 1. [fols. 5–7] Brüssel, den 4. März 1916, Streng vertraulich! Niederschrift über den wesentlichen Inhalt der Besprechung des Unterzeichneten mit dem Abteilungschef im Kriegsministerium, Oberst Ritter und Edler von Braun, und dem Referenten im Kriegsministerium A.Z. (S) Herrn Sichler am 2. März 1916 im Kriegsministerium in Berlin," signed Scherenberg, Anlage 1 to Bethmann to Bissing, R.K. 7601 K.H., Berlin, April 17, 1916, BAB R 1501/102797.

185. Anlage V. Zu Nr. 228 16.g.A.Z.(S), signed v. Braun and Sichler. "Streng geheim! Niederschrift über eine Besprechung zwischen dem Chef des Stabes des Generalgouvernements in Belgien, Oberstlt. Scherenberg, dem Oberst und Abteilungschef Ritter und Edler v. Braun und dem Referenten Sichler am 2. März 1916 im Kriegsministerium, Berlin," appendix 5 to ibid. Cf. Thiel's interpretation: Thiel, *"Menschenbassin Belgien,"* 80–81.

186. Bissing to Bethmann, Brussels, Mar. 14, 1916, in Köhler, *Staatsverwaltung,* 149. Bissing was referring to an agreement from 1914 that Belgians returning home from Holland would not be deported to Germany.

Bissing's views; after consulting with the war minister, Bethmann instead postponed a decision.[187]

So, Bissing turned elsewhere for support. He arranged for a large interdepartmental meeting in mid May 1916 involving the GG, the war ministry, the Reich and Prussian interior ministries, Prussian ministries of public works and trade and commerce, the naval office, the Reich treasury, and the AA. These offices did endorse the GG's plain statement that deportation to Germany of forced civilian laborers was unlawful: "Each violation of international-legal authority raises discord among the neutrals. Forcing Belgians against their will to work in Germany is impossible for both legal and practical grounds." The chair summarized the results: "The idea of using *force* to get Belgians to emigrate to Germany is given up."[188]

In return for this concession, Bissing sharpened his order on the unemployed (May 15, 1916), making them liable both for forced labor and deportation to Germany and giving military courts jurisdiction over their cases. However, he explained that his ordinance could only be applied "so long as there are no legitimate international-legal objections on the type of work [they will be forced to do]," that is, article 52's prohibition on "taking part in military operations."[189] The May decree on the one hand upheld international law (and therefore vastly reduced its usefulness to the war ministry), but on the other, it developed and extended Germany's coercive abilities. Although Bissing, like Schwarzhoff at The Hague in 1899, was clearly thinking of deporting only individuals, his decrees in fact laid the legal groundwork for mass deportation, just as the war ministry in March had rehearsed the arguments and methods (security, criminalization, withholding food) that shortly were to reverse Bissing's victory.[190]

At the seemingly lowest point in Germany's wartime fortunes, the Kaiser appointed the wildly popular generals Ludendorff and Hindenburg to lead Germany's military effort (August 29, 1916). Their fantastical efforts to boost munitions production ran into Germany's chronic labor shortage, as industrialists warned them in September.[191] The same haste, gigantism, and impatient command tone of Wandel's demand in March now returned, preceded this time by a firm rejection of international law. Ludendorff informed Bissing (September 14) that "international-legal objections must absolutely yield" to necessity. Ludendorff was not alone. Two days later, the architect of Germany's economic war effort, Walther Rathenau, said the same thing: "the solution to the labor problem can only be achieved by disregarding international prestige."[192] Rathenau's euphemism for

---

187. Bethmann to Bissing, Apr. 17, 1916, *UA* 3:1, 336; Ritter, *Sword and Scepter*, 3:362; Thiel, "*Menschenbassin Belgien*," 82–83.

188. "Aufzeichnung über die Sitzung im Reichsamt des Innern vom 13. Mai 1916," R 1501/102797, fols. 27–30.

189. Governor general to all military governors, the commandants of Beverloo and Maubeuge, and the county head, Brussels, May 20, 1916, III T.L. no. 4840, in *UA* 3:1, 431.

190. Köhler, *Staatsverwaltung*, 150–51; *UA* 3:1, 235–37, 431, and Bissing to Hindenburg, Ia Nr. 7793, Brussels, Sept. 15, 1916, ibid., 342; Thiel, "*Menschenbassin Belgien*," 85–86.

191. "Fantasy": Feldman, *Army, Industry, and Labor*, 150.

192. Ludendorff to Bissing, Sept. 14, 1916, in Köhler, *Staatsverwaltung*, 151, also cited in Bethmann to state secretary of interior, Nr. 11242, Berlin, Jan. 24, 1917 (with two exclamation points next to it in the margin), BAB R 901 84024; Rathenau to Ludendorff, Sept. 16, 1916, *UA* 3:1, 383.

law recognized, and rejected as irrelevant, the immense harm to Germany's international reputation that such a violation was bound to incite.

The next day, Bissing again explicitly rejected these views. Bissing's tenacity forced the internal argument to occur inside the legal realm, or at least in legal language. It unfolded in a step-by-step process in which Bissing laid out his position, which was then undercut by the Kaiser, tweaked by the AA, negotiated at two large interdepartmental meetings, and ultimately abandoned by the chancellor.

Bissing began by telling Hindenburg of the May 1916 agreement among high-ranking officials, including from the war ministry, that Germany must avoid open violation of the Hague Rules. He noted that OHL was now proposing a different violation. "If one has already recognized that the *forcible* transportation of Belgian workers *to Germany* violates the Hague Convention, this is even truer for the *forcible* use [of such labor] for building trenches in Northern France." Bissing added that he considered the Hague Rules binding for himself, and that if he were overruled (by the Kaiser, the only leader to whom he answered as governor general), all sorts of political misfortune would befall Germany.[193] Bissing went further. He noted that "no means of forcing unwilling workers has till now been customary in a civilized state," and that "in any case, I cannot assume responsibility for the results." This letter is valuable for several reasons. First, Bissing took international law seriously as an order that he was bound to uphold—recall that, thanks to the AA, the Hague Rules were part of the guidelines for occupation. That is, Bissing was doubly bound by law, and that doubtless strengthened his spine in the ensuing fight. Second, when confronted with a determined stand in favor of law, other officials, even the war ministry, were more prepared to abide by it, at least for a time. Third, the content of the Hague Rules was clear to everybody: they forbade using forced enemy civilian labor except in the civilians' own state, and they forbade forced labor anywhere, in the home occupied zone or in the rear zone, for directly military purposes. Fourth, to a military officer who took law seriously, forced labor of the kind envisaged was such a serious violation that it disqualified the state whose policy it was from membership in the legal community of civilized states.

The next day (September 16), Bissing departed for headquarters in Pless to make his case before the Kaiser. It did not go well. In the course of the meeting, Bissing submitted his resignation, which the Kaiser did not accept. Clearly, the Kaiser had not endorsed Bissing's defense of international law, though he did not decide definitively in favor of OHL's counterview that international law was simply not binding. Leaders ducked the stark choice, and it took several meetings to work out an acceptable compromise. As a contemporary subsequently observed, "no one was anxious to take responsibility."[194] Why not? Here, we must speculate. The claim of military necessity that Bethmann had used to cover the violation of Belgian neutrality had been unsuccessful in pacifying world (and particularly British) opinion. That opinion had been aroused again by the "Belgian atrocities" and once more (in April 1916) by deportations in Lille, Roubaix, and Tourcoing undertaken by the

---

193. Bissing to Hindenburg, Ia Nr. 7793, Brussels, Sept. 15, 1916, *UA* 3:1, 342–43; emphasis in original.
194. Dr. Levi, *UA* 3:1, 367.

local quartermaster general.[195] As Bissing wrote in a subsequent letter to the chancellor, forced-labor deportations would exacerbate the negative "world-political situation" for Germany by appearing to confirm that it pursued "a ruthless policy of power."[196] So long as German leaders cared about world opinion, they must also care about international law, for law was the lingua franca of international relations. Furthermore, deportation for forced labor violated not just the Hague Rules, but also bilateral agreements Germany had concluded during the war. One was an official assurance by General Ernst von Hoyningen, genannt Huene (October 17, 1914) that Germany would not intern Belgian refugees returning from Holland.[197] Another was an agreement with the Allies not to subject interned enemy civilians to forced labor (an accord Germany had meant to protect Germans interned in France and Britain).[198] All participants thus knew that forced-labor deportations violated both treaty law and solemn pledges. If one still wanted to use forced labor in Germany, then Bissing's principled stand forced one either openly to embrace criminal status (as Ludendorff did in internal documents), or to find legal subterfuges. The latter became Germany's actual policy. Subsequent meetings thus were not about discovering what the law would permit or forbid—which even in the rudimentary state of international law and treaties on civilian internees was clear—but what one could contend in public.

OHL's actual legal position was either Ludendorff's—military necessity suspended or nullified law (including in non-battlefield areas like occupied zones)—or the argument that OHL offered at the meeting in Pless. To Bissing's contention that no civilized state customarily did anything like this, OHL had replied that "the entire war is unprecedented."[199] Translated into legal terminology, this argument equates to the adage *rebus sic stantibus*—that is, circumstances have changed so much that they nullify outdated laws.[200] The navy had already heavily argued *rebus sic stantibus* to cover submarine warfare, and it was a favored position of all who embraced a social-Darwinistic vision of constant, struggle-induced change that must break the sclerotic confines of positive law.[201] Either way, OHL thought law negligible. Its indifference to Germany's growing reputation as uncivilized simplified its position.

Once he was deprived of the legal grounds on which his opposition had rested, Bissing was forced to restrict himself to listing the (many) political disadvantages to such a policy.[202] Of course, those smuggled the law back into the discussion, since political disadvantages were in fact sanctions upholding international law. Throughout, Bissing himself remained deeply concerned about law. For example, he retracted his fleeting agreement

195. Hull, *Absolute Destruction*, 254–55.

196. Bissing to Bethmann, IV 5120, Brussels, Sept. 26, 1916, BAB R 901 84022.

197. Foreign minister of the Netherlands to German government, The Hague, Nov. 29, 1916, IIIb 45895, BAB R 901 84023. The assurance was given to the Belgian international lawyer and politician Louis Franck, but it was on that basis that Holland permitted refugees to return to Belgium.

198. "Ergebnis der Verhandlungen mit dem AA (Dr. Dr. Kriege, Geh LR Eckardt u. WLR Dr. v. Keller, vom 16. und 18. September 1916)" GHQ, Sept. 21, 1916, BAB R 901 84022.

199. OHL memorandum, no date, but after Sept. 24, 1916, *UA* 3:1, 347–48.

200. See chapter 2 of this volume for discussion of *rebus sic stantibus*.

201. Erich Kaufmann, *Das Wesen des Völkerrechts und die clausula rebus sic stantibus* (Tübingen, 1911), 56, 231.

202. Bissing to Bethmann, Brussels, Sept. 26, 1916, BAB R 901 84022.

at Pless to deport only draft-age men—a measure he had thought was permissible—when aides informed him that it, too, contravened the Hague Rules.[203]

It is significant that the legal experts at the AA played a merely ancillary role in deciding this important legal question. They worked out details, but did not set basic principles, though once the deportations had actually begun, official correspondence tended to run through the AA's legal section, which became a kind of coordinating instance for policy. On the same day that Bissing presented his case to the Kaiser at Pless, legal section chief Johannes Kriege and his assistants, *Geheimrat* Paul Eckardt and *Wirklicher Legationsrat* Dr. Friedrich von Keller, began two days of meetings with representatives of the OHL. The basis for negotiation was a draft order that the quartermaster general had circulated to army groups in July 1916.[204] It sought to regularize the volunteers and forced work columns that the army was already using to replace ad hoc conscription of civilians for maintenance tasks in the communes. The order still operated within the legal restrictions that Bissing had insisted on in March and May 1916. It understood civilian labor as protected by Hague article 52. Although it defined three types of forced-work columns consisting of criminals, draft-age men, and others, including women and especially the unemployed, it still noted that work columns fell under article 52 and that draft-age men (seventeen to fifty-five) enjoyed the same protections accorded to prisoners of war.

The brief prepared by Kriege and his assistants after the meeting mostly clarified the different categories of civilians liable to forced labor. It was most helpful in offering OHL a legal cover for forced labor and deportation via a tortured construction of Hague article 43.[205] Article 43 held the occupant to provide law and order in the occupied zone; by construing mass unemployment as a security threat and issuing an ordinance permitting forced labor for those receiving welfare, the German authorities might round up masses of jobless civilians without going through the Belgian-administered communes. They also claimed that article 43 permitted wider use of "men, women, and adolescents" in any measure construed as "preventing an emergency [*Notstand*] for the population," including working in coal mines far from their homes (paragraph 3). Finally, those myriads of civilians falling afoul of "military-police coercive measures" (not the stricter criminal laws) were liable to deportation to Germany or elsewhere in the occupied area. The AA noted that draft-age men were civilians, not prisoners of war, and suggested conscripting their labor under another category instead. Unfortunately, none of this solved OHL's problem. The AA's lawyers correctly read Hague article 52 and Germany's bilateral agreements on interned civilians: forced civilian labor in Belgium was lawful, but not for trench building, and expanded criminalization permitted deportation to Germany, but deportee labor there was restricted to light work in camps. The best solution, the AA concluded along

---

203. Bissing to Hindenburg, n.d. but circa Sept. 24, 1916, in *UA* 3:1, 346–47; Ritter, *Sword and Scepter,* 3:364.

204. Generalquartiermeister, "Entwurf," II c Nr. 11816, GHQ, July 1916, BAB R 901 84022.

205. GHQ, Sept. 21, 1916, "Ergebnis der Verhandlungen mit dem AA...vom 16. und 18. September 1916," BAB R 901 84022.

with Bissing, remained volunteers who could work "at all jobs," including those "in other theaters of war."

OHL now hastened to increase the numbers of those it might deport by drafting an ordinance against "anti-German" behavior (September 24, 1916).[206] It criminalized the whole range of possible reactions to a vast scheme of forced or voluntary labor: hindering others from following German orders, encouraging them not to do so, slandering or threatening people exhibiting pro-German behavior, trying to stop someone from working for the Germans, or quitting one's job without a good reason. These infractions would be handled by military courts.

As of September 28, the chancellor, who had earlier deferred a decision, agreed with Bissing that Germany should avoid forced labor, but he wanted volunteers "encouraged with all conceivable means."[207]

On that same day, representatives of the OHL, the war ministry, the imperial ministry of the interior, the general governments of Belgium and Poland, and the AA met in Berlin to determine final policy. They operated within the limits set at Pless; in Gerhard Ritter's words, "the emphasis was on finding some legal pretext for the deportations that would not contravene the Hague convention too flagrantly."[208] Speaking for OHL, former military governor of Brussels Brigadier General von Sauberzweig thus tried to keep within the legal language of the AA's brief. He did not simply call on law-stopping military necessity, but instead cited security.[209] He followed the AA's lead in deriving Germany's actions from article 43 rather than the inconvenient article 52, and hence he claimed that masses of unemployed posed a danger to the army's rear (*Etappe*). Max von Sandt, head of the civil administration in Belgium, immediately contradicted him—the Belgian public was completely quiet. Sauberzweig repeated himself and then made a second legal-seeming suggestion. He warned that "one must guard against an overly anxious interpretation of the [Hague] Rules, since our enemies" did not do so. Director Theodor Lewald of the Reich interior ministry concurred, informing the group that his ministry and General von Moltke had already agreed in 1915 that it was best not to be "too narrow" in construing Hague restrictions on using foreign workers "in military works [*bei kriegerischen Bauten*]." If one translated "*opérations de la guerre*" as "*Operationen*," Lewald continued, then the Hague restriction would apply "only to warlike acts in the narrowest sense of the word," that is, battle. Sauberzweig also received assistance from the general government of Poland, which favored using forced labor, and when von der Lancken objected to applying the same standards to Belgium, Sauberzweig replied that all occupation areas should be treated equally. Still operating within the AA's brief, Sauberzweig seemed to agree that Germany's accord with the Allies on civilian detainees precluded forcing them to work in munitions factories in Germany. Perhaps this was why OHL and the Prussian war ministry now pressed instead to use two hundred thousand civilian forced laborers in the rear

---

206. "Verordnung betr. deutschfeindliches Verhalten," draft, GHQ, Sept. 24, 1916, BAB R 901 84022.

207. Bethmann note, Sept. 28, 1916, to Bissing to Bethmann, Sept. 26, 1916, BAB R 901 84022.

208. Ritter, *Sword and Scepter*, 3:366.

209. Protocol of the meeting of Sept. 28, 1916, in *UA* 3:1, 349–54.

zones (presumably to build the Siegfried line). Colonel Ernst von Wrisberg, director of the general war department of the Prussian war ministry, and Colonel Max Bauer, Ludendorff's amanuensis, both thought deportation to the rear much easier than overcoming the legal obstacles connected with deportation to Germany. Astonishingly, Eckardt (of the AA), who until now had repeated the formulas of the AA's preliminary brief and thus emphasized the protections of article 52, replied that his office had no objections to using Belgian forced labor in the rear zone. Eckardt might not have known that OHL intended to use deportees to build trenches, and/or he might have been focusing on deportation, which the AA thought legal *within* Belgium's own borders. Without reaching a conclusion, the meeting adjourned.

Bissing now tried to stop this latest OHL plan. He informed Hindenburg that forced civilian labor went "against my conscience."[210] He offered again to raise volunteers and to continue individual, but not mass, deportation of the unemployed who refused work (under Bissing's decree of May 16, 1916).

Two days later (October 6, 1916) in Brussels, Bissing and his military and civilian staff went at it again with representatives of the OHL. This turned out to be the decisive meeting. Hindenburg had meanwhile dropped the demand for forced labor in the rear (which OHL now carried out secretly) and substituted deportation to Germany, so that was the focus. OHL's representative Lieutenant Colonel von Schwartzkoppen, citing the AA's advice, said that deportation to Germany on the basis of the decree of May 16, 1916, was useless, because Germany was bound by its agreement with the Allies to use captive civilians only for light work. This meeting threatened to be as inconclusive as the preceding one, until chief of the civil administration von Sandt broke ranks and "corrected" the AA's legal judgment. He argued that persons deported under Bissing's unemployment decrees were no longer civilians (or equivalent to prisoners of war, if they were draft-age men); they were criminals (*Strafgefangene*) liable to forced labor under *Belgian* law. This redefinition removed them from all protection: they could be deported to Germany and from there, moreover, directly into the rear zones. Bissing, who after all had issued criminalization decrees in order to deport individuals and to encourage "volunteers," accepted von Sandt's views. But he remained firmly opposed to deportation to the rear zone; such a violation, he warned, would bring reprisals and destroy the CRB. He ended by repeating that his duty was to run his office according to international law. Those present now decided to ask the chancellor whether deportees could be regarded as prisoners, rather than as civilians.

In a letter that appeared to cross this request for advice, Bethmann stuck to the AA's legal brief. He suggested another way to legalize deportation to Germany or Poland—by claiming that Germany and its occupied zones formed a single economic unit, thus making the borders irrelevant, a scheme that the earlier Berlin meeting had also contemplated.[211]

---

210. Bissing to Hindenburg, Brussels, Oct. 4, 1916, in *UA* 3:1, 356.

211. Professor of law Richard Schmidt (Leipzig) had worked out the theory of "interim community of interest" in a report for the jurists' conference sponsored by the general government in Brussels on Sept. 29–30, 1916. According to this theory, lengthy occupation created shared "life interests" between the occupant and occupied, enabling the former to legislate over vast areas of life that the Hague Rules assumed were off-limits

Meanwhile, the military continued to press the line of complete nullification of law on the basis of military necessity. Von Wrisberg, who directed the department in charge of munitions at the war ministry, said bluntly (October 7, 1916), "Objections founded on international law must not hold us back; they must give way before the inexorable necessity of finding the most productive employment in war industry for all labor under German control."[212]

Two days later, the chancellor approved deportations.[213] He wrote to Bissing that both deportation and forced labor were "internationally-legally justified" against the unemployed who were receiving public aid (CRB) because there was no work in Belgium; but it was only legal so long as their labor was not "exclusively war-related" (article 52). Although he construed Bissing's decree of May 15, 1916, as a mere administrative measure, it sufficed—outright criminalization (that is, being sentenced to prison) was not necessary.[214] The chancellor confined himself to warning against "unnecessary severity," and he called for "appropriate wages," which however should be less than what volunteers received. Thus, Bethmann did not consider the measures legal, merely justified. He continued to recognize article 52, but he weakened it ("exclusively"). Above all, he hoped that efficient execution would mollify critics. In fact, the deportations were calamitous.

After the war, when the Reichstag inquired into the resulting fiasco, Bethmann defended his decision by saying that "the argument of inexorable military necessity" had coerced him, and that was true; military necessity was the framework for decision making.[215] Nevertheless, that was not Germany's public claim, as it had been for the violation of Belgian neutrality. Nor had it been possible to use reprisal to cover its illegal action, as Germany did with draconian measures taken against prisoners of war and with unrestricted submarine warfare.[216] Officials had explored that avenue, and in public Germany argued that Belgian unemployment was caused by the Allied blockade. Colonel Hans von Haeften, OHL's liaison with the AA, even suggested offering to return deportees if the Allies permitted raw material imports into Belgium, a suggestion consonant with genuine reprisal. Jagow thought it "a good idea," but he was brought down to earth by *Legationsrat* Ludwig Kempff of the Belgian general government and former German consul to Belgium. He reported that "actually we requisitioned and took away raw materials from the very beginning. So,

---

and still under the sway of local law: A. Willeke, ed., *Protokolle der Tagung richterlicher Militärjustizbeamter in Brüssel am 29./30. September 1916, samt einigen vorbereitenden Gutachten* (N.p., 1916), 147–49. Pirenne and Vauthier assume that Bissing had called this conference in order to clear the legal way for deportations. But that is probably untrue. The conference was planned in June 1916 at a time when Bissing had just successfully beaten back attempts by the war ministry to inaugurate forced deportation; furthermore, none of the lectures or reports concerned deportation directly: ibid., 13; Pirenne and Vauthier, *Législation*, 51–52.

212. Wrisberg to war ministry, Oct. 7, 1916, in Erich Ludendorff, *The General Staff and Its Problems: The History of the Relations between the High Command and the German Imperial Government as Revealed by Official Documents* (London, 1919), 156.

213. Bethmann to Bissing, Oct. 9, 1916, in Köhler, *Staatsverwaltung*, 152; Ritter, *Sword and Scepter,* 3:367–68.

214. The quartermaster general's "Entwurf" of July 1916 had considered a sentence necessary for criminalization: Sect. III-1, BAB R 901 84022.

215. German National Constituent Assembly, *Official German Documents Relating to the World War,* trans. Division of International Law Carnegie Endowment for International Peace (New York, 1923), 1:419, 412.

216. Kempff (political section of GG-Belg.) to Köpke, Brussels, Dec. 31, 1916, IIIb 47827, BAB R 901 84023.

our position is hardly wonderful, if we want to be honest with ourselves. Furthermore, in the last half year we've taken immense quantities of machines and factory parts to Germany."[217] OHL had successfully opposed the general government's repeated proposals to revive Belgian industry, in favor of expropriation. Reprisal would therefore not cover the deportations.

With both reprisal and military necessity off the table, and faced with Bissing's stubborn devotion to his orders to uphold international law, Germany was left with the claim of justification, however lame. But this episode shows that when an independent military commander directly responsible to the Kaiser found international law a critical factor in decision making, that forced the chancellor and the various departments to negotiate on that basis. Admiral von Pohl briefly set off a similar process in autumn 1914 regarding submarine warfare. It is striking how long Bissing fended off deportation (from March to October 1916). In the end, he was worn down by his own and everyone else's (von Sandt, the AA) desire to stretch the occupant's coercive power through legal-seeming mechanisms (the decrees, shifting attention from article 52 to article 43). When these did not reach far enough, they resorted to redefinition. The internal discussions clearly show that the decision makers knew what the law was (*opinio juris*) and felt forced by OHL's arguments of military necessity to break it. The reluctance to claim military necessity and the effort to find a legalistic cover both acknowledged the validity of the rules being broken.

The deportations electrified Europe. The neutrals (the United States, Spain, Switzerland, the Netherlands, and the pope) issued vociferous protests. Popular demonstrations broke out in Italy, France, neutral Ireland, and the United States.[218] Holland condemned the policy as a violation of the Martens Clause and also of the 1914 Huene agreement.[219] Exactly as Bissing had done, the United States expressed the widespread view that Germany had taken leave of the civilized world.[220] Secretary of State Robert Lansing had hitherto adhered strictly to "the policy of avoiding all protests on account of inhuman methods of warfare by belligerents which are in violation of international law."[221] But he was deeply, personally, shocked, both at the policy and at the fact that Germany openly admitted it. The Belgian deportees, he wrote privately to President Wilson,

> are to all intents in a state of involuntary servitude. To use a more ugly phrase, they are slaves under a system of slavery which has not been practiced in regard to civilian enemies by civilized nations within modern times. It arouses in me, as I am sure it must arouse in every liberty-loving man, an intense feeling of abhorrence

217. Jagow marginalium on note by v. d. Bussche, IIIb 47316, Dec. 11, 1916, BAB R 901 84023; Kempff to Köpke, Brussels, Dec. 31, 1916, IIIb 47827, ibid.

218. Thiel, "*Menschenbassin Belgien*," 216–17, 229–37.

219. Dutch ministry of foreign affairs to the German government, The Hague, Nov. 29, 1916, IIIb 45895, BAB R 901 84023.

220. Typed copy of State Department statement, handed to Bethmann by Joseph Grew on Dec. 5, 1916, IIIb 46302, BAB R 901 84023; cf. Grey to Secretary of State, Berlin, Dec. 5, 1916, *FRUS*, Suppl. 1916, 868 and Sec. of State to Grew, Washington, Nov. 29, 1916, ibid., 71.

221. United States, *Lansing Papers*, 1:43.

and a desire to find some way to prevent the continuance of a practice which is a reversion to the barbarous methods of the military empires of antiquity.[222]

Under these circumstances world opinion found it galling that Germany officially clung to the story that the deportations were legal.[223]

Civilian Forced Labor in the Zone of Fire

More shocks were to come. If the chancellor, Bissing, and the AA thought that they had compromised with OHL, trading deportations to Germany in order to stop forced civilian labor in the rear zone, they were mistaken. This issue raises the question of how successful other decision makers could be against the institutionalized relentlessness of OHL, particularly once they had weakened their own ground by compromising on basic principles. Even before the final decision to permit deportations to Germany, OHL had issued an order regulating (forced) civilian work battalions (ZABs), claiming to the rest of the government that they were legal under international law.[224] Ludendorff notified the AA of his intention to use ZABs in the rear zone at the beginning of January 1917, but in fact, OHL had apparently been using them long before: in January 1917 Reichstag member Matthias Erzberger already informed the AA of reliable information about "numerous forced laborers in the operation zone for a long time."[225] Beside the distastefulness of forced labor, there were two illegalities here: civilians were doing forbidden military work (on the Siegfried line), and some were doing it under fire.[226] Confronted by both the catastrophic public relations mess of the deportations and flagrant proof that OHL had gone behind their back, the AA swung into action.

The AA first tried to make permanent the temporary halt of deportations that Germany had announced (January 9, 1917) in face of the international uproar and widespread evidence of incompetent military and industrial execution; Reich Interior Minister Helfferich had reported that "the people [deportees] are frighteningly skinny and the number of deaths is large."[227] The AA finally succeeded (February 24, 1917), but not before Ludendorff, during long negotiations, had insisted on weakening Germany's

---

222. Ibid.

223. That is what Bethmann told Grew, and these were Zimmermann's instructions to the AA: Grew to Sec. of State, Berlin, Dec. 5, 1916, *FRUS,* Suppl. 1916, 868; Montgelas note to Sec. of State to Grew, Nov. 29, 1916, IIIb 46302, BAB R 901 84023.

224. "Dienstanweisung für die Aufstellung und Verwendung von Zivil-Arbeiter-Bataillonen (Z.A.B.)," n.d., but Oct. 3, 1916, IIc Nr. 30070, BAB R 901 82946, defended to the AA as legal in [by order of] Hahndorff to AA, IIc Nr. 33931, GHQ, Sept. 4, 1917, ibid.

225. War ministry / war office to AA, Nr. 30/1. 17 AZS 3b, Berlin, Jan. 3, 1917, BAB R 901 84023; Erzberger to Gesandter Baron v. Bergen im AA, Berlin, Jan. 5, 1917, BAB R 901 84024.

226. French sources reported civilians building trenches as early as May 1915 near La Fère and Cambrai: Special commissar of Annemasse to ministry of war, etc., May 11, 1915, SHAT 5N 87.

227. Helferrich to Bethmann, Berlin, Feb. 15, 1917, BAB R 901 84025.

public announcement by leaving open the possibility of renewed deportations ("temporarily stopped"). The chancellor wanted to hold out for permanent stoppage, but the AA representative at GHQ telegraphed: "I assure you that it is impossible to get L[udendorff] to accept different wording for the Kaiser's announcement. The meeting lasted three hours. If the whole thing were given up now...we would lose the entire battle and the impression here would be dreadful."[228] Part of the package deal involved insisting to the Kaiser that the whole enterprise had followed international law.[229]

The AA's partial success in stopping deportations to Germany was not repeated regarding forced civilian labor in the fire zone, however. Foreign Secretary Arthur Zimmermann insisted (February 1, 1917) that Ludendorff stop using civilian forced labor just behind the front because it violated both international law and OHL's promise to the AA/chancellor when they had acquiesced to deportations to Germany.[230] The AA saw through Ludendorff's claim that only "volunteers" worked on military projects in the rear (*Wirklicher Legationsrat* Dr. Köpke: "the free will [that Ludendorff claimed] isn't worth much").[231] The AA knew how little voluntarism there was among "volunteers" everywhere, since it was coauthor of the policy to produce them by force, either by lower wages for non-volunteers (as it preferred), or by criminalization (Bissing's method), or as camp commanders did, by giving them less food and worse conditions.[232] Historians agree that most "volunteers" in East and West were in fact disguised forced laborers—as General Wilhelm Gayl said, "volunteering is to be encouraged by all means according to the motto: 'if you don't come, we'll come get you.'"[233] After claiming that all those doing military work in the rear or in the fire zone were volunteers, Ludendorff and his aides in the succeeding months dredged up one explanation after another to silence the AA and general government: Belgian deportees returning from Germany were sent to the rear only "if they fulfilled the legal conditions"; or, civilians already living in the area (i.e., non-deportees) could be used legally for emergency (military) work; or, workers in the fire zone were kept only in areas that were not regularly shelled; or, removing laborers would harm German authority; or, Ludendorff simply denied everything.[234] The quartermaster general's office always hid behind the AA's legal brief, claiming in September 1917 that there were "hundreds of thousands of volunteers" and a declining number of ZABs working legally at the front.[235] That same report

228. Lersner to Grünau, Kreuznach, Feb. 21, 1916, BAB R 901 84025. See other correspondence, ibid.

229. Chancellor to Kaiser, personal report [*Immediatvortrag*], Berlin, Feb. 28, 1917, BAB R 901 84025.

230. Zimmermann to Grünau, Berlin, Feb. 1, 1917, BAB R 901 84024.

231. Grünau to AA, Nr. 77, Pleß, Feb. 7, 1917, BAB R 901 84024; Köpke note of Feb. 13 to same.

232. It was Köhler's suggestion to incarcerate Belgians at the overcrowded camp in Holzminden to encourage them to volunteer: *UA* 3:1, 354.

233. Cited in Elsner, "Ausländerbeschäftigung," 540. "Volunteers" really forced laborers: Herbert, *Geschichte der Ausländerbeschäftigung,* 89–91; Zunkel, "Die ausländischen Arbeiter," 295, 298, 301, 310; Liulevicius, *War Land,* 74; Gromaire, *L'occupation allemande en France,* 208, 220. Cf. Ritter, *Sword and Scepter,* 362, 369; Thiel, "*Menschenbassin Belgien,*" ch. 8; Westerhoff, *Zwangsarbeit im Ersten Weltkrieg,* 25–30, 45n41, 107–8, 202–3, 207–8, 215, 263.

234. Lersner to AA, GHQ, May 24, 1917, BAB R 901 84026; Ludendorff to AA, GHQ, May 23, 1917, ibid.; Lersner to AA, GHQ, May 25, 1917, ibid.; Falkenhausen to chancellor, Brussels, June 4, 1917, ibid.; Ludendorff to Friedrich, July 16, 1917, ibid. R 901 82946; Ludendorff to Friedrich, Aug. 2, 1917, ibid.

235. On instructions of Hahndorff to AA, IIc Nr. 33931, GHQ, Sept. 4, 1917, BAB R 901 82946.

clearly shows that OHL used civilian forced workers to substitute for prisoners of war whom the Germans by agreement with the Allies had had to withdraw from within thirty kilometers of the front.[236] These forced laborers were so valuable that in April 1918 OHL opposed extending the thirty-kilometer limit to civilians, an open admission of its long-standing policy.[237]

In the end, both the OHL and Bissing were right. Although lethal mismanagement and international protest halted the deportations after only seventy-five days, their frightful example did substantially increase the number of "volunteers" available for OHL's military projects and munitions work. Nevertheless, the political-international cost was enormous. Both President Wilson's plan for mediation and Bethmann's peace offer occurred simultaneously with the deportations, which discredited them both. The general government's patient work trying to build favorable sentiment toward Germany was destroyed. And Germany's reputation as unscrupulous scofflaw seemed once again confirmed.

236. See chapter 9. The report admitted using workers only eighteen kilometers from the front; ibid.
237. Keller and Romberg tel. to Eckart, Bern, April 23, 1918, IIIb 15159, BAB R 901 84193.

5

Great Britain and the Blockade

Great Britain's "blockade" was its most controversial method of warfare during the First World War.[1] Controversy at the time focused primarily on its legality and only secondarily on the ethics of potentially starving enemy civilians, though that issue grew in importance. We will begin with the legal dilemma. As the world's preeminent naval, maritime, financial, and commercial power, Britain, in its use of that power, provides an apposite comparison to Germany's use of its preeminent army. Britain's methods were often hard to square with international law, and they therefore raise a number of questions: How much did the British government value international law when it seemed to clash with its interests as a belligerent? How important was international law to its decision-making process and to its decisions? When it broke the law or went beyond it into uncharted territory, was it simply violating the law, or was it making new law? What kind of universal principles followed from its policies and the assumptions within them? These are the questions this chapter and the next pursue. We must begin with the legal situation in which Britain found itself in 1914.

The Laws of Sea Warfare and the Declaration of London

The policy of economic warfare that Britain discussed before 1914 and adopted thereafter aimed to strangle the German economy by blocking all seaborne trade. Such a policy

---

1. What became known at the time and ever since as "the blockade" was not a proper blockade under law. Sometimes to remind the reader of that fact, I shall use quotation marks.

faced two knotty problems: one geographical and the other legal. Although the British Isles blocked Germany's easy access to the ocean, it was almost impossible to stop trade between Germany and neutral Sweden or Norway because of their proximity to Germany via the narrow Skagerrak and Kattegat waters. Worse, Germany could import supplies overland via Denmark or especially Holland with its great international port, Rotterdam. All were neutral nations and therefore were legally entitled to trade non-contraband goods with any belligerent power. Stopping supplies to Germany thus required interfering with neutral trade and squaring that interference with international law.

The legal problem lay in the indeterminacy of the maritime laws of war. The rules of land warfare had been hammered out through repeated conflicts among four relatively evenly matched powers: France, Russia, Prussia/Germany, and Austria(-Hungary). There were areas of disagreement and "blank spots," but there were sufficient shared practices and customs to have made substantial codification of the laws of land warfare possible at the Hague Peace Conferences of 1899 and 1907. The naval situation differed fundamentally, because of Britain's centuries-long dominance at sea and the existence in every naval war of neutral states whose interests in continuing trade with Britain's enemies clashed directly with Britain's interest in stopping it. Until 1856 no basic agreement could be reached. But the Crimean War had brought together the two old naval enemies, France and Britain, and at the peace conference in Paris they agreed on these minimal rules: non-contraband enemy goods on neutral ships were free from seizure; non-contraband neutral goods aboard enemy ships were free; and to be legal, blockades must effectively "prevent access to the coast of the enemy," that is, they had to be real, not paper blockades. The mere announcement of a blockade without the means to enforce it was a fiction binding no power to observe it as lawful.[2] The Paris Declaration of 1856 was the first codification of international law. It was a major British concession, regarding both blockade and seizure, the two major belligerent rights and, together with capturing enemy merchant ships, the only ways to exercise economic warfare at sea. These concessions partly reflected Britain's increasingly complex position at sea. It was both the dominant naval power *and* the world's largest trader, financier, and insurer of ships; and it more and more depended on imported food that it no longer produced at home. Furthermore, without territorial aspirations in Europe, Britain could imagine that in many major wars it would remain neutral. Therefore, protection of neutral trade and insistence on genuine, effective blockades seemed as much in its interests as upholding the belligerent rights of blockade and capture.

At the 1907 Hague Peace Conference states had tried and failed to extend codification of the laws of war from land warfare to the sea, but they had agreed to establish an International Prize Court to adjudicate maritime disputes. Except for the Declaration of Paris, however, it had no law code to apply. Fearing that the new court might reject many customary British practices at sea because most of its judges would be from neutral or Continental countries, the British government invited the world's naval powers to London to

2. 1856 Paris Declaration in Adam Roberts and Richard Guelff, eds., *Documents on the Laws of War* (Oxford, 2004), 48–49.

set down in writing customary maritime law. The Admiralty and the Foreign Office were equally interested in a clear set of laws for naval warfare. Britain hoped

> to set out as definitely as possible the points of law in which the principles upheld by all the Powers—and also...their practice—are in agreement....The main task of the Conference will not therefore be to deliberate *de lege ferenda* [that is, to develop new, binding law by recognizing as law emerging norms or practices that hitherto were not considered obligatory].... The proposed Declaration should...place on record that those Powers which are best qualified and most directly interested, recognize...that there exists in fact a common law of nations of which it is the purport of the Declaration, in the common interest, to set out the principles.[3]

The result was the Declaration of London of 1909 (DoL). Befitting the inherently confused state of maritime law, however, the delegates in London were forced to go beyond mere codification of custom; the DoL contained new law based upon a set of compromises among the participants. Consequently, article 65 required states to accept the entire document; they could not exercise the usual right to reserve individual sections.[4]

Concerning commercial warfare, the DoL "not only gives greater definiteness to the rights of neutrals but actually takes away certain powers against them which the Anglo-American Prize Law has hitherto vested in the belligerents." That was the summary of Sir Herbert William Malkin, one of the Foreign Office's lawyers, writing during the war.[5] The DoL tightened the rules on maintaining and notifying blockade. Regarding contraband, the 1909 agreement contained two innovations with great significance for the World War. For the first time it specified lists of contraband in the traditional three categories of absolute (strictly military items), conditional (goods that might be used by the military), and free (goods with no military value that consequently were free from seizure). These lists turned out to be far too restrictive to apply adequately to industrial warfare. Second, the DoL recognized as legal an important commercial weapon, the doctrine of "continuous voyage," but restricted its application. The United States had used this practice during the Civil War when it had stopped ships and seized cargo ostensibly heading for neutral ports in cases where the cargo was actually going to be transshipped overland to the enemy. Continuous voyage thus used the ultimate destination of goods to permit interdiction of contraband trade even to neutral countries. The doctrine in Anglo-American law would have allowed Britain to stop neutral vessels carrying any contraband to the Netherlands bound ultimately for Germany. However, the DoL compromise permitted interdiction under cover of continuous voyage to apply only to absolute contraband (article 30),

---

3. Foreign Minister Grey to British ambassadors to the invited countries, Nov. 10, 1908, in James Brown Scott, ed., *The Declaration of London* (New York, 1919), 18–19.

4. James Brown Scott, *Declaration of London,* also available in the Human Rights Library of the University of Minnesota at http://www1.umn.edu/humanrts/instree/1909b.htm.

5. H. W. Malkin, "Anglo-American Prize Practice and the Declaration of London," unsigned, undated memorandum in FO 800/904, Malkin Papers, Contraband, 1855–1914, pt. 1.

not to items on the conditional contraband list or to blockade. Blockaders could not apply the doctrine, regardless of the ultimate destination of the cargo, if the vessel was "on her way to a non-blockaded port" (article 19) and neutral ports were not subject to blockade.

Thus, in Malkin's words, the DoL "restricts the flexibility which has hitherto characterized the English and American practice as regards conditional contraband."

Germany was highly satisfied with the DoL because it virtually guaranteed that Germany could continue to import necessary supplies through neutral Holland. The conditional contraband list contained foodstuffs, clothing, money, vehicles, boats, railway materials, planes, fuel, lubricants, powder and explosives "not specially prepared for use in war," barbed wire, horseshoes and equipment, field glasses and other optical equipment (article 24). None of these could be seized under continuous voyage. Germany was also pleased at the new rules of blockade. Its chief legal negotiator at the London Conference, Johannes Kriege, reported back to Berlin: "In the rules of blockade the German suggestions have by and large been accepted, and it is now particularly clear that a blockade-line must not cut off neutral ports. An enemy fleet trying to blockade the German North Sea ports could not simply block the Channel and the line running from the Shetland Islands to Norway, but must come much closer to the German coast."[6] In fact, those were exactly the lines the British Admiralty adopted in the First World War, to protect its ships from German mines, torpedo boats, and submarines.

The DoL was therefore much more advantageous to Britain as a neutral power than as a belligerent. But, according to Cecil J. B. Hurst, the chief legal adviser to the Foreign Office, protection of neutral trade was not Britain's primary object at the London Conference. Instead, the first secretary of the Committee of Imperial Defense (CID), Sir George Sydenham Clarke (later Lord Sydenham), had concluded from the Boer War (1899–1901) that seizing contraband antagonized neutral powers too much to be used effectively and that Britain should give up that method of commercial warfare and stick purely to blockade. His views were approved by an interdepartmental committee that included the Admiralty. In 1907 Britain had even tried unsuccessfully to abolish the right to seize contraband altogether, thus leaving blockade and the seizure of enemy merchant vessels as the sole maritime (economic) belligerent rights. So great was Britain's interest in "curbing the pretensions of belligerent prize courts" through establishing a permanent international prize court of appeal with a firm code of law that it was willing to compromise as it did in 1909.[7]

It has puzzled historians why the Admiralty would so lightly have relinquished previous rights to seizure. The answer may lie in the trade-offs affecting the rules of blockade. In exchange for tightening the rules of notification (special notification) that France wanted, Britain (and the United States) received implicit recognition of the legality of distant blockade. In place of the old rule of line blockade that had required blockaders to be stationed close to the targeted ports, the Continental nations acknowledged that defensive weapons such as torpedo boats and automatic contact mines now made close

---

6. Kriege to Chancellor Bernhard v. Bülow, Berlin, Jan. 5, 1909, AA/PA, Akten betr. Staats- und Völkerrecht, Bd. 7, R 19582.

7. Hurst memo, undated, but probably 1927, in ADM 116/3619.

blockade too hazardous. They recognized a "sphere of action" *(rayon d'action)* of up to eight hundred miles in which a blockade could operate, so long as it was effective.[8] Britain's delegate, Vice Admiral Sir Edmond J. W. Slade, underscored that it was impossible to set an exact distance, "so long as the effectiveness of the blockade were assured and the main squadron did not block neutral ports."[9] Although the British Admiralty would have liked to retain the Anglo-American interpretation of continuous voyage (that is, that it applied to all categories of contraband, not just absolute), it was not necessary, because an effective (distant) blockade permitted the belligerent to seize all goods anyway. Blockade was a stronger weapon than capture, so it did not matter if Sir Edward Grey gave up the wider, British doctrine of continuous voyage, as the Germans insisted, so as to save the codification.[10]

Thus, the Foreign Office and the Admiralty both supported the DoL.[11] They were greatly embarrassed when the House of Lords refused to ratify it, largely owing to fears that it did not adequately protect Britain's own food supply in wartime.[12] Grey intended to get the House of Commons to override the Lords' veto, but the war intervened.[13] The other signatories (Austria-Hungary, France, Germany, Italy, Japan, the Netherlands, Russia, Spain, and the United States) had all waited for British ratification before declaring their own. As of August 1, 1914, no state had registered ratification of the DoL.[14] The DoL therefore never actually came into effect, and in its entirety it bound no signatory, least of all Britain, which had refused ratification.[15]

Yet the legal status of the DoL was uncertain. Where it embodied customary law, it was certainly binding. That was not the case for those articles that followed mere usages (that

---

8. Georges Kaeckenbeeck, "Divergences between British and Other Views on International Law," *Grotius Society, Problems of the War: Papers Read before the Society in the Year 1918* 4 (1918): 237–38; "Instructions to the British Delegates by Sir Edward Grey," Dec. 1, 1908, in Scott, *Declaration of London,* 222; John W. Coogan, *The End of Neutrality: The United States, Britain, and Maritime Rights, 1899–1915* (Ithaca, NY, 1981), 99.

9. Cited in Alexander Freiherr Hold von Ferneck, *Die Reform des Seekriegsrechts durch die Londoner Konferenz 1908/09,* Handbuch des Völkerrechts (Berlin, 1914), 69n1.

10. Christopher Martin, "The Declaration of London: A Matter of Operational Capability," *Historical Research* 82, no. 218 (November 2009): 731–55; Nicholas A. Lambert, *Planning Armageddon: British Economic Warfare and the First World War* (Cambridge, MA, 2012), 85–87, 135–37.

11. There were dissenting voices in the Admiralty, and Lambert reads their slowness in producing the new Prize Manual as indication of second thoughts; nonetheless, with a few exceptions where Britain kept its old rules, the Prize Manual was identical to the DoL: ADM 116/1232; Lambert, *Planning Armageddon,* 94–98.

12. Coogan, *End of Neutrality,* 125–47.

13. Ibid., 136.

14. The U.S. Senate had "advised and consented" to the DoL, but the State Department withheld that agreement from deposit in London; thus, the United States never fully ratified the DoL: *New York Times,* Oct. 27, 1914; James Wilford Garner, *International Law and the World War* (London, 1920), 1:30.

15. The modern trend to require signatories to do nothing to defeat the purpose of a treaty that has not yet been ratified developed in international law after the First World War and in any case applies to treaties that ultimately do come into effect and excepts signatories that subsequently decline ratification or withdraw from the treaty: Martin A. Rogoff, "The International Legal Obligations of Signatories to an Unratified Treaty," *Maine Law Review* 32 (1980): 263–99.

is, national practices not yet recognized by other states as binding law),[16] or which were the result of innovation or compromise. These last categories included the contraband lists and the sections on continuous voyage. Yet the DoL had considerable prestige. Its preamble stated that it "correspond[ed] in substance with the generally recognized principles of international law."[17] Germany and France had incorporated it wholesale into their respective prize laws, and the navies of Britain and Italy had adopted it with small modifications.[18] During the war, states and international lawyers, belligerent and neutral alike, cited portions of the DoL as law, yet disagreed about its legal status generally.[19]

The DoL remains a legal puzzle. It epitomizes the modern legal dilemma of *lex ferenda,* or soft law in the era of codification. Enough states and legal scholars thought it authoritative that it seemed to reflect *opinio juris* in the modern sense of obligation arising not from consistent state practice, which was missing in the maritime sphere, but rather from agreement that the law ought to develop in this direction.[20] However, unlike the multilateral conventions that ground the modern, more extensive understanding of *opinio juris,* the DoL was never ratified, so it lacked the substance of treaty law. Instead, contemporaries understood that it mixed customary law and innovation for the "near future." The Austrian international jurist Alexander Hold von Ferneck acknowledged that at the conference Austria-Hungary and Germany had both "emancipated themselves thoroughly from their national laws and took the position of *de lege ferenda.*"[21] That is, they considered that they were forming, at least partly, new international law.[22] During the war, Britain's position down to mid-1916, when it ceased referring to the DoL at all, was to sift the preexisting customary law from the innovations. In February 1915 Lord Charles Beresford asked in Parliament whether the DoL "has the authority of international law." The

---

16. Charles de Visscher, "Les lois de la guerre et la théorie de la nécessité," *Revue général de droit international public* 24 (1917): 106–8.

17. Scott, *Declaration of London,* 114.

18. Joachim Schröder, *Die U-Boote des Kaisers; Die Geschichte des deutschen U-Boot-Krieges gegen Großbritannien im Ersten Weltkrieg* (Bonn, 2003), 73. On France: Adm. Slade note of Aug. 7, 1914, in ADM 116/1233.

19. The Netherlands thought it "a significant step forward" in legal development, but not binding law, whereas Sweden, Norway, and Denmark pronounced it a "precipitate [*Niederschlag*] of the current state of international law." A French internal document stated that the DoL "lacked the character of an international contract with reciprocal obligation." Loudon to Gevers, Nov. 19, 1914, containing note, *BPNL* 4, doc. 252; Arno Spindler, *Der Handelskrieg mit U-Booten* (Berlin, 1932), 1:48; "Note pour le Président du Conseil," end of Dec. 1915, *DDFr* 1915, 3: doc. 726; this same note carries a different date in the archive: June 11, 1916, MAE Blocus 45. Cf. J. Perrinjaquet, "La guerre européenne et les relations commerciales des belligérants et des neutres. L'application des théories de la contrebande de guerre et du blocus," *Revue générale de droit international public* 22 (1915): 128, 138, 175; Paul Fauchille, "La guerre sous-marine allemande," *Revue générale de droit international public* 25 (1918): 80; Hugh H. L. Bellot, "War Crimes: Their Prevention and Punishment," *Grotius Society, Problems of the War: Papers Read before the Society in the Year 1916* 2 (1917): 35–36; Dr. Neukamp's contribution to "Der Lusitania-Fall," *Zeitschrift für Völkerrecht* 9 (1916): 193. Even sometimes the truculent Churchill: Lambert, *Planning Armageddon,* 244.

20. On the modern view: Brian D. Lepard, *Customary International Law: A New Theory with Practical Applications* (Cambridge, 2010), 112, 118 for list of scholars agreeing with him.

21. Hold von Ferneck, *Die Reform des Seekriegsrechts,* 15.

22. *De lege ferenda:* see discussion in chapter 3.

first Foreign Office draft reply, by W. A. Stewart, noted that the DoL "was intended...to embody...generally recognized principles of international law" and was binding "insofar as this intention was fulfilled." Hurst rewrote this reply to say that the DoL "forms a convenient summary of many of the rules of international law on the questions with which it deals." Foreign Minister Grey rewrote Hurst's version to say: "The authority that attaches" to it "is that of the previously existing rules of international law embodied in it."[23] Grey and Cecil repeated that position numerous times.[24] In autumn 1914, international opinion on the legal status of the DoL was split. If one believed that the DoL was hard law, then Britain's "blockade" was from the beginning unlawful; if one judged the DoL a mix of *lex ferenda* and binding customary law, then the picture was much more complicated.

The uncertainties of naval law make it hard to compare Britain's prewar naval planning against the Schlieffen Plan's cavalier dismissal of unquestionable treaty law. Therefore, in the next section we focus on process: how decisions were made, who made them, and the importance of legal considerations in planning.

Prewar Naval Planning

British prewar military planning is not the clearest of subjects. Military and naval leaders disagreed on the wisdom of sending an expeditionary force to the Continent, while naval leaders weighed battle against economic warfare, and among those favoring the latter, they argued over what method to use (commercial warfare, close or distant blockade). Civilian leaders, including the prime minister and influential cabinet members, always saved the final decision for the moment when circumstances would finally be clear. Consequently, "plans" shifted continually, and their reality is always questionable. Recently, Nicholas A. Lambert has offered a well-researched and clear, though controversial, interpretation of prewar naval plans.[25] He argues that instead of sending the British Expeditionary Force (BEF), Britain intended to launch a full-scale economic/commercial war designed to destroy the German economy quickly by disrupting its credit, insurance, and commercial lifelines. Because at the same time planning for the BEF continued, and more so because the BEF was actually deployed, historians are likely to continue to debate this issue. However, Lambert's detailed account of the maritime planning that preceded the actual measures taken in 1914 is helpful in revealing naval and civil leadership thinking about international law. That thinking is revealed in three policy areas: distant blockade, ratification of the DoL, and immediate prewar planning for economic warfare.

---

23. Stewart note of Feb. 2, 1915, Hurst of Feb. 3, 1915, Grey, n.d., in FO 372/752, file 751, no. 16815 and no. 18254. Ultimately, Mr. Primrose answered Beresford's question differently. He said, "The Declaration has not been ratified, and has therefore not the same authority as a universally ratified code of law."

24. Grey, Oct. 28, 1915, no. 161757; Cecil, Dec. 23, 1915, no. 200398, both FO 372/752, file 751. Cecil, Mar. 9, 1916, FO 382/1126, no. 47202, file 1639.

25. Lambert, *Planning Armageddon.*

Beginning in 1905 during the First Moroccan Crisis, Director of Naval Intelligence Captain Sir Charles L. Ottley developed ideas for a distant blockade of German seaports. In the following two years his ideas were elaborated upon by a secret committee set up by the first sea lord (Lord Tweedmouth) and the assumptions behind the campaign later set down in a long memorandum, "The Economic Effect of War on German Trade." Reginald McKenna, the first lord of the Admiralty, circulated the paper in December 1908 to the Committee of Imperial Defense, the inter-ministerial body charged with military planning. The CID was an advisory committee only—the cabinet held the final decision, but CID deliberations were important for working out basic problems of policy so that later, concrete decisions could be made quickly. "The Economic Effect of War" proposed to bring the full weight of Britain's maritime, financial, and communications power to bear against Germany's economic vulnerabilities. Targeting primarily industry and finance, and secondarily food, trade on German and British merchant ships was to be completely stopped, together with credit, insurance, and other financial instruments that were the lifeblood of the modern economy. The ensuing credit panic, it was thought, would freeze the economy and cause Germany's swift collapse. Whereas blockade was normally a slow weapon effective only in long wars, Admiralty authors believed that the interconnection of modern industrial economies and their resulting fragility made any significant disruption immediately fatal. Thus modern blockade could actually substitute for sending the BEF.[26]

All of the navy's economic war plans down to 1912 assumed that neutral trade flowing into Germany through neutral ports in Scandinavia and the Netherlands was negligible because the neutrals possessed too few merchant ships and too limited port facilities to handle the surge of goods that might be redirected on account of the blockade. Because 74 percent of oceangoing merchant ships were either British- or German-owned, seizing enemy ships and blocking trade on one's own would effectively stop most trade. Consequently, until 1912 Britain's plans all envisioned letting neutral ships continue their legal trade to neutral ports.[27]

The Admiralty believed that its plans for distant blockade of the North Sea German ports were legal under international law, even after the DoL. Director of Naval Intelligence Rear Admiral Alexander Bethell set down the navy's legal theory on October 7, 1911.[28] He held that the DoL's large *rayon d'action* of eight hundred miles permitted a distant blockade that included the Channel and, in the north, Scapa Flow, so long as it was effective. He argued that it would violate neither article 18 ("The blockading forces must not bar access to neutral ports or coasts") nor article 19 ("Whatever may be the ulterior destination of a vessel or of her cargo, she cannot be captured for breach of blockade, if, at the moment, she is on her way to non-blockaded port"), since neutral vessels would be permitted to proceed to neutral ports.[29] Bethell felt that Britain would win its case before the Hague Prize Court on grounds that these articles were ambiguous. Bethell's views on law were

---

26. Ibid., 40–43, 77–79, 121–24.

27. Ibid., 40, 77–79, 238–39.

28. Ibid., 133–37, 217–18, 559n231.

29. Bethell minute, Oct. 7, 1911, "Blockade of the North Sea Coast of Germany," ADM 1/8132; G. Hope minute of Sept. 8, 1911, ibid.

accepted by Admiral Sir Arthur K. Wilson, Sir William Graham Greene (the assistant to the Admiralty secretary), and naval planners. In August 1914, Attorney General John Simon rejected them.

Some historians have seen in the struggle of a few officers to prevent ratification of the DoL proof that Britain outright planned to break international law. In early 1911, two successive secretaries of the CID squared off against each other. Admiral Charles Ottley (secretary from 1907 to 1912), who had been a delegate to the London Conference, defended the DoL, while Captain Maurice Hankey (secretary from 1912 to 1938) excoriated it. Hankey told a colleague, Major Adrian Grant Duff, of their meeting with First Lord of the Admiralty Reginald McKenna. Grant Duff's diary noted:

> 22 February 1911: The "worry over the Declaration of London" still goes on—and Hankey has now turned against it and denounced it as equivalent to tying up our right arm in a war with Germany.
>
> [Former First Sea Lord Admiral John "Jacky"] Fisher apparently allowed it to be negotiated with the deliberate intention of tearing it up in the event of war. Characteristic.
>
> 24 February: McKenna's standpoint seems much the same—the Germans are sure to infringe it in the early days of the war, then with great regret we tear it up—If they don't infringe it we must invent an infringement.[30]

Avner Offer has interpreted these lines as evidence of Britain's, or at least Fisher's, perfidy—especially shocking since Fisher had been a delegate to the Hague Convention of 1899.[31] We are already acquainted with Fisher's vituperations on international law. They should be taken seriously as impatience common among military men generally, but not as automatic national policy, since, as Lambert notes, Fisher knew he did not set policy himself and "understood the constitutional limitations of his office."[32]

Hankey's notes on their meeting show that McKenna accorded international law greater purview than did Hankey.[33] "If the question were entirely untrammeled by previously existing international obligations, he [McKenna] would feel bound to adopt" Hankey's view, McKenna told him. The first lord tried to appease Hankey by saying that "international treaties are easily evaded," either by a large British naval victory that would lessen neutrals' power to object, or by finding "some ~~excuse~~ pretext...for our acting contrary to the provisions of the Declaration of Paris and the Declaration of London," a pretext he thought the Germans would supply themselves. But when Hankey pressed on and suggested a formal Admiralty statement that "we had no intention of adhering to it [the DoL] if it did not suit our purpose," McKenna flatly rejected that idea. The Foreign Office "would never permit such a record to be made," he replied. He acknowledged that Britain might find it necessary in

---

30. Cited in Avner Offer, *The First World War: An Agrarian Interpretation* (Oxford, 1989), 280.

31. Ibid., 278–80.

32. Lambert, *Planning Armageddon*, 100.

33. Memorandum of a conversation on Feb. 23, 1911, between Hankey, McKenna, and Ottley (in Hankey's hand and with his corrections), CAB 17/87.

wartime to violate the declarations, but in that case "neutrals would be fully indemnified."[34] In other words, McKenna (and Ottley) held open the possibility that circumstances might permit Britain to kick loose of the DoL, either through reprisal (in the event of German violations), or by an overwhelming naval victory. But Britain still would recognize the validity of law by paying an indemnity. Lambert believes that Hankey's intemperate opposition to the DoL came from misunderstanding the Admiralty's plans for economic warfare, which the Admiralty thought could be applied effectively within legal bounds.[35]

While the DoL continued to be the framework within which naval planning occurred, after the Second Moroccan Crisis (1911) it seemed ever more likely that Britain might be drawn into a major Continental war in which economic warfare would be critical. The CID's deliberations became more urgent. Subcommittees studied many aspects of economic war policy: "local transportation and distribution of supplies; treatment of enemy and neutral ships; treatment of aliens; press and postal censorship; aerial navigation; wireless stations throughout the Empire; submarine cable communications; trading with the enemy; insurance of British shipping; resources and economic position of London; co-ordination of departmental action."[36] In most of these areas, legal constraints played a central role in discussions, and lawyers provided expert advice and were instrumental in reaching conclusions. In the case of "Trading with the Enemy," Prime Minister Herbert Asquith chose as chair Hamilton Cuffe, fifth Earl of Desart, an expert in international maritime law, former member of Britain's commissions preparing for both the Hague and the London conferences, and Britain's senior plenipotentiary to the latter.[37] Offering expert advice was Professor Lassa Oppenheim, Britain's foremost international lawyer, "as it was considered important to ascertain our law and, so far as possible, the law and the state of opinion in other countries."[38] The actual meetings of that subcommittee bristled with lawyers: John Paget Mellor (the procurator general), A. H. Dennis (the Treasury's solicitor), Cecil J. B. Hurst (the Foreign Office's legal adviser), and J. S. Risley (legal adviser to the Colonial Office).

Britain's prewar discussions also reveal a broad understanding of belligerence going far beyond the mere military. A 1908 Admiralty paper, "The Economic Effect of War on German Trade," discusses population, raw materials, shipping, freight costs, shifts in commerce due to war, credits and loans, etc. It recognized that Britain's ability to raise wartime loans depended "largely on the attitude which we maintain with other nations."[39] The CID subcommittee on "Trading with the Enemy" foresaw that policy might have to be tailored

---

34. Ibid. Coogan says this conversation remained entirely private, known only to the three: Coogan, *End of Neutrality,* 139. Hankey's memo says that Ottley brought the matter before the Admiralty.

35. Ottley: Lambert, *Planning Armageddon,* 148. Misunderstanding: 147.

36. Offer, *First World War,* 293n33.

37. Lambert, *Planning Armageddon,* 93–94, 142–43.

38. "Report and Proceedings of the Standing Sub-Commitee of the Committee of Imperial Defence on Trading with the Enemy 1912 (*Secret*)" 1912, 1, CAB 16/18A.

39. "Report and Proceedings of a Sub-Committee of the Committee of Imperial Defence on the Military Needs of the Empire 1909," appendix 5, ADM memo, Dec. 12, 1908, "The Economic Effect of War on German Trade" (CID Paper E-4), CAB 16/5.

to these considerations: the outcome of military operations, "the number of powers engaged in the war; the extent of neutral territory which might be violated by one or the other belligerent; the attitude of allies towards the question of trading with the enemy; the experience gained of the effect on trade of the prohibitions, and of the extent to which they might be evaded; and the trend of public opinion."[40] British planners went into the war with a sophisticated, multifaceted, and flexible conception of belligerence in which law and attitudes toward law in Britain, among its allies, among the neutrals, and even in public opinion, played an important part.

By 1912, the Admiralty recognized the importance of transshipment, the likelihood that Dutch (and possibly Belgian) neutral ports would provision Germany indirectly overland, regardless of a blockade of Germany's North Sea ports.[41] Extending blockade to cover neutral ports was unlawful. Blockade was a weapon used only against enemy states. That customary law principle was codified twice in the DoL: in article 1 ("a blockade must not extend beyond the ports and coasts belonging to or occupied by the enemy") and article 18 ("the blockading forces must not bar access to neutral ports or coasts"). In CID deliberations in February 1912, Lord Reginald Brett Esher for the first time proposed to break that principle and blockade the Belgian port of Antwerp if Germany overran Belgium. Doing so would have to violate Dutch territory because the Dutch river Scheldt ran on both sides of Antwerp. Esher defended his idea by citing reciprocal military necessity: "Our justification for violating the neutrality of Holland would be similar to Germany's justification for infringing the neutrality of Belgium." Hurst opposed Esher's proposal.[42]

The FO view on law is visible in notes that Hurst prepared for the CID subcommittee on various issues. One concerned an idea to prohibit British ships from carrying cotton (on the DoL free list) to neutral ports merely on suspicion that it was bound for Germany. Such a policy adopted at the outbreak of war, "resorted to in cold blood and not under the pressure of events as the war develops," might "entail political disadvantages which will outweigh the immediate naval advantages."[43] He thought that "the world at large" would see it as "an abuse of power" and an affront to the "supporters" of the DoL. British opinion too would resist it as "another violent departure from the established mode of conducting warfare." He continued,

> New rules must of course be made and new practices resorted to by belligerents to meet new circumstances where necessary, but the probable measure of neutral opposition and resentment must control the policy of resorting to any such new belligerent practice. The effect of pushing interference, which is technically legitimate, with neutral commerce too far is to drive the neutral into belligerence

---

40. "Report and Proceedings of the Standing Sub-Committee of the Committee of Imperial Defence on Trading with the Enemy 1912 (*Secret*)" 1912, 5, CAB 16/18A.

41. Graham Greene (ADM) to CID, enclosing V. W. Baddeley to Commanders-in-Chief at Home and Abroad on "treatment of neutral and enemy merchant ships in time of war," Oct. 18, 1911: "For the purpose of preparing the necessary action it may be assumed that the Declaration [of London] has been ratified." 115, CAB 17/86. By 1912: Lambert, *Planning Armageddon,* 164.

42. Minutes of 6th Meeting, Jan. 23, 1912, "Trading with the Enemy," 85, CAB 16/18A.

43. Appendix 26, "Trading with the Enemy," note by Hurst, 425, CAB 16/18A.

in self-defence, as happened in 1812 [when the previously neutral United States declared war on Great Britain].

Hurst's understanding of how international law worked was flexible and practical. Technical legality was an insufficient basis for sound policy because neutral anger had practical long-term consequences: the loss of Britain's standing in domestic and world opinion (as a hypocrite and bully). Even a powerful belligerent faced limits to changing the law. Changing circumstances during the war might legitimate such a move, but not at the outset. Creating new law, whether by innovation or violation, meant convincing "public opinion," overcoming "neutral opposition," and even mollifying supporters of the DoL, regardless of its uncertain legal status.

Hurst's moderation did not convince Esher. In a separate memorandum, Esher presciently outlined Germany's wartime strategy of quickly overrunning France, a disaster that he thought could be countered only by "pressing Germany by vigorous attack on her land frontiers and to blockade every avenue of approach to Germany by sea." "It is obvious," he continued, "that Britain could not venture to hesitate, whatever the political cost might be, to include Rotterdam and Antwerp in the area of blockaded ports."[44] But like Fisher and Hankey, Esher presented these dire possibilities as a deterrent: "So fatal would the pressure be, that I for my part can hardly conceive that Germany, except by an act of madness, would embark upon a war under such conditions."[45] In the law-abiding culture of Liberal Britain, "deterrent" might have been the only way to cloak such radical suggestions, even subjectively for the ambivalent thinker of such thoughts. But they were nonetheless a thought experiment that might have made it easier to adopt extreme policies later on. And of course for a deterrent to work, the enemy must know it; Fisher wanted to publicize the navy's plans for commercial/economic warfare, but that was never done.[46]

If blockading neutral states was illegal, there always remained the possibility of extending the contraband list—the method Britain ultimately chose. Articles 23 and 25 of the DoL permitted additions to both the absolute and conditional lists upon declaration. The "Trading with the Enemy" report (1912) recommended that route.[47]

The last important prewar meeting of the CID to discuss economic war measures occurred on December 6, 1912.[48] It focused on the "Trading with the Enemy" report and especially on Britain's Achilles' heel: Dutch (and Belgian) neutral ports and their transshipments to Germany. The Congress of Vienna in 1815 had made the Rhine River free for navigation and established an international commission to supervise and guarantee it. It produced the Rhine Conventions of 1831 and (revised) 1868, permitting goods arriving in Rotterdam, Amsterdam, and Dordrecht to be declared "in transit" upon their arrival and

---

44. Appendix 20, memorandum by Lord Esher, "Trading with the Enemy" (1912), 411, CAB 16/18A.

45. Ibid. Fisher, Hankey, and Esher thinking in terms of deterrent: Offer, *First World War,* 239, 240, 250, 295, 298, 303.

46. Lambert, *Planning Armageddon,* 168–69.

47. Appendix 3 (Note by the Secretary on Considerations of Policy), "Trading with the Enemy," 257, CAB 16/18A.

48. Minutes of CID Meeting Nr. 120, Dec. 6, 1912, CAB 2/3.

immediately sent on to Germany or Switzerland.[49] That made the major Dutch ports virtual extensions of Germany's own. At the meeting, Chancellor of the Exchequer David Lloyd George worried that trade via neutral Dutch ports would destroy the efficacy of blockade by half; he called for preventing them from importing "anything in excess of their own average internal consumption of any particular commodity." Colonel Seely of the War Office supported Lloyd George in this first imagining of statistical rationing of neutrals. Prime Minister Asquith objected that such a policy amounted to blockading neutrals, and thus "treat[ing] them as belligerent"—the same legal argument that Hurst had used against Esher.[50] Lloyd George responded by softening his position; he proposed to allow imports based on the prewar average "with a reasonable margin added." He dodged the issue of legality by declaring, "It is not necessary to treat them as hostile." Asquith summarized the proposed policy as either blockading the Netherlands and Belgium if they were hostile, or "limit[ing] their overseas trade" if they were friendly, and in that case "compensating them for their loss of the transit trade by a subsidy." The CID then adopted that position. The subsidy and the added "reasonable margin" were backhanded recognition of the position's illegality and were designed to reduce damage and mollify the neutrals. But, as it turned out, this policy recommendation was not immediately adopted when war broke out.

The prewar "War Books" contained two further preparations of importance. One gave the Admiralty the power to set contraband lists, but required it to consult with the Foreign Office, the War Office, and the Board of Trade. Of far greater significance was the role assigned to the Foreign Office. It, not the navy, was the administrative nerve center of economic warfare at sea. The policies, communications (to British offices and foreign nations), and oversight all lay with the Foreign Office.[51]

August 1914

On August 4, when Britain joined the war, the Admiralty activated elements of its prewar plans. It set its contraband list, it pressured British-owned merchant ships to call at British ports where it off-loaded food and forage, and it began capturing German merchant ships or forcing them to stay in neutral ports. Within one week, with the exception of

---

49. Convention…October 17, 1868 (Act of Mannheim), G. F. Martens, *Nouveau recueil générale de traités* (Göttingen: 1843–1875), 20:355–74, available online: http://babel.hathitrust.org/cgi/pt?id=mdp.39015023068706#view=1up;seq=369.

50. Minutes of 6th Meeting, Jan. 23, 1912, "Trading with the Enemy," 85, CAB 16/18/A.

51. CID, Co-ordination of Departmental Action, War Book (1914 edition), May 30, 1914, CAB 15/5; Zara S. Steiner, "The Foreign Office and the War," in *British Foreign Policy under Sir Edward Grey,* ed. F. H. Hinsley (Cambridge, 1977), 516; K. G. Robbins, "Foreign Policy, Government Structure and Public Opinion," in Hinsley, *British Foreign Policy under Sir Edward Grey,* 539. Lambert stresses the "pre-delegation" of authority to the Admiralty without acknowledging the authority given to the Foreign Office: Lambert, *Planning Armageddon,* 178–81.

the Baltic Sea, no German traders plied the waters.[52] But the most controversial aspects of economic warfare required cabinet approval before adoption, and the ensuing lengthy and acrimonious debates (despite the fact that seven cabinet members had attended the critical December 1912 CID session), the policies approved, and the continuing disagreements on naval strategy at the highest levels of the Admiralty clearly show that the prewar CID meetings had been just what they were designed to be: advisory, not policy-setting.[53]

The Admiralty immediately asked permission to do two contradictory things. It wanted Britain to conclude alliances with Norway, Belgium, and the Netherlands: "The advantages wh[ich] their alliance w[oul]d offer us in blockading Germany and in controlling his naval movements cannot be over-estimated."[54] And it wanted to blockade Rotterdam, one can only presume, if the alliances failed to materialize. In other words, the navy first wanted a diplomatic solution, before it grasped for force. The cabinet and the FO were divided about the wisdom of alliances, and in any event, the Netherlands turned down diplomatic soundings. But a small subset of the cabinet, led by Grey and Lewis Harcourt (Colonial Office), rejected blockading Rotterdam as inconsistent with the reasons for which Britain had gone to war: to uphold the law and to protect small nations.[55]

The parameters of Britain's naval war depended on whether one accepted the rules of the DoL. Grey's first instinct was to jettison the DoL altogether. On August 6 the United States had asked the belligerents whether they intended to apply the DoL in their naval warfare.[56] On August 7 Grey told the U.S. representative that Britain probably would not adhere to it because the Germans had sown "unanchored, floating" mines in the North Sea, and Britain must reserve the right to do the same.[57] This was an odd response, since the DoL contained no provision about mines. It was article 2 of Hague Convention VIII that forbade laying "automatic contact mines off the coast and ports of the enemy, with the sole object of intercepting commercial shipping."[58] Under the impact of Germany's violation of Belgian neutrality, Grey might have reacted emotionally by lumping together different legal codes and finding Germany afoul of them all. Grey mentioned Germany's offense several times that August, and his decisions were obviously affected by his judgment of it.[59]

---

52. In all, 245 ships were captured, 221 were shut up in the Baltic, and 1,059 more languished in neutral ports: Lambert, *Planning Armageddon*, 212. Ian F. W. Beckett, *The Great War* (New York, 2007), 242, agrees with Lambert. Other estimates: Ferro gives the number as 734 ships in neutral ports, Marc Ferro, *The Great War, 1914–1918* (London, 1991), 106; Herwig writes 623: Holger Herwig, *The First World War: Germany and Austria Hungary, 1914–1918* (London, 1997), 288.

53. Both Offer and Lambert emphasize policy setting: Offer, *First World War;* Lambert, *Planning Armageddon*. Seven: Lambert, 217.

54. Memorandum sent by Churchill to Grey, Aug. 3, 1914, cited in Lambert, *Planning Armageddon*, 205.

55. Lambert, *Planning Armageddon*, 206.

56. Bryan to Page, Aug. 6, 1914, *FRUS* 1914, Suppl., 216.

57. Grey to Barclay, Foreign Office, Aug. 7, 1914, *BD*, ser. H, 5: doc. 1.

58. Roberts and Guelff, *Documents*, 105.

59. Archibald C. Bell, *A History of the Blockade of Germany and of the Countries Associated with Her in the Great War, Austria, Bulgaria, and Turkey, 1914–1918* (London, 1937), 39.

Excursus: Automatic Contact Mines

Like the *levée en masse* and insurrection, automatic contact mines were another important legal issue preprogrammed to cause major disagreement when war broke out. Mines were a new invention (first used in the Russo-Japanese War) whose effectiveness and cheap cost permitted small countries with no navy to wreak significant damage even on major naval powers. As indiscriminate weapons, they threatened all neutral commerce. They could shift the balance of power at an extremely low cost. Not surprisingly, Britain, with the largest navy and the largest commercial fleet, had tried to outlaw them almost entirely at the Hague Convention of 1907. It wanted to prohibit all unanchored contact mines; all anchored mines that did not immediately become harmless upon drifting; and the use of mines "to establish or maintain a commercial blockade."[60] Britain was prepared to accept only anchored mines, and then only inside a belligerent's own territorial waters. Many small states rejected Britain's position because mines were a cheap form of defense against stronger naval powers.

But the main opposition to limiting automatic contact mines came from Germany. In a famous statement, former German foreign minister and now delegate to the Hague Conference Adolf Freiherr Marschall von Bieberstein countered the British position:

> I have no need to tell you that I entirely recognize the importance of the codification of rules to be followed in war. But it would be a great mistake to issue rules the strict observance of which might be rendered impossible by the law of facts. It is of the first importance that the international maritime law which we desire to create should only contain clauses the execution of which is possible from a military point of view—is possible even in exceptional circumstances. Otherwise the respect for law would be lessened, and its authority undermined.[61]

Marschall thus reiterated Germany's view on "the law of facts" and "exceptional [military] circumstances," which barred limiting too strictly this new weapon. Germany and France both reserved article 2, which forbade automatic contact mines "off the coast and ports of the enemy, with the sole object of intercepting commercial shipping." Germany objected to the word "sole."[62] Eyre Crowe, one of Britain's most influential representatives at the Hague Conference, was disgusted. He wrote to his wife: "This morning we finished off the mines and neutral rights in naval war. The result is so unsatisfactory that we made a protest in both cases. As regards mines, Marschall committed the folly of making a personally rude retort. Germany's attitude about the use of these mines is generally condemned."[63]

---

60. C. H. Stockton, "The Use of Submarine Mines and Torpedoes in Time of War," *American Journal of International Law* 2, no. 2 (April 1908): 279.

61. Kaeckenbeeck, "Divergences," 246n.

62. Stockton, "Use of Submarine Mines," 280.

63. Eyre Crowe to his wife, Oct. 8, 1907, Bodleian Library, Oxford University, Eyre Crowe Papers, MS. Eng. d. 2902, fols. 84–85.

British authorities concluded from these sessions that Germany intended in the next war to use mines alone to blockade its enemy's ports. Indiscriminate mining would also sink neutral ships and neutral goods aboard enemy ships, thus contravening the Declaration of Paris.[64] In short, British leaders were primed to expect German violations. Moreover, at the signing of Hague Convention VIII, Britain's delegates had announced that "the mere fact that this convention does not prohibit a particular act or proceeding must not be held to debar His Britannic Majesty's government from contesting its legitimacy."[65]

Given this prehistory, it is not surprising that the British Admiralty should have misinterpreted Germany's first belligerent act of the naval war. On August 4, 1914, the auxiliary warship *Königin Luise,* a converted passenger liner, laid a string of 180 mines thirty miles off the coast of Suffolk. The British light cruiser *Amphion* sank the *Königin Luise* the next day, before itself becoming a victim of the German mines on August 6. One hundred and thirty persons, including prisoners saved from the *Königin Luise,* died.[66] The Admiralty interpreted Germany's mine-laying as indiscriminate and its mines as unanchored, and thus illegal. In addition, Britain had pressed at the Hague in 1907 for codification of the customary three-mile limit to territorial waters; it was prepared to accept even ten miles, but neither Convention VIII on mines nor Convention XIII on the rights and duties of neutral powers in naval war defined the distance from shore of territorial waters or forbade laying mines in the open sea. Nevertheless, thirty miles was clearly beyond territorial waters (even today only a twelve-mile limit is recognized), and British authorities rejected as frankly illegal mining the open seas. Admiral Sir Reginald Yorke Tyrwhitt spoke for many when he denounced Germany's action as "indiscriminate" and "distinctly barbaric."[67]

However, the British navy had also been tempted to use the cheap new weapon. In 1905, Captain Ottley had wanted to use them in the open sea, but, more alive to law and public opinion than his German colleagues, he shrank at the thought of neutral and domestic disapproval; Ottley pressed to have the subject regulated at The Hague. In the unsatisfactory aftermath of those negotiations the Admiralty (February 11, 1913) had approved in principle a mine blockade for its allegedly moral effect in deterring neutral shipping and raising insurance rates, both of which aided interdiction of trade to contiguous neutral states; but it lacked the mines to do it.[68] On August 11, 1914, in retaliation against the German mines, including mines in the North Sea, the Admiralty warned shippers that Britain was "at liberty to adopt similar measures in self-defence," making the North Sea doubly dangerous.[69] The cabinet took up the matter after the instant U.S. protest against using

---

64. Stockton, "Use of Submarine Mines," 280.

65. Cited in Garner, *International Law,* 1:344.

66. Arthur J. Marder, *From the Dreadnought to Scapa Flow: The Royal Navy in the Fisher Era, 1904–1919* (Oxford, 1961–70), 2:71; Times (London), *The Times Documentary History of the War* (London, 1914–18), 3:54–57; F. Maynard Bridge, *A Short History of the Great World War* (London, 1919), 55.

67. Adm. Tyrwhitt to Beauchamp Tyrwhitt, Aug. 9, 1914, cited in Marder, *From the Dreadnought,* 2:72.

68. Lambert, *Planning Armageddon,* 53–55, 181.

69. Grey to Sir Rennell Rodd, Foreign Office, Aug. 10, 1914, no. 37812, and to twelve other neutral states, FO 371/2164 file 30342, no. 37812. Grey had changed Churchill's original wording, which was "at liberty to retaliate by setting mines where they are likely to damage the enemy," Churchill to Grey, Aug. 10, 1914, ibid.

methods "contrary to the terms of the Hague Convention."[70] The cabinet learned that the navy's goal was to "make an effective blockade of Rotterdam," a plan it rejected because of the neutral protest and because Asquith and several others, like Admiral Tyrwhitt, thought the practice "barbarous."[71] In mid-August, the cabinet judged using mines "a last resort." After German mines sank three British cruisers in September, the cabinet sanctioned reciprocal use of mines in the North Sea, but admonished the Admiralty to "carefully consider" the difficulties the measure raised. Only at the end of September, after the United States had failed to protest Germany's mine-laying and German submarines had appeared in the Channel, did the cabinet approve "in principle" mine barrages, though in fact none were laid until the following year.[72] In short, Britain's actual use of mines in the First World War occurred belatedly and only as reprisal/reciprocity.

If Grey opposed accepting the DoL because of Germany's mine-laying, the Admiralty's position was more complicated. Eyre Crowe, who favored adopting the DoL because of neutral states' attachment to it, had asked the Admiralty on July 30 to adhere to the declaration. It refused, though it had already issued instructions on the basis of its own Naval Prize Manual, which had been revised in 1909 to accord substantially with the DoL; the Admiralty Board approved the Prize Manual in 1913, even after the House of Lords had refused to ratify the DoL.[73] The new Prize Manual made several "concessions to continental opinion not actually required by British Law," as an internal report put it.[74] The most important concerned blockade and capture of contraband. The new Prize Manual accepted the DoL's stricter rules of blockade notification and limited the area within which blockade breakers could be seized. More important, whereas Britain's 1904 Prize Manual had permitted the application of continuous voyage to conditional contraband, the new Prize Manual did not. And the previous manual allowed seizure of merchant vessels carrying contraband bound for neutral ports with "nothing to suggest that the goods are to be forwarded to the enemy," while the new manual required at least proof that the articles were destined for a government agent.[75] In other words, pre-1909 British law permitted the very measures that would solve the Rotterdam problem now seemingly barred by its own Prize Manual.

However, the new Prize Manual was a confidential handbook of practice, not a law book. As the 1913 report said, "both [the 1904 and the 1909 manuals] may be within the law as understood in Great Britain." "Unless and until the Declaration of London is ratified,

---

70. Bryan to Barclay, Washington, Aug. 13, 1914, *FRUS* 1914, Suppl., 455–56.

71. "Effective blockade": Harcourt cabinet notes, Aug. 7, 1914; "barbarous": Asquith, cited in Lambert, *Planning Armageddon,* 222.

72. Cabinet meeting of Aug. 17, 1914, CAB 41/35/31; meeting of Sept. 23, 1914, CAB 41/35/47; and meeting of Sept. 30, 1914, CAB 41/35/48; Lambert, *Planning Armageddon,* 261–62.

73. ADM 116/1232.

74. "Interim Report of the Committee on the Revision of the Naval Prize Manual," June 9, 1913, ADM 116/1232.

75. Ibid.

there is on certain points no law which can be said to be univerally recognised, different nations entertaining different views."[76] When the Admiralty Board approved the new manual, its intention was "that the Prize Manual shall continue to be a confidential handbook for the guidance of Naval Officers...it does not affect the power of the Admiralty or His Majesty's Government to vary them if for any reason modifications should be necessary," so long as the modifications followed international law as Britain interpreted it.[77] Although the Admiralty sent copies of the Prize Manual to France and Russia in August 1914, it opposed publication because that would tie its hands "in issuing special instructions in particular cases which are not in exact accordance with the Manual."[78]

Nevertheless, the Admiralty worried that, without a public declaration that Britain had adopted the DoL, the British Prize Court would judge cases according to older international law rather than the new, secret Prize Manual. It might rebuff certain of the navy's actions.[79] Britain's ally France also pressed it to recognize the DoL, which, as Robert Cecil pointed out two years later, "represents to them an important victory gained by Continental ideas of the rules which should govern the exercise of sea power over the ideas of naval powers like England and the United States."[80] The government therefore inclined to accept the DoL in some form.

But, as we have seen, the DoL did not permit seizing conditional contraband, including food, that could reach the enemy through neutral ports. Without continuous voyage, the economic weapon against Germany was powerless. The resulting "difficult questions of law and policy," as Prime Minister Asquith called them, absorbed government attention for the entire second week of the war.[81] Beginning on August 13, the cabinet devoted itself to establishing the legal basis for prosecuting the war.

On that day, Grey proposed a distant blockade "across the North Sea and the Channel" plus "the treatment of food sent in by way of Rotterdam as conditional contraband, i.e., liable to seizure when it was destined, directly or indirectly, for the German armies."[82] Grey's proposal combined the new DoL permission of distant blockade *(rayon d'action)*, the older Anglo-American doctrine of continuous voyage, and the new scheme of rationing that Lloyd George had first broached in the December 1912 CID meeting. His proposal touched off a long debate on international law. Grey insisted on the legality of the entire package. Citing the DoL, Attorney General Simon disagreed.[83] Concerning food, Grey's position was unchanged from his 1908 instructions to the British delegates to the London Conference—continuous voyage applicable to all classes of contraband was recognized

---

76. Ibid.

77. Report of the Admiralty Board, July 14, 1913, ibid.

78. Hurst memo of Aug.10, 1914, FO 372/588, no. 39497, file 711.

79. Ibid.

80. Robert Cecil minute, June 5, 1916, in FO 372/1126, no. 108016, file 1639. Despite the French judgment, the United States also pressed for Britain to follow the DoL.

81. Asquith to George V., Cabinet letter, Aug. 13, 1914, CAB 41/35/29, cited in Coogan, *End of Neutrality,* 155.

82. "North Sea": memo of John Simon, Aug. 14, 1914; "Treatment of food": Asquith to king, Aug. 13, 1914, both cited in Lambert, *Planning Armageddon,* 217.

83. John Simon memorandum, Aug. 4, 1914, FO 800/89, pp. 18–21.

in international law. Rationing provided a way to continue feeding both the neutral and enemy civilian populations while denying food to the armed forces without formal proof of destination: "we cannot make contraband of food for the *civil* population of the enemy, but we can make *excessive* food beyond past average, conditional contraband as being intended for the German army," as Lewis Harcourt's note summarized it.[84] Former war minister and now lord chancellor Richard Burdon, Viscount Haldane, backed Grey, betting that the Prize Court would uphold rationing, while Prime Minister Asquith and the attorney general demurred. The discussion was acrimonious, and at least six cabinet members opposed Grey's plan (Simon, Harcourt, Postmaster General Sir Charles Hobhouse, Commissioner of Works Lord Alfred Emmott, President of the Board of Education Joseph Pease, and President of the Board of Trade Walter Runciman).[85]

In the next days, the legal and strategic debate continued. The cabinet worked its way to approving the pre-1912 CID position of permitting distant blockade while allowing some neutral merchant vessels through, and it considered diverting neutral trade by buying it up. The sticking point continued to be continuous voyage, with its high-handed treatment of neutrals and their trade, its threat of enemy civilian starvation, and the high standard of proof required by Britain's Prize Court.

In the meantime, Cecil Hurst, the Foreign Office's chief lawyer, had worked out a compromise with the Admiralty on the DoL. His draft order-in-council, the legal document setting out the rules Britain would follow in conducting the war, announced that Britain would adhere to the DoL with five modifications.[86] One of these (on the contraband list) was approved by Attorney General Simon, and the others (notably reinstituting continuous voyage) were approved by Grey, First Lord of the Admiralty Winston Churchill, and Lloyd George.[87] Senior admirals, however, raised legal and practical objections. Vice Admiral Slade, formerly director of naval intelligence and delegate to the DoL, doubted that Britain could prove its case before the Prize Court. He noted that conditional contraband

cannot be condemned unless the destination can be proved to be without question the armed forces of the enemy, a fortified place or some person who is supplying the enemy Government with such articles. This is no new rule, but is part of the customary law which will be administered in our Courts. Unless the vessels are condemned and declared to be good prize, heavy compensation has to be paid and neutral Powers are needlessly irritated.

Chief of Staff Admiral Doveton Sturdee doubted "whether the time has yet arrived to attempt to reimpose the doctrine of continuous voyage. In the past, this doctrine has raised the animosity of powerful neutrals without sufficient compensatory advantages."[88]

---

84. Harcourt, cabinet notes, Aug. 13, 1914, cited in Lambert, *Planning Armageddon,* 218.

85. Lambert, *Planning Armageddon,* 218, 559n233.

86. Draft order-in-council, Aug. 14, 1914, FO 372/588, no. 39497, file 711. See discussion of the modifications, below.

87. Hurst memo of Aug. 10, 1914; Crowe minute to same; FO 372/588, no. 39497, file 711.

88. Sturdee minute, Aug. 16, 1914, ADM 116/1233.

On August 17 the Cabinet discussed the draft order-in-council. Grey and Lloyd George defended it. Attorney General Simon rejected it as illegal and bound to inflame neutrals. Churchill withheld the negative views of his admiral colleagues, but even so, the Cabinet could not bring itself to overcome its legal scruples. It sent the matter back to a subcommittee for further discussion.[89]

On August 19 that discussion took place at the Foreign Office. Present were Foreign Minister Grey, Lord Chancellor Haldane, Home Secretary Reginald McKenna, Churchill, President of the Board of Trade Runciman, Attorney General Simon, Admirals Battenberg, Slade, and Sturdee, Permanent Secretary of the Admiralty Sir William Graham Greene, and Hurst.[90] They discussed the three most pressing issues: conditional contraband, continuous voyage, and blockade. The senior lawyer for the FO, Sir William E. Davidson, had ruled previously that food could not be classified as absolute contraband and therefore simply seized.[91] That judgment must have made it easier for the subcommittee to accept the DoL's conditional contraband list, which included food. But at the same time, they agreed to take "all possible steps" "to prevent foodstuffs in particular from being imported into Germany in neutral vessels whether directly or through Dutch ports." Doing so required reasserting the application of continuous voyage to conditional contraband. After days of individual deliberation, returning to the older Anglo-American usage had become easier, presumably because it enjoyed legal precedent and therefore, though controversial, was not an obvious violation of law.

The real focus of the meeting was on proof—that is, whatever policy they decided on had to be acceptable to the Prize Court. As conditional contraband, food could be captured only if it were "destined for the use of a belligerent in war."[92] The DoL had specified proof of enemy destination as consignment "to enemy authorities" or their "contractor," "to a fortified place belonging to the enemy," or to a port serving as a base of supply (article 34). The new Prize Manual substantially followed the DoL (article 39).[93] The meeting had the attorney general redraft article 3 of the order-in-council, in order to widen the kinds of evidence admissible to prove enemy destination ("any sufficient evidence").[94] But in addition, the home secretary cited "reliable reports" that the German government had assumed control of the nation's food supply.[95] If that were true, the burden of proof would be easy. Furthermore, Holland had blocked exports of food, "and therefore imports into Holland itself could not reach Germany so long as this embargo continued. Accordingly it was decided to approve of Article 5 of the Order in Council" (which applied the old rule of continuous voyage to conditional contraband).

---

89. Coogan, *End of Neutrality,* 158–59.

90. Minutes of the Conference, Aug. 19, 1914, FO 372/588 no. 42603, file 711.

91. Lambert, *Planning Armageddon,* 224.

92. Oppenheim's précis of customary international law before the DoL, Lassa Oppenheim, *International Law: A Treatise* (London, 1905), 2: para. 395.

93. Naval Prize Manual, Being a Manual for the Guidance of Naval Officers in Time of War, Admiralty 1913, ADM 116/1232.

94. The attorney general's emendations are in ADM 116/1233.

95. Minutes of Aug. 19, 1914, FO 372/588 no. 42063, file 711.

Finally, regarding blockade, the participants agreed to accept the new rules of the Naval Prize Manual, which embodied those of the DoL. The DoL gave blockading squadrons wider latitude than did the previous British rules.[96] However, the subcommittee recommended modifying article 61 of the Prize Manual, which the attorney general had pointed out prohibited a distant blockade that barred neutral ships from proceeding to neutral ports.[97] The subcommittee decided to abide by that prohibition, but believed that "if steps were taken . . . to see that neutral vessels did not deviate from their course to run to a German port," then distant blockade was lawful.

After another "protracted discussion" the cabinet finally approved the order-in-council, which was published immediately, on August 20.[98] It did not declare a blockade. Instead, it spelled out the modifications of the DoL that, on the one hand, gave Britain greater latitude in announcing and maintaining a blockade, had it chosen that course, and on the other, made it easier to seize certain cargoes presumed headed for the enemy. The method of commercial warfare Britain chose was capture, not blockade. Despite the conclusions of the meeting of the nineteenth, the final order did not keep the absolute and conditional contraband lists of the DoL, but substituted those the Admiralty had announced on August 4. Nevertheless, the cabinet restricted the definition of contraband food, thus permitting more through-shipments, part of its expressed "desire not to starve the [enemy] civilian population" but instead to pressure the German government to give up the war.[99]

Lambert interprets the deliberations leading to the first order-in-council as a search for a "convenient pretext" or "legal rationalization" for British measures.[100] On that view, one might compare them to the German meetings preceding the Belgian deportations. The structural differences are striking, however. Germany lacked a cabinet, so the legal issues were vetted only once before the Kaiser; thereafter, decision making devolved to lower instances, with the military taking the lead and ultimately determining policy. In Britain, the cabinet returned to the legal dilemmas again and again. The subcommittee consisted of six cabinet members, four representatives of the Admiralty, two lawyers (one the attorney general), and two opponents of the plan under discussion (Simon and Runciman). Subsequent orders were drafted by the navy together with Hurst, the FO's lawyer.[101] The Admiralty did not run the show.

The legal differences were also marked. Deportation for slave labor was entirely unprecedented and contrary to clear treaty law (the Hague Rules). The first order-in-council

---

96. "Report of the Delegates of the United States to the International Naval Conference Held at London, December 4, 1908, to February 26, 1909" (Mar. 2, 1909), and Annex C of that report; "Instructions Addressed to the British Delegates," Grey to Lord Desart, Dec. 1, 1908; and "Report of the British Delegates," Mar. 1, 1909, in Scott, *Declaration of London*, 198, 207–8, 222, 237.

97. Simon memorandum of Aug. 14, 1914, FO 800/89.

98. All orders-in-council are published in Bell, *History of the Blockade*, 712–19. "Protracted": Pease diary, Aug. 28, 1914, cited in Lambert, *Planning Armageddon*, 225.

99. Hankey to Asquith, July 20, 1915, cited in Lambert, *Planning Armageddon*, 226; restricted definition: ibid., 223.

100. Lambert, *Planning Armageddon*, 224–25. Also, Coogan, *End of Neutrality*, 160.

101. Minute of Aug. 22, 1914, "Proposed Order in Council bringing into force the main principles of the Declaration of London," ADM 116–1233.

accepted the DoL but modified six of its articles (15, 22, 24, 33, 35, 38) in ways favorable to Great Britain.[102] How far did these changes violate existing law? The order-in-council specified the conditions under which neutral vessels were presumed to know of a blockade; it returned to British law permitting capture of blockade breakers during their return voyage; and it expanded slightly the evidence permitted to prove enemy destination of contraband cargo. These were relatively minor matters. In weighing the changes to the contraband lists, one should recall that specifying items was one of the DoL's innovations (done at Britain's insistence!) and therefore not binding law because of nonratification. Even so, the Admiralty's changes of August 4, 1914, were minor. It shifted balloons from conditional to absolute contraband and added aircraft of all kinds. To the conditional contraband list it added "powder and lubricants not specially prepared for use in war."[103] These changes correctly anticipated the predominantly military uses of these items in wartime. However, they did prepare the way for new lists that were announced as soon as September 21, October 29, and December 23, 1914; in the end they expanded almost without limit.[104] Still, the August beginnings were very slight.

Legally most controversial were continuous voyage and its application to seizing food. The preparatory documents for the London Conference show clearly that the British government was convinced that continuous voyage was entirely legal under international law. Grey's instructions to the British delegates said, "The principle underlying the doctrine of continuous voyage is not of recent origin, and may be regarded as a recognized part of the law of nations." Furthermore,

> His Majesty's Government believe the more widely established rule to be that the destination of the contraband cargo, and not that of the vessel by which it is conveyed, is the decisive factor.... This principle may rightly be extended not only to cases where the contraband is to be carried on to the enemy after transshipment, but also to cases where the goods are forwarded by land transit through neutral territory.[105]

The Report of the British Delegates contains a long and faintly shamefaced account of how the British view on the law of continuous voyage was whittled down. "To obtain the advantages" to British commerce by listing contraband items, "some concession had to be made to the Powers which have hitherto refused to recognize the doctrine of continuous voyage." "Ultimately, a compromise was arrived at," in which continuous voyage was restricted to absolute contraband. The report makes clear that the delegates sacrificed some of Britain's belligerent rights in order to strengthen its neutral rights. "It was for these reasons...that we felt justified in applying for your assent to the compromise above

---

102. The order-in-council modified five articles of the new Prize Manual (31, 37, 38, parts of 39, and 41): draft explanatory telegram M. 15497, August ___, 1914, ADM 116/1233.

103. Proclamation, Aug. 4, 1914, printed in Bell, *History of the Blockade,* 722.

104. Fifteen contraband proclamations from Aug. 4, 1914, to July 2, 1917, printed in Bell, *History of the Blockade,* 722–44.

105. "Instructions," Grey to Desart, London, Dec. 1, 1908, in Scott, *Declaration of London,* 218, 223.

described."[106] That is, the restriction of continuous voyage to absolute contraband was a compromise nonbinding in the absence of ratification.

Grey had reason to think that continuous voyage was covered by international law. It was neither new nor purely an Anglo-American usage or doctrine. French courts had applied it during the Crimean War, it appeared in the Prussian Regulations of 1864, in those of Sweden, and Italy had applied it in 1896.[107] At the DoL, alongside Britain and the United States, France, Japan, and Italy recognized it.[108] Thus it was a more than merely domestic British usage. Furthermore, restricting continuous voyage to absolute contraband, as the DoL had done, was a greater innovation than the doctrine itself. It was also illogical. As James Brown Scott pointed out before the war, both absolute and conditional contraband "are liable to capture and confiscation, if directed to an enemy port. The intent in each case is the same; namely, to supply the enemy with objects useful in war, and the fact that some commodities are perhaps not so useful to the enemy as others is no reason why they should not be captured...if the ultimate destination is an enemy port." He characterized the DoL compromise as one "rather of fact than of law."[109] These considerations help to explain why Grey must have felt that returning to continuous voyage was not a breach of law. An inter-ministerial meeting of high officials in Berlin (August 28, 1914) agreed with Grey. It concluded that Britain's reintroduction of the application of continuous voyage to conditional contraband "probably violated" the DoL, but not "generally recognized international law," since the DoL remained unratified.[110]

Hurst disagreed with Grey not on continuous voyage, but on the broad language concerning destination. In 1916 he wrote that making conditional contraband "liable to capture to whatever port the vessel is bound and at whatever port the cargo is to be discharged," as the August 1914 order-in-council had done, "exceeded anything warranted by the practice of the past." Hurst thought it treated neutrals unjustly. When, after neutral protests, Britain modified that wording in the second order-in-council (October 29, 1914), Hurst thought it went too far in the opposite direction.[111] In any event, the robust doctrine of continuous voyage was legally precedented and defensible and in the eyes of many important decision makers was therefore not a violation of law.[112] Its application to food destined for enemy civilians was more controversial.

---

106. Report of the British delegates, Scott, *Declaration of London,* 241–43.

107. Garner, *International Law,* 2:297–98; Hold von Ferneck, *Die Reform des Seekriegsrechts,* 130; Oppenheim, *International Law,* 2:440. Sir William Grant enunciated the principle in 1806: James Brown Scott, "The Declaration of London of February 26, 1909," *American Journal of International Law* 8, no. 2 (April 1914): 314–15.

108. Bell, *History of the Blockade,* 41–42.

109. Scott, "Declaration of London," 315.

110. Delbrück to Bethmann, Berlin, Aug. 28, 1914, A. 21778, AA/PA R 21362, fols. 61–64.

111. Memo by Hurst on Art 1 (iii) of DoL, Jan. 1, 1916, FO 382/1125, no. 1639, file 1639; Lambert, *Planning Armageddon,* 226.

112. Even Adm. Slade, who raised the difficulty of proving enemy destination, recognized the doctrine of continuous voyage for contraband was legal, insofar as it had only been "abandoned as part of the compromise with Germany": Slade minute of Aug. 15, 1914, on "Proposed Order in Council," ADM 116/1233.

Starvation of Enemy Civilians

Starving enemy civilians is the Allied war policy that probably most strongly repels modern readers. At the time, Imperial Germany's argument that it violated the "law of war and every dictate of humanity" was the Kaiserreich's most popular propaganda appeal to neutral public opinion.[113] Immediately after the war, British public and governmental opinion began to shift, too; revulsion against the food blockade was a potent force pressuring the government to appease German demands for revision of the Treaty of Versailles even while it was being negotiated. The law of nations on this point was in flux; it was changing from unquestioned acceptance of enemy (civilian) starvation as a legitimate weapon of war to the (current) position that very few circumstances excuse such a policy.

Until the mid-nineteenth century, the laws of war had unproblematically sanctioned starvation of the enemy. Francis Lieber's United States code of 1863 succinctly stated the principle: "It is lawful to starve the hostile belligerent, armed or unarmed, so that it leads to the speedier subjection of the enemy."[114] Many modern writers thought this entitlement derived from the usages of siege warfare; in any case, permitting the stoppage of food shipments to enemy civilians was a recurrent feature of European warfare and a staple of the international law of siege, blockade, and contraband.[115]

But one can observe the advent of change in Britain's own actions. In 1793 and 1795, 1812–14, and as late as the Crimean War, Britain had stopped food shipments to the enemy.[116] By 1885, British leaders had begun to argue that food should only be seized if destined for the military. Lord Salisbury reacted to France's attempt to stop rice shipments to northern China by laying down stringent conditions: "Foodstuff with a hostile destination can be considered contraband of war only if they are supplies for the enemy's forces. It is not sufficient that they are capable of being so used; it must be shown that this was in fact their destination at the time of the seizure."[117] Britain retreated from Salisbury's injunction during the Boer War, when it declared food contraband and seized it going through the neutral port of Lourenço Marquès. After the United States protested the status of contraband (but

---

113. Gerard to Bryan, Berlin, Feb. 17, 1915, enclosing German note to the U.S., *FRUS* 1915, Suppl., 112–13; Gerard to Lansing, Berlin, July 8, 1915, enclosing German note, 463–64. Germany had changed its tune. In 1885 and 1892, Chancellors Otto v. Bismarck and Leo v. Caprivi had both defended seizing foodstuffs as a natural right of war: Grey to Page, Mar. 15, 1915, *BD*, ser. H, 5:50, doc. 41.

114. Francis Lieber, *Instructions for the Government of Armies of the United States in the Field, General Orders No. 100, 24 April 1863*, in *The Laws of Armed Conflicts: A Collection of Conventions, Resolutions and Other Documents*, ed. Dietrich Schindler and Jiri Toman (Geneva, 1988), art. 17. Lieber restricted that right to the militarily necessary: Charles A. Allen, "Civilian Starvation and Relief during Armed Conflict: The Modern Humanitarian Law," *Georgia Journal of International and Comparative Law* 19, no. 1 (1989): 19, 33–35.

115. See the précis of Perrinjaquet, "Guerre européenne," 149n1; Garner, *International Law*, 2:337–38; J. E. G. De Montmorency, "The Principles Underlying Contraband and Blockade," *Grotius Society, Problems of the War: Papers Read before the Society in the Year 1916* 2 (1917): 29; George Alfred Mudge, "Starvation as a Means of Warfare," *International Lawyer* 4, no. 2 (1969–70): 268.

116. Perrinjaquet, "Guerre européenne," 146; Eric W. Osborne, *Britain's Economic Blockade of Germany, 1914–1919* (Portland, OR, 2004), 20.

117. Cited in Garner, *International Law*, 2:291.

not the use of continuous voyage to seize it), Britain returned to Salisbury's principle, and applied that rule again in its protest when Russia declared food absolute contraband in 1904 during the Russo-Japanese War.[118] The doctrine of "special destination," as Salisbury's principle was known, was widely enough held in British governmental circles that in 1911 Admiral Ottley of the CID could incorrectly imagine that stopping food to civilians "runs counter to the policy to which we have ourselves adhered for the last hundred years."[119]

Although the DoL listed food as conditional contraband (article 24.1), that article papered over much disagreement. Pitt Cobbett, writing in 1913 from a standpoint sympathetic to Salisbury's position, nonetheless concluded that, regarding the status of food as conditional contraband, "there was neither consistent theory nor harmonious practice."[120] France's position at the London Conference was that "food and raw materials intended for non-combatants are not in principle considered as contraband of war, but can be declared such according to circumstances of which the Government is judge and in virtue of an order emanating from it."[121] Consequently, in August 1914 Rear Admiral Frédéric Paul Moreau wanted to place food on the absolute contraband list, thus permitting its seizure regardless of destination. After conferring with the French foreign office's chief lawyer, Henri Fromageot, the foreign minister discreetly asked Grey if that were possible; Britain categorically refused, following the opinion of the FO's chief lawyer Davidson.[122] France's request suggests that this strong devotee of the DoL thought either that it could be thus elastically interpreted, or that this modification did not significantly damage its principles. Indeed, Foreign Minister Théophile Delcassé described to President Raymond Poincaré the "diverse additions and modifications" contained in the August 20, 1914, order-in-council as still basically consistent with the DoL.[123] And France exerted tremendous pressure on Britain during the autumn of 1914 and afterward to tighten its interdiction of food.[124] After March 1915, that interdiction became more and more sweeping.

Grey publicly defended the principle allowing seizure of food destined for enemy civilians as a logical consequence of the belligerent right to blockade: "Inasmuch as the stoppage of all foodstuffs is an admitted consequence of blockade, it is obvious that there can be no universal rule, based on considerations of morality and humanity, which is contrary to this practice. The right to stop foodstuffs destined for the civil population

---

118. Perrinjaquet, "Guerre européenne," 146.

119. Note by Adm. Charles Ottley, Feb. 17, 1911, to "Treatment of Enemy and Neutral Ships in War, Decl. of London (1911)," CAB 17/87.

120. Pitt Cobbett, *Cases and Opinions on International Law; And Various Points of English Law Connected Therewith; Collected and Digested from English and Foreign Reports, Official Documents, and Other Sources; With Notes Containing the Views of the Text-Writers on the Topics Referred to, Supplementary Cases, Treaties, and Statutes,* vol. 2: pt. 2, War; pt. 3, Neutrality (published 1913) (London, 1909–13), 2:439. Cf. Mudge, who writes that since Grotius, food was conditional contraband in customary law: Mudge, "Starvation," 248.

121. Scott, *Declaration of London,* 29.

122. MAE, Paris, Aug. 5, 1914, 14vr, Corr. polit. vol. 1132; Paul Cambon to Minister of Foreign Affairs (MFA), London, no. 209, Aug. 5, 1914, MAE Direction de blocus, Contreband, vol. 33.

123. Delcassé to Poincaré (pres.), n.d., his covering preamble to the new order-in-council of Oct. 29, 1914, *DDFr 1914,* doc. 486.

124. See, for example, *DDFr 1914:* docs. 230, 256, 422.

must, therefore, in any case be admitted if an effective 'cordon' controlling intercourse with the enemy is drawn, announced, and maintained."[125] Grey received support from the international lawyers writing in the *Grotius Society,* who otherwise did not shrink from criticizing their own country's violations of law. Two carefully researched and reasoned articles on maritime law never questioned the legality of stopping food imports destined for civilians.[126] Antoine Pillet, a leading French international lawyer and the close associate of Louis Renault, the dean of international lawyers before the war, dismissed Germany's argument for a right to food out of hand: "This pretention is new and has little chance of success."[127]

Not until the 1949 revision of the Geneva Convention was the matter revisited. Convention IV, article 23, ordered belligerents to "permit the free passage of all consignments of essential foodstuffs, clothing and tonics intended for children under fifteen, expectant mothers and maternity cases." In addition to narrowing the right to food to sections of the civil population, article 23 made it conditional on the belligerent's judgment that "there are no serious reasons for fearing" that food shipments would be diverted, uncontrolled, or would "accrue to the military efforts or economy of the enemy through…substitution."[128] As one scholar writes, "This is hardly language which creates a binding obligation under international law."[129] At the urging of Britain and Belgium, the Additional Protocol I to the Geneva Conventions enunciated in 1977 for the first time the principle that "starvation of civilians as a method of warfare is prohibited."[130] Even so, twenty-one years later the United Nations blocked food shipments to Iraq and Kuwait. To this day, pressuring governments by interdicting food to civilian populations remains unsettled in international law.[131]

The late twentieth-century / early twenty-first-century view is expressed in the 1994 San Remo Manual on International Law Applicable to Armed Conflicts at Sea. However, even it does not bar every blockade of food. Article 102 prohibits blockade if "a) it has the sole purpose of starving the civilian population or denying it other objects essential for its survival; or b) the damage to the civilian population is, or may be expected to be, excessive

125. Grey to Page, Mar. 15, 1915, *BD,* ser. H, 5:49–50, doc. 41.

126. John Macdonell, "Some Notes on Blockade," *Grotius Society, Problems of the War: Papers Read before the Society in the Year 1915* 1 (1916): 93–104; De Montmorency, "Principles."

127. Antoine Pillet, "La guerre actuelle et le droit des gens," *Révue générale de droit international public* 23 (1916): 411; Martti Koskenniemi, *The Gentle Civilizer of Nations: The Rise and Fall of International Law, 1870–1960* (Cambridge, 2001), 282; Burleigh Cushing Rodick, *The Doctrine of Necessity in International Law* (New York, 1928), 76.

128. 1949 Geneva Convention IV, in Roberts and Guelff, *Documents,* 309–10.

129. Mudge, "Starvation," 253; also René Provost, "Starvation as a Weapon: Legal Implications of the United Nations Food Blockade against Iraq and Kuwait," *Columbia Journal of Transnational Law* 30 (1992): 592–93.

130. 1977 Geneva Protocol I Additional to the Geneva Conventions of August 12, 1949, and Relating to the Protection of Victims of International Armed Conflicts, art. 54, para. 1, in Roberts and Guelff, *Documents,* 450. Britain and Belgium: Provost, "Starvation," 602–3.

131. The reader may judge the arguments that food interdiction is now prohibited in customary international law: Provost, "Starvation"; Allen, "Civilian Starvation."

in relation to the concrete and direct military advantage anticipated from the blockade."[132] Although it is bad practice to apply anachronistic standards to the past, the exercise is instructive because it suggests that the Allied "blockade" of World War I would probably have passed them.

Starvation was never the sole object of Britain's economic measures; in fact, it was not the object at all.[133] Some navy planners wanted to use blockade to lure the German fleet out of its own ports and into a battle on Britain's terms in the North Sea.[134] Civilian leaders and naval officers who championed economic warfare, whether by blockade or capture, always targeted the entire German economy: its war and domestic industries, trade, finances, credit, communications, and food supply. The object was to make it impossible for Germany to conduct the war and force it to sue for peace. A 1906 memorandum by G. S. Clarke that formed part of an internal argument on retaining the right of capture put forward by some of those most involved in forming actual British policy in 1914 (including Cecil Hurst) described the kind of damage aimed for: "clearly such [economic] stress would be severely felt throughout the whole commercial and industrial structure, and all the elements of the population depending thereon." Credit would collapse and "there would be failure of banks and industrial establishments on a large scale."[135]

In any case, no one before the war or until late 1915 or even 1916 believed that it was possible to halt enough food to cause starvation or even significant deprivation in Germany. A memorandum on capture prepared for Grey in May 1914 concluded, "We cannot starve out an enemy on the Continent but we can secure that a powerful and influential section of his community shall normally be in favour of peace from fear of the great losses that war would cause them."[136] In October 1916, as Germany was sliding into its worst subsistence crisis of the war, the man detailed to collect and analyze reports on the economic situation inside the Central Powers was still writing that "the Germans are not starving and it is very doubtful whether they ever will be, however closely the blockade may be tightened."[137] It was indeed extremely hard to tell what impact the blockade was having.[138]

A glance at the contraband lists, continuously updated during the war, shows that industrial goods of all kinds, oils, metals and minerals, chemicals, precious metals, and

---

132. San Remo Manual, in Roberts and Guelff, *Documents*, 573–606, here 592. Art. 150(c) puts "essential foodstuffs" for civilians on the free list.

133. Much less the absurd suggestion that Britain threatened neutrals with starvation, as Coogan maintains: Coogan, *End of Neutrality*, 162, 167–68.

134. Marder, *From the Dreadnought*, 1:381–83. That was the primary goal of prewar blockade planning: Enclosure 2: "Secret." "Blockade of North Sea Coast of German Empire," "Remarks by the Vice Admiral Commanding 1st and 2nd Divisions, Home Fleet," Aug. 31, 1911, ADM 1/8132.

135. G. S. Clarke, Memorandum of May 14, 1906, titled "The Capture of the Private Property of the Belligerents at Sea," appendix B to "Right of Capture of Private Property at Sea," a memo by Desart, Ottley, Howell, Cockerill, Clarke, Davison, Hurst, and Crowe, CAB 37/86/14, p. 16.

136. Prof. Acland (undersecretary of state for foreign affairs), "Right of capture of private property at sea," May 7, 1914, FO 372/549, no. 20393, file 876, p. 15; Osborne, *Britain's Economic Blockade*, 38–39.

137. W. G. Max Müller, "The Economic Situation in Germany during September 1916," Oct. 14, 1916, *BD*, ser. H, 10:295, doc. 23.

138. Bell, *History of the Blockade*, 242–44; FO 371/2679 collects reports from various sources and records the confusion and skepticism of the Foreign Office analysts.

financial instruments were central to Britain's economic measures.[139] Similarly, the monthly economic reports on the effect of the blockade on the Central Powers provide a measure of the importance of each aspect of the policy.[140] Averaged over the war, the pages devoted to foodstuffs take up just under 50 percent of the reports; the rest were devoted to the industrial and financial impact. Not surprisingly, the percentage tops fifty when the blockade of food seemed most successful, in autumn 1915 and throughout 1916. In any event, it is clear that the attempt to starve the civilian population was never the "sole" object.

Nevertheless, when it seemed in 1915 and again in 1916 that, against all expectations, the measures were indeed succeeding, Britain kept up the pressure.[141] Internal discussion of the ethics of starvation was strongest in the first weeks of war when the cabinet (August 20, 1914) said that its object was "not to starve the civilian population."[142] That ethical idea ebbed thereafter—Arthur Balfour remarked in February 1915 that it was "unlikely that we shall starve Germany into submission; and I am not sure that I would do it if I could."[143] The ethical issue is at least part of the second, modern consideration of legality of blockade, weighing the damage done to civilians against the "concrete and direct military advantage." This is the doctrine of proportionality, an important principle in international law before 1914 and since 1945 enjoying the status of customary law.[144]

Modern armies try to judge whether the use of a weapon (for example, an air strike or artillery bombardment) is legal, by estimating the likelihood of civilian versus enemy soldier deaths or against the concrete military advantage in using the weapon. Such a calculation, however macabre, is the only practical way to try to apply the proportionality principle. It is only barely possible to attempt this sort of assessment for World War I, because neither the civilian death toll nor the exact effectiveness of the blockade is known.

Turning to the first problem, even if we simplify the question by ignoring the civilian victims among Germany's allies and in the occupied areas, it is difficult to reckon how many civilians died because of the blockade. We confront complex methodological issues (for example, the effect of nutrition on disease, the interplay of indirect factors on mortality) and difficult interpretive judgments, especially concerning the role of the German government's mismanagement of supplies and of its policy choice to redirect food, coal, clothing, and raw materials away from civilians to the military. For example, cotton that might have gone to much-needed clothing was used instead for detonators, and vegetable

---

139. These are listed in Bell, *History of the Blockade,* 722–44.

140. Most of these are printed in *BD,* ser. H, vols. 9–12.

141. House diary, May 26, 1915, Edward Mandell House, *The Intimate Papers of Colonel House: Arranged as a Narrative by Charles Seymour* (Boston, 1926), 1:453; Osborne, *Britain's Economic Blockade,* 123–24; Bell, *History of the Blockade,* 115–17, 569.

142. Hankey to Asquith, July 20, 1915, cited in Nicholas A. Lambert, "Strategic Command and Control for Maneuver Warfare: Creation of the Royal Navy's 'War Room' System, 1905–1915," *Journal of Military History* 69, no. 2 (April 2005): 226.

143. Balfour to Hankey, Feb. 17, 1915, cited in Lambert, *Planning Armageddon,* 370.

144. Judith Gail Gardam, "Proportionality and Force in International Law," *American Journal of International Law* 87, no. 3 (July 1993): 391–413.

fat, critical to civilian survival, became glycerine for explosives and propellants.[145] A major research project on the effect of the blockade on German industry and civilian life would be most welcome.

The first estimate (December 18, 1918) of excess civilian mortality due to the blockade in Germany was 762,796.[146] This figure was the National Health Service's (Reichsgesundheitsamt) hasty statistical contribution to the "innocence campaign" of the German Foreign Office. An order on December 10, 1918, enlisted the Health Service to help reduce the expected Allied demands for postwar reparations based on Germany's violations of international law, in this case by arguing that the blockade was equally illegal and equally deadly.[147] A subsequent German study in 1928 reduced this figure by 44 percent, to 424,000.[148] Since then, Jay Winter has proposed 300,000.[149] But the largest number is still often repeated.[150] Unfortunately, recent social histories have not helped test the validity of the aggregate claims, which are entirely statistical.[151] Although even the earliest studies admitted that outright starvation was rare, nevertheless, widespread hunger and malnutrition certainly killed many people before their time. The question then is, was the blockade effective enough to justify these deaths?

The effectiveness of the blockade was a subject of major controversy in Britain during the war. Proponents of hitting Germany harder and who therefore objected to solicitude for law or neutral rights claimed in Parliament and in the press that the Foreign Office's leadership had made the blockade nugatory.[152] Echoes of that charge are visible in the defensiveness of the blockade's official historian, A. C. Bell, and perhaps also in the hyperbole of writers like Basil Liddell Hart, who claimed that the blockade "ranks first" in

---

145. C. Paul Vincent, *The Politics of Hunger: The Allied Blockade of Germany, 1915-1919* (Athens, OH, 1985), 128; Bell, *History of the Blockade*, 310.

146. Reichsgesundheitsamt Germany, "Schädigung der deutschen Volkskraft durch die völkerrechtswidrige feindliche Handelsblockade," in *Das Werk des Untersuchungsausschusses der Verfassunggebenden Deutschen Nationalversammlung und des Deutschen Reichstages 1918-1919,* vol. 6, Reihe 4 (Berlin, 1928), 398. The author of this section was Dr. Max Rubner: Corinna Treitel, "Max Rubner and the Biopolitics of Rational Nutrition," *Central European History* 41, no. 1 (2008): 22n72. Rubner's figure omits deaths from the influenza pandemic.

147. Die Reichsregierung, Berlin, Dec. 10, 1918, copy, establishing the Commission to Determine Violations of Law [Kommission zur Festsetzung von Rechtsverletzungen], whose task was "to refute actual enemy allegations, *especially those that could support claims for reparation,* and to undergird our own allegations" (emphasis in the original), BAB, R 901 86399.

148. Dr. Roesle, "Die Geburts- und Sterblichkeitsverhältnisse," in *Deutschlands Gesundheitsverhältnisse unter dem Einfluss des Weltkrieges,* ed. Franz Bumm (Berlin, 1928), 28. Offer seems to accept Roesle's estimate: Offer, *First World War,* 33–34.

149. Jay Winter, "Some Paradoxes of the First World War," in *The Upheaval of War: Family, Work and Welfare in Europe, 1914-1918,* ed. Richard Wall and Jay M. Winter (Cambridge, 1988), 30.

150. Including by myself: Isabel V. Hull, *Absolute Destruction: Military Culture and the Practices of War in Imperial Germany* (Ithaca, NY, 2005), 320; Gerhard Hirschfeld, Gerd Krumeich, and Irina Renz, eds., *Enzyklopädie des Ersten Weltkrieges* (Paderborn, 2002), 665; Dirk Bönker, "Ein German Way of War? Deutscher Militarismus und maritime Kriegführung im Ersten Weltkrieg," in *Das Deutsche Kaiserreich in der Kontroverse. Eine Bilanz,* ed. Sven Oliver Müller and Cornelius Torp (Göttingen, 2009), 320.

151. Roger Chickering, *The Great War and Urban Life in Germany: Freiburg, 1914-1918* (Cambridge, 2007), esp. ch. 5; Belinda J. Davis, *Home Fires Burning: Food, Politics, and Everyday Life in World War I Berlin* (Chapel Hill, NC, 2000).

152. On the origins of this campaign: Lambert, *Planning Armageddon,* ch. 11.

the causes of German defeat.[153] Too few modern historians of the war devote much attention to the blockade or venture a view about its efficacy. But the best recent summary, by B. J. C. McKercher, is unequivocal. He calls its success "undeniable": "The Allied blockade policies pursued from August 1914 to April 1917 [when the United States entered the war and made the blockade airtight—IVH] had disrupted the German economy, increased food shortages, and created domestic unrest."[154] Historians feel more comfortable citing the effect on morale, rather than on the actual fighting. Gary Sheffield writes that "blockade complemented the defeat of the Central Powers on the battlefield but it could not have replaced it."[155] That is true, but one might turn this statement around and ask if the Allies could have won the war simply on the battlefield? If Germany had had the luxury of full resupply from abroad, in food and raw materials, an Allied victory seems far from possible. The World War was a war of attrition, and the blockade was surely a fundamental weapon in winning such a war. That was certainly the unanimous opinion among Allied leaders in 1918–19. Informed that Marshal Ferdinand Foch thought the blockade was 50 percent responsible for the victory, U.S. general Tasker Bliss replied that "he would give the blockade the greater percentage."[156] In Lloyd George's view, "Germany has been broken almost as much by the blockade as by military methods."[157] A subcommittee of the Supreme Blockade Committee meeting at Versailles in February 1919 "decided that the blockade had been so effectively carried out and so comprehensive during the period of hostilities," that it could not be improved on.[158] In autumn 1918 the confidence of Allied leaders in blockade seemed greater than in their military arms; they relied on the continuing blockade as the major bludgeon to force Germany to uphold the Armistice and later to sign the peace treaty. After November 1918, the blockade became the main guarantor of Allied victory. From the standpoint of contemporary expert opinion, the blockade did indeed provide a "concrete and direct military advantage" that would qualify as proportionate to the civilian losses it caused.

The Controversy over Interdicting Food during the War

The controversy over interdicting food came to a head in the spring of 1915. How Britain actually managed its policy, how it responded to neutral and enemy protest, and the fate

---

153. Bell, *History of the Blockade*, 117, 673–74; Liddell Hart cited in Gary Sheffield, *Forgotten Victory; The First World War: Myths and Realities* (London, 2001), 76.

154. B. J. C. McKercher, "Economic Warfare," in *The Oxford Illustrated History of the First World War*, ed. Hew Strachan (Oxford, 1998), 125, 132. Gary Sheffield agrees: Sheffield, *Forgotten Victory*, 76; also Michael Howard, *The First World War: A Very Short Introduction* (Oxford, 2002), 87; and Osborne, *Britain's Economic Blockade*, 153.

155. Sheffield, *Forgotten Victory*, 77.

156. Vance C. McCormick diary, April 27, 1919, in Suda Lorena Bane and Ralph Haswell Lutz, eds., *The Blockade of Germany after the Armistice, 1918–1919: Selected Documents of the Supreme Economic Council, Superior Blockade Council, American Relief Administration, and Other Wartime Organizations* (Stanford, CA, 1942), 412–13.

157. House, *Intimate Papers*, 163–64.

158. Minutes of Superior Blockade Council, Feb. 11, 1919, in Bane and Lutz, *Blockade*, 109.

of the American proposal to stop the food war all reveal how international law worked during the war.

Britain's actions in the first nine months of war took place within a legal framework. That is, it adjusted its food "blockade" policy according to how it read the law and to neutral protest and intervention, which were also framed in legal terms. One can see this even in the period marked by those "reliable reports" of August 1914 (erroneously) reporting that the German government had assumed control of the entire food supply. The Admiralty consequently ordered the seizure of food shipments only to Germany but not to its allies.[159] Almost simultaneously, however, Hurst received information that the reports were mistaken, and Crowe recognized that the potential error was "important."[160] A week later, Valentine Chirol's report on the economic situation in Germany noted that the capital city, Berlin, had centralized wheat purchases, suggesting that the initial reports might have been correct after all.[161] Three weeks later the Foreign Office canvassed its representatives in the neutral states neighboring Germany for "all possible evidence" supporting its legal contention, and by mid-October their disappointing results had begun to arrive: although some cities had followed Berlin's example, there was no sign that the German government had done so.[162] W. A. Stewart's immediate reaction was that the policy "will have to be revised."[163] By October 23, it was clear that the "reliable reports" were false. Hurst advised that "if there is a chance of this wholesale government control of foodstuffs coming to pass, it would be better not to make any premature attempt to treat all foodstuffs on their way to Germany as contraband."[164]

Two days later, the second order-in-council (October 29, 1914) was issued, the product of two months of negotiation between Britain and the United States. The inability to prove that the German government controlled food supplies contributed to Britain's willingness to rescind the sweeping claim of the August 20, 1914, order-in-council to capture all conditional contraband headed to the enemy.[165] It now restricted capture to conditional contraband consigned to "order," to an unclear consignee, to one living in an enemy country, or where it could be shown that the goods were headed for the armed forces. Under these rules much food continued to flow into Germany.[166]

---

159. Admiralty War Orders, Aug. 26, 1914, no. 15498, confirming Adm. teleg. of Aug. 19, 1914, FO 368/1183, no. 44721, file 72873. Cf. Coogan's interpretation that the policy "far exceeded the limits of international law" and broke "customary British law," suggesting that Britain ceased regarding international law: Coogan, *End of Neutrality,* 163–64.

160. Hurst minute, Aug. 25, 1914; Crowe minute, Aug. 27, 1914, FO 372/588, no. 43294, file 711.

161. Sir Valentine Chirol, "The Economic Situation in Germany during the First Month of the War," Sept. 4, 1914, *BD,* ser. H, 9: doc. 1.

162. Foreign Office to representatives in the Hague, Christiania, Stockholm, and Agent of the Committee on Restriction of Enemy Supplies, Sept. 29, 1914, FO 372/601, no. 52750, file 35250; Sir Alan Johnstone to Grey, Oct. 19, 1914, ibid., Nr. 61854.

163. Stewart minute to Johnstone to Grey, Oct. 19, 1914, FO 372/601, no. 61854, file 35250.

164. Hurst minute of Oct. 27, 1914 to Johnstone to Grey, Oct. 23, 1914, FO 372/602, no. 63267, file 35250.

165. Bell, *History of the Blockade,* 53–54.

166. Some authors interpret this order-in-council as eviscerating the "blockade": Lambert, *Planning Armageddon,* 268–78; Osborne, *Britain's Economic Blockade,* ch. 4.

The Foreign Office withstood several temptations that might have covered a return to the original, more sweeping order. One concerned the German Bundesrat decree empowering the government to take over food supplies. Hurst read it fairly and noted that it did not require them to do so, so "it affords no adequate ground for varying the policy as to foodstuffs at present."[167] The second concerned control of grain by Prussia through the establishment of the Grain Society in January 1915. Crowe rejected taking advantage of this, too: "our refusal to do so may eventually stand us in good stead."[168]

Eventually was not long in coming. On January 25, 1915, the Bundesrat decreed the governmental control over food supplies for which the Foreign Office had waited. Realizing the implications, however, the German government speedily amended the decree so it did "not apply to grain or flour imported from abroad," which, it reassured neutrals, would only go to civilian use.[169]

The Bundesrat's amendment coincided with a major German campaign to enlist the United States in its effort to guarantee food deliveries to German civilians, which would have freed up domestic production for the exclusive use of the military. This campaign had two prongs: a legal test case, the *Wilhelmina*, and a diplomatic maneuver culminating in the U.S. proposal that Britain and Germany compromise on their conduct of the war. Both prongs were blindsided by the German declaration on February 4 of unrestricted submarine warfare. These three things then became entangled.

Let us begin with the *Wilhelmina*. It was a U.S. steamer carrying food to Hamburg consigned to the American owners of the cargo, W. L. Green. Both the U.S. State Department and Britain strongly suspected that the German government had financed the operation.[170] Indeed, lawyers for the shippers notified Secretary of State William Jennings Bryan on the day the *Wilhelmina* sailed (January 22, 1915) "confirming their understanding of the proposition of international law...namely, that they had the right to ship foodstuffs" intended only for civilian use.[171] On February 7, two days before the *Wilhelmina* put into Falmouth harbor to escape bad weather, German ambassador Johann Heinrich Count Bernstorff not only guaranteed that the cargo would feed only civilians, but offered to leave "the sale and distribution" of all such foodstuffs "to American organizations."[172] The *Wilhelmina* thus became a legal test case of the right to interdict food.

Law was the framework within which the Foreign Office debated what to do. A junior clerk argued that "the supply of corn [grain] available for military uses depends on the total supply in Germany and the more corn imported the more there will be for military

---

167. Hurst minute, Nov. 11, 1914, FO 372/602, no. 69407, file 35250. Gesetz über die Ermächtigung der Bundesrats zu wirthschaftlichen Maßnahmen und über die Verlängerung der Fristen des Wechsel- und Scheckrechts im Falle kriegerischer Ereignisse, Germany, *Reichsgesetzblatt*, 75 vols. (Berlin, 1871–1945), 1914: Nr. 52, pp. 327–28.

168. Crowe minute, Jan. 13, 1915, to Lowther to Grey, no. 1, Jan. 4, 1915, FO 382/184 no. 3934, file 3934.

169. Johnstone to Grey, no. 158, Feb. 7, 1915, FO 382/184, no. 15719/2786; *Frankfurter Zeitung*, Feb. 7, 1915, ibid., no. 16882.

170. Spring Rice to Grey, no. 145, Feb. 23, 1915, FO 382/184, no. 21585/8445.

171. Hays, Kaufmann, and Lindheim to Bryan, New York, Jan. 22, 1915, *FRUS* 1915, Suppl., 313–14.

172. Bernstorff to Dept. of State, Washington, Feb. 7, 1915, ibid., 95. Bernstorff had guaranteed that only civilians would have access to the *Wilhelmina*'s cargo already on Jan. 28, *FRUS* 1915, Suppl., 317–18.

uses"; he brushed off the importance of the Bundesrat's amendment.[173] Crowe, however, instantly recognized that the Bundesrat amendment undercut the argument for seizing the *Wilhelmina* on grounds the food was headed for the enemy government. But the DoL also permitted capture if conditional contraband were headed for a "fortified place" or one "serving as a base for the armed forces" (article 34). Crowe pleaded for capture on these two grounds and labeled the distinction between civilian and military goods "a transparent subterfuge."[174] He wanted the Prize Court to decide, because either way, Britain won; if the Prize Court rejected the government's case, "we should gain American esteem for the fairness of our judicial decision."[175] Both the procurator general and the FO legal adviser Malkin thought that "fortified place" supplied the stronger argument, and the Admiralty supplied the necessary information.[176]

Meanwhile, the German campaign had won over Secretary Bryan, who suggested that the United States broker a deal in which Britain would permit food shipments to German civilians (guaranteed by U.S. organizations), in exchange for Germany canceling unrestricted submarine warfare.[177] Bryan thought Britain's position "without justification," but the U.S. note was careful to avoid any suggestion that Britain's food interdiction was illegal; it argued instead that it "will create a very unfavorable impression throughout the world," and even "revulsion."[178] The second U.S. note diluted its legal significance further, calling its own proposal a mere "*modus vivendi* based upon expediency rather than legal right," which did not recognize or deny "any belligerent or neutral right established by the principles of international law."[179] Robert Lansing, legal counselor to the State Department, was inclined to agree with Bryan that a starvation policy was against humanitarian principles, but he interpreted Germany's submarine declaration as blackmail—"an effort to compel neutrals by threats to force Great Britain to change her policy."[180]

Grey, who added as a condition of acceptance that Germany cease mining open waters, seems to have considered the American proposal favorably, but he was alone.[181] Hurst thought the proposal amounted to Germany "ensur[ing] the safety of her food supplies in return for the discontinuance of the illegal methods of warfare which she is now adopting." Like Lansing, Hurst thought Germany's object was to guarantee food supplies "by the indiscriminate sinking of merchant ships with their non-combatant crews." "There is no reason why [Britain] should enter into an agreement for relieving Germany of the

173. H. M. Knatchbull-Hugessen minute to Johnstone to Grey, no. 158, Feb. 7, 1915, FO 382/184, no. 15705, file 2786; Knatchbull-Hugessen minute of Feb. 15, 1915, to Lowther to Grey, no. 3, Feb. 8, 1915, ibid., no. 17314.

174. Crowe minute, Feb. 16, 1915, to Lowther to Grey, no. 3, Feb. 8, 1915, FO 382/184, no. 15705, file 2786.

175. Crowe minute, Jan. 31, 1915, FO 382/184, no. 11800, file 8554.

176. Memo of procurator general, n.d., Crowe minute, Feb. 16, 1915, FO 382/184, no. 17556, file 8554.

177. Coogan, *End of Neutrality,* 228; Bryan to Page, Washington, Feb. 16, 1915, *FRUS* 1915, Suppl., 107.

178. Bryan to Wilson, Washington, Feb. 15, 1915, United States, *Papers Relating to the Foreign Relations of the United States: The Lansing Papers, 1914–1920* (Washington, DC, 1939), 1:353; Bryan to Page, Washington, Feb. 16, 1915, *FRUS* 1915, Suppl., 107.

179. Bryan to Page, Washington, Feb. 20, 1915, *FRUS* 1915, Suppl., 119–20.

180. Lansing comments on the newspaper text of Germany's note of Feb. 16, 1915, United States, *Lansing Papers,* 1:357.

181. Bell, *History of the Blockade,* 231–33; Bryan to Wilson, Feb. 18, 1915, United States, *Lansing Papers,* 1:362.

consequences of her own illegalities."[182] This was essentially the position of Crowe, Senior Clerk Victor A. H. Wellesley, and Malkin, and the cabinet received their opinions in its deliberations.[183]

The cabinet ultimately rejected the modus vivendi, preferring instead to use Germany's U-boat campaign to cover as reprisal a much stiffer "blockade" of the Central Powers. A draft memorandum to U.S. ambassador Page on the *Wilhelmina* laid out Britain's legal thinking. First, it adduced reciprocity. It pointed out that at the beginning of August 1914 Germany had stopped and sunk the Dutch freighter *Maria,* with grain bound for Dublin, on the grounds, upheld by the German Prize Court, that Dublin was a base of supply. In the autumn of 1914 Germany had bombarded West Hartlepool, Scarborough, Yarmouth, and Whitby, none of them naval ports, on the basis that they were fortified places. Applying Germany's own rules ("The German government cannot have it both ways"), Britain observed that Hamburg was therefore clearly a fortified place. But, second, Grey's memorandum used retaliation to lay the legal basis for declaring food absolute contraband. The distinction between absolute and conditional contraband "has to all intents and purposes been swept away by the novel doctrines proclaimed and acted upon by the German government." Adverting to a long series of German violations of the laws of war and of humanity, the memo claimed that it was now open to Britain "to take retaliatory measures, even if such measures were of a kind to involve pressure on the civil population." Grey here had struck out Crowe's clearer draft language: "such as interfering with the oversea food supply of the German civil population."[184] In fact, Britain never declared food to be absolute contraband, though as the blockade got tighter, it mattered less and less in practice.[185]

The decision to pursue a retaliatory "blockade" (a policy we will examine in detail below) robbed the *Wilhelmina* of its test case status; it became simply irrelevant. Its cargo was withdrawn from the Prize Court and purchased by the government for a price commensurate with the profit its owners would have made in Hamburg. The decision to compensate the owners had been taken before the *Wilhelmina* even reached Britain, because it had set sail before the German government assumed control of foodstuffs, and thus could not have known of the change in its legal situation.[186]

Britain rejected the American modus vivendi because German government control of food supplies together with unrestricted submarine warfare gave Britain the legal cover it needed to enforce much stronger interdiction of all goods, including food, than it could

---

182. Hurst minute, Feb. 22, 1915, to Page to Grey, London, Feb. 22, 1915, FO 372/761, no. 20133, file 13659.

183. Grey minute, FO 372/761, no. 20133, file 13659.

184. Draft memorandum from Grey to Page, Feb. 19, 1915, FO 382/184, no. 18427, file 8554. Final memorandum: Grey to Page, Feb. 19, 1915, *FRUS* 1915, Suppl., 335–37.

185. Contraband lists always categorized food as "conditional contraband," Bell, *History of the Blockade,* 722–44. Cf. Robert Cecil's call to make food absolute contraband because "the whole German nation is now in arms against us," and thus "modern developments have made it absolute contraband." Cecil to Hurst, July 8, 1915, FO 382/462, no. 91022.

186. Page to Bryan, tel. London, Apr. 8, 1915, *FRUS* 1915, Suppl., 363–64; Page to Bryan, tel., London, Jan. 27, 1915, ibid., 317.

have done before within the legal strictures that it had accepted for itself. There was no "advantage" for Britain to accede to such a proposal.[187]

The failure of the modus vivendi on the German side shows that its leaders valued food for civilians much less than other wartime considerations. After private *pourparlers* with Britain and Germany, the United States had amended its original proposal so that in the end the deal traded food for civilians in exchange for dropping unrestricted submarine warfare and mining the open seas. In a sense, the deal reiterated the DoL and the Hague Convention on automatic contact mines: food remained conditional contraband subject to the restrictions laid down in DoL articles 33 and 35, submarines were subject to "cruiser rules" of operation that forbade them to sink any merchant ship without warning (articles 48–50), and unanchored automatic contact mines were forbidden entirely, while anchored mines could only be laid defensively, in one's own territorial waters.[188]

Foreign Secretary Jagow realized that the final American proposal

> would put England in a very difficult position; it would either have to reject it or be forced to admit that its previous conduct of war was contrary to international law, and it must declare itself ready to give up its plan to starve Germany under pressure of our U-boat campaign. It would be a moral victory over England's claim to mastery of the sea. And we would secure the provisioning of Germany.[189]

But apparently this was not enough. He added that Germany must insist on lifting capture of "raw materials for industrial purposes." He also added, but then crossed out, that "the prohibition of offensive mine war also appears unacceptable."[190] Naval leaders insisted successfully that both offensive mining of the open sea and the prohibition of arming merchant vessels and resistance of any kind by merchant vessels be added to Germany's conditions. The chancellor and his allies beat back Admiral von Tirpitz's attempt to include a further demand for the return to service of Germany's merchant ships, which in order to escape confiscation had transferred to neutral flags at the start of war. Bethmann Hollweg rejected the idea because it violated long-standing international law and therefore undercut the basis of the U.S. proposal, which was to return to law.[191] Tirpitz insisted that if Germany must give up unrestricted submarine warfare, it had to receive a "recognizable equivalent, otherwise it would appear weak"; the "citation of an entirely obsolete

---

187. Hurst minute, Feb. 22, 1915, FO 372/761, no. 20133, file 13659.

188. The modus vivendi also forbade the controversial, but nonetheless old practice whereby threatened enemy merchantmen would fly neutral flags. We will discuss this controversy in the next chapter.

189. Jagow memorandum to Gerard to Jagow, no. 2371, Feb. 22, 1915, IIIa 4258, BAB R 901 85914.

190. Ibid.

191. As the Austro-Hungarian delegation to the London Conference summarized, "According to the practice of almost all States, the sale of an enemy vessel made in the course of voyage and after the outbreak of hostilities can not prevent the capture of the vessel." The summary observation at the conference stated "the common principle" that "the transfer of a vessel can not be admitted when the object in view is to escape the consequences to which its character of enemy vessel exposes it." That principle was then embodied in DoL art. 56. Scott, *Declaration of London*, 100, 103, 172–73.

international law was not valid."[192] Tirpitz lost this fight, but the final German reply still contained the other demands, which permitted Britain to observe that Germany still intended to sink armed enemy merchantmen without notice by submarine and to sink other vessels by mines, so that it had in fact rejected the U.S. proposal.[193] From our perspective, the German response is noteworthy because it explicitly ranked in importance industrial raw materials and certain weapons or techniques of war ahead of food for civilians.

Although Wilson's go-between, Colonel Edward M. House, tried to revive the modus vivendi in May 1915, by then poison gas had joined submarines and automatic contact mines as impediments to an agreement.[194] From the spring of 1915 onward, the interdiction of food steadily expanded as one of the main instruments of warfare for both sides.

Neutral Responses and British Management

It would be convenient if one could use neutral protests to measure the extent of a belligerent violation of the laws of war. Unfortunately, both neutral protests and neutral silence were multicausal.[195] The United States passed over major breaches of treaty law and the laws of war because it did not wish to be drawn into the conflict nor to become a "chronic critic" of the belligerents.[196] Many diplomatic notes were drawn up for domestic public consumption, or were carefully edited to fulfill the widely held, but mechanistic standard of neutrality that called for protesting against one side only if one issued a simultaneous protest against the other. And neutrals close to the fighting, especially the Netherlands and Denmark, which abutted Germany but whose food exports were important to Britain, balanced precariously between both sides. Lack of coordination limited the impact neutrals might have had in upholding international law. Although both the United States and the Netherlands occasionally flirted with the idea of joint neutral protests, only the Scandinavian states actually issued them now and again.[197] But while Sweden and Norway

---

192. Tirpitz and Adm. Bachmann memorandum for the Immediatvortrag of Feb. 28, 1915, Alfred von Tirpitz, *Politische Dokumente: Deutsche Ohnmachtspolitik im Weltkriege* (Hamburg, 1926), 324.

193. German reply (of Feb. 28, 1915) contained in Gerard to Bryan, Berlin, Mar. 1, 1915, *FRUS* 1915, Suppl., 129–130; Grey memorandum, London, Mar. 15, 1915, *FRUS* 1915, Suppl., 140–41. Lansing had already recognized that any "exception made as to danger from mines" was unacceptable. Lansing comment on German note of Feb. 16, 1915, United States, *Lansing Papers,* 1:360. In May 1915 Jagow summed it up: "This proposition of permitting passage of food in return for cessation of submarine methods already made and declined." Gerard to Bryan, Berlin, May 25, 1915, *FRUS* 1915, Suppl., 415.

194. Page to Bryan, London, May 19, 1915, *FRUS* 1915, Suppl., 400–401; Bryan to Gerard, Washington, May 23, 1915, ibid., 406; Gerard to Bryan, Berlin, May 25, 1915, ibid., 415.

195. Cf. Anthony A. D'Amato, *The Concept of Custom in International Law,* foreword by Richard A. Falk (Ithaca NY, 1971), 98–102.

196. Wilson to Bryan, Washington, Sept. 4, 1914, *FRUS* 1914, Suppl., 33.

197. Lansing to Bryan, Washington, May 10, 1915, United States, *Lansing Papers,* 1:391; Loudon to Limburg Stirum, Oct. 21, 1914, *BPNL,* 4: doc. 211.

shared some economic interests, their political views were quite opposed: Norway was pro-Allied, while Sweden's court, military, and government were pro-German.

Nevertheless, neutral protests do provide some indication of world reaction to belligerent conduct. Regarding British economic measures, the neutral response in 1914 and 1915 was remarkably tame. The United States tried to get Britain to accept the entire DoL as the basis of its war measures, but abandoned the effort in October 1914 as hopeless.[198] Both the United States and the Netherlands essentially accepted the "blockade" as a system and issued mostly private protests on a case-by-case basis.[199] Britain's ambassador to Holland, Sir Alan Johnstone, described Dutch protests as having merely "academic character."[200] Indeed, the Dutch government wanted Britain to extend the absolute contraband list, which would make it easier for the Netherlands to block reexports to Germany.[201] Widespread neutral acquiescence to Britain's blockade-like measures made Germany restive. It issued its first protest against British maritime conduct in a memorandum to neutrals on October 10. Nine days later, the Scandinavian states began formulating a joint protest that appeared on November 12, 1914.[202] The Netherlands refused to join the Scandinavians, citing an earlier note of its own. The United States sent its first formal protest on December 26, 1914.[203]

The legal claims made in these protests differed. Neither the United States nor Holland assumed that the DoL was binding. The United States, realizing Britain would never agree to adopt the entire document, announced that henceforth "the rights and duties of the United States and its citizens in the present war [will] be defined by the existing rules of international law and the treaties of the United States irrespective of the provisions of the Declaration of London."[204] The Dutch foreign minister, John Loudon, told his ambassador in Germany that the DoL, "although not ratified by any of the participating powers and thus at the moment not part of generally recognized international law, is a large step forward in the development of that law."[205] Both Germany and the Scandinavian states based their protests on the premise that, despite its non-ratification, the DoL was "the most authoritative expression of the juridical conscience of nations, depicting…the existing status of international law," and that "full and entire validity must henceforth be conceded to nearly all its provisions."[206] Therefore, they listed the application of continuous voyage to conditional contraband and the extension of the contraband lists as violations of law. But all neutrals agreed that Britain was interfering with neutral-neutral trade in

---

198. Lansing to Wilson, Washington, Oct. 20, 1914, United States, *Lansing Papers,* 1:255–56; Lansing to Page, Washington, Oct. 22, 1914, *FRUS* 1914, Suppl., 257–58.

199. Coogan, *End of Neutrality,* chs. 9–10; Marc Frey, *Der Erste Weltkrieg und die Niederlande: Ein neutrales Land im politischen und wirtschaftlichen Kalkül der Kriegsgegner* (Berlin, 1998), 104, 68.

200. Johnstone to Grey, Dec. 16, 1914, Frey, *Erste Weltkrieg und die Niederlande,* 96.

201. Frey, *Erste Weltkrieg und die Niederlande,* 117.

202. *BNPL,* 4: docs. 192, 208, 235, 242; Sweden to German, French, British, and Russian ministers, Stockholm, Nov. 12, 1914, *FRUS* 1914, Suppl., 360–61.

203. *FRUS* 1914, Suppl., 372–75.

204. Lansing to Page, Washington, Oct. 22, 1914, *FRUS* 1914, Suppl., 258.

205. Loudon to Amb. to Germany Gevers, Nov. 19, 1914, *BPNL,* 4: doc. 252.

206. Swedish Foreign Minister Wallenberg to German, French, British, and Russian ministers, Stockholm, Nov. 12, 1914, *FRUS* 1914, Suppl., 361.

a way injurious to neutral sovereignty and therefore illegal. Especially vexatious was the diversion of neutral vessels to British ports upon mere suspicion and with lack of proof of enemy destination (particularly for food).[207]

Neutral protests were worrisome enough to cause Britain to tinker with its first order-in-council, issuing another on October 29, 1914. It specified and therefore narrowed somewhat the grounds for capture under continuous voyage. But that did not mollify the United States, for it created "the apparent indecision" and "uncertainty" in trade relations that the U.S. note particularly deplored.[208] On the whole, however, neutral states continued to acquiesce in British measures. Neutral acquiescence was a top priority of British policy, and its achievement was due more to how Britain managed the blockade than to the mere exercise of its maritime power. Even after March 1915, when it had frankly taken leave of the law, the policy was to cajole, pressure, and reward neutrals for their compliance. For example, the cabinet ordered (March 10, 1915) that neutral ships "should be detained long enough to make them feel the inconvenience of carrying such [enemy or contraband] goods, and the advantage of not doing so, but they should be given the benefit of the doubt when the case is not clear."[209] Admiral Slade of the War Trade Advisory Committee cautioned (June 1915) that "it is necessary to avoid making their [neutrals'] legitimate commerce suffer too much."[210] Even at the height of the "blockade" in 1917, Hurst was careful to build in "incentive[s]" for neutral cooperation.[211] An internal report from the end of 1916 summed up British policy: "A ruling consideration throughout has been the desire to impose on neutral shipping as little inconvenience as is consistent with the interception of the enemy's sea-borne commerce."[212]

Britain's success was the product of many factors. The blockade was run by civilian experts in diplomacy, who worked with their counterparts in commerce and trade. Grey attended to many of the controversial details and note-writing himself. Eyre Crowe was head of the Contraband Committee; he was succeeded by Robert Cecil (a lawyer), who became minister of blockade, when that office was established in February 1916. The senior government lawyers, like Hurst, John P. Mellor, and Frederick Smith, were deeply involved in decision making. The cabinet oversaw it all and decided the most controversial legal issues.[213] The decision-making process was not generally hindered by the Admiralty, which

---

207. Loudon to Johnstone, Nov. 13, 1914, *BNPL*, 4: doc. 248; Bryan to Page, Washington, Dec. 26, 1914, *FRUS* 1914, Suppl., 372–75; Wallenberg to ministers, Nov. 12, 1914, *FRUS* 1914, Suppl., 360–61.

208. "Unwarranted as such detentions are, in the opinion of this Government, American exporters are further perplexed by the apparent indecision of the British authorities in applying their own rules to neutral cargoes": Bryan to Page, Washington, Dec. 26, 1914, *FRUS* 1914, Suppl., 373.

209. Cited in Bell, *History of the Blockade*, 249.

210. Marjorie M. Farrar, *Conflict and Compromise: The Strategy, Politics and Diplomacy of the French Blockade, 1914–1918* (The Hague, 1974), 71.

211. Hurst memo of Feb. 5, 1917, "Proposed Order in Council for Further Reprisals against the Enemy," Malkin Papers, FO 800/913.

212. Report to the Foreign Office Secretary, the First Lord of the Admiralty, and the President of the Board of Trade, Nov. 4, 1916, *BD*, ser. H, 7:321, doc. 176.

213. Lambert, *Planning Armageddon*, 303–4; J. A. Spender and Cyril Asquith, *Life of Herbert Henry Asquith, Lord Oxford and Asquith* (London, 1932), 131.

continued to have a very broad conception of belligerence and whose representatives on the various blockade committees, such as Admiral Slade, had extensive experience in intelligence and diplomacy at the prewar legal negotiations at the Hague Convention and the London Conference.

Britain used many methods to achieve its goal; perhaps the most important was negotiation. The model for negotiations was Holland. In 1914, Britain at first opened talks with the Dutch government, trying to get its officials to ban transshipments to Germany. Although the Dutch might have liked to comply, they were far too vulnerable to German pressure to do so.[214] Britain then turned to private traders, who with government blessing set up cartel-like organizations like the Netherlands Overseas Trust (NOT), which offered the guarantees Britain sought. Separate agreements were laboriously worked out with the Swiss Société de Surveillance, the Danish Chamber of Manufacturers, and the Copenhagen Merchants' Guild.[215] These deals were especially useful because, as Bell says, they were "business agreements, which impinged upon no legal doctrine, or rule of policy."[216] They sidestepped the vexatious legal issues that ensnared the Foreign Office. More important, these agreements involved those most affected by policy in its formation. Britain certainly applied pressure—more as the war went on. For example, Holland had compensated Germany for Dutch cooperation with the British by exporting to Germany most of the food it raised or fished itself. In an effort in 1916 to get the Dutch to agree to redirect half of that amount to Britain, the navy detained twenty grain ships and seized Dutch fishing vessels. When the Dutch remained hard, Crowe and Cecil considered reducing forage imports, coal for Dutch ships, and even cutting Dutch overseas cables. Ultimately, they did none of these things, because in the end Britain favored negotiations, in which it made compromises and recognized limits to coercion. In this case the compromise was to reckon Dutch food shipments to the Committee for the Relief of Belgium as part of the Allied allotment. And Britain subventioned the (Allied) customers for Dutch fish, so that the fishermen would not suffer economically.[217]

In its negotiations, Britain was sensitive to neutral vulnerability to German military power. Attempting a similar redirection of Danish food, Britain took account of possible German retaliation. Cecil, who energetically pushed for harsher measures, nonetheless concluded it was better to adhere "to the present more cautious policy" that worked "by gradual and elastic pressure without driving Germany to retaliation."[218] Similarly, Britain overlooked massive shipments across Holland of sand and gravel destined for the German trenches, as well as the widespread use of Dutch riverboats for German military supply transports. Both were clearly unneutral behavior and thus quite illegal, but after energetic protests, Britain let them be, because it knew that the Netherlands was coerced by a German general staff threat of invasion.[219]

---

214. See the account of Holland: Frey, *Erste Weltkrieg und die Niederlande*, 113.

215. *BD*, ser. H, 5:xix.

216. Bell, *History of the Blockade*, 403.

217. Frey, *Erste Weltkrieg und die Niederlande*, 153, 170–80.

218. Foreign Office to Admiralty, Dec. 9, 1916, *BD*, ser. H, 8: doc. 10.

219. Frey, *Erste Weltkrieg und die Niederlande*, 254–57, 274–81; Garner, *International Law*, 2:449.

Money also played a big role in mollifying neutrals. When Britain shifted to an undeclared blockade in March 1915, it confiscated neither ships nor goods. Enemy goods aboard neutral ships were returned to the owners; requisitioned cargos were compensated. The owners of ships being diverted to British ports that sank on the way were paid in full plus 5 percent.[220] Cecil offered compensation to any ship sunk outside the war zone by a mine laid by the Allies.[221] Britain went beyond legal requirements: even when the British Prize Court upheld as legal its capture of the *Kim,* for example, the government compensated the owners.[222] It had taken to heart the maxim offered by one international jurist: "Compensation to neutrals is, and must be, no small part of the normal cost of a modern naval war."[223]

In addition to monetary subsidies and compensation, Britain provided safety. As article 3 of Hague Convention VIII required, Britain notified neutrals of its minefields, on condition they kept the information secret. It furnished safe lanes for their vessels.[224]

Britain also provided legal recourse. Neutral shipowners could appeal British actions before the Prize Court; if the Crown lost the case, the owners were indemnified. Britain's Prize Court distinguished itself from many others by its relative independence from the government. In a famous decision from 1916, the *Zamora* case, Sir Samuel Evans ruled that the Prize Court would follow international law, not the innovations contained in orders-in-council. The attorney general assembled a committee to discuss the effects of the *Zamora* decision. It concluded that they were far-reaching: "The King, i.e., the Executive, cannot alter the law of the Court. Orders in Council which purport to do so are *ultra vires* [beyond the power authorized by law] and *pro tanto* [to that extent] a nullity"; only changes favoring neutrals, not harming their interests, would be acceptable to the court; and, finally, "The Government *cannot* by executive act alter international law in its favour."[225] The British Prize Court was therefore a genuine legal venue where neutrals affected by blockade could have their cases heard. Appeals went to the Privy Council.

The Prize Court was also open to enemy owners. During the prewar CID planning sessions, Lassa Oppenheim had strongly recommended dropping the old rule barring enemies from appearing before the king's courts. He argued that that rule had been outstripped by legal developments generally, most other European nations granted standing to enemies, and the Hague rules of land warfare seemed to do the same.[226] Although the government did not follow Oppenheim's advice, the Prize Court did. In November 1914 Sir Samuel Evans ruled that enemy owners could be heard in cases involving the 1907

---

220. Marder, *From the Dreadnought,* 2:374.

221. *Berliner Lokal-Anzeiger,* July 6, 1917.

222. Garner, *International Law,* 2:308.

223. Macdonell, "Notes on Blockade," 102–3.

224. Chilton to Grey, no. 80, Aug. 11, 1914, FO 371/2164, no. 38134, fols. 207–8; Circular telegram from Foreign Office, Nov. 2, 1914, FO 372/633, no. 66775, file 39810; Julian S. Corbett, *Naval Operations* (London: Longmans, Green & Co., 1920–28), 1:188; Garner, *International Law,* 1:332.

225. Report of the "Zamora" Committee, in Malkin Papers, "Maritime Rights, Prize Orders in Council and Papers Relating to Withdrawal of Declaration of London, 1914–1917," FO 800/918.

226. Appendix 9, "Report and Proceedings," CAB 16/18A; and for Grey's rejection of this view, appendix 4, F. A. Campbell (FO) to Oppenheim, Mar. 27, 1911, ibid.

Hague Rules relating to merchant ships in time of war, if the enemy's government had not reserved those articles.[227]

Finally, and perhaps most important for businessmen, Britain offered certainty. Certainty came from the contracts negotiated with the private consortia or directly with firms, from instruments invented later in the war like "navicerts" (which guaranteed swift handling in British ports), from regularized procedures of search and visit, and from the Prize Court. Most of all it came from efficacy. The blockade ultimately worked.[228] The Contraband Committee each day pored over the manifests of every ship arriving from overseas. It ordered ships detained or cargo unloaded in some percentage of these cases—for example, in January 1915 in 27 percent, but by July 1915, in 42 percent of arrivals.[229] These are staggering numbers. With the advent of navicerts and greater neutral accommodation, the numbers detained fell, but not the numbers of ships overseen.[230]

Effectiveness, which translated into business certainty, helped to legitimate British measures. Britain well understood the relation between efficacy and acceptance. Its tinkering with the orders-in-council in October 1914 was designed "to assure their efficacy in reducing risks to neutrals and calming their irritation."[231] In the midst of sharp legal arguments about the "blockade" with the United States, Lord Eustace Percy minuted (February 1916) that "the finest legal arguments" would be unconvincing. "They don't want to have our 'blockade' justified to them; they want to see it work. They will judge of its 'effectiveness' by whether it shows signs of really bringing Germany to her knees, not by its compliance with legal definitions."[232] He was doubtless gratified by reports in May that the U.S. press had indeed come to accept the reality and the legality of the "blockade."[233]

Britain's success in getting neutral acquiescence to the blockade was in the end due to the nature of its government and to the breadth and depth of its power. The cabinet and FO kept the blockade firmly within a strategic context that factored legal, diplomatic, economic, coalition, public opinion, and other considerations into military policy. Britain's purely naval strength enabled it to monitor virtually all shipping and to divert a large number of vessels to British ports for visit and search. But its vast commercial reach permitted it to put together, with the help of neutral traders, for the first time in history a huge statistical base of world trade information without which the its measures could never have functioned.[234] Britain's knowledge of and importance to insurance, finance,

---

227. Evans ruling in the *Möwe* (Nov. 9, 1914), cited in Garner, *International Law*, 1:133–34.

228. Scholars impatient with the FO's consideration for international law and neutral opinion stress the inefficacy of the "blockade," particularly compared to what they believe an unlimited blockade might have accomplished: Osborne, *Britain's Economic Blockade*; Lambert, *Planning Armageddon*, esp. ch. 11.

229. Bell, *History of the Blockade*, 250.

230. For a description of the procedure for visit and search see Bell, *History of the Blockade*, 34–35.

231. Paul Cambon to Delcassé, no. 942, London, Oct. 28, 1914, *DDFr* 1914, doc. 437.

232. Lord Eustace Percy memo, ca. Feb. 3, 1916, FO 382/1099, no. 21163, file 302. Secretary of State Lansing said something similar: W. G. M. Müller, Report of Sept. 8, 1915, *BD*, ser. H, 9: doc. 20.

233. W. G. Max Müller, "Economic Situation in Germany during May 1916," June 15, 1916, *BD*, ser. H, 10: doc. 13.

234. Lambert stresses the difficulty of building the statistical base; it was indeed unprecedented, but ultimately British officials succeeded; Lambert, *Planning Armageddon*, ch. 9.

and credit positioned it to offer favors to those who cooperated and to punish those who did not. Its deep pockets (and after those were emptied, later creditworthiness) helped it to buy collaborators, with money, coal, subventioned customers, etc. Its diplomatic skills eased negotiation. And its form of government predisposed it to favor negotiation over pure force and permitted it to offer administrative regularity (once the blockade got going) and some legal guarantees, in the form of the Prize Court or compensation, to those who felt wronged by its actions.

Breaking and Making International Law

The Blockade, 1915–1918

O n February 26, 1915, Sir Edward Grey, referring to the blockade, said, "We believe that up to the present all we have done has been sanctioned by precedent, including that of the United States."[1] Two weeks later, he could not have said the same, for on March 11, 1915, Britain used the cover of reprisal to launch policies that were quite unprecedented.

The Declaration of the "War Zone"

The Admiralty had actually begun this course on November 2, 1914, when it unilaterally declared the North Sea a "war zone."[2] The readiness to adopt such a course might have been prepared almost two weeks earlier when First Lord of the Admiralty Winston Churchill proposed to the cabinet a scheme to close the North Sea to all vessels. Churchill had been discussing the possibility of a German landing in Great Britain; the cabinet approved the war zone plan in principle.[3] Although no archival documents on the Admiralty's decision survive, Nicholas Lambert has pieced together the story from personal correspondence.[4]

1. Grey to Cecil Spring Rice, no. 145, Feb. 26, 1915, FO 382/185 no. 22391, file 22076.

2. Circular telegram, Foreign Office, Nov. 2, 1914, FO 372/633, no. 66775, file 39810; enclosure, Grey to Spring Rice, Nov. 3, 1914, *FRUS* 1914, Suppl., 464.

3. Asquith to King, Oct. 22, 1914, CAB 41/35/54.

4. Nicholas A. Lambert, *Planning Armageddon: British Economic Warfare and the First World War* (Cambridge, MA, 2012), 297–99. On the outside of the relevant file is this sentence: "Statement (August 1915) that the notice issued to the Press on 3rd Nov. 1914 warning neutrals of the closure was issued by the First Lord

In the wake of naval blunders in the first months of the war, Prime Minister Herbert Asquith reappointed Admiral John "Jacky" Fisher as first sea lord on November 1, 1914. Always a champion of economic warfare, Fisher immediately set about strengthening the blockade with characteristic force and legal insouciance. In doing so, he presented the FO with the kind of dilemma that their German colleagues more often faced.

The day after his appointment, Fisher met with Asquith, Churchill, War Minister Herbert H. Kitchener, Foreign Minister Sir Edward Grey, and Admiral Sir John Jellicoe. Fisher pushed through three policies designed to give the British navy a stranglehold over the North Sea. Britain was to announce that foreign fishermen were henceforth banned from British coastal waters, and that the navy would lay minefields (recall that the cabinet had authorized these "in principle" in August) and change navigational buoys. Fisher's recommendations were probably partly in reaction to continued German mining of the North Sea (which had claimed twenty ships in the first two months of war and had sunk the dreadnought *Audacious* just one week before) and the Admiralty's erroneous belief that Germans illegally used neutral cover to disguise their mine-laying (and hospital ships and fishing trawlers for spying).[5] But they were mostly designed to force neutral ships into designated safety lanes and thence if necessary to British ports, where they could be searched for contraband. "We shall now be able to control effectively the neutral traffic now so remunerative to Dutch and Scandinavian pockets in feeding Germany," Fisher predicted.[6] Asquith was pleased; Grey was opposed, but unable to stop the effervescent Fisher.[7]

The Admiralty's war zone declaration on November 2 sarcastically claimed that "the ordinary features of German naval warfare" were illegal and produced "novel conditions" to which the British Navy must respond.[8] It stated that "the whole of the North Sea must be considered a military area" and added that Britain would now be forced to lay mines itself. It routed shipping through the Channel, but in response to vehement Norwegian protests it soon guaranteed a safe route to the north off Scotland.[9]

Despite the declaration's threat of mines and vigilant warships, Britain did not sink neutral vessels, nor did it intend to; it provided safe routes and pilots.[10] But it was not

---

and no papers exist to shew how it was discussed and decided on." ADM 1/8403/425. Also, Archibald C. Bell, *A History of the Blockade of Germany and of the Countries Associated with Her in the Great War, Austria, Bulgaria, and Turkey, 1914–1918* (London, 1937), 63.

5. Grey's explanation for Parliament, Nov. 24, 1914: FO 372/611, file 35888, no. 74685; Julian S. Corbett, *Naval Operations* (London, 1920–28), 1:257–58; Gerd Hankel, *Die Leipziger Prozesse: Deutsche Kriegsverbrechen und ihre strafrechtliche Verfolgung nach dem Ersten Weltkrieg* (Hamburg, 2003), 406; James Wilford Garner, *International Law and the World War* (London, 1920), 1:330n1; Arthur J. Marder, *From the Dreadnought to Scapa Flow: The Royal Navy in the Fisher Era, 1904–1919* (Oxford, 1961–70), 2:72.

6. Lambert, *Planning Armageddon*, 298.

7. K. G. Robbins, "Foreign Policy, Government Structure and Public Opinion," in *British Foreign Policy under Sir Edward Grey*, ed. F. H. Hinsley (Cambridge, 1977), 539–40.

8. British Foreign Office to Cecil Spring Rice, Nov. 3, 1914, *FRUS* 1914, Suppl., 464.

9. Amb. Schmedemann to Bryan, Christiania, Nov. 9, 1914, *FRUS* 1914, Suppl., 466.

10. Coogan is wrong in imagining that Britain had replaced search and visit with "explode and sink." John W. Coogan, *The End of Neutrality: The United States, Britain, and Maritime Rights, 1899–1915* (Ithaca, NY, 1981), 213–14, 235–36; and Dirk Bönker, "Ein German Way of War? Deutscher Militarismus und maritime Kriegführung

legal. Although Russia had barred neutral ships with wireless equipment from a large "war zone" in 1904–5, Britain's declaration was legally a novel extension of the doctrine of war zone and dubious because it was too big and not the site of actual military engagement.[11] The war zone was also unprepared legally and diplomatically. France was unpleasantly surprised and basically opposed the move.[12] The Norwegian protest decried this "attack" on the international-legal principle of freedom of the seas, though it "was persuaded of the good intentions of the British government."[13] Grey, evidently embarrassed at his own role, did not inform his FO colleagues; they first learned of it to their horror on November 25. They reacted in two ways. The senior legal adviser, W. E. Davidson, thought it too late to fix, and assumed "that those who are directly responsible in such matters consider that it is absolutely necessary for the safety of the state to take these measures whether they are legally justifiable or not."[14] In effect, Davidson argued war necessity (*Kriegsnotwendigkeit*) or self-preservation for a matter that was clearly one of mere military convenience. Sir Eyre Crowe, head of the FO's Contraband Department and an otherwise forceful advocate of economic warfare, nevertheless pressed to bring the matter before the cabinet; he thus took the political route to try to reverse the policy. That process was in the works when it was cut short by Germany's declaration of unrestricted submarine warfare (February 2, 1915) in its own war zone around the British isles. Fisher's move had thus provided Germany with a precedent, which it determined to follow, though operating by quite different principles.[15]

The March 11 (Reprisal) Order-in-Council

Under the cover of reprisal against Germany's declaration, Britain now introduced a series of innovations that contravened even the Declaration of Paris of 1856. The order-in-council of March 11, 1915, established a blockade in fact, but not in name. It targeted German exports (which could not count as contraband) as well as imports, and it removed goods of enemy origin (regardless of ownership) or enemy property from neutral ships heading to neutral ports. Two subsequent orders-in-council (October 20, 1915, and March 30, 1916) further whittled down the DoL, until it was formally dropped on July 7, 1916. Two final orders-in-council applied the previous measures to Germany's allies

---

im Ersten Weltkrieg," in *Das Deutsche Kaiserreich in der Kontroverse. Eine Bilanz,* ed. Sven Oliver Müller and Cornelius Torp (Göttingen, 2009), 321n36. Cf. "Navigation in the North Sea and English Channel," enclosure to Consul General Skinner to Bryan, London, Dec. 11, 1914, *FRUS* 1914, Suppl., 470–72.

11. Dr. J. Pawley Bate, memorandum for the historical section of the Foreign Office, n.d., FO 372/1186, no. 184425, file 539; Garner, *International Law,* 1:351–53; John Macdonell, "Some Notes on Blockade," *Grotius Society, Problems of the War: Papers Read before the Society in the Year 1915* 1 (1916): 104; Hankel, *Leipziger Prozesse,* 407–8.

12. Crowe note of Mar. 14, 1915, FO 371/2362, file 30717.

13. Norway to MAE, Nov. 5, 1914, Kristiania, no. 43889, MAE Corr. Polit. vol. 1132.

14. Cited in Lambert, *Planning Armageddon,* 299.

15. Unrestricted submarine warfare is the subject of chapters 7 and 8.

(January 10, 1917) and then (February 16, 1917) forced all neutral ships heading for neutral ports adjacent to an enemy to call at Allied ports under penalty of detention before the Prize Court or possible confiscation (if they carried enemy goods). Administratively, that is, outside the official orders-in-council, Britain and France perfected the rationing of neutrals using statistical measures of prewar imports, they made blacklists of firms trading with the enemy, and they extended the contraband lists until these included practically everything. The last contraband list contained 238 goods (counting foodstuffs as a single item). Nothing escaped scrutiny; officials fretted over German-made dolls and hairnets imported from China.[16]

Beginning in March 1915 then, Britain abandoned some of the legal framework it had worked out in August 1914 to cover its maritime conduct. But it did not abandon international law altogether. The decision-making process preceding the March 1915 order-in-council reveals how both Britain and France interpreted law and how they weighed it against belligerent convenience. It took six weeks to work out a policy acceptable to the cabinet and to France. Cabinet members hesitated at first because they could not believe that Germany truly meant to sink neutral merchant vessels, and only such a drastic violation of neutral rights would outweigh the damage to neutrals caused by a British reprisal blockade.[17] And there was the matter of starvation. Although Arthur Balfour thought it "unlikely that we shall starve Germany into submission," he added that "I am not sure that I would do it if I could."[18] Prime Minister Asquith and Grey were the last holdouts, both motivated equally by legal considerations and fear of neutral (especially U.S.) reaction;[19] indeed, those were synonymous, because neutrals framed their protests in the legal language of rights. Under the press of parliamentary and public opinion, Asquith gave way, announcing to the House of Commons that, because of Germany's repudiation "both of law and humanity, we are not going to allow our efforts to be strangled in a network of juridical niceties. We do not intend to put into operation any measures which we do not think effective, and I need not say we shall carefully avoid any measures which violate the rules either of humanity or of honesty."[20] That was a clear statement that Britain intended to break the law, covered by reprisal. But in fact the legal situation was not so straightforward.

A week after the German announcement of unrestricted submarine warfare around the British Isles, French representatives were already in London discussing a British draft. The personnel were naval officers with international-legal experience and lawyers. France sent Admiral Frédéric Paul Moreau, Henri Fromageot (the senior legal counsel at their foreign ministry), and A. C. de Fleuriau (longtime counselor at the French embassy); their English counterparts included Rear Admiral Edmond Slade (Britain's naval representative at

---

16. "Classified list of articles treated as absolute and conditional contraband from July 1917 to armistice," in Bell, *History of the Blockade,* 740–44; MAE Blocus 44, passim.

17. J. A. Spender and Cyril Asquith, *Life of Herbert Henry Asquith, Lord Oxford and Asquith* (London, 1932), 131; Lambert, *Planning Armageddon,* 361–62.

18. Balfour to Hankey, Feb. 17, 1915, cited in Lambert, *Planning Armageddon,* 370.

19. Lambert, *Planning Armageddon,* 365, 367.

20. Cited ibid., 367.

the London conference in 1909), Cecil J. B. Hurst (legal adviser to the Foreign Office), and Attorney General John Simon, and, at later meetings, Sir Francis Hopwood (a lawyer and civil lord of the Admiralty), Sir Graham Greene and Captain Webb from the Admiralty, and John Mellor (the procurator general).[21]

The French tended to favor more clear-cut legal approaches than the British. As they had done in August 1914 and did again several times later, the French pressed for a declared, legal blockade of Germany's North Sea coast.[22] The British Admiralty turned down that idea probably for the same reasons they rejected it in 1914; the French naval minister remarked that such a blockade could only be done by submarine, putting the Allies on a par with Germany.[23] When the discussion turned to whether Hague Convention VI might keep the Prize Court from condemning neutral ships under the new order, Fromageot "objected to any action which implied that the Hague Conventions were not binding, as France had appealed to them frequently."[24] But at home, both Foreign Minister Delcassé and his chief adviser, Pierre de Margerie, felt that Germany's entire war conduct, plus neutral pusillanimity in failing to condemn German violations, authorized a strong, extralegal, but principled response. They advocated mitigating neutral economic suffering as far as possible (for example, by compensating them with sales of confiscated enemy property), but at the same time making clear that the neutrals' failure to hold Germany to international law had created a situation in which "the Declaration of Paris and other international acts had become null and void [*caducs*] and the Allies consequently retained their full liberty of action."[25] No such startling language appeared in the final order, however.

In fact, both Britain and France were concerned with the neutrals' response; they discussed getting advance neutral approval or acquiescence to a new order, but Britain dropped that idea.[26] Instead, Grey opted to send diplomatic cover notes explaining the Allies' new policy. He carefully inserted the word "blockade" three times into the note to the United States, a ploy that Robert Lansing saw through but called "very adroit," since it sought "apparently to have this Government adopt the idea that it is a blockade and to discuss it from that standpoint."[27] A declared blockade would have legitimated seizing German property, including exports, and Grey knew that the United States was more likely to accept a customary belligerent weapon than a resort to reprisal to cover an otherwise illegal act. But the order-in-council did not declare blockade, and France distanced itself entirely from any use of that word to describe what the Allies were doing.[28]

21. Paul Cambon to Minister, no. 226, London, Feb. 12, 1915, MAE Blocus 44; Hurst memo, Mar. 1, 1915, FO 382/185 no. 26073, file 22076; Crowe memo, Feb. 13, 1915, FO 382/185 no. 19838, file 19838.

22. Paul Cambon to Minister, no. 238, London, Feb. 12, 1915, MAE Blocus 44.

23. Delcassé to P. Cambon, Paris, no. 517, Feb. 15, 1915, MAE Blocus 44.

24. Malkin memo, Feb. 27, 1915, FO 382/185, no. 23349, file 22076.

25. P. de Margerie to Paul Cambon, n.d., handwritten, MAE Blocus 44, final copy printed as Delcassé to Paul Cambon, tel. no. 479, Paris, Feb. 13, 1915, *DDFr*, 1915, 1: doc. 203.

26. Paul Cambon to Minister, no. 274, Feb. 18, 1915, MAE Blocus 44.

27. Fleuriau to Minister, no. 450, London, rec'd Mar. 14, 1915, MAE Blocus 44; United States, *Papers Relating to the Foreign Relation of the United States: The Lansing Papers, 1914–1920* (Washington, DC, 1939), 1:281.

28. Fleuriau to Minister, no. 450, London, Mar. 14, 1915, MAE Blocus 44.

Margerie repeated that position in June 1915: "Actually, the only and true justification for [the order-in-council] is [the Allies'] right to have recourse for their legitimate defense to all the means of fact and of reprisal [that] respect the life of non-combatants and the interests of innocent neutrals, against the methods of naval war begun by the Germans...in violation of the laws and customs of war at sea."[29]

A policy of pure reprisal would at least have been clear, but in fact the legal foundations of the order-in-council were blurred, not just on the question of blockade, but even on reprisal. The final language refers to "an unquestionable right of retaliation."[30] We will discuss the international law of reprisal more fully in chapter 9, but here suffice it to say that retaliation was an imprecise term in international law as interpreted by British writers. John Westlake held retaliation to be a species of retorsion, in which a state responded to injury by creating mirror-image damage on the offending state; pure retorsion was any action taken "to compensate [a state] for some damage" done by another. Oppenheim used "retaliation" to refer to both retorsion and reprisal; in his usage, retorsion was retaliation for a legal, but unfriendly act. Most writers agreed that reprisals were, in Oppenheim's formulation, "otherwise illegal acts performed by a State for the purpose of obtaining justice for an international delinquency by taking the law into its own hands."[31] Reprisal justified the use of illegal means to bring a violator back to the law. It was in the nature of reprisal that innocent third parties (in this case neutrals) might be hurt. However, reprisal was not unlimited: it was supposed to be proportionate to the original offense, and increasingly the international community insisted that legal reprisal must be done within "the laws of humanity."[32] Because legal reprisal merely justifies the extraordinary use of an illegal means, reprisal is a legal sanction but does not create a legal precedent. In other words, it breaks the law, but cannot remake it.

The earliest drafts of the March 1915 order-in-council proposed a genuine reprisal blockade with a sunset clause saying it would remain in force until Germany rescinded its unrestricted submarine campaign.[33] The preamble to the final order-in-council cited Germany's "violation of the usages of war," and thus presumably constituted reprisal (not retorsion). Indeed, all the British drafters had concluded "that the Prize Court might refuse to uphold the order-in-council except as a measure of retaliation, because it was quite inconsistent with the Declaration of Paris, which is binding on this country."[34] Certainly,

---

29. Cabinet of Minister, Paris, June 26, 1915, *DDFr*, 1915, 2: doc. 163; handwritten draft, dated June 25, 1915, in MAE Blocus 44.

30. Bell, *History of the Blockade*, 714–15.

31. John Westlake, *International Law; Part II: War* (Cambridge, 1907), 2:6–8, 69–70, 112–13; Lassa Oppenheim, *International Law: A Treatise* (London, 1905), 2:31–41. The British Manual of War also used "reprisal" and "retaliation" interchangeably: Colonel J. D. Edmonds and Lassa Oppenheim, *Land Warfare: An Exposition of the Laws and Usages of War on Land, for the Guidance of Officers of His Majesty's Army* (London, 1912), para. 456.

32. See Russian proposal to limit reprisal at the Brussels Conference of 1874, arts. 69–71 (not passed), and the Manual of the Institute of International Law (Oxford), art. 85, cited in Westlake, *International Law*, 2:112–13; and discussion in chapter 3.

33. Draft Order in Council, "Confidential. Reprisals against Germany," Feb. 26, 1915, and Mar. 1, 1915, Malkin Papers, FO 800/89.

34. Hurst's memo of the meeting of Feb. 27, 1915 (dated Mar. 1, 1915), FO 382/185 no. 26073, file 22076.

that is how the French Prize Court construed it.[35] But neither the words "blockade" nor "reprisal" occur in the final order, and "retaliation" was used only once. The earlier phrase "frame retaliatory measures" was changed to "adopt further measures."[36] And the sunset clause disappeared; such a sentence should have characterized a true reprisal.[37]

The linguistic peculiarities, which somewhat obscured the order's legal bases, suggest several possible interpretations. One is that reprisal was a legal fig-leaf covering an illegal policy that Britain wished to pursue regardless of how the Germans waged war (recall First Lord of the Admiralty Reginald McKenna's remark that the Germans were sure to infringe the law, permitting Britain to discard it). President of the Privy Council Lord Robert Crewe explained that avoiding reprisal language would permit Britain to continue the "blockade" even if Germany suspended unrestricted submarine warfare.[38] For these reasons a further extension of the contraband list that originally was to be appended to the order was intentionally published separately.[39] A second possibility is that the order was tailored to mollify the well-known American prejudice that acts of reprisal were simply illegal.[40] If so, it failed; the Americans repeated that allegation in protests of October and November 1915. Grey replied that Britain was "quite unable to admit the principle that to the extent that these measures are retaliatory they are illegal.... They do not, in reality, conflict with any general principle of international law, of humanity, or civilisation; they are enforced with consideration against neutral countries, and are, therefore, juridically sound and valid."[41] Third, although reprisal was the only way to get the Prize Court to accept the irregular "blockade," avoiding the word increased distance between Britain and Germany, for its foe's diplomatic correspondence and public announcements frequently used it. The British drafters did not wish to emphasize the objective illegality of the "blockade," or, more important, to flesh out arguments that might seem to undermine the status of law in general.[42] That was, of course, the chief danger in adverting to reprisal, and the main reason that Oppenheim, for example, had written that it was "an imperative

---

35. Fromageot note of Dec. 5, 1916, MAE Blocus 45.

36. Confidential print, Mar. 4, 1915, "Retaliation against Germany, Draft Order in Council," in MAE Blocus 44.

37. Paul Cambon after speaking with Crowe, reported to Paris that the Prize Court "did not want the Declaration of Paris abrogated, but only suspended due to exceptional circumstances and only so long as those circumstances continue." Cambon to Minister, no. 131, Mar. 5, 1915, MAE Blocus 44. The cabinet discussed the order-in-council at length in several sessions, but the reason for dropping both "blockade" and "reprisal," which occurred in the draft of March 4, are unclear: draft order-in-council, "Retaliation against Germany," Mar. 4, 1915, Malkin Papers, FO 800/89; cabinet discussions of Feb. 10, 17, 19, 24, Mar. 2: CAB 41/36/3–8.

38. Crewe to Bertie, July 13, 1915, *BD*, ser. H, 5: doc. 262.

39. Hurst's memo of the meeting of Feb. 27, 1915 (dated Mar. 1, 1915), FO 382/185 no. 26073, file 22076.

40. Crewe to F. Bertie, July 13, 1915, *BD*, ser. H, 5: doc. 262; Grey note, Jan. 4, 1916, FO 382/1099, no. 3545, file 302.

41. Spring Rice to Lansing with enclosed memorandum, Apr. 24, 1916, *FRUS* 1916, Suppl., 377, replying to Lansing to Page, Washington, Oct. 21, 1915, *FRUS* 1915, Suppl., 578–89, esp. 589.

42. The French ambassador to the United States, Jusserand, argued strongly against using German arguments to justify the March order-in-council: Jusserand to Delcassé, no. 395, Washington, June 2, 1915, *DDFr*, 1915, 2: doc. 55. The FO's lawyer, Malkin, called the March order "a vast development of the principle of continuous voyage": "Notes on the Order in Council March 1915," Malkin Papers, FO 800/89.

necessity" to limit its use as much as possible.[43] When Grey said that using reprisal "with consideration" did not violate "general principles," he was repeating the views of Margerie and Delcassé, that by respecting "lives" and "interests" of neutrals, the Allies' "blockade" was justified and thus, while not legal, not illegal either. Indeed, Britain's administration of the blockade continued to follow the same legal forms as before; capture depended on solid evidentiary proof of enemy destination (or origin) and was presented before the Prize Court as usual.[44] Britain continued to pay indemnities where necessary and to buy cargoes where possible. Thus, these three possible interpretations of the reprisal order-in-council were not mutually exclusive; they would all probably have been present and would have contributed to the somewhat opaque language of the order.

In October 1915 France again tried to clarify the legal situation and to put Allied policy on an unquestionably legal foundation by persuading Britain to proclaim a genuine blockade of all of Germany, including the North Sea and the Baltic. Crowe responded that the Allies would have to use submarines, just as the Germans were doing, and that was what the Allies had been protesting the entire time.[45] Margerie pressed on, explaining that Allied submarines would turn neutral vessels back to their own ports, only sinking them if they resisted. The point was "not to capture the ships, but to isolate the blockaded country."[46] France was not only trying to make the blockade more effective. It was primarily trying to meet neutral protests that all cited law. An internal note explained the proposition like this: "The measures taken under the decree of 13 March [1915] are an innovation in international law, and the neutrals have reproached it for having the effects of blockade without actually being one." "A declaration of a regular blockade would put the Allies in a much better position to respond to the neutrals, especially to the United States." It would permit the application of continuous voyage, the restriction of all enemy commerce, and the capture of enemy correspondence aboard neutral ships—all points of law that the neutral states had protested.[47] The French arguments apparently convinced the British Foreign Office, but the Admiralty declined on technical grounds (too few submarines, icy conditions, and the close proximity of Sweden to Denmark), and Russia rejected the proposal for fear that Sweden would retaliate by stopping transshipments to Russia across its territory.[48] The neither-fish-nor-fowl quality of the March 1915 order-in-council therefore continued.

---

43. Oppenheim, *International Law,* 2:262–63.

44. Bell, *History of the Blockade,* 249; Lambert, *Planning Armageddon,* 375.

45. Paul Cambon to Viviani, no. 583, London, Oct. 17, 1915, MAE Blocus 46.

46. De Margerie to Paul Cambon, no. 3502, Paris, Oct. 24, 1915, MAE Blocus 46.

47. Handwritten "Note," unsigned, Nov. 2, 1915, and Fromageot, "Résumé sommaire du projet de déclaration du blocus du côte de l'Allemagne par la France, l'Angleterre, et la Russie," Nov. 2, 1915, MAE Blocus 46. The French version of the March 11, 1915, order-in-council was a slightly different decree of March 13, which took account of differences in French and British law: *FRUS* 1915, Suppl., 150–51. Neutral protests: Bryan to Page, Washington, Mar. 30, 1915, *FRUS* 1915, Suppl., 152–56; Loudon to Rappard, Mar. 10, 1915, *BPNL,* 4: doc. 340; Netherlands Foreign Office to its Legation in Washington, Mar. 23, 1915, *FRUS* 1915, Suppl., 149. On mail aboard neutral ships: *FRUS* 1915, Suppl., 590, 734–42.

48. A. de Fleuriau to Minister, Nr. 639, London, Nov. 5, 1915, MAE Blocus 46; Thiébault to Minister, no. 378, Stockholm, Nov. 2, 1915, ibid.

More tinkering with the DoL occurred in orders-in-council of October 20, 1915, and March 30, 1916, each time making the legal situation more obscure. Crowe noted that even the Foreign Office disagreed about which articles of the DoL were now actually in force, and the Admiralty fought the Foreign Office over whether to use the word "blockade" to describe Britain's measures.[49] Cecil thought "the argumentative difficulties in which we are placed by the adoption of the DoL... sufficiently serious to make it desirable to re-cast our Orders and merely say that we propose to act on the rules of international law as they existed at the outbreak of war, adding certain declarations with respect to points which were not then clear."[50] Thus Cecil did not believe that by overthrowing the DoL, Britain was entering a law-free zone.

In July 1916 Britain and France cut the Gordian knot by renouncing the DoL altogether. Since the "blockade" was steadily tightening, the July 7, 1916, order-in-council might appear to be merely another step in that process. But neither the orders to the cruisers enforcing the blockade nor the actions of the vast blockade apparatus changed.[51] Robert Cecil, head of the newly created (February 1916) Ministry of Blockade, aimed instead to clarify the legal basis of Britain's measures and thereby reduce neutral opposition. The Prize Court's *Zamora* decision (April 7, 1916) accelerated matters, because it undermined the legal status of the DoL. The court had held that it was bound by international law, not by orders-in-council. It was only via orders-in-council that the unratified DoL had seemed to be recognized as binding by the government, and it now seemed that the court would not recognize it. The way was clear to jettison the DoL.

Neither the British Admiralty nor France wished to do so.[52] France championed the DoL as a victory of Continental principles over Anglo-American ones.[53] While the British Admiralty was apparently happy to continue with current practice without principled statements, France wanted clear rules of procedure. If the DoL were to be disavowed, France wanted it replaced with another, public declaration of principles.[54] Even after the March 1915 order-in-council, the Foreign Affairs Committee of the French Senate had asked the MAE (the French foreign office) to specify "the new law" on blockade that had resulted. Léon Bourgeois had tried to do so, but had given up because changes in warfare and ongoing legal debates between neutrals and belligerents made any formulation of principles "premature."[55] In May 1916 the top legal, blockade, and naval experts of both countries met in Paris.[56] Both French foreign office lawyers, Fromageot and Gout,

---

49. Crowe minute, Jan. 5, 1916, Malkin Papers, FO 800/918; G. Greene to Grey, Mar. 13, 1916, FO 382/682, no. 48657, file 88.

50. Cecil to Howard, draft, Mar. 12, 1916, FO 382/1125, no. 42644, file 3369.

51. Draft Admiralty Order, Aug. 1, 1916, Malkin Papers, FO 800/913; Bell, *History of the Blockade*, 463.

52. Bell, *History of the Blockade*, 463–64.

53. Robert Cecil minute, June 5, 1916, in FO 372/1126, no. 108016/1639. Despite the French judgment, the United States pressed, too, for Britain to follow the DoL.

54. Marjorie M. Farrar, *Conflict and Compromise: The Strategy, Politics and Diplomacy of the French Blockade, 1914–1918* (The Hague, 1974), 36–37.

55. Bourgeois to the President of the Republic, Paris, July 27, 1915, MAE Blocus 44.

56. Minister of Blockade and lawyer Robert Cecil, Adm. Slade, and Hurst, meeting with Naval Minister Adm. Lucien Lacaze, Léon Bourgeois, Denys Cochin (minister of blockade), and the two Foreign Office lawyers, Fromageot and Gout, May 1916 (from Cecil minute of June 5, 1916, FO 372/1126, no. 108016, file 1639).

defended the DoL as one of the few codifications of maritime law, but they acceded to a compromise suggested by French naval minister, Admiral Lucien Lacaze. The text of the renunciation would be merely a clear statement of "blockade" practice, but the cover note to neutrals explained that the DoL "could not stand the test of a continuous development of unforeseen circumstances."[57] The rest of the note went to great lengths to assure neutrals that the Allies would follow international law.

> These successive modifications [of the DoL] may have led to misinterpretations of the intentions of the Allies; who have therefore come to the conclusion that they must adhere exclusively to the application of the rules of international law as recognised in the past.
>
> The Allies declare solemnly and without reserve that they will continue to observe these principles, both so far as the action of their cruisers is concerned, and in the judgments of their prize courts; that, faithful to their word, they will duly observe the international conventions regarding the laws of warfare; that, respecting the laws of humanity, they repudiate all idea of threatening the existence of non-combatants; that they will inflict no unjustifiable injury on neutral property, and that, if any injury should be caused by their action at sea to *bona fide* merchants, they will always be ready to examine claims, and to grant such compensation as may be justly due.

The note makes five statements: (1) the Allies are returning to older international law (not abrogating law); (2) they will follow the Hague Conventions; (3) they will follow "the laws of humanity," meaning that, unlike the Germans, they will not kill passengers or crews at sea; (4) they will make only justifiable injury to neutral property (that statement upheld the practices so far); but (5) they will compensate damages that a court holds unjustifiable.

The order-in-council itself returned to British law on capturing contraband-carrying vessels on their return voyage; it returned to U.S. law applying continuous voyage to all contraband and to blockade; it adopted the more stringent rule of the DoL (unnamed!) that permitted confiscation of a neutral vessel for carrying contraband making over 50 percent of its cargo (rather than the older, more lenient British rule); and it announced wider criteria for proving enemy destination so as to target blacklisted firms.

Britain issued two further retaliatory orders-in-council. The first (January 10, 1917) extended the measures of March 1915 to Germany's allies. It was made retroactive in order to cover the Admiralty's illegal seizure of "several million pounds" worth of Austrian property, "under the supposition" that the March 1915 order had authorized it.[58] When the Foreign Office learned what the Admiralty had been doing, Cecil contacted the French for advice. Fromageot reported that since the March 1915 order had been covered by reprisal, it must refer only to Germany, thus making the Admiralty seizures unlawful. But he pointed out that the

---

57. Farrar, *Conflict and Compromise*, 37–38. Text of cover note and excellent discussion in Bell, *History of the Blockade*, 463–65.

58. Several million: F. Leverton Harris to F. E. Smith, Dec. 23, 1916; supposition: Hurst to President of the Prize Court, Jan. 9, 1917, Malkin Papers, FO 800/913.

Central Powers' extension of unrestricted submarine warfare to the Mediterranean might "justify" extending reprisal to Germany's allies. However, he thought it imprudent to do so because it would disturb the United States.[59] Nonetheless, Britain went ahead. The procurator general then pointed out that the Prize Court would not accept a retroactive law, so Hurst wrote privately to the president of the Prize Court, explaining the embarrassing situation.[60]

The last order-in-council of February 16, 1917, was even more difficult to cover legally. It was designed to force neutral vessels to call at Allied ports by threatening them with confiscation if they did not. Confiscation would have been permitted under the law of regular blockade; it was the standard penalty for blockade-runners. So, once again, the Foreign Office contemplated declaring a blockade, and once again pulled back on the advice of the international lawyers and Lord Chancellor Robert Finlay, who feared that the British Prize Court would not accept its validity.[61] They recommended the "principle of retaliation" plus a positive incentive: ships containing contraband or enemy goods would not be confiscated, if they had called at an Allied port. Foreign Minister Aristide Briand had legal and political qualms: such a reprisal contradicted both French domestic law and the Declaration of Paris. And it would anger the United States at just the moment when that country seemed about to enter the war on the Allied side precisely because of Germany's illegal unrestricted submarine warfare, whose recommencement Germany had announced on January 31, 1917.[62] Informed of the British proposal, the French ambassador to the United States, Jean Jules Jusserand, was even more pointed in his rejection. Britain's project "would reduce to the state of a 'scrap of paper' one of the most important international acts that has ever been signed, that is, the Declaration of Paris. One should either proclaim a regular blockade or renounce these aggravations [of the neutrals]."[63] Jusserand repeated his opposition several days later, and again, law and France's self-understanding as a law-abiding power were paramount considerations.

> Such a project is in my view unacceptable. If there is a country which must respect an act as solemn as the Declaration of Paris, it is ours. It would be a paltry excuse to say that, because the Germans had violated it to the detriment of neutrals, that we were going to do the same.

He then continued:

> I have always been convinced that, beyond all questions of principle, it is in our material interest to conform as strictly as possible to international law. There is no

---

59. Fromageot handwritten note, Dec. 5, 1916, MAE Blocus 45.

60. Mellor to Hurst, Dec. 26, 1916, and Hurst to President of the Prize Court, Jan. 9, 1917, Malkin Papers, FO 800/913.

61. Paul Cambon to Minister, no. 191–92, received Feb. 9, 1917, MAE Blocus 45; British Embassy, Paris, Feb. 6, 1917, MAE Blocus 46; Bertie to French Foreign Minister, Feb. 11, 1917, MAE Blocus 45. Hurst memo, Feb. 5, 1917, "Proposed Order in Council for Further Reprisals against the Enemy," confidential, Malkin Papers, FO 800/913.

62. Briand to Jusserand, no. 374, Paris, ca. Feb. 14, 1917, MAE Blocus 46.

63. Jusserand to Briand, no. 457, Washington Mar. 11, 1917, MAE Blocus 46.

way to render the enemy odious while keeping our popularity without which, for example, we would never be able to raise the American loans which have been so useful to us.[64]

For the experienced diplomat, Jusserand, law and material interest went together because France's (and the Allies') respect for law and the identification of their fight with upholding the law made possible the goodwill of the American neutral and all its bounty.

Inside the French Foreign Office, the influential head of the minister's cabinet, Pierre de Margerie, took a less principled stand, at least in correspondence with Britain. He wrote that France "is not in principle opposed to the new Order in Council," but thought it "impolitic," until the United States had actually entered the war.[65] In fact, France was indeed opposed in principle. A note to the foreign minister in March explained the French dilemma. The order-in-council was "in manifest contradiction" with the Declaration of Paris. "Nevertheless, in order not to undermine the unity of action with our ally," French lawyers had prepared a similar decree. It lay unapproved, at first ostensibly because France feared the possible U.S. reaction.[66] However, France learned of the mild U.S. response by February 25. More significantly, even after the United States entered the war on the Allied side on April 7 and material interest played no further role, France never joined Britain in its final order-in-council.[67] French legal objections were simply too strong.

Britain's Understanding of International Law

No modern state has a single understanding of law. Discerning "Britain's" views means identifying a spectrum of opinion that crystallized into action. But action is not merely policy. In international law, the arguments and justifications used to explain or defend policy are potentially as important as the acts themselves, for they indicate what one thinks binding law is (*opinio juris*), how one thinks it is formed and changed, and how important it is to guiding the contours of policy.

It should be clear from the foregoing that Britain took law enormously seriously, even when it was breaking it. Providing for independent legal views was encouraged even in the appointment process: the legal advisers in the different ministries were appointed not from within, but by the attorney general himself (except in the Admiralty, where the navy consulted with the attorney general and the treasury solicitor).[68] The belligerent measures

64. Jusserand to Minister, Nr. 153, Washington, received Feb. 16, 1917, MAE Blocus 46.

65. Margerie to Paul Cambon, Paris, Feb. 15, 1917, MAE Blocus 46.

66. "Note pour le ministre," Paris, Mar. 29, 1917, MAE Blocus 46; "Projet de Decret," MAE Blocus 45, indicating that Louis Renault, Adm. Moreau, Fromageot, Gout, and another, illegible, had drafted it.

67. Jusserand to Minister, no. 188, Washington, received Feb. 25, 1917, MAE Blocus 45; Minister of Blockade, Section d'information, "Note pour le ministre," Nov. 22, 1939, MAE Blocus 46.

68. Attorney General John Simon memo, Oct. 13, 1914; draft memo of reply from McKenna, Nov. 8, 1914; and Treasury Solicitor John Mellor to Greene, Nov. 21, 1914: ADM 1/8400/399.

of "blockade" were all formed after extensive discussions of law among the main legal advisers, often including the highest law officers of the land, the attorney general and the procurator general, together with naval officers who had been delegates to the prewar international-legal conferences. Repeated joint Anglo-French meetings of the respective foreign offices' lawyers wrestled with the legal issues raised by innovations such as rationing, and perfected the actual methods used to put policy into action.[69] These discussions have left behind an enormous documentation that attests to the huge effort the Allies expended trying to pour their conduct of the naval war into legal bottles.

This task was made somewhat easier by certain assumptions that Britons typically transferred from the common law to international law. The British delegates to the London Conference of 1908–9 described what distinguished Britain's view of law. They noted the problem that some Continental powers precluded "a rule being described as part of the existing law, because it was not strictly covered by the letter of their prize legislation. Such a hard-and-fast criterion of classification may, according to the British view of international law as a living thing, capable of development and adaptation from time to time to new conditions, seem inconveniently rigid and defective."[70] Attorney General Frederick Smith wrote that international law long antedated its codification. "It is well to remember that laws of war and customs of the sea were known, like the law merchant, long before the system of modern international law was framed. All these were conceived as deriving their authority from natural reason evidenced by the common consent of mankind or the classes of men specially concerned."[71] Leaving aside for a moment the question of authority, Smith's words indicate the high regard in which customary, unwritten law was held in Britain. The difficulties with the DoL only confirmed the British view that premature codification hindered the development of "the true principles" of law.[72]

Custom, state practices, and Prize Court decisions were the kinds of precedents that indicated law. "What is a rule of international law without precedent?" Crowe once asked.[73] Precedents did not speak for themselves or produce doctrine, however; they required interpretation.[74] In Grey's instructions to the delegates to the London Conference we find his assessment of the dangers of doctrinal clarity. In his view, it was responsible for obscuring underlying agreement on international norms. Differences between Anglo-American and Continental views were not so much the result of "differing practices," he wrote, "as of theories constructed by jurists in order to justify the executive measures adopted by belligerents, and of deductions somewhat hastily drawn from the language employed in the decisions of the Prize Courts." "In course of time these systems appear to have

---

69. Memorandum, enclosure of Board of Trade to Foreign Office, July 19, 1915, *BD*, ser. H, 5: doc. 286; Delcassé to Paul Cambon, no. 2396, Paris, Aug. 8, 1915, *DDFr*, 1915, 2: doc. 365.

70. Report of the British Delegates, Foreign Office, March 1, 1909, in James Brown Scott, ed., *The Declaration of London* (New York, 1919), 235–57, here 253.

71. Sir Frederick E. Smith, "First Interim Report from the Committee of Enquiry into Breaches of the Laws of War," Jan. 13, 1919, p. 54, Bodleian Library, Pollock Papers, MS ENG. Hist. d. 431.

72. Report of the "Zamora" Committee, Malkin Papers, FO 800/918.

73. Crowe to his wife, Feb. 22, 1911, The Hague, Oxford, Bodleian Library, Crowe Papers.

74. International Law Committee, Dec. 18, 1918, "Freedom of the Seas," 43, *BD*, ser. I, 1: doc. 10.

become stereotyped by jurists to such an extent that the reasons for their existence and the practices from which they were deduced have been lost sight of," leading to unwarranted claims.[75]

Such a skeptical view of doctrine predisposed British decision makers to adapt flexibly to changes in practices or circumstances. That predisposition partly explains the common claim in orders-in-council, contraband lists, and elsewhere that changed conditions had required adjustment in British practice.[76] A cabinet leader explained to the Dutch ambassador that "the adjustment of old principles to new conditions is of the essence of legal progress."[77] But one searches in vain among the British documents, internal and external, for the etiquette *rebus sic stantibus* to label such flexibility. That term was never used, and its absence is important. *Rebus* is the tag used especially by international-legal skeptics to justify violations or renunciation of treaties due to changed circumstances. British decision makers never overtly adduced *rebus,* despite their openness to the force of changing circumstance, because they did not wish to undermine the principle that treaties were generally valid (*pacta sunt servanda*) or that international law was binding.

Instead, Britain preferred to cover its changes to law by referring to general, underlying principles. A. Pearce Higgins, a law officer in the foreign office, wrote to the procurator general that the Prize Court would uphold the extension of belligerent rights "so long as these are not in violation of the fundamental principles on which rules of contraband are based."[78] Similarly, Grey answered U.S. qualms about the March 1915 order-in-council by emphasizing that "What is really important in the general interest is that adaptations of the old rules should not be made unless they are consistent with the general principles upon which an admitted belligerent right is based."[79] It was on this basis that Cecil justified before Parliament the picking and choosing of rules from the DoL: "But I cannot make it too clear... [that] the policy of the Government is to abide by the principles of international law whether they are in favour or against us, and to adhere to them, and them only, and it is only so far as the DoL embodies those principles that they have any intention of being bound by its provisions."[80] Both the private, internal and the public statements reveal the same view of preexisting, underlying principles.

The belief in general principles had another important consequence: Britain rejected the doctrine of *non liquet,* which held that there were gaps in the law, that is, areas simply

---

75. "Instructions Addressed to the British Delegates by Sir Edward Grey," Grey to Lord Desart, London, Dec. 1, 1908, in Scott, *Declaration of London,* 220–21.

76. For example, the orders-in-council of Oct. 29, 1914 ("special conditions") and July 7, 1916 ("changed conditions of commerce and diversity of practice"); the expanded contraband list of Apr. 12, 1916 ("The circumstances of the present war are so peculiar ..."), cited in Secretary of the Admiralty to the [International Law] Committee, Apr. 30, 1918, *BD,* ser. I, 1: doc. 10; Hurst note in appendix 26 of "Report and Proceedings" (1912) CAB 16/18A.

77. Van Swinderen to Loudon, London, Mar. 4, 1915, *BPNL* 4: doc. 328.

78. Dr. A Pearce Higgins, "Memorandum for H.M.'s Procurator-General on Conditional Contraband," *BD,* ser. H, 5: doc. 94, p. 126.

79. Grey to Page, July 23, 1915, *BD,* ser. H, 5: doc. 304, p. 399.

80. Minutes of Parliament, Mar. 9, 1916, col. 1797, FO 382/1126, no. 47202, file 1639.

uncovered by it, in which a state was free to act as it chose.[81] If both codification and practice failed to offer guides, as for example Higgins thought was the case regarding what sorts of supplies hospital ships might carry, then one could fill that omission "by means of analogy or logical deduction" from principle, in this case as enunciated in the Martens Clause.[82] But unwritten principle was just as binding. That was the basis for Britain's emphatic rejection of Germany's claim that submarines were uncovered by international law—in Britain's view all vessels were subject to the rules of humanity that dictated saving passengers and crew before sinking merchant ships.[83]

Such a flexible view of law might have encouraged unilateral lawmaking, but for the equally strong conviction in Britain that international law was made by the society of "civilized" states acting together. The British delegates to the London Conference ended their report on exactly this point; they laid down the criteria by which the "general validity and therefore...general respect" of the DoL would be judged: by its "conformity with the true law of nations, of which, according to the view always upheld by this country, it is an essential feature that it should flow from the recognition of the principles of right and of fair dealing common to all civilized peoples."[84] That included neutrals, and most authoritative writers believed that maritime law emerged from the weighing together of the rights of naval belligerents and of neutrals.[85] The response of neutrals to Britain's actions was therefore important to it not simply politically, or economically, but also legally. Neutral acquiescence to many of Britain's maritime innovations (like navicerts, the private trusts, and rationing) led to the conviction that Britain had changed the law. Francis Oppenheimer, the lawyer and consul who was centrally involved in developing both the NOT and the system of rationing, told a colleague in the Foreign Office in December 1917 that he deserved "a substantial honor" since his ideas had created a "New System in international law."[86]

---

81. *Non liquet* usually refers to gaps preventing a court from reaching a judgment, but it is a convenient shorthand for the larger argument that international law is incomplete. See the discussion in Hersh Lauterpacht, *The Function of Law in the International Community* (Oxford, 1933), 51–69; James Leslie Brierly, *The Law of Nations: An Introduction to the International Law or Peace,* ed. Humphrey Waldock (Oxford, 1963), 67–68; Martti Koskenniemi, *The Gentle Civilizer of Nations: The Rise and Fall of International Law, 1870–1960* (Cambridge, 2001), 365–69; Julius Stone, "*Non Liquet* and the Function of Law in the International Community," *British Yearbook of International Law* 35 (1959): 124–61.

82. A. P. Higgins to J. P. Mellor, Dec. 7, 1916, FO 383/1076, file 3804.

83. See next chapter. Sir H. Erle Richards's memo in H. Goudy et al., "Report of the Committee on the Legal Status of Submarines," *Transactions of the Grotius Society* 4 (1918): xlvii. Also, Grey's "Instructions," in Scott, *Declaration of London,* 226.

84. Report of the Delegates, in Scott, *Declaration of London,* 254–55.

85. The International Law Committee cited both William E. Hall and John Westlake to this effect: International Law Committee, Dec. 18, 1918, "Freedom of the Seas," *BD,* ser. I, 1: doc. 10, pp. 50–51.

86. Francis Oppenheimer, diary entry of Dec. 24, 1917, Oxford, Bodleian Library, Oppenheimer Papers, box 3: folder labeled "Dec. 17." Although the neutrals ultimately accepted rationing, in Jan. 1916 British legal experts questioned its legality: Lord Crewe circulated "The Policy of Rationing Neutral States Adjoining Germany and Its Relation to International Law," Jan. 25, 1916, CAB 37/141, 29, cited in Marc Frey, *Der Erste Weltkrieg und die Niederlande: Ein neutrales Land im politischen und wirtschaftlichen Kalkül der Kriegsgegner,* Studien Zur Internationalen Geschichte (Berlin, 1998), 171; Bell, *History of the Blockade,* 325, 531, 534, 537–38, 541.

The importance of neutrals—in other words, the coincidence of the diplomatic with the legal system—is too often ignored in scholarship on the war. Instead, one finds two commonplace assertions: that the only important neutral was the United States and that once it entered the war all consideration for neutrals simply stopped; and that legal language was either a British ploy or a cover for American material interests.

The United States was certainly the most important neutral for Britain; for Germany, though, Holland and the Scandinavian countries were more vital.[87] But for Britain, too, the continued goodwill or at least cooperation of the Netherlands was crucial. If this were not true, then neither the very gradual tightening of the blockade, which reaped the Foreign Office such opprobrium in the newspapers, Parliament, and from other sections of government, nor the tedious negotiations and delicate diplomatic interventions, which fill countless documents (many dating from after U.S. entry into the war), would have been necessary.[88] Every aspect of the "blockade"—its civilian-diplomatic control, its reliance on legal and economic experts, its contractual formulations, its compromises and subventions, its administrative and statistical innovations—was due to the effort to mollify as far as possible all the neutral states affected most deeply by Britain's maritime measures. Because of the proximity of the Netherlands and Scandinavia, more of the actual negotiations were focused on those states than on the United States. Moreover, the neutrals were inextricably tied to each other because the same rules applied to them all. Thus, to give one example, we find Walter Langley minuting in 1915 (about seizing enemy parcels aboard neutral merchant vessels), "We must be careful how we word our protest as the inability of Norway to defend her neutrality would not justify us in disregarding the neutrality of the Netherlands or the U.S."[89]

How seriously ought we to take the legal arguments that characterized the belligerent/neutral wartime correspondence? Some historians believe that Britain framed the issues in legal terms and thus "entangled" (*verwickelte*) the United States in legal debates that hindered energetic protests about sovereignty or national rights.[90] Others judge the highly legalistic U.S. notes as window-dressing for economic interest.[91] If law were just a ploy, then we should discover a discrepancy between internal and external correspondence, the first circulating around the "real" issues, and the second for show. But that is not the case, either for the neutrals or for Britain and France. Of course, not every legal argument rehearsed behind closed doors was used in public, but I hope the numerous citations from internal documents above have clearly shown how central regard for law was to Allied policy making in both Britain and France. Concerning the American fondness for legal argumentation, it was not Britain, but State Department counselor and later secretary Robert Lansing who recommended the strictly legal approach to U.S. foreign policy. He

---

87. Hurst memo, Jan. 1, 1916: "We intend to exercise all the rights of capture which the admitted principles of international law give us—not more, or we shall be brought into conflict again with the U.S., not less, because we cannot afford to sacrifice any belligerent right." FO 382/1125, no. 1639, file 1639.

88. Frey chronicles some of this activity: Frey, *Erste Weltkrieg und die Niederlande.*

89. Langley minute to Wardrop (Bergen) to FO, no. 38, Aug. 18, 1915, FO 372/780, file 112241.

90. Frey, *Erste Weltkrieg und die Niederlande,* 125; Arthur S. Link, *Wilson the Diplomatist: A Look at His Major Foreign Policies* (Chicago, 1965), 42.

91. For example, Lambert, *Planning Armageddon,* 357–58, 344.

found law the best way to fulfill President Wilson's goal of keeping the United States out of the war. Lansing asked (January 1, 1915), "While the argument of legal right is perhaps narrow, can we safely go further" without being drawn into war for moral or emotional reasons?[92] Lansing's approach was congenial to Wilson, and both surely agreed, as a Lansing memo of November 1914 put it, that "law is the sole measure of neutrality and of the government's duty to preserve it."[93] Lansing's devotion to law *for its own sake* caused him to draft notes strictly in order to clarify legal issues for the future.[94] As for Wilson, the president explained in a private note to Bryan (July 1915) that "[we] conceive ourselves as speaking for the rights of neutrals everywhere, rights in which the whole world is interested and which every nation must wish to see kept inviolable."[95] These memoranda and letters, and there are many more like them, were not for public consumption; they represented the private views of the writers.

Wilson's conviction about neutral rights was certainly shared. The Netherlands and the Scandinavian states all expressed their protests in legal form. The Dutch ambassador to Britain, Maree van Swinderen, carefully monitored the legal arguments he heard being used in any venue, public or private. He quoted the English original of Asquith's alarming statement to Parliament concerning the March 1915 order-in-council, that "we are not going to allow our efforts to be strangled in a network of juridical niceties."[96] "Juridical niceties" were of course the main protection of neutrals' sovereignty and economies, short of leaving neutrality and becoming a belligerent oneself.

The question whether solicitude for neutrals equates to care for the law or their legal right, or whether it is merely a cover for political or economic expediency, poses a false dichotomy. The material interests of a belligerent (in getting munitions, food, or credit from neutrals) and the material interests of neutrals (in staying out of war, in continuing trade and commerce) are inextricably bound up with their legal rights; international law expresses and protects their material interests. Furthermore, neutral anger at belligerent violations is a form of international-legal sanction, even when it stops short of going to war. It increases the "cost" of the war; it embarrasses one before the world, hinders cooperation, disrupts normal expectations, threatens postwar relations, and so forth. Due regard for neutral sanctions is thus part of how the international-legal system, which is a central aspect of the diplomatic world, operates and polices itself. Political expediency can help uphold international law because of a state's interest in remaining part of the society that has created the law. Thus, when Hurst wrote (1912) that "the probable measure of neutral opposition and resentment must control the policy of resorting to any such new belligerent practice," he was being as good a lawyer as he was a practical planner.[97]

---

92. United States, *Lansing Papers*, 1:192.

93. Reply to Hugo Münsterberg to Wilson, Cambridge, MA, Nov. 19, 1914, United States, *Lansing Papers*, 1:169. On Wilson, for example, "Outline Sketch by President Wilson of a Note to Great Britain," Mar. 19, 1915, United States, *Lansing Papers*, 1:278–79; Link, *Wilson the Diplomatist*, 36–37.

94. Lansing to Bryan, Washington, May 5, 1915, United States, *Lansing Papers*, 1:385.

95. Wilson to Bryan, July 13, 1915, United States, *Lansing Papers*, 1:455–56.

96. Van Swinderen to Loudon, Mar. 2, 1915, *BPNL* 4: doc. 327.

97. Hurst memo, "Trading with the Enemy," appendix 26 to "Report and Proceedings," p. 426, CAB 16/18A.

Britain's self-image as law-abiding and as a leader in the world community of "civilized" states cannot be overemphasized in understanding its devotion to law for its own sake. Lord Granville had famously expressed this conviction in mid-century:

> It is the duty and the interest of this country, having possessions scattered over the whole globe, and priding itself on its advanced state of civilisation, to encourage moral, intellectual and physical progress among all other nations. For this purpose the foreign policy of Great Britain should be marked by justice, moderation and self-respect, and this country should in its relations with other States do by others as it would be done by.[98]

Britain's "self-respect" was thus anchored to international law as the expression of justice among civilized states.

A good way to measure the extent to which this conviction had been internalized by British decision makers is their striking interest in consistency, that is, in keeping one's word. In late 1915 Britain's ambassador to the United States had made a verbal commitment to permit shipment of medical supplies to U.S. Red Cross personnel in Germany. Everyone in London considered Cecil Spring Rice's promise a major faux pas. But Crowe, Lord Percy, and Alwyn Parker (of the Ministry of Blockade) felt they were stuck. In Percy's view, neither Britain's allies nor the Admiralty could justify reneging: "We have assumed an obligation and even if our Allies were to demur [which France did], we should have to redeem our pledge."[99] Similarly, Hurst felt that having used the word "blockade" in diplomatic correspondence, Britain had awakened certain expectations: "We cannot eat our words or forget them," he minuted.[100] W. E. Davidson, chief legal adviser to the Foreign Office, responded exactly the same way to an error in claiming the status of a hospital ship under the wrong article, a claim that allowed the Germans to argue correctly that it had no such protection. Davidson wrote, "I presume that the American Ambassador at Berlin passed on that Note to the German Government, and if so, it is rather difficult for us now to change our ground and to argue that the definition in Art. 1 does not apply."[101] The documentary record is replete with similar examples.

The censorship of neutral mail provides another case where we can examine how law figured in British decision making. The 1907 Hague Convention XI introduced for the first time the protection of "postal correspondence of neutrals or belligerents, whatever its official or private character may be, found on the high seas aboard a neutral ship or enemy ship," except "in case of violation of blockade." "If the ship is detained, the correspondence is forwarded by the captor with the least possible delay" (article 1).[102]

---

98. Jan. 12, 1852, cited in Georg Schwarzenberger, *The Frontiers of International Law* (London, 1962), 132–33.

99. Percy minute, Jan. 2, 1916, FO 382/682, no. 217141, file 88.

100. Hurst minute, Mar. 23, 1916, FO 382/1100, no. 51537, file 302.

101. Davidson minute, Mar. 25, 1916, FO 372/918, no. 53818, file 389.

102. Convention (XI) Relative to Certain Restrictions with Regard to the Exercise of the Right of Capture in Naval War, in *Documents on the Laws of War,* ed. Adam Roberts and Richard Guelff (Oxford, 2004), 119–26, here 121.

In early August 1915 several incidents tested the validity of the law. The most famous one concerned the German U-boat that stopped the Norwegian freighter *Haakon VII*. Showing "politeness and restraint," as a Danish observer later testified, the U-boat commander examined and threw overboard parcels containing contraband, but, discovering in one a wreath, repacked and forwarded it to its recipient. He then took twenty bags of mail.[103] Two similar incidents at about the same time suggest the German navy was trying out a new intelligence scheme based on reading confiscated mail. On August 18 the Norwegian foreign minister threatened to stop carrying all German mail if the practice continued. An AA official noted that that would be "unpleasant";[104] he doubtless also recognized that Germany was on the short end of the rope, since the Allies had far more to gain, and far more sea power by which to gain it, from violating Hague Convention XI than had Germany. On August 21, representatives of the AA, the federal office of Justice, Interior, and Post, and the Admiralty met; the view of the legal advisers to the AA, Walter Simons and Johannes Kriege, prevailed: "In the case of the 'Haakon VII' confiscation of letters cannot be covered under international law and therefore such confiscations will not be repeated and the letters shall be sent on."[105] Germany assured Norway it would not happen again, but it held the door open for the future by arguing, first, that the Hague Convention XI had not been signed by all belligerents in the war and thus was not valid, and, second, that the Allies had already held up mail and Germany reserved the right to do the same. It is not clear whether the Admiralty in Berlin insisted on these reservations; in any case, it approved the wording.[106]

The cat was now out of the bag, and the War Office in London was determined to chase it. Significant information about blockade evasion and the Central Powers' economic situation and adaptations could be gained by reading their mail. The War Office hoped that Sir Edward Grey would stand down from his position that censoring mail from neutral ships violated Convention XI.[107] The British meeting was an almost perfect counterpart to the German one: in Cecil's room at the Foreign Office representatives of the Admiralty, War Office, Home Office, Treasury, War Trade Department, and Post Office met. All but one were lawyers. Their first order of business was "whether we should have a good case for imposing this censorship."[108] That is, law was the framework. They thought their case rather weak, a merely "technical case" based on retaliation for the *Haakon VII*. Nevertheless, they thought the advantages to censorship significant but stopped in their tracks when the Admiralty representative mentioned that Britain had publicly taken the

---

103. Army report, Newcastle, Aug. 19, 1915, FO 372/780, no. 116335, file 112241; War Office confidential report, n.d., no. 115575, ibid.

104. Oberndorff to Foreign Office, Nr. 512, Kristiania, Aug. 18, 1915, and (Lentze?) note, Aug. 19, 1915, IIIa 15866, BAB R 901 85964.

105. Simons note, Aug. 21, 1915, IIIa 15339 and 15490, BAB R 901 85964.

106. German verbal note to Norway, Berlin, Aug. 23, 1915, BAB R 901 85964.

107. He had said so in a note of May 7, 1915, on the *Naartenskijk*. Cubitt (War Office) to Foreign Office, no. 53/3274, Aug. 25, 1915, FO 372/780, no. 119590, file 112241.

108. Minutes of the Interdepartmental Meeting on Censorship of the Mails, Oct. 5, 1915, FO 372/781, no. 149963, file 112241.

position that "the privileges of Mails which are protected by the Hague convention will continue to be carefully observed."[109] The meeting broke up. Afterward, Grey again held his legal ground.[110]

Three weeks later the War Office returned with French backing and a lengthy, well-researched legal argument.[111] It began from the standpoint (shared by Germany) that Hague Convention XI, because it was not ratified by all the belligerents, was not valid. It then rehearsed the state practice and legal writings of the nineteenth century and admitted that there was indeed a movement toward safeguarding correspondence, but claimed it had never accreted "into an accepted alteration of Customary Law, nor has it in practice met with universal approval."[112] Protection was, in short, not obligatory. They ended with Henri Fromageot's 1907 summary of customary law, from which they concluded that, "if carried out with due care and speed," censorship of mailbags on neutral vessels was legal and ought to be acceptable to neutrals. The War Office's conviction that important contraband information was being smuggled via letters seemed borne out by Germany's quick reversal. One clerk minuted, "It is so unlike Germany to be penitent unless she can gain something directly or indirectly by such a course."[113]

The lawyers now weighed in. Malkin agreed with the legal situation as the War Office had outlined it, but he emphasized a limit: censoring genuine neutral-to-neutral letters was not legitimate.[114] He also wondered if denouncing the Hague Convention were a wise policy. Hurst also approved of the memo's appraisal of law. But he argued that the Hague Convention was simply irrelevant, since it did not apply to blockade, and the March 1915 order-in-council had been justified as a type of blockade. "Consistency is of the essence of blockade; we weaken our case from the legal point of view by every exception that we make," he wrote.[115]

Crowe, as always, pursued the most forceful line. He wanted to renounce the Hague Convention XI and retract Britain's earlier announcement. But even he had legal qualms, because "we cannot easily point to any material change of the circumstances since the assurance [was] given."[116] Cecil thought Hurst's view of the law "no doubt" correct, but he still found covering censorship by blockade "a rather technical ground." So, he suggested canvassing the neutrals to see how upset they would be if Britain adopted the measure.[117] Grey reluctantly agreed to the canvass and ordered a memo prepared for the cabinet and for the French government.[118] The canvass was not encouraging. The Dutch foreign minister replied that "such action would be...another serious blow to international law and

---

109. Foreign Office circular of Sept. 23, 1915, FO 372/781, no. 149953, file 112241.

110. G. L. (G. Locock?) to Cecil, Oct. 6, 1915, FO 372/781, no. 149953, file 112241.

111. B. B. Cubitt to Foreign Office, Oct. 29, 1915, FO 372/781, no. 160751, file 112241.

112. War Council Memorandum on "Mail Bags on Neutral Vessels: Note on the State of International Law as to the Violability," enclosed with B. B. Cubitt to Foreign Office, Oct. 29, 1915, FO 372/781, no. 160751, file 112241.

113. Illegible signature on note War Council memo, FO 372/781, no. 160751, file 112241.

114. Malkin note, Nov. 2, 1915, FO 372/781, no. 160751, file 112241.

115. Hurst minute, Nov. 3, 1915, FO 372/781, no. 160751, file 112241.

116. Crowe minute, Nov. 4, 1915, FO 372/781, no. 160751, file 112241.

117. Cecil to Grey, Nov. 4, 1915, FO 372/781, no. 160751, file 112241.

118. Grey minute, n.d., FO 372/781, no. 160751, file 112241.

he should have to register a strong protest."[119] Grey, Cecil, and Permanent Undersecretary Sir Arthur Nicolson all continued to have grave doubts about adopting the course.[120] The War Office and the Foreign Office advisers spent December thinking of ways to make censorship more clearly legal or at least palatable to neutrals. They came up with two. The first was to construe article 1 narrowly, so that its purview reached only ships on the "high seas," as its text said, but not those that had "voluntarily" come to British ports, where Britain had the acknowledged right to supervise mail on its own territory. The second way was inducements for neutral merchant vessels to show up "voluntarily": bunkering (that is, providing coal over which Britain had a near monopoly) only to ships promising not to trade with Germany. The Foreign Office's W. A. Stewart minuted that Britain should spare no expense in inducements that permitted it to go ahead without renouncing Hague Convention XI.[121]

As the navy had done in the fall of 1914, when it continued to seize food cargo from merchant ships after the changed October 29 order-in-council (these shipments were then released by the Foreign Office), it now (December 1915) simply went ahead and seized mail.[122] Apprised of the navy's actions by a Dutch protest, Stewart noted that it had happened so often that "it is difficult for us to suggest that the action was due to inadvertence."[123] Grey was thus forced to approve the examination of mail on ships voluntarily stopping in British ports.[124]

As France had done regarding the DoL and "blockade," it pressed to clarify the legal basis for the measures. The French ambassador to Denmark suggested a formal announcement, but both he and the French government recognized that it required a pretext. "The wished-for opportunity may I suppose come by the Germans shocking civilisation by some further striking outrage," Stewart noted.[125] But, for once, Germany did not do the Allies the favor. Unable to use reprisal, the Allied announcement on censorship, drafted in February but not published until April 1916, argued that international law was unsettled, it applied in any case only to letters, and letters seized aboard the Dutch ship *Tubantia* showed that Germany had shifted its contraband from parcels to letters, in this case 174.5 pounds of finest rubber.[126] In its protest note, the United States expressed relief that Britain was not claiming the extension of blockade rights to cover its postal censorship

---

119. Johnstone to Foreign Office, no. 1231, the Hague, Nov. 27, 1915, FO 372/781, no. 180110, file 112241.

120. Grey note to Johnstone to Foreign Office, no. 1231, The Hague, Nov. 27, 1915, FO 372/781, no. 180110, file 112241; Nicolson minute of Dec. 3, 1915, ibid., no. 181901.

121. B. B. Cubitt to Foreign Office, Dec. 13, 1915, FO 372/781, no. 190641, file 112241; Stewart minute, Dec. 8, 1915, ibid., no. 186465; Stewart minute, Dec. 17, 1915, ibid., no. 190641; Stewart draft of Foreign Office to War Office, Dec. 30, 1915, ibid.

122. Bell, *History of the Blockade,* 358–59.

123. Stewart minute, Dec. 17, 1915, to Dutch ambassador to Foreign Office, no. 4514, Dec. 15, 1915, FO 372/781, no. 192564, file 112241.

124. Stewart draft of Foreign Office to War Office, Dec. 30, 1915, FO 372/781, no. 192564, file 112241.

125. Stewart minute, Dec. 23, 1915, to Bertie to Foreign Office, Dec. 20, 1915, FO 372/781, no. 196615, file 112241; Findlay to Foreign Office, Christiania, Dec. 20, 1915, ibid., no. 195479.

126. Memorandum Relative to Postal Correspondence on the High Seas, Feb. 15, 1916, *FRUS* 1916, Suppl., 599–601.

(Hurst's previous argument), but it rejected anyway a belligerent's right to search all ships in British ports.[127]

The Allies waited five months to reply.[128] Their answer was characteristically cautious. It insisted on the voluntary nature of ships in British ports, and argued that Convention XI applied only on the "high seas." Thus, the right to censor mail aboard ships voluntarily in British ports was covered by the domestic law of Britain. The Allies did not renounce the convention, but doubted its validity in the present war because six belligerents had failed to sign or ratify it. Nevertheless, the Allies would be "guided" by its principles, although they "can not admit that there is therein a final provision legally binding them, from which they could not possibly depart." As to ships on the high seas, the memorandum rehearsed state practice and discovered "no general rule...prohibiting" censorship. On the contrary, a long list of precedents, the last of which occurred during the Russo-Japanese War of 1904–5, established a belligerent right of "supervision granted them by international law to impede any transportation intended to aid their enemy." It read the famous *Peterhoff* case of the U.S. Civil War to show that it was only innocent correspondence that was protected in wartime, and it promised to forward such letters "with as little delay as possible." "Abuses, grave errors, or derelictions" would be made whole "in accordance with the principles of law and justice which it never was and is not now their intention to evade."

The Allied reply thus followed a familiar template: it stayed firmly within a legal framework; it preferred to construe a law narrowly, rather than to renounce it altogether; it kept future legal options open; it adverted to general principles that it promised to uphold; it relied on precedent to cover its actions; it read legal cases carefully; it promised cooperation; and, if it ended up breaking the law, it promised indemnification.

All the significant neutrals protested postal censorship, but their ire diminished as the censorship apparatus finally reduced delays to forty-eight hours.[129] By November 1916 Britain could process nine thousand letters per day.[130] Once again, the Allies' regularity and effectiveness contributed to the acceptance of measures that, in this case, extended the conception of contraband to apply to letters.

We shall see, in other chapters, similar examples of the legal discussions behind policy formation regarding reprisals and the use of prisoner-of-war labor, but the pattern should now be clear. Policy decisions, even when they ultimately broke the law, took place inside a legal framework. From the junior clerks to the foreign minister, the arguments were always also about what the law would allow, what arguments were most effective, what principles were most fundamental. The law was certainly used as a tool to achieve one's ends, but it was not thought infinitely malleable. Real concern was given to what one could prove before the Prize Court, to the likely response of neutral states, to internal consistency, and to the legal status of enemy policy. The latter continued to play a hugely important role, and

---

127. Lansing to Jusserand, Washington, May 24, 1916, *FRUS 1916*, Suppl., 604–8.

128. Memorandum, enclosed in Jusserand to Lansing, Washington, Oct. 12, 1916, *FRUS 1916*, Suppl., 624–28.

129. Garner, *International Law*, 2:353, 362.

130. Page to Lansing, London, Nov. 8, 1916, *FRUS 1916*, Suppl., 630, my calculations.

not just as a sought-after pretext to cover expanding Allied belligerent policy. G almost guaranteed that British policy makers would be, as Crowe minuted, "on our gua against the declarations or assurances given by the German government."[131] The anger visible in the sudden lurch toward retaliation in March 1915 was stoked not just by the shock of unrestricted submarine warfare, but by the fact that it occurred simultaneously with the German appeal on behalf of noncombatants' right, and by the fact that it had announced the beginning of sinkings on February 18, several days after a German U-boat had sunk the British merchant vessel *Dulwich*.[132] These coincidences convinced the British again and again that they were dealing with an entirely lawless government.

The point is that when Cecil remarked that he wished to avoid leaving Britain open "to the observation that we were making a change in international law for our own purposes during the war," or when Higgins noted that "the only possible official view is that our actions have been in accordance with the bedrock principles of international law," or when Hurst warned that "we ought to be careful about 'scraps of paper,'" they were not simply engaging in propaganda.[133] They were expressing basic assumptions identifying Britain with lawfulness. Contravening the law was more than simply embarrassing; it was an affront to a fundamental self-image held by British decision makers.

Nevertheless, sometimes they broke the law. Britain's leaders recognized the validity of military necessity, and the Foreign Office okayed various military actions taken on that basis. But the British conception of military necessity was narrower than the German. Lord Reginald Brett Esher, one of the most bellicose planners, seems to have covered his recommendation to violate Dutch neutrality by reference to a probable German violation of Belgium, that is, by reciprocity or retaliation. Hurst, arguing against him, had seen military necessity as operating not by plan, but in response to "the pressure of events as the war develops."[134] In a later, wartime memo, Hurst seems to have seen military necessity as operating primarily in the sphere of weapons development or methods: "New measures on the part of the belligerent must be countered by new measures on the part of his opponent."[135] Crowe cited it as the only justification for the last order-in-council of 1917.[136] The international-legal writers closest to the Foreign Office—for example the Grotius Society (which it had asked to prepare a report on postwar international law), G. G. Phillimore, and F. E. Smith, the attorney general—all agreed with the usual view among British jurists that military necessity must be severely limited in application.[137] Unlike in

---

131. Crowe minute, Feb. 16, 1915, to Page to Grey, Feb. 16, 1915, FO 382/184, no. 18427, file 8554.

132. Ibid.

133. Cecil to Lord Crewe, Feb. 29, 1916, FO 382/1125, no. 42065, file 6339; Higgins report, Dec. 14, 1918, cited in Erik Goldstein, *Winning the Peace: British Diplomatic Strategy, Peace Planning, and the Paris Peace Conference, 1916–1920* (Oxford, 1991), 222; Hurst minute, Feb. 8, 1916, FO 382/1099, no. 15779, file 302.

134. Esher, minutes of CID meeting of Jan. 23, 1912, CAB 16/18A, p. 85; Hurst memo, appendix 26, "Report and Proceedings," ibid., p. 425. Admiral Fisher's view seems also to have been one of reprisal: Avner Offer, *The First World War: An Agrarian Interpretation* (Oxford, 1989), 283.

135. Hurst minute, Apr. 9, 1915, to Page to Grey, Apr. 2, 1915, FO 382/186, no. 38783, file 22076.

136. Paul Cambon to Minister, Nr. 256, London, Feb. 17, 1917, MAE Blocus 46.

137. "Report of the Committee on the Legal Status of Submarines," Jan. 30, 1918; G. G. Phillimore, "Bombardments," *Grotius Society* 1 (1916): 66; Smith: Garner, *International Law*, 2:472n2.

...itary necessity exempted the actor from liability, in Britain it might ... the act remained illegal and thus required indemnification.[138]

...etween a junior clerk, F. E. F. Adam, and his boss, Lord Percy, in 1916 is ...ndary in which British decision makers found themselves. The issue was ...ical supplies, a small list of which Britain had offered to excuse by permit. ... "urgent military necessity" would allow Britain to requisition these items ...p them from reaching Germany. Percy replied irritably, "Either we have a rig... ... Red Cross articles or we have not. If we have not, we equally have no right to make their shipment subject to permits." Percy preferred arguing that "circumstances having changed," Britain would withdraw its offer of permits and advert instead to the old belligerent right of blockade by which all goods, including medical supplies, were stopped.[139] Although Britain sometimes acted on the basis of military necessity, it never liked citing that precept; it preferred the cover of older international law.

Violating the law was an embarrassment, and, for the most part, the British knew when they were doing so. Hurst, Mellor, and Malkin opposed the reprisal order-in-council of March 1915.[140] Apparently, only a single international lawyer in all of Britain thought it legal.[141] In November 1915 the Subcommittee of the War Trade Advisory Committee, asked to report on the legality of rationing the neutrals, concluded that "it would be difficult to answer their contention that such a rule was not justified by international law." It therefore wished to avoid a public proclamation of the policy, hoping instead for a "series of Prize Court decisions" that might uphold rationing on U.S. Civil War precedents.[142] Attorney general F. E. Smith summed up the situation since March 1915 in a note to Hurst, who was struggling to draft the last reprisal order-in-council of February 1917. "We are trying to do—I think for good reasons—a flagrantly illegal thing. Such matters cannot easily be expressed in a legal form. I think your last formulae as little objectionable as any I can suggest and I am prepared to support them in the Prize Court. As to the Privy Council we must take our chance—a poor one."[143]

If we recall that France never did join Britain in this last order, we may use Smith's remarks to summarize the forces tending to restrain Britain from wholesale violation of international law: its self-conception as a law-abiding state, its domestic government, its sense of international law as a product of a society of states to which Britain belonged and aspired to lead, its consequent recognition of other states and their interests as formative of law, its understanding that its own interests varied over time and circumstance (as a

138. Georges Kaeckenbeeck, "Divergences between British and Other Views on International Law," *Grotius Society, Problems of the War: Papers Read before the Society in the Year 1918* 4 (1918): 228.

139. F. E. F. Adam, minute, Feb. 12, 1916, and Percy minute, Feb. 15, 1916, to Buchanan to Grey, Petrograd, no. 4, Jan. 26, 1916, and draft telegram from Foreign Office to War Office and Admiralty, FO 382/682, no. 24155, file 88.

140. Bell, *History of the Blockade,* 237; John P. Mellor to Hurst, Treasury, Jan. 13, 1916, Malkin Papers, "American Protest, Civil War Precedents, Etc. 1915," FO 800/917.

141. Hurst minute, Dec. 12, 1916, on Sir Francis Piggott to Lord Sydenham, Eshurst, Surrey, Jan. 19, 1916, FO 382/1099, no. 32327, file 302.

142. Report of the Subcommittee, *BD,* ser. H, 6: doc. 208.

143. F. E. Smith to Hurst, Feb. 7, 1917, Malkin Papers, FO 800/913.

neutral trader or as a belligerent),[144] its awareness of the independence of the Prize Court and of the Privy Council as appeals court, and its concern for the often different views of its own allies. The alacrity with which Britain offered indemnities is the final indication of its adherence to the idea of law, even when it broke it.

Making International Law

The main legal foundation for the blockade was the March 1915 order-in-council whose text adverted to retaliation but whose supplementary diplomatic notes justified it as "a legitimate adaptation of the old right of blockade."[145] Beginning in 1918, Britain began planning to clarify the legal situation on this and other matters by establishing an International Law Committee (ILC) to advise how the law should be reformed at the treaty negotiations in Versailles. Its representatives came from the Admiralty, the Air Ministry, and the War and Foreign Offices; its chair was Viscount George Cave, the home secretary. Nine of its fifteen members were lawyers: Hurst, Higgins, Mellor, Stewart, John Macdonell, H. Erle Richards, T. W. H. Inskip (Admiralty), C. R. Brigstocke (Air Ministry), and R. F. Roxburgh (one of the secretaries).[146]

The ILC began its deliberations under a salvo from the Lords of the Admiralty aimed at the doctrine of "freedom of the seas" and the entire apparatus that, as the later report said, had so "embarrassed the navy in the prosecution of the present war, and, but for the illegal conduct of Germany, which enabled HM's Government to justify its action as reprisals, would have made the Order in Council of the 11th March, 1915, difficult, and that of the 16th February 1917, impossible to justify."[147] The Admiralty argued straightforwardly that "all Conventions and Declarations which place limitations on the exercise of sea power are to the disadvantage of the country which has the strongest Naval Force, and therefore so long as we maintain our superiority on the seas the provisions of the Declaration of Paris are necessarily to our disadvantage when we are at war."[148] They urged renunciation of the Declaration of Paris, which would have returned the world to an entirely non-codified state of maritime law.

Two of the lawyers argued strenuously against the Admiralty. They pointed out that the Declaration of Paris was widely regarded as customary law; Britain routinely followed three of its four articles and had abrogated the fourth (protecting enemy goods in neutral ships) only in an unusual, total war; Britain's peacetime and neutral interests were better covered by the declaration than by its abrogation; and Britain's allies all supported

---

144. A. P. Higgins, "Memorandum for HM's Procurator-General on Conditional Contraband," *BD*, ser. H, 5: doc. 94, p. 127.

145. Draft reply to U.S. note, Jan. 24, 1916, FO 382/1099, no. 16664, file 302.

146. Its other members were Viscount Cave, Rear Adm. G. P. W. Hope, Rear Adm. Sir Reginald Hall, Brig. Gen. G. K. Cockerill, Sir Eyre Crowe, and Col. E. H. Davidson (Air Ministry). *BD*, ser. I, 1: doc. 10.

147. ILC, Dec. 18, 1918, "Freedom of the Seas," *BD*, ser. I, 1: doc. 10.

148. O. Murray (ADM) to Foreign Office, Apr. 30, 1918, FO 372/1185, no. 76209, file 539.

it. Higgins doubted that the practices Britain had introduced under the March 1915 order-in-council would be upheld by Prize Courts as law (having been covered by reprisal)—that is, there was no ready-made substitution for the declaration; and Macdonell ended by pointing out that Britain would be open to claims "that she is treating a long-standing engagement as a 'scrap of paper.'"[149]

At a meeting on October 11, 1918, the ILC rejected this advice and voted in favor of the Admiralty. Why? The committee explained "that the paramount consideration was the interest of this country as a belligerent, rather than as a neutral, and that, from the point of view of the conduct of war, the opinion of the Admiralty...must prevail."[150] Thus, this extraordinary victory for the military over all other points of view occurred just as the war was coming to a victorious conclusion, when the navy could imagine that Britain still possessed the "strongest naval force," and when war, not peace, seemed the proper measure of law. Even so, the ILC was obviously ill at ease. Its draft memorandum for the War Cabinet admitted that abrogation would "be a step ill according with the present trend of opinion outside this country," and that it could hardly be announced as policy, as a unilateral abrogation, but would have to be handled in a gingerly diplomatic fashion.[151]

As it was, this drastic recommendation went nowhere. During the inter-Allied armistice negotiations, Britain reserved its right to interpret "freedom of the seas" differently from President Wilson, and that was the chief issue at stake.[152] No mention of the Declaration of Paris occurred at Versailles. By 1927 it was clear that Britain's supremacy at sea had vanished. A secret report in November 1927 to the cabinet on "Belligerent Rights at Sea" recognized that the rise of American naval power and the costs of modern warfare had changed Britain's position and therefore its views on law.[153] The enclosed memo by R. L. Craigie of the Foreign Office, who had participated in the Anglo-French negotiations to renounce the DoL, cautioned that, given the new naval balance, both the United States and Britain in their war plans must be careful not to abjure the Declaration of Paris, lest the enemy do the same.[154] Hurst's position was succinct: "The existing rules of international law give us all we want."[155]

This episode, which perhaps belongs under the heading "power corrupts, and absolute power corrupts absolutely," illustrates vividly the evanescence of legal positions taken on a one-sided basis, as if any state's "interests" could be boiled down to a single condition or frozen at a particular constellation of relations of power as they exist at one moment, and are inevitably gone the next.

---

149. Higgins memo, May 20, 1918, FO 372/1185, no. 98306, file 539; Macdonell note, n.d., ibid., no. 140995.

150. Minutes of ILC meeting of Oct. 11, 1918, FO 372/1185, no. 176616, file 539.

151. Draft memo, FO 372/1185, no. 176416, file 539, also W. A. Stewart memo of Oct. 24, 1918, ibid.

152. R. F. Roxburgh memo, n.d., on Wilson's idea of "freedom of the seas," FO 372/1186, no. 182809, file 539; minutes of ILC meeting of Nov. 26, 1918, ibid., no. 198687.

153. "Belligerent Rights at Sea and the Relations between the United States and Great Britain, November 1927, Printed for the Cabinet," C.P. 258 (27), ADM 116/3619.

154. R. L. Craigie memo, Oct. 17, 1927, to "Belligerent Rights at Sea and the Relations between the United States and Great Britain, November 1927, Printed for the Cabinet," C.P. 258 (27), ADM 116/3619.

155. Hurst memo, n.d., replying to Hankey memo, "Belligerent Rights at Sea and the Relations between the United States and Great Britain, November 1927, Printed for the Cabinet," C.P. 258 (27), ADM 116/3619.

Determining how far Britain's practices in World War I actually did change international law is not easy. Although there was widespread agreement in 1918 that maritime law needed reform, only the submarine was the object of interwar international codification. At Washington in 1922 and in London in 1930 (repeated in 1936), many powers agreed that submarines were subject to the same rules of warfare governing surface ships, meaning that they could not sink merchant vessels without warning and without saving passengers and crew.[156] To this day there is no maritime equivalent to the Hague rules of land warfare. The 1994 San Remo Manual on International Law Applicable to Armed Conflicts at Sea is the closest approximation to a modern code. It is the work of international lawyers and naval officers, but unlike the Declaration of London, their draft occurred not under the auspices of governments, but under that of the International Institute of Humanitarian Law; like the DoL, the San Remo Manual has never been ratified. Its status is therefore uncertain.[157] In addition, it reflects practices and technologies perfected in the Second World War and afterward, obscuring the impact of World War I on the rules it contains. Nevertheless, the San Remo Manual is the best measuring stick we possess to judge which of Britain's policies, including those contrary to the DoL, changed international law.

Already by April 1915 the United States had recognized two of Britain's innovations as legal: distant blockade (so long as it was effective and did not amount to blockading neutral ports), and the diversion to Allied ports of neutral merchant vessels suspected of carrying contraband.[158] The San Remo Manual goes much further. Its articles approve many of the most controversial British "blockade" practices: distant blockade (article 96); diversion to port (article 121); the expanded doctrine of continuous voyage (contraband need only be "ultimately destined for territory under the control of the enemy," article 184); the lack of distinction of conditional from absolute contraband (though it does recognize a free list) (article 148); the extension of contraband lists (article 149); the use of navicerts (articles 122–23); and the declaration of a war zone in exceptional cases, so long as the "same body of law applies both inside and outside the zone," neutral rights are respected, and "safe passage" for neutrals is provided—requirements that Britain, but not Germany, fulfilled (articles 105 and 106).[159] We have discussed earlier how, despite the stricter rules developed since 1919 to protect enemy civilians, the "hunger blockade" might have passed legally through the exceptions noted in article 102(a) ("sole purpose") and 102(b) (proportionate to "military advantage"). The San Remo Manual does not mention mail, but an eminent contemporary international lawyer writes that today, "public mail from or to an enemy

---

156. "Treaty relating to the Use of Submarines and Noxious Gases in Warfare," Washington, Feb. 6, 1922, and "Procès-verbal relating to the Rules of Submarine Warfare set forth in Part IV of the Treaty of London of 22 April 1930" (art. 22), and repeated in London, Nov. 6, 1936. Both available on the International Committee of the Red Cross (ICRC) website, and the latter in Roberts and Guelff, *Documents*, 169–73.

157. Roberts and Guelff, *Documents*, 573–606.

158. Page to Grey, Apr. 2, 1915, *BD*, ser. H, 4: doc. 63, enclosure to doc. 62; Bryan to Page, Washington, Mar. 30, 1915, *FRUS* 1915, Suppl., 152–56.

159. Wellesley on the difference between Britain's war zone and Germany's: "The point is what method of warfare is to be carried on within that area. We propose to abide by the recognized rules. Germany has declared her intention to sink every enemy merchant vessel at sight." Minute of Feb. 9, 1915, FO 376/760, no. 14908, file 13659.

destination would probably be treated as contraband, while the private mail would be subjected to censorship."[160] The one section where the San Remo Manual definitely rejects British practice concerns medical supplies, which now may not be stopped (article 104).

But many issues raised in World War I remain unresolved, often reappearing in the San Remo Manual verbatim from the DoL. The manual therefore gives only an approximate indication that subsequent legal and naval experts have judged Britain's blockade to have been on the whole a reasonable modern adaptation of the principles of maritime warfare.[161]

---

160. Leslie C. Green, *The Contemporary Law of Armed Conflict* (Manchester, 1993), 165.

161. Compare the different views of Green, *Contemporary Law,* 154–72; Michael G. Fraunces, "The International Law of Blockade: New Guiding Principles in Contemporary State Practice," *Yale Law Journal* 101, no. 4 (Jan. 1992): 893–918; Wolff Heintschel von Heinegg, "Naval Blockade," in *International Law across the Spectrum of Conflict: Essays in Honour of Professor L. C. Green on the Occasion of His Eightieth Birthday,* ed. Michael N. Schmitt (Newport, RI, 2000), 203–30.

Germany and New Weapons

Submarines, Zeppelins, Poison Gas, Flamethrowers

The Allies believed that Imperial Germany was simply lawless. But German decision makers did weigh law as a factor in policy. However, their interpretation of law was fundamentally different from that of the Allies, not just in its substance, but more important in how law worked, and in its importance for its own sake.

No decisions better reveal the German understanding of international law than those concerning submarine warfare. For one thing, the decision-making process stretched from September 1914 to January 1917 and thus left behind a large documentary record. But submarine warfare was also one of the few issues of war conduct that produced a decision-making process comparable to what was routine among the Allies. In Wilhelm Deist's words, it "was the only decision made by the German leadership that was comprehensively coordinated."[1] The chancellor, Auswärtiges Amt (AA), Admiralty, Naval Office, high command, often the Kaiser, and sometimes other federal secretaries took part in deliberations. Similar decision processes did not occur regarding land warfare, though they sometimes did concerning occupation. Why was submarine warfare different? For one thing, the Kaiser took his personal right to command (*Kommandogewalt*) vis-à-vis the navy seriously; he had created the battle fleet, and he identified with it. But perhaps more important, naval leaders recognized that submarine warfare clearly affected foreign affairs, and therefore it fell also within the purview of the chancellor and the AA. The navy knew from the beginning that law was critical to forging submarine policy. In many

---

1. Wilhelm Deist, "Strategy and Unlimited Warfare in Germany: Moltke, Falkenhayn, and Ludendorff," in *Great War, Total War: Combat and Mobilization on the Western Front, 1914–1918,* ed. Roger Chickering and Stig Förster (Cambridge, 2000), 275–76. Arguably, the Belgian deportations was another.

ways, the submarine decision, especially in the first six months of the war, shows Imperial Germany at its most sensitive toward international law, a sensitivity doubtless enhanced by the international uproar over the violation of Belgian neutrality and the "Belgian atrocities."

Although the building of the German battle fleet was one of the proximate causes of the war, in August 1914 it was quite unready to challenge Britain.[2] The Kaiser and Chancellor Theobald von Bethmann Hollweg therefore decided to keep the fleet from battle and save it as an asset for the postwar period or for peace negotiations. The inaction of battleships created the vacuum that the new and untried submarine then filled.

The Imperial German Navy entered the war with two contradictory theories of international law. One was a theory by implication, visible in Admiral Alfred von Tirpitz's position in preparation for the Hague Convention of 1907. Alive to Germany's economic vulnerability during a naval war, everyone but Tirpitz favored restricting belligerent rights as much as possible. That is, Germany's maritime weakness meant that strengthened neutral rights protected its interests. Tirpitz opposed diminishing in any way the belligerent threat that Germany posed to Britain; in case of a British blockade, he wanted, in the words of one historian, "a ruthless war on [British] trade and the bombardment of coastal towns and harbors."[3] Tirpitz believed that law did not protect Germany, it fettered it. His view was consonant with a trend in German naval strategic thought set down in a 1903 memo by the chief of the Admiralty, Vice Admiral Wilhelm Büchsel. It overturned the previous strategic assumption that Germany could rely on neutrals and allies to use international law to curb Britain's full display of belligerent power.[4] Büchsel reckoned according to a more lawless universe in which power was Germany's only real protection.

Despite these intimations, the second understanding of law was dominant in the navy. The Declaration of London (DoL) safeguarded Germany's food and raw material imports, it was clearly in Germany's interest, and naval leaders expected that it would be the basis of naval conduct, including their own, during the war. Germany's Naval Prize Manual of 1909 had essentially taken over the DoL.[5]

Although the submarine was a new weapon (it was first used in 1904–5) and was unmentioned in the DoL and the Hague Conventions of 1907, the DoL and the customary law behind it had major implications for submarine warfare. The submarine raised the question whether a belligerent could lawfully destroy merchant ships, and if so, under what circumstances?

---

2. Historians disagree whether Tirpitz ever meant to use the fleet militarily against Britain, or rather as a political fulcrum to extract far-reaching concessions from it without going to war. Volker R. Berghahn, *Der Tirpitz-Plan; Genesis und Verfall einer innenpolitischen Krisenstrategie unter Wilhelm II* (Düsseldorf, 1971); Jonathan Steinberg, *Yesterday's Deterrent: Tirpitz and the Birth of the German Battle Fleet* (London, 1965); Rolf Hobson, *Imperialism at Sea: Naval Strategic Thought, the Ideology of Sea Power, and the Tirpitz Plan, 1875–1914* (Boston, 2002). See Keith Bird, "The Tirpitz Legacy: The Political Ideology of German Sea Power," *Journal of Military History* 69 (July 2005): 821–32.

3. Hobson, *Imperialism at Sea*, 282.

4. Ibid., 274–76.

5. Josef Diehl, *Die Londoner Seerechtsdeklaration von 1909 und die deutsche Prisenordnung von 1909: Ein Vergleich* (Coburg, 1929).

As with starvation of the enemy, the law on sinking merchant ships was changing in the years before 1914. Because enemy merchant vessels were subject to confiscation, they were also liable to be destroyed, following the principle that a state may dispose of its property as it wills. However, since only a prize court ruling effected the transfer of the ship to the captor, destruction at sea ought in principle not to take place; instead, captured enemy vessels were to be brought to the prize court. State practice recognized exceptions to this rule, but those exceptions described a wide range from "imperative necessity" to mere convenience, as the international lawyer Lassa Oppenheim noted.[6] In 1882 the Institute of International Law listed five exceptions permitting the destruction of enemy merchant vessels at sea:

1 when the condition of the vessel and the weather make it impossible to keep the prize afloat;
2 when the vessel navigates so slowly that she cannot follow the captor and is therefore exposed to an easy recapture by the enemy;
3 when the approach of a superior enemy force creates the fear that the prize might be recaptured by the enemy;
4 when the captor cannot spare a prize crew [without endangering its own safety];
5 when the port of adjudication to which the prize might be taken is too far.[7]

If sometimes enemy merchant ships might be sunk, until 1869 no European country permitted sinking *neutral* merchant vessels under any conditions. In that year Russia changed its naval rules, followed by the United States in 1898, and by Japan in 1904, responding to Russia. But until 1904 no state actually acted on its new rules; in that year, during the Russo-Japanese War, Russia sank the British steamship *Knight Commander*—"a very serious breach of international law," as Foreign Minister Henry, fifth Marquess of Lansdowne, called it.[8] Russia then retreated from its unprecedented act, explaining a further sinking as an accident. But its prize court upheld the destructions as legal.[9]

This issue was heatedly debated in 1907 at the Hague and again in 1909 at the London Conference. Britain's position, enshrined in its pre-1913 prize regulations, was that neutral vessels were never to be sunk; if a captor was incapable of bringing them safely to port, it must release them. By 1909, Britain's traditional view was clearly superseded. It was forced into a compromise that it later regretted.[10] Article 48 of the DoL stated the traditional

---

6. Lassa Oppenheim, *International Law: A Treatise* (London, 1905), 2:200.

7. Section 50 of the Règlement international des prises maritime, trans. by Oppenheim, cited in Oppenheim, *International Law*, 2:201, my corrections in brackets, from Jan Helenus Ferguson, *Manual of International Law, for the Use of Navies, Colonies and Consulates* (The Hague, 1884), 2:509.

8. Hugh H. L. Bellot, "Destruction of Merchantmen by a Belligerent," *Grotius Society, Problems of the War: Papers Read before the Society in the Year 1915* 1 (1916): 55.

9. Ibid.

10. H. Goudy et al., "Report of the Committee on the Legal Status of Submarines," *Transactions of the Grotius Society* 4 (1918): xxxvii–xxxviii; memo by J. Pawley Bate, prepared for the Historical Section of the Foreign Office, FO 372/1186, no. 184425, file 539.

general principle: "A neutral vessel which has been captured may not be destroyed by the captor; she must be taken into such port as is proper for the determination there of all questions concerning the validity of the capture."[11] Article 49 then declared, "As an exception, a neutral vessel which has been captured by a belligerent war-ship, and which would be liable to condemnation, may be destroyed if the observance of Art. 48 would involve danger to the safety of the warship or to the success of the operations in which she is engaged at the time." "Success of operations" is a much broader category than the five exceptional conditions admitted by the Institute of International Law a quarter century earlier. Britain agreed to this weakening of principle because it thought that three other articles curbed the misuse of article 49. Article 51 required the captor to prove "exceptional necessity"; if he could not, he owed full compensation, even if the prize were valid (for example, if the vessel really did carry contraband). Article 52 required full compensation in cases of invalid capture, and article 53 did the same for neutral goods not liable to condemnation that were destroyed in the process. These sanctions were explicitly designed to underscore the exceptional nature of the destruction of neutral merchant vessels. As a result, Britain's new Prize Manual (1913) followed the DoL (article 77, articles 141–50).[12]

As we know, the DoL was of doubtful international validity. Beyond a doubt, however, was the customary law repeated in article 50 of the DoL: "Before the vessel is destroyed all persons on board must be placed in safety, and all ship's papers and other documents... relevant for the purpose of deciding on the validity of the capture must be taken on board the war-ship." It was unanimous state practice in all cases before 1914 of destruction of merchant vessels of any kind to save the passengers and crew.[13] The Russian naval prize regulations ordered commanders to "take off all persons on board, and as much of the cargo as possible, and [to] arrange for the safety of the vessel's papers."[14] The German Naval Prize regulations did the same: "The safety of all persons on board, and so far as possible their effects, is to be provided for, and all ship's papers and other evidentiary material... of value."[15] The saving of all persons aboard enemy and neutral vessels subject to destruction was so self-evident that it was simply assumed at the Hague deliberations in 1907 and in the silence of U.S. regulations.[16]

While the German prize regulations of September 1909 recognized the obligation to remove all persons aboard before sinking, it recognized a wider spectrum of necessity

---

11. James Brown Scott, ed., *The Declaration of London* (New York, 1919).

12. Naval Prize Manual (1913), ADM 116/1232. Cf. Frederick E. Smith, Law Officers opinion on "Destruction of Merchant Ships at Sea in Time of War," Feb. 12, 1917, TS 25–2023.

13. James Wilford Garner, *International Law and the World War* (London, 1920), 2:257.

14. Ibid., 2:258.

15. Charles Henry Huberich and Richard King, *The Prize Code of the German Empire as in Force July 1, 1915* (New York, 1915), art. 116, p. 68, cited in Goudy, "Report of the Committee," xxxvi.

16. Cf. Henri Fromageot's report, in Netherlands, Ministry of Foreign Affairs, *Actes et documents, Deuxième conférence internationale de la paix, La Haye 15 juin–18 octobre 1907* (The Hague, 1908), 1:262–64, 268, hereafter *Actes* (1907); Charles H. (Captain) Stockton, *The Laws and Usages of War at Sea: A Naval War Code* (Washington, DC, 1900), arts. 14, 6, 11; Alexander Freiherr Hold von Ferneck, *Die Reform des Seekriegsrechts durch die Londoner Konferenz 1908/09*, Handbuch des Völkerrechts (Berlin, 1914), 165–66; British Naval Prize Manual (1913), art. 144, ADM 116/1232.

excusing destruction. Article 113 permitted the sinking of neutral prizes because of danger to the captor's ship or to its operations; it gave as examples, "among other things,"[17] if "the vessel, on account of its defective condition or by reason of deficiency of supplies, cannot be brought into port; or the vessel cannot follow the war vessel, and is therefore liable to recapture; or the proximity of the enemy forces gives ground for fear of recapture; or the war vessel is not in a position to furnish an adequate prize crew."[18] Thus, the German prize regulations applied to neutral ships the exigencies previously thought to cover the destruction of enemy merchantmen as well, in essence erasing the distinction between the two. But Germany was hardly alone in doing so. At the Hague in 1907, Russia had been the prime mover of permission to destroy, because "the absolute prohibition of destruction [of neutral prizes] would have established an unjustifiable inferiority for the country not having ports close to its metropole."[19] In other words, the weaker naval powers and/or those with unfavorable geographies or fewer colonies sought, and found, a way to diminish their deficit as belligerents.

The Decision for Submarine Warfare: Autumn 1914

Submarines proved their military value on September 22, 1914, when a single U-boat sank three old British cruisers in the North Sea, two of which had stopped to rescue survivors from the first.[20] But, slow and vulnerable, submarines were ill-equipped for primarily military use against modern warships. However, the soft targets of merchant shipping were another matter. At the very end of September, Captain Heinrich von Hennig of *U-18* observed the "many freighters" going to and from England and noted, "In my opinion sinking a few merchantmen with U-boats would make an unexpected commotion in public opinion and disturb England's economic life. It would be easier to do this than to lay minefields."[21] The original impetus for sinking merchantmen thus came from below.

On October 2, 1914, Lieutenant Commander Hermann Bauer, head of the submarines under the command of the high seas fleet, began pressing his superior, Admiral Friedrich von Ingenohl, chief of the high seas fleet, to permit submarine warfare on merchantmen. Bauer repeated his request on October 8 and declared it could be covered as reprisal for the British navy's announcement that it was mining the Dover Straits, even though he

---

17. "u.a.," "Die Prisenordnung vom 30. September 1909 in ihre Fassung vom 1. Juli 1915," contained in Huberich and King, *Prize Code of the German Empire*, 135.

18. Huberich and King, *Prize Code of the German Empire*, 66–67. These articles remained the same from the Prize Regulations of Sept. 30, 1909.

19. Netherlands, *Actes* (1907), 1:263. Britain and the United States supported an outright prohibition of destruction of neutral prizes.

20. Arthur J. Marder, *From the Dreadnought to Scapa Flow: The Royal Navy in the Fisher Era, 1904–1919* (Oxford, 1961–70), 2:55.

21. Archibald C. Bell, *A History of the Blockade of Germany and of the Countries Associated with Her in the Great War, Austria, Bulgaria, and Turkey, 1914–1918* (London, 1937), 203.

admitted that Britain's measure was "not explicitly" forbidden by the Hague Convention, and that it was directed primarily "against our U-boats."[22] Bauer was right on both counts. Mining the Dover Straits was not part of the "blockade." It was a purely military response to the submarine threat posed to military transports and communication by the *U-18*, which had slipped into the Channel just as the Allies fought to defend Antwerp.[23] As an anchored and announced minefield in a military area, it was quite legal. Bauer's search for a legal cover for unrestricted submarine warfare indicates that he recognized its intrinsic illegality, particularly since he foresaw the likelihood that neutral vessels might be sunk, too.[24]

Admiral von Ingenohl refused on legal and humanitarian grounds to forward Bauer's first suggestion.[25] But in under a week, sentiment inside the naval officer corps favoring energetic action had reached the point where Ingenohl now passed Bauer's second try along to his boss, Chief of the Admiralty Admiral Hugo von Pohl. Rear Admiral Paul Behncke, the vice-chief of the Admiralty and head of its staff, advised Pohl that "current conditions do not justify this strong [*scharfe*] violation of international law," which would kill "non-combatants, neutrals, and [destroy] neutral property."[26] Pohl adopted Behncke's standpoint, recognizing that Britain's mines were not sufficient justification, especially since Germany had done the same in the waters around Denmark ("den Belt").[27] He told the High Seas Fleet (October 24) that he rejected the proposal "at least for the time being."[28] But in fact, he seems to have embraced it.

Pohl was at general headquarters with the chancellor when Bauer's request reached him. On the same day that Pohl held back Ingenohl and Bauer, Bethmann Hollweg telegraphed Foreign Minister Gottlieb von Jagow with the news that

> the navy seems to intend to blockade the English coast with mines and submarines and to sink without warning all the enemy [*sic*] merchant ships nearing the coast. The announcement would be made known after completion of the mine barrage. The navy covers departure from the rules of sea warfare by arguing that these were regulated at a time when submarines were not known and their possible uses were not taken into account.

The chancellor thus (mis)understood the navy's plan as targeting only enemy merchant ships. Bethmann then gave his own opinion.

---

22. Arno Spindler, ed., *Der Handelskrieg mit U-Booten*, Der Krieg Zur See 1914–1918 (Berlin, 1932–34), 1:2; Alfred von Tirpitz, *Politische Dokumente: Deutsche Ohnmachtspolitik im Weltkriege* (Hamburg, 1926), 281, citations from appendix 1, 177–78.

23. Julian S. Corbett, *Naval Operations* (London, 1920–28), 1:188.

24. Spindler, *Handelskrieg*, 1:178.

25. Ibid., 1:4.

26. Ibid., appendix 3, 1:181.

27. Ibid., 1:8–9.

28. Ibid., 1:10.

In view of the conduct of war *à outrance* that England intends, I also consider it advisable [*geboten*] to break England's resistance with the most radical means. Shortening the war by these means is entirely in our interest. One need not consider English reprisals, such as the possible destruction of German [merchant] ships in English ports, because in the event of victory, we would enforce compensation. Please reply immediately by telegraph how much the navy's proposal may be justified by law. Perhaps it could be based as retaliation [*Gegenmaßregel*] for the English principle of continuous voyage?[29]

If anything, the chancellor was more enthusiastic than the Admiralty chief. Nine days after the chancellor asked his question and while the AA deliberated, the British navy announced the "military zone" in the North Sea, giving Pohl the cover he needed.

Given the British navy's declaration and Britain's "continuous" violations, Pohl asked his staff (November 4) to investigate the possibility of a U-boat and mine blockade of Britain that would threaten "every merchant ship" near a British harbor with sinking "without being able to pick up its crew."[30] Like almost all non-submariners (that is, the vast majority of the naval officer corps in Germany and elsewhere), Pohl assumed that submarines were incapable of following the customary rules of commercial warfare at sea, the "cruiser rules" that required saving everyone on board. At this stage, Pohl favored a "blockade," because it would permit sinking all blockade-breakers. Sinking neutral merchantmen "without previous warning" was thus part of the plan from the beginning.[31]

Pohl's advisers saw many problems. Chief of Staff Behncke, Captain Kurt von Graßhoff (political section) and Lieutenant Commander Ernst Vanselow (legal section) worried that Germany lacked sufficient submarines, and the "far-reaching effects" of the measure on neutrals were such that they recommended the fulfillment of four conditions before proceeding.[32] First, only "a complete chance of success" justified the risks; but knowing that the navy was too weak to create a genuine food crisis in Britain, they measured success psychologically, as the effect on public morale. Second, in order to minimize neutral losses, they advocated a warning so drastic "that neutrals will not even try to reach English harbors." Third, in order to bolster the effect, they called for simultaneous air attacks and mine laying. But, finally, they believed that only a previous major land victory would keep neutral states from declaring war. Their memorandum is noteworthy for its mixture of bluff, caution, and extremism. They obviously attached more importance to neutrals' reaction than did Pohl, but they proposed to handle it by bluff (the warning) and military victory. Germany's naval weakness, which meant that the blockade would be ineffective (and thus illegal), was to be made good by other illegal means (air attack). Legal considerations were absent, or rather present only in their concern for the neutrals' reaction.

---

29. Bethmann to Jagow, GHQ, Oct. 24, 1914, Tel. Nr. 79, AAHQ e.o. Nr. 1822 pr., AA/PA, Akten des Auswärtigen Amtes im Generalhauptquartier, 1914–16 no. 5, Bd. 2, R 22383; also as IIIa 17692 in BAB R 901/85910.

30. Pohl to Admiralty staff, GHQ, Nov. 4, 1914, in Spindler, *Handelskrieg*, appendix 10, 1:195.

31. Pohl to Admiralty staff, GHQ, Nov. 7, 1914, in Spindler, *Handelskrieg*, appendix 11, 1:196–97.

32. Memo of Nov. 13–14, 1914, excerpted in Spindler, *Handelskrieg*, 1:28–29.

Meanwhile, the AA had answered the chancellor, not surprisingly striving to give him the legal weapons he had requested. Surprisingly, however, the answer was not drafted by the main legal adviser to the AA, Johannes Kriege (who approved it without emendation), but by a more junior clerk, Privy Councillor Walter Simons.[33] The chancellor was advised that a blockade by U-boats and anchored mines was "unobjectionable" (*unbedenklich*) because Russia had never signed the Hague Convention on automatic contact mines, so it was not in effect. A mine and/or U-boat blockade could therefore be used "also vis-à-vis neutrals" so long as it was effective and publicly declared. Simons therefore did not distinguish mines from U-boats, an equation that Bethmann had originally put in his query, but then struck out.[34]

Simons then continued:

> No treaty regulations are valid against the proposal to sink every enemy merchant vessel nearing the English coast. But our enemies would probably advert to the general international-legal principle that civilians in an undefended area are not to be directly attacked with weapons. The difference between mines and U-boats is that with mines, the merchant ship sinks as the result of its own activity, whereas with U-boats it is done with the conscious activity of our forces. If the proposal only affected English citizens, that would be justified by England's illegal maritime measures and especially by its attempt to starve Germany via illegal stoppage of neutral trade.

After warning of possible reprisals by England, bad relations with neutrals, and reclamations by the United States, he offered two ways to make the measure more palatable.

> One could uphold the measure vis-à-vis neutrals either if one destroyed English ships after first ordering quick departure from the vessel, or a general warning to neutrals not to travel on English ships preceded it. Without consulting with the naval authorities it is impossible to judge if such a procedure would sap the measure of too much energy. If so, then the advantages and disadvantages of the proposal must be weighed against each other.

Simons's draft, which Kriege and Jagow approved, reveals a number of assumptions about international law that, taken together, tilted strongly in favor of military considerations. After a narrow, but defensible, reading of the validity of the 1907 Hague regulations, Simons unproblematically asserted that a blockade enforced only by automatic contact mines would be legal if it were effective and announced. Nothing in treaties, usages, or

---

33. Draft of Undersecretary to Chancellor, Nr. 72, tel., Berlin, Oct. 27, 1914, IIIa 17692, BAB R 901/85910. Simons later represented Germany at the peace negotiations in Versailles and in subsequent reparations conferences; he served briefly as president of the Weimar Republic in 1925. My thanks to Dieter Gosewinkel for pointing out Simons's later career.

34. "U-boats are actually to be seen as mines," crossed out, Bethmann to Jagow, GHQ, Oct. 24, 1914, no. 79, BAB R 901/85910. In pencil someone has written "Actually, the effect of mines and U-boats is the same."

custom (mines being too new) upheld such a view, which would have meant that all ships of whatever kind would have been automatically blown up as blockade breakers. This is a much stronger interpretation of blockade than the great blockader, Britain, held, because it equated the right of confiscation with immediate, universal destruction.

Simons then indicated the preference for treaty law typical of the Continental powers (by beginning with the observation that no treaties forbade sinking all enemy merchantmen during blockade), leaving it to the "enemies" to advert to general principles (of not killing noncombatants). Simons answered the chancellor's query in the positive: Germany could cover a U-boat and/or mine blockade as reprisal for Britain's "illegal maritime measures." In his view, the killing of enemy civilians in such a reprisal was legal. But there were also neutral persons and goods aboard those enemy ships. Simons suggested solving that dilemma either by following customary law and thus removing all persons from the ships before they were sunk, or by issuing a "general warning." This last is another surprising suggestion for two reasons. Simons erased the binding quality of customary law by claiming that a mere warning could substitute for it. And the warning he suggested was quite deficient. It appears to be fashioned after the notification required for blockades and minefields, but in both of those cases the Hague Rule required announcing the exact location.[35] Finally, Simons ended his report by suggesting that if following the law weakened the measures too much, then the government must decide whether to break the law on the basis of political advantage. Simons's views passed the muster of his superiors, Kriege and Jagow, so they cannot have been unusual inside the AA.

As Admiral von Pohl pushed harder for the U-boat blockade, Chancellor Bethmann instructed the AA in mid-November to meet with the Admiralty and to present his doubts about the naval plan because of the danger of neutral anger and enemy retaliation, especially the halting of food supplies to the Committee for the Relief of Belgium and a Russian potential blockade of the Baltic Sea. Given those possibilities, the chancellor thought that a U-boat blockade should probably only occur either if Germany enjoyed "a very positive military situation in east and west...or if in extreme necessity the blockade were our last resort." Bethmann apparently felt that in either extreme, victory or defeat, international law could be more easily abandoned. He also noted that "Admiral v. Pohl admits that in executing the blockade the destruction by our U-boats of neutral merchant vessels, even if forbidden, is nevertheless not impossible, indeed, [it is] likely."[36]

After the joint meeting, Simons again drafted the précis, and Kriege and Jagow approved it.[37] It is a fascinating document. The navy had admitted that "the U-boats would probably not be able to execute the blockade all the time," meaning it would be ineffective by legal standards. The plan was "that all merchant ships going to or from the English coast would be destroyed without warning and without consideration for the destruction of human

---

35. Hague Convention VIII (automatic contact mines), arts. 3 and 4, in *Documents on the Laws of War*, ed. Adam Roberts and Richard Guelff (Oxford, 2004), 105–6. The Declaration of London set much stricter standards for notification of blockade: arts. 8–12; see also "observations," Scott, *Declaration of London*, 61–62, and the general report, 140–41.

36. Bethmann to Jagow, no. 113, Nov. 20, 1914, IIIa 20172, BAB R 901/85910.

37. Zimmermann to Bethmann, Berlin, Nov. 30, 1914, IIIa 20172, BAB R 901/85910.

life. Neutral ships, if they could with certainty be identified as such, would be spared, [but] these cases would probably only occur exceptionally," because the navy expected enemy merchant vessels to fly neutral flags, and "U-boats cannot do close searches."

The AA concluded that the navy's plan was unlawful regarding sinking "both English and neutral ships," for the former, because submarines would not follow cruiser rules that required saving passengers and crews. Regarding neutral ships, the illegality consisted, first, in the ineffectiveness of the blockade, and second, in the inability to declare it correctly, since it would be active now in one place and now in another, depending on the availability of submarines. "Therefore, Germany can only establish the planned measures...as reprisal [*Vergeltung*]." Against Britain the reprisal would be for its attempt "via the illegal paralysis of legitimate neutral trade to hit the national economy of Germany and in the end to destroy the entire German people via starvation." But the plan was also to undertake reprisals against the neutrals for accepting Britain's measures, thus allegedly violating their neutrality, and for their own embargo decrees that forbade the export of food to Germany. "Naturally it would not be admitted that neutral ships, people, or goods would be intentionally targeted by German warships." They concluded, "It is undeniable that this rationalization of our procedures against the neutrals stands on clay feet [*auf schwachen Füßen*] and that neither the governments nor public opinion in neutral countries would be liable to accept it." After listing possible enemy reprisals, they wrote that the strength of neutral reaction would depend on the military situation: if Germany were winning, the neutrals would likely not declare war.

The AA advised Bethmann that a U-boat blockade should only be attempted if it could be effective "at least for several weeks in a row," and if neutrals would not declare war. Therefore, the number of U-boats should be larger, and Germany should be militarily successful at least on the western front, meaning "the Channel coast ports of Dunkirk, Calais, and Boulogne should be in German hands." These territorial goals were Bethmann's own, as outlined in his memorandum of September 9, 1914.[38]

The AA thus gave Bethmann the advice he had asked for. The AA underscored the illegality of the whole project and the difficulty of justifying it even as reprisal. Everyone was aware that neutral ships would be sunk and neutral persons killed. Like the chancellor, the AA concluded that military considerations, not legal ones, were paramount in making the decision. It is therefore all the more surprising that Admiral von Pohl's response to this disappointing news was to send the chancellor a long memorandum on "sea law and the conduct of war."[39]

Pohl's memorandum is vivid testament to the navy's bitter disappointment that the DoL had not, after all, been able to protect Germany's belligerent interests. The DoL, he wrote, had given Germany "the possibility of covering its entire needs of raw materials, food, oils, and fuel" through neutrals, "so that an economic starvation of the German Empire through England was not to be feared." Pohl's basic assumption was that the DoL was

---

38. Fritz Fischer, *Germany's Aims in the First World War* (New York, 1967), 104.

39. Pohl memo, "Seerecht und Kriegführung," GHQ, Dec. 24, 1914, ad A.H. 2779, BAB R 901 85910, also in AA/PA, R 22385.

indeed law, and Britain had broken it. "The well-meaning intention to limit the severities of sea warfare, to bring sea law into a form appropriate to the spirit of our age...has failed. *Sea law has not withstood the severe demands of war, the power and existential questions.*" Not just Britain, but also the neutrals were responsible for this failure, because their fear caused them to placate Britain. But the island nation was vulnerable because it depended on imports of raw materials and food more than Germany did. Law having failed, force was the only remedy left. "It would be false consideration for the enemy and for the neutrals, if we were to remain on the defensive...and not go on the offensive. After the experiences which Germany has had with the concepts of law [*Rechts*] and honesty in years-long effort, this [offensive] is a command of self-preservation [*ein Gebot der Selbsterhaltung*]." One could "justify" going on the offensive via "a blockade which is recognized in international law in all its effects." But it could not be done by mines and surface cruisers alone. "Modern technology" had handed Germany a weapon that "would lead to a complete revolution in the conduct of war." That weapon was the submarine. "*But new means require new forms* and one cannot demand of the U-boat that it announce its presence" (by surfacing to remove crews and passengers).[40] Therefore, a general warning must suffice. "The more severe effects of a U-boat blockade we can accept in good conscience. The life of a few daredevil merchant crews...need not count more than those of many thousands of our countrymen." "England has pushed aside the law of the sea in this war when it was a hindrance." Now Germany should do the same. "What we do in this regard, occurs because of political considerations."

Pohl's memorandum is deeply ambivalent about international law. Its language reads in parts like that of a disappointed suitor. The fact that Pohl chose a legal, rather than a purely military tack with which to argue suggests either that, despite the chancellor's words, Pohl could not believe that the main civilian leaders' objections to U-boat blockade were not legal in nature, or that Pohl's own legal qualms, evident in his immediate rejection of U-boat blockade at the beginning of October, still irked him and he busily tried to argue them into oblivion.

Pohl's condemnation of Britain as the great (naval) criminal was widespread in Germany and inverted the Allied judgment of Germany. However, once Pohl had decided that the DoL was a lost cause, he jettisoned law altogether. He used four arguments. First, international law had been wiped out by the grim realities of war—a version of the military necessity argument. Second, law was not in Germany's self-interest; it clashed with the imperatives of self-preservation. Third, Germany's weapon, the submarine, was not covered by law because it was too new ("new means require new forms"). Finally, Britain's previous violation of the law was taken to nullify it altogether—in other words, to create a law-free zone. These are among the most common arguments to which naval and military men recurred in later policy debates.

Three days later, on December 27, 1914, Bethmann and Jagow answered Pohl's memorandum and set down for posterity the legal position of the AA and the chancellor on submarine warfare; they sent a copy of this foundational statement to the Supreme

---

40. Emphases in original.

Command.[41] Its first sentence laid down the legal assumption undergirding policy: "Proceeding from the standpoint that we can use those measures of war against the enemy that seem most appropriate to defeat him and to end the war quickly, we may entirely ignore taking consideration of England, especially also regarding the purely utilitarian maxims of its conduct of war and the ruthless pressure that it exerts on neutrals under the pretext of stopping contraband." That is, military necessity and only secondarily reprisal justified unrestricted submarine warfare. They twice admitted "that torpedoing neutral ships is not entirely compatible with the general rules of international law." The bulk of the document concentrated on possible neutral reactions, especially those of the United States, Italy, and Romania. It concluded, "The hesitations [*Bedenken*] of the Auswärtiges Amt against the planned U-boat blockade are thus not of a legal nature, but result from considerations of military-political opportunity. The question is not if, but *when* the measure—without harming our position—may be taken."[42]

The legal position of the civilian leadership was therefore explicitly not one. The chancellor and the foreign minister rejected international law as a significant factor in decision making. And both recognized that unrestricted submarine warfare (that is, sinking merchant ships without saving those aboard) was illegal. Arno Spindler, the author of the official history of the submarine campaign, writing in the 1920s, argued against interpreting the memo as proof that Bethmann and Jagow regarded the submarine issue as "purely a question of power." He believed that they also regarded it as a "legal question," one that they had answered positively: "under the existing circumstances of the war," unrestricted submarine warfare was legal.[43] But their language strongly suggests that Bethmann and Jagow were not satisfied that reprisal adequately justified the measure, otherwise they would not have adverted primarily to military necessity, and only secondarily to reprisal, almost as an afterthought. Simons's advisory draft had pointed out the clay feet on which the reprisal argument stood, especially regarding neutrals. In the memorandum both leaders clearly made the decision conditional on Germany's "military position on the Continent," and only when that was "so secure, that the decision [i.e., victory] is seen as certain," could the submarine weapon be used. If Bethmann and Jagow had indeed emphasized law instead of power, they would have greatly strengthened their own position in the decision-making process to come, for questions of legality were in their bailiwick, while the military was the acknowledged expert in deciding "military-political" questions.

We have seen that already in October Bethmann was anxious in principle to unleash the submarine, so it is not surprising that from mid-November 1914 into January 1915 the AA and Admiralty hammered out the legal form that submarine warfare would eventually take. Pohl had originally favored blockade, but Jagow and the AA preferred a war zone, as Pohl summarized, "because we cannot fulfill the formalities that are generally recognized

---

41. "Standpunkt des Auswärtigen Amtes in der Frage der U-Boots-Blockade," signed Bethmann and Jagow, sent to Pohl on Dec. 27, 1914, zu A.H. 2779, AA/PA R 22385, also published in Tirpitz, *Politische Dokumente*, 292–95; Spindler, *Handelskrieg*, 1:56.

42. Emphases in original.

43. Spindler, *Handelskrieg*, 1:57.

as necessary for a blockade to meet international law."[44] Tirpitz thought a war zone was an error because it was more extreme than a blockade and would upset the neutrals even more.[45] On January 26, 1915, Pohl explained to the commander of the high seas fleet, who also favored blockade, why a war zone was preferable: "A blockade would force us to follow exactly the recognized international-legal principles that appear in our own Prize Manual as binding, without giving us the right to sink blockade breakers whose crews have not been warned or saved. Blockade would thus only burden us with duties that we cannot fulfill without giving us greater rights."[46]

Germany lacked the requisite number of submarines to fulfill the Prize Manual's definition of effectiveness. (Bauer had reckoned that a mere four submarines would suffice, and given repairs, other assignments, and travel to and from the British coast, not much more than this absurdly small number was actually available.)[47] Because so few U-boats could only cover part of the area at any time, the exact boundaries of the blockade would have to be continually redeclared. "These formalities would hinder us from hitting quickly and hard." The requirement of exact notification would force Germany to declare a much larger blockade than its tiny number of submarines could cover. And, finally, "the blockade breaker may only be destroyed after the crew had been brought to safety. This cannot happen when one uses submarines." Therefore, "the waters around England and Ireland will be declared a war zone on the English model, and enemy and neutral ships will be warned of the danger for ship, persons, and goods, if they travel in these waters, outbound or inbound."

The reasons Pohl listed were not simply his own; they were the reasons that he and the AA had been mulling over for two months. They are remarkable for three things in particular. First, German leaders knew what international law required, and they straightforwardly admitted to themselves that Germany was too weak to fulfill it, not so much because of (erroneous) assumptions about what submarines could not do, but because Germany simply did not have enough of them. In other words, the main impetus to throw over international law was Germany's own weakness as a belligerent.

Second, the leaders apparently thought of the war zone as a law-free area. Whereas blockade required one to save persons aboard ships, the war zone, apparently, did not. This remarkable idea had two sides. One denied that the rule was truly a general principle applicable to sea warfare regardless of where it was fought or with what means. The rescue of passengers and crew was so deeply and unanimously embedded in customary law that denying it amounted to rejecting the existence of general principles altogether. And if

---

44. Pohl to Jagow, B. 106751, Berlin, Dec. 19, 1914, "Ganz geheim!" AA/PA R 22385; also Pohl to Bethmann, B. 10671 I, BAB R 901, 85910. A copy went to Kriege, the legal adviser.

45. Tirpitz to Pohl, Berlin, Dec. 16, 1914, Tirpitz, *Politische Dokumente*, 288.

46. Pohl to Ingenohl, Jan. 26, 1915, in Spindler, *Handelskrieg*, 1:72–73.

47. Bericht des Führers der U-Boote vom 27. Dezember 1914 an das Kommando der Hochseestreitkräfte, Wilhelmshaven, in Spindler, *Handelskrieg*, 1:217–22, appendix 18. In May/June 1914, an internal study by Lt. Ulrich-Eberhard Blum of the Submarine Inspectorate had estimated that Germany would need 222 submarines for a successful blockade of England: Holger Herwig, "Total Rhetoric, Limited War: Germany's U-Boat Campaign, 1917–1918," in Chickering and Förster, *Great War, Total War*, 204.

general principles did not exist, they could not be applied to new situations. In short, there were gaps in the law that could not be filled by extrapolating from general principles. This is the doctrine of *non liquet,* which we have examined previously.[48]

The third remarkable aspect of Pohl's summary was its contention that Germany's war zone followed the British model. But of course Britain did not sink neutral merchantmen in the North Sea, with or without warning. Pohl's contention might have come from his reading of the British Admiralty's stern warning that merchant vessels would "be exposed to the gravest dangers from mines which it has been necessary to lay and from warships searching vigilantly by night and day for suspicious craft." Pohl cited this phrase in a letter to Tirpitz.[49] The draft AA announcement for the future submarine measure, written in November 1914, was more cautious; it merely said that Britain "endangered" neutral vessels.[50] It is hard to tell whether Britain's war zone was merely a convenient cover, whether the tendency of many writers to equate mines and U-boats made the equation of Britain's war zone with Germany's seem logical, or whether Germany's leaders projected their own readiness to embrace unprecedented, lethal measures onto their enemy.

Once the chancellor and AA had interpreted the law and decided on reprisal, and once they and the navy had chosen war zone over blockade, the legal parameters of submarine warfare were set. Civilian decision makers did not reexamine them. Only through concern about the reactions of neutral states did international law obliquely affect later decision making. German state behavior thus still moved within the orbit of the community of law only insofar as the Kaiserreich believed that it remained dependent on the neutrals.

Imperial Germany's decision-making process also differed from Britain's. As the foundations for submarine warfare were being laid, joint meetings were unusual. Instead, positions and arguments were traded back and forth in correspondence. Inside agencies, the normal routine of business went ahead uninterrupted by the gravity of the issue; at least in the AA, legal advice originated with lower clerks, and the surviving documents show little editing by their superiors. There was no joint prewar planning, and sometimes no planning at all, to set the template for later decisions, which then occurred under the press of war.

Other New Weapons: Aerial Warfare, Incendiaries, and Poison Gas

At the same time that Imperial Germany's decision makers were fashioning submarine policy, they were also debating whether or how to use other new weapons such as the

---

48. See chapter 6.

49. Foreign Office to Spring Rice, Nov. 3, 1914, *FRUS* 1914, Suppl., 464; Pohl to Tirpitz, Berlin, Dec. 19, 1914, in Tirpitz, *Politische Dokumente,* 290.

50. Denkschrift über deutsche Gegenmaßnahmen gegen die völkerrechtswidrigen Maßnahmen Englands zur Unterbindung des neutralen Seehandels mit Deutschland, appendix to Zimmermann to Bethmann, Berlin, Nov. 30, 1914, IIIa 20172, BAB R 901 85910, printed in Tirpitz, *Politische Dokumente,* 290–92.

zeppelin, the flamethrower, and poison gas. Their discussions reveal further patterns in how international law affected policy making.

Without preliminary discussion inside the government, the German army on the night of August 24–25, 1914, used a zeppelin to drop six shrapnel bombs on Antwerp. Twelve civilians died. Britain's representative to Belgium telegraphed the next day, "This atrocious act has intensified bitter indignation which brutality of Germans has aroused."[51] In the Foreign Office indignation mixed with confusion over which laws applied to such an act. The Hague Convention XIV of 1907 prohibited "the discharge of projectiles and explosives from balloons or by other new methods of a similar nature."[52] But many of the belligerents, including France, Germany, Italy, Japan, and Russia, never signed or acceded to it, so it was not technically binding during the war. However, the rules of bombardment seemed applicable. The Hague rules of land warfare forbade "bombardment, by whatever means, of towns, villages, dwellings, or buildings which are undefended" (article 25). Except where the object was actually to capture the place, the commander "must...do all in his power to warn the authorities" (article 26), and historic and medical buildings and the like were supposed by spared "as far as possible" (article 27). The Hague Convention IX (1907) attempted to apply the same standards to naval bombardment (articles 1, 5, and 6) but in fact offered greater latitude, for, in addition to military works and depots, it included workshops and plants "which could be utilized for the needs of the hostile fleet or army" as legitimate military targets (article 2). The main issues raised by bombardment were, then, whether a place was undefended, whether advance notification was possible, and whether the attacker had aimed at military targets.

On August 30, 1914, the army began a series of night zeppelin raids on Paris.[53] But only in September, when OHL, seconded by the Admiralty, pressed to bomb London did the chancellor and the AA become aroused.[54] From general headquarters, Foreign Secretary Jagow asked (via his assistant, Werner Freiherr von Grünau) for clarification about the status of military targets that were explicitly open to aerial bombardment in the Hague naval rules (Convention IX), but not mentioned in the Hague land rules.[55] The next day, Undersecretary Arthur Zimmermann telegraphed back that neither Hague convention was applicable because neither "wanted to regulate aerial warfare."[56] Therefore, belligerents

---

51. Sir F. Villiers to Foreign Office, Antwerp, Nr. 128, Aug. 25, 1914, FO 372/495, no. 42977, file 38720.

52. Declaration XIV Prohibiting the Discharge of Projectiles and Explosives from Balloons. The Hague, October 18, 1907, available on the International Committee of the Red Cross website, http://www.icrc.org/ihl.nsf/FULL/245?OpenDocument.

53. Raymond Poincaré diary, Aug. 30, 1914, in *The Memoirs of Raymond Poincaré, 1914*, trans. George Arthur (Garden City, NY, 1929), 119–20; Susan R. Grayzel, "'The Souls of Soldiers': Civilians under Fire in First World War France," *Journal of Modern History* 78, no. 3 (September 2006): 596–98.

54. Pohl diary, Sept. 2, 1914, Hugo Pohl, *Aus Aufzeichnungen und Briefen während der Kriegszeit* (Berlin, 1920), 43–44; Albert Hopman diary, Sept. 23, 1914, Albert Hopman, *Das ereignisreiche Leben eines "Wilhelminers,"* ed. Michael Epkenhans (Munich, 2004), 444, 444n403.

55. Jagow to AA, GHQ, Sept. 27, 1914, zu AH 1272, AA/PA R 22383.

56. Zimmermann to Jagow, Berlin, Nr. 591, Sept. 28, 1914, AA/PA R 22383. Grünau thought the Hague rule applied to aerial bombing; *Geheimrat* Lentze thought the matter unclear: Grünau minute Sept. 29, 1914, on Nr. 591.

were "not bound by treaty, but only insofar as provisions of general international-legal principles may apply." These would surely permit targeting military objects, he thought; "that this is the general view of belligerent signers is shown by the fact that the provisions calling for previous warning in article 26 of the Hague Land Rules and article 2 of Convention XI were never followed." It is not clear which state practices of aerial warfare Zimmermann had in mind: perhaps those of the Tripolitanian War (1911), or the Balkan Wars (1912–13), for since the outbreak of hostilities, the Allies had barely taken to the air—just a few days before, Britain had tried to bomb the zeppelin hangar in Düsseldorf.

The matter came to a head in early November. On the third, German cruisers, without first informing the chancellor, shelled Yarmouth, a seaside resort on Britain's east coast. Bethmann angrily informed Admiral von Pohl that the bombardment had an enormous impact on "the entire political and military situation of Germany in the current war."[57] "That this act was not reported to the chief imperial official responsible for the overall politics of the empire is incompatible with politics and with the constitution [*geltenden Staatsrecht*]." Either Bethmann's legal remonstrance had an effect, or the new chief of the general staff, Erich von Falkenhayn, was more cautious than his predecessor. In any event, on November 11, Falkenhayn asked the AA to warn France and Britain that Germany would shortly bomb defended places "that are not directly in the area of operations."[58] He had London in view. Forewarned, Bethmann tried to stop the operation. His first argument was legal: London was not a fortified city.[59]

> Dropping dynamite bombs on London would be condemned by all neutrals, especially in America, as a complete disregard not only of every international law, but also as an act of inhumanity; it would turn all sympathy against us and probably bring further harsh consequences in its train.... At the conclusion of peace, especially one that is not *very* favorable to us, the sympathy of neutrals (like America and Italy) will be extremely valuable. And our enemies would doubtless use a bombardment of London seen as "barbaric" to saddle us with the most onerous conditions. Your Excellency knows how the violation of Belgian neutrality has been used everywhere against us; a bomb attack on the "open" city of London would call forth further bitterness against us, and we must reckon with such imponderables. Finally, our enemies would doubtless hold themselves justified in following our example and bombing *German* open cities.[60]

Bethmann ended by asking, what military use would such an act have?

The chancellor's first salvo was thus extremely powerful. Significantly, it was based entirely on law, even though Bethmann put the voice of law into the mouths of neutrals (not the German government). But his list of negative consequences amounts to

---

57. Bethmann to Pohl, Nov. 5, 1914, in Tirpitz, *Politische Dokumente,* 151–52.

58. Falkenhayn to Jagow, GHQ, Nr. 375, Nov. 11, 1914, AA/PA R 22384.

59. Bethmann to Falkenhayn, GHQ, Nov. 12, 1914, AAHQ Nr. 2266, AA/PA R 22384.

60. Emphases in original.

international-legal sanctions: economic reprisal, loss of neutral support, disadvantageous peace terms, possible reparations, and military reprisals in kind. His final query on military effectiveness raised both the legal question (if an attack cannot succeed, its very gratuitousness would seem to make it illegal), and the policy question (if you are to break the law, then the gain must outweigh the damage). Bethmann's remark about the violation of Belgian neutrality suggests that he had learned a lesson about the potential cost of breaking international law for purely military reasons.

While the navy and army continued preparing for an early December bombing run on London using ten-to-fifteen-kilogram incendiaries, the AA scurried to prove that London was undefended.[61] Consistent with Zimmermann's advice, Bethmann's fallback position was to limit aerial attacks to clearly military objects, and he began to prepare the Kaiser's entourage to influence Wilhelm II in that direction.[62] Meanwhile, Falkenhayn had shown that London was indeed "occupied by troops and equipped with extensive defensive measures."[63] Grünau incorporated Falkenhayn's information into a revised legal memorandum that circulated up to the chancellor.[64] It repeated the observation that only general principles governed aerial bombardment. The main question now concerned the fortified or defended status of targets. The memorandum noted that Germany, Britain, France, and Japan had reserved article 1, paragraph 2, which had exempted from bombardment coastal cities defended by automatic contact mines. That meant that such cities were valid targets, and so were those with analogous defenses against aerial attack. Concerning previous warning, the memorandum concluded that "it appears both from the nature of aerial war and from...practice in the current war" that warnings were unnecessary. The belief that aerial war had a "nature" that might shape law we will examine in detail below, but its appearance in a memorandum drafted by the AA is significant. Finally, the memorandum expanded legitimate targets from purely military facilities to "the bombardment of the city itself." It was contended that the city lost its "open" status because of three forts and ten redoubts to the city's south, artillery pieces, and antiaircraft measures.

Zimmermann now strongly advised Falkenhayn not to give advanced warning of air attacks. Warnings were not precise enough, he wrote, to fulfill the requirements of the Hague conventions; they were unnecessary, as Grünau had pointed out; they were useless to save civilians; and they would only cause greater anger.[65]

Having lost the legal battle, Bethmann was left to weigh military effectiveness against neutral anger. On January 9, 1915, a meeting with the Kaiser laid down policy on the

---

61. Hopman diary, Nov. 13, Nov. 18, 1914, Hopman, *Das ereignisreiche Leben*, 498, 498n562, 503; Jagow to German embassy in the Netherlands, Nov. 13, 1914, no. 2312, AA/PA, R 22384; Zimmermann to Jagow, Berlin, Nov. 13, 1914, no. 1055, ibid.

62. Hans v. Plessen diary, Nov. 16, 1914, Charleville, in *Kaiser Wilhelm II. als Oberster Kriegsherr im Ersten Weltkrieg; Quellen aus der militärischen Umgebung des Kaisers 1914–1918*, ed. Holger Afflerbach (Munich, 2005), 696; Hopman diary, Nov. 19, 1914, Hopman, *Das ereignisreiche Leben*, 503.

63. Falkenhayn to Bethmann, GHQ, Nov. 17, 1914, no. 2684P, AA/PA R 22384.

64. Aufzeichnung über die Zulässigkeit der Beschießung Londons durch Luftstreitkräfte, no. 2349 pr., Nov. 26, 1914, AA/PA R 22834. Bethmann read the memo on Nov. 15. Grünau's authorship: Zimmermann to Jagow, Berlin, Nov. 22, 1914, no. 1135, ibid.

65. Zimmermann to Jagow, Berlin, Nov. 22, 1914, no. 1135, AA/PA R 22834.

aerial bombardment of Britain and the opening of submarine warfare. Present were the chancellor, Admiralty Chief Pohl, and the military and naval cabinet chiefs, General Hans von Plessen and Admiral Georg Alexander von Müller. Bethmann won both his points. Unrestricted submarine warfare was postponed until it could be militarily effective, "as the last trump card."[66] Concerning aerial bombardment, Pohl had argued for "no restraint" (*Schonung*); he believed that bombardment was important not just for military reasons but for its negative effect on civilian morale, "the moral impression."[67] But Pohl, who previously had discussed matters with the chancellor, said that historical buildings and private property would be respected if possible. Pohl recorded in his diary that the Kaiser thought it "dreadful to kill innocent women and children by bombs."[68] Kaiser and chancellor thus agreed with one another, though possibly for different reasons. The resulting decision was to target only military objects, at first in coastal towns and only later in London.[69]

Raids on the Norfolk coast began on the night of January 20. Theodor Wolff, the liberal editor of the *Berliner Tageblatt,* recorded the results: "a few harmless adults and children killed. Senseless! Naturally now renewed cries about the barbarians. Otherwise, the effect is zero."[70] Germany's ambassador reported that U.S. public opinion considered the raids "superfluous and barbaric."[71] Substantiated, Bethmann sprang into action. He told Pohl that raids "on open places are making the worst possible impression, especially in the U.S. Serious circles here [in Berlin] also are raising doubts because the military purpose and success seems inapparent." He demanded "the fastest possible clarification."[72] Despite Bethmann's concerted opposition, he was unable to stop the policy of zeppelin bombardments.

This seesaw battle between the navy and the AA continued sporadically throughout the war. In April 1915 Zimmermann sent to the AA's man at general headquarters, Karl Georg von Treutler, a Baedeker guide to London ("the best available map of London in the AA"), to help him try to locate areas off-limits to air attacks.[73] In September 1915 the AA tried again, but what had been a secondary defense with Admiral von Pohl ("moral impression") was now the main measure of military success.[74] The new chief of the Admiralty, Henning von Holtzendorff, championed bombing civilians because it "produce[s] among the people a feeling of powerlessness and helplessness. The sense of security that England's insular

66. Plessen diary, Jan. 9, 1915, Charleville, in Afflerbach, *Kaiser Wilhelm II. als Oberster Kriegsherr,* 721–22.

67. Pohl diary Jan. 9, 1915, Pohl, *Aufzeichnungen,* 100–101; Pohl memorandum for the meeting of Jan. 9, 1915, Tirpitz, *Politische Dokumente,* 192.

68. Pohl, diary Jan. 9, 1915, Pohl, *Aufzeichnungen,* 100–101.

69. Plessen diary, Jan. 9, 1915, Afflerbach, *Kaiser Wilhelm II. als Oberster Kriegsherr,* 721–22.

70. Wolff diary, Jan. 21, 1915, *Theodor Wolff. Tagebücher 1914–1919; Der Erste Weltkrieg und die Entstehung der Weimarer Republik in Tagebüchern, Leitartikeln und Briefen des Chefredakteurs am "Berliner Tageblatt" und Mitbegründer der "Deutschen Demokratischen Partei,"* ed. Bernd Sösemann (Boppard am Rhein, 1984), 1:150.

71. Bernstorff to AA, no. 101, Jan. 23, 1915, AA/PA R 20890–1.

72. Bethmann to Pohl, no. 201, Berlin, Jan. 21, 1915, AA/PA R 22385.

73. Zimmermann to Treutler, Berlin, April 28, 1915, A.S. 1849, AA/PA R 22386.

74. Jagow to German ambassadors in the Netherlands and Scandinavia, Berlin, Sept. 20, 1915, A.S. no. 5057, AA/PA R 22174.

position has encouraged among the people and which has made them not experience war as terrifying [*Schrecknis*], is gone."[75] The purpose of the zeppelin raids was now openly terror; that is, the Imperial German Navy, over the objections of the AA and chancellor, had embraced strategic bombing. Holtzendorff said he tried to spare the poor and hit the rich, whose influence on government was greater. In the end, Britain's new, secret phosphorous bullets, which caused the vulnerable zeppelins to burn up and which a senior air official described as "not in accordance with the Hague Convention," stopped large-scale aerial attacks, though isolated ones continued intermittently into 1918.[76]

The flamethrower was another new weapon whose legality seemed questionable. This device had been invented and patented by R. Fiedler, director of the Fiedler Flammen-Apparate-Gesellschaft in Berlin. In the last week of August 1914, the Prussian war ministry had contracted for four hundred flamethrowers. Three weeks later, Fiedler informed Reichstag representative and leader of the Catholic Center Party Matthias Erzberger that he could provide much greater destruction.[77] Besides a bigger edition of the flamethrower, he proposed a large incendiary bomb filled with the same, sticky inflammable substance. Fiedler explained why the flamethrower was such a powerful weapon. "The flames have a terrible effect; either they kill hundreds or... they make them completely incapable of fighting.... Moreover, the moral effect is monstrous, quite incomparable with any other close-combat weapon," because the victims "come flooding back as living pillars of fire," producing "a paralyzing horror" on the soldiers behind them.

Fiedler's bomb was even better. Dropped by zeppelin, it could be ignited before impact, creating "a rain of fire on the target, smashing through roofs and igniting everything flammable." A single bomb "could cover an area of several thousand square meters." Fiedler imagined zeppelins dropping his invention over "Antwerp, London, Portsmouth, Paris, Bordeaux." It would bring "the highest amount of dread and horror [*Grauen und Entsetzen*] upon our enemies and must destroy their power of resistance to its innermost core." He promised to have some ready by month's end. Just in case, Fiedler enclosed a self-drawn sketch of a bomb raining down orange flames upon an urban parish with its church in the center.

Erzberger enthusiastically forwarded Fiedler's letter to the chancellor. He thought the apparatuses would be "possible to use to become master over over-mighty England. Doubts that one could derive from alleged international law [*angeblichen Völkerrecht*]

---

75. Holtzendorff report, Berlin, Sept. 25, 1915, A. 19418.IV, AA/PA R 22174. Similar statements: Plessen diary, Sept. 28, 1915, Charleville, "Der moralische Eindruck auf die Bevölkerung sehr stark," Afflerbach, *Kaiser Wilhelm II. als Oberster Kriegsherr,* 832; Pohl diary, Oct. 14, 1915, Wilhelmshaven, "das wird großen Eindruck gemacht haben," Pohl, *Aufzeichnungen,* 140.

76. Hague Convention: Lt. Gen. Sir D. Henderson, War Cabinet #102, Mar. 22, 1917, CAB 23/2; Hopman, *Das ereignisreiche Leben,* 929n472; Garner, *International Law,* 1:452n2; Walter Alexander Raleigh and H. A. Jones, *The War in the Air, Being the Story of the Part Played in the Great War by the Royal Air Force* (Oxford, 1922–37), 3:147 and 5: appendix 1.

77. Fiedler to Erzberger, Berlin, Sept. 14, 1914, AA/PA R 22383.

collapse entirely in view of the foe's conduct of war, and doubts based on humanity can nowadays be decisive only in Berlin salons, not on the field of battle."[78]

Bethmann was less cavalier. He had Grünau draw up a legal opinion and then send it to the war minister for his views. Grünau's memorandum draws interesting distinctions.[79] It began by noting that Germany (like France, Japan, and Russia) had not signed the Hague Declaration XIV (1907) prohibiting dropping explosives from balloons or other conveyances. Nonetheless, there were two other limits to such bombing: the St. Petersburg Declaration that forbade small explosive devices under four hundred grams, and, more to the point, article 23(e) of the Hague rules of land warfare, forbidding belligerents "to employ arms, projectiles, or material calculated to cause unnecessary suffering." Grünau doubted that Fiedler's devices could pass that test. "From the legal point of view and in the interest of our reputation [*Ansehen*] in the world," Grünau said that they should be used only against buildings or warships, where fire-grenades were already allowed.[80] He "decisively" rejected using them against troops. But he named an exception. "Such a use [against troops] could only come into question if we faced such an overwhelming superiority of enemy forces that we could not otherwise avert the destruction of our own forces." Recall that Bethmann had made the same exception regarding submarine warfare. Bethmann, Jagow, Treutler, Bethmann's secretary Kurt Riezler, and Expert Counselor (*vortragender Rat*) Wilhelm von Radowitz all approved Grünau's draft.

Colonel Heinrich Scheüch, who replied on behalf of the war ministry, was made of sterner stuff. Although the army had originally bought Fiedler's flamethrowers for defensive purposes, he now foresaw offensive uses, if the weight of the mobile flamethrowers could be brought down.[81] He rejected Grünau's automatic assumption that the device violated article 23(e). Death by fire might indeed be more painful than other sorts of battlefield deaths, he acknowledged, but was this suffering "unnecessary?" That would be true only if there were another, equally useful weapon causing less suffering. One also had to consider "the horror that such a weapon causes especially to the uncivilized peoples with whom we have to deal in the east and west [referring to colonial troops fighting in Europe]. Forgoing such a useful weapon for reasons of humanity would mean being inhumane to one's own soldiers." Besides, a quick war is most humane. From this standard litany Scheüch then reached his crowning argument: "Such a conduct of war is a military necessity and as such cannot be a violation of international law." He thought it very dangerous to wait until the bitter end to use the weapon, because one might wait too long, and if the weapon were then ineffective, it would indeed be a violation of article 23(e). And, besides, even if one waited, the enemy would still never admit "that a weapon that is in itself a violation of international law would lose that character if it were used only in the moment of greatest danger."

Grünau himself had opened the door to the military necessity argument but had tried to limit it to an extreme situation. Scheüch's response showed how vain limitation was

---

78. Erzberger to Bethmann, Berlin, Sept. 17, 1914, Nr. 1080, AA/PA R 22383.

79. Grünau draft letter to war minister and naval minister, GHQ, Sept. 21, 1914, zu A.H. 1080, AA/PA R 22383.

80. An analogous use to Britain's phosphorous bullets against airships.

81. Scheüch to Bethmann, GHQ, Oct. 18, 1914, no. 1870, "Geheim," AA/PA R 22383.

against the norms prevailing inside military culture.[82] Most of Scheüch's justifications were standard issue (quick war, inhumanity to one's own troops, military necessity). But his legal gyrations are notable for using international law against itself: by capitalizing on the vagueness of "unnecessary" and by using the effectiveness criterion to argue for quicker use of the new weapon. This tactic is akin to the Admiralty staff's recommendation to bolster the weak submarine blockade with mines and aerial bombing, and it often reappears in the arguments of Tirpitz and other naval officers against following cruiser rules in submarine warfare.

Gas

Poison gas was perhaps the most shocking new weapon of the war. Revulsion against poison as inhumane and cowardly was an unbroken tradition in European culture reaching back to antiquity; using poison gas in war was unprecedented.[83] The first Hague Convention (1899) produced a "Declaration (2) concerning Asphyxiating Gases," "derived," as Adam Roberts and Richard Guelff write, "from the general principles of customary international law prohibiting the use of poison and materials causing unnecessary suffering."[84] It said, "The contracting Powers agree to abstain from the use of projectiles the sole object of which is the diffusion of asphyxiating or deleterious gases." Although it was signed or ratified by all the belligerents in the war and was therefore clearly valid, the declaration, by specifying "projectiles" and "sole object," may inadvertently have narrowed a customary prohibition that was much broader. But if that were true, the Hague rules of land warfare (1899) also forbade belligerents "to employ poison or poisoned weapons" (article 23a) or "To employ arms, projectiles, or material calculated to cause unnecessary suffering" (article 23e). The law prohibiting poisonous weapons was comparatively clear, and in any event, in August 1914, no power possessed lethal gas, a way to deliver it, or plans to do so.

The historiography of gas warfare in World War I is too often marred by technological determinism and a consequently dismissive attitude toward international law. Technological determinism has fed on the facts that the militaries of Germany, Britain, and France all engaged in desultory and unsuccessful chemical experiments before the war, and France in August 1914 requisitioned thirty thousand 26-millimeter tear gas shells from the French police, using them without effect in the fall campaign.[85] France's action is then said to have made it "psychologically easier" for the Germans to go ahead; it was "a prelude to chemical warfare," and "it is not unreasonable to think that [gas warfare] would

---

82. For military culture and its precepts see chs. 4, 6, and 7 in Isabel V. Hull, *Absolute Destruction: Military Culture and the Practices of War in Imperial Germany* (Ithaca, NY, 2005).

83. J. M. Spaight, *War Rights on Land* (London, 1911), 101; Olivier Lepick, *La grande guerre chimique 1914–1918* (Paris, 1998), 18–19.

84. Roberts and Guelff, *Documents,* 59. The declaration is on 60–61, and the signers and ratifiers on 65–66.

85. Dieter Martinetz, *Der Gaskrieg 1914/18: Entwicklung, Herstellung und Einsatz chemischer Kampfstoffe: Das Zusammenwirken von militärischer Führung, Wissenschaft und Industrie* (Bonn, 1996), 9.

probably have occurred elsewhere later under the impulse of another protagonist."[86] This is the familiar tit-for-tat explanation with its consequent tendency to equalize all the belligerents. Once everyone is equally at fault, "indignation" at the first use of poison gas looks like hypocrisy, and law becomes a chimera.[87] The account that follows emphasizes the differences among the belligerents, especially regarding the alacrity with which they pursued the development and use of lethal gas, their decision-making processes, and their regard for international law.

Gas is the only aspect of Germany's war conduct that is now almost completely devoid of documentation, a condition that has encouraged the acceptance of ex post facto rationalizations for accounts of why decisions were made. Internal army records, if they still existed, likely would have been destroyed with the Heeresarchiv in the Allied bombing of April 1945.[88] But it is curious that no documents survive in the AA, whose archive was not destroyed in the Second World War, and which otherwise contains important information on army and navy decisions, and especially on those that were controversial inside the government. Johannes Kriege, the AA's chief legal counsel, wrote Germany's postwar legal brief defending itself against Allied charges that Germany had violated the Hague Declaration; but his notes are likewise missing. There are two possible explanations for this complete absence of documentation. Either Kriege culled every scrap from the AA records and then deposited that material elsewhere (for example, in the army archive) or destroyed it, or else there were no records to begin with—that is, the army never consulted the chancellor or the AA on its plans to use poison gas. Arguing from absence is hazardous, but memoirs and secondary literature based on surviving reports do not indicate that a high-level government discussion of poison gas ever took place.[89]

The driving force behind Germany's gas warfare was War Minister and, after mid-September, Chief of the General Staff Erich von Falkenhayn. He acted toward the end of September 1914—that is, immediately after the Schlieffen Plan's failure at the Marne, but before trench warfare had solidified. By the beginning of October his subordinate, Major Max Bauer, had contacted chemists, chief among them Fritz Haber; and by October 24, 1914, shells containing a type of tear gas had already been tried out at Neuve-Chapelle—to no effect.[90] It is unknown if Falkenhayn knew of the French tear gas shells; in any case Germany did not protest their use.

Besides the enormous rush, the German effort stands out for its quick leap to lethality. By October 23, 1914, Falkenhayn had contacted the leaders of Germany's chemical

---

86. Ulrich Trumpener, "The Road to Ypres: The Beginning of Gas Warfare in World War I," *Journal of Modern History* 47, no. 3 (1975): 463; Lepick, *La grande guerre chimique*, 58, 65; Ludwig Fritz Haber, *The Poisonous Cloud: Chemical Warfare in the First World War* (Oxford, 1986), 280.

87. Lepick, *La grande guerre chimique*, 3–4; Haber, *Poisonous Cloud*, 316–17; Trumpener, "Road to Ypres," 461.

88. Lepick, *La grande guerre chimique*, 9.

89. Max Bauer's semiofficial account mentions no internal discussion of the legality of gas warfare: "Denkschrift betr. den Gaskampf und Gasschutz" (1919), BA-Koblenz, Nachlaß Bauer, Nr. 35.

90. Rolf-Dieter Müller, "Total War as the Result of New Weapons? The Use of Chemical Agents in World War I," in Chickering and Förster, *Great War, Total War*, 96–97.

industry in search of a gas that would result in the "complete poisoning of the enemy."[91] In the face of disappointing results, he kept up the pressure, in mid December 1914 demanding a gas that produced "lethal poisoning."[92] Neither France nor Britain was conducting research along these lines at this time. Haber homed in on chlorine as the agent, while Carl Duisburg focused on phosgene in January 1915.[93] While the Kaiser in early November approved using smoke bombs dropped from aircraft, there is no record that Falkenhayn consulted him on poison gas.[94] It appears that artillery-range testing for both tear gas and lethal gas occurred in early January 1915, and Falkenhayn had decided by mid-January that both should actually be used at the front.[95] Improved tear gas shells were tried out against the Russians on January 31, 1915.[96] Several weeks later, at the end of February 1915, special troops began installing canisters of lethal chlorine gas in the Ypres section of the western front.[97] They were finished by March 10; only bad weather (westerly winds that would have blown the gas back at the Germans) postponed the first use of lethal gas until April 23, 1915.

This timeline strongly suggests that Falkenhayn decided to use lethal gas for internal reasons, not in reaction to France. In late fall 1914 France developed a second form of tear gas and fitted it to hand grenades that Marshal Joffre approved for use on January 7, 1915. Instructions for their use were printed on February 21, and the grenades may actually have been used on March 3 in the Argonne.[98] These instructions quickly fell into German hands, and both they and the Argonne attack were subsequently used as proof that Germany's own use was covered by reprisal.[99] But, obviously, Falkenhayn's decision was made weeks before either event. Moreover, the French used tear gas, not lethal gas, as contemporary German soldiers' accounts attested.[100]

What role did international law play in the German decision? Germany's ex post facto justifications all adduced reprisal, not even military necessity, which indicates the widespread conviction that poison gas was illegal. There was indeed significant opposition to the weapon in the officer corps. Falkenhayn began informing the first military commanders of the impending use of chlorine gas in mid-January. Their reactions reflected traditional conceptions of honorable fighting and customary warfare—they found gas "disgusting," or

91. Emil Fischer to Carl Duisberg, Dec. 20, 1914, in Martinetz, *Gaskrieg,* 18–19.

92. Ibid.

93. Smoke bombs: Timo Baumann, "Giftgas und Salpeter: Chemische Industrie, Naturwissenschaft und Militär von 1906 bis zum ersten Munitionsprogramm 1914/1915" (PhD diss., Universität Köln, 2008), 239.

94. Ibid.

95. Trumpener, "Road to Ypres," 465, 467–68.

96. German troops used tear gas again in March 1915 in the West, Martinetz, *Gaskrieg,* 17; Lepick, *La grande guerre chimique,* 63–64. If Germany used tear gas in retaliation or reprisal, then its first use ought to have been against France, not Russia: cf. the inconclusive arguments in Baumann, "Giftgas," 335.

97. Trumpener, "Road to Ypres," 471.

98. Martinetz, *Gaskrieg,* 9; Lepick, *La grande guerre chimique,* 56.

99. Crown Prince Rupprecht of Bavaria, diary, March 1, 1915, Rupprecht Kronprinz von Bayern, *Mein Kriegstagebuch,* ed. Eugen von Frauenholz (Munich, 1929), 1:304–5; Kriege, Memorandum, *UA* 3. Reihe, 4:41.

100. Lepick, *La grande guerre chimique,* 56.

"entirely awful."[101] Some of them must have expressed their revulsion in legal terms, for one scholar reports that "their doubts were relieved by Haber and diverse international lawyers," and some were lied to and told that chlorine gas was not lethal.[102] It is unclear who these lawyers were or to which institution they were attached. Bauer reported (1915) that OHL's legal position at the time was not based on reprisal, but on three other arguments. First, (lethal) gas was not a "poison" in the sense of article 23a of the Hague Rules, because gas fell instead under Hague Declaration (2) concerning Asphyxiating Gases (1899). That made it possible to take advantage of the declaration's narrow language and argue, second, that canisters were not "projectiles," and in any case, since Germany used shrapnel shells to deliver its tear gas (and later its lethal gases), its "sole" purpose was not poisoning. For good measure, OHL added that the suffering of victims was not "unnecessary" because the weapon was useful, a contention we have encountered before.[103] The disingenuousness of these arguments should be clear. One might add that the canisters were used not in order to "comply" with the law, but because they were plentiful, shells were in short supply, and containers worked better at the close distances characterizing the Ypres front.[104]

Obviously, international law was barely a hindrance to Falkenhayn's decision. Fear of retaliation was a much stronger deterrent.[105] Haber and other chemists assured Falkenhayn that Germany's industrial-chemical supremacy guaranteed that the Allies would be unable to strike back. It was in that sanction-free atmosphere that Falkenhayn went ahead.

What did Falkenhayn expect of the new weapon? General Fritz von Loßberg recalled that at Verdun in June 1916, Falkenhayn pinned his last hopes for success on gas, and Bauer in late 1916 considered it "the only means for defeating England."[106] Thus at some point in the war, poison gas enjoyed the status of a wonder weapon, like unrestricted submarine warfare.[107] But Ulrich Trumpener's careful dissection of its early use suggests that in the beginning Falkenhayn and his commanders used gas merely for tactical reasons, to achieve minor advances, at most to take Ypres.[108] If this is true, its introduction is even stronger testimony to the small regard the army command held for international law, for

---

101. Einem to his wife, Feb. 1, 1917, Adolf Wild von Hohenborn, *Briefe und Tagebuchaufzeichnungen des preußischen Generals als Kriegsminister und Truppenführer im Ersten Weltkrieg,* ed. Helmut Reichold and Gerhard Granier (Boppard a.R., 1986), 167n22; Thaer, letter of April 28, 1915, Albrecht von Thaer, *Generalstabsdienst an der Front und in der O.H.L.,* Abhandlungen der Akademie der Wissenschaften in Göttingen, philologisch-historische Klasse, Dritte Folge, Nr. 40, ed. Siegfried Kaehler (Göttingen, 1958), 33; Plessen diary, April 23, 1915, Afflerbach, *Kaiser Wilhelm II. als Oberster Kriegsherr,* 764.

102. Martinetz, *Gaskrieg,* 20–21, no source given.

103. Bauer, "Denkschrift betreffend den Gaskamp und Gasschutz," cited in Trumpener, "Road to Ypres," 468.

104. L. F. Haber suggests that canisters were partly chosen for the legal argument (see *Poisonous Cloud,* 28) but elsewhere says the reason was lack of howitzer shells (25, 280); Trumpener, "Road to Ypres," 467.

105. Müller, "Total War," 97; Holger Afflerbach, *Falkenhayn: politisches Denken und Handeln im Kaiserreich,* Beiträge zur Militärgeschichte, vol. 42 (Munich, 1994), 261; Trumpener, "Road to Ypres," 470.

106. Fritz von Loßberg, *Meine Tätigkeit im Weltkriege 1914–1918* (Berlin, 1939), 213; Hopman, *Das ereignisreiche Leben,* 925.

107. Lepick, *La grande guerre chimique,* 233, 245; Müller, "Total War," 101; Haber, *Poisonous Cloud,* 259–84. On its successful tactical uses: Joseph Palazzo, *Seeking Victory on the Western Front: The British Army and Chemical Warfare in World War I* (Lincoln, NE, 2000).

108. Trumpener, "Road to Ypres," 474–75.

it is quite clear that most officers knew that poison gas was a major taboo breaker. General Wild von Hohenborn referred to his own use of phosgene later in the war as "my internationally illegal grenades—but what are the Hague agreements now?" he asked; "scraps of paper blowing in the wind!"[109]

On April 23, 1915, German troops at Ypres, finally enjoying an easterly wind, opened canisters filled with chlorine gas, which drifted over to the Allied lines and caused many stunned soldiers there to flee their trenches. German troops advanced four kilometers, but they did not take Ypres, and they did not achieve breakthrough, if that had indeed been the goal.[110] Germany used gas five more times in the next month, but neither then nor later did poison gas amount to more than an occasionally useful tactical device.[111] Most historians conclude that gas was a failure—it did not end the stalemate, it did not shorten the war. But it did completely shock the Allies and neutrals.[112]

French president Raymond Poincaré called it "organized crime"; British commander in chief Sir John French, "a mean and dastardly practice, hitherto unheard of in civilized warfare"; Chief of Staff Lieutenant Colonel Maxime Weygand, "an inhumane form of warfare"; and Sir Henry Rawlinson feared that his soldiers would henceforth refuse to take Germans prisoner.[113] These expressions were immediate, unanimous, and expressed in private documents; they were not propaganda.[114] But even stronger proof that Allied military leaders found the use of poison gas simply incredible is their utter inability to read the many warning signs they received in the weeks during which the Germans waited for the winds to shift. Ten days before the attack, a German deserter revealed the plan; both French and British troops found dead German soldiers equipped with gas masks; and a week beforehand the Belgian army informed the French high command of the German gas masks.[115] When Captain Maurice Hankey, secretary of Britain's War Council, asked British general headquarters if this information meant that Germany was planning a chemical attack, he was told that "the Germans were notoriously preparing something of this kind, but it was believed to be intended for use in trenches captured by us, and not for offensive purposes."[116] That is, the British expected them to use tear gas, not poison gas. If the Allies themselves had been planning to use poison gas, they would likely have

---

109. Wild note, June 22 1916, Charleville, Wild von Hohenborn, *Briefe,* 167.

110. Plessen diary, April 23, 1915, Charleville, in Afflerbach, *Kaiser Wilhelm II. als Oberster Kriegsherr,* 764.

111. Lepick, *La grande guerre chimique,* 65n2.

112. Ibid., 297–98.

113. Ibid., 86, 107; Palazzo, *Seeking Victory,* 43.

114. Marion Girard, *A Strange and Formidable Weapon: British Responses to World War I Poison Gas,* Studies in War, Society, and the Military (Lincoln, NE, 2008), 81.

115. Robert A. Doughty, *Pyrrhic Victory: French Strategy and Operations in the Great War* (Cambridge, MA, 2005), 149; Lepick, *La grande guerre chimique,* 76; Service historique de l'armée de terre France, *Les armées françaises dans la Grande Guerre* (Paris, 1922–37), 2:699.

116. Hankey to Asquith, Apr. 25, 1915, "secret," CAB 21/83, cited in Lepick, *La grande guerre chimique,* 76. Also, on previous judgment of the "remote contingency" of a German gas attack: Hankey to Lt. Col. E. D. Swinton, May 5, 1915, CAB 21/83.

interpreted correctly the substantial intelligence they possessed. As it was, they were simply unable to imagine what Germany was about to do.[117]

We might return to the Allies and tear gas for a moment. At the beginning of the war, Britain and France disagreed about its legality under the Hague Conventions. French army policy, apparently developed without consulting French civilian leaders, distinguished irritants from poisons, which they defined by their lethality. After the German gas attack at Ypres, civilian leaders asked about the army's response and were informed that "since the beginning of the war, the French army has used devices that hinder breathing but do not asphyxiate [*engins suffocants, mais non asphyxiants*], made of chloracetone and bromoacetate ethyl. These products, particularly the last, are very effective but harmless: they conform completely to the stipulation of the Hague and Geneva Conventions."[118] After the war, Kriege claimed that France's use of bromoacetate ethyl contravened international law because, unlike the German shells used in October 1914 and January 1915, French shells did not also produce shrapnel and therefore constituted "sole" use of gas.[119] Beneath Kriege's technical argument was the assumption that all gas, even tear gas, violated the law. The French army's view seems to have been that tear gas of the kind one would use on one's own population was permissible in war against others, but it drew the line at obvious poisons: on August 30, 1914, for example, the French war ministry rejected a chemist's suggestion to use sulfur dioxide and chlorine.[120]

The British War Ministry and Admiralty were of different mind. Although the Foreign Office judged that gas not causing permanent damage was lawful, in October 1914 the Admiralty and the War Office nonetheless rejected using tear gas in shells on the grounds that they were "if not actually contrary to the letter of The Hague Conventions are opposed to its spirit."[121] Although First Lord of the Admiralty Winston Churchill encouraged continued chemical experimentation, neither his idiosyncratic actions nor the naval interest in developing smoke screens in spring 1915 indicate that the British government had abandoned its early view, which is also notable for its rejection of technical legalism.[122] Robert Cecil's remark to Parliament summed up the government's astonishment: "The most terrible [violation of international law] is the barbarous use of poisonous gases. I am quite certain no one would have thought that credible or possible six months ago."[123]

---

117. Thus, their response is not a "singular enigma," but evidence of their own limited intentions: Lepick, *La grande guerre chimique,* 77.

118. Ministry of war, "Note au sujet des mesures prises à la suite de l'emploi des produits asphyxiants par l'armée ennemie," Paris, April 28, 1915, SHAT 6N 21 Fond Buat Carton 20, also cited in Lepick, *La grande guerre chimique,* 57; emphasis in original.

119. Kriege report to Parliament, in *UA,* 3rd ser., 4:41.

120. Martinetz, *Gaskrieg,* 19.

121. Hankey to Asquith, Apr. 25, 1915, "secret," CAB 21/83; War Office, "Section I: Offensive Chemical Warfare Prior to the Formation of the Scientific Advisory Committee on 23rd June 1915," typed ms., WO 142/240. Cf. Lepick, *La grande guerre chimique,* 60; Haber, *Poisonous Cloud,* 22.

122. Lepick, following Haber (almost verbatim), seems to think otherwise: Haber, *Poisonous Cloud,* 23; Lepick, *La grande guerre chimique,* 60.

123. Parliamentary Debates, Commons, vol. 71 (April 14–May 19, 1915), col. 1205, cited in Girard, *Strange and Formidable Weapon,* 33.

In its response to the Ypres gas attack, France remained closer to Germany than to Britain. The army instantly moved to launch reprisals in kind. Three days after Ypres, the war ministry contacted French industrialists to ensure that France possessed enough chemicals "to be used in reprisals against the enemy," and it purchased many kilometers of iron pipe "in anticipation of the widespread use of asphyxiants at the front analogous to those of the Germans."[124] There seems to have been no high-level discussion of reprisals in kind or their legality; the civilian leadership approved the army's default response without demur.[125] As we shall see, the use of exactly reciprocal reprisal was a long-standing French policy that seems to have predetermined how it responded to gas warfare.

The reaction at the British front was just like that of the French war ministry. Sir John French called for immediate retaliation in kind, but the war minister, General Hubert H. Kitchener, pulled him back. "The use of asphyxiating gases," he wrote to French, "is as you are aware contrary to the rules and usages of war....Before therefore we fall to the level of the degraded Germans I must submit the matter to the Government."[126] Kitchener therefore categorized the problem as a legal one, making it a matter of higher government policy. He also shared the widespread distaste inside the government of using methods that contradicted Britain's self-understanding as law-abiding and civilized. The cabinet nevertheless approved reprisal on May 4. Throughout the war, Britain experimented with and developed gases of increasing lethality, but its policy was never to use them first, but only in reprisal. For example, the Scientific Advisory Committee recommended jellite shells (containing cyanide) in May 1916, and the Ministry of Munitions prepared to manufacture them, but only after Germany had used highly lethal phosgene gas in June at Verdun did the government approve their use.[127] The tendency in Britain was to try to restrict reprisal by keeping the final decision in the cabinet's hands; and that larger reprisal policy also determined how Britain handled gas warfare.

New weapons confronted decision makers with central legal questions. None of the three belligerents, Britain, France, or Germany, had an institutional mechanism to vet new weapons against law.[128] Inventions usually came to the attention of military authorities from inventors or go-betweens. The decision to test or develop them rested with the military and was made on practical grounds: Did they work? Did one have the raw materials and industrial infrastructure to produce them economically? Therefore, it was only late in the game that higher-level oversight came into play. The German government faced relatively more such decisions than did its foes, though it is hard to say whether Germany's strengths in chemistry and engineering or greater openness to invention was the cause. Occasionally, the Prussian war ministry would ask the chancellor about the legality of new weapons, as it did in February 1914 concerning a scheme to blast enemy telephone lines

---

124. Ministry of war, "Note au sujet," Paris, April 28, 1915, SHAT 6N 21 Fond Buat Carton 20.

125. Lepick, *La grande guerre chimique*, 106–7.

126. Kitchener to French, April 24, 1915, WO 142/240, cited in Girard, *Strange and Formidable Weapon*, 34. Also the discussion in Lepick, *La grande guerre chimique*, 94–96.

127. Girard, *Strange and Formidable Weapon*, 38–40.

128. For Germany see: BAB R 901 81901 through 81906 on military inventions, April 1914 to Oct. 1926. For France: 10 N (Ministry of Armaments) 81 and 82: Proposition d'inventions, 1915–18.

with bursts of electricity.[129] But during the war, once a new weapon existed, the pattern of decision making seems clear. Civilian leadership, which was chiefly in charge of applying legal considerations, faced especially strong undertow from military institutions: from the junior, and then quickly from the senior naval officer corps regarding submarines; from the war ministry, which had already bought flamethrowers without advance discussion; and from OHL, which had already bombed civilian targets from the air. Within the German constitutional system, those military institutions were privileged, because military matters, especially those dealing with weaponry, were the province of military experts. As the chancellor admitted in February 1915, "[Whether submarine blockade can actually be done] is a purely technical question, I don't understand any of it. But the technical experts say it can be done."[130]

The chancellor set the legal tone for the AA, which was not a genuinely independent institution—that is, the foreign secretary was merely the mouthpiece of the chancellor, who set foreign policy. That subordinate position was reflected in the foreign secretary's lesser rank compared to equivalent secretaries of other departments.[131] Bethmann's tilt toward submarine warfare in October 1914 therefore strongly influenced the legal advice the AA outlined for him. It is also clear that Bethmann was significantly less concerned about law than was Edward Grey; throughout his tenure, Bethmann attached greater importance to the opinion of important neutral states, and that was the avenue by which international law usually entered his consideration. But it is surely true that Bethmann must have been discouraged by the military intransigence he faced, for even when he deployed the strongest panoply of legal arguments, as against the aerial bombing of London, he lost.

The legal arguments that surfaced in the course of the deliberations of autumn 1914 are also revealing. Submarine warfare and poison gas were covered as reprisal, an implicit acknowledgment of their illegality; in neither case was reprisal genuine, in the sense that its object was not to force the foe to return to legal behavior. Reprisal covered methods of warfare desirable for military reasons, as was probably the case with the British March 1915 order-in-council. The difference is the alacrity with which German leaders adverted to reprisal. Where no cover for reprisal could be found, as with the flamethrower, military necessity filled the bill, circumscribed by more limitations when advised by the AA, and none at all according to the war ministry. Aerial warfare was justified by analogy to artillery or naval bombardment, that is, as a mere extension of normal military practice. The elasticity of that argument is well illustrated by two examples rationalizing poison gas. In May 1915 the Ninth Army official war diary regretted the loss of "chivalry" in warfare, but insisted that "actually [poison gas] is just the logical development of the usual practice of all armies."[132] After the war, the war ministry defended poison gas by claiming that "by

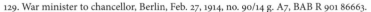

129. War minister to chancellor, Berlin, Feb. 27, 1914, no. 90/14 g. A7, BAB R 901 86663.

130. Theodor Wolff diary, Feb. 9, 1915, Wolff, *Tagebücher,* 1:163.

131. Lamar Cecil, *The German Diplomatic Service, 1871–1914* (Princeton, NJ, 1976), 154–57.

132. Ninth Army command official diary, May 14, 1915, cited in Martinetz, *Gaskrieg,* 22.

reviving at Ypres the historical method of smoking out in the modern form of chlorine gas, we neither used a more harmful substance, nor did we create a new method of warfare."[133]

Finally, the legal advisers in the AA recognized the existence of general principles behind treaty law, but their language seldom identified Germany with those principles. Instead, they are put in the mouths of neutrals arguing against possible German war policies. Such larger principles appeared to AA writers as revocable in cases where the enemy himself violated law (the law-free zone), or where he threatened "destruction of our own forces"—Grünau's phrase does not make clear whether he was thinking of loss of the war, or merely a smaller military defeat. The legal discussions of autumn 1914 inside Imperial Germany reveal no identification with international law and no sense that law might be, intrinsically, a good worth upholding or in Germany's interest to strengthen. On the contrary, it mostly appears either as an impediment to necessary action, or at most as a tool one might instrumentalize. Nevertheless, Imperial Germany had certainly not left the field of law altogether; it debated law seriously at the beginning of the war, and it remained in the purview of law so long as neutrals remained important to it, for whatever reasons.

133. Prussia, Kriegsministerium, and Oberste Heeresleitung, *Die deutsche Kriegführung und das Völkerrecht; Beiträge zur Schuldfrage* (Berlin, 1919), 23.

Unrestricted Submarine Warfare

The Decision to Launch Unrestricted Submarine Warfare, February 1915

In contrast to the careful deliberations of the fall, the actual launching of submarine warfare occurred in a rather ad hoc fashion. Three separate initiatives, none of which qualified as national policy, shaped the strong drift within the navy toward using the new weapon against commerce. First, in October and November 1914, two submarines commanders on their own initiative sank three enemy merchant vessels, saving the crews each time.[1] Then, in January 1915, Lieutenant Commander Bauer ordered the U-boats under his command to enter the Irish Sea "and by sinking one or more vessels introduce insecurity into shipping and harm trade."[2] Four enemy merchantmen were sunk under this order, all attacks following cruiser rules. Finally, on January 15, acting on his own, the chief of the high seas fleet ordered one U-boat to haunt the French Channel coast and to sink merchant vessels without warning. Three ships fell to this order.[3] The navy was thus drifting into submarine warfare without the imprimatur of higher orders. The potential political risks were already obvious: the October 1914 sinking of the *Amiral Ganteaume*, filled with Belgian refugees whom the submarine commander mistook for enemy troops; and the February 1, 1915, attack on the hospital ship

---

1. Arno Spindler, ed., *Der Handelskrieg mit U-Booten*, Der Krieg Zur See 1914–1918 (Berlin, 1932–34), 1:31. The commandants followed Germany's prize rules: Joachim Schröder, *Die U-Boote des Kaisers; Die Geschichte des deutschen U-Boot-Krieges gegen Großbritannien im Ersten Weltkrieg* (Bonn, 2003), 91.

2. Spindler, *Handelskrieg*, 1:60.

3. Ibid., 1:64.

Asturias, saved because the torpedo was defective.[4] Both incidents foreshadowed the crises one could expect submarine warfare to produce.

Pressure from the navy and public opinion to open an unlimited submarine campaign was building up throughout January 1915. On February 1, literally the day before Admiral Hugo Pohl left the Admiralty to become chief of the high seas fleet, he met with Chancellor Theobald von Bethmann Hollweg, State Undersecretary of the Foreign Office Arthur Zimmermann, Chief of Staff Erich von Falkenhayn, and Secretary of the Interior Klemens von Delbrück, and presented the navy's case again; Bethmann thought the matter over that evening and, the following day, approved submarine warfare. Two days later, Pohl got the Kaiser's imprimatur during a short boat trip in which he happened to find himself alone with Wilhelm and Admiral Alfred von Tirpitz. He might have faced more resistance if Chief of the Naval Cabinet Georg Alexander von Müller, an opponent of submarine warfare, had been present. But Bethmann was counting on the Kaiser's approval, one way or the other.[5] There were no minutes to either of these meetings, and scholars have since puzzled over what the principals thought they were doing. From our perspective the most important question concerns the sinking of neutral vessels without warning: Was this naval policy, and did Bethmann and the AA understand it correctly?

Many years later, Zimmermann recalled that the navy had assured Bethmann that neutral ships would not be sunk.[6] The official naval historian found Zimmermann's recollection impossible to believe, because Pohl knew perfectly well that submarines could not necessarily distinguish neutral from enemy ships, so neutrals were bound to be sunk. Instead, he surmises that Pohl must have argued what the navy as a whole hoped, namely, that if the campaign sank many enemy vessels right from the first day and neutrals received a two-week warning, they would simply stay away and thus avoid danger.[7] In other words, Germany could have its extreme policy without political risk. More recently, Joachim Schröder has argued that Pohl simply lied to the civilians and the Kaiser.[8] This is possible; everyone agrees that Pohl was unpleasantly careerist, not especially careful of the truth, and hell-bent to launch the popular panacea on his watch.[9] But there are reasons to be cautious about accepting an interpretation that saddles Pohl with sole responsibility.

We have seen that the chancellor and his AA advisers had been aware for months that submarine warfare would inevitably kill neutrals (aboard enemy ships) and sink neutral ships. They had agreed that this fact would be glossed over: "Naturally it would not be admitted that neutral ships, people, or goods would be intentionally targeted by German

---

4. Ibid., 1:64, 65n1.

5. Jagow note to Kriege, Feb. 3, 1915, on Behncke to Bethmann, A. 2264, Berlin, Feb. 2, 1915, BAB R 901 85910.

6. Spindler, *Handelskrieg,* 1:79. Foreign Secretary Gottlieb v. Jagow recorded the same memory: "Politische Aufsätze," AA/PA Jagow Papers, vol. 8, pt. 1, p. 134.

7. Spindler, *Handelskrieg,* 1:79, 83.

8. Schröder, *U-Boote des Kaisers,* 103.

9. Cf. Adm. v. Müller's diary, Apr. 20, 1915, in Georg Alexander von Müller, *Regierte der Kaiser? Kriegstagebücher, Aufzeichnungen und Briefe des Chefs des Marine-Kabinetts, 1914–1918,* ed. Walter Görlitz (Göttingen, 1959), 92.

warships."[10] Reprisal was going to be based partly on the charge that neutral acquiescence to the British blockade constituted un-neutral acts and therefore opened those states and their nationals to legitimate reprisal; that claim would hardly have been necessary if they were not to be targeted, too. The chancellor and AA were both at ease with the legal foundations they had laid for future submarine policy; their hesitations were "not of a legal nature."[11] Their legal consciences might also have been somewhat assuaged by the petition that many of the most prominent Berlin professors sent to the chancellor on January 26, urging him to unleash the submarine; among them was the distinguished international lawyer and expert on maritime law Heinrich Triepel.[12] But it is doubtful how necessary such reassurance might have been, given how far the chancellor and the AA had already moved. Tirpitz quoted Bethmann's own words from a conversation between the two men on January 27, 1915: "He [Bethmann] would not care about international-legal qualms concerning submarine blockade, if he could only be assured that it would be effective, and that was essentially a naval-technical question."[13] It was surely the naval-technical side that Pohl guaranteed (incorrectly) at the February 1 meeting. Bethmann's chief misgivings had always been political, and these will also have been diminished by the large military victories that Germany had won in the east in December 1914.

Without waiting for the Kaiser's approval, which all the participants appeared to take for granted, Rear Admiral Paul Behncke at the Admiralty drafted a brief announcement of the new policy that was barely emended at the AA.[14] To it was appended a longer explanatory memorandum that the AA and Admiralty had jointly worked out already in November 1914 to be presented to the world.[15] Neither document mentioned that submarines and mines would be the weapons that Germany would use to enforce its "war zone." The short Admiralty announcement said that in "the waters surrounding Great Britain and Ireland including the whole English Channel" "all enemy merchant vessels" after February 18 "will be destroyed although it may not always be possible to save crews and passengers." Neutral vessels were exposed to "danger" because "the British Government" had "ordered" its merchantmen to fly neutral flags in order to escape attack.[16]

The memorandum was almost identical with the November draft, save for the addition of Britain's "misuse of neutral flags" as another source of peril for neutral ships. Otherwise, its legal argumentation remained the same. It accused Britain of breaking the DoL by extending the contraband list, erasing the distinction between absolute and conditional contraband ("continuous voyage"), violating the Declaration of Paris by removing

---

10. Zimmermann to Bethmann, Berlin, Nov. 30, 1914, IIIa 20172, BAB R 901 85910.

11. "Standpunkt des Auswärtigen Amtes in der Frage der U-Boots-Blockade," signed Bethmann and Jagow, sent to Pohl on Dec. 27, 1914, zu A.H. 2779, AA/PA R. 22385, also published in Alfred von Tirpitz, *Politische Dokumente: Deutsche Ohnmachtspolitik im Weltkriege* (Hamburg, 1926), 292–95.

12. Schröder, *U-Boote des Kaisers*, 97.

13. Tirpitz note, Jan. 27, 1915, Tirpitz, *Politische Dokumente*, 301.

14. "Bekanntmachung," zu A 2264, Berlin, Feb. 2, 1915, BAB R 901 85910; Spindler, *Handelskrieg*, 1:86.

15. Anlage to Zimmermann to Bethmann, Berlin, IIIa 20172, Nov. 30, 1914, BAB R 901 85910.

16. Gerard to Bryan, Berlin, Feb. 4, 1915, *FRUS* 1915, Suppl., 94; German version printed in Spindler, *Handelskrieg*, 1:87.

German goods on neutral ships, seizing draft-age German males from neutral ships, declaring a war zone in the North Sea, which amounted to a blockade of neutral ports—all these things with the aim of starving the German nation. It accused neutral states of acquiescing in these measures and adding to them by their own embargoes. If the neutrals had accepted Britain's "vital interests" (*Lebensinteressen*), then they must do the same for Germany. It warned neutrals against entrusting themselves or their goods to British merchant ships and warned neutral ships "urgently" against entering the war zone. Although it used reprisal as legal justification, it did not say that Germany would rescind these measures if Britain returned to the DoL.[17]

The orders given to submarine commanders reflected the navy's original intention to sink all ships found in the declared war zone. The first order, of February 4, 1915, did not distinguish enemy from neutral merchant vessels; indeed it gave no instructions on how to treat neutral ships.[18] Before these orders could be acted upon, however, Germany was inundated by a quick and strongly negative response from neutral newspapers and diplomats. Germany's first reaction to the neutral response, however, was to toughen the measure. When the Dutch foreign minister remarked that he assumed Germany would indemnify neutral losses, Foreign Secretary Gottlieb von Jagow minuted that "if we did that, we would ruin the effect of the U-boat blockade, whose goal is to scare neutral shipping from Britain's coast."[19] Johannes Kriege, chief of the AA's legal section, agreed and repeated to his subordinate Walter Simons that promising indemnities would "significantly reduce the deterrent effect."[20] Consequently, Admiral Gustav Bachmann, Pohl's successor as Admiralty chief, drafted a second announcement, which the AA accepted, designed to be clearer and more frightening.

It justified destruction without warning by claiming that "visit and search are put out of the question" because Britain was arming its merchant fleet and urging ships to resist Germany's methods by ramming submarines. "English merchant vessels in the designated waters are therefore no longer to be regarded as undefended, and so may be attacked by the Germans without previous warning or visit." That is, armed merchant ships and unarmed resisting vessels were tantamount to warships and could be sunk accordingly. The inability of the submarine to defend itself during visit and search dictated that "there can be no further assurance for the safety of neutral shipping in the English naval war zone." Germany admitted that "it is intended to make the most extensive use of mines in all parts of the war area," which increased the danger for neutrals. Germany thus now admitted a

---

17. Enclosure to Bernstorff to Bryan, Washington, Feb. 7, 1915, *FRUS* 1915, Suppl., 96–97; German version in Spindler, *Handelskrieg,* 1:87–89.

18. Spindler, *Handelskrieg,* 1:95. Recall the similar temptation to scare away neutral shipping using mines, a method contemplated and initially in August 1914 rejected by the British cabinet as "barbarous," but later admitted in principle. Admiral John Fisher pressed for such a policy again after rejoining the Admiralty and in January 1915 admitted that neutral vessels would be sunk, which he planned to blame on the Germans: see Nicholas A. Lambert, *Planning Armageddon: British Economic Warfare and the First World War* (Cambridge, MA, 2012), 222, 311–17.

19. Jagow note, n.d., to Müller to AA, den Haag, Nr. 67, Feb. 6, 1915, IIIa 2818, BAB R 901 85910.

20. Kriege to Simons, IIIa 2818/2855, Berlin, Feb. 15, 1915, BAB R 901 85910.

policy that Britain had alleged since August 1914—that it "strewed the high seas" with unanchored, unreported, automatic contact mines in breach of the Hague Convention VIII. The declaration repeated the claim of "misuse of neutral flags" and the conclusion that "the new German method of naval warfare is...justified by the murderous character" of Britain's hunger blockade. But it added something new: Germany's measures would be rescinded if Britain returned voluntarily to the Declaration of Paris and the DoL, "or...she is compelled to do so by the neutral powers."[21]

The second announcement thus made it clearer that neutrals would surely be sunk, if not by submarines then by mines. The covering précis addressed to Germany's representatives in the neutral states said: "We must count on the fact that neutral ships in the English war zone will mostly not be recognized as such by our U-boats and will therefore be immediately destroyed."[22] Therefore, the announcement beefed up the legal grounds for this *novum* by arguing that armed merchantmen, resistance, and the flag ruse made it impossible for submarines to fulfill the requirements of visit and search. By adding a sunset clause, Germany came closer to clothing submarine warfare as genuine reprisal.

On February 12, 1915, Admiral Bachmann issued new orders to U-boat commanders that specified sinking enemy merchant and passenger ships ("their loss will make the biggest impression of all"), but not neutral merchant ships. Nevertheless, the strong bias toward sinking all ships is evident in the caveats Bachmann added. "The security of the U-boat is primary." "Misidentifications will be inevitable, if neutrals want to sail in the war zone despite every warning. A [submarine] commandant who makes such a mistake [i.e., who sinks a neutral ship] will be covered." As Tirpitz summarized the order, "In case of doubt, the decision is to be made in favor of attack."[23] However, when Pohl learned that neutrals were to be spared, he lamented that it ruined any chance of success.[24]

The navy's bloody-mindedness should not be interpreted as a desire to sink all neutral ships for their own sake. Both the navy and the AA doubtless preferred to cut off Britain without destroying neutral vessels. Their aim was to deter neutrals from entering the war zone in the first place, a goal to be accomplished with warnings if possible, but with a few exemplary sinkings if necessary.[25] It was essentially the same tactic as shelling a seaside resort, or dropping occasional bombs on cities, or affecting the psychology of soldiers by the threat of poison gas or death by fire—it was designed to offset one's own strategic weakness (in this case, the inability to uphold a genuine blockade) by demonstrative, or eerie destruction that worked on the enemy's (or his neutral abettors') morale and psychological steadfastness. Exemplary destruction for these purposes is, of course, terror. It is the weapon of the weaker in a struggle. And law, including international law, is tilted against it, precisely because of its irregularity and its lack of conventional effectiveness.

---

21. Bernstorff to Bryan, Washington, Feb. 15, 1915, *FRUS* 1915, Suppl., 104–5; German version in Spindler, *Handelskrieg*, 1:103–04.

22. AA to German embassies in neutral countries, Berlin, IIIa 3111, Feb. 12, 1915, précis written by Simons, passed by Kriege and Jagow, BAB R 901 85910.

23. Bachmann order and Tirpitz's summary: Tirpitz, *Politische Dokumente*, 308.

24. Ibid., 311.

25. See Pohl's statement of Feb. 10, 1915, ibid., 310.

The neutrals, with the exception of pro-German Sweden, responded negatively to Germany's campaign even before it started.[26] All of them rejected the charge of complicity in Britain's blockade; three tried to demonstrate their innocence by noting their opposition to Britain's use of the flag ruse. Denmark and Italy, like the United States since the beginning of the war, explicitly refrained from making any judgments about the legality of methods that the belligerents used against each other. They seem to have considered diplomatic agnosticism the price of neutrality. However, they did not shrink from making fundamental statements about international law. Germany's closest neighbors explicitly rejected its main legal justification. Holland said that it had always rejected the proposition that "vital interests of belligerents excused every kind of conduct in war." Denmark repeated its repudiation of "the justification for violations of international law grounded in the necessities of war." Italy made three points: the law permitting the destruction of neutral merchant ships under exceptional circumstances was controversial; it could not be effected by a mere warning; nor could reprisals be directed against neutrals. The United States, as always, was much more specific. It noted that, since Germany was not claiming to blockade, its sole belligerent rights at sea consisted of visit and search, and before destruction, Germany must determine the ship's nationality and whether it contained contraband. Sinking without warning was "an act so unprecedented in naval warfare that this Government is reluctant to believe that the Imperial Government ... contemplates it as possible." That sentiment echoed former Italian prime minister Sidney Baron Sonnino's spontaneous reaction when informed of Germany's announcement: "The destruction of a neutral ship under neutral flag without investigation would be a monstrous thing [*une chose énorme*], an impermissible thing."[27] Both Italy and the United States threatened further steps if Germany proceeded.

In order to forestall these steps, which might include entering the war, Bethmann began his almost two-year-long effort to rein in the navy. Before considering the legal implications of his struggle, we should pause and examine the two issues that the German announcement had entangled with submarine warfare: the flag ruse and armed merchant vessels.

The Flag Ruse

Germany's first announcement cited the flag ruse, and its second cited both it and the arming and resistance of enemy merchant vessels as reasons why submarines could not be expected to save the crews and passengers aboard merchant ships that they sank. From the long discussions in the fall of 1914 (and, as we shall see, from those during the next two years), it is clear that the navy thought surfacing, searching, and saving were incompatible

---

26. The protests of the Netherlands (Feb. 12), Denmark (Feb. 16), Italy and Spain (both Feb. 17) are reprinted in Spindler, *Handelskrieg,* 1:260–69. The first U.S. note (Feb. 10) is in *FRUS* 1915, Suppl., 98–100.

27. Cited in Spindler, *Handelskrieg,* 1:133.

with the nature of the submarine anyway, and had thought so even before British merchant ships used the flag ruse or began resistance. Pohl's plan from the beginning was to sink without warning; the flag rule and armaments or resistance were simply covers. But both struck many observers as plausible arguments against British conduct at sea.

Between January 21 and 30, 1915—that is, before the scheduled opening of unrestricted submarine warfare on February 18—German U-boats sank seven British merchant vessels in the Channel and the Irish Sea.[28] As a result, on January 31 the British Admiralty sent a wireless message advising merchant captains to use neutral flags to disguise themselves while in submarine-infested waters; the Germans picked up this message.[29] Since at least November 1914, the German navy had expected the British to use the neutral flag ruse to counter submarines.[30] It was an old practice, though one more common for warships than for merchantmen. The rule was that warships might use neutral flags to lure an enemy vessel, but had to hoist their own flag before they began hostilities.[31] There is some indication that, in the years before 1914, the extrapolation of principles from land warfare to naval conflicts was causing the practice to become more controversial; U.S. warships used the ruse in 1898 against Spain, but the U.S. Naval Code of 1900 dropped it.[32] Since the eighteenth century, merchantmen had rarely used the ruse, and the first reaction of the landlubbers in the British diplomatic corps was to deny that it was Admiralty policy.[33] The Admiralty swiftly corrected them, pointing out that the Merchant Shipping Act of 1894 listed it as a normal procedure, and Britain offered the safety of its flag to other nations' vessels seeking to escape harm.[34]

The neutral protests confirmed backhandedly the legality of the flag ruse; none of them charged that it violated international law, just that it now endangered neutral ships.[35] The United States confined itself to requesting that it be used only in emergencies, which seems to have been the intent and which Grey repeated in a notice to British embassies.[36] From the legal standpoint, the most interesting part of the controversy was that it occurred at all. As the British Admiralty noted, "The whole idea of using false colours [by merchant vessels] is to ensure that the laws of war will be recognized," that is, that warships will stop, search, and visit.[37] It was not the flag ruse that potentially endangered neutral ships, but unrestricted submarine warfare. Neutral protests seem designed to prove to Germany that neutrals were not supinely acquiescing to Britain's measures, as it had alleged, and thus

---

28. Ibid., 1: fig. 3.

29. Tirpitz, *Politische Dokumente,* 300. Bell writes that the message was sent on February 2 and only to steamers on the Dutch route: Archibald C. Bell, *A History of the Blockade of Germany and of the Countries Associated with Her in the Great War, Austria, Bulgaria, and Turkey, 1914–1918* (London: HMSO, 1937), 222.

30. Zimmermann to Bethmann, Berlin, Nov. 30, 1914, IIIa 20172, BAB R 901 85910.

31. Lassa Oppenheim, *International Law: A Treatise* (London, 1905), 2:217–18, para. 211.

32. Oppenheim, *International Law,* 2:217n2.

33. Johnstone to Foreign Office, The Hague, Feb. 4, 1915, no. 17, FO 376/760, no. 13659, file 13659.

34. Foreign Office to Johnstone, Feb. 6, 1915, no. 6, FO 376/760, no. 14078, file 13659.

35. Bell, *History of the Blockade,* 223–24.

36. Foreign Office to British embassies, no. 6, Feb. 16, 1915, with addition in Grey's hand: "a neutral flag should only be used for the sole purpose of escaping capture." FO 376/760, no. 17630, file 13659.

37. Admiralty memo, "The Use of Neutral Flags by British Merchantmen, 1915," Malkin Papers, FO 800/941.

should not be put in harm's way. It was a roundabout argument that accepted the German parameters, while simultaneously trying to escape from them.

Resistance by Enemy Merchant Vessels

The right of enemy, but not of neutral merchant vessels, to resist search and visit by fleeing or by using force was well anchored in old naval practice and in international legal writings throughout the nineteenth century.[38] For this reason, until 1907 captured crews and officers of enemy merchant vessels were treated as prisoners of war; at the Hague Conference in that year, Belgium suggested and the other states agreed as a humanitarian gesture to release the crews if they gave their written word not to contribute to war operations after their repatriation.[39] The right of enemy merchantmen to resist capture followed the rule, as Lassa Oppenheim expressed it, that "unless attacked they must not commit hostilities, and if they do...they are liable to be treated as criminals just like private individuals committing hostilities in land warfare."[40] In other words, legal resistance was purely reactive. Resisting enemy merchantmen were therefore not the equivalent of converted merchant vessels being used in wartime as auxiliary cruisers to seek out and attack the foe's shipping—force could be initiated by genuine merchantmen only in self-defense, though resistance could theoretically end in the legal capture of the enemy's warship by the merchantman.[41]

This uncontroversial subject was not discussed at the Hague Convention of 1907 or at the London Conference (1909). It became contentious only in 1913 in the wake of a dispute, very like that concerning automatic contact mines, on the conversion of merchant vessels to auxiliary warships. Conversion allowed lesser naval powers to augment their fleets by arming their merchant vessels and placing them under naval authority in time of war. The dispute, which pitted Germany against Britain, concerned whether one could convert ships on the high seas (the German position), or only in one's own home waters (the British view, which of course advantaged the large colonial powers). Britain feared that swift German liners could enjoy the privileges of a merchantman in neutral ports, convert secretly at sea, and then strike British shipping lanes. Neither in 1907 nor in 1909 could unanimity be reached on the rules of conversion. The DoL reporter observed that "up to the present this question, of relatively recent origin, has been decided by the Governments

---

38. James Wilford Garner, *International Law and the World War* (London: Longmans, Green & Co., 1920), 1:400 and 400n5 for bibliography.

39. Netherlands, Ministry of Foreign Affairs, *Actes et documents, Deuxième conférence internationale de la paix, La Haye 15 juin–18 octobre 1907* (The Hague, 1908), 1:267–68.

40. Oppenheim, *International Law,* 2:96, para. 85.

41. Ibid.; Ferdinand Perels, *Das internationale öffentliche Seerecht der Gegenwart* (Berlin, 1903), 175, as cited in Heinrich Triepel, "Der Widerstand feindlicher Handelsschiffe gegen die Aufbringung," *Zeitschrift für Völkerrecht* 8 (1914): 391n8.

according to their own particular views and there does not at present exist any common principle in this regard recognized by all."[42]

To counteract this new threat, Churchill told Parliament on March 26, 1913, that the Admiralty had contacted "leading shipowners" and offered "to lend the necessary guns, to supply ammunition, and to provide for the training of members of the ship's company to form the gun's crews" of "first-class British liners."[43] The owners would pay the cost of structural conversion. The defensive intent was clear: the context of Churchill's speech was "trade protection"; he was responding to the problem that "a considerable number of foreign merchant steamers may be rapidly converted into armed ships." The goal was to offer "defence," and Churchill said that these ships had "a wholly different status from that of the regularly commissioned merchant cruisers," that is, Britain's own liners destined to become auxiliary ships of the navy. By August 1914 there were either twenty-four or thirty-nine armed ships.[44]

Five months after Churchill's announcement, the Institute of International Law met in Oxford to draft a succinct, up-to-date, and complete statement of maritime law. The participants debated the legality of resistance, and a majority upheld the old rule that non-warships "could not commit acts of hostility against the enemy" but could "use force to defend themselves against the attack of an enemy vessel."[45] The main voice against this view belonged to Heinrich Triepel, distinguished professor at the University of Berlin, who had come to international law via municipal constitutional law. His argument dovetailed exactly with that of Georg Schramm, Admiralty privy councillor in the German Naval Ministry, whose book on prize law had just appeared.[46] Schramm's work was not a response to Churchill's speech. It was a principled attack on the right to resistance per se.[47]

Schramm's arguments were theoretical; that is, they were based not on history, treaty, or practice (all of which opposed him), but on extrapolation from four principles. First, Schramm equated neutral and enemy merchantmen; their rights and duties were the same, he argued. Second, resistance by either was "an attack against the rights of a belligerent."[48] Schramm did not explain how one ought to weigh clashing rights, or why a belligerent's

---

42. James Brown Scott, ed., *The Declaration of London* (New York, 1919), 99.

43. Churchill before the House of Commons, Mar. 26, 1913, in Great Britain, Parliament, *House of Commons Debates (Hansard)*, 4th ser., vol. 50, cols. 1776–77, accessed online http://hansard.millbanksystems.com/commons/1913/mar/26/mr-churchills-statement.

44. Twenty-four armed merchant vessels: Schröder, *U-Boote des Kaisers,* 133, citing Churchill, *The World Crisis, 1911–1914,* 287; thirty-nine: Arthur J. Marder, *From the Dreadnought to Scapa Flow: The Royal Navy in the Fisher Era, 1904–1919* (Oxford, 1961–70), 1:366; Erich Raeder, *Der Kreuzerkrieg in den ausländischen Gewässern,* Der Krieg zur See 1914–1918 (Berlin, 1922), 1:51.

45. Institute of International Law, "Manual of the Laws of Naval War," in *The Laws of Armed Conflict,* ed. Dietrich Schindler and Jiri Toman (Dordrecht, 1913), art. 12.

46. Carl Bilfinger, "Heinrich Triepel 1868–1946," *Zeitschrift für ausländisches öffentliches Recht und Völkerrecht* 13 (1950): 1–13; Georg Schramm, *Das Prisenrecht in seiner neuesten Gestalt* (Berlin, 1913).

47. Garner writes that Schramm also responded to the arming of merchantmen, but it is unlikely, since he thought arming was legal (and so was flight to avoid capture): Schramm, *Prisenrecht,* 310; Garner, *International Law,* 1:401–3.

48. Schramm, *Prisenrecht,* 308.

rights outranked those of neutrals or of enemy non-warships. Third, the old arguments grounding international law were now surpassed by the "modern conception of the legal norm of war as an armed conflict between states," in which rights and duties adhered not to individuals, but to the states to which they belonged. And fourth, that modern view held that "in land as in sea wars only the organized armed forces of states are permitted to use force for attack or defense."[49] Schramm denied that enemy merchantmen had a right to self-defense (*Notwehr*), because that applied only where illegal force was used against one, but belligerent search and visit were perfectly legal.

Triepel set down his detailed, lawyerly arguments in a subsequent article.[50] They are mostly noteworthy for the learned lengths to which he had to go in order to discount evidence of the legality of resistance from prize court rulings on cargoes of resisters, prize court rulings altogether, the law of treatment of crews, the bulk of international-legal writing, and naval prize law. Although Triepel rejected Schramm's use of *Notwehr* and his equation of neutral with enemy merchantmen, he agreed with Schramm on the main points. Visitation was a belligerent right. "The generally accepted tendency of the modern law of war was to limit hostile acts...to *state* armed forces," and Triepel could cite approvingly the fourth "vow" of the 1907 Hague Conference "to bring the rules of war at sea as close as possible to those of the *land*."[51]

The arguments of Schramm and Triepel were extrapolations from a certain neo-Hegelian view of the state and from the principles of land warfare as enunciated by major land powers. They recapped for the sea the arguments Imperial Germany had been making since 1874 regarding occupation of enemy territory and popular resistance to it. In a sharp review of Schramm, Lassa Oppenheim rehearsed the grounds for upholding the right to resist: long state practice, two hundred years of customary law, its reconfirmation at Oxford in 1913, and its traces at the Hague.[52] Oppenheim concluded that "the right to capture a ship does not include the duty of that ship to submit willingly to the capture" (161). For an enemy merchantman, but not for a neutral, visitation automatically means capture and confiscation, therefore "visitation, though legal, is a hostile act that...may be countered with armed resistance" (169). Garner, following the same line, later wrote that the proper analogy was to unoccupied territory and the right of citizens to resist an invader.[53]

Regarding resistance to capture at sea, the Imperial German legal conception was new, categorical, and different from that shared by most other states and international-legal authorities. On June 22, 1914, the German Admiralty added to its prize rules the paragraph: "armed resistance by an armed enemy merchantman is to be broken with all means. The responsibility for the damage to ship, cargo, and passengers belongs to the enemy

---

49. Ibid., 308–9.

50. Triepel, "Widerstand Feindlicher Handelsschiffe."

51. Ibid., 405; emphasis in original.

52. Lassa Oppenheim, "Die Stellung der feindlichen Kauffarthschiffe im Seekrieg," *Zeitschrift für Völkerrecht* 8 (1914): 154–69.

53. Garner, *International Law,* 1:411.

government. The crew is to be treated as prisoners of war."[54] This paragraph did not go as far as Schramm's or Triepel's theory would have permitted, especially since granting prisoner-of-war status kept German prize law within the European norm; if resistance were truly illegal, then resisters ought to have been treated as francs-tireurs. The work of Schramm and Triepel showed the drift of German legal policy, which only reached its completion during the war.

Armed Enemy Merchantmen

The disagreement between Germany and Britain on the status of armed merchantmen put the neutrals in a difficult spot. Only the Netherlands prohibited armed merchantmen from entering Dutch ports, in effect treating them like warships. The Dutch walked a fine legal line. They rejected the German contention that resistance was illegal, but they classed armed resistance as a (legal) act of war, concluding that strict neutrality required closing Dutch ports to belligerent armed merchant vessels, just as it would to regular warships.[55]

But the U.S. roller-coaster ride shows growing unease about the institution of arming vessels. On August 25, 1914, British Ambassador Cecil Spring Rice assured the United States that armed British merchant ships "will never be used for purposes of attack," their armament was purely defensive, and "they will never fire unless first fired upon" nor "under any circumstances attack any vessel."[56] A longer memorandum of September 9 set out the reasons why Britain had returned to the "very old" practice of arming. It cited historical precedents and legal writings (including those of Ferdinand Perels, the former legal adviser to the German Admiralty), and then gave criteria for distinguishing armed merchantmen from auxiliary cruisers: armed merchant vessels "engaged in ordinary commerce and embark[ed] cargo and passengers in the ordinary way"; they did not seek out enemy ships.[57] Ten days later, the State Department compiled its own list of ten criteria by which it would judge the bona fides of armed merchant vessels.[58] Germany protested the American decision, repeating its insistence that "resistance is contrary to international law" and "would give the warship the right to send the merchant ship to the bottom with crew and passengers." "The distinction between offensive and defensive arms is irrelevant," the protest continued; "the destination of the ship for use of any kind in war is conclusive," and defensive arms could just as well "be used for offensive purposes."[59] Despite its acceptance of the British view, the United States seems to have remained inhospitable

---

54. Cited in Raeder, *Kreuzerkrieg*, 41–42. The last sentence was: "Passengers are to be released unless it is shown that they have engaged in resistance, in which case they are to be placed before an extraordinary court-martial."

55. Minister of Foreign Affair to Amb. Kühlmann, The Hague, no. 37051, Sept. 7, 1915, BAB R 901 86271.

56. Spring Rice to Bryan, Washington, Aug. 25, 1914, *FRUS* 1914, Suppl., 604.

57. Memorandum, Sept. 9, 1914, *FRUS* 1914, Suppl., 607–8.

58. "The Status of Armed Merchant Vessels," Sept. 19, 1914, *FRUS* 1914, Suppl., 611–12.

59. Gerard to Bryan, Berlin, Oct. 16, 1914, *FRUS* 1914, Suppl., 613.

to armed merchant vessels; otherwise it is hard to explain why, between September 10, 1914, and January 16, 1916, none arrived at U.S. ports.[60]

By mid-September 1915 Secretary of State Robert Lansing found the German view persuasive. Given the vulnerability of the small U-boats, he wrote, weapons intended to be defensive "may now be employed for offensive operations."[61] He proposed revising the U.S. position and treating armed merchantmen as warships. Wilson agreed, but the matter stalled until the diplomatic impasse over the submarine sinkings of the *Lusitania* and the *Arabic* had been resolved. At the beginning of January 1916, Lansing returned to the issue, suggesting that the United States broker an exchange along the lines of the failed swap of food deliveries for the cessation of unrestricted submarine warfare. This time, Britain was to stop arming merchant ships and Germany would cease unrestricted submarine warfare.[62] Lansing reasoned that "the rule of visit...could hardly be required justly of a submarine, if the observation of the rule compels the submarine to expose itself to almost certain destruction by coming to the surface." In order to keep the old cruiser rules intact, armed merchant ships should be reclassified as warships. Wilson found this position "reasonable, and thoroughly worth trying."[63] It took Lansing a week to realize what he was actually asking. His exchange, he now saw, "only required [of the Central Powers that they] conform to the rules of international law, while it required their enemies to modify a present practice which might be construed [as] a legal right."[64] Lansing pulled back, and the U.S. official position remained what it had been.

In March 1916 the United States issued a solomonic statement that "There is no settled rule of international law" defining armed merchant vessels as warships; the decision must rest with each neutral state.[65] It recognized the "right to arm for the purpose of self-protection," and rejected the German view that warships enjoyed exclusive belligerent rights: "the right to capture and the right to prevent capture are recognized as equally justifiable." But if an armed merchant vessel attacks first, or flees, then the belligerent "can properly exercise force to compel surrender." If a defensively armed merchantman was "certain of attack," it could legally act preemptorily, but if it had a commission or order "to attack in all circumstances," or if it were "entitled to receive prize money" for doing to, or was "liable to a penalty for failure to obey the orders," then its status was clearly that of an auxiliary warship. This was an admirable summary of the difficult judgments neutrals had to make.

Lansing's perplexity was in part caused by British Admiralty instructions to merchant ships that Austria had found aboard the *Woodfield* (November 9, 1915) and then published (February 14, 1916) in order to justify the new naval policy of sinking without warning all armed enemy vessels.[66] The instructions, dated February 25, 1915, were for "vessels carrying

---

60. *New York Times,* Jan. 28, 1916, IIIa 19102, BAB R 901 86272.

61. Lansing to Wilson, Washington, Sept. 12, 1915, United States, *Papers Relating to the Foreign Relation of the United States; The Lansing Papers, 1914–1920* (Washington, DC, 1939), 1:331.

62. Lansing to Wilson, Jan. 7, 1916, ibid., 1:334.

63. Wilson to Lansing, Jan. 10, 1916, ibid., 1:335.

64. Lansing to Wilson, Washington, Jan. 17, 1916, ibid., 1:336.

65. Memorandum on the status of armed merchant vessels, March 25, 1916, *FRUS* 1916, Suppl., 244–48.

66. *Note verbale* IIIa 1909/26921, enclosed in Gerard to Lansing, Berlin, Feb. 14, 1916, *FRUS* 1916, Suppl., 187–98.

a defensive armament"; they advised that if a ship were actively pursued by a submarine, it "should open fire in self-defence, notwithstanding the submarine may not have committed a definite hostile act such as firing a gun or torpedo."[67] It added, "Before opening fire, the British Colours should be hoisted. It is essential that fire should not be opened under Neutral Colours." Those instructions were enlarged upon in April 1915, and masters were told to let the submarine come within eight hundred yards for a better shot.[68] The State Department ultimately decided that anticipatory action was justified by standards of effectiveness and was legal as self-defense; nevertheless, firing first contravened the British ambassador's pledge of August 1914. German officials, naval and civilian, interpreted the instructions as offensive. One of them summarized them as "consequently, attack!"[69] That interpretation reflected the new German legal view of 1913 that judged the old right of resistance as illegitimate belligerent action.[70] If was therefore useless for Britain to publish subsequent Admiralty instructions of October 20, 1915, which reiterated the right of enemy merchantmen to resist search and visit forcibly and which repeated yet again that "the armament is supplied for the purpose of defence only, and the object of the master should be to avoid action whenever possible."[71] This disagreement on the right to defend produced two famous cases, those of Captain Fryatt and Captain Blaikie.

Captain Fryatt

On March 28, 1915, the unarmed British steamer *Brussels,* on its way to the Netherlands, encountered *U-33.* The commander of the U-boat, Lieutenant Konrad Gansser, later recalled that he had surfaced, but the *Brussels* did not stop and instead speeded toward him. He submerged and escaped.[72] The *Brussels* and her captain, Charles Fryatt, arrived safely in Amsterdam. Fryatt later denied that he had ever spoken to the press, but the *Amsterdamer Telegraaf* immediately published a story claiming that the *Brussels* had rammed the U-boat; that story became embellished as it was reprinted in other papers.[73] Back in London, MP and former commander of the Channel fleet Charles Beresford had asked the

---

67. Instructions regarding submarines applicable to vessels carrying a defensive armament, confidential, Feb. 25, 1915, BAB R 901 86273.

68. Instructions regarding submarines applicable to vessels carrying a defensive armament, Apr. 1915, BAB R 901 86273.

69. Chief of Admiralty to Chancellor, B. 1831 I, IIIa 1908, Berlin, Jan. 23, 1916, "Ganz Geheim," Marginalium to Instructions to British Merchant Vessels passing through the Mediterranean Sea, Malta, June 1915, "You are to carry out the procedure recommended by the Admiralty in their printed instructions if a hostile Submarine is sighted." BAB R 901 86273.

70. Cf. Garner, *International Law,* 1:395–96, 397n2.

71. Instructions for defensively armed merchant ships (Oct. 20, 1915), enclosed in Spring Rice to Lansing, Washington, Apr. 28, 1916, *FRUS* 1916, Suppl., 250–51.

72. Report on the attempted ramming of "U.33" by the s.s. "Brussels" on March 28, 1915, Annex 2 of the English translation of the Report of the Reichstag Commission of Inquiry, FO 383/497.

73. Reichstag report, FO 383/497, 598, 569.

Admiralty for a list of merchant captains who had "baffl[ed]" German submarines. Fryatt's name came on that list; he received a gold watch from the Admiralty "for conspicuous bravery in saving his ship from a German U-boat."[74] Note that neither Beresford nor the Admiralty mentioned ramming.

It was Fryatt's bad luck to be captured along with his ship a year later, June 22, 1916. Taken at first to the civilian detention center at Ruhleben, Fryatt wound up on July 27, 1916, in Bruges before a court-martial of the marine corps (Flanders). Notified ten days in advance of the impending trial, the Foreign Office enlisted the help of the American ambassador in Berlin, James W. Gerard. Gerard contacted the AA on the twentieth and twenty-second; the AA requested that the Admiralty postpone the trial to allow Gerard to arrange for special counsel. Despite the intervention of both the AA and the Admiralty, the court-martial proceeded on schedule. It found Fryatt guilty of attempted ramming and thus of having engaged in hostilities while a civilian; it executed him the same day.[75] Admiral Reinhard Koch explained the verdict to the AA. The U-boat had followed cruiser rules, and Fryatt tried "suddenly and insidiously [*hinterlistigerweise*] to ram and destroy it."[76] Because he was not a member of the armed forces, Fryatt was a "*franc-tireur*," who justly deserved to die. "As the law of war on land protects the members of the army from assassination by guerrillas, the same law of war protects members of the navy from assassination at sea." Koch thus argued that the rules of land warfare applied directly to the sea.

The international éclat surrounding Fryatt's execution was tremendous.[77] Captain Fryatt joined Nurse Cavell as a celebrated victim of German "frightfulness." Britain entered "the most formal protest" of "the judicial murder...in direct violation of the law of nations and the usages of war."[78] Fryatt's death confirmed everything negative British leaders believed about Imperial Germany. Horace Rumbold, who had served in Britain's Berlin embassy in the last two years of peace, interpreted the AA's verbal responses to Gerard as evidence that "the Germans are reluctant to put anything down on paper"; the hasty execution, he thought, was clear "proof that the Germans knew they were committing an illegal act and that they wished to forestall the outcry which was soon to follow."[79] Robert Cecil prepared remarks for Parliament. His original words indicated the depth of his feelings; he described the government's "horror" (changed to "indignation") at the plain "murder" ("judicial" was struck out). "It is impossible to guess," he wrote, "to what further atrocities they may proceed." The government "when the time comes will endeavour to bring to justice the criminals whoever they may be and whatever their station. In such cases as this the man who authorises the system under which such crimes are committed may well be

---

74. Ibid., 598, 567.

75. On Fryatt case see FO 383/195, file 123628.

76. Koch to Zimmermann, Berlin, July 31, 1916, no. B. 19565, AA/PA R 21471.

77. Ambassador Richard v. Kühlmann reported the "almost univocal" rejection of Germany's legal arguments by the Dutch press: Kühlmann to AA, The Hague, Aug. 3, 1916, no. 1052, AA/PA R 21471.

78. J. Masterton Smith to Eric Drummond, approved by Balfour, Aug. 5, 1916, FO 383/195, no. 149202, file 123628.

79. Horace Rumbold minute, Aug. 1, 1916, FO 383/195, no. 149202, file 123628.

the most guilty of all."[80] Once again, it would be quite mistaken to dismiss these words as propaganda. On a *Weekly Dispatch* article of July 30, 1916, calling for the execution of the Kaiser "for the accumulated horror of the crimes" for which he was allegedly responsible, C. H. Montgomery minuted that it was "useless stuff at the present time," but Rumbold replied, "Perhaps so, but it reflects the views of most of us."[81] The Fryatt case helped spark a principled debate taken up to the War Committee on the efficacy of reprisal versus postwar trials, a subject we shall examine later.

Because the Fryatt case was part of the Allies' demand that Germany submit to postwar war-crime trials, a commission of German lawyers and naval officers reviewed the case in April 1919.[82] Among its members was Captain Ernst Vanselow, who had been in charge of legal affairs for the Admiralty. The commission concluded that the trial and execution did not violate international law. The legal basis for the verdict was the Imperial Edict (AKO) of August 21, 1900, the naval version of the Imperial Edict of December 28, 1899, which criminalized hostile actions taken by "a foreigner who did not belong to the forces of the enemy" (561). Of course, that order referred to actions taken in the occupied zone during land warfare. In order to apply it to the sea, the commission had to deny the right of resistance to capture, which, they admitted, "a majority of foreign governments" upheld (576). Citing Schramm, Triepel, and some wartime German writers, they nevertheless concluded that international law on the issue was unsettled (581). As to the penalty, death, the commission recognized the court-martial's right to apply the "unwritten Laws of Warfare born of the hard necessities of that state," since no other penalties were prescribed elsewhere (584). The commission found the haste of execution "regrettable" but within the law, for the AKO called for "immediate" execution (559, 585). In short, the postwar commissioners upheld the unilateral extension of Germany's land-warfare laws to the sea.[83]

The commission was also aided in reaching its conclusion by a tendentious reading of the Admiralty's instructions (February 10, 1915) to merchant vessels upon sighting a submarine.[84] It reproduced in Annex A the first two paragraphs of the instructions, which admonished merchantmen never to "tamely surrender to a submarine," but always to try to escape because "a vessel which surrenders is certain to be sunk."[85] It advised keeping the submarine astern, since torpedoes shot from that position were easily avoided. The commission suppressed the third paragraph, which instructed captains, if a submarine suddenly surfaced close ahead, to "steer straight for her at your utmost speed, altering course as necessary to keep her ahead. She will probably then dive, in which case you will have ensured your safety, as she will be compelled to come up astern of you." This paragraph

---

80. Cecil minute to R. O. Houston, July 31, 1916, FO 383/195, no. 150417, file 123628.

81. Rumbold minute of Aug. 3, 1915, FO 383/195, no. 150473, file 123628.

82. Report of the Reichstag Commission of Inquiry, FO 383/497.

83. See Hankel's interesting interpretation: Gerd Hankel, *Die Leipziger Prozesse: Deutsche Kriegsverbrechen und ihre strafrechtliche Verfolgung nach dem Ersten Weltkrieg* (Hamburg, 2003), 442–51; and Garner, *International Law,* 1:407–13.

84. Section 2, Procedure if an Enemy Submarine is Sighted, copy, FO 383/497, p. 682.

85. Annex A of the Report of the Reichstag Commission of Inquiry, English translation, FO 383/497, 609. My thanks to Michelle Moyd for this document.

made clear that ramming was not the object of such maneuvers; since the *Brussels* had not touched the U-boat, Captain Fryatt's defensive intentions should have been clear.[86]

In a closely reasoned article from 1917, Franz W. Jerusalem drew much more interesting conclusions from the Fryatt case.[87] He reasoned that the principled disagreement between the British and German views showed that "the law of war in one fundamental point [i.e., who may fight] lacks international character; it is municipal law" (568). Like Schramm and Triepel, Jerusalem found British law retrograde because it did not limit legal warfare to members of the armed forces. From this viewpoint, "the German principle of the law of war is the more complete, since it comes closer to the unachievable, but in the Kantian sense desirable ideal of perpetual peace" (570). But the clash of the more complete or civilized with the retrograde created a paradox, Jerusalem wrote:

> The side that possesses the more developed law of war will have to have recourse more often to reprisals, because the enemy does not know which obligations his opponent's law of war requires of him, and is convinced of the absolutely binding nature of his own laws of war. The result is that [the more civilized] must advert in the course of reprisal to a conduct of war that must seem quite cruel to the enemy. (572)

Jerusalem's piece is by no means a whitewash of German war conduct. He went on to argue that Germany's subsequent unrestricted submarine campaign after January 1917 was *not* reprisal, and thus Germany had agreed to fight the war on Britain's basis; consequently, merchantmen now did have the right to defend themselves (584–85). This was an exceedingly unpopular argument among Jerusalem's colleagues.[88] Instead, one should understand Jerusalem as voicing an increasingly common view among German international lawyers that World War I was a clash of civilizations, visible in fundamental disagreements about international law. Germany represented superior, modern principles of law and order that paradoxically must be enacted by the ancient and seemingly cruel means of reprisal.

Captain Blaikie

On December 4, 1916, the armed British merchant transport *Caledonia* encountered a U-boat southeast of Malta. Spotting its periscope, the *Caledonia* zigzagged, the U-boat torpedoed it, and, sinking, the *Caledonia* hit the submarine, but never fired a shot. Captain James Blaikie, the master, was rescued by the U-boat commander, who told him, "You

---

86. The Admiralty instructions of Feb. 10, 1915, were not among the supporting documents that the AA distributed in explanation of Germany's campaign to sink armed merchantmen without warning, because they referred to unarmed merchantmen (*Note verbale*, Berlin, Feb. 14, 1916, IIIa 1909/26921, *FRUS* 1916, Suppl., 187–98). But their inclusion in the postwar commission report shows that Germany possessed them during the war.

87. Franz W. Jerusalem, "Der Fall Fryatt," *Zeitschrift für Völkerrecht* 10 (1917/1918): 563–85.

88. See Kohler's vehement attack on him: ibid., 585n1.

tried to ram me," whereupon Blaikie replied, "Well, you tried to sink me, and you did it, and it's all in the game isn't it?"[89]

Primed by Fryatt's fate, the Mercantile Marine Service Association, the Chamber of Shipping, Parliament, and the press instantly demanded that the Foreign Office stop the Germans from executing Blaikie, too. They need not have worried, because the Foreign Office immediately wanted to threaten reprisals and found the Admiralty much more timid than the diplomats.[90] Moving even faster than the British Foreign Office, Zimmermann assured the American go-betweens that Blaikie was safe, because "the *Caledonia* was an armed cruiser...and thus he was only doing his duty."[91] Blaikie's case coincided with Bethmann's peace proposal; it would have been highly inopportune to repeat the Fryatt fiasco. But more than this, because the *Caledonia* was armed, she and her master fell under the June 22, 1914, addendum to the prize rules categorizing armed merchant crews as prisoners of war (not civilians). Germany's announcement (February 11, 1916) that armed merchant vessels would be treated like warships (and thus subject to sinking without warning) paradoxically saved their captains and crews from execution by assimilating them to the military.

The controversy over whether armed merchant vessels were warships was more interesting as a sign of the cleft between Germany's view of law and Britain's than it was consequential for the war. Armed merchant vessels sank no submarines during the First World War.[92] Of course, despite what Germany alleged, that was not their purpose. Instead, their armament allowed merchant vessels to escape by forcing threatened submarines to dive. At this they were successful.[93] "Q-ships" were much closer to what Germany protested: they were *ruses de guerre,* outfitted by Britain to look like neutral merchant ships but actually on the prowl for submarines. When they were first introduced in 1915, they took the Germans by surprise and sank six U-boats. Afterward, however, though there were two hundred of them, they sank only eight more.[94]

The Tergiversations of the Submarine Campaign

We have seen that, once German leaders had decided on the form of the submarine campaign (war zone, not blockade), legal considerations played no role in their further

---

89. W. Graham Greene to Secretary of POW Dept, FO, Dec. 13, 1916, FO 383/205, no. 252671, file 250207.

90. Newton to Admiralty, Dec. 11, 1916, FO 383/205, no. 253239, file 250207.

91. Page to Foreign Office, London, Dec. 18, 1916, no. 1735, FO 383/205, no. 256152, file 250207.

92. Schröder, *U-Boote des Kaisers,* 166, 407. Appendix 4 of the German note to the neutral powers of Feb. 8, 1916, claimed that of nineteen cases where armed merchant vessels had fired on submarines, one had been sunk: "Bewaffnete Kauffahrteischiffe," *Zeitschrift für Völkerrecht* 9 (1916): 527–29.

93. Appendix 4, "Bewaffnete Kauffahrteischiffe": of nineteen cases of clashes between armed merchant vessels and submarines, fifteen ships escaped, and three were sunk; the appendix does not explain what happened to the last vessel.

94. Schröder, *U-Boote des Kaisers,* 169–70.

decisions. Nevertheless, the opposition of neutrals, especially the United States, impressed legal strictures onto Germany gradually and unevenly, but in the end successfully forcing U-boats to abide entirely by cruiser rules from May 1916 through January 1917. Beginning in February 1917 and lasting until almost the end of the war, Imperial Germany then disregarded neutral sanctions and threw over the law entirely. Submarine warfare was the most intricate and confusing aspect of belligerent conduct in the First World War; this is not the place to rehearse it once again.[95] Instead, the following discussion focuses on three things: (1) the general pattern of decision making as an orientation for (2) the handling of crises that reveal the working assumptions about law, and (3) the hidden theory of law peculiar to the German navy, visible in its extraordinary behavior behind the scenes.

Bethmann's concern remained constant: he feared that sinking neutral vessels, or enemy passenger ships with neutrals aboard, would bring the United States into the war against Germany. The U.S. position was clear from its very first protest note of February 10, 1915: U.S. merchant ships must be spared, and passengers and crews aboard other vessels must always be saved. Almost all accounts of submarine warfare overlook the fact that the U.S. view, which was the most stringent and legalistic of all the neutral protests, made a huge concession to Germany from the beginning. For customary law dictated that sinking merchant vessels, even enemy ones, was *exceptional*; but in submarine warfare it was *policy*. It may be that the very extremity of Germany's announcement induced the world to adopt a compromise position from the outset.

In any event, Bethmann's struggle with the navy began immediately, before the campaign had even started in February 1915, with his attempt to spare Italian and American merchantmen, that is, the ships of the two countries whose protest had threatened some form of greater retaliation. He succeeded, and in April was able to add Dutch vessels to the list.[96] Bethmann was moving to get all neutral shipping spared, when the *U-20* sank the *Lusitania* on May 7, 1915, ushering in the first big crisis with the United States. At a Crown council at the end of the month, Bethmann succeeded in getting his principle accepted that all neutral merchant vessels should be spared. That principle did not cover the *Lusitania*, however, which was an enemy passenger ship. The next day Bethmann belatedly persuaded Wilhelm to add enemy passenger liners to the off-limits list, but in a measure of the navy's strength and its sensitivity to appearing to compromise, the passenger ship order was kept secret.[97]

The sinking of the British liner *Arabic* in mid-August 1915 moved the process along by a notch: Bethmann forced the Admiralty to reveal the previously secret order and to issue a new one treating all enemy passenger ships according to cruiser rules. By September 1915 new orders specified that enemy merchant ships inside the declared war zone would be

---

95. The newest account, with many excellent insights and information, but also with occasional errors, is Schröder, *U-Boote des Kaisers*. Still useful is especially vol. 1 of Spindler, *Handelskrieg*. The older, succinct accounts by Assmann and Stegemann are also still worthwhile: Kurt Assmann, *Deutsche Seestrategie in zwei Weltkriegen*, Die Wehrmacht im Kampf, vol. 12 (Heidelberg, 1957); Bernd Stegemann, *Die deutsche Marinepolitik 1916–1918* (Berlin, 1970).

96. Spindler, *Handelskrieg*, 1:139, 2:100.

97. Ibid., 2:166n1.

sunk without warning, but neutral ships and enemy passenger ships would be sunk using cruiser rules.

The navy chafed under these limitations and in December 1915 received powerful support from Army Chief of Staff Falkenhayn, who now favored unrestricted submarine warfare, regardless of possible U.S. entry, as part of his plans to attack Verdun in the spring. The Admiralty, now under Admiral Henning von Holtzendorff, pressed to apply unrestricted warfare to armed enemy merchant ships, arguing that they were in effect warships. The navy thus took advantage of German law to open a (large) category of British ships to unrestricted submarine warfare.[98] Wilhelm agreed on January 24, 1916, and, surprisingly, so did the chancellor, without consulting the AA. As the campaign began in February, the navy and OHL pressed for unlimited submarine warfare altogether and clashed directly with Bethmann. Wilhelm wavered, postponing the start of unlimited war to April 1, but the sinking of the liner *Sussex* on March 24, 1916, and the ensuing diplomatic struggle with the United States, canceled the navy's and OHL's plans. The chancellor had always argued that submarine warfare by cruiser rules was the safest route, harming Britain but not antagonizing the United States, and he finally won. On May 1, 1916, Wilhelm declared that Germany would henceforth follow cruiser rules in all its submarine activities. For reasons we will examine shortly, the navy did not actually act on these instructions until October 1916.

In the meanwhile, in August 1916 Falkenhayn had been replaced by Erich Ludendorff and Paul von Hindenburg, who favored unrestricted submarine warfare. Public pressure in the press and the Reichstag to unleash the submarines continued to build, held in check only by Bethmann's preparations for a peace proposal in December 1916. Bethmann lost an ally in late November when Arthur Zimmermann, a U-boat enthusiast, replaced Jagow as director of the AA, and when both Bethmann's peace plan and Wilson's failed, Bethmann acquiesced to unrestricted submarine warfare in January 1917. It first targeted only armed merchant vessels, but swiftly expanded to all ships encountered in the war zone. Unrestricted submarine warfare remained in effect until October 20, 1918, when it was finally withdrawn as a precondition for the Armistice.[99]

Bethmann's odyssey began and ended with the problem that Simons had outlined in his first memo, "the general international-legal principle that civilians in an undefended area are not to be directly attacked with weapons."[100] Once Germany had canceled that legal principle by reprisal, Bethmann's first limiting position was to spare neutral vessels; his second was to spare enemy passenger ships. Not until the summer of 1915 did he arrive at his final policy: submarines must abide by cruiser rules. This was the compromise German diplomats worked out with the United States. It was a compromise because it sacrificed the customary rule that enemy non-warships and all neutral craft were to be sunk only under exceptional circumstances, in order to keep the general principle that

---

98. Schröder, following V. E. Tarrant, *Kurs West: Die deutschen U-Boot-Offensiven,* writes that by the end of 1915 766 British merchant vessels were armed: Schröder, *U-Boote des Kaisers,* 166.

99. German reply to Wilson's second note, Oct. 20, 1918, *FRUS* 1918, Suppl., 1:379–81.

100. Draft of Undersecretary to Chancellor, Nr. 72, tel., Berlin, Oct. 27, 1914, IIIa 17692, BAB R 901 85910.

noncombatants must not be the direct targets of hostile action. In other words, submarines would be accepted as new weapons if they abided by (part) of the old rules. Unlike the civilian leadership, the German navy never accepted this compromise.

The Crises: *Lusitania, Arabic, Sussex*

The sinking of the *Lusitania* horrified the world because 1,195 civilians (123 of them American) died. The continuing fascination of the public unfortunately often focuses on whether the ship contained contraband (it did: 18 fuse cases, 125 cases of empty shrapnel shells, 4,200 cases of safety cartridges, and 189 cases of infantry equipment), or whether it was armed (it was not, despite Germany's initial claim).[101] These issues are irrelevant; the law demanded visit, search, and safety of those aboard, regardless.

The first U.S. note (May 13, 1915) was extremely cordial but stayed consistent with the position enunciated in the first protest note of February, that the United States would hold Germany "to a strict accountability for any infringement" of U.S. neutral rights (Wilson: "We defined our position at the outset and cannot alter it").[102] The note was the product of a long, internal discussion in Washington of how to respond to several other, previous sinkings involving American victims. Wilson chose "to put the whole note on very high grounds...on the interests of mankind which are involved...on the manifest impropriety of a single nation's essaying to alter the understandings of nations," and on Germany's choice of a weapon that could not possibly follow the law.[103] The sometimes wavering president was stiffened by State Department legal counselor (soon to be secretary) Robert Lansing, who interpreted successive sinkings of merchant vessels as proof "that the German naval policy is one of wanton and indiscriminate destruction of vessels regardless of nationality."[104] Lansing specified what "full accountability" meant: apology, repudiation, and full reparation. Lansing also insisted on discussing the legal issues for their own sake.[105] Although other American interests were reflected in it position, the law was genuinely the crux of the matter for the United States.

The initial German reply pushed responsibility for the *Lusitania* onto Britain, for forcing Germany "to resort to retaliatory measures."[106] While Germany inquired behind the scenes how best to answer the first U.S. note, it sent a place-holder reply that addressed none of the legal concerns. Instead, it disputed factual matters and claimed that, since

---

101. Cargo: *New York Times,* August 26, 1918, reporting on the evidence from civil damage suits, BAB R 901 85950 IIIa 20649. Cf. Schröder, *U-Boote des Kaisers,* 128, 134. Arming: Garner, *International Law,* 1:361; Spindler, *Handelskrieg,* 2:91–92.

102. Wilson to Bryan, Washington, May 11, 1915, United States, *Lansing Papers,* 1:392; Bryan to Gerard, Washington, May 13, 1915, *FRUS* 1915, Suppl., 393–96.

103. Wilson to Bryan, Washington, April 22, 1915, United States, *Lansing Papers,* 1:378.

104. Lansing to Bryan, May 1, 1915, United States, *Lansing Papers,* 1:381.

105. Lansing to Bryan, May 5, 1915, United States, *Lansing Papers,* 1:384–5.

106. German note of May 10, 1915, enclosed in Gerard to Bryan, Berlin, May 10, 1915, *FRUS* 1915, Suppl., 389.

Britain had armed its merchant fleet and instructed it to attack, Germany could no longer consider any British merchant vessels "undefended territory."[107] While Admiral von Pohl liked the German reply for "ignoring the American impudence," Lansing, Bryan, and the cabinet found the tone offensive; it renewed their conviction that the United States must insist that Germany return to legal warfare.[108] Wilson complained to Bryan that the German foreign office "always misses the essential point involved, that England's violation of neutral rights is different from Germany's violation of the rights of humanity" (i.e., property was less important than lives).[109]

The frosty U.S. counter-reply of June 9, 1915, repeated the U.S. position and unleashed a protracted, wide-ranging negotiation inside Germany that involved not just the chancellor, the AA, and the navy, but also prominent private citizens such as Albert Ballin, the owner of the Hamburg-Amerika line, and the German-born reporter for the Hearst papers, Karl von Wiegand.[110] The resulting reply was more tactical maneuvering—even Bryan acknowledged the "sarcastic tone of certain phrases," which he attributed to the German government's need to placate domestic public opinion.[111] After rehearsing at great length Germany's history of lawfulness, and at equal length, Britain's of lawlessness in this war, Germany offered to safeguard U.S. ships and passengers. American citizens could travel to Europe aboard preannounced and specially marked vessels, if necessary, even enemy ones.[112]

But Germany had refused to admit wrong, to pay reparation, or to address its obligations under the law. The third American note (July 21, 1915) insisted that it do all three things.[113] But in return, the United States made two remarkable concessions. It offered to recognize the submarine as a legitimate weapon, adverting to the "extraordinary conditions" and "radical alterations of circumstance and method of attack" introduced into naval warfare, which

> the nations of the world can not have had in view when the existing rules of international law were formulated, and [the United States] is ready to make every reasonable allowance for these novel and unexpected aspects of war at sea; but it can not consent to abate any essential or fundamental right of its people because

---

107. German note of May 28, 1915, enclosed in Gerard to Bryan, Berlin, May 29, 1915, *FRUS* 1915, Suppl., 419–21.

108. Pohl diary, Wilhelmshaven, May 31, 1915, Hugo Pohl, *Aus Aufzeichnungen und Briefen während der Kriegszeit* (Berlin, 1920), 130; Lansing to Bryan, June 1, 1915, United States, *Lansing Papers,* 1:417; J. Perrinjaquet, "La guerre commerciale sous-marine; Les torpillages du *Lusitania,* de l'*Arabic,* de l'*Ancona,* et du *Persia;* Les protestations des États-Unis et les concessions de l'Allemagne," *Revue générale de droit international public* 23 (1916): 151.

109. Wilson to Bryan, Washington, June 2, 1915, United States, *Lansing Papers,* 1:421.

110. Tirpitz, *Politische Dokumente,* 374–75. U.S. note of June 9, 1915, *FRUS* 1915, Suppl., 436–38.

111. Bryan to Wilson, Washington, July 14, 1915, United States, *Lansing Papers,* 1:457. Cf. on the sarcasm: Perrinjaquet, "La guerre commerciale," 167–71.

112. Gerard to Lansing, no. 2565, Berlin, July 8, 1915, *FRUS* 1915, Suppl., 464–66.

113. Lansing (now secretary of state) to Gerard, Washington, July 21, 1915, *FRUS* 1915, Suppl., 480–82.

of a mere alteration of circumstance. The rights of neutrals in time of war are based upon principle, not upon expedience, and the principles are immutable.

In the past two months, German submarine commanders had shown that they could indeed follow "the accepted practices of regulated warfare." Germany could therefore "lift the whole practice of submarine attack above the criticism which it has aroused." If Germany accepted cruiser rules for submarines, disavowed the attack on the *Lusitania,* and paid reparation, the United States offered cooperation with Germany in pursuing "freedom of the seas." In less veiled language, the United States offered to mediate an exchange whereby Germany gave up unrestricted submarine warfare and Britain the most objectionable aspects of its blockade. However, if Germany continued along its illegal path, the United States would regard that act as "deliberately unfriendly."

The U.S. offer was the greatest diplomatic opportunity that Germany received in the war, for it promised to end Germany's Continental isolation, move the United States away from Britain, and open further benefits from American cooperation. It was an important and genuine offer.[114] The price was forgoing unrestricted submarine warfare forever by admitting that it violated international law. Germany's skilled ambassador to the United States, Johann Heinrich Count Bernstorff, outlined Germany's choice. "If [unrestricted submarine warfare] is a goal in itself and we have the reasonable hope of using it to defeat England, then it is more advantageous not to answer the U.S. note and to execute [unlimited] submarine warfare without regard to neutrals. If submarine warfare is a means to an end, i.e., lifting or diminishing the British blockade," then Germany should accept the U.S. offer.[115]

Germany never answered. Its silence was not the product of coordinated deliberations, however. Instead, while the AA attempted several drafts and Naval Cabinet Chief Admiral von Müller (who was skeptical of U-boats) suggested offering to put the matter of compensation before the Hague arbitration court,[116] the rest of the navy and public opinion pulled sharply in the other direction. The navy's line was consistent throughout. As Tirpitz put it, disavowing the sinking of the *Lusitania* was unthinkable, because "this was done legally and it is outrageous [*unerhört*] to demand apology or concessions on that basis."[117] Nothing was worth relinquishing the legal right to use the submarine in its most powerful way, namely, without limit.[118] The American demand for apology equaled an admission of criminality, and both the navy and public opinion found that humiliating. Even the liberal *Berliner Tageblatt* favored a "quick, short, decisive answer, putting the responsibility for any loss of American lives onto the American government."[119]

---

114. Assmann, *Deutsche Seestrategie,* 83; Schröder, *U-Boote des Kaisers,* 156–57.

115. Bernstorff report of July 28, 1915, cited in Spindler, *Handelskrieg,* 2:180–81.

116. Schröder, *U-Boote des Kaisers,* 159–60.

117. Note of June 22, 1915, Tirpitz, *Politische Dokumente,* 364.

118. Tirpitz, note of June 29, 1915, ibid., 374.

119. Theodor Wolff diary, July 28, 1915, in *Theodor Wolff. Tagebücher 1914–1919; Der Erste Weltkrieg und die Entstehung der Weimarer Republik in Tagebüchern, Leitartikeln und Briefen des Chefredakteurs am "Berliner*

Despite naval opposition, by the beginning of August, the AA had worked itself up to a two-part compromise: Germany's submarines would follow cruiser rules if Britain stopped arming its merchantmen and disavowed the right to resist; if the United States got Britain to return to the DoL, Germany would stop torpedoing merchantmen, though it insisted on the legality of "the principle of the U-boats."[120] In a sense, this offer repeated the food/submarine swap proposal that had already failed in February 1915. Germany would cease its unprecedented policy that clearly violated customary law, while Britain was asked to relinquish two policies, one a revival of an older legal practice (arming), and the other well founded in current international practice and disputed mainly by Germany, alone. As to the second offer, if the DoL were accepted, submarines would be unnecessary to guarantee food and raw material imports to Germany. In February, during the previous exchange proposal, Britain had also insisted that Germany must stop mining the open sea and, in June 1915 when the exchange offer was renewed, stop using poison gas; the AA draft was silent on these weapons. And it did not admit illegality or take responsibility (for compensation).

Germany was still honing its inadequate answer to the U.S. offer when on August 19, Captain Rudolf Schneider of *U-24* spotted the British liner *Arabic* outbound from Liverpool. Apparently thinking it was going to ram him, he sank it without warning, killing forty-seven civilians, two of them Americans.[121] This new crisis brought matters to a head, and Bethmann finally won against his chief naval opponents. On August 30, 1915, the Kaiser removed Tirpitz as official war adviser and Bachmann as navy minister; as Bethmann wanted, he ordered that submarines treat enemy passenger ships according to cruiser rules. Nonetheless, even under these circumstances, the first German note on the *Arabic* (September 7) refused "to acknowledge any obligation to grant indemnity...even if the commander should have been mistaken," and, while it proposed to submit the matter "as being a question of international law" to the Hague arbitration tribunals, it did so under condition that the decision would not rule on the legality of German submarine warfare.[122] The chancellor thus held on to the navy's sine qua non, that Germany must not admit that unrestricted submarine warfare was illegal. Lansing judged the note "cold and uncompromising"; it forced the United States either to repeat yet again its demand for apology, repudiation, and indemnity, or to break diplomatic relations.[123]

Bernstorff now urgently advised Germany simply to accept cruiser rules and repudiate Captain Schneider.[124] The AA and navy returned to the drafting table, but once again they could not go that far. Their directive to Bernstorff alluded to "stringent instructions" to

---

Tageblatt" und Mitbegründer der "Deutschen Demokratischen Partei," ed. Bernd Sösemann (Boppard am Rhein, 1984), 1:263.

120. Entwurf zu einer Note an die Vereinigten Staaten von Amerika, Berlin, Aug. 9, 1915, AA/PA R 21545, frames 139–45; partly cited in Schröder, *U-Boote des Kaisers,* 163.

121. Schröder, *U-Boote des Kaisers,* 171–72; FO 372/783 file 153865, no. 191292; *FRUS* 1915, Suppl., 516–20, 524–33, 547–48.

122. Note of Sept. 7, 1915, *FRUS* 1915, Suppl., 539–40.

123. Lansing to Wilson, Washington, Sept. 11, 1915, United States, *Lansing Papers,* 1:479–80.

124. Spindler, *Handelskrieg,* 2:271–72.

U-boat commanders that would surely avoid future incidents, but did not embrace cruiser rules. They construed Captain Schneider as having disobeyed orders, and they agreed to pay an indemnity, without, however, admitting that it was required. That is, they neither disavowed submarine policy nor admitted its illegality. Bernstorff knew this was inadequate, so he added the words "regrets and disavows this act," and he omitted the phrase "without acknowledging the international-legal obligation" to pay indemnity.[125] On that basis, the United States accepted Germany's note, but the *Lusitania* matter remained open.

The *Lusitania* was never formally settled because the United States continued to insist that Germany admit that unrestricted submarine warfare was illegal, and Germany steadfastly refused, even though Bethmann and the AA were increasingly anxious to have the United States intercede with Britain about the blockade and even about peace.[126] German leaders found such an admission "impossible," "not tolerated," a "humiliation," a "sign of weakness," and "unreasonable and dishonorable."[127] This emotional language reflected their rejection of what such an admission seemed to mean. Illegality was dishonorable, and German leaders were hypersensitive to Allied propaganda that had successfully labeled the Kaiserreich a criminal state. Yet, at the same time, their own arguments seemed to confirm that impression. Zimmermann told Ambassador Gerard (January 30, 1916) "that there was no longer any international law," and Bethmann and Wilhelm told him the same thing (May 3, 1916).[128] During the same conversation Kaiser and chancellor somewhat inconsequentially used Pohl's original argument, that "anyway the coming of the submarine has made a change in international law necessary."[129] And they repeated the navy's conviction that "Germany could not surrender the submarine," that it would fight against the American attempt at "wrenching the submarine weapon from our hands."[130] The navy had succeeded in convincing the civilian leadership and the Kaiser that abiding by cruiser rules effectively nullified submarines.

On February 16, 1916, Bernstorff delivered Germany's much-delayed reply to the third U.S. *Lusitania* note of seven months before. Still arguing that retaliation policies were legal, it said that Germany had limited its use of the submarine after the *Lusitania* was sunk, it regretted the sinking, and accepted liability for it.[131] Lansing, to whom Bernstorff had revealed Germany's probable reply, would have assented—though he found Germany's

---

125. Cf. Ibid., 2:272 with Bernstorff to Lansing, Washington, Oct. 5, 1915, *FRUS* 1915, Suppl., 560.

126. Lansing to Gerard, Washington, Jan. 26, 1916, *FRUS* 1916, Suppl., 150–51.

127. Botho Wedel (AA), cited by Wolff in his diary of Feb. 4, 1916, Wolff, *Tagebücher*, 1:345; Zimmermann, cited by Gerard, Gerard to Lansing, Berlin, Jan. 29, 1916, *FRUS* 1916, Suppl., 154; Bethmann in interview with Wiegand, Feb. 8, 1916, *FRUS* 1916, Suppl., 161–62; Tirpitz, *Politische Dokumente*, 335, 403; Karl von Einem, *Ein Armeeführer erlebt den Weltkrieg; persönliche Aufzeichnungen*, ed. Junius Alter (Leipzig, 1938), 213–14.

128. Gerard to Lansing, Berlin, Jan. 30, 1916, *FRUS* 1916, Suppl., 155; Gerard to Lansing, Berlin, May 3, 1916, ibid., 253–54.

129. Zimmermann, cited by Gerard to Lansing, Berlin, Jan. 30, 1916, *FRUS* 1916, Suppl., 155; Jagow, cited by Gerard to Lansing, Feb. 1, 1916, ibid., 156; Bethmann and the Kaiser, Gerard to Lansing, Berlin, May 3, 1916, ibid., 254.

130. Zimmerman, cited in Gerard to Lansing, Berlin, Feb. 7, 1916, *FRUS* 1916, Suppl., 160; Bethmann interview of Feb. 8, 1916, ibid., 161.

131. Bernstorff to Lansing, Feb. 16, 1916, *FRUS* 1916, Suppl., 171–72.

position not "satisfactory" but merely "acceptable"—had Germany not announced unrestricted submarine warfare against armed enemy ships (February 8, 1916).[132] That policy seemed to undo Germany's pledge of August 1915 to spare enemy passenger ships. As Bernstorff struggled with damage control, the *U-29* on March 23, 1916, mistakenly torpedoed the unarmed French passenger ship *Sussex,* which, despite fifty fatalities aboard, limped to port with easily identifiable pieces of torpedo wreckage in her hull.[133] Germany's first suggestion that an English mine might have been the culprit seemed a mockery.[134]

The *Sussex* was the last straw. The United States interpreted the attack as proof of a policy of system and deception. America, its note said, had waited for Germany to "square its policy with the recognized principles of humanity as embedded in the law of nations," but this latest incident had proved that the submarine was "utterly incompatible with the principles of humanity, the long-established and incontrovertible rights of neutrals, and the sacred immunities of non-combatants."[135] In short, the United States had withdrawn its recognition of the submarine as a legitimate weapon. If Germany did not stop unrestricted submarine warfare, the United States would break diplomatic relations.

In January 1916 Bethmann had given his imprimatur to Admiral Holtzendorff's sharpened warfare against armed merchant ships, and he had done so without consulting the AA.[136] Faced with unyielding U.S. opposition, he now retreated. Once again, a crisis gave him the leverage to defeat the navy and OHL; the Kaiser wavered, but in the end backed his chancellor. Before setting pen to paper, Bethmann made sure he understood exactly what the United States demanded.[137] In reply, the United States set down the customary rules.[138] Whereas the U.S. note on armed enemy merchantmen, released at the same time, amounted to new legislation, the U.S. reply on cruiser warfare as applied to submarines basically repeated the customary law. But it is noteworthy for two things. First, it emphasized the higher standard that warships must apply to neutral vessels before sinking them. An enemy merchantman might be sunk because "it is impossible to take it into port," but a neutral vessel "must not be sunk in any circumstances, except of gravest importance to the captor's state." The United States therefore restated the exceptional limit to destruction of neutral vessels that had been lost since February 1915. Second, the U.S. note specified what "bringing to safety" meant for the crews and passengers aboard both enemy and merchant vessels. Safety was fulfilled only if passengers were discharged within sight of land, and not in conditions of strong wind, rough seas, or thick or cold weather, nor if the lifeboats were open, overcrowded, small, unseaworthy, or insufficiently manned. Significantly, the

---

132. Lansing memorandum of conversation with Bernstorff, Feb. 17, 1916, *FRUS* 1916, Suppl., 172.

133. Statement of fact in *Sussex* case, accompanying note to German government of April 18, 1916, *FRUS* 1916, Suppl., 234–37.

134. First German *Sussex* note, April 10, 1916, *FRUS* 1916, Suppl., 227–29.

135. Lansing to Gerard, Washington, April 18, 1916, *FRUS* 1916, Suppl., 232–34.

136. Spindler, *Handelskrieg,* 3:86–87.

137. Gerard to Lansing, Berlin, April 25, 1916, *FRUS* 1916, Suppl., 244.

138. Memorandum on the status of armed merchant vessels, written on March 25, 1916, but made public on April 27, *FRUS* 1916, Suppl., 244–48. Memorandum on conduct of naval vessels toward merchant ships, enclosed in Lansing to Gerard, Washington, April 28, 1916, ibid., 252.

German note accepting cruiser warfare for all merchant ships, enemy and neutral (May 4, 1916), did not list these terms, though Lansing made sure that Germany had received them.[139] Instead, after a long prelude on the "illegal conduct of British warfare," Germany announced that its submarine commanders had received this order: "In accordance with the general principles of visit and search and destruction of merchant vessels recognized by international law, such vessels, both within and without the area declared as naval war zone, shall not be sunk without warning and without saving human lives, unless these ships attempt to escape or offer resistance."[140] This order applied cruiser rules to all merchant vessels, armed and unarmed, enemy and neutral, passenger liner and freighter, inside and outside the war zone. And it recognized that these rules were indeed "general principles" of international law, an admission that finally seemed to accept the constant U.S. contention that Germany's retaliatory decree of February 1915 had always been illegal. Actually, however, the German note remained consistent with the course Bethmann had outlined since October 1914, that Britain's hunger blockade justified unrestricted submarine warfare. Germany's consent to abide by cruiser rules was conditional on U.S. success in getting Britain to "observe the rules of international law universally recognized before the war," as the United States had expressed them in its notes of December 28, 1914, and November 5, 1915. Those notes were the first and the most complete protest it had filed against the British "blockade" and, if followed, would have nullified Britain's measures.[141] Although the United States explicitly rejected Germany's condition, it remained Germany's position, expressed at the end of its note, reserving to "itself complete liberty of decision" should Britain remain adamant.[142]

Behind its long dispute with the United States, and behind the even longer struggles inside the German government, there was a hidden theory of law that dictated Germany's intransigence, the inability of the civilian leadership to take advantage of diplomatic opportunity, and the unwillingness of the navy to use the U-boat to its best advantage. That theory might be called "weapons positivism."

Weapons Positivism

The navy always claimed that visit and search was impossible for submarines: in Tirpitz's succinct words, in practice accepting cruiser rules "means the complete abandonment of effective submarine warfare."[143] Not only was it possible, however—cruiser warfare was

---

139. Gerard to Lansing, Berlin, May 7, 1916, *FRUS* 1916, Suppl., 262.

140. German note of May 4, 1916, enclosed in Gerard to Lansing, Berlin, May 4, 1916, *FRUS* 1916, Suppl., 257–60.

141. The dates Germany cited were those when the protests were delivered. They were actually sent from Bryan to Page, Dec. 28, 1914, *FRUS* 1914, Suppl., 372–75; and Lansing to Page, Oct. 21, 1915, *FRUS* 1915, Suppl., 578–89.

142. Gerard to Lansing, Berlin, May 4, 1916, *FRUS* 1916, Suppl., 259–60; Lansing to Gerard, Washington, May 8, 1916, ibid., 263.

143. Tirpitz's report to Kaiser, Sept. 7, 1915, in Tirpitz, *Politische Dokumente,* 425; see also the long list of reasons given by submarine chief Bauer, submarine chief of the Flanders flotilla Lt. Karl Bartenbach, and Lt.

more successful for Germany's submarines than sinking without warning. Torpedoes often ran low and missed the target altogether; their sinkage rate was about 40 percent.[144] Deck guns were much more accurate. In the first and second U-boat campaigns (that is, February to September 1915 and February to May 1916), 85 percent of merchant sinkings followed cruiser rules. In the third campaign (October 1916 through January 1917), the percentage was 98.5.[145] Because by October 1916 Germany had many more, and improved, U-boats, the third campaign was very successful. Altogether, before Germany launched truly unrestricted submarine warfare in February 1917, its submarine commanders followed cruiser rules 94 percent of the time—actually, higher, since many ships were searched and then released without being sunk. In short, the celebrated cases of the *Lusitania, Arabic,* and *Sussex* were genuinely exceptional, yet Germany refused publicly to adopt legal methods as policy until May 1916, a stance that reaped worldwide infamy for over a year.

Even more shocking, perhaps, is the fact that when Germany publicly threw over the law and enforced on its U-boat captains sinking without warning, the sinkage rate climbed a mere 11.2 percent.[146] For this 11.2 percent, Imperial Germany brought the United States into the war against it.

Not only was Germany's stated policy at odds with its actual warfare, but the navy made matters much worse by refusing to use submarines under the limited, but entirely workable conditions of the law. Twice—once after the chancellor forced through the prohibition on sinking passenger liners (September 1915), and again after his victory in publicly accepting cruiser rules (May 1916)—the navy suspended submarine warfare altogether in the war zone.[147] This altogether ten-month suspension occurred without notice to the Kaiser and actually in defiance of his orders in the months from July to October 1916.[148] Extrapolating statistically from the U-boats' success after October 1916, scholars have estimated that the navy's enforced abstinence saved one million tons of shipping to Britain—approximately the amount that might have made the difference to the success of the unrestricted U-boat campaign after February 1917.[149]

It could be said that the German navy sank Germany's (slim) chances for victory twice: once by bringing the United States into the war, and once by refusing to use its submarines in their most successful method, that is, (almost) legally. These dysfunctional decisions were based on a quixotic clinging to unrestricted submarine warfare. That stance was due to more than stubbornness, ignorance, prestige, careerism, or anger at Britain's violations

---

Klaus Hansen (commander of *U-41*), June 28, 1915, in Spindler, *Handelskrieg*, 2:168–72; Bachmann's report to the Kaiser, Aug. 29, 1915, ibid., 279; the report of the chief of the Admiralty to the Kaiser, Berlin, Feb. 22, 1915, in Tirpitz, *Politische Dokumente*, 319; and Scheer's memorandum, "The meaning of our U-boat war," Sept. 30, 1915, ibid., 443–48.

144. Spindler, *Handelskrieg*, 2:184.

145. Schröder, *U-Boote des Kaisers*, 152, 203, 241.

146. Stegemann, *Deutsche Marinepolitik*, 72.

147. Spindler, *Handelskrieg*, 2:286–87; Schröder, *U-Boote des Kaisers*, 219–21.

148. Schröder, *U-Boote des Kaisers*, 228.

149. Assmann, *Deutsche Seestrategie*, 91; Stegemann, *Deutsche Marinepolitik*, 49–51, 64–48; Schröder, *U-Boote des Kaisers*, 407.

of law.[150] It reflected above all a fundamental assumption about the relation of war to law. Let us briefly analyze what amounted to the legal theory behind naval policy. It had three parts.

The grounding assertion was, as Tirpitz put it, that "submarine warfare is something completely new and thus outside of old international law; it is the same thing with aerial attacks," he added.[151] As we have seen, this conviction followed the doctrine of *non liquet,* or the postulate of gaps in the law. If you likewise believed either that there were no general principles from which one could extrapolate to fill those gaps, or you denied that principles such as humanity, discrimination, or proportionality were applicable, then you created a law-free zone in which whatever was not expressly forbidden was permitted. Germany acknowledged once the existence of general principles (which it expressed narrowly as "general principles of search and visit," rather than of saving noncombatant lives), in its note of May 4, 1916, but even then it held open the possibility of the law-free zone via reprisal for Britain's misdeeds. Reprisal was how civilian leaders created the *non liquet,* and navy officers, too, often used it to cover their actions.

Either way, the law-free zone cleared the path for the second stage in the argument, that a belligerent had the *right* to use the submarine weapon. Civilian leaders tended to establish that right by reference to self-preservation, or defending the homeland from starvation. Jurists often adduced the narrower German legal doctrine of self-defense (*Notwehr*). But the navy had a more appropriately martial idea. Tirpitz expressed it pithily like this: "Only such firmness [in insisting on unlimited warfare] can convince [other nations] of the existing, perfect right to use this form of war conduct, and elicit the impression of a decisive will to victory."[152] Unwavering, concentrated force came closest to creating the impact and (often only psychological, rather than strictly military) effectiveness that produced the presumption of legality. It was for this reason that Tirpitz had wanted to wait for a much larger submarine fleet before launching the submarine "blockade." It was for this reason that Behncke, Vanselow, and Graßhoff had called for extensive automatic contact mining and surprise aerial assaults to accompany unrestricted submarine warfare. And we have seen the same argument from Colonel Scheüch regarding flamethrowers and incendiary bombs. The right to use a particular weapon or method depended on the military might and will behind it.

But it would be incorrect to conclude that the navy was interested only in might and not in right. Quite the contrary. The navy was determined to get the submarine and what they took to be its essential manner of warfare recognized by the world as legal. Tirpitz's associate, Rear Admiral Albert Hopman, confided to his diary in September 1916: "It is essential to work with all political means on the USA so that it recognizes the justice and necessity of our unrestricted submarine policy."[153]

---

150. These are some of the reasons given in Schröder, *U-Boote des Kaisers,* 406; Stegemann, *Deutsche Marinepolitik,* 33.

151. Note of Tirpitz and Bachmann, Feb. 28, 1915, Tirpitz, *Politische Dokumente,* 324.

152. Tirpitz, mid- to late Feb. 1915, Tirpitz, *Politische Dokumente,* 312.

153. Hopman diary Sept. 2, 1916, Albert Hopman, *Das ereignisreiche Leben eines "Wilhelminers,"* ed. Michael Epkenhans (Munich: R. Oldenbourg, 2004), 865; repeated in his "Über die Weiterentwicklung der Marine,"

Vice Admiral Reinhard Scheer (future chief of the high seas fleet and future chief of the naval staff) provided the most detailed exposition of the navy's legal views in a high seas fleet memorandum of September 30, 1915, directed against the chancellor's recent victory sparing enemy passenger liners. The weakness of Germany's battleship fleet, he wrote, made the U-boat "the decisive weapon against England."[154] "Existing international law reckons only with surface warships. The essence of the U-boat is, like that of the mine, surprise underwater attack. Surface actions like stopping, searching papers, ship, and cargo, saving the crew in case of destruction, can only be done in rare cases without an obvious self-alienation [*Selbstentäußerung*]. Therefore they cannot be required of submarines." Scheer then drew the legal conclusions:

> The new being needs a new law. That is a natural development of law, as it is recognized in every area of human progress. It is not illegal. But the new law naturally produces resistance fed by contrary interests, and overcoming that requires work and energy. It is said that "international law can only be made by those with power." We have the power, if we defeat England. If we relinquish the only means by which we can defeat England, England will make sure that legal chains are attached to the submarine for all time, making it harmless to the English position of power.

The new weapon, law, and world power were thus inextricably tied together. Only by using the (currently) illegal weapon could one break the (British) system that made it illegal. Hopman at the naval ministry said the same thing. "The goal of the navy was to stop England's power-veto [*Machteinspruch*] of the development of Germany's sea- and world-power." That was why it was so critical to "press most energetically for international recognition of an international-legal principle [permitting unrestricted submarine warfare]."[155]

This is the reason that the navy emphatically rejected any limits to the submarine. As Scheer argued,

> We would saddle ourselves with the most dangerous encumbrance to our legal position if we—even only temporarily—tried to conduct submarine warfare by surface [cruiser] rules. We would thus be admitting that submarines can follow these rules and we would undermine our previous legal position. Because the impossibility of requiring submarines [to follow] these rules is the single moral ground for departing from them and for demanding new law for submarines.[156]

This is why the navy unilaterally stopped submarine warfare on the two clear occasions when the civilian leadership instituted variants of cruiser rules. It is why the navy opposed

July 7, 1916, in which he demanded "international recognition of the international-legal principle" covering unrestricted submarine warfare, 79–80. Spindler, *Handelskrieg,* 2:185: all naval officers agreed.

154. Scheer, "Die Bedeutung unseres U-Bootskrieges," Wilhelmshaven, Sept. 30, 1915, in Tirpitz, *Politische Dokumente,* 443–48.

155. Hopman memorandum for State Secretary of the Navy Eduard von Capelle, "Über die Weiterentwicklung der Marine," July 7, 1916, in Hopman, *Das ereignisreiche Leben,* 2:830–39, here 830, 837.

156. Scheer, "Die Bedeutung unseres U-Bootskrieges," in Tirpitz, *Politische Dokumente,* 446.

admitting publicly that German U-boats actually followed the rules. And it is why the navy hid the success of limited submarine warfare from the chancellor and the Kaiser. Only twice were Germany's leaders able to force the navy to divulge the statistics that proved that submarines could indeed follow the law and be effective; that knowledge helped the chancellor move public policy closer to the law (sparing passenger ships in September 1915, postponing unrestricted submarine warfare in February 1916, and ultimately accepting cruiser rules in May 1916).[157]

In Scheer's comment about "the essence" of the submarine, and its "self-alienation" if limited, the reader will recognize a narrow variant of war positivism. Recall that jurist Carl Lueder had written (1889) that "the formation of the law of war...flows from the nature of war"; "all warlike measures of violence which are required by the goal of war, must be used unlimitedly and cannot be restricted by a legal commandment."[158] Where Lueder had derived the law (of military necessity) from the alleged nature of war, the Wilhelminians derived it from the nature of weapons. This represents in the sphere of law the same technical trivialization visible in Imperial Germany's conduct of war—for example, in Erich Ludendorff's conception of the final March offensive of 1918 as essentially tactical, rather than strategic or even operational ("I forbid the word 'operation'").[159] Like the legal positivism dominant in Bismarckian Germany, weapons positivism rejected moral considerations as outside the purview of law, and it retained legal positivism's obeisance to state authority, which wielded the weapon in its own name and right.[160] But unlike legal positivism, which regarded written law (treaties) as solely valid and which therefore tended to be static, weapons positivism was radically fluid. Technological progress completely undermined and displaced written law. The engineer replaced the legislator.

Under the circumstances, one might expect that weapons positivism would have appealed mainly to military men. But the radicalization of the World War made it acceptable even to major German jurists like the preeminent constitutional lawyer and exemplar of legal positivism, Paul Laband. Concerning the *Lusitania,* Laband defended the submarine, arguing (1915) that "the use of a weapon is determined by its characteristics [*Beschaffenheit*], and the rules that arose for battle with other weapons, cannot be applied unchanged to the new weapon."[161] Weapons positivism, in addition to undercutting existing law, negated the principle of discrimination, whose development was one of the main features of international law in this period and which was taken to be fundamental to the existing laws of war. G. G. Phillimore's position (1915) was typical of jurists, including earlier

---

157. Schröder, *U-Boote des Kaisers,* 178–79, 196–97.

158. Carl Lueder, "Krieg und Kriegsrecht im Allgemeinen," in *Handbuch des Völkerrechts,* ed. Franz von Holtzendorff (Hamburg, 1889), 187.

159. See Hull, who explains the dysfunctional technicity of Wilhelminian military decision making in terms of its organizational culture: Isabel V. Hull, *Absolute Destruction: Military Culture and the Practices of War in Imperial Germany* (Ithaca, NY, 2005) for Ludendorff's words: 302.

160. On legal positivism, see Wolfgang Friedmann, *The Changing Structure of International Law* (New York, 1964), ch. 7; Leslie Green, "Legal Positivism," in *The Stanford Encyclopedia of Philosophy,* ed. Edward M. Zalta (Stanford, CA, 2009), http://plato.stanford.edu/archives/fall2009/entries/legal-positivism/.

161. "Der Lusitania-Fall," *Zeitschrift für Völkerrecht* 9 (1916): 181. This edition of the journal contains similar articles written by nineteen German jurists.

German writers, who rejected weapons positivism: "The nature of the warlike instrument should not be allowed to affect the duty of observing established rules of war."[162]

Weapons positivism has another important legal feature. Part of the allure of new weapons is that, for a time at least, only one party possesses them. If weapons determine law, then so does the first user, unilaterally. President Wilson expressed the widespread rejection of that principle, calling it "the manifest impropriety of a single nation's essaying to alter the understandings of nations."[163] Yet the conviction that a single nation could do precisely that was widespread among German leaders. It was part of a revolutionary view of law that held that the winner in war determined subsequent international law by itself; weapons positivism was only an indicator of this larger belief. We have seen Scheer's conviction that the winner of the World War would dictate future naval law: if Germany won, the submarine was safe; if Britain won, it was forever fettered. Tirpitz (and Hopman) thought the same; that is why they were so intent on not giving away the "right" of unlimited submarine warfare, for doing so would affect "the further conduct of the war and for all future time."[164] Ludendorff ended his account of total war (1935) with the sentence: "The policy of might, too, will finally decide what are, and what are not 'law and usages.'"[165]

One might interpret these utterances of military men as mere convenience, a legal-seeming way of discarding legal limits altogether. Bethmann Hollweg was a lawyer, not a military man, yet the conditions he set for safe violation of international law (military victory or impending defeat) suggest that, for the former case, he expected a victorious Germany to be able to dictate its version of the law to neutrals and of course to the defeated Allies.[166] The conviction among German jurists that Germany's views of the laws of war exemplified progress, as against those of the backward British, was widespread, but never so vehemently expressed as by Josef Kohler, the founding editor of the *Journal of International Law* (*Zeitschrift für Völkerrecht*). In 1916 he wrote that most nations had disqualified themselves from participating in the (re-)establishment of international law.[167] He rejected what the Allies insisted was valid international law because it rested on treaties and the "soap bubbles" of the Hague Conventions, both of which were illusory. "This mirage [*Wahngebilde*] of a community of nations which dictates the norms of international law and which as a rule decides conflicts, so that the house of nations is only now and again shaken by war, is long gone" (6). The hypocritical Allies and the un-neutral behavior of Norway, Holland, and Denmark meant that they could not be

---

162. G. G. Phillimore, "Bombardments," *Grotius Society* 1 (1916): 66; Franz von Holtzendorff, *Handbuch des Völkerrechts. Auf Grundlage europäischer Staatspraxis*, vol. 1, *Einleitung in das Völkerrecht* (Berlin, 1885), 133.

163. Wilson to Bryan, Washington, April 22, 1915, United States, *Lansing Papers*, 1:378.

164. Tirpitz's immediate report to the Kaiser, Berlin, Sept. 7, 1915, Tirpitz, *Politische Dokumente*, 424.

165. Erich Ludendorff, *The Nation at War*, trans. of *Der totale Krieg*, trans. A. S. Rappoport (London, 1936), 141.

166. Cf. Ernst Stenzel, *Die Kriegführung des deutschen Imperialismus und das Völkerrecht; zur Planung und Vorbereitung des deutschen Imperialismus auf die barbarische Kriegführung im Ersten und Zweiten Weltkrieg, dargestellt an den vorherrschenden Ansichten zu den Gesetzen und Gebräuchen des Landkrieges (1900–1945)* (Berlin, 1973), 30–34.

167. Josef Kohler, "Das neue Völkerrecht," *Zeitschrift für Völkerrecht* 9 (1916): 5–10. Hereafter cited parenthetically in text by page number.

regarded as "equal brother nations" (7). "Under no circumstances can these nations join us in an Areopagus in which every state has equal rights to dictate to the world the rules of international law" (8). Only German (neo-Hegelian) legal science was able to construe the law correctly and to recognize "that the real is also the rational" (6). "Science operates here like a legislator" (9). Kohler, like most other German legal writers during the war, identified three "great ideas" that would serve as the foundation for the new international law. These were: "[1] war is not fought between peoples, but between states, and thus only state organs are permitted to fight; [2] war may destroy, but destruction must be justified [*geheiligt*] by the end, it must only happen in order to defeat the enemy and all unnecessary injury must be avoided; [3] war must never put the civilian population in a lawless situation—occupied territory must be given a state order as soon as possible" (9). The reader will recognize the first and third of these as areas of major disagreement between Germany and most other European states since the 1870s. The second point was a fundamental principle of the Hague Rules (article 23e), but we have seen how easily expansive notions of military necessity canceled it. Kohler's rejection of previous treaties (meant to cover Germany's violation of Belgian neutrality[168]) and of international conventions cleared the field of existing law. The resulting tabula rasa was not to be filled by reference to custom or the practice of nations, that is, precedents: "when peoples like the English or the Americans, because they cannot analyze [*construiren*], work with precedents, they must renounce participation in the development of [legal] science and restrict themselves to supplying material" (10). Instead, the new international law would be the province of Germany. "After a victorious war, Germany will be so strengthened that we can take over the protection of international law" (10).

Kohler's language was more emotional and stark than others', but his legal position was the norm among German jurists.[169] The widespread fear that international law had broken down, interpreted by others to be a result of Germany's own policies and actions, was interpreted by German legal writers as evidence that no international community actually existed. On the model of the Bismarckian sovereign state of neo-Hegelian interpretation, they reasoned that international law would henceforth be created by the realities of power, that is, by a single authority whose predominance, created and assured by its military power, established its utter sovereignty (unlimited by external law) and at the same time proved its alignment with human progress. In short, Germany was, or after its victory soon would be, the monadic, sovereign lawgiver to the world.

Actual policy makers did not think in such lofty terms. But their assumptions about state sovereignty, state self-preservation, military necessity, weapons positivism, and their chafing at the strictures laid on them by international laws developed by a community

---

168. Josef Kohler, "Die Neutralität Belgiens und die Festungsverträge," *Zeitschrift für Völkerrecht* 9 (1916): 298–309.

169. Martti Koskenniemi, *The Gentle Civilizer of Nations: The Rise and Fall of International Law, 1870–1960* (Cambridge, 2001), 229. The jurists were themselves typical of the educated bourgeoisie; historian Georg v. Below 1917 wrote "the ideas of liberty, equality, and fraternity have been transcended by the German ideas of 1914, duty, order, justice," cited in Klaus Böhme, *Aufrufe und Reden deutscher Professoren im Ersten Weltkrieg* (Stuttgart, 1975), 24.

of states with interests different from their own made their policy decisions and their public justifications of them consonant with the jurists' doctrines, even though they were not based on them.[170] The countervailing pressure exerted by the chancellor and the AA, mostly primed by their fear of the political consequences of illegal actions, was ultimately not strong enough to win out against the military view backed by vocal (and often orchestrated) public opinion.

Imperial Germany did not win the war, so this experiment in revolutionary international law was not carried out. But Germany's methods, weapons, arguments, and justifications were facts; they elicited reprisals in kind (that is, the use of the same methods or weapons), counterarguments, and new developments. How much did Germany's conduct make or affect later international law?

Postwar International Law

In the Washington Treaty of 1922 the principal Allies (the United States, Britain, France, Italy, and Japan) set down their view of the law regarding submarines and poison gas.[171] "Asphyxiating, poisonous or other gases, and all analogous liquids, materials or devices" were prohibited outright (article 5). The treaty applied the same cruiser rules to enemy and neutral merchant vessels, making them subject to attack only if they resisted visit and search, and liable to destruction only after the crew and passengers were saved (article 1[1]). Submarines were explicitly held to the "universal rules" of cruiser warfare (article1[2]). But the Washington Treaty was never ratified, nor was a kind of successor to it, the Treaty of London of April 22, 1930, whose article 22 subjected all naval warships, including submarines, to cruiser rules. Those rules were therefore repeated once again in the Treaty of London of November 6, 1936.[172] Both London treaties contained the U.S. specifications of "safety," holding that favorable "sea and weather conditions," "proximity of land, or the presence of another vessel" were required before the ship's lifeboats met the "safe" criterion (rule 2).

The interwar codes therefore ratified the U.S.-German compromise of May 1916: the submarine was recognized as a legitimate weapon, so long as it followed cruiser rules; but the conditions under which destruction was permitted, the status of armed merchantmen, and the other questions remained open.

---

170. "No other power showed as little understanding for the legal order among nations as did Germany": Hankel, *Leipziger Prozesse,* 153.

171. Treaty Relating to the Use of Submarines and Noxious Gases in Warfare, Washington, February 6, 1922, full text at http://www.icrc.org/ihl.nsf/WebPrint/270-FULL?Open Document.

172. Procès-verbal relating to the Rules of Submarine Warfare set forth in Part IV of the Treaty of London of April 22, 1930 [and] London, November 6, 1936, full text at http://www.icrc.org/ihl.nsf/WebPrint/330-FULL?OpenDocument.

World War II swiftly returned to the cycle of reprisal and unrestricted sinkings on both sides.[173] The intervention of the Second World War (and subsequent conflicts) makes it hard to discern the lingering effects of the First World War on the law. We must again return to the San Remo Manual of 1994, which, though it is not binding law, provides the fullest international discussion and codification of the modern law of sea warfare.

With the exception of the treatment of armed enemy merchantmen, the San Remo Manual generally upholds the Allies' view of the rules of naval warfare. The submarine is a legitimate weapon against commercial vessels only if it abides by the cruiser rules as specified by the United States in 1916 and in the London Treaties of 1930 and 1936 (paragraphs 45, 139, 151).[174] Neutral merchant vessels are liable to destruction only under extraordinary circumstances of un-neutral service or resistance (paragraph 67). Enemy merchant vessels may be sunk (following cruiser rules) with somewhat more latitude, but the participants concluded that "mere reference to military exigencies does not suffice to justify the destruction."[175] In short, a *policy* of destruction would not seem to have been upheld. Enemy passenger ships may not be destroyed unless they carry military personnel or material (paragraph 140), and neutral passenger ships may not be sunk under any circumstances (paragraph 152). Ruses of war are permitted (paragraphs 109, 110). Armed neutral merchantmen are not liable to attack solely by virtue of their armament (paragraph 69). War zones are legal, but all the rules of sea warfare still apply within them; they must be proportionate to military needs and capabilities, they must be notified, and legitimate neutral shipping must be provided with safe routes (paragraphs 105, 106).[176] Regarding automatic contact mines, San Remo repeats and slightly strengthens the Hague Rules of 1907, thus requiring that belligerents exercise control, make uncontrolled mines harmless, notify, and provide safe routes for neutral shipping (paragraphs 80–92). Neutral compliance with war zones, blockades, navicert systems, and the like may not be construed as un-neutral behavior (paragraphs 107, 122). San Remo says nothing explicit about the right of enemy merchantmen to resist capture, but seems to uphold it, since the crews are considered prisoners of war (paragraph 165d).[177]

In addition to these specific rules, San Remo expresses the general principles behind them and which limit all belligerent actions. These are: the methods or weapons of warfare are not unlimited; civilians and other protected persons and nonmilitary property must be distinguished from combatants and military objects; military objectives must be limited to those offering "a definite military advantage"; reasonable precautions must be

---

173. Richard Dean Burns, "Regulating Submarine Warfare, 1921–41: A Case Study in Arms Control and Limited War," *Society for Military History* 35, no. 2 (April 1971): 56–63.

174. 1994 San Remo Manual on International Law Applicable to Armed Conflicts at Sea, in *Documents on the Laws of War,* ed. Adam Roberts and Richard Guelff (Oxford, 2004), 573–606.

175. Louise Doswald-Beck, ed., *San Remo Manual on International Law Applicable to Armed Conflicts at Sea* (Cambridge, 1995), 210.

176. On proportionality: ibid., 182–83.

177. However, so are crews of neutral merchantmen engaging in hostilities (para. 165e).

taken in targeting; unnecessary suffering must be avoided; and indiscriminate methods or weapons are prohibited (paragraphs 38–46).[178]

Both the specific and the general rules make up a very lengthy list in effect refuting the Imperial German arguments of World War I. Although the First World War rarely seems to have surfaced in the discussions, the fundamental issues it raised are addressed again and again and developed in the direction of the Allied views.

The one exception in naval warfare concerns armed enemy merchant vessels. These are now legitimate military objectives, if they are "armed to an extent that they could inflict damage to a warship" (paragraph 60f). Discussants acknowledged that this paragraph changed the traditional rule, and it was controversial. Some representatives argued that since targeting armed enemy merchantmen was done under cover of reprisal in both world wars, "the belligerent States themselves had considered [such] attacks...illegal."[179] Others made the Imperial German argument that a nation with an inferior surface fleet must be allowed to take other measures. In the end, the change was approved not on that ground, but because it was "unrealistic" to expect enemy forces to distinguish offensive from defensive armament.[180] Lansing had thought the same thing.[181]

Concerning the use of other new weapons, subsequent law is mixed. There is no current codification of air war, including the rules regarding aerial bombardment.[182] In 1923 the principal Allies and the Netherlands drafted a code for the Hague that was never ratified.[183] It prohibited bombing "for the purpose of terrorizing the civilian population" or forcing the payment of requisitions or contributions to an occupant (articles 22, 23); it restricted bombing to military targets (article 24). The massive bombings on both sides during the Second World War, in part to instill terror, overlaid the slender beginnings of the First World War.

Poison gas is much more definitively rejected and has a much clearer lineage to the First World War. Article 171 of the Treaty of Versailles stated that "asphyxiating, poisonous or other gases and all analogous liquids, materials or devices" were prohibited, and that same phrase was repeated in the 1922 Washington Treaty and in the 1925 Geneva Protocol prohibiting poison gas and bacteriological weapons, written under the auspices of the League of Nations.[184] Although Fascist Italy and Imperial Japan used poison gas, the 1925 Geneva Protocol has been ratified and followed to a much greater extent than any other rule of warfare. Since 1970 a further sixty-three states have adhered to the Geneva Protocol.[185]

---

178. Newer prohibitions in this list include the unnecessary damage to the natural environment and ordering that an action will result in no survivors.

179. Doswald-Beck, *San Remo Manual,* 149.

180. Ibid., 150–51.

181. The Committee on the Legal Status of Submarines had originally recommended that arming of merchant ships cease, but it dropped that view after Sir John Macdonell's objections: H. Goudy et al., "Report of the Committee on the Legal Status of Submarines," *Transactions of the Grotius Society* 4 (1918): xlii, xliv.

182. William Hays Parks, "Air War and the Law of War," *Air Force Law Review* 32 (1990): 1–225.

183. 1923 Hague Rules of Aerial Warfare, in Roberts and Guelff, *Documents,* 140–53.

184. Roberts and Guelff, *Documents,* 155–67, including the 1925 Geneva Protocol for the Prohibition of the Use in War of Asphyxiating, Poisonous or Other Gases, and of Bacteriological Methods of Warfare.

185. Ibid., 157. This discussion follows Roberts and Guelff.

It remains uncertain whether the protocol applies to tear gas as well. In 1930, Britain interpreted it as doing so, and France joined it, thus abandoning its position in the Great War. The modern trend seems to be in strengthening the prohibition: including tear gas and other nonlethal gases, and in banning not just first use, but subsequent use covered by reprisal. Indeed, first use of poison gas is now considered prohibited by customary law and thus applicable to non-signatories.

If Germany's use of poison gas has been entirely rejected, the flamethrower and similar incendiaries have been permitted for use against troops and military targets, but not against civilians or their property. That is the essence of Protocol III of the prodigiously titled 1980 UN Convention on Prohibitions or Restrictions on the Use of Certain Conventional Weapons Which May Be Deemed to Be Excessively Injurious or to Have Indiscriminate Effects.[186]

Despite the uncertain status of some of these rules, the trend in legal development has clearly been to expand the principles of the pre-1914 Hague and Geneva rules. This development has occurred not because of victor's justice, though the victors certainly pressed for them at Versailles and in postwar conventions, but because these rules and principles are seen by most nations as protecting them from the effects of warfare pursued with few or no limits.

---

186. Protocol III, ibid., 515–60.

Reprisals

Prisoners of War and Allied Aerial Bombardment

Reprisal is the most direct means by which a belligerent may try to force an opponent to behave within the law. International-legal skeptics of the time believed that reprisal was the only sanction upholding international law, but even proponents of international law agreed that "reprisals cannot be dispensed with, because without them illegitimate acts of warfare would be innumerable."[1] But reprisals could just as easily destroy the law as uphold it: they hit the innocent, rather than the guilty; they used methods otherwise held to be illegal, they were hard to distinguish from mere revenge; and they could lead to vicious spirals of counter-reprisal. Lieber's first modern code of war law (1863) thus cautioned that retaliation, as he called it,

> will therefore never be resorted to as a measure of mere revenge, but only as a means of protective retribution, and, moreover, cautiously and unavoidably; that is to say, retaliation shall only be resorted to after careful inquiry into the real occurrence, and the character of the misdeeds that may demand retaliation. Unjust or inconsiderate retaliation removes the belligerents farther and farther from the mitigating rules of a regular war, and by rapid steps leads them nearer to the internecine wars of savages.[2]

---

1. Lassa Oppenheim, *International Law: A Treatise* (London, 1905), 2:259; cf. Germany, Großer Generalstab, *Kriegsbrauch im Landkriege,* Kriegsgeschichtliche Einzelschriften (Berlin, 1902), 2–3.

2. Francis Lieber, *Instructions for the Government of Armies of the United States in the Field, General Orders No. 100, 24 April 1863,* in *The Laws of Armed Conflicts: A Collection of Conventions, Resolutions and Other Documents,* ed. Dietrich Schindler and Jiri Toman (Geneva, 1988), art. 28.

Lieber's language reminds us to distinguish reprisal from the other three R's: retorsion, retaliation, and reciprocity, for many authors used these loosely or interchangeably.[3] Retorsion involves a legal, though unpleasant, response to a legal but unfriendly state action. Retaliation and reciprocity are closer to each other. In the seventeenth century, retaliation meant an exact, mirror response to an act, but that meaning was later displaced by the looser sense of "any action taken in response to the earlier conduct of another State."[4] Reciprocity fulfills the original meaning of an exact mirroring of treatment. While retorsion uses legal means, retaliation and reciprocity may drift into the illegal. Reprisal differs from all three by always employing illegal means, but doing so with the aim of returning a scofflaw to legal behavior. The aim therefore excuses the illegality of the method.[5] The distinction among mere retaliation with no legal object, exact reciprocity, and justified reprisal is critical to understanding what happened in the World War.

In 1914 the law of reprisal remained uncodified.[6] The Russian draft code that provided the basis for discussion at the Brussels Conference of 1874 included three articles designed to reduce reprisals in several ways: by making them exceptional, restricting them to humane means "as far as shall be possible," and requiring that they be initiated only on the basis of firm proof, under order of the commander in chief, and in proportion to the offense.[7] Fundamental disagreements among the European states prevented the approval of any articles regulating reprisal, an impasse continuing right through the two Hague conferences. The law of reprisal remained customary.

Nevertheless, the law continued to develop in the direction of greater limitation, a trend visible in the prewar writings of jurists. British writers were most punctilious. The official manual on land warfare (1912) specified in detail when and how reprisals were to be used. Though its authors considered reprisals "indispensable as a last resource," they believed that elaborate investigation should precede them, and even afterward it might be wiser to refrain. And they underscored that reprisals must cease immediately with the infraction.[8] French writers detailed less and thus limited less. Robert Jacomet (1913), following the Hague example, omitted a section on reprisal, while Antoine Pillet (1901) confined himself to arguing that reprisal should not be used against civilians as the Germans had done in 1870.[9]

---

3. See John Westlake, *International Law; Part II: War* (Cambridge, 1907), 2:6–8, 69–70, 112–13; Oppenheim, *International Law,* 2:31–41. The British manual of war also used reprisal and retaliation interchangeably; see Colonel J. D. Edmonds and Lassa Oppenheim, *Land Warfare: An Exposition of the Laws and Usages of War on Land, for the Guidance of Officers of His Majesty's Army* (London, 1912), para. 456.

4. Shane Darcy, "The Evolution of the Law of Belligerent Reprisals," *Military Law Review* 175 (2003): 186.

5. The best account is Frits Kalshoven, *Belligerent Reprisals* (Leiden, 1971).

6. See chapter 3.

7. Arts. 69–71 of the Russian draft: Geoffrey Best, *Humanity in Warfare: The Modern History of the International Law of Armed Conflicts* (New York, 1980), 171. The final Declaration of Brussels (1874): Dietrich Schindler and Jiri Toman, eds., *The Laws of Armed Conflicts* (Geneva, 1988), 25–34.

8. Edmonds and Oppenheim, *Land Warfare,* 97–98; similarly, Thomas Erskine Holland, *The Laws of War on Land* (Oxford, 1908), 60–61.

9. Robert Jacomet, *Les lois de la guerre continentale* (Paris, 1913); Antoine Pillet, *Les lois actuelles de la guerre* (Paris, 1901), 209–12.

Despite the fact that they allowed greater sway to reprisal, German writers, including the most pro-military Carl Lueder (1889), recognized that custom and "civilization" were hedging reprisal through the requirement of proportionality, prior investigation, control by a high-level commander, and distinguishing between individual atrocity (which ought to be exempt from reprisal) and government policy (its proper target). However, Lueder concluded that the demands of war (*Kriegsräson*) were paramount and "not to be excluded by considerations of humanity," where reprisal was concerned.[10] The German government never printed an official war manual, but the closest thing, the 1902 General Staff compendium, simply quoted Lueder.[11] Nevertheless, Christian Meurer, writing after the Second Hague Conference, regretted the lack of codified limits or even prohibition of reprisal and favored the humanitarian standards of the Brussels Conference.[12]

The Great War was disfigured by wave after wave of violent reprisals exercised with lethal stubbornness, particularly against prisoners of war. The reprisal policies of Britain, France, and Germany differed from one another, and generally they reflected the spectrum expressed by their national prewar writers. These policies reveal basic assumptions about international law, its operation via sanctions in wartime, and the degree of self-identification with the "civilized" standards inherent in it. But reprisal was also strongly governed by state decision-making structures, especially the strength of military versus civilian leaders, the independence of unit and camp commanders, and the integration or disorder of policy making at the center. We will focus on those points that the states themselves had raised: (1) Did reprisals genuinely aim to reestablish the law? (2) Were they based on proof of wrongdoing? (3) Who made the decision? (4) How quickly were they adopted as policy? and (5) Were they proportionate?

Expectations

The belligerents entered the war with clear expectations about how prisoners of war should be treated. The Hague rules of land warfare of 1899, slightly amended in 1907, had merely set down these expectations without extending protections, except for requiring each state to set up a central office to collect and coordinate information on prisoners.[13] The gist of the rules was that prisoners were to be "humanely treated," the captor state being responsible for their maintenance and charged with providing food, lodging, and clothing "on the same footing" as the captor's own troops (articles 4 and 7). These same principles were

---

10. Carl Lueder, "Das Landkriegsrecht im Besonderen," in *Handbuch des Völkerrechts*, vol. 4, ed. Franz von Holtzendorff (Hamburg, 1889), 437, 392.

11. Germany, *Kriegsbrauch*, 16.

12. Christian Meurer, *Die Haager Friedenskonferenz*, vol. 2, *Das Kriegsrecht der Haager Konferenz* (Munich, 1907), 123, 135, 152n6.

13. Annex to the Convention (1907), arts. 14–16, in *Documents on the Laws of War*, ed. Adam Roberts and Richard Guelff (Oxford, 2004), 73–84.

contained in the manuals of all three nations and should have been uncontroversial.[14] Although the Hague Rules pronounced the principles, they did not specify the details. They also allowed captors to use non-officer prisoner labor, though it must "not be excessive and shall have no connection with the operations of the war" (article 6), which were not defined. Furthermore, wages from that work could be deducted for "the cost of their maintenance," a provision that contradicted the captor state's responsibility for upkeep. Every vagueness and loophole provided grounds for misbehavior, suspicion, and reprisal.

Despite their expectations, none of the belligerents had actually prepared for their prisoners in 1914. There were no camps, logistical plans, or organization. The immediate burden of prisoners was much greater on Germany, for the partial success of the Schlieffen Plan netted over 650,000 prisoners by December 1914; France had only about 46,000.[15] But even in France and Britain, lodging and conditions were inadequate for some time.[16] However, these failings did not spark reprisal. Reprisal developed from policy.

Beginning the Cycle

The dictates of presumed "military necessity" operated from the beginning in Germany's prisoner-of-war policies. An August 31, 1914, order of the German Eighth Army noted that "feeding the [Russian prisoners of war being transported back from the front lines] is not possible because, due to the uncertainty of the eastern army's supply lines, all food to hand must be reserved for the German troops....Prisoners must be treated strictly....They are not to be given water at first; while they are in the vicinity of the battlefield it is good for them to be in a broken physical condition."[17]

Meanwhile, treatment of POWs already in Germany at first followed the Hague standard, but swiftly drifted away from its protections. On August 19, Bavarian War Minister Otto Freiherr Kress von Kressenstein interpreted the Hague rules on prisoners to his subordinates. "Prisoners of war are to be treated humanely," he wrote, "but without inappropriate consideration." Their parcels were to be limited, so that they did not enjoy "plenty,

---

14. Edmonds and Oppenheim, *Land Warfare,* arts. 66, 88, in general: 54–116; French instruction of March 21, 1893, discussion in Georges Cahen-Salvador, *Les prisonniers de guerre (1914–1919)* (Paris, 1929), 21–26; Germany: "Regulativ über die Behandlung, Verpflegung pp. der Kriegsgefangenen nach erfolgtem Eintreffen in den Gefangenendepots" (July 30, 1870), and "Bestimmungen über die Unterbringung der Kriegsgefangenen" (April 23, 1896), printed in *UA,* 3rd ser., vol. 3, pts. 1 and 2, 865–71; see discussion in Uta Hinz, *Gefangen im Großen Krieg. Kriegsgefangenschaft in Deutschland 1914–1921,* Schriften der Bibliothek für Zeitgeschichte (Essen, 2006), 65–69.

15. Jochen Oltmer, "Unentbehrliche Arbeitskräfte: Kriegsgefangene in Deutschland 1914–1918," in *Kriegsgefangene im Europa des Ersten Weltkriegs,* ed. Jochen Oltmer (Paderborn, 2006), 75; Cahen-Salvador, *Prisonniers,* 45–46.

16. For comparative conditions and treatment: Heather Jones, *Violence against Prisoners of War in the First World War: Britain, France, and Germany, 1914–1920* (Cambridge, 2011).

17. Cited in Alan Kramer, *Dynamic of Destruction: Culture and Mass Killing in the First World War* (Oxford, 2007), 63.

while our troops in the field suffer want."[18] Eleven days later, his mild admonition was far exceeded by orders from Berlin. The newly created Quarters Department (Unterkunftsdepartement), which was in effect the prisoner-of-war department, expected to capture over half a million more prisoners.

> Because of the terrible atrocities that our troops face in enemy territory (poisonings, boiling water, dumdum bullets) and especially because of bitterness that Russians in East Prussia have hacked off or shot through the right arms of youngsters fourteen to seventeen years old, so that they may never serve in the army, the following principle was adopted: "Only the most necessary attention will be given to prisoner health, and none at all to their comfort." If many of them die [*Wenn größere Abgänge bei ihnen entstehen*], it cannot be helped. There is no problem that they will camp without tents or shelter in the autumn; our troops in 1870/71 had to do the same.[19]

This order was taken from revenge, not as reprisal.[20] The Prussian war ministry never sent it to the Auswärtiges Amt, nor did it notify the Allies. It was based on the hysterical rumors of the war's beginning, uninvestigated and, as it turned out, false. It was also taken at the height of Germany's military success.

The flush of presumed victory was the background for another enunciation of principles on September 11. Colonel Emil von Friedrich, head of the Unterkunfts-Departement and thus chief administrator of Germany's prisoners of war, noted that the "sharpest discipline" was to be maintained in the camps; "food is to be kept as plain as at all possible."[21] "The principle for all measures is consideration for the health of our own land, and insofar as that principle requires, to pay attention to the health of the prisoners, but all further measures for better treatment and comfort are out of the question." Friedrich then informed his readers of potential plans in the event of victory to transfer French and British prisoners to German-occupied Russia, and Russian prisoners to occupied Belgium and France. That would permit "exploitation of enemy territory for their provisioning" and then their direct transport home via the sea, thus "sparing and protecting our own land against using up food and against epidemics and infectious disease."

These examples show that virtually from the beginning of the war, Germany's application of the Hague principles was provisional.[22] Not only military necessity could weaken or cancel them, but also the army's unverified suspicions about the enemy's behavior, and the imperative (that grew ever stronger) to spare Germany's own slender resources (of food, personnel, clothing, medicine, doctors, heating coal, and transportation infrastructure—the lack of all of which directly affected prisoner welfare). Friedrich's report of the

---

18. Kress to the deputy commanders in Bavaria, Munich, Aug. 19, 1914, BayKrA, M Kr. 1630.

19. Von Bucher to Kress, Berlin, no. 3076, Aug. 30, 1914, BayKrA, M Kr. 1630.

20. Cf. Heather Jones, *Violence against Prisoners,* 73.

21. Friedrich, Nr. 784/9/9.14.U3, Berlin, Sept. 11, 1914, BayKrA, M Kr. 1631.

22. See the excellent discussion in Hinz, *Gefangen im Großen Krieg,* 61–70, and Heather Jones, *Violence against Prisoners,* 73–78.

deliberations inside the war ministry suggests that Imperial Germany would not have behaved more magnanimously in victory—indeed, all of these examples come from the time when Germany's leaders thought they were about to win the war.

By mid October 1914, neutral inspection visits to POW camps began. These provided more systematic information than did the accidental accounts of escaped prisoners or letters that had somehow evaded censorship. As a consequence of the inspection reports, on October 28 the French army reduced its German prisoners' meat ration by 100 grams, and on December 15, it began mirroring German treatment by reducing the wages it had hitherto paid to officer prisoners.[23] From these small beginnings reprisals between France and Germany proliferated. Responding to German conditions, some of them reprisals themselves for (sometimes alleged) French conditions, France reduced and delayed mail, confiscated letters of complaint, reduced food rations, blocked aid packages, held noncommissioned officers to work like troops, stopped paying medical corps members, docked pay, invoked bread-and-water punishment for prisoners sentenced for infractions, refused to reveal lists of prisoners working in factories or to explain court judgments against prisoners, etc. The reprisals on the German side were more severe, but mirroring food and clothing restrictions harmed the health of Germans held prisoner and made their (long) captivity hellish.

The French System of Reciprocal Reprisal

The French internal discussion on reprisal policy began on August 10, 1914, with the capture of a German medical corps major who was carrying five boxes of bullets with exposed lead cores. Such "dumdum" ammunition was likely to mushroom upon impact and for that reason was prohibited by Hague Declaration 3 (1899).[24] An early French war ministry draft (August 14), never sent or acted upon, disclosed a first reaction. It cited the use of illegal ammunition and other "criminal acts" by German soldiers and called for "executing without delay the same number of German prisoners...as the French victims, choosing the prisoners from among the highest-ranking officers and beginning with the most senior."[25] That phrase was crossed out and followed by one calling for the punishment of the responsible senior commanders. Two weeks later, a similar draft, this time by the French foreign office, was contemplated on the basis of information that the "Belgian atrocities" of August 1914 "are not the result of isolated acts of indiscipline, but instead *a system ordered by the commanders themselves.*" To stop the descent into "barbarism," the draft threatened

---

23. Reduction from 350 grams/day to 250 grams/day: Ministry of war report no. 29, May 20, 1916, SHAT 6N 111; Cahen-Salvador, *Prisonniers*, 47. Some French POW-camp commanders evidently on their own had reduced bread and meat rations in late August; the minister of war countermanded the bread order, but permitted a reduction in meat portions that were then made standard by the order of Oct. 28: Minister of War Millerand to commanding generals of regions 9 through 19, no. 10.091-I/II, Bordeaux, Sept. 18, 1914, 7N 161.

24. 1899 Hague Declaration 3 concerning Expanding Bullets, in Roberts and Guelff, *Documents*, 63–66.

25. War minister to foreign minister, Aug. 14, 1914, MAE Corr. Polit. 1097.

to execute one interned civilian German for each noncombatant French citizen killed; for each burned village, "one or more" German officer prisoners; and for other crimes, such as killing the wounded or shooting at ambulances, "analogous reprisals according to the gravity of each case."[26] Again, the threatened reprisals were crossed out, and, again, the note was never sent—"impractical" is written on the top. Instead, Henri Fromageot, the chief international lawyer at the foreign ministry, began systematically collecting "authentic testimony" of German violations for worldwide publication and for official protests to Germany and to the neutral signatories of the Hague Conventions.[27] Protests began on August 16 and were repeated, always citing new incidents, every few days.

Rather than kill Germans in their hands, the French government instead adopted the policy of (limited) reciprocity. Where possible, it aimed at "an exact reciprocity" of treatment, as in most of the instances listed above.[28] But there were limits—for example, in rationing. When French authorities greatly reduced the meat (and later, bread) ration in December 1915, those calories were made good by substituting legumes: German prisoners apparently gained weight on the new diet.[29] The desire to extract prisoner labor was probably dominant, though perhaps not exclusive, in such decisions.[30] As German treatment of POWs worsened in 1916, the French ministry of war was also cautious "to avoid carefully all useless meanness or vexation that might have unfortunate consequences on the lot of our compatriots in Germany."[31] Until the waning months of the war, Germany held more French prisoners than France did German, making fear of counter-reprisal an active factor in policy making. Beyond considerations of utility, France may also have limited its reciprocation for higher reasons: it never followed Germany in erecting entire camps dedicated to reprisal, for example.[32] And even its most potentially lethal reprisal, aerial bombing of German cities, was hedged with restraints.

Aerial Bombing Reprisals

In June 1915 the Allies began the occasional aerial bombing of German urban areas as reprisal against German air attacks on French and British towns, which had begun in

---

26. Handwritten draft memo from foreign minister to Kaiser Wilhelm II and Secretary Jagow, Aug. 28, 1914, MAE Corr. Polit. 1098.

27. Foreign ministry (in Fromageot's hand) to interior, finance, and naval ministries (justice crossed out), Aug. 13, 1914; For. Min. memorandum, Aug. 16, 1914, MAE Corr. Polit. 1097.

28. The phrase "une exacte réciprocité" occurs frequently in reprisal documents: SHAT 6N 100.

29. Ministry of war report no. 29, May 20, 1916, SHAT 6N 111; Min. of War Galliéni to all commanders, no. 23.310 6/10, Paris, Dec. 3, 1915, 7N 161.

30. C. Vérand (min. of war, prisoner division) to commanding generals of Paris, Lyon, and Regions, no. 36.218, Paris, Apr. 19, 1916, 7N 161; Commission Interministerielle de prisonniers de guerre, protocol of the meeting of Jan. 10, 1916, 7N 1993.

31. Weekly journal of the inspectorate of prisoners of war, Sept. 10–16, 1916, 6N 110.

32. Jean Cahen, "Note pour le cabinet militaire du président du conseil," min. of war, Paris, Sept. 5, 1918, 6N 111.

August 1914.[33] From January 1916 to November 1917 France launched thirty-nine reprisal air raids on Germany.[34] The pace accelerated in 1918, partly due to increased capability, partly in response to continuing German raids on London and Paris—the last attack on Paris was during the night of September 15, 1918.[35] Altogether, Allied bombs killed 746 Germans; in Britain to mid-February 1918, 1,284 people had been killed by German raids; in Paris alone 275 had died from forty-five German air attacks (not counting the 1,600 killed by the "Big Bertha" artillery shelling).[36] In all cases, most of the dead were civilians. The comparison shows that aerial bombardment was relatively limited during World War I, and that Germany engaged in it first, longer, and produced about twice as many casualties as did Allied bombing. However, assessing the relative meaning of aerial bombardment requires that we look at the law, expectations, motives, and goals. These show that France was the most restrained belligerent.

In 1914 international law governing aerial bombardment was underdeveloped. The 1907 Hague Declaration (XIV) prohibition of launching projectiles or explosives from balloons was never signed by France, Germany, Russia, Italy, and Japan, so it was not binding during the war.[37] In its place, states reckoned by analogy from the Hague rules of land warfare, which prohibited attacking or bombarding undefended towns, villages, and buildings (article 25). The extension of that principle to naval warfare (Convention IX, 1907) contained an important exception for "military works," depots, and factories that could be used for war (article 2). "Unavoidable damage" to civilian lives or property while targeting those objects was justified, though the article admonished commanders to "take all due measures" to reduce harm.

Just before the war, Britain and Germany had completed a mutual agreement to interpret "defended area" to mean "a locality supplied with military works that can protect it effectively against enemy attack. Thus a commercial port may not be considered as a fortified place by the sole fact that there are forts or batteries designed to defend its maritime approaches."[38] This note had not been signed by August 1914, but Britain assumed Germany would abide by it. When Germany did not, proved by its naval bombardment of

---

33. See chapter 7 for a discussion of Germany's decision to bomb civilian areas. On the first Allied reprisal raids: Christian Geinitz, "The First Air War against Noncombatants: Strategic Bombing of German Cities in World War I," in *Great War, Total War: Combat and Mobilization on the Western Front, 1914–1918*, ed. Roger Chickering and Stig Förster (Cambridge, 2000), 212.

34. Andrew Barros, "Strategic Bombing and Restraint in 'Total War,' 1915–1918," *Historical Journal* 52, no. 2 (2009): 421.

35. Paris: Susan R. Grayzel, "'The Souls of Soldiers': Civilians under Fire in First World War France," *Journal of Modern History* 78, no. 3 (Sept. 2006): 613. Hankel judges the 1918 raids on Paris as strictly for purposes of terror: Gerd Hankel, *Die Leipziger Prozesse: Deutsche Kriegsverbrechen und ihre strafrechtliche Verfolgung nach dem Ersten Weltkrieg* (Hamburg, 2003), 477.

36. Germany: Hankel, *Leipziger Prozesse,* 478; Geinitz, "First Air War," 207. Britain, based on the *Times:* James Wilford Garner, *International Law and the World War* (London, 1920), 1:462n6. Paris: Grayzel, "Souls of Soldiers," 595; Garner, *International Law,* 1:492n2.

37. Roberts and Guelff, *Documents,* 139.

38. Draft Note for Signature (5th Draft), Nr. 29865, Confidential Print, July 9, 1914, FO 372/752, file 751, no. 14144; W. A. Stewart minute of Jan. 26, 1915, ibid.

Yarmouth on November 3 and of Whitby, Hartlepool, and Scarborough in December 1914, the agreement was null. The principle remaining was that belligerents were to take "due measures" to spare civilians in their attacks on military objectives.

The law of reprisal could have been construed to dispense with "due measures" and simply let bombs fall where they might. But whether reprisals might be taken against civilians was a different and highly controversial matter. The French international jurist Antoine Pillet argued that they could not; German writers, by accepting the legality of hostage taking, implicitly recognized that they could. French air war policy, including its air reprisals, hewed closely to Pillet's position.

Although the doctrine of strategic bombing was not really developed until the interwar years, both Britain and Germany set the foundations for it during the First World War. Strategic bombing targets more than just obvious military objectives located in cities, thus accepting a high possibility of "collateral damage"; it directly targets civilian morale as well, reckoning popular support as a critical asset in modern warfare. That is why General Hugh Trenchard, commander of Britain's Independent (Air) Force and a founder of strategic doctrine, argued to the French in July 1918 that "the word 'reprisal' should be removed from the military vocabulary."[39] For reprisal—the use of illegal means to combat illegal means—underscored that targeting civilians violated international law. Every time the Allies cited reprisal as the reason for aerial bombardment, they strengthened the principle that civilians were protected by law. Despite Trenchard's arguments, seconded by some voices within the French army and industrial circles, France rejected strategic bombing. It focused its growing air force on supporting the ground war at the front.[40] Even after France possessed the world's largest air force (1918), and the collapsing German lines made striking targets inside Germany much easier, France did not abandon its position. Its non-reprisal bombing targets remained railroads, railway stations, depots, batteries, convoys, and hangars.[41]

French reprisal attacks targeted the same military objects behind the lines in German towns and cities.[42] In other words, French reprisal did not aim directly at enemy civilians, but instead accepted the greater likelihood of civilian deaths during air strikes on military objectives. France did not directly aim at civilian morale, though French planners trusted that spirits would decline as military strength collapsed.

Several facts underscore that French raids were genuine legal reprisals. With their bombs, French planes always dropped leaflets naming the French town for which the reprisal attack was being made. The government kept a firm hand on reprisal raids. Army leaders always rejected pilots' pleas to conduct reprisal attacks against symbolic centers

39. Cited in Barros, "Strategic Bombing," 424.

40. This process is well described in Barros, "Strategic Bombing," and Philippe Bernard, "À propos de la stratégie aérienne pendant la Première Guerre Mondiale: Mythes et réalités," *Revue d'histoire moderne et contemporaine* 16 (Apr.–June 1969). See also the reports in SHAT 16N 1757.

41. See the many reports in SHAT 16N 1757.

42. Barros, "Strategic Bombing," 420–21; Louis Rolland, "Les pratiques de la guerre aérienne dans le conflit de 1914 et le droit des gens," *Revue générale de droit international public* 23 (1916): 562.

like Berlin, Hamburg, or Cologne.[43] When in February 1916 Field Marshal General Joseph Joffre slipped and called for non-reprisal raids on German towns west of the Rhine, he was quickly jerked back; within two days, he countermanded his order and called instead for striking the usual military objectives.[44] Until March 1917, reprisal raids were left in the hands of the army command (France had no independent air force and, unlike Britain, refused to create one during the war). In that month, fearing escalation, the government (war minister) took complete control over air reprisals; it approved each on a case-by-case basis only.[45] In September 1917, that policy was loosened. Although War Minister Paul Painlevé hesitated for four months, he finally approved an army command proposal for automatic, tit-for-tat reprisal raids in case open French towns were attacked. Apparently, a shift in German air strategy meant that that policy never went into effect.[46]

Nevertheless, the Allies seemed to consider, but not necessarily to adopt, aerial bombardment more and more frequently as the reprisal of choice against German war conduct in the latter part of the war. In the spring of 1917, the French government decided on "serious reprisals against German open villages," in case German submarines should purposely sink Allied hospital ships; British and French aircraft bombed Freiburg as a consequence of this decision.[47] In October 1918, the Allies considered air attacks to stop Germany's systematic destruction of Northern France and Belgium during its retreat, but decided that heavy postwar reparations were preferable.[48] Aerial bombing reprisals remained controversial in both Britain and France, as discussions in the House of Lords in June 1917 and in the French Chamber of Deputies in March 1918 showed.[49]

French air reprisals were a striking example of controlled, limited reciprocity. Executing reciprocity correctly required excellent internal government coordination and also enhanced that coordination. This aspect of reciprocity is perhaps best illustrated by returning to the main arena of reprisal, prisoners of war.

French governmental centralization and efficiency made precise reciprocity possible. Representatives of the war ministry and the foreign office met three times a week to discuss prisoner and reprisal issues.[50] The two ministries traded information swiftly and easily, and both enjoyed a high degree of personnel continuity that lasted throughout the war. In order to make sure that reciprocity was exactly executed, the central government issued frequent, exact, identical orders to the regional commanders (who were in charge of the prisoner-of-war camps), and ultimately established a tight system of inspection to make

---

43. Barros, "Strategic Bombing," 422.

44. Joffre to État-Major, Neuf Chateau, no. 1713 M., Feb. 1, 1916, and Joffre to same, no. 1835, Feb. 3, 1916, SHAT 16N 1757.

45. Bernard, "À propos de la stratégie aérienne," 362; Barros, "Strategic Bombing," 420–21.

46. Barros, "Strategic Bombing," 421.

47. General Commander to naval ministry, tel. Apr. 26, 1917, MAE Corr Polit. 1139. Barros writes that War Minister Hubert Lyautey had earlier rejected such proposals, but had agreed to call regular raids against military objectives "reprisal" attacks: Barros, "Strategic Bombing," 422. See also Garner, *International Law,* 1:490.

48. Garner, *International Law,* 1:326.

49. Ibid., 1:490, 492.

50. Vérand to war minister (cabinet), no. 41004 PG, Paris, June 3, 1916, SHAT 6N 111.

sure those orders were carried out.[51] The Inspector General's office was established in February 1915, commanded throughout the war by the energetic General C. Vérand, assisted by another general, H. Jacquillat.[52] They appointed inspectors-colonels whose "frequent and objective visits" to camps produced detailed and sometimes hard-hitting reports, such as the one describing one camp commandant as "not very intelligent and tired," and the camp buildings as "mediocre" and in parts "unacceptable."[53] More important, inspectors-colonel had the power to issue orders immediately to fix deficiencies.[54] The inspectors general themselves regularly visited camps; in fact, their inspections averaged seven per week in the period from March to December 1916.[55] Active oversight produced the kind of uniformity that the policy of "exact reciprocity" required.

The French system was also notable for the remarkable degree of cooperation among departments, despite inevitable friction. At various points control of reprisal shifted among agencies, as we have seen in 1917 when the war minister took over air reprisal from army command. In June 1916, the minister of war readily acceded to the foreign office desire to place prisoner-of-war reprisals in the hands of the council of ministers in order to prevent incidents that might provoke Germany to counter-reprisals against their much more numerous French prisoners.[56] When reprisals involved political-diplomatic issues, control shifted to the foreign office or higher, for example when the sentence that courts-martial had meted out to Lieutenant Erler for war crimes resulted in reprisals against ten French officers in German hands.[57]

Such inter-ministerial coordination greatly improved the chances that French reprisals avoided being capricious or misdirected. The record reveals that France generally acted on information coming from the neutral (Spanish) or Red Cross observers of camps inside Germany—that is, not on the basis of newspaper accounts or (solely) prisoner complaints; and most of that information was current—that is, it did not involve conditions long since addressed.[58] The influence of the foreign office was also apparent in distinguishing atrocity from policy. In June 1917, the foreign office's legal adviser, Henri Fromageot, was consulted about whether to complain about evidence that German soldiers had killed French wounded.[59] Fromageot advised against it, warning that France must make sure that French soldiers had never done the same, but more important, that "this is not a

51. Millerand to commanding generals in the regions, Paris, Lyon, North Africa, and Morocco, Sept. 25, 1915, Nr. 17.744 6/10, 7N 161.

52. Cahen-Salvador, *Prisonniers*, 46.

53. Their duties: Vérand to regional commanding generals, no. 39.393 PG, Paris, May 19, 1916, SHAT 6N 110. Inadequate camp commandant: Hardy, "Note pour le Chef de Cabinet," Paris, Jan. 12, 1916, ibid.

54. Vérand to regional commanding generals, no. 42.449 PG, Paris, June 15, 1916, SHAT 6N 110.

55. See the *journaux hebdomadaire* for 1916: SHAT 6N 110.

56. Roques (min. of war) to foreign minister, June 6, 1916, SHAT 6N 111.

57. Cahen, *Bordereau d'envoi* to cabinet of foreign office, no. 4(?)974 PG3, Paris, July 10, 1916, SHAT 6N 111. Lt. Willi Erler was tried and sentenced to twenty years imprisonment and degradation for having followed orders on September 4, 1914, to burn a Belgian farm, resulting in one civilian death, in retaliation for alleged francs-tireurs activity.

58. See SHAT 6N 110.

59. On that practice, including among Allied soldiers: Heather Jones, *Violence against Prisoners*, 82–83.

case of orders given by superior authorities but of isolated acts of German soldiers in the course of combat."[60] The war provided many temptations to confuse atrocity with policy; Fromageot had to set down the distinction several times.[61] But on the whole, French reprisals were directed against government policies, not individual acts. And, despite some slip-ups, exact reciprocity, not escalation, was the hallmark of France's reprisal policy.[62]

Germany's Reprisal Policy

From the beginning of the war, the Prussian war ministry, the high command (OHL), and the AA battled over what principles should govern Imperial Germany's use of reprisal. The AA was much more cautious than military leaders. In October, the AA delayed action pressed by the general staff and the Kaiser to incarcerate British enemy aliens, until it was sure that Britain really had done the same, after which it relented.[63] It similarly delayed war ministry–ordered reprisals against Allied prisoners of war in January 1915. Zimmermann accepted the reports of the U.S. observers that the bad conditions in French and British camps were due to "poor organization and inadequate infrastructure," not to perfidy.[64] There was thus no ground for reprisal measures that would "doubtless lead to similar reprisals on the French side and consequently to continuous further measures on both sides."

In the course of 1915, the AA lost leverage over the army, many of whose commanders had initiated local "reprisals" independently from the beginning. By mid 1916, the reprisal cycle had reached such an extent that Bethmann Hollweg tried to reassert AA authority. On June 25, 1916, the chancellor set out his case to both the war minister and the OHL. Citing the reprisal that the war ministry had taken in the case of Lieutenant Erler, Bethmann complained that its 10:1 ratio (ten French officers arrested) "goes way over the framework of reprisal measures."[65] It was the "beginning of a fateful road" whose "final end would be a war of destruction against defenseless prisoners." It nourished the "hatred against Germany" that helped the French government keep up war morale. Foreign Minister von Jagow had already conferred with Prussian War Minister Adolf Wild von Hohenborn to get his agreement to contact the AA in every case of reprisal against foreigners, which "are in no way purely military measures," as Bethmann argued. "On the contrary, under

60. Fromageot note, June 29, 1916, MAE Corr. Polit. 1112.

61. Notes of n.d. (ca. Nov. 1914), MAE Corr. Polit. 1103; of n.d. (ca. Apr. 5, 1915) ibid. no. 1108, Aug. 14, 1917 (ibid., no. 1112),

62. The Commission de la main-d'oeuvre de prisonniers de guerre occasionally discussed measures that exceeded those against which they were confronted: see protocol of the meeting of Feb. 16, 1917, SHAT 16N 2455.

63. Zimmermann to Jagow, tel. Oct. 22, 1914, AAHQ Nr. 1793, AA/PA R 22387; Zimmermann to Jagow, Nr. 834, Oct. 27, 1914, ibid., R 22384.

64. Zimmermann to Jagow, Nr. IIIb 23925.14/3772, Berlin, Jan. 13, 1915, AA/PA R 22385.

65. Bethmann to Adolf Wild v. Hohenborn (war min.) and Falkenhayn, Berlin, June 25, 1916, IIIb 19817/113306, AA/PA R 22213.

certain conditions they extend in goal and effect deep into the constitutional responsibility of the AA for the protection of Germans in foreign lands and the relations to foreign states, even in time of war." Wild had agreed to Jagow's request, but nothing had come of it. Bethmann cited reprisals against Russian officers, the jailing of fifteen French civilians in reprisal for the (alleged) treatment of five Germans in Morocco, and the public announcement of four more reprisals just in the last few days. None of these had occurred with AA knowledge or approval, which Bethmann now demanded both for reprisals and for their publication in the press.

The Prussian war minister rejected Bethmann's arguments for co-control over the "use and proportion" of reprisals.[66] Wild claimed that reprisal belonged exclusively to the war ministry because of its responsibility for prisoners of war. An investigation of the German decision on the Erler case had proved that "there is a deep-seated fundamental difference of opinion" on reprisal that would make "cooperation between the two offices extraordinarily difficult. The AA is fundamentally opposed to using reprisal," he claimed, and its opposition caused delays that undermined their effectiveness. Wild made five arguments that summarized the basic assumptions operating among the military. First, reprisal was a purely military matter. Second, reprisals were effective. In Wild's view, France had capitulated to Germany in the cases of the imprisonment of Lieutenant Schierstädt, the evacuation of German civilian prisoners from Dahomey and from North Africa, the end of the ban on mail to colonial German prisoners, and the Franco-German agreement on food for prisoners. Each one of these cases, he argued, was preceded by "months of fruitless negotiation, finally resorting to reprisals and immediately afterward the relenting of the French government." Third, there was no legal limit to reprisal; whatever was effective was legal. "A reprisal is only useful if it is able to exert a palpable pressure on the opponent." "The experiences with France show that only the use of sharper measures" works. Thus, effectiveness, not proportion or mere reciprocity, was the proper criterion. Fourth, Germany was stronger than France and could thus exert more force: "thanks to our successes in the war [i.e., the greater number of prisoners and the occupation of French territory with its captive civilians], we have more effective and sensitive means to apply in reprisal." Fifth, using Germany's greater force for the protection of Germans was Wild's "duty," which outweighed the "probably more theoretical fears of a...war of destruction and Your Excellency's political reservations." On the basis of these five arguments, Wild retained the right to make the final decision, though he begrudgingly agreed to contact the AA before ordering reprisals or their publication.

The chancellor apparently hoped that he might have better luck with Wild's successor, General Hermann von Stein. Two days after Stein assumed office in the war ministry, Bethmann renewed the argument.[67] This time, he pointed out that military reprisals affected civilian prisoners, who were the AA's responsibility, but more fundamentally, all reprisals were notified through the office of the AA and thus "under its responsibility." That and their undoubted political effects on pending negotiations and the views of neutrals

---

66. Wild to Bethmann, GHQ, July 6, 1916, AA/PA R 22213.

67. Bethmann to War Min. Hermann v. Stein, Berlin, Oct. 31, 1916, AA/PA R 22213.

placed them also under the AA's constitutional purview. He denied that the AA was fundamentally opposed to reprisal. On the contrary, it had willingly worked to execute many of them. But it had done so following principles "that have largely proved themselves and in general have been supported by the war ministry and the overwhelming majority of the Reichstag."

Bethmann then listed these principles, which correctly summarized customary international law: (1) the violation against which the reprisal is directed must be "clearly proved"; (2) it must have been committed by the government, "not merely by a subordinate organ"—that is, Fromageot's rule of high policy, not atrocity; (3) it must be proportionate ("like must be retaliated with like"); and (4) "obvious barbarities must be out of the question." The fourth point was a clear statement that Germany's civilian government rejected Lueder's old argument that "questions of humanity" did not limit reprisal.

Stein's emphatic reply proved that Wild's stance was firm military policy.[68] Stein denied that civilian prisoners were under civilian administration. Even civilians had a military importance "for military intelligence and war industry"—reprisals were "a purely military matter." He repeated that reprisals "were the best means" of protecting German prisoners. It simply took too long to prove allegations; "under some circumstances, reprisals must already be taken on the basis of believable information." While nodding at the principle of proportionality, Stein overrode it: "It is also my view that like must be met with like. However, I will use in reprisal all the advantage that Germany's weapons have won in the higher number of enemy prisoners if special circumstances make it seem necessary to me." The exceptional remained an important escape from binding principle. Like Wild, Stein agreed to receive the AA's opinion on reprisals and their publication, but not necessarily to follow it.

That was in mid November. By January 27, 1917, the Allies had rejected Bethmann's peace proposal, the chancellor had run out of delaying tactics, and Germany's military leaders and the Kaiser launched unrestricted submarine warfare, the wonder weapon they hoped would guarantee victory in six months, even if the United States did enter the war. That mixture of military hubris and desperation, the fixation on the victory of pure force, was the background to War Minister von Stein's astonishing letter of that date to the chancellor.[69] Stein began by breaking the official agreement that Germany had offered in March 1916 and France had accepted in July to begin no reprisals without four weeks' notice.[70] He argued changed circumstances (*rebus sic stantibus*). "In my view," wrote Stein, "this arrangement no longer fits the current situation. The coming decisive battle demands of every German the utmost exertion of energy. The German people thus have a right to expect that German civilian and military prisoners everywhere will be helped wherever necessary immediately and with full power." If necessary, reprisals would now be launched "immediately" and "without previous notice." Furthermore, Stein retracted his promise

---

68. Stein to Bethmann, Berlin, Nov. 19, 1916, "Geheim," AA/PA R 22213.

69. Stein to Bethmann, Nr. 39/17.6 U5/1, Berlin, Jan. 27, 1917, Geheim, AA/PA R 22213.

70. Spanish embassy to AA, Berlin, Apr. 28, 1916, containing French *note verbale* of Mar. 6, 1916, BAB R 901 84647; French note of Aug. 2, 1916, ibid.

to receive the AA's views. "In the present high point of the war," when the enemy had rejected "with scorn" Germany's peace proposal, "concern for the views of neutrals must be completely subordinated to caring for life and limb of Germans in the enemy's hands and for upholding in the army and at home the will to victory to the end. That is in the first place the responsibility of the war minister." In short, the military planned to use reprisal to mobilize domestic morale.

In a lengthy memorandum, the AA rejected all of these claims and repeated its earlier arguments.[71] It emphasized four important objections: (1) the Franco-German agreement reserved reprisal for proven instances of violations due to government policy; (2) the AA was constitutionally responsible for civilian prisoners and for any action with political consequences, (3) "at a time when we are using a method of war [unrestricted submarine warfare] that harms neutral interests in the highest degree, we must not offend them unless absolutely necessary," and (4) "the agreement with France occurred at our initiative and thus should not be renounced without a compelling reason. Furthermore, the agreement fulfills the suggestions of important neutrals and the Reichstag." No better statement could be made of the imbrication of legal principle, politics, and international community. The AA was also shocked by the army's frank avowal that it could unilaterally renounce an official agreement concluded between two governments. The matter was so important, the memorandum concluded, that it must be referred to the Kaiser.

Yet nothing happened immediately. It took one final push for the chancellor and the AA to go to the Kaiser and insist on their own legal right, which in turn upheld international legal principle. The issue concerned Germany's proclamation in January 1917 of reprisals that put French and British prisoners of war into the firing zone under conditions of brutality and ill-treatment so horrific that neutral voices began to be raised. We shall handle this episode in more detail shortly. But for now we must focus on the letter sent by Germany's envoy to Switzerland, Konrad Freiherr von Romberg, in early April 1917.

Romberg's post in Bern opened him to the flood of information available to the Swiss government as neutral observer of belligerent prisoner-of-war and civilian camps, as mediator between the belligerents, and to reports and behind-the-scenes views of the International Committee of the Red Cross. As a result, Romberg was the German diplomat most sensitized to world opinion and consequently to international law; he frequently adverted to both in his dispatches to Berlin. On this occasion, the director of the French-Belgian section of the Office of Assistance to Prisoners of War had given Romberg a detailed letter from a French prisoner, describing conditions in the reprisal camps in the zone of fire. The director, who in his official capacity knew how German prisoners were treated, said that the condition of German prisoners in Allied hands "could not compare with the miserable conditions" outlined in the letter; these were "so cunningly cruel [*raffiniert grausam*] that they exceeded every measure" and had nothing to do with "measures of reciprocity."[72]

---

71. Aufzeichnung über die vom Kriegsministerium beabsichtigte Verschärfung der Vergeltungsmaßnahmen wegen schlechter Behandlung deutscher Krieg- und Zivilgefangenen, Feb. 7, 1917, BAB R 22213.

72. Romberg to AA, Nr. Kr. I.B. 1833, Bern, Apr. 7, 1917, BAB R 901 84147.

Romberg told the AA that he hoped this latest wave of reprisals, launched mainly on the testimony of a single repatriated former prisoner, would end. He continued, "If Austria-Hungary has a tolerable reputation in the Entente countries, this is partly due to the fact that it has managed its prisoners with a lighter hand and no reprisal controversies relating to prisoners of war have poisoned its relations with the Entente. But after this war we shall receive streams of hatred for the dramatic reversals [*Peripetien*] of our prisoner policy, made worse by the lies of our foes." He ended with the director's observation that diplomats were much more likely than narrow-minded military men to appreciate the "many circumstances that accumulate to cause at present the division and hatred among peoples."

Romberg's letter was one of the weapons that the AA used to force a royal audience behind the back of the war minister. The AA's man at OHL headquarters, Werner Freiherr von Grünau, had first to overcome the objections of the chief of the military cabinet, General Moritz Freiherr von Lyncker, who wanted Wilhelm to hear the military's objections. But Lyncker, who was "personally offended at the rough tone of the war minister's last letter," finally relented; the meeting took place on May 6, 1917. Wilhelm, it seems, was easy to persuade. An agreement with France to keep all prisoners of war (not civilians, as it turned out) farther than thirty kilometers from the front lines was approved, and the AA was included into reprisal decisions. "I am happy this business is finished," Grünau told Romberg, "I'm just curious to see the war minister's face!"

Apparently, OHL knew little about this long-running battle between the AA and the war ministry.[73] But OHL now became the greater problem. Chief of Staff Erich von Falkenhayn had ordered reprisals unilaterally, including at least one that called for burning three villages to every one destroyed by Russia as tsarist troops retreated through Russia's own territory.[74] The situation deteriorated under the much more energetic and mercurial General Erich Ludendorff. After his and Paul von Hindenburg's appointments in August 1916, the OHL inserted itself into negotiations, ruined official agreements, and, like the Prussian war ministry, amassed to itself the right to decide, launch, and publicize reprisals. Even the war ministry later clashed with the Third OHL on things like ratifying agreements on treatment of prisoners of war and permitting neutral observers to visit camps in the occupied zone. However, most (but not all) reprisals pushed by OHL still went through the AA on their way to enemy governments, giving the AA the opportunity to lengthen deadlines so that they fulfilled bilateral agreements to wait one month or, in particular pressing cases, fifteen days before beginning with reprisals. The AA also softened tough, undiplomatic language.

The AA never exercised genuine control over Germany's reprisal policies. That rested with the various, uncoordinated branches of the military, not just OHL and the Prussian war ministry, but individual unit and camp commanders. They operated on several assumptions, some of which we have already observed: reprisals were the only effective

---

73. Lersner to Kriege, Nr. 344, GHQ, Mar. 19, 1917, AA/PA R 22214.

74. AAHQ, Nr. 1124 Jagow to Bethmann, Nr. 31, Berlin, Mar. 20, 1915, enclosing a letter from Matthias Erzberger, AA/PA R 22386.

way to affect their enemy's (putative) behavior; effectiveness was the only criterion; therefore, disproportion was acceptable or even sometimes required. As we shall see below, Ludendorff's reprisal order of December 11, 1917, showed that the military recognized no intrinsic limits based on humanitarian considerations.[75] Reprisal policy was also strongly affected by the military's hypersensitivity to "dignity and prestige," especially regarding the officer corps.[76] It reacted allergically to rumors of slights directed against officers and was quick to overreact.

Germany's information strategy also skewed reprisal policy. The most objective, accurate information on the treatment of prisoners came from the neutral observers (in Germany, the Spanish embassy inspected for France and Russia, the United States and later the Netherlands for Great Britain; in France and Britain, the United States and later Spain and sometimes Switzerland visited German prisoners). All the belligerents complained about neutral observers and questioned their impartiality and bona fides from time to time, but Germany made the most determined efforts to control neutral visits, censor prisoner testimony, and bar neutral inspections altogether.[77] French reciprocity forced the Prussian war ministry to countermand orders such as deducting prisoner letters to neutral observers from their spartan monthly limit, suppressing all letters containing complaints that the Germans judged calumnious, and requiring all prisoner testimony to neutrals to be made in the presence of a German listener—though the war ministry sometimes returned to these practices, and the reprisal cycle began again.[78] Some of these actions were at least covered as reprisal, but barring neutral observers altogether was policy.

Neutral visits to regular prisoner-of-war camps had begun in autumn 1914, but the war ministry threw up more and more hurdles against them, until by August 1916 the Spanish ambassador announced he was ready to quit because of constant chicanery.[79] The preceding month, the war minister had made it clear he would prefer all such visits to stop. After OHL had forbidden U.S. inspections of the reprisal camp at Libau, where five hundred British prisoners were held in a reprisal, the AA remonstrated with the war minister because the diplomats feared that Britain would reciprocate. The war ministry was not afraid, it informed the AA: "the army administration would welcome [the opportunity, by counter-reprisal] to stop future camp visits by Americans in Germany."[80]

Reprisal camps were entirely off-limits, and so were all the camps in the zone of operations and the rear (*Etappe*). This policy was so fundamental that the war ministry stuck to it even when, in January 1916, it jeopardized the Stockholm Agreement (with Russia)

75. Copy of order, signed Hahndorff, GHQ, Dec. 11, 1917, Nr. 48660, BAB R 901 84149.

76. Zimmermann to Grünau, Nr. 1437, Berlin, Nov. 23, 1916, citing War Min. Stein, Nov. 17, 1916, AA/PA R 22213.

77. Hinz, *Gefangen im Großen Krieg*, 76–80.

78. C. Vérand to regional commanding general, no. 73680 PG3, Paris, Jan. 11, 1917, SHAT 7N 161; Cahen-Salvador, *Prisonniers*, 84–86; Hinz, *Gefangen im Großen Krieg*, 78–79.

79. Treutler to Grünau, Nr. 1055, Berlin, Aug. 5, 1916, AA/PA R 22213.

80. War ministry, signed Hoffmann, to AA, Ref. IIa 19540, Berlin, July 8, 1916, AA/PA R 22213; testimony of Friedrich to Reichstag main committee, Oct. 12, 1916, *Der Hauptausschuss des Deutschen Reichstags 1915–1918*, Quellen zur Geschichte des Parlamentarismus und der politischen Parteien, ed. Reinhard Schiffers, Manfred Koch, and Hans Boldt (Düsseldorf, 1981–83), 2:878.

on prisoners of war that the war ministry desperately wanted.[81] The matter arose again in January 1917 when Germany insisted on bilateral agreements with France and Britain barring the use of prisoner labor in a zone within thirty kilometers from the front. France made neutral visits part of its counterproposal. The war ministry rejected them "for military reasons," which were apparently so unintelligible to the AA that it changed the wording to read that since it was "a temporary measure," no visits were necessary.[82] In the next months, France permitted Swiss observers to monitor prisoners and camps in its army zone, while Germany continued to refuse.[83] The war ministry admitted to the AA that OHL was behind the refusal.[84] In October 1917, OHL gave permission for a single Spanish colonel to visit the army zone, but in fact, no visit ever took place. Instead, OHL finally in December 1917 removed the French prisoners from the zone, and thus, the war ministry informed the AA, "an inspection...would not be necessary."[85] No inspections ever took place. Five days before the Armistice, the war ministry again repeated that no neutral visits in the army zone were permitted, "because of the military situation," but the war ministry assured the AA that "the question will be benevolently reviewed as soon as possible."[86] Army commanders of all three states opposed neutral visits, but only in Germany did the military successfully block them in face of civilian leadership opposition.

We may assume that German military commanders truly feared that neutral observers in the zone of military operations might see and reveal operational secrets—both the French and British commands feared the same thing.[87] It is hard to see why the same criterion would apply to camps in the rear or in Germany, however. Imperial Germany's penchant for secrecy went beyond the military. In November 1916, the AA instructed the army to call the camps to which Belgian civilian workers were deported anything but "camp" (*Lager*), so that they would be off-limits by definition to neutral observers.[88] The Americans and Spanish insisted anyway, and the war ministry made sure that they saw only the workplaces, but not the camps themselves.[89] It remains unclear how much Imperial Germany's strong preference for secrecy was simply part of the wartime mentality of

---

81. "Bemerkungen der deutschen Heeresvewaltung zu dem Schlußprotokoll der Konferenz von Delegierten der Vereine des Deutschen, Österreichischen, Ungarischen und Russischen Roten Kreuzes in Stockholm," Berlin, Jan. 31, 1916, BAB R 901 86664.

82. Friedrich (war ministry) to chancellor, no. 2521/17.U.5./1, Berlin, Jan. 22, 1917, BAB R 901 84146.

83. Spanish ambassador to AA, Berlin, July 25, 1917; Spanish embassy to AA, Aug. 25, 1917; BAB R 901 84147.

84. Von Sabel (in war ministry) to chancellor (AA), Nr. 524/8.17 U.5/1, Berlin, Aug. 30, 1917, BAB R 901 84147.

85. War ministry to AA, Nr. 2481/11.17.U5/1, Berlin, Dec. 3, 1917, BAB R 901 84148.

86. War ministry, signed Hartog, to AA, no. 4853.10.18.U5/3, Berlin, Nov. 6, 1918, BAB R 901 84149. The issue this time concerned British soldiers.

87. État-major général, Direction de l'arrière, GQG, no. 5352, Jan. 10, 1917, referring back to a his letter no. 7904/DA of Oct. 27, 1916, SHAT 6N 111.

88. Typescript, signed Lewald, "Ergebnis der unter Beteiligung der Reichs- und Preußischen Ressorts am 17. Okt. 1916 im Reichsamt des Innern abgehaltenen kommissarischen Besprechung, betr. Versorgung der Kriegsindustrie mit Arbeitskräften," BAB R 901 84022.

89. Lancken to AA, tel. Nr. 215, Brussels, Nov. 11, 1916, BAB R 901 84022; Spanish Ambassador Polo to Jagow, no. 1294, Berlin, Nov. 17, 1916, ibid.; Kriegsamt to AA, Jan. 24, 1916, Nr. 39/12.16.A.Z.S., in connection with IIIb 47728, Spanish Embassy to AA, no. 1463, Berlin, Dec. 12, 1916, BAB R 901 84023.

secrecy for its own sake, or meant to curb challenges to state authority, or to hide horrendous conditions.

Germany's information policy also clashed with the accepted principles governing reprisal: the incident must be proved, must be the result of government policy and not the work of individuals, and must be recent. Whereas France's reciprocal reprisals were overwhelmingly based on Spanish observer reports, Germany's were frequently the result of unsubstantiated testimony by single persons. Sometimes the results were simply embarrassing, as when Germany had to recall a reprisal threat based on the lurid testimony (under oath and a year after the alleged events) of a sergeant who turned out to be a "liar."[90] Sometimes such testimony started brutal reprisals that affected thousands of men.[91] The war ministry often threatened or actually took reprisal on the basis of outdated information—for example, concerning camps that did not exist at all or had been closed for months, or, as in the case of medical corpsman Josef Scheel, on events that allegedly occurred nine months earlier.[92] France protested Germany's habitual "invocation of old facts"—a habit that caused the Allies to suspect that Germany used them as excuses to cover exploitative and illegal behavior toward prisoners of war actually motivated by the desire to use prisoner labor.[93]

There was also a striking imbalance between German and Allied complaints concerning prisoner-of-war treatment, which fed the tendency toward disproportion in Germany's reprisals. In one of the first big reprisals launched against British prisoners, Colonel Friedrich, head of the war ministry's prisoner-of-war department, listed the following deficiencies in the treatment of German soldiers, taken by the British, but used by France to unload ships at Le Havre and Rouen: the floors were dusty; there were no desks, chairs, or benches; there was no place to exercise; the wounded were not given enough time to heal before they were made to work hard; the work was too hard, for it required unloading two hundred 150-to-200-pound flour sacks per day; the food was inadequate to the work; prisoners reporting in sick were given seven to fourteen days "strict arrest"; the civil population misbehaved toward the prisoners who were not adequately protected by guards; at Rouen the washing and toilet facilities were inadequate; and "altogether the treatment...must be described as utterly disrespectful [*unwürdig*]."[94] Some of these were serious allegations, and if they were true, they certainly required fixing. But they pale in comparison to what happened to the five hundred British reprisal prisoners sent

---

90. War minister to chancellor (AA), Nr. 3971/9.17.U.5/1, Berlin, Oct. 1, 1917, BAB R 901 84148; war ministry, signed Hartog, to AA, no. 401/10.17.U5/1, Berlin, Oct. 3, 1917, ibid.

91. Romberg to AA, no. Kr. I.B. 1833, Bern, Apr. 7, 1917, BAB R 901 84147.

92. Cahen and Jacquillat, "Note pour le Secrétaire particulier de Ministre," no. 40187 PG, Paris, May 26, 1916, SHAT 6N 111; *journal hebdomadaire* of Oct. 15–21, 1916, SHAT 6N 110; war minister to AA, no. 4909.3.18.U5/1, Berlin, Apr. 26, 1918, BAB R 901 84148.

93. French note, P.G. 53.334, Paris, Apr. 12, 1918, enclosed in Spanish embassy to AA, Berlin, Apr. 30, 1918, BAB R 901 84148.

94. Friedrich (war min.) to chancellor (AA), Nr. 16318/17U5/3, Berlin, May 4, 1917, BAB R 901 84147; also Heather Jones, *Violence against Prisoners*, 137–40.

to Libau in the east. After two months, 80 percent were no longer capable of work, and twenty-three were dead.[95]

The dismal German record on reprisal was also worsened by poor organization. Unlike in France, where the regional commanders in charge of prisoner camps were subordinate to the war ministry and where after July 1916 interned enemy civilians were under the authority of the interior minister, in Imperial Germany, all camps were run by military commanders subordinate to the deputy corps commanders who were immediate to the Kaiser. The prisoner-of-war department of the war ministry could make suggestions, or even orders, but it had no authority to enforce compliance. U.S. ambassador James W. Gerard, who oversaw the neutral inspections of British prisoners in Germany, described the impossibility of his task: "I did not find the Germans at all efficient in the handling of prisoners of war. The authority was so divided that it was hard to find who was responsible for any given bad conditions." The independence of the commanders undercut central administration: "Cases came to my attention where individual corps commanders on their own initiative directed punitive measures against the prisoners in their districts, on account of the rumours of the bad treatment of German citizens in England....It required constant vigilance to seek out instances of this kind and cause them to be remedied."[96] War Minister Wild seems to have been completely oblivious to the problem. When AA representative Treutler confronted him in June 1916 about catastrophic conditions in the camps, Treutler reported that Wild "was visibly uninformed...he believes that the...'Camp Inspectorate' together with war ministry directives had cleared up the defects in question."[97]

Divided authority meant that Colonel (later Major General) Friedrich, who directed the Unterkunfts-Departement from August 1914 to his death at the beginning of September 1918, entered into official agreements and made promises that could be sabotaged by OHL or any of the camp commanders. It is hard to assess Friedrich's own bona fides. On the one hand, he was capable of writing to the Red Cross that in times of emergency the "phrase 'necessity knows no law' becomes law," yet on the other, he was a tireless negotiator and advocate of the law-like agreements on prisoners with France and Britain.[98] The Janus-faced quality of Friedrich, or perhaps better of his position, is epitomized by the internal conference he called in April 1915 to improve the catastrophic food situation Allied prisoners faced as a result of the measures taken in autumn 1914 (before the "hunger blockade" had had an effect). The elaborate menus and instructions leave no doubt that Friedrich was genuinely determined to improve matters, yet instead of contacting a nutritionist or medical doctor to set the new standards, he invited...a professor of animal husbandry.[99] These sorts of contradictions provoked Thomas Legh, second Baron Newton, who negotiated with Friedrich several times in Newton's capacity as head of the British Foreign

---

95. Hankel, *Leipziger Prozesse*, 382; Heather Jones, *Violence against Prisoners*, 140–43.

96. James W. Gerard, *My Four Years in Germany* (New York, 1917), 121.

97. Treutler to state secretary of AA, no. 398, GHQ, June 30, 1916, AA/PA R 22213.

98. Friedrich to ICRC, April 6, 1916, cited in Hinz, *Gefangen im Großen Krieg*, 266. Cf. Keller/Romberg tel. to Eckart, Bern, Apr. 23, 1918, R 901 84193; v. Hindenburg to Hertling, Kr. IX A 2082, Bern, Apr. 20, 1918, ibid.

99. Hinz, *Gefangen im Großen Krieg*, 209–13; Gerard, *My Four Years*, 126–28.

Office's Prisoners of War and Aliens Department (FOPD), to the following equivocal conclusion: "General Friedrich is, I expect, speaking the truth for once in a way."[100]

The complexities of German policy making are nicely summed up in the worst problem that most prisoners faced: lack of food. Food rations were reduced and simplified from the beginning, for example, by orders from the Bavarian war minister without reference to reprisal, and then by Berlin as immediate, unnotified "reprisal." Apart from reprisal, the sixty-pfennig daily allotment per prisoner was very small in any case, although the Prussian war ministry wondered if it could not be reduced.[101] The improvements of April 1915 were sometimes undercut by camp commanders. The blockade then produced a genuine food shortage that only Allied food packages made good; without them, Allied prisoners would have starved.[102] France provided approximately one-third of the food consumed by French prisoners of war, thus shifting the legal burden of upkeep from the captor nation (as the CRB had done for civilians).[103] In this situation, Germany then initiated a six-month-long reprisal that stopped bread packages to French prisoners, based on the incorrect assumption that the lower French bread allotment to German prisoners had not been entirely made good by substitution.[104] Once this reprisal ended, however, Germany sporadically withheld food packages in order to force reluctant prisoners to work or to punish them for other reasons.[105] And despite the overall German policy of delivering food parcels, their arrival was uncertain, owing to their sheer number, infrastructure problems, but also to the insistence on using prisoners in the army zone and rear where the unalterable priority of military transports infinitely delayed or stopped the food and clothing packages upon which prisoners relied for their survival.[106] It is politically understandable that Germany shrank from feeding prisoners of war better than it could feed its own civilians (France, too, ultimately put nonworking German prisoners on the same ration as French civilians).[107] However, at no time, even when it could have done so in 1914 and early 1915, did any German leader, civilian or military, insist that prisoners of war be treated on a par with German soldiers, as customary and written law required. The military culture of Imperial Germany placed prisoners very low on the

100. Newton minute of June 19, 1917, in Townley to FO, no. 1730, The Hague, June 18, 1917, FO 383/268, file 235, no. 121179.

101. Gerard, *My Four Years,* 126; Wandel to Kress, Nr. 908/10.14.B 2, Berlin, Nov. 8, 1914, BayKrA, M Kr. 6547.

102. Kramer, *Dynamic of Destruction,* 65.

103. I have calculated 28 percent on the basis of figures given in Cahen-Salvador, *Prisonniers,* 112.

104. Hinz, *Gefangen im Großen Krieg,* 215. Germany did the same to Romanian prisoners of war, 228. Germany halted bread packages again in March 1918: German *note verbale* to France, no. IIIb 9793/39876, Mar. 12, 1918, BAB R 901 84647.

105. Friedrich approved of the punitive withholding of food: "Notizen über die Besprechung seitens des Preußischen Kriegsministers im Preußischen Abgeordnetenhaus am May 26, 1916," BayKrA, M Kr. 1650.

106. French *note verbale* of Jan. 15, 1917, concerning the admission that the distribution camp for the rear and zone (Wahn) was unable to ship bread packages to prisoners there, BAB R 901 84146. On German general policy: Heather Jones, *Violence against Prisoners,* 266–68.

107. Art. 27 of Bern Agreement II equalized rations of German prisoners of war and French civilians: Édouard Ignace (undersecretary of state for military justice) to regional commanding generals and camp commandants, no. 2477, Paris, June 15, 1918, SHAT 7N 1993.

priority list; the assumptions regarding reprisal pushed them lower still, and apparently no intrinsic regard for law or humanitarian standards was strong enough to overcome these pressures.[108]

Britain and Reprisal

Compared to France and Germany, Britain shrank from using reprisals. Nevertheless, it did resort to them. Its internal discussions reveal considerable concern for Britain's reputation as a law-abiding and "civilized" nation, for the vulnerability of British prisoners in German hands, and doubts that Britain could ever use reprisal effectively against the stubborn Kaiserreich.[109] In the course of the war, two conflicting opinions developed inside government: one favored reprisal bombing of German civilians as the only method likely to force Germany to abide by law; the other rejected reprisal altogether in favor of postwar trials. Both methods were tried during the First World War and its aftermath, and they laid the foundations for strategic bombing and for the Nuremberg Trials of the Second World War, respectively.

Apparently the first call for drastic reprisals came in December 1914 from Admiral John Fisher in response to the zeppelin raids on British towns. He wanted Britain to take and threaten to execute one German hostage (enemy aliens residing in Britain) for every British civilian killed. His civilian chief, Winston Churchill, contemplated circulating Fisher's idea to the cabinet, but then demurred, fearing it would be both ineffective and damaging to Britain's reputation. In the end, the cabinet simply reserved the liberty to take German enemy aliens hostage.[110]

This incident might have primed Churchill to force through Britain's first act of reprisal in March 1915.[111] He ordered that the captured crew members of the *U-8* and *U-12* submarines be placed in naval detention instead of prisoner-of-war camps. The Admiralty explained that because U-boat crews engaged in "wantonly killing non-combatants, they cannot be regarded as honourable opponents"; their offenses were "against the law of nations and contrary to common humanity."[112] The Foreign Office doubted the wisdom of Churchill's move. Horace Rumbold noted that "it is difficult to see where such reprisals would stop."[113] The cabinet approved differential treatment, but ordered that care be taken

---

108. For Imperial Germany's military culture and prisoners see Isabel V. Hull, *Absolute Destruction: Military Culture and the Practices of War in Imperial Germany* (Ithaca, NY, 2005), 70–90, 121, 145–48, 152–57.

109. Heather Jones, *Violence against Prisoners,* 228.

110. Arthur J. Marder, *From the Dreadnought to Scapa Flow: The Royal Navy in the Fisher Era, 1904–1919* (Oxford, 1961–70), 2:151.

111. Of course, Britain's orders-in-council of August 1914 and March 1915 were also covered by reprisal, but these have been examined earlier. On Churchill's initiative: Heather Jones, *Violence against Prisoners,* 83–87.

112. W. Graham Greene to Foreign Office, Mar. 29, 1915, FO 383/32 file 263, no. 36804.

113. Rumbold minute, Mar. 30, 1915, to W. Graham Greene to Foreign Office, Mar. 29, 1915, FO 383/32 file 263, no. 36804.

"to observe the provisions of the Hague Convention of 1907," which prohibited treating prisoners of war like criminals.[114] Grey personally edited the Admiralty statement, dropping additional threats of investigations and not rescuing U-boat survivors, but he kept the phrase about "honourable opponents."[115]

After getting confirmation from the Americans, Germany retaliated by placing thirty-nine British officers in penal detention. Germany's reprisal was thus an expansion in two ways: first, because it incarcerated only officers (the thirty-nine Germans included crew members), and second, because penal conditions in some German camps were harsher than those in Britain, though this discrepancy was probably not intentional. In those camps, British officers were held in isolation, deprived of tobacco, had less opportunity for exercise, and were forbidden to speak to their fellow Englishmen. The U-boat crews and officers were held (separately) under the same conditions as regular prisoners of war, but in prisons rather than in camps. April and May passed in disputes about comparative conditions, a dispute Churchill needlessly lengthened by insisting that U.S. inspectors should visit the German camps before he would permit their counterparts in Britain to do the same.[116] Meanwhile, pressure from the men's families and in Parliament mounted to break the deadlock. By early June, the Foreign Office intervened to get the cabinet to reverse the policy. Churchill's replacement at the Admiralty, Arthur J. Balfour, announced the reversal to Parliament and hinted at trials: "the general question of personal responsibility should be reserved until the end of the war."[117]

The contretemps had caused the Foreign Office to consider reprisal more fully. The new parliamentary undersecretary of state for foreign affairs (and future blockade minister), Robert Cecil, wrote a long memo on the subject less than two weeks after taking office.[118] Based on the U.S. inspection reports, Cecil concluded that the Germans really had tried to respond reciprocally to Britain's actions. The Americans thought Germany would rescind its reprisal as soon as Britain did so. "We owe so much to the efforts of the American Embassy in Berlin to secure better conditions for our prisoners that it would be foolish to disregard this expression of opinion." After considering diplomacy, Cecil, a lawyer by training, then examined the law. He followed Lassa Oppenheim's (unusual) opinion that superior orders exonerated soldiers and threw responsibility instead onto the order-givers; thus, in his view, the U-boat crews and officers had not violated international law. "No doubt we can justify their special treatment upon the ground of reprisals," but reprisal "can only be justified" if they are effective. That test remained doubtful, since the Germans found Britain's action "insulting" (the charge of dishonourable conduct), but it would hardly deter submarine warfare. Therefore "on a strictly legal point of view...it is difficult to justify the action we have taken, and it would be better to seek for some other method of expressing our disapproval of this particular German atrocity."

114. Asquith to King, Apr. 24, 1915, CAB 41/36/18.

115. Foreign Office to U.S. Amb. Page, April 1, 1915, FO 383/32, file 263, no. 36804.

116. Greene to Foreign Office, April 28, 1915, FO 383/60, no. 51579, file 48319. This same file contains the information on conditions in Britain and Germany.

117. Cecil to Page, June 9, 1915, FO 383/61, no. 76883, file 48319.

118. Cecil memo of June 8, 1915, FO 383/61, no. 74605, file 48319.

Effectiveness was a stringent criterion for reprisal. It cut out purely symbolic or emotional uses ("this should bring home to the German Government what we think of them").[119] The addition of diplomatic and coalition concerns further limited how decision makers calculated "the balance of advantage."[120] So, for example, after Britain had cajoled France into arresting a German consul in hopes of prying loose one of their own whom the Germans held, it had to back down when Germany threatened its ally with reprisal.[121] Effectiveness also kept Britain's reprisals genuine, that is, aimed at returning the foe to the law. That criterion even the most vociferous Germanophobes in the Foreign Office, such as Robert G. Vansittart, kept in mind.[122]

The summer of 1916 saw the execution of Captain Fryatt (July 27) and initiatives by both the pope and the International Committee of the Red Cross to halt all reprisals against prisoners of war. All three events caused Britain to reconsider the policy of reprisal. The Foreign Office Prisoners of War and Aliens Department had "prepared [in February] a list of German officers whose imprisonment or even execution would have caused the maximum effect in Germany," to deter possible German reprisals in the *Baralong* case.[123] Now, in summer, that department revisited the issue and decided that executing German officers would not have saved Captain Fryatt, because German policy was "to terrorise our merchant captains." Besides, Germany would probably have shot twice as many Britons in return, "and we may thus embark on a series of executions following the principles of arithmetical progression." That left postwar trials and economic and travel restrictions as better suggestions.[124] The cabinet's War Committee, presided over by the prime minister, rejected executions and suggested instead investigating property confiscation,

---

119. CFD (C. F. J. Dormer?) minute, Mar. 30, 1915, FO 383/32, no. 36804, file 263.

120. This phrase used by Grey in rejecting confiscation of German merchant ships, and by Cecil rejecting reprisal against Denmark for the violations that Germany forced it to undertake: Grey note to Lord Charles Beresford query of April 22, 1915, FO 376/762, file 13659, no. 50545; Foreign Office to Admiralty, Dec. 9, 1916, *BD*, ser. H., vol. 8, doc. 10.

121. Page to Grey, April 19, 1916, FO 383/128, no. 75736, file 1647, and Grey to French ambassador, April 24, 1916, ibid., no. 74651. Similarly, concerning reprisals on property: Lord Granville to Grey, Paris, Aug. 11, 1916, FO 373/195, no. 15890, file 123628.

122. For example, Vansittart minute, Feb. 14, 1918, to Townley to Foreign Office, no. 661, Feb. 13, 1918, in which Vansittart typically called for "strong" reprisal threats "in order that they [the Germans] may if possible be induced to climb down before we have to act." FO 383/411, no. 28318, file 15210. Also, memorandum for War Cabinet, Secret G.T. 5931, Oct. 8, 1918, initialed by Balfour, 116, CAB 24/66/31.

123. The *Baralong* was a British warship, disguised as a merchantman and flying the U.S. flag when, on August 19, 1915, it came upon a U.S. merchant vessel, the *Nicosian,* being searched by a German U-boat before it was to sink her. Thereupon, the *Baralong* either did, or did not, raise the British war flag before sinking the U-boat, and its boarding crew either murdered eleven German survivors on orders from the *Baralong*'s captain, or else killed them in revenge for the sinking of the *Arabic,* about which the British crew had recently been informed. Either way, the *Baralong* case was an atrocity, not government policy, but I am unaware that either the British captain or the boarding party was ever brought to trial. The German account: "Der Baralong-Fall," sixty-four-page white book published by the AA, AA/PA R 22387. The behind-the-scenes discussion in the FO: FO 372/783, file 153865, and FO 372/923, file 903. A British view: Julian S. Corbett, *Naval Operations* (London, 1920–28), 3:131–34.

124. Memorandum of FOPD, ca. July 30, 1916, FO 383/195, no. 151547, file 123628.

postwar trials, and reparations as punishment; it also wanted to ask France and Russia for their views.[125]

Not surprisingly, France proposed "a uniform [Entente-wide reprisal] regime" of treatment for German prisoners.[126] Strong opposition within the Foreign Office stopped any joint policy because, as Eyre Crowe wrote, the Russians had misbehaved in East Prussia and the French "treat their prisoners less well than we do."[127] Britain did not wish to be tainted by either one. The permanent undersecretary, Lord Charles Hardinge, suggested replying that Britain was "opposed in principle to the adoption of reprisals as a means to secure better treatment"; they would only "provoke the Germans to maltreat our prisoners even more." Grey agreed and added that reprisals entailed "increasingly harsh treatment of prisoners...which it would become repugnant to inflict."[128] Lord Newton, head of the FOPD, concurred, but warned against saying "anything which precluded us from any form of retaliation. Retaliation may under certain circumstances be unavoidable."[129]

The British position of 1916 had been worked out in discussions inside government and in response to pressure exerted by the press and in Parliament. As in France and Germany, public pressure came on both sides of the issue: patriots, the despairing, and hotheads demanded acute retaliation, while the families of suffering prisoners pleaded to end reprisals. The archives contain bales of letters tugging in both directions, and debates in Parliament reflected that split. Unquestionably, public opinion was important to official decision making; for example, the Foreign Office's rush to threaten retaliation in the Blaikie case was clearly due to its desire to avoid the public censure it had received for "allowing" Captain Fryatt to be executed.[130] Indeed, preemptory threats of this kind became "general policy" thereafter (December 1916).[131] But Grey made clear to Parliament that, whatever the public thought, "the question of retaliation or reprisals involves considerations both of principle and policy which can hardly be decided departmentally," that is, they were the province of the highest levels of government, the War Committee, and, after Lloyd George's reorganization of December 1916, the War Cabinet.[132] Thus, Britain kept a higher level of governmental oversight over reprisals than did France, and certainly, than Germany.

Recommendations for reprisal reached the War Committee or War Cabinet after they had been worked out between the Foreign Office and War Office, and sometimes the Admiralty. But the final decision on all reprisals, including those involving prisoners of war,

---

125. War Committee meeting 104, Aug. 1, 1916, CAB 22/39; Hardinge minute, Aug. 1, 1916, Grey to Bertie and Buchanan, Aug. 2, 1916, FO 383/195, no. 151547, file 123628. Draft telegram in CAB 22/39.

126. Cambon to Grey, Sept. 6, 1916, FO 383/195, no. 177588, file 123628.

127. Crowe minute, Earl Granville to Grey, no. 826, Aug. 9, 1916, FO 383/195, no. 157823, file 123628.

128. Grey to Cambon, Oct. 2, 1916, FO 383/195, no. 177588, file 123628.

129. Hardinge minute, Cambon to Grey, Sept. 6, 1916; Grey minute; Newton minute of Sept. 13, 1916, FO 383/195, no. 177588, file 123628.

130. FO 383/205, file 250207.

131. War Cabinet Nr. 23, Dec. 30, 1916, Nr. 18, CAB 23/1; Vansittart minute, Jan. 31, 1917, to Page to FO, no. 2227, Jan. 11, 1917, FO 383/283, file 3241, no. 10479.

132. Grey in reply to Major Hunt, May 31, 1916, FO 383/155, no. 108738, file 463; spoken in the House of Commons June 1, 1916, *Hansard*, vol. 82:2879.

was taken by the War Cabinet "on a case-by-case basis."[133] By June 1917 the cycle of reprisals concerning prisoners of war had reached overwhelming proportions. The secretary of war, Edward Lord Derby, was "reluctant to trouble the War Cabinet with every individual case," yet he did "not feel that I am authorised to deal with them all on my own responsibility." The cases he had in mind ran the gamut from "callousness" to delay, to potentially lethal "brutality," and to the ever-expanding counter-reprisals. In effect, prisoner-related reprisals now landed before a small committee consisting of representatives of the War Office, Foreign Office, and Admiralty, presided over by a member of the War Cabinet, Lord Privy Seal George Nathaniel Curzon.[134] Curzon's position meant that reprisal policy still was set by the central government.

Reprisals taken against German prisoners in their hands had always troubled the British government. As Grey had said, they were "repugnant to inflict," and there was widespread opinion both inside government and out that, in the words of Lord Newton, a competition of ill treatment was "a policy for which the enemy are better adapted by temperament and tradition than ourselves."[135] That self-understanding became a problem as Germany's methods became more extreme. In November 1916 German U-boats sank two British hospital ships, the prelude to its policy of doing so deliberately on (incorrect) grounds that Britain used its hospital ships to transport troops and war matériel to the front. The Foreign Office's legal adviser, Cecil Hurst, thought that some method of retaliation must be found, "but personally I admit I cannot think of one."[136] His colleague, the senior clerk Victor A. Wellesley, who was not usually a hard-liner, minuted, "It is difficult to retaliate effectively against savages. You can only kill them."[137]

Wellesley's conclusion pointed to what became Britain's chief reprisal policy: the bombing of "open towns" in Germany. The scholarly literature on this aspect of the war is hard to decipher, for it is primarily interested in the origins of later strategic bombing doctrine, and no author distinguishes which raids on towns were undertaken explicitly as reprisal and which were not.[138] Furthermore, many authors assume that reprisal raids are defined as purposely targeting civilians, whereas France's and Britain's aerial reprisals always

---

133. Minute of Lord Derby (secy. of state for war) to War Cabinet, June 6, 1917, marked "secret," FO 383/267, no. 112396, file 235.

134. Ibid.

135. Newton's draft response to Major Hunt's inquiry in Parliament, Mar. 15, 1917, FO 383/265, file 235, no. 59001; similarly, Cecil and Lloyd George, War Committee meeting Nr. 104, Aug. 1, 1916, CAB 22/39.

136. Hurst minute, Nov. 24, 1916, to Buchanan to Grey, Petrograd, no. 71 treaty Nov. 12, 1916, FO 372/918, file 389, no. 236272. Hurst's words referred to the sinking of two Russian hospital ships off Greece, but they occurred simultaneously with the British sinkings, and the minuters were responding to the principle of torpedoing hospital ships.

137. Wellesley minute, n.d., to Buchanan to Grey, Petrograd, no. 71 treaty Nov. 12, 1916, FO 372/918, file 389, no. 236272. Not a hard-liner: Wellesley minute, July 22, 1916, to Buchanan to Foreign Office, July 21, 1916, FO 372/918, no. 142423, file 389.

138. Neither do the German lists: Verzeichnis der feindlichen Luftangriffe auf deutsches Gebiet, BAB R 901 86397.

targeted military objectives in German towns.[139] The inherent inaccuracy of these early attacks makes it impossible to reckon the purpose from the results.

The French historian René Martel writes that the first Allied aerial reprisal (by French planes on Karlsruhe, June 15, 1915) was undertaken among other reasons because "the British government had demanded a vigorous response" to zeppelin raids on nonmilitary targets in England.[140] It is not clear when Britain flew its first reprisal air raids against German towns, or what the targets were. Garner believes that Britain (and France) began first in the summer of 1916 to adopt these reprisal measures with regularity.[141] In December 1916, the prospect that Captain Blaikie might be executed moved the War Cabinet to discuss using aerial reprisal raids, but apparently it rejected them "on grounds of humanity and because it was unduly wasteful of airmen and air machines."[142] Nevertheless, by February 1917 influential people in the Foreign Office like Hardinge and Newton, disgusted by the sinking of hospital ships, favored air raids on German "open towns" as "the only reprisals that the German Government and public will understand."[143] France had decided to put German officers aboard its hospital ships as a deterrent and recommended that Britain follow its example, but the Foreign Office feared German reprisals against British officers.[144] By the beginning of April 1917, six hospital ships had been sunk by mines or torpedoes, killing 247 and wounding 73.[145] Consequently, the War Cabinet (April 12, 1917) finally decided that it had "no other alternative": aerial attacks on towns were "the only practicable form of reprisals...and the only one that had proved most effective in the past."[146] Two days later the Allies bombed Freiburg, killing twelve.[147]

Continued misgivings over aerial bombardment were evident in parliamentary debates, where some speakers condemned aerial bombing of civilians, and in the government's

---

139. Cf. Neville Jones, *The Origins of Strategic Bombing: A Study of the Development of British Air Strategic Thought and Practice up to 1918* (London, 1973), 123; Walter Alexander Raleigh and H. A. Jones, *The War in the Air, Being the Story of the Part Played in the Great War by the Royal Air Force* (Oxford, 1922–37), 6:125–26, 138–52.

140. René Martel, *French Strategic and Tactical Bombardment Forces of World War I*, ed. Steven Suddaby, trans. Allen Suddaby (Lanham, MD, 2007), 53–56.

141. Garner, *International Law,* 1:488.

142. Newton minute, Feb. 8, 1917, to Carlin to Balfour, Feb. 14, 1917, FO 383/1076, no. 35968, file 3804. Cf. Hayward, who seems to believe that Britain was set to do so: Joel Hayward, "Air Power, Ethics, and Civilian Immunity during the First World War and Its Aftermath," *Global War Studies* 7, no. 2 (2010): 15. Adm. Jellicoe observed to the War Cabinet on Dec. 13, 1916, that Britain "had not hitherto resorted" to "attacks by aircraft on open towns," War Cabinet no. 6, CAB 23/1.

143. Hardinge, undated minute, and Newton minute of Feb. 18, 1917, both to Carlin to Balfour, Feb. 14, 1917, FO 383/1076, no. 35968, file 3804.

144. Bertie to Foreign Office, Paris, no. 329, April 8, 1917, and minutes by Orde, Langley, Stewart, and Newton, FO372/1077, no. 72820, file 3804. To the British threat (Jan. 31, 1917) of immediate, unspecified reprisals should Germany sink more hospital ships, Germany had counter-threatened with exactly reciprocal measures. Balfour to Page, Jan. 31, 1917, FO 383/1076, no. 24894, file 3804; Carlin to Balfour, Feb. 14, 1917, no. 35968, ibid.

145. Admiralty secretary's answer to query of Mr. Gilbert in Parliament, April 5, 1917, FO 372/1077, no. 73860, file 3804.

146. War Cabinet minutes of April 12, 1917, CAB 23/40, cited in Hayward, "Air Power," 15–16.

147. Roger Chickering, *The Great War and Urban Life in Germany: Freiburg, 1914–1918* (Cambridge, 2007), 102.

hesitation for some time to publicize its reprisal air raids.[148] But large German raids on London in June and July 1917, using ninety-two and twenty-one bombers respectively and killing 216 people, confirmed the War Cabinet in its aerial reprisal policy.[149] But it took four months and further German air raids on London for the War Cabinet to adopt reprisal raids as more than just "a temporary measure."[150] Several considerations came together: reprisal, prophylactic air defense (German planes needed for its own air defense would be unavailable to bomb Britain), boosting civilian morale despondent because of German raids, and striking German war industry (the Admiralty had embraced industrial bombing since summer 1916, and the War Cabinet in September 1917 "felt that we must carry the aerial war into Germany, not merely on the ground of reprisal").[151] British reprisal raids consequently became much more common after October 1917, probably resulting in more civilian casualties than military damage, though the raids always targeted military objects.[152] The creation of the Royal Air Force in April 1918 and an "Independent Force" of bombers (commanded by Hugh Trenchard, later credited as the founder of British strategic bombing theory) whose sole task was aerial reprisal bombing, showed that aerial bombing of civilian urban spaces had taken institutional hold in Britain. Nevertheless, these were relatively slight beginnings. Trenchard commanded less than 8 percent of RAF aircraft, all aircraft in France remained under General Foch's command, and most bombers were used to support the ground war.[153] Reprisal bombing of urban areas remained a minor part of the war effort. But during 1918, civilians at the Foreign Office became the most fervent lobbyists for reprisal bombing, far outstripping the War Office and the Admiralty. To understand why, we must turn to the treatment of prisoners of war in the zone of armies.

In the "Zone"

The zone of armies stretched from the active front to the officially designated "rear" (*Etappe*); both areas were run by the army commands. Danger from artillery shelling was particularly acute in the first ten or more kilometers. All armies sometimes used recently

---

148. Remarks of Major Chapple, April 26, 1917, FO 372/1077, no. 36956, file 3804; Garner, *International Law,* 1:490–91; Malcolm Cooper, *The Birth of Independent Air Power: British Air Policy in the First World War* (London, 1986), 42–43.

149. Neville Jones, *Origins of Strategic Bombing,* 133–35; Cooper, *Birth of Independent Air Power,* 97–108, 131.

150. Raleigh and Jones, *War in the Air,* 5:29, 38–39, 58, 64–65, 85–91.

151. Ibid., 5:64–65, 86–87, 91, 116–19, 493; War Cabinet meeting, Sept. 5, 1917, CAB 23/4.

152. War Cabinet meeting no. 366, Mar. 18, 1918, CAB 23/5/58; Air Ministry memorandum "Proposed Bombing Reprisals for Acts of Devastation," Oct. 14, 1918, CAB 24/66/87; CID, "Air raids on open towns. Memorandum prepared in the Historical Section of the CID in accordance with War Cabinet 358," Minute 9, Mar. 12, 1918, cited in Hayward, "Air Power," 21; Geinitz, "First Air War," 214, 214n37; Raleigh and Jones, *War in the Air,* 6:125–26, 138–52.

153. Neville Jones, *Origins of Strategic Bombing,* 178, 186; Cooper, *Birth of Independent Air Power,* 136; Geinitz, "First Air War," 213–14.

captured prisoners to help remove the wounded and dead from the front, before sending these prisoners to triage camps farther back, and ultimately to prisoner-of-war camps in the interior. Keeping prisoners in the zone permanently began as part of the general trend of using prisoner labor, but it became entangled with reprisal and ended in the systematic exploitation to death of masses of Allied prisoners in 1917 and especially 1918.[154]

Because of the security risks posed by the large numbers of prisoners they had taken, Germany hesitated at first to use POWs for labor. France took the lead in employing them in "public works," but its latitudinarian interpretation included unloading ships carrying war matériel at Channel ports, and working on railroads, or in mines.[155] Apparently, the French army and government interpreted the Hague Convention's injunction against work in "connection with the operations of war" (article 6) to mean handling munitions, which it always expressly forbade.[156] That narrow interpretation was close to the standard view of large military powers as expressed at the Brussels Convention in 1874.[157] France also did not view the zone as automatically off-limits to POW laborers. There may have been prisoners interned there as early as July 1915. After France decided to use large numbers of prisoners for labor in the zone in May 1916, it forbade them to handle munitions or to be kept within artillery range, it ordered conditions to be on a par with those of camps in the interior, it permitted neutral inspections, and it moved prisoners in and out of the zone depending on its general labor needs (especially of agriculture). France obviously regarded the zone and the interior as interchangeable. Being interned in the zone was not a punishment, which is clear from the army's list of jobs meant to punish the recalcitrant—zone work was not included.[158] In short, France's premium was to exploit prisoner labor reliably over the long haul in the widest geographical area outside artillery range. It supplemented a wide interpretation of the legally permissible by recourse to the opportunity for reprisal that Germany offered it.

That opportunity had come in 1915. In February the Prussian war ministry revoked its earlier strict interpretation of the limits of using prisoner-of-war labor, claiming it had been "outstripped by circumstances." In April it ordered that "the use of prisoners of war

---

154. Heather Jones, "The German Spring Reprisals of 1917: Prisoners of War and the Violence of the Western Front," *German History* 26, no. 3 (2008): 335–56; Heather Jones, *Violence against Prisoners,* chs. 3–5.

155. "Note sur la main d'oeuvre des prisonniers de guerre, juillet 1916," SHAT, 6N 111; Commission interministerielle des prisonniers de guerre, "État du travail des prisonniers de guerre," April 1, 1915, SHAT 6N 23.

156. Compte-rendu de la séance de la commission de la main-d'oeuvre des prisonniers de guerre, Jan. 24, 1917, SHAT 16N 2455.

157. Spanish representative and Jomini, Brussels, Conference, *Actes de la Conférence de Bruxelles (1874)* (Brussels, 1899), 72.

158. It is unclear whether those interned in the zone in 1915 were in temporary or permanent camps: Cahen-Salvador, *Prisonniers,* 54. Order on conditions in the zone: C. Vérand to Commanding Generals of the regions in the zone of armies, no. 40.555 P.G. Paris, May 30, 1916, SHAT 7N 161; *journal hebdomadaire,* Aug. 5–12, 1916, and Sept. 17–23, 1916, SHAT 6N 110; main d'oeuvre, Zone des Armées, fin Dec. 1916–Jan. 1917, book 2, SHAT 16N 2441; Maj. Gen. Debeney (GQG) to Min. of War, no. 5959/DA, GQG, June 22, 1917, vol. 6, doc. 93, SHAT 16N 2442; *journal hebdomadaire,* Sept. 24–30, 1916, SHAT 6N 110.

for work *of every kind* must be advanced with all means."[159] In June and August 1915 France and Germany traded protests that the other was using prisoners for war work.[160] When Germany failed to respond promptly to the French protest note of August 31, 1915, France leapt to its advantage. In October 1915, France declared that "it considers itself from now on released from all international obligations on this point."[161] This French policy was much more radical than mere reprisal, for reprisal seeks to uphold law by punishment, whereas being released from all obligation simply nullifies it. Reprisal would have had a time limit; nullification provided a permanent labor supply, and that goal appears to have dictated French policy.

The French argument that violation nullified obligation was tempting, but controversial. During the war some French jurists defended it by analogy to contract or on grounds of reciprocity—the foundation of French reprisal policy.[162] This interpretation was also widespread, though not universal, inside the German government and among German jurists.[163] In Britain, it was different. Although Edward Grey once remarked that "some new departure from all recognized rules of humanity and civilized war" might "justify us in declaring all ordinary rules abrogated in dealing with Germany," his basic view, common to government and jurists alike, was, as Hugh Bellot put it: "it is childish to argue that because one side breaks the rules there should be no rules at all."[164]

Of course, the French decision did retain some rules (no handling munitions, no work or lodging inside artillery range), and so did German policy at first. The Prussian war ministry decree of May 15, 1915, exempted prisoners from work that bore "a direct relation to warlike actions in the battle zone."[165] But just a month later, the war ministry dropped these legal limitations, "if necessity demands it. In a war aimed publicly at the starvation of our people, the dictate of self-preservation trumps all international law."[166] This statement succinctly combined three arguments: military necessity, state self-preservation, and

159. Erlaß of Feb. 22, 1915, and Prussian War Ministry memorandum on "Beschäftigung der Kriegsgefangene," April 15, 1915, cited in Hinz, *Gefangen im Großen Krieg*, 262–63.

160. *Note verbale* from AA for France, Nr. IIIa 10996/35190, draft signed Lentze, Berlin, June 21, 1915, AA/PA, R 22387; French foreign office, *note verbale*, no. 243, Paris, Aug. 31, 1915, annex to République Française, document relatifs à la guerre 1914–1915–1916, SHAT 6n 1.

161. "Note sur la main d'oeuvre des prisonniers de guerre, juillet 1916," SHAT 6N 111.

162. J. Perrinjaquet, "La guerre européenne et les relations commerciales des belligérants et des neutres. L'application des théories de la contrebande de guerre et du blocus," *Revue générale de droit international public* 22 (1915): 128; A. Méringhac, "De la sanction des infractions au droit des gens commises, au cours de la guerre européenne, par les empires du centre," *Revue générale de droit international public* 24 (1917): 16.

163. Reinhard Koch (Admiralty) to AA, B. 32182 I., Berlin, Sept. 20, 1917, AA/PA, R 20906; Holtzendorff to AA, B. 14787 I., Berlin, May 30, 1917, ibid., R 20903; Otto Nelte, "Die belgische Frage," *Zeitschrift für Völkerrecht* 8 (1914): 754; Dr. Neukamp, "Die Haager Friedenskonferenzen und der Europäische Krieg," *Zeitschrift für Völkerrecht* 8 (1914): 556; Lueder, cited in Best, *Humanity in Warfare*, 174.

164. Grey to Spring Rice, no. 82, Jan. 30, 1915, FO 382/184, no. 11379, file 8554; Hugh H. L. Bellot, "War Crimes: Their Prevention and Punishment," *Grotius Society, Problems of the War: Papers Read before the Society in the Year 1916* 2 (1917): 52; Westlake, *International Law*, 114.

165. Cited in Hinz, *Gefangen im Großen Krieg*, 262–63.

166. Prussian war ministry, "Erläuterungen oder Änderungen zu dem Erlaß vom 15 Apr. 1915," cited in Hinz, *Gefangen im Großen Krieg*, 264.

(implicitly) retaliation (for starvation of civilians). It laid down a fundamental position that some army commanders seem independently to have adopted without reference to it, at the latest in February 1916 at Verdun. Many French prisoners were not sent back to camps, but instead were kept for months near the firing line building trenches and railroads, and unloading munitions. Germany later reported that the army commanders had done so on their own initiative, though standard reports to the general staff surely must have enumerated the number of prisoners taken and described the work they did.[167] These retained prisoners were visible from the French side, and that knowledge, together with the public reprisals against French prisoners beginning in April 1916 (for alleged mistreatment of German captives in North Africa), prepared the way for the next descent down the spiral of violence.[168]

In May 1916 the French war minister approved the army's request to use POWs in greater numbers in the zone. Their food, pay, and dress were to be the same as in the interior; their bedding (five kilograms of straw) was to be changed "if possible" every fifteen days; "as much as possible" they were to be lodged in barracks, not tents; "proper" hygiene and medical care were to be provided. Although no set distance from the front lines was spelled out, it seems that circa fifteen kilometers was imagined as safe from artillery fire.[169] In short, the policy's intention was to use prisoner labor under conditions as close to those in the interior as possible; this was not a reprisal. Logistical shortfalls and lack of inspection in the first six months meant conditions in fact were uneven and often worse than the policy specified. In the Verdun sector, the commander of the Second Army, General Georges Robert Nivelle, secretly contravened policy by initiating his own "reprisal" that mirrored and then surpassed what French prisoners endured across the lines in German hands.[170] The results were appalling. Men were lodged in muddy hovels too small to stand in or stretch out; only when incapable of work were they permitted to go to the hospital, where, one German orderly recalled, they arrived "with fully frost bitten feet … eaten all over their body by vermin and as most were suffering from diarrhea, they soiled themselves over and over with their own feces."[171] They died of dysentery and artillery shelling.[172] When he became commander in chief, Nivelle was prepared to go farther and create entire reprisal camps in the firing zone on the German model. Asked directly by the French government, which until late winter 1917 knew nothing of the true

---

167. "L'emploi des prisonniers français à des travaux en rapport avec les opérations de la guerre sur le front russe et sur le front français," no date, SHAT 6N 111; Friedrich to chancellor (AA), no. 3276/17.U5/1., Berlin, Jan. 30, 1917, BAB R 901 84146.

168. On conditions in Northern Africa: Heather Jones, *Violence against Prisoners*, 110–16.

169. C. Vérand to commanding generals of the regions in the zone of armies, no. 40.555 P.G. Paris, May 30, 1916, SHAT 7N 161; on distance: GQG of Armies of North and North-East, État-Major, 2e Bureau, "Emploi par les allemands de prisonniers de guerre et de prisonniers civils à proximité du front," GQG, Jan. 8, 1917, SHAT 6N 111 (complaining that Germans use prisoners less than 12–13 km from the front); État-major général, Direction de l'arrière, GQG, no. 5352 DA, GQG, Jan. 10, 1917, ibid. (noting that the 12,000–15,000 German prisoners in the French zone were held between 15–30 km from the front).

170. Heather Jones, "German Spring Reprisals," 343–46; Heather Jones, *Violence against Prisoners*, 145–50.

171. Heather Jones, "German Spring Reprisals," 345.

172. A later note to the Germans claimed that, in one instance, "only" 8 of 141 dysentery victims died in the hospital at Amiens, *Note verbale* of Jan. 15, 1917, IIIb 3356 BAB R 901 84146.

conditions in the zone, Nivelle lied about holding prisoners under fire.[173] But by then, the damage had been done.

Unaware of Nivelle's retaliation order, the British army in July 1916 asked to follow French precedent and use prisoner labor in the zone. The War Office approved it as a "temporary measure" on July 17 and, like France, ordered that the prisoners were to do "no defence work" nor to be held "within range of enemy fire."[174] The original two thousand German prisoners quickly climbed to twelve thousand; France kept about twenty-three thousand Germans in its zone, almost six thousand of them in the Verdun sector.[175] In August, Lieutenant General Herbert E. Belfield, director of prisoners in the War Office, inspected the British zone camps and found the men "reasonably well housed, well fed and clothed and the conditions are generally good." But he feared German reprisals nonetheless, for British army command, like their German colleagues, opposed neutral (American) inspections on grounds of proximity to the front and poor transportation.[176] Belfield suggested covering denial of neutral visits by claiming reprisal, since Germany refused visits to its reprisal camps in the East where it currently held British prisoners; but that was never the official position. Until October 1916, when General Haig relented on neutral visits, there was no way to prove to Germany that its men were well treated. The Foreign Office had wanted inspections, but War Secretary David Lloyd George seems to have upheld the army command's entire plan, saying at one point (September 30, 1916) that "purely military considerations must determine the employment of prisoners of war in France."[177]

On the last day of 1916, Belfield's fear materialized. Germany protested French POW policy in the zone and threatened exact reciprocity if all German prisoners were not removed to thirty kilometers from the front lines and their mail regularized by January 15, 1917. France received Germany's note on the twelfth, replied by the fifteenth, but its reply arrived in Berlin on the eighteenth. Citing noncompliance, Germany launched its reprisal, adding British prisoners in late February. Its measures lasted until mid-May for French prisoners and mid-June for the British. Negotiations to end the reprisals revealed interesting patterns. Both the French and British army commands pleaded military necessity to keep prisoners working eight (Britain) or twenty (France) kilometers behind the front. As Lloyd George had done in the summer of 1916, incoming prime minister Alexandre Ribot at first backed his generals (Nivelle, once more).[178] But French public opinion forced

---

173. Heather Jones, "German Spring Reprisals," 348.

174. War Office to A.G. [Adjutant General], GHQ, France, July 17, 1916, secret, WO 32/5098, doc. 69A; Belfield to Newton, Jan. 28, 1918, FO 383/406, no. 19077, file 2209.

175. GHQ to WO, tel. no. 171, July 26, 1916, WO 32/5098, doc. 74; Belfield handwritten note of Oct. 9, 1916, WO 32/5098, doc. 15B; Heather Jones, *Violence against Prisoners*, 145.

176. Belfield to Army Council, Aug. 30, 1916, WO 32/5098; the order specifying conditions: "Formation of Prisoner of War Companies, Provisional Orders and Instructions," no. A.G. (b) 2006/4, July 27, 1916, ibid., doc. 1B.

177. Haig: Fowke, Adjutant General, writing for Haig, to WO, B/2006/26, Oct. 19, 1916, WO 32/5098, doc. 28A; Newton to WO, 158907/1218/P. Aug. 19, 1916, ibid., doc. 6A; H. G. Creedy[?], Army Council, note of Sept. 30, 1916, ibid.

178. "Extract from Procès Verbale of the Anglo-French conference held in London on 12 and 13 March 1916 [*sic*]," actually 1917, WO 32/5098, doc. 90A.

him to accede to Germany's demands. Once France had given in, Britain could no longer maintain its rigid stance; both governments finally agreed to the thirty-kilometer limit.[179] Lord Newton of the FOPD drew two lessons from the affair. "One, that we ought never to tie ourselves up by association with the French, or any other ally, over prisoner questions. The other, that no important decisions should be taken without consultation with the competent authorities. If the War Cabinet had taken the opinion of General Belfield, or of this Department, this deplorable incident would never have occurred."[180]

On the German side, we must examine two issues: was the 1917 policy a genuine reprisal? and what was reciprocity? On the first question, there were real grounds for reprisal. War Minister von Stein's draft letter listed every type of violation or complaint that the war ministry had received since August 1914, ranging from the trivial to the lethal.[181] Concerning the zone, the incidents he cited were mostly, but not exclusively, around Verdun. He originally wanted prisoners removed to fifty kilometers from the front, and when France began to acquiesce in the negotiations, Stein held out the possibility of removing prisoners from the rear areas as well.[182] Furthermore, the German reprisal numbers matched the number of German soldiers laboring in the zone.[183] These are all indications that he was serious in using reprisal to improve prisoners' conditions.

But the timing of Germany's protest is curious. The bundled nature of the complaints, some of them stretching back to 1914, suggests a clearing of the decks before the anticipated last push to victory that German military and naval leaders expected to happen with the opening of unrestricted submarine warfare (January 1917). Jettisoning law in this final effort was, in fact, Stein's position once the submarine decision was made.[184] Reprisal was also the wrong tool, given that Stein himself admitted that German army commanders had used prisoners in the fire zone in the spring of 1916 and that the practice had apparently been greatly extended during the summer of 1916, without official recourse to reprisal.[185] Finally, General Ludendorff's order seems purely, indeed extravagantly, punitive.

His wire of January 20, 1917, to all commanding generals in the west ordered that all newly made French (and later British) prisoners were to be held

> in open pens, [with] the least possible food and water, no utensils for eating or drinking, no protection against the weather, officers held separately but not better treated, to remain in the pens for fourteen days. Interrogations to be carried out

---

179. Heather Jones, "German Spring Reprisals," 350–52.

180. Newton minute, Feb. 3, 1918, to Belfield to Newton, Jan. 28, 1918, FO 383/406, no. 19077, file 2209.

181. Stein to Chancellor, Nr. 35487/16.U.5./1, Berlin, Dec. 18, 1916, IIIb 48502, BAB R 901 84146.

182. Ribot to War Minister, no. PG 2839, Paris, Apr. 14, 1917, copy, SHAT 6N 111.

183. Heather Jones, *Violence against Prisoners*, 145, 152, 153, 155.

184. Stein to Bethmann, Nr. 39/17.6 U5/1, Berlin, Jan. 27, 1917, Geheim, AA/PA R 22213. See above, 289–90.

185. Stein to Chancellor, Nr. 35487/16.U.5./1, Berlin, Dec. 18, 1916, IIIb 48502, BAB R 901 84146. Both France and Britain later dated the widespread use of prisoners in the zone to July/August 1916: French *note verbale* in Spanish embassy to AA, no. 350/172, Berlin, Oct. 3, 1917, BAB R 901 84148 (IIIb 43989); see much testimony by escaped British prisoners in FO 383/406, no. 38519, file 2209; Justice Robert Younger, "Report on the Treatment by the Enemy of British Prisoners of War behind the Firing Lines in France and Belgium," Mar. 4, 1918, ibid., no. 36365.

sharply: isolation, tied-to-post, wire cages, denial of food as means of coercion are permitted. No physical mistreatment [meaning, presumably, beating]. The collection camps: the most makeshift accommodations, tents, the most primitive barracks or earthen huts, no heat, no light, straw sacks not necessary, the most minimal provision of eating utensils and soap. The simplest opportunity for washing and laundry, complete isolation from the population, strict limits of movement, scanty food, no hot water, no opportunity to cook, no cantine. Religious service permitted.... Work commandos: accommodations as you like, protection from weather not necessary, hygienic arrangements dispensable, scanty food, long and strenuous work without any limit, including transport of munitions and trench work under enemy fire.[186]

Outgoing mail was to be sped up, so that France learned of the conditions quickly, but incoming mail, including food packages, were to be delayed by four weeks.

Ludendorff's order makes clear that labor was not the object, but instead exemplary punishment on a massive scale. His order was carried out. The resulting death rate was high; for example, in four months one-third of the original 580 men of one reprisal unit died of starvation, disease, or shooting. Survivors were typically so emaciated and exhausted that they had to be carried into camps when they were finally released to the interior.[187] Ludendorff's order took the very worst, probably exceptional, treatment reported by German prisoners and made it the norm. B. B. Cubitt of the War Office was astonished at Germany's actions, because it must have known from prisoner letters (and after October 1916 from neutral inspection reports) that conditions in the British sector generally were nothing like what Germany alleged.[188] Ludendorff's construal of reciprocity was certainly effective in forcing France and Britain to comply with Germany's demands, but its extremism also confirmed their belief in Imperial Germany's unregenerate ruthlessness and inhumanity.

Worse, Ludendorff's order lowered the bar for prisoner treatment thereafter. For while Germany did remove French and British prisoners from the fire zone after the thirty-kilometer agreement, it did not return them to camps in Germany, but kept them working in the rear zones.[189] Believable reports indicated that some unit commanders violated the thirty-kilometer rule throughout 1917. That and extreme exploitation in the rear zones produced prisoners who were "in the same shocking condition" as during the reprisals.[190]

As Germany prepared for its last effort to win the war, the March 1918 offensives, it once again removed all limits to the mistreatment of prisoners of war. But this time it did not claim reprisal. It thus repeated the pattern of submarine warfare, which had originally been launched under cover of reprisal (February 1915), but then simply decreed

---

186. Ludendorff to AA, tel. Jan. 20, 1917, IIIb 3200, BAB R 901 84146.

187. Heather Jones, "German Spring Reprisals," 352.

188. Cubitt to Foreign Office, 0103/8472, Feb. 2, 1917, WO 32/5098 doc. 68A.

189. Heather Jones, *Violence against Prisoners*, 160–61.

190. Thirty-kilometer zone: Cubitt of WO to FO, Nr. 0103/1/154 Jan. 10, 1918, FO 383/406, no. 6185, file 2209; same condition: testimony of Private Alfred Fountain, interned in Soltau Feb. 19, 1917–Jan. 7, 1918, FO 383/406, no. 20622, file 2209.

as war policy (January 1917). Over two weeks before the offensive began, the Prussian war ministry announced that prisoners capable of work would be retained at the front; thus, retention of prisoners was part of the plan, not simply an expedient resorted to under pressure of events.[191] It violated Germany's bilateral agreements with France and Britain, both regarding the thirty-kilometer limit and the Hague and Bern Agreements of 1917 on prisoners of war. Britain and France had scrupulously upheld those agreements.[192] OHL's intention was to use prisoner labor, but conditions at the front and the habit of using coercion to overcome resistance, illness, and inability relaunched the punitive treatment of 1917.[193] Despite OHL's repeated orders beginning on May 17, 1918, rescinding the policy, the situation deteriorated as unit commanders followed the logic of lethal military necessity.[194] Throughout May, June, and July 1918 information poured into London and Paris of horrendous, deadly abuse of tens of thousands of Allied prisoners at the western front and in labor camps in the occupied zone. We lack precise statistical data, but two reports suggest extraordinary levels of mortality, at least in some areas. Red Cross doctors who directly after the war cared for French prisoners from the occupied zone described them as suffering from "intense anemia, extreme emaciation, with loss of forty percent of their original weight.... The mortality rate is up to fifty percent of cases."[195] In October 1918 the Dutch minister in Brussels reported a POW camp near Charleville in which, of 350 British prisoners, 190 had died since June (in four months, a mortality rate of 54 percent).[196] War Cabinet member Robert Borden called Germany's policy "slow assassination."[197]

From Reprisals to Trials

Under the sway of Germany's treatment of British prisoners, the Foreign Office, especially its Prisoners Department, became probably the strongest advocate of reprisal inside the government. The FOPD had opposed the (German) proposal to meet in The Hague and work out an agreement on prisoner exchanges and treatment in June 1917. Lord Newton,

---

191. Prussian war minister to all deputy general commanders, Mar. 2, 1918, in Hinz, *Gefangen im Großen Krieg,* 32n106. Cf. Jones's interpretation of the order as improvisation: Heather Jones, *Violence against Prisoners,* 178, 183.

192. Heather Jones, *Violence against Prisoners,* 160, 183.

193. Heather Jones, "The Final Logic of Sacrifice? Violence in German Prisoner of War Labor Companies in 1918," *Historian* 68, no. 4 (2006): 770–83; Heather Jones, *Violence against Prisoners,* ch. 4.

194. Ludendorff's order of May 17, 1918, repeated at least eight times, Heather Jones, *Violence against Prisoners,* 183–85.

195. Heather Jones, "Final Logic," 790.

196. Robertson to Foreign Office, no. 3450, Oct. 4, 1918, FO 383/408, no. 114586, file 2209. For prisoners in the zone: Report of prisoner of war department, 71.01 (received in Bern Aug. 15, 1918), enclosed in Swiss Foreign Office to German Foreign Office, Bern, Aug. 16, 1918, IIIb 27850, "Urgent," BAB R 901 84149; Misc. no. 19 (1918): Robert Younger, "Report on the Treatment by the Germans of Prisoners of War Taken during the Spring Offensives of 1918," Cd. 9106, Oct. 1918, FO 383/408, no. 115782, file 2209.

197. War Cabinet minutes, July 28, 1918, FO 383/416, no. 110248, file 65313.

head of the FOPD, admonished Curzon that "such a meeting is now impossible until assurances have been received that this disgraceful state of things has terminated."[198] The War Cabinet, like France, pressured by public opinion, overrode Newton and opted for negotiations.[199] The government, as Newton noted, was "indisposed to take strong reciprocal action," and the most indisposed was the War Office.[200] The Foreign Office files are replete with complaints of War Office timidity. Even General Belfield sighed that "the War Office always seem to find some excuse for not taking any strong action."[201] Vansittart, the most vehement fire-breather in the FOPD, thought them "spineless."[202] Newton noted that, "as far as I can see, the War Office are against reprisals, whereas the Admiralty desire to threaten them."[203] Britain had thus developed the opposite constellation from Germany, where the war ministry and general staff pursued reckless reprisal against the wishes of the AA. In Britain, the War Office had concluded that reprisals were ineffective or, given the Germans' proven readiness to go to any extreme, inconceivable. As B. B. Cubitt, writing for the War Office, confessed regarding one typical incident, "it is difficult to know what really drastic action can be taken."[204]

When in 1918 a second round of Hague negotiations with Germany over prisoner issues was suggested, the Foreign Office became even more vociferous. Vansittart noted that "the Germans have violated every consideration of humanity and every agreement as well," so there was no point in negotiation. H. B. Warner favored bombing "the civilian population of the Rhine towns, making known this intention and its reasons by leaflets dropped over these towns." Newton agreed that bombing was best.[205] The Foreign Office now bypassed the minions at the War Office and wrote directly to its new chief, Alfred Milner, summarizing the murderous conditions and urging "drastic reprisals."[206] The government overrode the Foreign Office again, preferring the second round of Hague negotiations, which concluded in July 1918. Despite the agreement, news of abuse and death continued to flood the Foreign Office, and the War Office continued to reject reprisal.[207]

Finally, on September 24, 1918, the FOPD sat down with two representatives of the War Office and reviewed the situation. They agreed that "reprisals in some form must be proposed to the War Cabinet."[208] But before proceeding they canvassed the War Office, Admiralty, Air Ministry, and Colonial Office. They summarized the facts: the Germans "systematically" held at the front all prisoners capable of working, keeping many of them in the zone of fire. Their work directly aided the operations of war. Worse, inhumane treatment,

---

198. Newton memorandum to Curzon, June 5, 1917, FO 383/267, no. 113137, file 235.

199. Newton memorandum of June 12, 1917, FO 383/267, no. 114982, file 235; Cecil draft of dispatch to Bertie, June 15, 1917, FO 383/268, no. 122454, file 235.

200. Newton memo of June 1, 1917, FO 383/267, no. 110298, file 235.

201. Belfield minute, Oct. 22, 1917, FO 383/273, no. 202231, file 235.

202. Vansittart minute, Oct. 23, 1917, FO 383/273, no. 202231, file 235.

203. Newton minute, Jan. 2, 1918, FO 383/275, no. 240098, file 235.

204. Cubitt to Foreign Office, no. 0103/1/735, Oct. 26, 1917, FO 383/273, no. 205970, file 235.

205. Vansittart minute, May 22, 1918; Newton minute, May 23, 1918, FO 383/407, no. 90590, file 2209.

206. Foreign Office to War Office, May 24, 1918, FO 383/407, no. 90590, file 2209.

207. See the many documents in FO 383/407, file 2209.

208. Minutes of conference of Sept. 24, 1918, FO 383/407, no. 11303, file 2209.

starvation, and artillery fire had killed "a large number." Prisoners were sent to camps and actually reported as captured only after "they have become useless, owing to weakness or disease." The FOPD recommended five types of reprisal. Three were exactly reciprocal: non-notification of capture, denial of mail, and use in the fire zone. One was thought to be reciprocal: reprisals in future would be automatic (that is, the Germans would not be specially notified, nor would the month-long waiting period specified in the two Hague agreements be observed).[209] The final reprisal broke new ground: German officers were to be treated like common soldiers as to billeting and work. This idea was probably inspired by observing Germany's sensitivity to dishonorable treatment of its officers (the French hospital-ship reprisal had successfully exploited this characteristic).

Almost simultaneously, the Foreign Office pursued another tack: postwar trials. On October 3, 1918, Newton suggested to the home secretary charging individual Germans with war crimes after the war.[210] This new idea had steadily gained momentum. It might first have been suggested publicly in October 1914 by the *Edinburgh Review* regarding Germany's violation of Belgian neutrality.[211] A joint Allied note of May 24, 1915, had declared that Britain, France, and Russia would "hold personally responsible...all members of the Ottoman Government and those of their agents who are implicated" in the mass murder of the Armenians.[212] Two weeks later, Balfour had hinted the same when he declared to the House of Commons that "the general question of personal responsibility [for unrestricted submarine warfare] should be reserved until the end of the war."[213] On July 31, 1916, Prime Minister Asquith told the House of Commons, regarding the execution of Captain Fryatt, that Britain was "determined to bring to justice the criminals, whoever they may be, and whatever their station. In such cases as this the man who authorizes the system under which such crimes are committed may well be the most guilty of all."[214] In all these cases, Britain judged that a system or policy was behind the deeds, but it could not immediately respond in an appropriate way. Postwar trials was a kind of public place-holder for more drastic action.

Inside the Foreign Office, postwar trials also seemed a useful threat, especially against German reprisals.[215] At the same time, everyone believed that certain aspects of German war conduct constituted crime, a conviction visible in Robert Cecil's language when in August 1915 he urged the War Office to discover "if possible further particulars of the grosser forms of ill treatment with names of the criminals."[216] By mid 1916, support for war crimes trials was clearly growing inside the Foreign Office. Responding to reports that

---

209. The Foreign Office had long complained that Germany launched reprisals without notification and without observing the waiting period.

210. Newton minute, Oct. 3,1918, FO 383/407, no. 114359, file 2209.

211. Louis Renault, "De l'application du droit pénal aux faits de guerre," *Revue générale de droit international public* 25 (1918): 23.

212. Amb. Sharp to Bryan, Paris, May 28, 1915, *FRUS* 1915, Suppl., 981.

213. Cited in Cecil to Page, June 9, 1915, FO 383/61, no. 76883, file 48319.

214. New York Times, *Current History: The European War* (New York, 1917), 1018.

215. For example, Wellesley minute of Dec. 9, 1915, and Langley minute on same document, FO 372/783, no. 185503, file 153865.

216. Cecil, minute Aug. 30, 1915, FO 383/43, no. 119237, file 1061.

German soldiers and administrators had violated article 7 of the Hague Convention (on treatment of prisoners of war), the junior-most clerk suggested "bring[ing] the guilty to trial and punishment," and his superiors, Horace Rumbold, and Lord Newton agreed.[217] Newton wanted the matter presented to the cabinet. But as the document rose higher in the chain, doubts increased. Permanent Undersecretary Arthur Nicolson merely signed with no comment, while Grey felt that "the question of punishing those German officers should stand over till the terms of peace."[218] That is, Grey was not opposed to war crimes trials, but did not want them to occur during the war. But Grey let Newton present the suggestion to the Army Council.

The Army Council quickly rejected the idea.[219] It feared setting a "precedent which might involve us in difficulties in similar cases in the future," and eliciting German reprisals, if its soldiers were convicted. The second fear was realistic, since Germany had retaliated against French war crimes trials of German officers. Like Grey, the Army Council wanted trials postponed until the peace, "when we can consider the question of 'war crimes' committed by Germany as a whole." The Foreign Office accepted this view. That was June 1916. The following month, the execution of Captain Fryatt reopened the issue, and the War Committee once again put Britain on record for holding "those in authority" responsible.

Postwar trials raised many difficult questions. No codification of international law specified penalties. Should trials be held by national courts, or (nonexistent) international ones? Could soldiers or even officers hide behind superior orders? Were heads of state liable? Was violation of treaties a criminal act? Allied legal experts disagreed on these and other questions. It is perhaps notable that the dean of French international lawyers, Louis Renault, rejected trying heads of state or extending criminal law to encompass "political" offenses, such as beginning a war of aggression or breaking international treaties. That would be "the law of the future, a future which I shall not see."[220] Where Renault thought that national courts were the proper venue of such trials, Hugh H. L. Bellot did not shrink from advocating a new Hague Court of Criminal Appeal.[221] Renault's colleague Paul Pic saw no reason why law should stop before "the most highly placed, sovereigns, chiefs of state or of the army"—they all deserved "punishment proportionate to their crime."[222] All three lawyers understood that international law and the mechanisms to enforce it had to expand beyond their current limits in order to be adequate to the circumstances of the World War. That was necessary because its alternative, reprisal, had reached its own outermost limits. "The Allies would dishonor themselves" if they responded in kind to the massacre of civil-

---

217. W. O'Reilly, Rumbold, Newton minutes of May 23, 1916, to Union of South Africa, Defence Department, "Report of Commission of Enquiry into the Treatment of Prisoners of War by the German Protectorate Authorities during the Late Hostilities," FO 383/168, no. 97578, file 629.

218. Ibid.

219. Cubitt to Foreign Office, June 10, 1916, ibid., no. 112727.

220. Renault, "Application," 23.

221. Bellot, "War Crimes," 51.

222. Paul Pic, "Violation systematique des lois de la guerre par les Austro-allemands. Les sanctions nécessaires," *Revue générale de droit international public* 23 (1916): 260.

ians; they would descend to the level of the purveyors of "'Kultur.'"[223] Reprisals had reached the end of their effectiveness; they no longer prevented evil precedents, they set them, and thus they corroded the law rather than sustaining it.[224]

The internal debate over reprisal versus trials occurred one last time as the Foreign Office reprisal recommendation reached the various ministries on September 25, 1918. Since the Air Ministry had been established around a core of bombing units dedicated to aerial reprisal, it almost always supported reprisal policy. The Foreign Office took "it for granted that the Air Ministry will agree," and the fliers did not disappoint.[225] They immediately assented, adding that they hoped the "over lenient treatment now given to prisoners of war in this country" would be modified to permit "the fullest use being made of their power to labour."[226] But the RAF was alone. The Admiralty rejected the toughest recommendation, the plan to make officers work.[227] That was "not a true reprisal, but a new measure" guaranteed to cause German retaliation. Worse, "abrogation of one of the few provisions of the Hague Conventions which have been observed on both sides during the present war should only be made in the very last resort." The navy recommended sticking to exact reciprocity with the customary four-week warning. The War Office continued to think reprisals ineffective, and they rejected forcing officers to work as a violation of article 6 of the Hague Convention that all belligerents had so far upheld. It seemed "inadvisable that a departure from it should be initiated by Her Majesty's Government."[228] The India Office was content to leave the decision to others, but preferred a "solemn warning" that "all officials and persons concerned will be held responsible 'morally, penally and pecuniarily' for all breaches of international law," quoting from a recent announcement of the French government.[229]

On October 11, 1918, the War Cabinet debated the issue. The problem with trials was that "no nation, unless it was beaten to the dust, would accept such terms."[230] War Minister Milner advocated harsher treatment for German officers, but Undersecretary of State for Foreign Affairs Robert Cecil countered that "he could not recall a single instance when the carrying out of reprisals had obtained good results." However, the *threat* of reprisals did occasionally work. Furthermore, "the Germans were very sensitive to outside opinion." They might be embarrassed by publication of their horrendous treatment of POWs, especially since the new chancellor, Prince Max von Baden, had been so active in trying to improve the lot of internees. In the end, the War Cabinet decided on publication and the threat of postwar trials.

---

223. Pic, "Violation systematique," 264; Renault, "Application," 29.

224. Bellot, "War Crimes," 54.

225. Barnett Hall minute of Sept. 13, 1918, to J. A. Corcoran to Foreign Office, Sept. 12, 1918, FO 383/401, no. 113062, file 368. This minute referred to a different reprisal suggestion than the one of the Sept. 24 meeting.

226. W. A. Robinson (Air Ministry) to Foreign Office, Sept. 26, 1918, FO 383/407, Nr. 114024, file 2209.

227. Charles Walker (Admiralty) to Foreign Office, Oct. 1, 1918, FO 383/407, Nr. 1140384, file 2209.

228. Cubitt to Foreign Office, Oct. 5, 1918, FO 383/407, Nr. 114662, file 2209.

229. H. V. Cox to Foreign Office, Oct. 1918, FO 383/407, Nr. 114944, file 2209.

230. War Cabinet minutes of Oct. 11, 1918, FO 383/474, no. 115762, file 114592.

This final debate is significant for several reasons. It reflected in real policy the widespread recognition among contemporary international-legal scholars that during wartime international law was broadly upheld by three forms of sanction: reprisal, trial (which most of them construed as occurring in national courts), and public opinion.[231] The FOPD embraced reprisal out of frustration and despair: that Germany would not uphold either international or bilateral agreements, that force was the only language it understood, and that Britain's own self-understanding as law-abiding and "civilized" hindered it from applying sufficient force to be effective. Indeed, even the "drastic action" it recommended in late September 1918 was tame considering the lethal practices it was supposed to counter. Frustration could predispose one to punitive vengeance, an attitude exemplified by Vansittart. Even the relatively equanimous Lord Newton routinely used the word "Hun" in internal correspondence after spring 1917. But there were limits. When Vansittart went on about the "*filthy*" German language, Hardinge jerked him back: "I am very much surprised at this sort of language being used in a minute. It is very unnecessary and even silly."[232] In fact, the reprisals advocated by the Foreign Office were genuine; they aimed at returning Germany to the law. The basic argument between the Foreign Office and the War Office concerned effectiveness. H. B. Warner, speaking for the FOPD, thought that the success of the recommendations of September 24, 1918, "was likely to be proportionate to their severity," whereas opponents, looking back at Germany's record of counter-reprisal, thought not.[233]

By the end of the war, Britain had largely rejected reprisal in favor of the two remaining classes of sanctions. One was expanding the instruments and reach of law through postwar trials, setting precedents for specific sentences for war crimes, and extending culpability to heads of state and chiefs of armies. The more Britain threatened these things publicly, the more it created pressure on itself to make them come true. Trials formed part of the panoply of other sanctions that were only possible after fighting had ended: reparations, indemnities, and economic and political disabilities that were hammered out in the Treaty of Versailles, together with the positive framework (the League of Nations and diplomatic cooperation) that the Allies hoped would make future sanctions less necessary.

But in October 1918, before the war ended, the War Cabinet decided to displace reprisal by an alternative sanction: harnessing public opinion. Of course, the Allies had done this successfully since the beginning of the war through public diplomacy and propaganda. It was logical to continue in this vein. Doing so acknowledged the importance of public opinion to the development of international law and, perhaps more important, the fact that law was the creation of a broad community of peoples (not just states, and certainly not just belligerents). Cecil's correct observation of German sensitivity to publicity is

231. Oppenheim, *International Law*, 1:14–15; Renault, "Application," 9; Bellot, "War Crimes," 54; Pic, "Violation systematique," 260.

232. Vansittart minute, June 12, 1917, Hardinge minute, undated, to Townley to Foreign Office, Hague, no. 1626, June 11, 1917, FO 383/267, file 235, no. 116654.

233. Warner minute, Oct. 3, 1918, to Walker to Foreign Office, Oct. 1, 1918, FO 383/407, no. 114384, file 2209.

important, for it shows that in Britain's view Germany was still tethered, however insecurely, to that broader world, for all the labeling of the nation as "barbarian."

In 1939, this same choice among sanctions recurred, but vis-à-vis a different Germany. Under those circumstances, the observation that successful trials could only occur when a nation was "beaten to the dust" became relevant and indicated the relation between protecting and extending international law and unconditional surrender.

Conclusion

10

International law defined most clearly what was at stake in the war: namely, for Europe, the continued existence or disappearance of a state system that allowed for nations organized as states to determine their own paths within a common framework. Treaties, conventions, and customary law were the products and the guarantors of this system. The laws of war were similarly the lowest common denominator of behavior *in extremis* that qualified a state for membership. The instant Imperial German breaches of treaty, convention, and customary law signaled, first, a strong challenge to the existence of this system and, second, Germany's estrangement from it. The Kaiserreich was largely operating on different principles, some of which it had announced previously at international conventions like Brussels and the Hague, and some of which it had not. It is uncertain how clearly German leaders in August 1914 saw that their actions required a complete reorganization of Europe, and hence of its (international) laws, though both things had become quite clear by the beginning of September 1914. Just as the Allies condemned Imperial Germany for violating law, German leaders applied their own criteria and judged German policy as justified by necessity or reprisal and their opponents as hypocritical scofflaws for violating the (unratified) Declaration of London and allegedly engaging in popular insurrection. The German position proposed a serious alternative to the laws and customs of Europe as they had evolved since 1815 and before.

Because law is both a fundamental guarantor and a sensitive expression of community and of the expectations that uphold social behavior, and because Germany was one of the five great powers of the European state system, its disagreements on international law were critically important. They were both material (they concerned the substance of rules) and interpretive (what law was and how it operated). The uniquely strong concept of military necessity held by military and civilian leaders and shared by German academics suspended the laws of war upon the subjective judgment of military officers. Non-German contemporaries identified military necessity as the main problematic feature of Imperial Germany's view of war. But a larger version of necessity, *Notstand*, applied imperative necessity prophylactically to political or diplomatic situations that had not (yet) occurred, thus covering or justifying preventive war and major treaty violations that then created the circumstances in which military necessity operated. Both subjective judgments of necessity were produced largely from within: military necessity by the Kaiserreich's military-organizational culture of risk, speed, and absolute victory or absolute destruction, on the one hand, and *Notstand* by the assumption of civilian leaders (supported by bourgeois public opinion) that Germany must either "develop" (expand) or die, a conviction that predisposed them to imagine that other powers sought to suffocate or even annihilate them.

Behind these ideas of necessity were theories of law with powerful consequences. What I have called war positivism claimed that the putative nature of force and violence unleashed in war produced the "natural" laws of war, which could not be limited by norms or binding laws external to them. War positivism was difficult, perhaps impossible to distinguish from the old saw that "might makes right." Weapons positivism was the reduced, tactical version in which the alleged nature of new weapons erased old laws and general principles in the interest of the untrammeled use of new technologies. Both forms of positivism introduced enormous dynamism into the law. Under them *rebus sic stantibus* became a principle of international law more fundamental than *pacta sunt servanda*. Both positivisms made it possible for a single belligerent exercising sufficient power or having developed a new weapon to "discover" new law or disqualify old laws unilaterally—in other words, to legislate. The ability of a single state to change law by itself spelled the effective end of legal community, both in the sense of a community bound by law and of one that legislates on the basis of shared interests, norms, or history.

Imperial Germany's brand of positivism had other effects, too. There are recurring indications that German leaders thought of silences in the law as unlegislated, law-free zones (*non liquet*). Similar zones might be created punctually when one's enemies violated a rule; in the opinion of Admiral Reinhard Koch, for example, violation by one enemy negated the rule for all belligerents.[1] Claiming reciprocity to free oneself from legal strictures tempted the Western Allies, too—Edward Grey wondered if Germany's violations would not "justify us in declaring all ordinary rules abrogated in dealing with Germany," and France did just that relating to prisoners of war in October 1915.[2] But the ultimate effect of the absence of a legal rule, whether by the assumption of *non liquet* or by prior violation, depended on whether the state thought general principles established binding limits even in that case. The Hague delegates intended the Martens Clause to be such a statement of

---

1. Reinhard Koch to AA, B. 32182 I., Sept. 20, 1917, Berlin, AA/PA R 20906. In Prof. Ebers's view, violation of one rule of international law also probably justified noncompliance "with other, related norms": Report of Prof. Dr. Ebers to Investigating Committee, *UA* 3:4, p. 404.

2. Grey to Spring Rice, no. 82, London, Jan. 30. 1915, FO 382/184, file 8554, no. 11379; "Note sur la main d'oeuvre des prisonniers de guerre, juillet 1916," SHAT 6N 111.

limits, and the Allies generally accepted that view. German leaders and academics were more inclined to interpret it as an empty phrase designed to paper over disagreement, and thus inoperative or very weak.[3] Similarly, the general principles to which the Western Allies frequently alluded, often connected with a phrase about "civilized" nations, were not a staple of official German notes during the war. In short, Imperial German leaders were much less likely to grant the existence of general principles or preexisting, binding customary laws that limited state action even in situations where for whatever reasons law was thought to be suspended or annulled.

We must ask how much Imperial Germany's challenge to the international-legal system was a product of its weakness. For Germany's risk of war in July 1914 and its consequently large role in starting the war were quixotic, insofar as the Entente's much greater strength made it almost impossible for Germany to win outright. The Kaiserreich repeatedly resorted to techniques to overcome its weakness (the Schlieffen Plan with its shortcut through Belgium, the forced retention of migrant workers, terror against civilians to speed victory, unrestricted submarine warfare in lieu of a dominant surface fleet, poison gas). Its extravagant exploitation of occupied areas was the only way that Germany could continue a war that it did not win in the first weeks. All of these methods were serious violations of existing international law. Furthermore, they weakened Germany rather than strengthening it, because moral authority is also a source of power, and it accrued to the Allies.

Eric Posner and others point out that many rules of international law favor the powerful, and that weaker states may be less inclined to accept or follow them.[4] But Germany was not objectively, but only relatively weak in comparison to its enemies' coalition. Imperial Germany was a great power, and it had been instrumental in codifying the laws of war and in helping to determine the law's silences. If in the end the Hague Rules and unwritten customary law seemed to Germany's leaders to be contrary to its interests as a belligerent, we must ask what those interests were. For law, both codified and customary, protects legitimate interests, not all interests. In granting the protection of legitimate interests, the international legal system creates a right to act in a certain way under certain circumstances, and, more important, grants that same right to all other states in the same community of law. Law's universality creates "the expectation of expectations" that build and maintain society.[5] The consequent regularity of state behavior creates stability, makes planning possible, enhances security, spreads the cost of enforcement, and regulates conflict. Because the acquisition of legal rights is reciprocal, this enhancement of a state's (legal) power at the same time "imposes significant constraints on states as they engage in

---

3. For example, Zimmermann to Jagow, GHQ, Nr. 230, Sept. 2, 1914, AA/PA R 22382. Zimmermann's dismissal of the clause is similar to that in Otto Nelte, "Die belgische Frage," *Zeitschrift für Völkerrecht* 8 (1914): 754; Karl Strupp, "Der belgische Volkskrieg und die Haager Landkriegsordnung," *Zeitschrift für Völkerrecht* 9 (1916): 284. Meurer is inconsistent: Christian Meurer, *Die völkerrechtliche Stellung der vom Feinde besetzten Gebiete* (Tübingen, 1915), 3, 23, 62–64, 71. See also Gerd Hankel, *Die Leipziger Prozesse: Deutsche Kriegsverbrechen und ihre strafrechtliche Verfolgung nach dem Ersten Weltkrieg* (Hamburg, 2003), 256.

4. Eric A. Posner, "A Theory of the Laws of War," *University of Chicago Law Review* 70, no. 1 (Winter 2003): 304–5.

5. Niklas Luhmann, *Rechtssoziologie* (Opladen, 1987), 38–39, 54, 80–94, 100, 108–10, and 129.

behavior that contributes to the maintenance, development, or change of rules of customary international law," in Michael Byers's words.[6] He continues, "by qualifying and constraining the application of state power in the customary process in this and other ways, the international legal system distinguishes the resulting rules of customary international law from the arbitrary commands of powerful states, and accords those rules the authority and compelling power of the entire international society of which the legal system is a part." There are two points here. First, law does indeed reflect the interests of powerful states. But, second, by granting the same interest-laden rights to other states, powerful and weaker, it simultaneously limits the powerful within the community of all states. This is how (and why) interest, power, law, and community interact and mutually reinforce and also limit one another.

As Hersh Lauterpacht writes, since "rights are conferred by the community...the community must see to it that the rights are not exercised in an anti-social manner. To deny this in regard to international law is to maintain that in the international sphere rights are faculties whose source lies not in the objective law created by the community, but in the will and the power of the State."[7] Although many of Germany's prewar international-legal writers had recognized the community of states as legislator, the lack of an overarching authority on the monarchist model seemed to many to reinforce the Hegelian concept of the individual state as the embodiment of will and power whose consent to rules was voluntary and thus revocable; that view made the single state, not the community, the basis of whatever law there was.[8] This self-described "realistic" interpretation of law dominated German constitutional legal theory (*Staatslehre*) after unification and strongly determined how legally trained officials understood international law.[9] Legal "realists"

6. Michael Byers, "Custom, Power, and the Power of Rules: Customary International Law from an Interdisciplinary Perspective," *Michigan Journal of International Law* 17 (1995–96): 122–23.

7. Hersh Lauterpacht, *The Function of Law in the International Community* (Oxford, 1933), 298.

8. The law-giving community: Emanuel von Ullmann, *Völkerrecht,* Das Öffentliche Recht der Gegenwart (Tübingen, 1908), 3–5; Franz von Liszt, *Das Völkerrecht systematisch dargestellt* (Berlin, 1913), 3–6. Some German jurists upheld this view even during the war, for example, Ludwig Dambitsch, "Völkerrechtsverletzung," *Zeitschrift für Völkerrecht* 10 (1917/18): 368–74. The contrary view, most famously expressed in Adolf Lasson, *Princip und Zukunft des Völkerrechts* (Berlin, 1871), 65–66, 73–74; Adolf Lasson, "Selections from *Das Culturideal und der Krieg* (Berlin, 1868) and *Princip und Zukunft des Völkerrechts* (Berlin, 1871)," in *A Survey of International Relations between the United States and Germany, August 1, 1914–April 6, 1917, Based on Official Documents,* ed. James Scott Brown (New York, 1917), l–liii, lxiii–lxv; Max Seydel, *Grundzüge einer allgemeinen Staatslehre* (Würzburg, 1873), 31–32; and Erich Kaufmann, *Das Wesen des Völkerrechts und die clausula rebus sic stantibus* (Tübingen, 1911), 199–200, 204, 212–14. Against the theory of state consent: James Leslie Brierly, *The Basis of Obligation in International Law and Other Papers,* ed. Hersch Lauterpacht and C. H. M. Waldock (Oxford, 1958), 12–17.

9. Michael Stolleis, *Geschichte des öffentlichen Rechts in Deutschland* (Munich, 1988), 2:435–36. Germany's foreign office had a higher percentage of lawyers than the foreign offices of Britain or France: "Just under one third of the 548 diplomats [in the AA] holding the rank of assistant or secretary of legation or above between 1871 and 1914 held the doctor juris degree." Lamar Cecil, *The German Diplomatic Service, 1871–1914* (Princeton, NJ, 1976), 27; Paul Gordon Lauren, *Diplomats and Bureaucrats: The First Institutional Responses to Twentieth-Century Diplomacy in France and Germany,* Hoover Institution Publications (Stanford, CA, 1976), 100n71, 101; Zara S. Steiner, *The Foreign Office and Foreign Policy, 1898–1914* (London, 1985), 17–18.

were convinced of two things: the primacy of the state, and the existential requirement of its constant, dynamic development. The "justified self-interestedness" of the state put international relations "in constant flux" (Adolf Lasson); when its interests clashed with those of another state, "the dichotomy of interest would seek its equalization in war" (Max Seydel).[10] Binding law shielded the weak and thereby hindered the development of the strong, which is why when such situations arose, war, not law, must decide, and, in Lasson's words, "for both sides war is rational and necessary in the nature of things, and thus also just."[11] In essence, this was Germany's wartime claim. Chancellor Bethmann Hollweg spoke for broad sections of the military and civilian elites (whose annexationism he later blamed for restricting his policy options) when he repeatedly identified Germany's interest as "the free development of our energies" so as "to extend the greatness of our empire."[12] On the Continent, Germany's development could occur only at the expense of other peoples.

It was that revolutionary endeavor that consequently destroyed international law in World War I. The size and extent of the war were largely due to the enormous stakes involved in the conflict. It was not "total war" that destroyed law, but rather the destruction of law (which meant the destruction of the European order) that produced total, or near total, war.[13] Law, at once the product of the prewar community, the symbol of its order, and its guarantor, was the first victim of a revolutionary project to overthrow the European state system. Historians have long recognized the revolutionary means that Imperial Germany used, some right from the beginning (for example, promoting Islamic jihad and colonial revolts), some later (most famously, sending Vladimir Lenin to the Finland station). These means fit the radical nature of Germany's goals. But the polycratic and frankly inefficient character of Imperial German government meant that the radical potential of its policies emerged without coordination, indeed almost haphazardly. So, although German leaders planned to violate Belgian neutrality, they did not set out deliberately to destroy the whole edifice of European law. That fell because it could survive neither the collapse of post-Napoleonic Europe nor the way of waging war that the German military had developed by 1914. Only after the war was begun did the requirements of victory become clearer. It is significant that the chancellor and others repeatedly identified both impending defeat *and* probable victory as the conditions under which they would openly adopt flagrant violations of current international law uncovered by reference to reprisal. In the first case, they had nothing to lose; in the second, they would be powerful enough to set the new legal foundations of the postwar order. When the Allies won,

---

10. Lasson, "Selections," lxvii–lxviii; Seydel, *Grundzüge*, 31–32.

11. Lasson, *Princip*, 69.

12. Bethmann Hollweg speech to Reichstag, Dec. 2, 1914, in *Sten.Ber.* vol. 306, 17–20. Bethmann mentioned "development" five times in his Reichstag speech explaining why Germany was at war, Aug. 4, 1914: ibid., 5–7. After the war: German National Constituent Assembly, *Official German Documents Relating to the World War*, trans. Division of International Law Carnegie Endowment for International Peace (New York, 1923), 1:348, 350, 427.

13. On the question of World War I's totality: Roger Chickering and Stig Förster, eds., *Great War, Total War: Combat and Mobilization on the Western Front, 1914–1918* (Cambridge, 2000).

they devoted enormous energy to reestablishing international law in the framework of the Treaty of Versailles and the new League of Nations, in trials of alleged war criminals, and in planning for revision of material law. They had interpreted the war from the beginning as a struggle over law, and so their victory was meant to institutionalize the rule of law in diplomatic and international-political affairs.

Allied Violations

Although Imperial Germany might be called a structural violator of international law during the war, it was not the only violator. The fact that breaches occurred on both sides has encouraged self-styled "realists," international-legal skeptics, cynics, and pacifists alike to claim that all states were equally guilty, either because lawbreaking is in the nature of states, or in the nature of war, or both. This study offers a more differentiated view.

Allied violations took place largely under the rubrics of reciprocity (especially for France, exemplarily concerning prisoners of war, and for both Allies regarding the use of gas after Ypres II) and reprisal (the British orders-in-council establishing a de facto blockade after March 1915). Neither cover, and especially not reprisal, claimed to create new law; citing reprisal actually acknowledges the illegality of the action and therefore vitiates any claim to change the law. Allied justifications for their illegal acts indicate how much they wanted to save the edifice of international law from the effects of their own violations. Although both Western Allies believed in a realm of legitimate military necessity, they rarely used that term to cover themselves. According to one German view, military necessity merely suspended law, leaving open the possibility that one could return to it later; according to the most robust German interpretation, however, military necessity actually created (new) law according to the real-existing exigencies of war.[14] The Allies mostly eschewed that route. Similarly, though both France and Britain acknowledged that new technical circumstances had made some older laws obsolete (such as those calling for close blockade), they asserted neither *rebus sic stantibus* nor weapons positivism. Instead, in both internal and public statements they argued that their innovations applied general principles of customary international law to new situations. This method came more easily to minds schooled in the common law than in Continental law.[15] Historical precedents and judicial decisions (of national and prize courts) offered a wealth of possibilities to change or tweak individual laws without seeming to harm the idea of law altogether. While the British Foreign Office especially had recourse to the great data bank of the past, France (like Germany) laid much more stock and store in positive treaty law. The French foreign office discovered general principles behind the letter of positive law and in debates and correspondence occasioned by international conventions. Achieving common Allied

14. One view: Karl Strupp, *Das internationale Landkriegsrecht* (Frankfurt, 1914), 4.

15. Franz von Holtzendorff, *Handbuch des Völkerrechts. Auf Grundlage europäischer Staatspraxis,* vol. 1, Einleitung in das Völkerrecht (Berlin, 1885), 121–22.

war policy involved a great deal of behind-the-scenes legal negotiation and did not always succeed (*vide* the last order-in-council and the treatment of prisoners of war). These and other abiding disagreements show that no completely uniform Allied interpretation of international law existed regarding individual laws, but the agreement on general principles was all the more striking for this. And beneath it lay a more fundamental accord that Allied war policy must never undermine the idea of a binding legal order coterminous with the European state system.

The one exception to that conviction occurred after the great, unexpected success of the blockade and the Allied victory in 1918. These emboldened British leaders, led by the Admiralty, to contemplate jettisoning every concession belligerent Britain had made in maritime law since 1856 on behalf of neutrals (including British neutral interests!). This pipe dream faced insuperable European and American opposition and was abandoned without being acted on. But it demonstrates how momentary power superiority and great security anxiety might tempt a state to engage in unilateral legal destruction (in this case of the Declaration of Paris, which most people recognized had become customary law). A mere nine years later, the power constellation had changed, and the navy understood again that security interest and law coincided more than they diverged.

Allied war policy-making, even when it broke the law, also differed from Imperial Germany's. With rare exceptions (such as the British Admiralty's unilateral announcement of the "war zone" in November 1914), major belligerent policy was set at joint meetings in which the leading governmental lawyers, usually from several different offices, played an energetic and independent role from the beginning. Legal issues were always important in deliberations, sometimes paramount. The British War Cabinet and the French Council of Ministers then reprised these arguments before reaching a decision. In the interest of Allied unity and because of national legal differences and/or different interpretations of international law, inter-Allied legal conferences were also common, particularly regarding the blockade. In Germany, inter-ministerial conferences were less frequent and often seem to have taken place inside narrower parameters—that is, the fundamental legal decision had already been made, and the conference worked out the details. Legal representatives rarely, if ever, functioned as autonomous members of the decision-making process. Bethmann's pointed request for legal cover for the submarine and mine blockade in 1914 typifies the use of lawyers primarily as technical aides. Of course, British and French lawyers provided plenty of technical cover, as their jobs dictated, but one discovers them offering inconvenient opinions in clear language much more frequently than in the German records. Internal documents show that British officials were highly aware, and embarrassed, when their policies broke the law; they were more likely than their German counterparts to admit their violations openly among themselves and not to dismiss them with the excuse that law was being broken everywhere and/or simply did not exist any longer. All of these things are subtle but significant indications of how important international law was to decision makers and policy formation.

The violations themselves differed, too. Concerning the largest issue, the blockade, it was much closer to previous practice than was unrestricted submarine warfare or the use of poison gas. Major blockades lasting for years were not new to Europeans. State and public opinion was shifting about the ethics of interdicting food to civilian populations, but that had been common practice before 1914. The demise of the close blockade seemed to be justified by the more important international criterion of effectiveness, which the distant blockade amply fulfilled. The major innovations—rationing neutrals, and, under the title of seizing contraband (rather than blockade), extending that definition to practically everything—were sweetened or softened by diplomatic gradualism, negotiation with firms and governments, payoffs and subsidies, business-oriented incentives (such as time-saving navicerts), the possibility of legal redress before the Prize Court, and the regularity and dependability that real effectiveness provided. Neutrals were angry, but they acquiesced to the blockade for these reasons; their acquiescence factored into the process by which some of these blockade innovations have since become recognized as lawful.

The manner in which the Foreign Office managed the blockade was hugely important to its success—success that depended equally upon the sheer naval ability to pull it off and the political/legal acumen in handling neutrals who were most disadvantaged by it. Diplomatic acuity twinned with power. Without power, Britain would have lacked the wartime "luxury" of long, tedious negotiations, the wherewithal to offer significant inducements, the dense network of consuls and business contacts to provide the information, and the ships and facilities to ensure efficient administration. When it comes to making international law, power is the ability to arrange circumstances so that many divergent interests may be brought, more or less, under one legal umbrella. Power is the long breath it takes to bring about change multilaterally and to exercise coercion obliquely and gingerly.

Imperial Germany did not possess this type of power. Its submarine and automatic contact mine "blockade," its surprise use of poison gas, its trek across Belgium, its exemplarily rough treatment of civilians were all shortcuts designed to vault into a position of world power without the breadth or depth of economic, fiscal, or diplomatic power to do so. Once it had failed to win in the fleeting window of opportunity that its resources could cover, it fell back on full-scale exploitation of the occupied territories to sustain its war effort. The violations resulting from the original attempt and then its longer follow-through destroyed international law far more completely than did Allied breaches, for they broke not just material rules of positive law, but long-standing principles of customary law—in the case of poison and the willful killing of civilians, centuries-long prohibitions. The already well-developed principles of *pacta sunt servanda,* proportionality, discrimination, and effectiveness were all nullified. These were the very foundations of international law, the meta-rules that governed its maintenance, modification, and extension.

Given this fundamental challenge, it is hardly a wonder that the Western Allies focused their war aims from the beginning on reestablishing the intrinsic value of law. They identified law with their own governmental forms, with the international state and economic systems that guaranteed their independence and prosperity, and with the norms that defined themselves—their word for this was "civilized." Fighting under the banner of law also constrained the Allies. It caused them to weigh carefully the consequences of policy and curbed the temptation to achieve immediate results through lawlessness; at the very least it meant avoiding the appearance of violating law without good cause. It meant paying close attention to world public opinion and to neutral governments especially when it conflicted with them; that attention in effect granted them some influence over policy and its justifications. In short, taking law seriously automatically made policy more sensitive to the outside world.

Paradoxically, the greater the monopoly that the Allies seemed to exercise over the legal by successfully branding the Germans as lawless in the eyes of world opinion, the less the Kaiserreich had to lose by acting lawlessly. Like the professors signing the October (1914) Manifesto who defiantly embraced the epithet "militarism," the government paid steadily less attention to the effects of its policies on foreign opinion.[16] The exception was Scandinavia, whose importance to Germany's war effort kept it as a factor in German policy making. Otherwise, losing the battle for world opinion freed it to behave as egotistically as its most radical jurists theorized was right (Erich Kaufmann: "every state...has the right to perform any international act that is necessary for its self-preservation").[17] After defeat, this same sense of being alone in the world mutated into the claim of victimhood against an unjust legal regime that served only the "interests" of Germany's enemies. This was, of course, the script of revisionism and the "innocence campaign."

What If Imperial Germany Had Won the War?

We must ask if Imperial Germany's theories of law could have produced a new, stable legal system. Many German voices called for such. The navy was out to produce "new law" based on Germany's unilateral use of the submarine weapon. The influential international jurist and editor Josef Kohler proposed that Germany lead an "Areopagus" of nations to refound international law now that the "soap bubble" of the Hague Rules had burst, a supreme court minus Britain, France, Italy, Russia, the United States, Norway, Denmark, and Holland.[18] Kohler identified the "three great ideas" that would found the new law: (1) war was between states, not peoples, who could under no circumstances take part in warlike activities; (2) only purposeful destruction was permitted; and (3) occupation must create as soon as possible ordered circumstances.[19] The more liberal Karl Strupp also wondered if Germany could work with a scofflaw like Britain, but thought that Germany would find some partners to revise international law on the basis of Grotius's phrase that "everything in war is allowed that is necessary to achieve the goal of war."[20] His colleague Ludwig Beer

---

16. Jürgen von Ungern-Sternberg and Wolfgang von Ungern-Sternberg, *Der Aufruf "An die Kulturwelt!" Das Manifest der 93 und die Anfänge der Kriegspropaganda im Ersten Weltkrieg* (Stuttgart, 1996).

17. Kaufmann, *Wesen des Völkerrechts*, 199. Lasson: "For as a reasonable natural being, the state is an absolutely selfish being, and like any other mere natural being, it is everywhere completely justified in its selfishness": Lasson, "Selections," liv.

18. Josef Kohler, "Das neue Völkerrecht," *Zeitschrift für Völkerrecht* 9 (1916): 6–7.

19. Ibid., 9.

20. Karl Strupp, "Gegenwartsfragen des Völkerrechts," *Niemeyers Zeitschrift für Internationales Recht* 25 (1915): 364. Strupp omitted Grotius's caveat, "which does not contravene positive law"—which Meurer retained in his postwar report to the Reichstag, *UA* 3:1, 320; Hugo Grotius, *The Rights of War and Peace Including the Law of Nature and of Nations*, A. C. Campbell (Chestnut Hill, MA, 2003), 291.

wrote that "*German* international law, that is, an international law in the incomplete form of external state law [*eines äußeren Staatsrechts*—this phrase describes the 'realistic' positivism of post-1871 German legal theory], will become *international* law; the international community of culture will develop and strengthen on a national basis."[21] There was thus no shortage of theories about how Imperial Germany might lead the postwar world to a new legal order. But Germany was already living and acting according to legal assumptions, and these were the real stuff out of which a postwar, German-dominated legal order would probably have developed. Were they capable of producing law?

Addressing this question requires asking what makes law-ness, what are the attributes of law? The anthropologist Leopold Pospisil has offered a summary of four qualities that he identified in the context of primitive law, that is, law as it operates absent an overarching state.[22] This is a useful perspective for students of international law, particularly for the period before the establishment of the League of Nations, the United Nations, and the various international courts. Pospisil's findings demonstrate that law is recognizable and operative even with a minimum of formal structure, so long as a community exists over time. His four attributes are authority, sanction, obligation, and intention of universal application. Applying these standards to the Kaiserreich is illuminating.

Imperial Germany had no problem supplying authority, but it was not of the kind defining the international community, nor did it promise to last long. The Wilhelminian conception of authority was that of a single state or of a hegemon extending its own law to others, as in the occupied zones, for example. The identification of self-preservation as the chief right of any state dissolved the idea of community by reducing every important clash to a non-judiciable arena to be decided by power.[23] In this view authority oscillated between the all-powerful and the evanescent. But the all-powerful was evanescent, too, since by disregarding the interests of others, it engendered constant conflict.[24] Continuous development meant that the hegemon, too, would someday pass away (Kaufmann: "the right of the state to exist and abide, so long as it 'can'" [but not longer]; Lasson: "In the great historical world process that which is weak succumbs because it is worthless, and that which is strong maintains itself because in *particular* events and at a *particular* time it is able better to serve the great mission of mankind").[25]

Sanction was also not missing from Imperial Germany's performance of law, but it was much narrower than the panoply of sanctions on which international law normally relies in practice. Nineteenth-century positivists commonly held that reprisal (or war, in

---

21. Ludwig Beer, "Krieg und Völkerrecht vor dem deutschen Reichsgericht," *Niemeyers Zeitschrift für Internationales Recht* 25 (1915): 338. On external state law: Brierly, *Basis of Obligation*, 35–36; Paul Laband, *Das Staatsrecht des deutschen Reiches* (Tübingen, 1901), 2:121n1.

22. Leopold Pospisil, "The Attributes of Law," in *Law and Warfare: Studies in the Anthropology of Conflict,* ed. Paul Bohannan (Garden City, NY, 1967), 25–41.

23. Contra the argument for non-judiciability: Lauterpacht, *Function,* 7–9, 139–65.

24. The AA recognized this problem regarding annexing Belgium: "Aufzeichnung über die Behandlung Belgiens nach dem gegenwärtigen Kriege im Falle eines entscheidenden Sieges," Anlage der Angabe zu IIIa. 18082.14, n.d., ca. Oct. 18, 1914, BAB R 901 85345.

25. Kaufmann, *Wesen des Völkerrechts,* 182; Lasson, "Selections," lxvii, emphasis mine.

peacetime) was the only sanction upholding international law; that view predominated in military thinking inside Germany.[26] It ignored the wide range of social and official sanctions that regularly influenced state action, ranging from losing reputation in public opinion through the full panoply of diplomatic, economic, symbolic and other slights and harms that states could inflict on lawbreakers short of an outright reprisal. In wartime, the threat of postwar reparation and indemnities and long-term economic disadvantages (announced by the Allies at the Paris Economic Conference in June 1916) might be major considerations.[27] And there was the new idea of trials. The failure of reprisals to curb illegal acts and the murderous spiral they unleashed moved the Allies to replace reprisal with postwar trials of alleged war criminals. Paul Pic, professor of law at Lyons, was one of the first to suggest using the International Court of Justice at The Hague for this purpose.[28] But it was a feature of the polycratic nature of German government that only the chancellor and AA were sensitive to this wide range of possible sanctions. They fought a losing battle to stop the overuse of reprisal, but more important, to reexert civilian political control over this legal tool. The salience of reprisal in internal policy-setting debates is clear from the most effective argument that the chancellor and the AA repeatedly deployed against military leaders in favor of upholding international law: fear of Allied or neutral reprisal. It is impossible to know how a victorious Kaiserreich would have wielded international-legal sanctions, but its wartime record would predict an overreliance on reprisal alone.

The third attribute of law is obligation; what distinguishes law from mere morality is its imperative, binding quality. That was precisely what the Imperial German concepts of military necessity, *Notstand,* and self-preservation so radically undercut. If a state could overthrow or suspend the law whenever it deemed it necessary, then no binding law was possible. The abrogation of the London Treaty of 1839 on Belgium, of numerous of the Hague Rules beginning almost immediately, and of the bilateral Hague and Bern Agreements of 1917 and 1918 on prisoners convinced the Allies that Germany believed that no form of positive treaty law was binding. That is a major reason why the Armistice contained unusually stiff demands and why the Treaty of Versailles was not negotiated. As the military representatives to the Allied Supreme War Council told the council in October 1918, "The Government of Germany is in a position peculiar among the Nations of Europe in that its word cannot be believed, and that it denies any obligation of honor," a conviction that President Wilson repeated directly to the German government: the world

---

26. Geoffrey Best, *Humanity in Warfare: The Modern History of the International Law of Armed Conflicts* (New York, 1980), 168.

27. On the range of sanctions: Paul Pic, "Violation systematique des lois de la guerre par les Austro-allemands. Les sanctions nécessaires," *Revue générale de droit international public* 23 (1916): 243–68; Hugh H. L. Bellot, "War Crimes: Their Prevention and Punishment," *Grotius Society, Problems of the War: Papers Read before the Society in the Year 1916* 2 (1917): 31–55; Louis Renault, "De l'application du droit pénal aux faits de guerre," *Revue générale de droit international public* 25 (1918): 6–29; A. Méringhac, "De la sanction des infractions au droit des gens commises, au cour de la guerre européenne, par les empires du centre," *Revue générale de droit international public* 24 (1917): 7, 26–28.

28. Pic, "Violation systematique," 267–68. See also "First Interim Report from the Committee of Enquiry into Breaches of the Laws of War, with Appendices," Presented to the Right Honourable Sir Frederick E. Smith, Bart., K.C., M.P., Jan. 13, 1919, p. 22, Oxford, Bodleian Library, Pollock Papers, MS ENG. Hist. d. 431.

"cannot trust the word of those who have hitherto been the masters of German policy."[29] The Imperial German interpretation of military necessity, its application of *Notstand* to international law, and its capacious understanding of self-preservation were capable of annulling legal obligation but not creating it.

The final attribute of law is intention of universal application. The meta-rule of equality of states does not refer to their power, wealth, or extent, which are obviously highly unequal, but to their equal membership in the law-creating community of states, which subjects all to the same writ of law, both in terms of rights and obligations. But Imperial Germany rejected the universality of international law in two important respects. First, it denied that small states were viable, much less equal. Kaiser Wilhelm's repeated flirtation with the future incorporation of Holland and Denmark, the Schlieffen Plan's assumption that Belgium would not fight because it was too small, the repeated, irritated astonishment of military leaders when it did so, and the numerous private expressions of the imminent disappearance of small states as independent entities are all indications of how very widespread was the social Darwinistic conviction of a constant struggle among power-states that would inevitably cause small states to die and be swallowed up by bigger ones. In such a world, equality of states (in law) was absurd. But beyond this assumption, the Kaiserreich's elastic conception of military necessity (illustrated by Colonel Groß von Schwarzhoff's demand that the exception be added to virtually every rule at the Hague Convention), *Notstand,* and weapons positivism all made the exception the rule, or they derived law from particular circumstances in a particular time. This radical particularism contradicted legal universalism fundamentally. It was only when Germany was defeated that it sought the international-legal protections that it had denied to other states. In the event of a German victory, the precepts and legal assumptions that had led its prewar politics and, especially, its wartime conduct could not have produced the meta-rules or the general principles of abiding international law, even as the hegemonic, single lawgiver, because its actions expressed legal assumptions that lacked the essential qualities of law, quite apart from the justifiable questions of fairness and the legitimate interests of other nations.

The Great War and the Law

Because of Imperial Germany's enormous challenge to the existing international-legal system, the actual operations of law during wartime—how well it succeeds in being obeyed and why, how it changes to fit new conditions, how it handles violators—are less clear during World War I than they would be in a "usual" war, one whose purpose was not to overturn the world order. The clearest role of international law in the Great War was as an indicator of what was at stake. The Allied victory was not complete enough to

---

29. Cited in Bullitt Lowry, *Armistice 1918* (Kent, OH, 1996), 19; third American note (Secretary of State to Swiss chargé), Washington, Oct. 23, 1918, *FRUS 1918*, Suppl. 1, 382.

stop the challenge, which was renewed in the Second World War, a war very different from 1914 but which raised the same fundamental questions of law and state order. International law, including the laws of war (now called international humanitarian law), has continued to develop in the general direction set out by the Allies in World War I, both regarding material law and general principles (such as discrimination, proportionality, binding treaties, effectiveness). The First World War directly produced these developments in international law: instead of reprisals, trials for war criminals, including heads of state; the condemnation of aggressive war; the strengthened prohibition of poison; and the elaboration of humane treatment for prisoners of war. The Second World War muddied the analytic waters by making it hard to tell which other post-1945 modifications are owed to the earlier war.

"Realists" claim that states only follow law when it is in their interest. That is the same claim of the earlier, German legal "realists." It is based on an interpretation of states as bundles of will and power involved in existential struggles to expand or die. Such states share few interests in common; free-existing monads, they give their consent to community and therefore to law provisionally at their convenience, and at their convenience they withdraw it. The law they recognize, if they do, is their own. As we have seen, this view of the state, state community, and law was unusual in 1914; in fact, it was unique to Imperial Germany. The international relations school of realism has therefore built its model for "the state" on an extreme outlier.

The acceptance of Imperial Germany as the norm has blinded "realists" to why the war started, why it was fought the way it was, and what it was about. In place of Germany's primary responsibility, we have instead "sovereign states equally determined to maintain their power and prestige" sliding into a war through entangling alliances, or falling prey to the inevitable conflicts "created by the anarchic system and resulting security dilemma"—these are the same arguments as those of the innocence campaign.[30] For decades now, most German historians have emancipated themselves from that script, yet it is alive and well in much English-language writing and predominant in political science theory. Its persistence causes the Great War to disappear in a haze of putative Wilsonian idealism; it becomes a senseless embarrassment better skipped for the robust narrative of the Second World War.[31] States might indeed have been "equally determined to maintain their power and prestige" in 1914, but Britain and France understood power and prestige in diametrically opposite ways to Imperial Germany. They understood themselves as part

---

30. "Sovereign states": Raymond Aron, *The Century of Total War* (Boston, 1955), 13; "security dilemma": Robert Jervis, "Systems Theories and Diplomatic History," in *Diplomacy: New Approaches in History, Theory, and Policy*, ed. Paul Gordon Lauren (New York, 1979), 217.

31. Despite their laudable attempt to resurrect the importance of international law to international politics and political theory, Kaplan and Katzenbach are good examples of how hard, perhaps impossible, it is to do so within the confines of conventional IR theory. Skipping World War I and omitting German and Japanese responsibility for World War II: Morton A. Kaplan and Nicholas deB. Katzenbach, *The Political Foundations of International Law* (New York, 1961), 42–44. For a detailed refutation of the Wilsonian idealism canard: Francis Anthony Boyle, *World Politics and International Law* (Durham, NC, 1985), esp. 7, 51–52. See also Keir A. Lieber, "The New History of World War I and What It Means for International Relations Theory," *International Security* 32, no. 2 (Fall 2007): 155–91.

of a European state community that rested on "a mutual consensus on norms and rules, respect for law, and an overall balance among the various actors [including small states] in terms of rights, security, status, claims, duties, and satisfactions rather than power."[32] International law was inextricably imbricated in this system as product, guarantor, operant, symbol, and language—indeed it was almost identical with it, which is why erasing international law from consideration of the "real" eviscerates the World War of meaning, and why restoring law recaptures the fundamental issues over which the war was fought.

In rejecting the view of historians that Germany had begun World War I, the famous realist political scientist Raymond Aron complained that this view was "irresistibly simple, disconcerting to those who want to penetrate beyond the superficial facts and root out the deep-seated forces of which the very participants themselves had no knowledge."[33] On the contrary, the historical view is anything but simple, especially if you add fundamental factors like international law that realism discards. It is hard to know which is more complex, the workings of international law replete with its subtleties, technicalities, and clashing interpretations, or the workings of the Imperial German government, with its polycracy, diagonals, zigzags, self-censorship, and self-deception. But one of the fruits of examining policy through the lens of law is that you do discover potent factors hidden from, or not entirely visible to, the decision makers. For, unlike the Nazi regime, the Kaiserreich had no all-encompassing racial theory to guide it—indeed, it had no theory at all that it could express coherently to the world; that is one reason it failed at propaganda. And, unlike the Nazi regime whose extremity was visible from the beginning (for those who wanted to look), the Kaiserreich's revolutionary violence was more emergent.

Imperial Germany's polycracy meant that different understandings of law might be located in different departments. That was partly true in Britain and France, too, where the militaries tended to be much more focused on the short term and consequently less interested in law. But strong civil leadership could curb military proclivities, though not always quickly or completely. In all three countries, the foreign offices were the primary location of the legal viewpoint. In Germany, reprisal against prisoners of war and curbing ineffective aerial bombardment of cities moved the AA to make the strongest case for following international law; its relative failure in both cases testifies to the predominance of military considerations over political/legal ones in policy making. But regarding *Notstand,* military necessity, *non liquet, rebus sic stantibus,* dismissal of the Martens Clause, and other issues as well, the AA and chancellor were very close to the military standpoint. They had already assimilated the military arguments, which was not surprising given the military's high status institutionally and in public opinion and its thorough penetration into German legal writing.

Although Imperial Germany acted in ways that reveal deeply held assumptions about states, law, community, rights, and obligations, no contemporary seems to have gathered

---

32. Paul W. Schroeder, "Did the Vienna Settlement Rest on a Balance of Power?" *American Historical Review* 97, no. 3 (1992): 694, cited in Jervis's interesting and welcome reconsideration of the relation of historical research to political science theory: Robert Jervis, "A Political Science Perspective on the Balance of Power and the Concert," *American Historical Review* 97, no. 3 (June 1992): 723.

33. Aron, *Century of Total War,* 14.

these together into a whole or discussed them critically. Germany's leaders seem to have regarded their actions as self-explanatory for a great power—they were repeatedly surprised by the shock and denunciations their policies caused, which is one reason they tended to dismiss these as propaganda. The basic assumptions behind German policies (and the institutional ways those policies were formed) were profoundly destructive of the legal order and incapable of replacing it with an abiding legal framework based on those assumptions. Yet neither Germany's leaders nor its jurists seem to have grasped this. They were affronted by charges of lawlessness; the innocence campaign was fueled not just by the desire to overturn the Versailles Treaty, but just as strongly by a sense of dishonor at being judged criminal. Yet Germany's legal counterarguments, its justifications and rationales, were often strikingly narrow and technical; they were somehow sharply lawyerly without partaking in the gravity or principled sweep characteristic of law. It is as if Imperial Germany could not speak the same legal language as the rest of Europe. That loss of language measures the distance the Kaiserreich had drifted away from the community and its estrangement from the consensus that the community had reached on the limits placed on war by law.

Bibliography

PRIMARY SOURCES

France

Archives du Ministère des Affaires Étrangères, La Courneuve (MAE)

Correspondance politique et commerciale Guerre 1914–1918

114–115	Allemagne/Autriche, dossier général
125	Allemagne/Autriche, dossier général
143–148	Allemagne, sujets ennemis
979–981	Opérations stratégiques
1097–1113	Droit de guerre, dossier générale
1114–1119	Droit de guerre
1132–1134	Droit de guerre sur la mer, règles

Blocus

33	Contrebande, Dossier général
46	Négociations entre la France et la Grande Bretagne de 1915–17 sur le blocus de l'Allemagne
365	Politique générale du blocus

Service historique de l'armée de terre, Chateau de Vincennes (SHAT)

5N 87	Cabinet du Ministre, Télégrammes, août 1914
5N 266	Gaz, 1915–20
5N 276	Cabinet du Ministre, Renseignements de Situation, Blocus, juil. 1914–janv. 1917
5N 284	Cabinet du Ministre, Renseignements de Situation, Guerre Économique, 1914–18

6N 1   Fonds Poincaré, Documents Généraux, 1914–18

6N 21   Fonds Buat

6N 23   Fonds Buat Correspondance, août 1914–oct. 1915

6N 27   Fonds Buat, Colonies, juil. 1914–oct. 1914

6N 46   Fonds Galliéni, Circulaires-Revues de Press, nov. 1915–mars 1916

6N 110   Fonds Clemenceau, vie aux armées 1914–18, Prisonniers de guerre, 1915–18

6N 111   Fonds Clemenceau Prisonniers de Guerre, 1915–18, Camp Retranché
            de Paris, 1915–18

7N 161   Conseil supérieur de guerre, État Majeure de l'Armée: Prisonniers de guerre, régime
            et emploi des prisonniers

7N 1993   3ème Bureau, 1914–19

7N 1976   État-Major de l'Armée, 3ème Bureau, 1914–19

10N 57   Ministère de l'Armament, Matériel chimique de guerre

10N 81   Proposition d'inventions, 1915–18

10N 82   Proposition d'inventions, 1915–18

16N 1757   Documents rélatifs à l'aéronautique, 1914–19

16N 2441   Grand Quartier Général, Direction de l'arrière, Main d'oeuvre et prisonniers de
            guerre, déc. 1916–févr. 1917

16N 2442   Grand Quartier Général, Direction de l'arrière, Section organisation, Main d'oeuvre
            et prisonniers de guerre, 1 mars 1917–5 mars 1918

16N 2455   Grand Quartier Général

16N 2456   Grand Quartier Général, Direction de l'arrière, Prisonniers de guerre,
            Organisation, Divers

16N 2459   Emploi des prisonniers de guerre dans la zone des armées, 1915–19

16N 839   Grand Quartier Général, État-Major, 1èr Bureau

19N 1326   7ième Army: "Plan d'évacuation de la population civile en Haute
            Alsace…," 1918

Germany

Auswärtiges Amt, Politisches Archiv, Berlin (AA/PA)
(RZ numbers are omitted in the footnotes)

RZ 201, R 181   Fragen betr. Haager Landkriegsordnung, vol. 1

RZ 201, R 182   Fragen betr. Seekrieg, vol. 1

RZ 201, R 19581–R 19582 Staats- u. Völkerrecht, vols. 6–7

RZ 201, R 20880–R 20913 Weltkrieg Nr. 9, Grausamkeiten, vols. 1–32

RZ 201, R 21362   Weltkrieg Nr. 14 b, vol. 1, Verwaltung Belgiens

RZ 201, R 21544–R 21547 Weltkrieg Nr. 18a, vols. 9–12, *Lusitania, Arabic*

RZ 201, R 21553   Weltkrieg Nr. 18a, vol. 18, *Lusitania, Arabic*

RZ 202, R 22172   Generalhauptquartier 9a, England Luftkrieg, vol. 1

RZ 202, R 22213–R 22214 Generalhauptquartier 16, Kriegsgefangenen, vols. 1–2

RZ 202, R 22354   Generalhauptquartier 42a, Ubootkrieg: Hospitalschiffe, vol. 1

RZ 202, R 22382–R 22388 Akten des Auswärtigen Amtes im Generalhauptquartier 5, vols. 1–6

RZ 202, R 22421   Akten des Auswärtigen Amtes im Generalhauptquartier 28, 1914–16,
                         vol. 1, "Verwaltung besetzter Gebiete," Aug.–Nov. 1914

Nachlaß Gottlieb von Jagow   vol. 8

Nachlaß Johannes Kriege   vols. 1, 3–5

Bundesarchiv Berlin-Lichterfelde (BAB)

R 901 28901–28904	Die Anwendung der Grundsätze der Genfer Konventionen auf den Seekrieg, Militärwesen Nr. 96a, Bde. 1–4, Mai 1901 bis 8 Jan. 1909
R 901 28905–28916	Akten betr. die Konferenz zur Revision der Genfer Konvention, Bde. 1–11, Feb. 1906 bis März 1914
R 901 74779	Haagerlandkriegordnung.
R 901 81901–81906	Akten betr. militärische Erfindungen, Bde. 8–13, Apr. 1914 bis Okt. 1926
R 901 82117–82120	Die Anwendung der Grundsätze der Genfer Konvention…auf den Seekrieg, Bde. 5–8, Feb. 1909 bis März 1920
R 901 82122–82129	Die Beschlagnahme des Hilfslazarettschiffes "Ophelia" durch englische Seestreitkräfte, Bde. 1–6, 1914–18
R 901 82146–82148	Akten betr. die Konferenz zur Revision der Genfer Konvention, Bde. 12–14, Apr. 1914–März 1920
R 901 82595–82598	Akten betr. deutsche und belgische Geiseln im Kriege, 1914–18
R 901 82600	Akten betr. englische Geiseln, 1914
R 901 82946	Akten betr. die Heranziehung von Zivilpersonen zur Arbeitsleistung in der Feuerzone, Aug. 1917–Mai 1918
R 901 84022–84028	Akten betr. die zwangsweise Heranziehung belgischer Arbeitsloser zur Arbeit, Bde. 1–7, Okt. 1916 bis 1920
R 901 84146–84149	Akten betr. die Verwendung deutscher Kriegsgefangener in der gegnerischen Feuerzone; Gegenmaßregeln der Deutschen Regierung, Bde. 1–4, Aug. 1916 bis Apr. 1919
R 901 84190	Akten betr. Protokolle, Aufzeichnungen pp. zur deutsch-englischen Gefangenenkonferenz im Haag vom Juni/Juli 1918, Bd. 2, Juni 1918–Juli 1918
R 901 84191–84195	Akten betr. Verhandlungen mit der Französischen Regierung über Gefangenenfragen, Bde. 1–5, Juli 1917 bis Dez. 1919
R 901 84636–84637	Verhandlungen mit Frankreich wegen Völkerrechtswidriger Behandlung des gefangenen Sanitäts-Personals
R 901 84647	Sondermaßnahmen gegen französische Kriegsgefangene, 1916
R 901 84750–84752	Verbringung der deutschen Gefangene aus Nord-Afrika nach Frankreich bzw. nach der Schweiz, Bde. 1–3, 1916–17
R 901 85156	Akten betr. die Bestellung oder Zulassung von Verteidigern vor den Militär-Gerichten, 1915–18
R 901 85223–85225	Heranziehung von Kriegsgefangenen zu Arbeiten, Bde. 1–3, 1914–15
R 901 85345	Auswärtiges Amt Abteilung IIIa, Geheime Akten, Die Haltung der Kriegführenden Mächte im Kriege 1914
R 901 85354	Akten betr. die Blockade Deutschlands im Weltkriege, Jan. 1915–Jan. 1920
R 901 85701	Akten betr. die Aufbringung des englischen Dampfers "Brussels" durch deutsche Seestreitkräfte
R 901 85721–85722	Belästigung des Schiffsverkehrs durch Deutschland, Allg., Bde. 1–2, 1917–18
R 901 85904	"Das Auslegen von Seeminen der kriegführenden Maechte…"

R 901 85910–85915	"Die Erklärung der Gewässer rings um Grossbritanien und Irland als Kriegsgebiet," Geheim, Bde. 1–6 (1914–15)
R 901 85942	Die Versenkung des englischen Passagierdampfers "Falaba," 1915
R 901 85949–85950	Akten betr. die Versenkung des englischen Dampfers *Lusitania* durch ein deutsches Unterseeboot im Kriege 1914/15, Bde. 1–2, Mai 1915–Dez. 1915
R 901 85964	"Haakon VII" Die Wegnahme der Postsachen durch ein deutsches U-Boot, 1915
R 901 85974–85975	Die Versenkung des Dampfers "Sussex," Bde. 1–2, 1915
R 901 86012–86013	Akten betr. Die Erklärung der Gewässer um Großbritannien, Frankreich und Italien sowie im östlichen Mittelmeer als Kriegsgebiet (verschärfter U-Boot-Krieg), Allgemeines, Bde. 1–2, 31 Jan. 1917—März 1920
R 901 86072–86073	Grausamkeiten auf den Kriegsschauplätzen, Bde. 1–2 (1914–15)
R 901 86238–86243	Völkerrechtswidrige Verwendung v. farbiger Truppen, Bde. 1–4 1914–16
R 901 86249	Akten betr. die den Städten Valenciennes und Roubaix aus Anlaß der Beschießung der Konsulate in Alexandrette, Haife und Jaffe durch französische Seestreitkräfte auferlegte Kontribution, Apr. 1915–Sept. 1917
R 901 86271–86277	Akten betr. Bewaffnung von Handelsschiffen im Kriege, Bde. 1–7, 16 Okt. 1914–Nov. 1921
R 901 86397–86398	Akten betr. Führung des Luftkrieges im Völkerkrieg 1914, Bde. 1–2, Aug. 1914–Jan. 1919
R 901 86399	Die Kommission zur Festsetzung der Rechtsverletzungen 1915
R 901 86587–86593	Die Verletzung der Neutralität Belgiens aus Anlaß des Krieges, 1914–20
R 901 86663–86664	Gesetze um Gebräuche des Landkriegs, Bde. 1–2, Apr. 1891 bis 1920
R 1501/102797	Reichsministerium des Innern, Gewinnung belgischer Arbeiter für die deutsche Kriegsindustrie, Band 1, Mai 1916–Apr. 1917
R 3003	OberReichsAnwalt (ORA) Reichsgericht bJ 642/20

Bundesarchiv-Koblenz

Nachlaß Max Bauer (N 1022), Nr. 35

Bayerisches Hauptstaatsarchiv-Kriegsarchiv, Munich (BayKrA)

Kriegsministerium

1630–1631	Kriegsgefangene, vom 1896–15 Sept. 1914
1634–1638	Kriegsgefangene
1650	Kriegsgefangene
1665	Kriegsgefangene
6547	Ernährung der Kriegsgefangene (auch der zurückgekehrten deutschen) 1914–Mai 1915
6549	Ernährung der Kriegsgefangene, 1 Jan. 1916–Okt. 1916
11171	Entscheidungen des Reichsmilitärgerichts, Bedarf, Verteilung, 1901–16

11172	Entscheidungen des Reichsmilitärgerichts, Bedarf, Verteilung, 1916–19
13439	Aus der Kriegsgefangenschaft zurückgekehrte Wehrpflichtige, Wiederverwendung, 12 Feb. 1915–7 Okt. 1919
13735	Kriegsgefangene Sanitätspersonal im Kriege, 1914–18
13736	Kriegsgefangenes Sanitätspersonal im Kriege, Bd. 2, 1 Aug. 1915–31 März 1916
13785	Sterbefälle der Kriegsgefangenen, 1914–19
13799	Feindliche Greueltaten im Kriege, 1914
14126–14128	Verletzungen des Kriegsrechts, 3 Bde., 1914–22
14160	Militärgefangenenkompanien, 1917–20
14171	Arbeitskommandos und Arbeiterkompanie bei den Artillerie-Depots 18 März 1915–8 Aug. 1919
14208	Kriegsamt: Ausländische Arbeiter 30 Okt. 1916–1920

Oberkommando der 6ten Armee (AOK6)

Bund 13	Armee Befehle, I. Satz, 20 Aug. 1914–23 Dez. 1918
Bund 13a	Armee Befehle, I. Satz, 20 Aug. 1914–23 Dez. 1918
Bund 21	Abt. 1a: Sammlung grundlegender Befehle, 15 Juni–20 Okt. 1917
Bund 28	Oberquartiermeister: Besondere Anordnungen, 1. Satz, 12 Aug. 1914–14 Dez. 1918

Heeresgruppe Kronprinz Rupprecht

1100	Registratur: Armeebefehle (1A, 7A, 2A, 18A) 1917–18
1101	Registratur: Abt. Iab, Heeresbefehle, 19 Jan. 1917–22 Jan. 1918
1102	Registratur: Abt. Iab, Heeresbefehle, 7 Mai 1917–26 Jan. 1918
1103	Registratur: Abt. Iab, Heeresbefehle, 18 Aug. 1917–2 Sept. 1917

General Kommando des 2. bayerischen Armee-Korps

Bund 177	III. Justiz-Pflege: Kriegstagebuch 7 Juli 1916–29 Nov. 1918; 1. Disziplinar-Sachen, Exzesse, und 1h: Verletzungen des Kriegsrechts, 1914–18)

2. bayerische Infanterie Division

Bund 118	Feldjustizbeamter; 1. Kriegstagebuch 2 Aug. 1914–13 Dez. 1918; 4. Behandlung feindlicher POWs, 1915–18; Spionage, Allg. 1915–18

5. bayerische Infanterie Division

Bund 63	Abt. 1 Registratur, Kriegsgefangene, 1914–18

United Kingdom

The National Archives, Kew (TNA)

ADMIRALTY (ADM)

ADM 1/8132
ADM 1/8396/345

ADM 1/8400/397
ADM 1/8400/399
ADM 1/8403/425
ADM 53/34792
ADM 116/1232
ADM 116/1233
ADM 116/3619
ADM 137/294
ADM 137/382
ADM 137/1096

CABINET (CAB)

CAB 2/3
CAB 15/5
CAB 16/5
CAB 16/18A
CAB 17/86
CAB 17/87
CAB 17/100
CAB 17/126
CAB 21/83
CAB 22/39
CAB 23/1–8
CAB 23/13
CAB 23/40
CAB 23/42
CAB 24/1
CAB 24/19/99
CAB 37/86/14
CAB 37/127/40
CAB 37/127/43
CAB 37/128/1
CAB 41/35
CAB 41/36

FOREIGN OFFICE (FO)

FO 368 (Commercial)
FO 369 (Consular)
FO 371 (General)
FO 372 (Prize Series)
FO 382 (Contraband)
FO 383 (Prisoners of War)
FO 800 (Private Papers)

WAR OFFICE (WO)

WO 32/4904
WO 32/5098
WO 32/5177

WO 32/5188
WO 32/5369
WO 32/5381
WO 32/5425
WO 32/5565
WO 32/5608
WO 142/240
WO 142/241

PUBLISHED DOCUMENT COLLECTIONS (CITED)

Albertini, Luigi. *The Origins of the War of 1914.* 3 vols. Oxford: Oxford University Press, 1952–57.

Bane, Suda Lorena, and Ralph Haswell Lutz, eds. *The Blockade of Germany after the Armistice, 1918–1919: Selected Documents of the Supreme Economic Council, Superior Blockade Council, American Relief Administration, and Other Wartime Organizations.* Stanford, CA: Stanford University Press, 1942.

BD: British Documents on Foreign Affairs: Reports and Papers from the Foreign Office Confidential Print. Part 2: From the First to the Second World War. General editors: Kenneth Bourne and D. Cameron Watt. Series H: The First World War, 1914–1918, ed. David Stevenson, 9 vols. Series I: The Paris Peace Conference of 1919, ed. M. Dockrill. Bethesda, MD: University Publications of America.

Belgium. Ministère de la justice. *Réponse au livre blanc allemand du 10 mai 1915, "Die völkerrechtswidrige Führung des belgischen Volkskriegs."* Paris: Berger-Levrault, 1916.

Belgium, and Official Commission of the Belgian Government. *Reports on the Violation of the Rights of Nations and of the Laws and Customs of War in Belgium.* 2 vols. London: HMSO, 1914.

BPNL: Bescheiden Betreffende de Buitenlandse Politiek van Nederland 1848–1919, Derde Periode 1899–1919, Vierde Deel, 1914–1917. R. G. P. 109, edited by C. Smit. The Hague: Martinus Nijhoff, 1962.

Brussels. Conference. 1874. *Actes de la Conférence de Bruxelles (1874).* Brussels: n.p., 1899.

Carnegie Endowment for International Peace. Division of International Law. *Official German Documents Relating to the World War.* 2 vols. New York: Oxford University Press, 1923.

———. *Violations of the Laws and Customs of War: Reports of the Majority and Dissenting Reports of American and Japanese Members of the Commission of Responsibilities, Conference of Paris, 1919.* Pamphlet no. 32. Oxford: Oxford University Press, 1919.

Cobbett, Pitt. *Cases and Opinions on International Law, and Various Points of English Law Connected Therewith, Collected and Digested from English and Foreign Reports, Official Documents, and Other Sources, with Notes Containing the Views of the Text-Writers on the Topics Referred to, Supplementary Cases, Treaties, and Statutes.* Vol. 2, Part II: War, and Part III: Neutrality (published 1913). London: Stevens and Haynes, 1909–13.

DDFr: France. Foreign Office. Commission de publication des documents diplomatiques français. *Documents Diplomatiques Français, 1914.* Paris: Imprimerie Nationale, 1999.

Doswald-Beck, Louise, ed. *San Remo Manual on International Law Applicable to Armed Conflicts at Sea.* Cambridge: Cambridge University Press, 1995.

France. Foreign Office. Commission de publication des documents diplomatiques français. *Documents Diplomatiques Français, 1915.* 3 vols. Paris: Imprimerie Nationale, 2002.

———. *Les violations des lois de la guerre par l'Allemagne.* Paris: Berger-Levrault, 1915.

FRUS: United States Department of State. *Papers Relating to the Foreign Relations of the United States; 1914–1918; Supplement: The World War.* Washington, DC: Government Printing Office, 1928–33.

German National Constituent Assembly. *Official German Documents Relating to the World War.* 2 vols. Translated by Division of International Law, Carnegie Endowment for International Peace. New York: Oxford University Press, 1923.

Germany. Auswärtiges Amt. *Die völkerrechtswidrige Führung des belgischen Volkskriegs.* Berlin: Verlag Stilke, 1915.

Germany. Nationalversammlung. *Das Werk des Untersuchungsausschusses der Verfassungsgebenden Deutschen Nationalversammlung und des Deutschen Reichstages 1919–1928, Verhandlungen/ Gutachten/Urkunden.* Ser. 1, vols. 3 (1927), 10 (1930), 11 (1930); ser. 3, vols. 2–4 (1927); ser. 4, vols. 1–7 (1925–28). Berlin: Deutsche Verlagsgesellschaft für Politik und Geschichte, 1925–30.

Germany. *Reichsgesetzblatt.* 75 vols. Berlin: Bureau des Bundeskanzlers, 1871–1945.

Germany. Reichsgesundheitsamt. "Schädigung der deutschen Volkskraft durch die völkerrechtswidrige feindliche Handelsblockade." In *Das Werk des Untersuchungsausschusses der Verfassunggebenden Deutschen Nationalversammlung und des Deutschen Reichstages 1918–1919,* vol. 6. Reihe 4, 387–442. Berlin: Deutsche Verlagsgesellschaft für Politik und Geschichte, 1928.

Germany. Reichsmilitärgericht. *Entscheidungen des Reichsmilitärgerichts.* Berlin: F. Vahlen, 1902–19.

Germany. *Strafgesetzbuch für das Deutsche Reich. Mit Commentar von Hans Rüdorff.* Berlin: J. Guttentag, 1871.

Gooch, G. P., and Harold Temperley, eds. *British Documents on the Origins of the War, 1898–1918.* London: HMSO, 1926–38.

GP: Germany. Auswärtiges Amt. *Die grosse Politik der Europäischen Kabinette, 1871–1914. Sammlung der Diplomatischen Akten des Auswärtigen Amtes.* Edited by Johannes Lepsius, Albricht Mendelssohn Bartholdy, and Friedrich Thimme. Berlin: Deutsche Verlagsgesellschaft für Politik und Geschichte, 1922–27.

Great Britain. *Great Britain and the European Crisis: Correspondence, and Statements in Parliament, together with an Introductory Narrative of Events.* London: HMSO, 1914.

Hansard's Parliamentary Debates. http://hansard.millbanksystems.com/.

Hertslet, Edward. *The Map of Europe by Treaty; Showing the Various Political and Territorial Changes Which Have Taken Place since the General Peace of 1814.* 4 vols. London: Butterworths, 1875.

Institute of International Law. "Manual of the Laws of Naval War." In *The Laws of Armed Conflict,* edited by Dietrich Schindler and Jiri Toman, 858–75. Dordrecht: Martinus Nijhoff, 1913.

Martens, G. F. *Nouveau recueil générale de traités.* Göttingen: Dieterich, 1843–75.

Matthias, Erich, and Rudolf Morsey, eds. *Die Regierung des Prinzen Max von Baden.* Vol. 2 of Quellen zur Geschichte des Parlamentarismus und der politischen Parteien, Erste Reihe. Düsseldorf: Droste, 1962.

Netherlands. Ministry of Foreign Affairs. *Actes et documents, deuxième conférence internationale de la paix, La Haye 15 juin–18 octobre 1907.* The Hague: Martinus Nijhoff, 1908.

———. *Conférence internationale de la paix, La Haye 18 mai–29 juillet 1899.* The Hague: Imprimerie nationale, 1899.

Prussia, and War Ministry. *Kriegs-Etappen-Ordnung (K.E.O.) (12 March 1914) (D.V.E. Nr. 90).* Berlin: Reichsdruckerei, 1914.

Roberts, Adam, and Richard Guelff. *Documents on the Laws of War.* 3rd ed. Oxford: Oxford University Press, 2004.

Schiffers, Reinhard, Manfred Koch, and Hans Boldt, eds. *Der Hauptausschuss des Deutschen Reichstags 1915–1918.* Quellen zur Geschichte des Parlamentarismus und der politischen Parteien. Düsseldorf: Droste, 1981–83.

Schindler, Dietrich, and Jiri Toman, eds. *The Laws of Armed Conflicts.* Geneva: Henry Dunant Institute, 1988.

Scott, James Brown, ed. *Diplomatic Documents Relating to the Outbreak of the European War.* Carnegie Endowment for International Peace. Division of International Law. New York: Oxford University Press, 1916.

———. *The Hague Conventions and Declarations of 1899 and 1907, Accompanied by Tables of Signatures, Ratifications and Adhesions of the Various Powers and Texts of Reservations....* Publications of the Carnegie Endowment for International Peace. Division of International Law, Washington, DC. New York: Oxford University Press, 1918.

Sten.Ber. Germany. Reichstag. *Stenographische Berichte über die Verhandlungen des Deutschen Reichstages* (Berlin). http://www.reichstagsprotokolle.de/rtbiiaufauf_k13.html.

Times (London). *The "Times" Documentary History of the War.* London: *Times,* 1914–18.

UA: Germany. National Constitutional Assembly. *Das Werk des Untersuchungsausschusses der Verfassunggebenden Deutschen Nationalversammlung und des Deutschen Reichstages, 1919–1928, Verhandlungen, Gutachten, Urkunden.* 4 Reihen (sections). Berlin: Deutsche Verlagsgesellschaft für Politik und Geschichte, 1919–28.

United States. *Papers Relating to the Foreign Relation of the United States: The Lansing Papers, 1914–1920.* 2 vols. Washington, DC: Government Printing Office, 1939.

Willeke, A., ed. Protokolle der Tagung richterlicher Militärjustizbeamter in Brüssel am 29./30. September 1916, samt einigen vorbereitenden Gutachten. N.p., 1916.

SECONDARY SOURCES, MEMOIRS, DIARIES, ETC. (CITED)

Adams, R. J. Q. *Bonar Law.* Stanford, CA: Stanford University Press, 1999.

Addison, Christopher. *Four and a Half Years: A Personal Diary from June 1914 to January 1919.* Vol. 1. London: Hutchinson & Co., 1934.

Adler, Selig. "The War-Guilt Question and American Disillusionment, 1918–1928." *Journal of Modern History* 23, no. 1 (March 1951): 1–28.

Afflerbach, Holger. *Falkenhayn: Politisches Denken und Handeln im Kaiserreich.* Beiträge zur Militärgeschichte, vol. 42. Munich: Oldenbourg, 1994.

———, ed. *Kaiser Wilhelm II. als Oberster Kriegsherr im Ersten Weltkrieg; Quellen aus der militärischen Umgebung des Kaisers 1914–1918.* Munich: Oldenbourg, 2005.

Allen, Charles A. "Civilian Starvation and Relief during Armed Conflict: The Modern Humanitarian Law." *Georgia Journal of International and Comparative Law* 19, no. 1 (1989): 1–85.

Aron, Raymond. *The Century of Total War.* Boston: Beacon Press, 1955.

Asquith, Herbert Henry. *Memories and Reflections, 1852–1927.* London: Cassell & Co., 1928.

Assmann, Kurt. *Deutsche Seestrategie in zwei Weltkriegen.* Die Wehrmacht im Kampf, vol. 12. Heidelberg: Kurt Vowinckel, 1957.

Baden, Prince Max von. *Erinnerungen und Dokumente.* Stuttgart: Deutsche Verlags-Anstalt, 1927.

Barros, Andrew. "Strategic Bombing and Restraint in 'Total War,' 1915–1918." *Historical Journal* 52, no. 2 (2009): 413–31.

Basler, Werner. *Deutschlands Annexionspolitik in Polen und im Baltikum 1914–1918.* East Berlin: Rütten & Loening, 1962.

Baumann, Timo. "Giftgas und Salpeter: Chemische Industrie, Naturwissenschaft und Militär von 1906 bis zum ersten Munitionsprogramm 1914/1915." PhD diss., University of Düsseldorf, 2008.

Bayern, Rupprecht Kronprinz von. *Mein Kriegstagebuch.* 3 vols. Edited by Eugen von Frauenholz. Munich: Deutscher National Verlag, 1929.

Beckett, Ian F. W. *The Great War.* New York: Longman, 2007.

Beer, Ludwig. "Krieg und Völkerrecht vor dem deutschen Reichsgericht." *Niemeyers Zeitschrift für Internationales Recht* 25 (1915): 321–38.

Bell, Archibald C. *A History of the Blockade of Germany and of the Countries Associated with Her in the Great War, Austria, Bulgaria, and Turkey, 1914–1918.* London: HMSO, 1937.

Bellot, Hugh H. L. "War Crimes: Their Prevention and Punishment." *Grotius Society, Problems of the War: Papers Read before the Society in the Year 1916* 2 (1917): 31–55.

Berghahn, Volker R. *Der Erste Weltkrieg.* Munich: C. H. Beck, 2003.

———. *Der Tirpitz-Plan; Genesis und Verfall einer innenpolitischen Krisenstrategie unter Wilhelm II.* Geschichtliche Studien zu Politik und Gesellschaft, vol. 1. Düsseldorf: Droste Verlag, 1971.

Bernard, Philippe. "À propos de la stratégie aérienne pendant la première guerre mondiale: Mythes et réalités." *Revue d'histoire moderne et contemporaine* 16 (April–June 1969).

Best, Geoffrey. "How Right Is Might? Some Aspects of the International Debate about How to Fight Wars and How to Win Them, 1870–1918." In *War Economy and the Military Mind,* edited by Geoffrey Best and Andrew Wheatcroft, 120–35. London: Croom Helm, 1976.

———. *Humanity in Warfare: The Modern History of the International Law of Armed Conflicts.* New York: Columbia University Press, 1980.

Bethmann Hollweg, Theobald von. *Betrachtungen zum Weltkrieg.* Vol. 2, *Während des Weltkrieges.* Berlin: Reimar Hobbing, 1922.

"Bewaffnete Kauffahrteischiffe." *Zeitschrift für Völkerrecht* 9 (1916): 521–45.

Bilfinger, Carl. "Heinrich Triepel 1868–1946." *Zeitschrift für ausländisches öffentliches Recht und Völkerrecht* 13 (1950): 1–13.

Bird, Keith. "The Tirpitz Legacy: The Political Ideology of German Sea Power." *Journal of Military History* 69 (July 2005): 821–32.

Bluntschli, Johann Caspar. *Le droit international codifié.* Translated by C. Lardy. Paris: Guillaumin et cie., 1874.

Böckenförde, Ernst-Wolfgang. *Gesetz und gesetzgebende Gewalt: Von den Anfängen der deutschen Staatsrechtslehre bis zur Höhe des staatsrechlichen Positivismus.* Berlin: Duncker & Humblot, 1981.

Boemeke, Manfred F. "Woodrow Wilson's Image of Germany, the War-Guilt Question, and the Treaty of Versailles." In *The Treaty of Versailles: A Reassessment after 75 Years,* edited by Manfred F. Boemeke, Gerald D. Feldman, and Elisabeth Glaser, 603–14. Cambridge: Cambridge University Press, 1998.

Böhme, Klaus. *Aufrufe und Reden deutscher Professoren im Ersten Weltkrieg.* Stuttgart: Universal-Bibliothek, 1975.

Bonfils, Henry. *Manuel de droit international public (droit des gens) aux étudiants des facultés de droit et aux aspirants aux fonctions diplomatiques et consulaires.* Paris: A. Rousseau, 1912.

Bonfils, Henry, and Paul Fauchille. *Manuel de droit international public (droit des gens).* 5th ed. Paris: Arthur Rousseau, 1908.

Bönker, Dirk. "Ein German Way of War? Deutscher Militarismus und maritime Kriegführung im Ersten Weltkrieg." In *Das Deutsche Kaiserreich in der Kontroverse. Eine Bilanz,* edited by Sven Oliver Müller and Cornelius Torp, 308–22. Göttingen: Vandenhoeck & Ruprecht, 2009.

Bonnevie, Victor. *La défense des Belges devant les tribunaux de guerre allemands.* Brussels: J. Lebègue & Cie., 1919.

Bower, Graham. "The Laws of War: Prisoners of War and Reprisals." *Grotius Society, Problems of the War: Papers Read before the Society in the Year 1915* 1 (1916).

Boyle, Francis Anthony. *World Politics and International Law.* Durham, NC: Duke University Press, 1985.

Bridge, F. Maynard. *A Short History of the Great World War.* London: H. F. W. Deane & Sons, 1919.

Brierly, James Leslie. *The Basis of Obligation in International Law and Other Papers.* Edited by Hersch Lauterpacht and C. H. M. Waldock. Oxford: Oxford University Press, 1958.

———. *The Law of Nations: An Introduction to the International Law of Peace.* 6th ed. Edited by Humphrey Waldock. Oxford: Oxford University Press, 1963.

Bülow, Bernhard von. *Denkwürdigkeiten.* 4 vols. Berlin: Ullstein, 1920.

Burns, Richard Dean. "Regulating Submarine Warfare, 1921–41: A Case Study in Arms Control and Limited War." *Society for Military History* 35, no. 2 (April 1971): 56–63.

Byers, Michael. "Custom, Power, and the Power of Rules: Customary International Law from an Interdisciplinary Perspective." *Michigan Journal of International Law* 17 (1995–96): 109–80.

Cahen-Salvador, Georges. *Les prisonniers de guerre (1914–1919).* Paris: Payot, 1929.

Carr, Edward Hallett. *International Relations since the Peace Treaties.* London: Macmillan, 1937.

———. *Propaganda in International Politics.* New York: Farrar and Rinehart, 1939.

Cecil, Lamar. *The German Diplomatic Service, 1871–1914.* Princeton, NJ: Princeton University Press, 1976.

Charmley, John. *Splendid Isolation? Britain and the Balance of Power, 1874–1914.* London: Houghton & Stoddard, 1999.

Chickering, Roger, and Stig Förster, eds. *Great War, Total War: Combat and Mobilization on the Western Front, 1914–1918.* Cambridge: Cambridge University Press, 2000.

Clark, Christopher. *The Sleepwalkers: How Europe Went to War in 1914.* New York: HarperCollins, 2012.

Coogan, John W. *The End of Neutrality: The United States, Britain, and Maritime Rights, 1899–1915.* Ithaca, NY: Cornell University Press, 1981.

Cooper, Malcolm. *The Birth of Independent Air Power: British Air Policy in the First World War.* London: Allen & Unwin, 1986.

Corbett, Julian S. *Naval Operations.* 5 vols. London: Longmans, Green & Co., 1920–28.

Curtis, Bradley, and Mitu Gulati. "Withdrawing from International Custom." *Yale Law Journal* 120 (2010–11): 202–75.

Dahn, Felix. *Das Kriegsrecht; Kurze, volksthümliche Darstellung für Jedermann zumal für den deutschen Soldaten.* Würzburg: A. Stuber, 1870.

D'Amato, Anthony A. *The Concept of Custom in International Law.* Ithaca, NY: Cornell University Press, 1971.

Dambitsch, Ludwig. "Völkerrechtsverletzung." *Zeitschrift für Völkerrecht* 10 (1917/18): 368–74.

Daniel, Ute. "Women's Work in Industry and Family: Germany, 1914–1918." In *The Upheaval of War: Family, Work and Welfare in Europe, 1914–1918,* edited by Richard Wall and Jay M. Winter, 267–96. Cambridge: Cambridge University Press, 1988.

Darcy, Shane. "The Evolution of the Law of Belligerent Reprisals." *Military Law Review* 175 (2003): 184–251.

Davis, Belinda J. *Home Fires Burning: Food, Politics, and Everyday Life in World War I Berlin.* Chapel Hill: University of North Carolina Press, 2000.

Deist, Wilhelm. "Strategy and Unlimited Warfare in Germany: Moltke, Falkenhayn, and Ludendorff." In *Great War, Total War: Combat and Mobilization on the Western Front, 1914–1918,* edited by Roger Chickering and Stig Förster, 265–79. Cambridge: Cambridge University Press, 2000.

De Montmorency, J. E. G. "The Principles Underlying Contraband and Blockade." *Grotius Society, Problems of the War: Papers Read before the Society in the Year 1916* 2 (1917): 21–30.

"Der Lusitania-Fall." *Zeitschrift für Völkerrecht* 9 (1916): 135–237.

De Schaepdrijver, Sophie. *La Belgique et la Première Guerre Mondiale.* New York: Peter Lang, 2004.

De Visscher, Charles. "Les lois de la guerre et la théorie de la nécessité." *Revue général de droit international public* 24 (1917): 74–108.

Dickmann, Fritz. *Die Kriegsschuldfrage auf der Friedenskonferenz von Paris 1919.* Munich: R. Oldenbourg, 1964.

Diehl, Josef. *Die Londoner Seerechtsdeklaration von 1909 und die deutsche Prisenordnung von 1909: Ein Vergleich.* Coburg: Tageblatt-Haus, 1929.

Dietz, Heinrich. "Das Militärstrafrechtswesen im Kriege." In *Der Weltkampf um Ehre und Recht.* Vol. 8, *Die Organisationen der Kriegführung, Dritter Teil: Die Organisationen für das geistige Leben im Heere,* edited by Max Schwarte, 136–45. Leipzig: E. Finking d. J., 1931.

Dixon, Martin. *Textbook on International Law.* 4th ed. Oxford: Oxford University Press, 2000.

Doughty, Robert A. *Pyrrhic Victory: French Strategy and Operations in the Great War.* Cambridge, MA: Harvard University Press, 2005.

Dülffer, Jost. *Regeln gegen den Krieg? Die Haager Friedenskonferenzen 1899 und 1907 in der internationalen Politik.* Berlin: Ullstein, 1981.

Dumberry, Patrick. "Incoherent and Ineffective: The Concept of Persistent Objector Revisited." *International and Comparative Law Quarterly* 59, no. 3 (2010): 779–802.

Edmonds, Colonel J. D., and Lassa Oppenheim. *Land Warfare: An Exposition of the Laws and Usages of War on Land, for the Guidance of Officers of His Majesty's Army.* London: HMSO, 1912.

Einem, Karl von. *Ein Armeeführer erlebt den Weltkrieg; persönliche Aufzeichnungen.* Edited by Junius Alter. Leipzig: V. Hase & Koehler, 1938.

Elsner, Lothar. "Ausländerbeschäftigung und Zwangsarbeitspolitik in Deutschland während des Ersten Weltkrieges." In *Auswanderer-Wanderarbeiter-Gastarbeiter; Bevölkerung, Arbeitsmarkt und Wanderung in Deutschland seit der Mitte des 19. Jahrhunderts,* edited by Klaus J. Bade, 527–57. Ostfildern: Scripta Mercaturae Verlag, 1984.

———. "Der Übergang zur Zwangsarbeit für ausländische Arbeiter in der deutschen Landwirtschaft zu Beginn des 1. Weltkriegs." *Wissenschaftliche Zeitschift der Wilhelm-Pieck-Universität Rostock, Gesellschafts- und Sprachwissenschaftliche Reihe* 26, no. 3 (1977): 291–98.

Elsner von Gronow, Kurt, and Georg Sohl, eds. *Militärstrafrecht für Herr und Marine des Deutschen Reichs; Handbuch für Kommando- und Gerichtsstellen, für Offiziere und Juristen.* Berlin: H. W. Müller, 1906.

Endres, Karl. *Die völkerrechtlichen Grundsätze der Kriegführung zu Lande und zur See.* Berlin: R. von Decker's Verlag, 1909.

Ernst, Carl. *Der große Krieg in Belgien; Beobachtungen seinen ehemaligen hannoverschen Landsleuten gewidmet.* Gembloux, Belgium: J. Duculot, 1930.

Erzberger, Matthias. *Erlebnisse im Weltkrieg, von Reichsfinanzminister a. d. M. Erzberger.* Stuttgart: Deutsche Verlagsanstalt, 1920.

Evans, Ellen L., and Joseph O. Baylen. "History as Propaganda: The German Foreign Ministry and the 'Enlightenment' of American Historians on the War-Guilt Question, 1930–1933." In *Forging the Collective Memory: Government and International Historians through Two World Wars,* edited by Keith Wilson, 151–77. Providence, RI: Berghahn Books, 1996.

Farrar, Marjorie M. *Conflict and Compromise: The Strategy, Politics and Diplomacy of the French Blockade, 1914–1918.* The Hague: Martinus Nijhoff, 1974.

Fauchille, Paul. "La guerre sous-marine allemande." *Revue générale de droit international public* 25 (1918): 75–84.

Fay, Sidney B. *The Origins of the World War.* 2 vols. New York: Macmillan Co., 1928.

Feldman, Gerald D. *Army, Industry, and Labor in Germany, 1914–1918.* Princeton, NJ: Princeton University Press, 1966.

Ferguson, Jan Helenus. *Manual of International Law, for the Use of Navies, Colonies and Consulates.* The Hague: Martinus Nijhoff, 1884.

Ferguson, Niall. *The Pity of War: Explaining World War I.* New York: Basic Books, 1998.

Ferro, Marc. *The Great War, 1914–1918.* London: Routledge, 1991.

Fiore, Pasquale. *Nouveau droit international public, suivant les besoins de la civilisation moderne.* Paris: A. Durand et Pedone-Lauriel, G. Pedone-Lauriel, successeur, 1885–86.

Fischer, Fritz. *Germany's Aims in the First World War.* New York: W. W. Norton, 1967.

Förster, Stig. "Im Reich des Absurden: Die Ursachen des Ersten Weltkrieges." In *Wie Kriege entstehen: Zum historischen Hintergrund von Staatenkonflikten,* edited by Bernd Wegner, 211–52. Paderborn: Schöningh, 2003.

France. Service historique de l'armée de terre. *Les armées françaises dans la Grande Guerre.* 11 vols. Paris: Imprimerie nationale, 1922–37.

Fraunces, Michael G. "The International Law of Blockade: New Guiding Principles in Contemporary State Practice." *Yale Law Journal* 101, no. 4 (January 1992): 893–918.

French, David. *British Strategy and Wars Aims, 1914–1916.* Oxford: Oxford University Press, 1986.

Frey, Marc. *Der Erste Weltkrieg und die Niederlande: Ein neutrales Land im politischen und wirtschaftlichen Kalkül der Kriegsgegner.* Studien zur Internationalen Geschichte. Berlin: Akademie Verlag, 1998.

Friedmann, Wolfgang. *The Changing Structure of International Law.* New York: Columbia University Press, 1964.

Fry, Michael Graham. "British Revisionism." In *The Treaty of Versailles: A Reassessment after 75 Years,* edited by Manfred H. Boemeke, Gerald D. Feldman, and Elisabeth Glaser, 565–601. Cambridge: Cambridge University Press, 1998.

Gallwitz, Max von. *Meine Führertätigkeit im Weltkriege 1914/1916: Belgien—Osten—Balkan.* Berlin: E. S. Mittler & Sohn, 1929.

Gardam, Judith Gail. "Proportionality and Force in International Law." *American Journal of International Law* 87, no. 3 (July 1993): 391–413.

Garner, James Wilford. *International Law and the World War.* 2 vols. London: Longmans, Green & Co., 1920.

Gatzke, Hans W. *Germany's Drive to the West.* Baltimore: Johns Hopkins University Press, 1966.

Gay, George I. *Public Relations of the Commission for Relief in Belgium: Documents.* Stanford, CA: Stanford University Press, 1929.

Gebele, Hubert. *Großbritannien und der Große Krieg: Die Auseinandersetzung über Kriegs- und Friedensziele vom Kriegsausbruch 1914 bis zu den Friedenschlüssen von 1919/1920.* Regensburg: S. Roderer Verlag, 2009.

Geinitz, Christian. "The First Air War against Noncombatants: Strategic Bombing of German Cities in World War I." In *Great War, Total War: Combat and Mobilization on the Western Front, 1914–1918,* edited by Roger Chickering and Stig Förster, 207–25. Cambridge: Cambridge University Press, 2000.

Geiss, Imanuel. *July 1914: The Outbreak of the First World War: Selected Documents.* New York: Scribner, 1968.

Gerard, James W. *My Four Years in Germany.* New York: Hodder and Stoughton, 1917.

Germany. Großer Generalstab. *Kriegsbrauch im Landkriege.* Kriegsgeschichtliche Einzelschriften. Berlin: E. S. Mittler, 1902.

Geyer, Michael. "Insurrectionary Warfare: The German Debate about a *Levée en Masse* in October 1918." *Journal of Modern History* 73 (September 2001): 459–527.

Gibson, Hugh. *A Journal from Our Legation in Belgium.* Garden City, NY: Doubleday, Page & Co., 1917.

Girard, Marion. *A Strange and Formidable Weapon: British Responses to World War I Poison Gas.* Studies in War, Society, and the Military. Lincoln: University of Nebraska Press, 2008.

Goldstein, Erik. *Winning the Peace: British Diplomatic Strategy, Peace Planning, and the Paris Peace Conference, 1916–1920.* Oxford: Oxford University Press, 1991.

Goudy, H., et al. "Report of the Committee on the Legal Status of Submarines." *Transactions of the Grotius Society* 4 (1918): xxxi–l.

Grayzel, Susan R. "'The Souls of Soldiers': Civilians under Fire in First World War France." *Journal of Modern History* 78, no. 3 (September 2006): 588–622.

Green, Leslie C. *The Contemporary Law of Armed Conflict.* Manchester: Manchester University Press, 1993.

———. "Legal Positivism." In *The Stanford Encyclopedia of Philosophy* (2009 edition), edited by Edward M. Zalta. Stanford, CA: Stanford University Press, 2009.

Grey, Edward (Viscount Grey of Fallodon). *Twenty-Five Years, 1892–1916.* 2 vols. London: Hodder and Stoughton, 1925.

Gromaire, Georges. *L'occupation allemande en France (1914–1918).* Paris: Payot, 1925.

Grotius, Hugo. *The Rights of War and Peace Including the Law of Nature and of Nations.* Edited by A. C. Campbell. Chestnut Hill, MA: Adamant Publishing, 2003.

Gumz, Jonathan E. *The Resurrection and Collapse of Empire in Habsburg Serbia, 1914–1918.* Cambridge: Cambridge University Press, 2009.

Gündell, Erich von. *Aus seinen Tagebüchern: Deutsche Expedition nach China 1900–1901, 2. Haager Friedenskonferenz 1907; Weltkrieg 1914–1918 und Zwischenzeiten.* Edited by Walter Obkircher. Hamburg: Hanseatische Verlagsanstalt, 1939.

Haber, Ludwig Fritz. *The Poisonous Cloud: Chemical Warfare in the First World War.* Oxford: Oxford University Press, 1986.

Hahn, Erich J. C. "The German Foreign Office and the Question of War Guilt." In *German Nationalism and the European Response,* edited by Carole Fink, Isabel V. Hull, and MacGregor Knox, 43–70. Norman: University of Oklahoma Press, 1985.

Hall, William Edward. *A Treatise on International Law.* Oxford: Clarendon Press, 1904.

Hamilton, Richard F., and Holger Herwig. *Decisions for War, 1914–1917.* Cambridge: Cambridge University Press, 2004.

Hankel, Gerd. *Die Leipziger Prozesse: Deutsche Kriegsverbrechen und ihre strafrechtliche Verfolgung nach dem Ersten Weltkrieg.* Hamburg: Hamburg Edition, 2003.

Hartmann, Julius von. "Militärische Nothwendigkeit und Humanität; ein kritischer Versuch." *Deutsche Rundschau* 13–14 (1877–78): vol. 13: 111–28 and 450–71; vol. 14: 71–91.

Hayward, Joel. "Air Power, Ethics, and Civilian Immunity during the First World War and Its Aftermath." *Global War Studies* 7, no. 2 (2010): 3–31.

Hazlehurst, Cameron. *Politicians at War, July 1914 to May 1915: A Prologue to the Triumph of Lloyd George.* London: Cape, 1971.

Heffter, August Wilhelm. *Das Europäische Völkerrecht der Gegenwart auf den bisherigen Grundlagen.* 5th ed. Berlin: E. H. Schroeder, 1867.

Heinemann, Ulrich. *Die verdrängte Niederlage; Politische Öffentlichkeit und Kriegsschuldfrage in der Weimarer Republik.* Göttingen: Vandenhoeck & Ruprecht, 1983.

Heintschel von Heinegg, Wolff. "Naval Blockade." In *International Law across the Spectrum of Conflict: Essays in Honour of Professor L. C. Green on the Occasion of His Eightieth Birthday,* edited by Michael N. Schmitt, 203–30. Newport, RI: Naval War College, 2000.

Henckaerts, Jean-Marie. "Study on Customary International Humanitarian Law: A Contribution to the Understanding and Respect for the Rule of Law in Armed Conflict." *International Review of the Red Cross* 87, no. 857 (March 2005): 175–212.

Henry, Albert. *Le ravitaillement de la Belgique pendant l'occupation allemande.* Publications of the Carnegie Endowment for International Peace, Belgian Series. Paris: Les presses universitaires de France, 1924.

Herbert, Ulrich. *Geschichte der Ausländerbeschäftigung in Deutschland 1880 bis 1980; Saisonarbeiter, Zwangsarbeiter, Gastarbeiter.* Berlin: J. H. W. Dietz Nachf., 1986.

Herwig, Holger. "Clio Deceived: Patriotic Self-Censorship in Germany after the War." In *Forging the Collective Memory; Government and International Historians through Two World Wars,* edited by Keith Wilson, 87–127. Providence, RI: Berghahn Books, 1996.

———. *The First World War: Germany and Austria Hungary, 1914–1918.* London: Arnold, 1997.

———. "Total Rhetoric, Limited War: Germany's U-Boat Campaign, 1917–1918." In *Great War, Total War: Combat and Mobilization on the Western Front, 1914–1918,* edited by Roger Chickering and Stig Förster, 189–206. Cambridge: Cambridge University Press, 2000.

Hinz, Uta. *Gefangen im Großen Krieg. Kriegsgefangenschaft in Deutschland 1914–1921.* Schriften der Bibliothek für Zeitgeschichte. Essen: Klartext, 2006.

Hirschfeld, Gerhard, Gerd Krumeich, and Irina Renz, eds. *Enzyklopädie des Ersten Weltkrieges.* Paderborn: Schöningh, 2002.

Hobson, Rolf. *Imperialism at Sea: Naval Strategic Thought, the Ideology of Sea Power, and the Tirpitz Plan, 1875–1914.* Boston: Brill, 2002.

Hoffmann, Max von. *Die Aufzeichnungen des Generalmajors Max Hoffmann.* 2 vols. Edited by Karl-Friedrich Nowak. Berlin: Verlag für Kulturpolitik, 1929.

Hoffmann, Stanley. "An American Social Science." In *Janus and Minerva: Essays in the Theory and Practice of International Politics,* edited by Stanley Hoffmann, 3–24. Boulder, CO: Westview Press, 1987.

Hold von Ferneck, Alexander Freiherr. *Die Reform des Seekriegsrechts durch die Londoner Konferenz 1908/09.* Handbuch des Völkerrechts. Berlin: W. Kohlhammer, 1914.

Holland, Thomas Erskine. *The Laws and Customs of War on Land, as Defined by the Hague Convention of 1899.* London: Harrison and Sons, 1904.

———. *The Laws of War on Land.* Oxford: Oxford University Press, 1908.

Holtzendorff, Franz von. *Handbuch des Völkerrechts. Auf Grundlage europäischer Staatspraxis.* Vol. 1, Einleitung in das Völkerrecht. Berlin: Carl Habel, 1885.

Hoover, Herbert. *An American Epic.* Vol. 1, *Introduction: The Relief of Belgium and Northern France, 1914–1930.* Chicago: Henry Regnery, 1959.

Hopman, Albert. *Das ereignisreiche Leben eines "Wilhelminers."* Edited by Michael Epkenhans. Munich: R. Oldenbourg, 2004.

Horne, John, and Alan Kramer. *German Atrocities, 1914: A History of Denial.* New Haven, CT: Yale University Press, 2001.

House, Edward Mandell. *The Intimate Papers of Colonel House: Arranged as a Narrative by Charles Seymour.* 4 vols. Boston: Houghton Mifflin, 1926.

Howard, Michael. *The First World War: A Very Short Introduction.* Oxford: Oxford University Press, 2002.

Huber, Max. "Die kriegsrechtlichen Verträge und die Kriegsraison." *Zeitschrift für Völkerrecht* 7 (1913): 351–74.

Huberich, Charles Henry, and Richard King. *The Prize Code of the German Empire as in Force July 1, 1915.* New York: Baker, Voorhis & Co., 1915.

Hull, Isabel V. *Absolute Destruction: Military Culture and the Practices of War in Imperial Germany.* Ithaca, NY: Cornell University Press, 2005.

———. "'Military Necessity' and the Laws of War in Imperial Germany." In *Order, Conflict, Violence,* edited by Stathis Kalyvas, Ian Shapiro, and Tarek Masoud, 352–77. Cambridge: Cambridge University Press, 2008.

Hutten-Czapski, Bogdan von. *Sechzig Jahre Politik und Gesellschaft.* Berlin: E. S. Mittler, 1936.

Jacomet, Robert. *Les lois de la guerre continentale.* 2nd ed. Paris: Fournier, 1913.

Jäger, Wolfgang. *Historische Forschung und politische Kultur in Deutschland; Die Debatte 1914–1980 über den Ausbruch des Ersten Weltkrieges.* Göttingen: Vandenhoeck & Ruprecht, 1984.

Jennings, R. Y. "The Caroline and McLeod Cases." *American Journal of International Law* 32, no. 1 (1938): 82–99.

Jerusalem, Franz W. "Der Fall Fryatt." *Zeitschrift für Völkerrecht* 10 (1917/18): 563–85.

Jervis, Robert. "A Political Science Perspective on the Balance of Power and the Concert." *American Historical Review* 97, no. 3 (June 1992): 716–24.

———. "Systems Theories and Diplomatic History." In *Diplomacy: New Approaches in History, Theory, and Policy,* edited by Paul Gordon Lauren, 212–44. New York: Free Press, 1979.

Joffre, Joseph. *The Personal Memoirs of Joffre, Field Marshal of the French Army.* 2 vols. Translated by T. Bentley Mott. New York: Harper & Bros., 1932.

Jones, Heather. "The Final Logic of Sacrifice? Violence in German Prisoner of War Labor Companies in 1918." *Historian* 68, no. 4 (2006): 770–83.

———. *Violence against Prisoners of War in the First World War: Britain, France, and Germany, 1914–1920.* Cambridge: Cambridge University Press, 2011.

Jones, Neville. *The Origins of Strategic Bombing: A Study of the Development of British Air Strategic Thought and Practice up to 1918.* London: William Kimber, 1973.

Kaeckenbeeck, Georges. "Divergences between British and Other Views on International Law." *Grotius Society, Problems of the War: Papers Read before the Society in the Year 1918* 4 (1918): 213–52.

Kalshoven, Frits. *Belligerent Reprisals.* Leiden: A. W. Sijthoff, 1971.

Kaplan, Morton A., and Nicholas deB. Katzenbach. *The Political Foundations of International Law.* New York: John Wiley & Sons, 1961.

Kaufmann, Erich. *Das Wesen des Völkerrechts und die clausula rebus sic stantibus.* Tübingen: J. C. B. Mohr, 1911.

Keynes, John Maynard. *The Economic Consequences of the Peace.* New York: Harcourt, Brace and Howe, 1920.

Kirschen, Sadi. *Devant les conseils de guerre allemands. Affaires: Cavell; Blanckaert; Boël; Franck-Backelmans; Parenté; Colon; Mus; Kugé; Freyling; Bosteels; Libre Belgique; Bril; Feyens; Monod.* Brussels: Rossel & fils, 1919.

Kohler, Josef. "Das neue Völkerrecht." *Zeitschrift für Völkerrecht* 9 (1916): 5–10.

———. "Die Neutralität Belgiens und die Festungsverträge." *Zeitschrift für Völkerrecht* 9 (1916): 298–309.

———. "Notwehr und Neutralität." *Zeitschrift für Völkerrecht* 8, no. 1 (1914): 576–80.

Köhler, Ludwig. *Die Staatsverwaltung der besetzten Gebiete. Volume: Belgien.* Carnegie Foundation for International Peace. New Haven, CT: Yale University Press, 1927.

Koskenniemi, Martti. *The Gentle Civilizer of Nations: The Rise and Fall of International Law, 1870–1960.* Cambridge: Cambridge University Press, 2001.

Kramer, Alan. *Dynamic of Destruction: Culture and Mass Killing in the First World War.* Oxford: Oxford University Press, 2007.

Krüger, Peter. *Deutschland und die Reparationen 1918; Die Genesis des Reparationsproblems in Deutschland zwischen Waffenstillstand und Versailler Friedensschluss.* Schriftenreihe der Vierteljahrshefte für Zeitgeschichte, Nr. 25. Stuttgart: Deutsche Verlags-Anstalt, 1973.

Laband, Paul. *Das Staatsrecht des deutschen Reiches.* 4 vols. 4th ed. Tübingen: J. C. B. Mohr, 1901.

Lademacher, Horst. *Die belgische Neutralität als Problem der europäischen Politik, 1830–1914.* Bonn: Ludwig Röhrscheid, 1971.

Lambert, Nicholas A. *Planning Armageddon: British Economic Warfare and the First World War.* Cambridge, MA: Harvard University Press, 2012.

Lancken-Wakenitz, Oscar, Freiherr von der. *Meine Dreissig Dienstjahre, 1888–1918, Potsdam—Paris—Brüssel.* Berlin: Verlag für Kulturpolitik, 1931.

Lasson, Adolf. *Princip und Zukunft des Völkerrechts.* Berlin: Wihelm Hertz, 1871.

———. "Selections from *Das Culturideal und der Krieg* (Berlin, 1868) and *Princip und Zukunft des Völkerrechts* (Berlin, 1871)." In *A Survey of International Relations between the United States and Germany, August 1, 1914–April 6, 1917, Based on Official Documents,* edited by James Scott Brown, l–lxx. New York: Oxford University Press, 1917.

Lauren, Paul Gordon. *Diplomats and Bureaucrats: The First Institutional Responses to Twentieth-Century Diplomacy in France and Germany.* Hoover Institution Publications. Stanford, CA: Hoover Institution Press, 1976.

Lauterpacht, Hersh. *The Function of Law in the International Community.* Oxford: Clarendon Press, 1933.

Lepard, Brian D. *Customary International Law: A New Theory with Practical Applications.* Cambridge: Cambridge University Press, 2010.

Lepick, Olivier. *La grande guerre chimique 1914–1918.* Paris: Presses Universitaires de France, 1998.

Lieber, Francis. *Instructions for the Government of Armies of the United States in the Field, General Orders No. 100, 24 April 1863.* In *The Laws of Armed Conflicts: A Collection of Conventions, Resolutions and Other Documents,* edited by Dietrich Schindler and Jiri Toman, 3–23. Geneva: Henry Dunant Institute, 1988.

Lieber, Keir A. "The New History of World War I and What It Means for International Relations Theory." *International Security* 32, no. 2 (Fall 2007): 155–91.

Lingelbach, William E. "Belgian Neutrality: Its Origin and Interpretation." *American Historical Review* 39, no. 1 (October 1933): 48–72.

Link, Arthur S. *Wilson the Diplomatist: A Look at His Major Foreign Policies.* Chicago: Quadrangle Books, 1965.

Lipkes, Jeff. *Rehearsals: The German Army in Belgium, August 1914.* Leuven: Leuven University Press, 2007.

Liszt, Franz von. *Das Völkerrecht systematisch dargestellt.* 9th ed. Berlin: O. Häring, 1913.

Liulevicius, Vejas. *War Land on the Eastern Front: Culture, National Identity, and German Occupation in World War I.* Cambridge: Cambridge University Press, 2000.

Lohr, Eric. *Nationalizing the Russian Empire: The Campaign against Enemy Aliens during World War I.* Cambridge, MA: Harvard University Press, 2003.

Loßberg, Fritz von. *Meine Tätigkeit im Weltkriege 1914–1918.* Berlin: E. S. Mittler, 1939.

Lowe, C. J., and M. L. Dockrill. *The Mirage of Power.* 3 vols. Boston: Routledge & Kegan Paul, 1972.

Lowry, Bullitt. *Armistice 1918.* Kent, OH: Kent State University Press, 1996.

Ludendorff, Erich. *The General Staff and Its Problems: The History of the Relations between the High Command and the German Imperial Government as Revealed by Official Documents.* London: Hutchinson, 1919.

———. *The Nation at War* [Der totale Krieg], translated by A. S. Rappaport (London: Hutchinson, 1936).

Lueder, Carl. "Das Landkriegsrecht im Besonderen." In *Handbuch des Völkerrechts,* vol. 4, edited by Franz von Holtzendorff, 371–545. Hamburg: A. G. Richter, 1889.

———. "Krieg und Kriegsrecht im Allgemeinen." In *Handbuch des Völkerrechts,* vol. 4, edited by Franz von Holtzendorff, 169–367. Hamburg: A. G. Richter, 1889.

Luhmann, Niklas. *Rechtssoziologie.* 3rd ed. Opladen: Westdeutscher Verlag, 1987.

Macdonell, John. "Some Notes on Blockade." *Grotius Society, Problems of the War: Papers Read before the Society in the Year 1915* 1 (1916): 93–104.

Mantoux, Étienne. *The Carthaginian Peace; or, the Economic Consequences of Mr. Keynes.* London: New York, 1946.

Marder, Arthur J. *From the Dreadnought to Scapa Flow: The Royal Navy in the Fisher Era, 1904–1919.* 5 vols. Oxford: Oxford University Press, 1961–70.

Martel, René. *French Strategic and Tactical Bombardment Forces of World War I.* Edited by Steven Suddaby, translated by Allen Suddaby. Lanham, MD: Scarecrow Press, 2007.

Martin, Christopher. "The Declaration of London: A Matter of Operational Capability." *Historical Research* 82, no. 218 (November 2009): 731–55.

Martinetz, Dieter. *Der Gaskrieg 1914/18: Entwicklung, Herstellung und Einsatz chemischer Kampfstoffe: Das Zusammenwirken von militärischer Führung, Wissenschaft und Industrie.* Bonn: Bernard & Graefe, 1996.

Mayerhofer, Lisa. *Zwischen Freund und Feind: Deutsche Besatzung in Rumänien 1916–1918.* Munich: Martin Meidenbauer Verlagsbuchhandlung, 2010.

McCoubrey, H. "The Nature of the Modern Doctrine of Military Necessity." *Revue de droit militaire et de droit de la guerre* 30, no. 1–4 (1991): 215–55.

McKercher, B. J. C. "Economic Warfare." In *The Oxford Illustrated History of the First World War,* edited by Hew Strachan, 119–33. Oxford: Oxford University Press, 1998.

McPhail, Helen. *The Long Silence: Civilian Life under the German Occupation of Northern France, 1914–1918.* New York: I. B. Tauris, 2000.

Méringhac, A. "De la sanction des infractions au droit des gens commises, au cours de la guerre européenne, par les empires du centre." *Revue générale de droit international public* 24 (1917): 5–56.

Messerschmidt, Manfred. "Völkerrecht und 'Kriegsnotwendigkeit' in der deutschen militärischen Tradition." In *Was damals Recht war. NS-Militär- und Strafjustiz im Vernichtungskrieg,* 191–230. Essen: Klartext, 1996.

Messinger, Gary S. *British Propaganda and the State in the First World War.* Manchester: Manchester University Press, 1992.

Meurer, Christian. *Die Haager Friedenskonferenz.* Vol. 2, *Das Kriegsrecht der Haager Konferenz.* Munich: J. Schweitzer, 1907.

———. *Die völkerrechtliche Stellung der vom Feinde besetzten Gebiete.* Tübingen: J. C. B. Mohr, 1915.

Mitrany, David. *The Effect of the War on Southeastern Europe.* Carnegie Endowment for International Peace. New Haven, CT: Yale University Press, 1936.

Mitrovic, Andrej. *Serbia's Great War, 1914–1918.* Central European Studies. West Lafayette, IN: Purdue University Press, 2007.

Moltke, Helmuth von. *Militärische Korrespondenz aus den Dienstschriften des Krieges 1870/71.* 1st section, 3rd part. Edited by General Staff Germany. Berlin: Ernst Siegfried Mittler & Sohn, 1896.

———. *Moltke; Vom Kabinettskrieg zum Volkskrieg: Eine Werkauswahl.* Edited by Stig Förster. Bonn: Bouvier, 1992.

Mombauer, Annika. *Origins of the First World War: Controversies and Consensus.* New York: Longman, 2002.

Montgelas, Max, and Walter Schücking, eds. *Die deutschen Dokumente zum Kriegsausbruch; Vollständige Sammlung der von Karl Kautsky zusammengestellten amtlichen Aktenstücke mit einigen Ergänzungen. Im Auftrage des Auswärtigen Amtes nach gemeinsamer Durchsicht mit Karl Kautsky.* 5 vols. Charlottenburg: Deutsche Verlagsgesellschaft für Politik und Geschichte, 1919.

Morgan, J. H. "War Treason." *Grotius Society, Problems of the War: Papers Read before the Society in the Year 1916* 2 (1917): 161–73.

Morgenthau, Hans J. *Politics among Nations.* New York: Alfred A. Knopf, 1954.

Morley, John Viscount. *Memorandum on Resignation August 1914.* London: Macmillan, 1928.

Mudge, George Alfred. "Starvation as a Means of Warfare." *International Lawyer* 4, no. 2 (1969–70): 228–69.

Müller, Georg Alexander von. *Regierte der Kaiser? Kriegstagebücher, Aufzeichnungen und Briefe des Chefs des Marine-Kabinetts, 1914–1918.* Edited by Walter Görlitz. Göttingen: Musterschmidt, 1959.

Müller, Rolf-Dieter. "Total War as the Result of New Weapons? The Use of Chemical Agents in World War I." In *Great War, Total War: Combat and Mobilization on the Western Front, 1914–1918,* edited by Roger Chickering and Stig Förster, 95–111. Cambridge: Cambridge University Press, 2000.

Munro, Dana C., George C. Sellery, and August C. Krey, eds. *German War Practices, Part 1: Treatment of Civilians.* Washington, DC: Government Printing Office, 1917.

Nelte, Otto. "Die belgische Frage." *Zeitschrift für Völkerrecht* 8 (1914): 745–54.

Neukamp, Dr. "Die Haager Friedenskonferenzen und der Europäische Krieg." *Zeitschrift für Völkerrecht* 8 (1914): 545–68.

"The Neutrality of Belgium." *American Journal of International Law* 9, no. 3 (July 1915).

New York Times. *Current History: The European War.* New York: New York Times Co., 1917.

Offer, Avner. *The First World War: An Agrarian Interpretation.* Oxford: Clarendon Press, 1989.

Oltmer, Jochen. "Unentbehrliche Arbeitskräfte: Kriegsgefangene in Deutschland 1914–1918." In *Kriegsgefangene im Europa des Ersten Weltkriegs,* edited by Jochen Oltmer, 67–96. Paderborn: Schöningh, 2006.

Oppenheim, Lassa. "Die Stellung der feindlichen Kauffarthschiffe im Seekrieg." *Zeitschrift für Völkerrecht* 8 (1914): 154–69.

———. *International Law: A Treatise.* 1st ed. London: Longmans, Green & Co., 1905.

———. "The Legal Relations between an Occupying Power and the Inhabitants." *Law Quarterly Review* 33, no. 4 (October 1917): 363–70.

———. "War Treason." *Law Quarterly Review* 33, no. 3 (1917): 266–86.

Osborne, Eric W. *Britain's Economic Blockade of Germany, 1914–1919.* Portland, OR: Frank Cass, 2004.

Otte, T. G. "A 'German Paperchase': The 'Scrap of Paper' Controversy and the Problem of Myth and Memory in International History." *Diplomacy and Statecraft* 18 (2007): 53–87.

Palazzo, Joseph. *Seeking Victory on the Western Front: The British Army and Chemical Warfare in World War I.* Lincoln: University of Nebraska Press, 2000.

Parks, William Hays. "Air War and the Law of War." *Air Force Law Review* 32 (1990): 1–225.

Perels, Ferdinand. *Das internationale öffentliche Seerecht der Gegenwart.* Berlin: E. S. Mittler & Sohn, 1903.

Perrinjaquet, J. "La guerre européenne et les relations commerciales des belligérants et des neutres. L'application des théories de la contrebande de guerre et du blocus." *Revue générale de droit international public* 22 (1915): 127–238.

Phillimore, G. G. "Bombardments." *Grotius Society* 1 (1916): 61–66.

Pic, Paul. "Violation systematique des lois de la guerre par les Austro-allemands. Les sanctions nécessaires." *Revue générale de droit international public* 23 (1916): 243–68.

Pickles, Katie. *Transnational Outrage: The Death and Commemoration of Edith Cavell.* Basingstoke: Palgrave Macmillan, 2007.

Pillet, Antoine. "La guerre actuelle et le droit des gens." *Revue générale de droit international public* 23 (1916): 5–31; 423–71.

———. *Les lois actuelles de la guerre.* 2nd ed. Paris: Arthur Rousseau, 1901.

Pirenne, J., and M. Vauthier. *La législation et l'administration allemandes en Belgique.* Publications of the Carnegie Endowment for International Peace, Belgian Series. New Haven, CT: Yale University Press, 1925.

Pohl, Hugo. *Aus Aufzeichungen und Briefen während der Kriegszeit.* Berlin: Karl Siegesmund, 1920.

Poincaré, Raymond. *The Memoirs of Raymond Poincaré, 1914.* Translated by George Arthur. Garden City, NY: Doubleday, Doran & Co., 1929.

Ponsonby, Arthur. *Faleshood in War-Time.* London: E. P. Dutton & Co., 1928.

Posner, Eric A. "A Theory of the Laws of War." *University of Chicago Law Review* 70, no. 1 (Winter 2003): 297–317.

Pospisil, Leopold. "The Attributes of Law." In *Law and Warfare: Studies in the Anthropology of Conflict,* edited by Paul Bohannan, 25–41. Garden City, NY: Natural History Press, 1967.

Preußen, Wilhelm Kronprinz von. *Meine Erinnerungen aus Deutschlands Heldenkampf.* Berlin: E. S. Mittler & Sohn, 1923.

Provost, René. "Starvation as a Weapon: Legal Implications of the United Nations Food Blockade against Iraq and Kuwait." *Columbia Journal of Transnational Law* 30 (1992): 577–639.

Prussia, Kriegsministerium, and Oberste Heeresleitung. *Die deutsche Kriegführung und das Völkerrecht; Beiträge zur Schuldfrage.* Berlin: Ernst Siegfried Mittler & Sohn, 1919.

Raeder, Erich. *Der Kreuzerkrieg in den ausländischen Gewässern.* Der Krieg zur See 1914–1918. Berlin: E. W. Mittler & Sohn, 1922.

Raleigh, Walter Alexander, and H. A. Jones. *The War in the Air: Being the Story of the Part Played in the Great War by the Royal Air Force.* 6 vols. Oxford: Clarendon Press, 1922–37.

Read, James Morgan. *Atrocity Propaganda, 1914–1919.* New Haven, CT: Yale University Press, 1941.

Reichsarchiv. *Der Weltkrieg 1914 bis 1918.* 14 vols. Berlin: E. S. Mittler & Sohn, 1925–44.

Renault, Louis. "De l'application du droit pénal aux faits de guerre." *Revue générale de droit international public* 25 (1918): 6–29.

———. *Les premières violations du droit des gens par l'Allemagne, Luxembourg et Belgique.* Paris: Receuil Sirey, 1917.

Ritter, Gerhard. *The Schlieffen Plan: Critique of a Myth.* London: Oswald Wolff, 1958.

———. *Staatskunst und Kriegshandwerk; Das Problem des "Militarismus" in Deutschland.* Vol. 2. Munich: R. Oldenbourg, 1964.

Robbins, K. G. "Foreign Policy, Government Structure and Public Opinion." In *British Foreign Policy under Sir Edward Grey,* edited by F. H. Hinsley, 532–46. Cambridge: Cambridge University Press, 1977.

Roberts, Adam. "Land Warfare: From Hague to Nuremberg." In *The Laws of War: Constraints on Warfare in the Western World,* edited by Michael Howard, George Andreopoulos, and Mark Shulman, 116–39. New Haven, CT: Yale University Press, 1994.

Roberts, Anthea. "Traditional and Modern Approaches to Customary International Law: A Reconciliation." *American Journal of International Law* 95, no. 4 (2001): 751–91.

Rodick, Burleigh Cushing. *The Doctrine of Necessity in International Law.* New York: Columbia University Press, 1928.

Roesle, Dr. "Die Geburts- und Sterblichkeitsverhältnisse." In *Deutschlands Gesundheitsverhältnisse unter dem Einfluss des Weltkrieges,* edited by Franz Bumm, 3–61. Berlin: Deutsche Verlagsanstalt, 1928.

Rogoff, Martin A. "The International Legal Obligations of Signatories to an Unratified Treaty." *Maine Law Review* 32 (1980): 263–99.

Röhl, John C. G. *Wilhelm II. Der Weg in den Abgrund 1900–1941.* Munich: C. H. Beck, 2008.

Rolland, Louis. "Les pratiques de la guerre aérienne dans le conflit de 1914 et le droit des gens." *Revue générale de droit international public* 23 (1916): 497–604.

Romen, A., and Carl Rissom, eds. *Militärstrafgesetzbuch für das Deutsche Reich vom 20. Juni 1872 nebst dem Einführungsgesetz.* 2nd ed. Berlin: Guttentag, 1916.

Samuel, Herbert Viscount. *Memoirs.* London: Cresset Press, 1945.

Sanders, Michael L., and Philip M. Taylor. *British Propaganda during the First World War.* London: Macmillan, 1982.

Satow, Ernst. "*Pacta Sunt Servanda* or International Guarantee." *Cambridge Historical Journal* 1, no. 3 (1925): 295–318.

Scheuerman, William E. *Morgenthau.* Malden, MA: Polity Press, 2009.

Schmitt, Carl. "Das Doppelgesicht des Genfer Völkerbundes (1926)." In *Positionen und Begriffe mit Weimar-Genf-Versailles 1923–1939,* 3rd ed., 48–50. Berlin: Duncker & Humblot, 1994.

———. "Der Begriff des Politischen (1927)." In *Frieden oder Pazifismus? Arbeiten zum Völkerrecht und zur internationalen Politik 1924–1978,* edited by Günter Maschke, 194–239. Berlin: Duncker & Humblot, 2005.

———. "Völkerrechtliche Formen des modernen Imperialismus (1932)." In *Positionen und Begriffe im Kampf mit Weimar-Genf-Versailles 1923–1939,* 3rd ed., 184–203. Berlin: Duncker & Humblot, 1994.

Schramm, Georg. *Das Prisenrecht in seiner neuesten Gestalt.* Berlin: E. S. Mittler & Sohn, 1913.

Schröder, Joachim. *Die U-Boote des Kaisers; Die Geschichte des deutschen U-Boot-Krieges gegen Großbritannien im Ersten Weltkrieg.* Bonn: Bernard & Graefe, 2003.

Schroeder, Paul W. "Did the Vienna Settlement Rest on a Balance of Power?" *American Historical Review* 97, no. 3 (1992): 683–706.

Schütze, Heinrich Albrecht. *Die Repressalie unter besonderer Berücksichtigung der Kriegsverbrecherprozesse.* Bonn: Ludwig Röhrscheid, 1950.

Schwabe, Klaus. "Versailles nach 60 Jahren." *Neue Politische Literatur* 24 (1979): 446–75.

Schwarzenberger, Georg. *The Frontiers of International Law.* London: Stevens & Son, 1962.

Scott, Charles Prestwich. *The Political Diaries of C. P. Scott, 1911–1928.* Edited by Trever Wilson. Ithaca, NY: Cornell University Press, 1970.

Scott, George Winfield, and James Wilford Garner, eds. *The German War Code Contrasted with the War Manuals of the United States, Great Britain, and France.* Washington, DC: Committee on Public Information, 1918.

Scott, James Brown. "The Declaration of London of February 26, 1909." *American Journal of International Law* 8, no. 2 (April 1914): 274–329.

Segesser, Daniel Marc. *Der Erste Weltkrieg.* Wiesbaden: Marixverlag, 2010.

Seydel, Max. *Grundzüge einer allgemeinen Staatslehre.* Würzburg: A. Stuber, 1873.

Sheffield, Gary. *Forgotten Victory; The First World War: Myths and Realities.* London: Headline, 2001.

Showalter, Dennis. "From Deterrence to Doomsday Machine: The German Way of War, 1890–1914." *Journal of Military History* 64 (July 2000): 679–710.

Spaight, J. M. *War Rights on Land.* London: Macmillan, 1911.

Spender, J. A., and Cyril Asquith. *Life of Herbert Henry Asquith, Lord Oxford and Asquith.* London: Hutchinson & Co., 1932.

Spindler, Arno, ed. *Der Handelskrieg mit U-Booten.* Der Krieg zur See 1914–1918. Berlin: E. S. Mittler & Sohn, 1932–34.

Stegemann, Bernd. *Die deutsche Marinepolitik 1916–1918.* Berlin: Duncker & Humblot, 1970.

Stein, Ted L. "The Approach of the Different Drummer: The Principle of the Persistent Objector in International Law." *Harvard International Law Journal* 26, no. 2 (1985): 457–82.

Steinberg, Jonathan. "A German Plan for the Invasion of Holland and Belgium, 1897." In *The War Plans of the Great Powers, 1880–1914,* edited by Paul J. Kennedy, 155–70. Boston: Allen & Unwin, 1985.

Steiner, Zara S. *The Foreign Office and Foreign Policy, 1898–1914.* London: Ashfield Press, 1985.

———. "The Foreign Office and the War." In *British Foreign Policy under Sir Edward Grey,* edited by F. H. Hinsley, 516–31. Cambridge: Cambridge University Press, 1977.

Stenzel, Ernst. *Die Kriegführung des deutschen Imperialismus und das Völkerrecht; zur Planung und Vorbereitung des deutschen Imperialismus auf die barbarische Kriegführung im Ersten und Zweiten Weltkrieg, dargestellt an den vorherrschenden Ansichten zu den Gesetzen und Gebräuchen des Landkrieges (1900–1945).* Berlin: Militärverlag der Deutschen Demokratischen Republik, 1973.

Stevenson, David. *French War Aims against Germany.* Oxford: Oxford University Press, 1982.

Stockton, Charles H. *The Laws and Usages of War at Sea: A Naval War Code.* Washington, DC: Government Printing Office, 1900.

———. "The Use of Submarine Mines and Torpedoes in Time of War." *American Journal of International Law* 2, no. 2 (April 1908): 276–84.

Stolleis, Michael. *Geschichte des öffentlichen Rechts in Deutschland.* 3 vols. Munich: C. H. Beck, 1988.

Stone, Julius. "*Non Liquet* and the Function of Law in the International Community." *British Yearbook of International Law* 35 (1959): 124–61.

Strachan, Hew. *The First World War.* Vol. 1, *To Arms.* Oxford: Oxford University Press, 2001.

Strazhas, Aba. *Deutsche Ostpolitik im Ersten Weltkrieg: Der Fall Ober-Ost, 1915–1917.* Wiesbaden: Harrassowitz Verlag, 1993.

Strupp, Karl. *Das internationale Landkriegsrecht.* Frankfurt: Joseph Baer & Co., 1914.

———. "Der belgische Volkskrieg und die Haager Landkriegsordnung." *Zeitschrift für Völkerrecht* 9 (1916): 281–97.

———. "Gegenwartsfragen des Völkerrechts." *Niemeyers Zeitschrift für Internationales Recht* 25 (1915): 339–82.

Taylor, A. J. P. *The Struggle for Mastery in Europe, 1848–1918*. Oxford: Oxford University Press, 1954.

Thaer, Albrecht von. *Generalstabsdienst an der Front und in der O. H. L.* Abhandlungen der Akademie der Wissenschaften in Göttingen, philologisch-historische Klasse, Dritte Folge, Nr. 40. Edited by Siegfried Kaehler. Göttingen: Vandenhoeck & Ruprecht, 1958.

Thiel, Jens. *"Menschenbassin Belgien": Anwerbung, Deportation und Zwangsarbeit im Ersten Weltkrieg*. Schriften der Bibliothek für Zeitgeschichte, vol. 20. Essen: Klartext, 2007.

Thirlway, Hugh W. A. *International Customary Law and Codification: An Examination of the Continuing Role of Custom in the Present Period of Codification of International Law*. Leiden: A. W. Sijthoff, 1972.

Thomas, Daniel H. *The Guarantee of Belgian Independence and Neutrality in European Diplomacy, 1830s–1930s*. Kingston, RI: D. H. Thomas, 1983.

Tirpitz, Alfred von. *Politische Dokumente: Deutsche Ohnmachtspolitik im Weltkriege*. Hamburg: Hanseatische Verlagsanstalt, 1926.

Toppe, Andreas. *Militär und Kriegsvölkerrecht: Rechtsnorm, Fachdiskurs und Kriegspraxis in Deutschland*. Munich: R. Oldenbourg, 2008.

Treitel, Corinna. "Max Rubner and the Biopolitics of Rational Nutrition." *Central European History* 41, no. 1 (2008): 1–25.

Triepel, Heinrich. "Der Widerstand feindlicher Handelsschiffe gegen die Aufbringung." *Zeitschrift für Völkerrecht* 8 (1914): 378–406.

———. *Völkerrecht und Landesrecht*. Leipzig: C. L. Hirschfeld, 1899.

Trumpener, Ulrich. "The Road to Ypres: The Beginning of Gas Warfare in World War I." *Journal of Modern History* 47, no. 3 (1975): 460–80.

Ullmann, Emanuel von. *Völkerrecht*. Das Öffentliche Recht der Gegenwart. Tübingen: J. C. B. Mohr, 1908.

Ungern-Sternberg, Jürgen von, and Wolfgang von Ungern-Sternberg. *Der Aufruf "An die Kulturwelt!" Das Manifest der 93 und die Anfänge der Kriegspropaganda im Ersten Weltkrieg*. Stuttgart: Franz Steiner, 1996.

Vattel, Emmerich de. *The Law of Nations, or, Principles of the Law of Nature, Applied to the Conduct and Affairs of Nations and Sovereigns*. London: G. G. and J. Robinson, 1797.

Vincent, C. Paul. *The Politics of Hunger: The Allied Blockade of Germany, 1915–1919*. Athens: Ohio University Press, 1985.

Wandt, Heinrich. *Etappe Gent*. Vienna: Agis-Verlag, 1926.

Wehberg, Hans. *Die Abkommen der Haager Friedenskonferenzen, der Londoner Seekriegskonferenz nebst Genfer Konvention*. Berlin: J. Guttentag, 1910.

———. "Pacta Sunt Servanda." *American Journal of International Law* 53, no. 4 (October 1959): 775–86.

Wende, Frank. *Die belgische Frage in der deutschen Politik des Ersten Weltkrieges*. Hamburg: Wissenschaftlicher Verlag Eckart Böhme, 1969.

Westerhoff, Christian. *Zwangsarbeit im Ersten Weltkrieg: Deutsche Arbeitskräftepolitik im besetzten Polen und Litauen 1914–1918*. Paderborn: Schöningh, 2012.

Westlake, John. *International Law; Part II: War*. Cambridge: Cambridge University Press, 1907.

Whitlock, Brand. *Belgium: A Personal Narrative*. 2 vols. New York: D. Appleton & Co., 1919.

Wieland, Lothar. *Belgien, 1914: Die Frage des belgischen "Franktireurkrieges" und die deutsche öffentliche Meinung von 1914 bis 1936*. Frankfurt: Peter Lang, 1984.

Wild von Hohenborn, Adolf. *Briefe und Tagebuchaufzeichnungen des preußischen Generals als Kriegsminister und Truppenführer im Ersten Weltkrieg*. Edited by Helmut Reichold and Gerhard Granier. Boppard am Rhein: Harald Boldt, 1986.

Williamson, John G. *Karl Helfferich, 1872–1924: Economist, Financier, Politician*. Princeton, NJ: Princeton University Press, 1971.

Williamson, Samuel R. "Joffre Reshapes French Strategy, 1911–1913." In *The War Plans of the Great Powers, 1880–1914*, edited by Paul M. Kennedy, 205–27. Boston: Allen & Unwin, 1985.

Wilson, Keith M. "Britain." In *Decisions for War, 1914*, edited by Keith M. Wilson, 175–208. New York: St. Martin's Press, 1995.

———. "The British Cabinet's Decision for War, 2 August 1914." *British Journal of International Studies* 1 (1975): 148–59.

Wilson, Trevor. "Lord Bryce's Investigation into Alleged German Atrocities in Belgium, 1914–1915." *Journal of Contemporary History* 14, no. 3 (July 1979): 369–83.

Winter, Jay. "Some Paradoxes of the First World War." In *The Upheaval of War: Family, Work and Welfare in Europe, 1914–1918*, edited by Richard Wall and Jay M. Winter, 9–42. Cambridge: Cambridge University Press, 1988.

Wittgens, Herman. "The German Foreign Office Campaign against the Versailles Treaty." Seattle: Ph.D. diss., University of Washington, 1970.

———. "Senator Owen, the Schuldreferat, and the Debate over War Guilt in the 1920s." In *Forging the Collective Memory: Government and International Historians through Two World Wars*, edited by Keith Wilson, 128–50. Providence, RI: Berghahn Books, 1996.

Wolff, Theodor. *Theodor Wolff. Tagebücher 1914–1919; Der Erste Weltkrieg und die Entstehung der Weimarer Republik in Tagebüchern, Leitartikeln und Briefen des Chefredakteurs am "Berliner Tageblatt" und Mitbegründer der "Deutschen Demokratischen Partei."* Edited by Bernd Sösemann. Boppard am Rhein: Harald Boldt, 1984.

Wrisberg, Ernst von. *Heer und Heimat, 1914–1918*. Leipzig: Koehler, 1921.

Xu, Guoqi. *China and the Great War: China's Pursuit of a New National Identity and Internationalization*. Cambridge: Cambridge University Press, 2005.

Young, Harry F. *Prince Lichnowsky and the Great War*. Athens: University of Georgia Press, 1977.

Zilch, Reinhold. *Okkupation und Währung im Ersten Weltkrieg: Die deutsche Besatzungspolitik in Belgien und Russisch-Polen 1914–1918*. Goldbach: Kiep Verlag, 1994.

Zorn, Albert. *Das Kriegsrecht zu Lande in seiner neuesten Gestaltung; Eine kritische Untersuchung*. Berlin: Carl Heymanns Verlag, 1906.

Zunkel, Friedrich. "Die ausländischen Arbeiter in der deutschen Kriegswirtschaftspolitik des 1. Weltkriegs." In *Entstehung und Wandel der modernen Gesellschaft; Festschrift für Hans Rosenberg zum 65. Geburtstag*, edited by Gerhard A. Ritter, 280–311. Berlin: Walter de Gruyter, 1970.

Index

Gromaire, Georges, 126–27

Grotius, Hugo, 26–27, 325

Grünau, Werner Freiherr von, 114–15, 225–27, 230, 239, 291–92

Gündell, Erich von, 82

guides, forced civilian, 65, 72, 97

Haakon VII, 201

Haber, Fritz, 232–33

Hague arbitration tribunal, 262

Hague art. 23(e) on unnecessary suffering, 230–31, 271

Hague art. 43: 98, 103, 104, 111, 115, 133–34, 137

Hague art. 52: 100, 124, 127, 130, 134–37

Hague Convention (1907): on mines, 155–57; on sinking merchant ships, 212–15; on enemy merchant crews, 247; on prisoners, 298

Hague Convention IV (1899) (Hague Rules), 55, 60, 73–76, 89, 93; German instructions concerning, 83; British and French incorporation into manuals, 83–86; incorporation into German domestic law, 87; Germany says Hague Rules (1907) are binding, 87; ignored by *Kriegs-Etappen-Ordnung*, 101; RMG rules they are subordinate to German domestic law, 109–10; prohibition of using prisoner labor for operations of war, 304

Hague Convention VIII (mines), 244

Hague Convention IX on naval bombardment, 225

Hague Convention XI on mail, 200–204

Hague Convention XIV on aerial bombardment, 225, 230

Hague Declaration 3 (dumdum bullets), 281

Hague International Prize Court, 142, 148

Hague Peace Conferences, 2, 57, 82, 96, 142, 270, 317

Haig, Douglas, 307

Haldane, Richard, 34, 39, 159–60

Hall, William Edward, 91

Hankey, Maurice, 149–50, 152, 235

Harcourt, Lewis, 36–39, 154, 159

Hardinge, Charles, 41, 300, 302, 315

Hartmann, Julius von, 45, 68–72, 76–77

Heffter, August Wilhelm, 91

Helfferich, Karl, 121, 138

Hershey, Amon S., 106

Higgins, A. Pearce, 196–97, 205, 207–8

Hindenburg, Paul von, 122–25, 130–38, 258, 291

Hohenlohe, Chlodwig von, 24

Hold von Ferneck, Alexander, 146

Holstein, Friedrich von, 24

Holtzendorff, Franz, 91

Holtzendorff, Henning von, 123, 228–29, 258, 264

Hötzendorf, Franz Conrad von, 58, 120

Hopman, Albert, 267–70

Horne, John, 56, 59

hospital ships: attack on the *Asturias*, 240–41; French reprisal for sinkings, 285, 302, 312; Britain contemplates reprisal for sinkings, 301

hostages, 52, 65, 72, 79, 81, 85, 101, 116, 284, 297

Huber, Max, 45, 49

Huene, Ernst von Hoyningen, genannt, 132, 137

Hurst, Cecil J.B., 144, 147, 150–53, 159–61, 163, 167, 171–73, 178, 187, 193, 199, 200, 202, 204–8, 301

imperial criminal code, German (RStGB), 104–5

Imperial Edict of December 28, 1899 (August 21, 1900 for the sea) (AKO): contradicts Hague Rules, 83; in occupied zones, 105, 109–10; Fryatt case, 254;

imperial military court (RMG), 109–10

incendiary bombs, 227, 267

incendiary bullets, 229

indemnities; Britain pays, 150, 180, 190, 192, 204, 206–7; Germany refuses, 243, 262–63; as sanctions, 315, 327

Ingenohl, Friedrich von, 215–16

"innocence campaign," 7–12, 329–31

Institute of International Law, 213, 248

insurrection: disagreement on civilian right to (1874), 62–64; in 1899, 74–75

intention to follow Hague Rules: German, 82–83, 87, 104; British and French, 83–86

International Committee of the Red Cross, 299, 310

International Law Committee (Britain), 207–8

interpreting international law, 10, 18, 20, 45–46, 59, 62, 66, 73–75, 84, 88–94, 97n6, 99–100, 111, 114, 120, 134, 145, 158, 165, 188–90, 195, 219, 252, 275, 279, 283–84, 304–5, 317–18, 321–23, 328, 330

Italy, 10, 13, 19, 54, 65, 100, 137, 145–56, 163, 222, 225–26, 245, 272, 274, 283, 325

Jacomet, Robert, 84–86, 277

Jaequemyns, Édouard Rolin, 73, 96, 98, 111